PARKIN ◆ BADE

MICROECONOMICS

CANADA IN THE GLOBAL ENVIRONMENT TENTH EDITION

Prepare, Apply, Assess and Develop Employability Skills with MyLab Economics

83%

of students said it helped them earn higher grades on homework, exams, or the course

*Source: 2016 Student Survey, n 10,263

MyLab™ Economics is an online homework, tutorial, and assessment program constructed to work with this text to engage students and improve results. It was designed to help students develop and assess the skills and applicable knowledge that they will need to succeed in their courses and their future careers.

See what students had to say about MyLab Economics:

"Usually when I do homework myself and don't get it I am stuck, but [MyLab Economics] provided the tools necessary to help me learn how to work my way through the trickiest problems."

— Zainul Lughmani, Binghamton University

Digital Interactives

Economic principles are not static ideas, and learning them shouldn't be either! Digital Interactives are dynamic and engaging assessment activities that promote **critical thinking** and **application** of key economic principles.

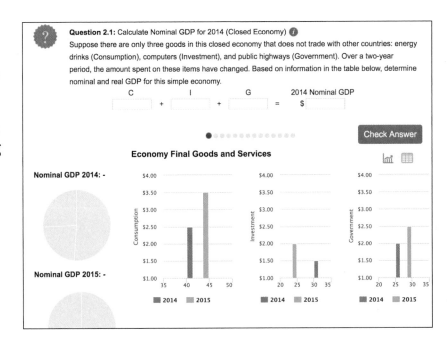

Question Help

MyLab Economics homework and practice questions are correlated to the textbook, and many generate algorithmically to give students unlimited opportunity for mastery of concepts. If students get stuck, Learning Aids including Help Me Solve This and eText Pages walk them through the problem and identify helpful information in the text, giving them assistance when they need it most.

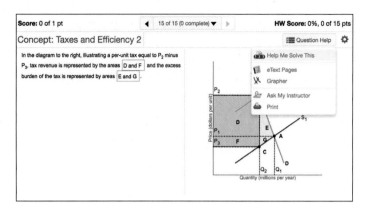

"[MyLab Economics] provides ample practice and explanation of the concepts at hand."
— Heather Burkett, University of Nebraska at Omaha

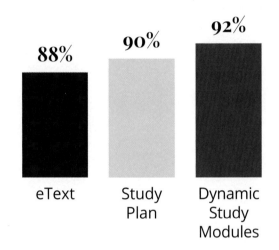

% of students who found learning tool helpful

Dynamic Study Modules help students study introductory economics topics effectively on their own by continuously assessing their **knowledge application** and performance in real time. These are accessible on smartphones, tablets, and computers.

Pearson eText 2.0 allows you to read and study anytime, anywhere. Using the same login and password as the MyLab, the Pearson eText 2.0 app gives you access to an interactive version of your textbook on your tablet or mobile phone, offline and online, so you can read and study as you move throughout your day.

The **MyLab Gradebook** offers an easy way for students and instructors to view course performance. Item Analysis allows instructors to quickly see trends by analyzing details like the number of students who answered correctly/incorrectly, time on task, and median time spent on a question-by-question basis.

87%

of students would tell their instructor to keep using MyLab Economics

For additional details visit: www.pearson.com/mylab/economics

PARKIN ◆ BADE

MICROECONOMICS

CANADA IN THE GLOBAL ENVIRONMENT   TENTH EDITION

MICHAEL PARKIN   ROBIN BADE

University of Western Ontario

Pearson

ACQUISITIONS EDITOR: Anne Williams
MARKETING DIRECTOR: Leigh-Anne Graham
CONTENT MANAGER: Emily Dill
PROJECT MANAGER: Avinash Chandra
MANAGER OF CONTENT DEVELOPMENT: Suzanne Schaan
DEVELOPMENTAL EDITOR: Leanne Rancourt
DIGITAL CONTENT MANAGER: Nicole Mellow
SENIOR MEDIA DEVELOPER: Olga Avdyeyeva
PRODUCTION SERVICES: Cenveo® Publisher Services

TECHNICAL ILLUSTRATOR: Richard Parkin
PERMISSIONS PROJECT MANAGER: Joanne Tang
PHOTO PERMISSIONS RESEARCH: iEnergizerAptara®, Ltd.
TEXT PERMISSIONS RESEARCH: iEnergizerAptara®, Ltd.
INTERIOR DESIGNER: Emily Friel, Integra Software Services/
Anthony Leung
COVER DESIGNER: Anthony Leung
COVER IMAGE: © Orangeline / Dreamstime
VICE-PRESIDENT, DIGITAL STUDIO: Gary Bennett

Pearson Canada Inc., 26 Prince Andrew Place, North York, Ontario M3C 2H4.

978-0-13-468684-4

2 18

Library and Archives Canada Cataloguing in Publication

Parkin, Michael, 1939-, author
        Microeconomics : Canada in the global environment / Michael Parkin, Robin
Bade. — Tenth edition.

Includes index.
Issued in print and electronic formats.
ISBN 978-0-13-468684-4 (softcover).—ISBN 978-0-13-488520-9 (loose-leaf).—
ISBN 978-0-13-483516-7 (PDF).—ISBN 978-0-13-488516-2 (HTML)

        1. Microeconomics—Textbooks. 2. Canada—Economic conditions—1991- —
Textbooks. 3. Textbooks. I. Bade, Robin, author II. Title.

HB172.P37 2018   338.5   C2017-906396-0
                                                 C2017-906397-9

TO OUR STUDENTS

Michael Parkin is Professor Emeritus in the Department of
Economics at the University of Western Ontario, Canada. Professor Parkin has
held faculty appointments at Brown University, the University of Manchester,
the University of Essex, and Bond University. He is a past president of the
Canadian Economics Association and has served on the editorial boards of
the *American Economic Review* and the *Journal of Monetary Economics* and
as managing editor of the *Canadian Journal of Economics*. Professor Parkin's
research on macroeconomics, monetary economics, and international
economics has resulted in over 160 publications in journals and edited
volumes, including the *American Economic Review*, the *Journal of Political
Economy*, the *Review of Economic Studies*, the *Journal of Monetary Economics*,
and the *Journal of Money, Credit and Banking*. He became most visible to the
public with his work on inflation that discredited the use of wage and price controls.
Michael Parkin also spearheaded the movement toward European monetary union.
Professor Parkin is an experienced and dedicated teacher of introductory economics.

Robin Bade earned degrees in mathematics and economics
at the University of Queensland and her Ph.D. at the Australian National
University. She has held faculty appointments at the University of Edinburgh in Scotland, at Bond University in Australia, and at the Universities
of Manitoba, Toronto, and Western Ontario in Canada. Her research on
international capital flows appears in the *International Economic Review*
and the *Economic Record*.
Professor Parkin and Dr. Bade are the joint authors of *Foundations of Economics* (Addison Wesley), *Modern Macroeconomics* (Pearson Education
Canada), an intermediate text, and have collaborated on many research and
textbook writing projects. They are both experienced and dedicated teachers of introductory economics.

BRIEF CONTENTS

PART ONE
INTRODUCTION 1

CHAPTER 1 What Is Economics? 1

CHAPTER 2 The Economic Problem 33

PART TWO
HOW MARKETS WORK 59

CHAPTER 3 Demand and Supply 59

CHAPTER 4 Elasticity 87

CHAPTER 5 Efficiency and Equity 109

CHAPTER 6 Government Actions in Markets 131

CHAPTER 7 Global Markets in Action 155

PART THREE
HOUSEHOLDS' CHOICES 181

CHAPTER 8 Utility and Demand 181

CHAPTER 9 Possibilities, Preferences, and Choices 205

PART FOUR
FIRMS AND MARKETS 227

CHAPTER 10 Output and Costs 227

CHAPTER 11 Perfect Competition 253

CHAPTER 12 Monopoly 279

CHAPTER 13 Monopolistic Competition 305

CHAPTER 14 Oligopoly 325

PART FIVE
MARKET FAILURE AND GOVERNMENT 353

CHAPTER 15 Externalities 353

CHAPTER 16 Public Goods and Common Resources 375

PART SIX
FACTOR MARKETS AND INEQUALITY 397

CHAPTER 17 Markets for Factors of Production 397

CHAPTER 18 Economic Inequality 423

Flexibility

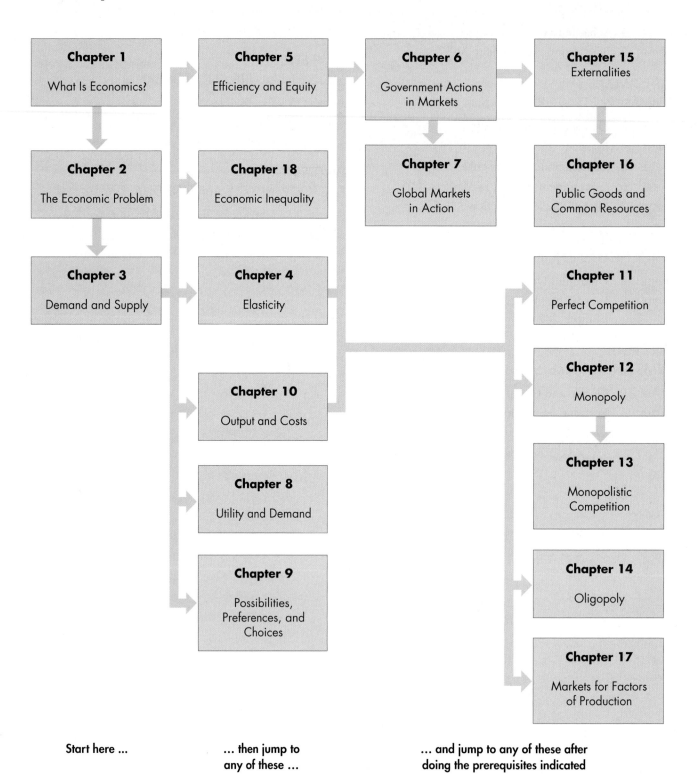

Chapter 1 — What Is Economics?

Chapter 5 — Efficiency and Equity

Chapter 6 — Government Actions in Markets

Chapter 15 — Externalities

Chapter 2 — The Economic Problem

Chapter 18 — Economic Inequality

Chapter 7 — Global Markets in Action

Chapter 16 — Public Goods and Common Resources

Chapter 3 — Demand and Supply

Chapter 4 — Elasticity

Chapter 11 — Perfect Competition

Chapter 10 — Output and Costs

Chapter 12 — Monopoly

Chapter 8 — Utility and Demand

Chapter 13 — Monopolistic Competition

Chapter 9 — Possibilities, Preferences, and Choices

Chapter 14 — Oligopoly

Chapter 17 — Markets for Factors of Production

Start here ...

... then jump to any of these ...

... and jump to any of these after doing the prerequisites indicated

PART ONE
INTRODUCTION 1

CHAPTER 1 ◆ **WHAT IS ECONOMICS?** 1

Definition of Economics 2

Two Big Economic Questions 3
What, How, and For Whom? 3
Do Choices Made in the Pursuit of Self-Interest
also Promote the Social Interest? 5

The Economic Way of Thinking 9
A Choice Is a Tradeoff 9
Making a Rational Choice 9
Benefit: What You Gain 9
Cost: What You *Must* Give Up 9
How Much? Choosing at the Margin 10
Choices Respond to Incentives 10

Economics as Social Science and Policy Tool 11
Economist as Social Scientist 11
Economist as Policy Adviser 11

Economists in the Economy 12
Jobs for an Economics Major 12
Will Jobs for Economics Majors Grow? 12
Earnings of Economics Majors 13
Skills Needed for Economics Jobs 13

Worked Problem, Summary (Key Points and Key Terms),
Study Plan Problems and Applications, and Additional Prob-
lems and Applications appear at the end of each chapter.

APPENDIX Graphs in Economics 17

Graphing Data 17
Graphing Economic Data 18
Scatter Diagrams 18

Graphs Used in Economic Models 20
Variables That Move in the Same Direction 20
Variables That Move in Opposite Directions 21
Variables That Have a Maximum or a
Minimum 22
Variables That Are Unrelated 23

The Slope of a Relationship 24
The Slope of a Straight Line 24
The Slope of a Curved Line 25

Graphing Relationships Among More Than
Two Variables 26
Ceteris Paribus 26
When Other Things Change 27

MATHEMATICAL NOTE
Equations of Straight Lines 28

■ AT ISSUE, 8

■ ECONOMICS IN THE NEWS, 6, 14

CHAPTER **2** ◆ **THE ECONOMIC PROBLEM** 33

Production Possibilities and Opportunity Cost 34
Production Possibilities Frontier 34
Production Efficiency 35
Tradeoff Along the *PPF* 35
Opportunity Cost 35

Using Resources Efficiently 37
The *PPF* and Marginal Cost 37
Preferences and Marginal Benefit 38
Allocative Efficiency 39

Gains from Trade 40
Comparative Advantage and Absolute
Advantage 40
Achieving the Gains from Trade 42
The Liz–Joe Economy and Its *PPF* 44

Economic Growth 45
The Cost of Economic Growth 45
A Nation's Economic Growth 46
Changes in What We Produce 46

Economic Coordination 48
Firms 48
Markets 48
Property Rights 48
Money 48
Circular Flows Through Markets 48
Coordinating Decisions 49

■ ECONOMICS IN ACTION, 46

■ ECONOMICS IN THE NEWS, 36, 50

PART ONE **WRAP-UP** ◆

Understanding the Scope of Economics
Your Economic Revolution 57

Talking with
Esther Duflo 58

PART TWO
HOW MARKETS WORK 59

CHAPTER **3** ◆ **DEMAND AND SUPPLY** 59

Markets and Prices 60

Demand 61
The Law of Demand 61
Demand Curve and Demand Schedule 61
A Change in Demand 62
A Change in the Quantity Demanded Versus a
Change in Demand 64

Supply 66
The Law of Supply 66
Supply Curve and Supply Schedule 66
A Change in Supply 67
A Change in the Quantity Supplied Versus a
Change in Supply 68

Market Equilibrium 70
Price as a Regulator 70
Price Adjustments 71

Predicting Changes in Price and Quantity 72
An Increase in Demand 72
A Decrease in Demand 72
An Increase in Supply 74
A Decrease in Supply 74
Changes in Both Demand and Supply 76

MATHEMATICAL NOTE
Demand, Supply, and Equilibrium 80

■ ECONOMICS IN THE NEWS, 73, 75, 78

CHAPTER **4** ◆ **ELASTICITY** 87

Price Elasticity of Demand 88
  Calculating Price Elasticity of Demand 88
  Inelastic and Elastic Demand 89
  The Factors That Influence the
    Elasticity of Demand 90
  Elasticity Along a Linear Demand Curve 91
  Total Revenue and Elasticity 92
  Your Expenditure and Your Elasticity 94

More Elasticities of Demand 95
  Income Elasticity of Demand 95
  Cross Elasticity of Demand 96

Elasticity of Supply 98
  Calculating the Elasticity of Supply 98
  The Factors That Influence the
    Elasticity of Supply 99

■ ECONOMICS IN ACTION, 93, 95, 96

■ ECONOMICS IN THE NEWS, 94, 97, 102

CHAPTER **5** ◆ **EFFICIENCY AND EQUITY** 109

Resource Allocation Methods 110
  Market Price 110
  Command 110
  Majority Rule 110
  Contest 110
  First-Come, First-Served 110
  Lottery 111
  Personal Characteristics 111
  Force 111

Benefit, Cost, and Surplus 112
  Demand, Willingness to Pay, and Value 112
  Individual Demand and Market Demand 112
  Consumer Surplus 113
  Supply and Marginal Cost 113
  Supply, Cost, and Minimum Supply-Price 114
  Individual Supply and Market Supply 114
  Producer Surplus 115

Is the Competitive Market Efficient? 116
  Efficiency of Competitive Equilibrium 116
  Market Failure 118
  Sources of Market Failure 118
  Alternatives to the Market 119

Is the Competitive Market Fair? 120
  It's Not Fair if the *Result* Isn't Fair 120
  It's Not Fair if the *Rules* Aren't Fair 122
  Case Study: A Generator Shortage in a
    Natural Disaster 122

■ ECONOMICS IN ACTION, 117

■ AT ISSUE, 123

■ ECONOMICS IN THE NEWS, 124

CHAPTER **6** ◆ **GOVERNMENT ACTIONS IN MARKETS** 131

A Housing Market with a Rent Ceiling 132
    A Housing Shortage 132
    Increased Search Activity 132
    A Black Market 132
    Inefficiency of a Rent Ceiling 133
    Are Rent Ceilings Fair? 134

A Labour Market with a Minimum Wage 135
    Minimum Wage Brings Unemployment 135
    Is the Minimum Wage Fair? 135
    Inefficiency of a Minimum Wage 136

Taxes 137
    Tax Incidence 137
    Equivalence of a Tax on Buyers and Sellers 138
    Taxes and Efficiency 139
    Tax Incidence and Elasticity of Demand 140
    Tax Incidence and Elasticity of Supply 141
    Taxes and Fairness 142
    The Big Tradeoff 142

Production Quotas and Subsidies 143
    Production Quotas 143
    Subsidies 144

Markets for Illegal Goods 146
    A Free Market for a Drug 146
    A Market for an Illegal Drug 146
    Legalizing and Taxing Drugs 147

■ ECONOMICS IN ACTION, 134, 142, 145

■ AT ISSUE, 136

■ ECONOMICS IN THE NEWS, 148

CHAPTER **7** ◆ **GLOBAL MARKETS IN ACTION** 155

How Global Markets Work 156
    International Trade Today 156
    What Drives International Trade? 156
    Why Canada Imports T-Shirts 157
    Why Canada Exports Regional Jets 158

Winners, Losers, and the Net Gain from Trade 159
    Gains and Losses from Imports 159
    Gains and Losses from Exports 160
    Gains for All 160

International Trade Restrictions 161
    Tariffs 161
    Import Quotas 164
    Other Import Barriers 167
    Export Subsidies 167

The Case Against Protection 168
    Helps an Infant Industry Grow 168
    Counteracts Dumping 168
    Saves Domestic Jobs 168
    Allows Us to Compete with Cheap Foreign Labour 168
    Penalizes Lax Environmental Standards 169
    Prevents Rich Countries from Exploiting Developing Countries 169
    Reduces Offshore Outsourcing that Sends Good Canadian Jobs to Other Countries 169
    Avoiding Trade Wars 170
    Why Is International Trade Restricted? 170
    Compensating Losers 171

■ ECONOMICS IN ACTION, 156, 162, 167

■ AT ISSUE, 170

■ ECONOMICS IN THE NEWS, 166, 172

PART TWO **WRAP-UP** ◆

Understanding How Markets Work
The Amazing Market 179

Talking with
Susan Athey 180

PART THREE
HOUSEHOLDS' CHOICES 181

CHAPTER **8** ◆ **UTILITY AND DEMAND** 181

Consumption Choices 182
  Consumption Possibilities 182
  Preferences 183

Utility-Maximizing Choice 185
  A Spreadsheet Solution 185
  Choosing at the Margin 186
  The Power of Marginal Analysis 188
  Revealing Preferences 188

Predictions of Marginal Utility Theory 189
  A Fall in the Price of a Movie 189
  A Rise in the Price of Cola 191
  A Rise in Income 192
  The Paradox of Value 193
  Temperature: An Analogy 194

New Ways of Explaining Consumer Choices 196
  Behavioural Economics 196
  Neuroeconomics 197
  Controversy 197

■ ECONOMICS IN ACTION, 194

■ ECONOMICS IN THE NEWS, 198

CHAPTER **9** ◆ **POSSIBILITIES, PREFERENCES, AND CHOICES** 205

Consumption Possibilities 206
  Budget Equation 207

Preferences and Indifference Curves 209
  Marginal Rate of Substitution 210
  Degree of Substitutability 211

Predicting Consumer Choices 212
  Best Affordable Choice 212
  A Change in Price 213
  A Change in Income 215
  Substitution Effect and Income Effect 216

■ ECONOMICS IN ACTION, 214

■ ECONOMICS IN THE NEWS, 218

PART THREE **WRAP-UP** ◆

Understanding Households' Choices
Making the Most of Life 225

Talking with
Steven D. Levitt 226

PART FOUR
FIRMS AND MARKETS 227

CHAPTER **10** ◆ **OUTPUT AND COSTS** 227

Economic Cost and Profit 228
  The Firm's Goal 228
  Accounting Profit 228
  Economic Accounting 228
  A Firm's Opportunity Cost of Production 228
  Economic Accounting: A Summary 229
  Decisions 229
  Decision Time Frames 230

Short-Run Technology Constraint 231
  Product Schedules 231
  Product Curves 231
  Total Product Curve 232
  Marginal Product Curve 232
  Average Product Curve 234

Short-Run Cost 235
  Total Cost 235
  Marginal Cost 236
  Average Cost 236
  Marginal Cost and Average Cost 236
  Why the Average Total Cost Curve
    Is U-Shaped 236
  Cost Curves and Product Curves 238
  Shifts in the Cost Curves 240

Long-Run Cost 242
  The Production Function 242
  Short-Run Cost and Long-Run Cost 242
  The Long-Run Average Cost Curve 244
  Economies and Diseconomies of Scale 244

■ ECONOMICS IN ACTION, 234, 245

■ ECONOMICS IN THE NEWS, 238, 246

CHAPTER **11** ◆ **PERFECT COMPETITION** 253

What Is Perfect Competition? 254
  How Perfect Competition Arises 254
  Price Takers 254
  Economic Profit and Revenue 254
  The Firm's Decisions 255

The Firm's Output Decision 256
  Marginal Analysis and the Supply Decision 257
  Temporary Shutdown Decision 258
  The Firm's Supply Curve 259

Output, Price, and Profit in the Short Run 260
  Market Supply in the Short Run 260
  Short-Run Equilibrium 261
  A Change in Demand 261
  Profits and Losses in the Short Run 261
  Three Possible Short-Run Outcomes 262

Output, Price, and Profit in the Long Run 263
  Entry and Exit 263
  A Closer Look at Entry 264
  A Closer Look at Exit 264
  Long-Run Equilibrium 265

Changes in Demand and Supply as Technology
Advances 266
  A Decrease in Demand 266
  An Increase in Demand 267
  Technological Advances Change Supply 268

Competition and Efficiency 270
  Efficient Use of Resources 270
  Choices, Equilibrium, and Efficiency 270

■ ECONOMICS IN ACTION, 263, 265

■ ECONOMICS IN THE NEWS, 267, 269, 272

CHAPTER **12** ◆ **MONOPOLY** 279

Monopoly and How It Arises 280
How Monopoly Arises 280
Monopoly Price-Setting Strategies 281

A Single-Price Monopoly's Output and Price Decision 282
Price and Marginal Revenue 282
Marginal Revenue and Elasticity 283
Price and Output Decision 284

Single-Price Monopoly and Competition Compared 286
Comparing Price and Output 286
Efficiency Comparison 287
Redistribution of Surpluses 288
Rent Seeking 288
Rent-Seeking Equilibrium 288

Price Discrimination 289
Two Ways of Price Discriminating 289
Increasing Profit and Producer Surplus 290
A Price-Discriminating Airline 290
Efficiency and Rent Seeking with Price Discrimination 293

Monopoly Regulation 295
Efficient Regulation of a Natural Monopoly 295
Second-Best Regulation of a Natural Monopoly 296

■ ECONOMICS IN ACTION, 281, 293

■ ECONOMICS IN THE NEWS, 294, 298

CHAPTER **13** ◆ **MONOPOLISTIC COMPETITION** 305

Monopolistic Competition and Other Market Structures 306
What Is Monopolistic Competition? 306
Identifying Monopolistic Competition 307
Measures of Concentration 307
Limitations of a Concentration Measure 308

Price and Output in Monopolistic Competition 310
The Firm's Short-Run Output and Price Decision 310
Profit Maximizing Might Be Loss Minimizing 310
Long Run: Zero Economic Profit 311
Monopolistic Competition and Perfect Competition 312
Is Monopolistic Competition Efficient? 313

Product Development and Marketing 314
Product Development 314
Advertising 314
Using Advertising to Signal Quality 316
Brand Names 317
Efficiency of Advertising and Brand Names 317

■ ECONOMICS IN ACTION, 309, 315

■ ECONOMICS IN THE NEWS, 318

CHAPTER **14** ◆ **OLIGOPOLY**   325

What Is Oligopoly?   326
　Barriers to Entry   326
　Small Number of Firms   327
　Examples of Oligopoly   327

Oligopoly Games   328
　What Is a Game?   328
　The Prisoners' Dilemma   328
　An Oligopoly Price-Fixing Game   330
　A Game of Chicken   335

Repeated Games and Sequential Games   336
　A Repeated Duopoly Game   336
　A Sequential Entry Game in a Contestable
　　Market   338

Anti-Combine Law   340
　Canada's Anti-Combine Law   340
　Some Major Anti-Combine Cases   340

■ ECONOMICS IN ACTION, 327, 334, 341, 342, 343

■ ECONOMICS IN THE NEWS, 337, 344

PART FOUR **WRAP-UP** ◆

　Understanding Firms and Markets
　Managing Change and Limiting Market Power   351

　Talking with
　Thomas Hubbard   352

PART FIVE
**MARKET FAILURE AND
GOVERNMENT**   353

CHAPTER **15** ◆ **EXTERNALITIES**   353

Externalities in Our Lives   354
　Negative Production Externalities   354
　Positive Production Externalities   354
　Negative Consumption Externalities   354
　Positive Consumption Externalities   354

Negative Externality: Pollution   356
　Private, External, and Social Cost   356
　Establish Property Rights   357
　Mandate Clean Technology   358
　Tax or Cap and Price Pollution   359
　Coping with Global Externalities   362

Positive Externality: Knowledge   363
　Private Benefits and Social Benefits   363
　Government Actions in the Face of External
　　Benefits   364

■ ECONOMICS IN ACTION, 355, 360, 362, 366

■ AT ISSUE, 361

■ ECONOMICS IN THE NEWS, 368

CHAPTER **16** ◆ **PUBLIC GOODS AND
                  COMMON RESOURCES**   375

Classifying Goods and Resources   376
    Excludable   376
    Rival   376
    A Fourfold Classification   376

Public Goods   377
    The Free-Rider Problem   377
    Marginal Social Benefit from a Public Good   377
    Marginal Social Cost of a Public Good   378
    Efficient Quantity of a Public Good   378
    Inefficient Private Provision   378
    Efficient Public Provision   378
    Inefficient Public Overprovision   379
    Two Types of Political Equilibrium   381
    Why Government Is Large and Growing   381
    Voters Strike Back   381

Common Resources   382
    Sustainable Use of a Renewable Resource   382
    The Overuse of a Common Resource   384
    Achieving an Efficient Outcome   385

■ ECONOMICS IN ACTION, 380, 382, 383, 387

■ ECONOMICS IN THE NEWS, 388

PART FIVE **WRAP-UP** ◆

    Understanding Market Failure and
    Government
    Making the Rules   395

    Talking with
    Caroline M. Hoxby   396

PART SIX
**FACTOR MARKETS AND
INEQUALITY**   397

CHAPTER **17** ◆ **MARKETS FOR FACTORS OF
                  PRODUCTION**   397

The Anatomy of Factor Markets   398
    Markets for Labour Services   398
    Markets for Capital Services   398
    Markets for Land Services and Natural
        Resources   398
    Entrepreneurship   398

The Demand for a Factor of Production   399
    Value of Marginal Product   399
    A Firm's Demand for Labour   399
    A Firm's Demand for Labour Curve   400
    Changes in a Firm's Demand for Labour   401

Labour Markets   402
    A Competitive Labour Market   402
    Differences and Trends in Wage Rates   404
    A Labour Market with a Union   405

Capital and Natural Resource Markets   409
    Capital Rental Markets   409
    Land Rental Markets   409
    Nonrenewable Natural Resource Markets   411

MATHEMATICAL NOTE
Present Value and Discounting   416

■ ECONOMICS IN ACTION, 404, 413

■ AT ISSUE, 407

■ ECONOMICS IN THE NEWS, 410, 414

CHAPTER **18** ◆ **ECONOMIC INEQUALITY**   423

Measuring Economic Inequality   424
  The Distribution of Income   424
  The Income Lorenz Curve   425
  The Distribution of Wealth   426
  Wealth or Income?   426
  Annual or Lifetime Income and
    Wealth?   427
  Trends in Inequality   428
  Poverty   429

Inequality in the World Economy   430
  Income Distributions in Selected
    Countries   430
  Global Inequality and Its Trends   431

The Sources of Economic
Inequality   432
  Human Capital   432
  Discrimination   434
  Contests Among Superstars   435
  Unequal Wealth   436

Income Redistribution   437
  Income Taxes   437
  Income Maintenance Programs   437
  Subsidized Services   437
  The Big Tradeoff   439
  A Major Welfare Challenge   439

■ ECONOMICS IN ACTION, 427, 428, 429, 438

■ ECONOMICS IN THE NEWS, 440

PART SIX **WRAP-UP**   ◆

  Understanding Factor Markets and Inequality
  For Whom?   447

  Talking with
  Raj Chetty   448

Glossary **G-1**
Index **I-1**
Credits **C-1**

New To This Edition

All data figures, tables, and explanations thoroughly updated to the latest available; four main content changes; 31 new Economics in the News items based on recent events and issues; almost 80 new news-based problems and applications; and all seamlessly integrated with MyLab Economics and Pearson eText: These are the hallmarks of this tenth edition of *Microeconomics*.

Main Content Changes

Chapter 1 now contains an entirely new section, "Economists in the Economy," which describes the types of jobs available to economics majors, their earnings compared with majors in other related areas, and the critical thinking, analytical, math, writing, and oral communication skills needed for a successful career in economics.

FIGURE 1.3   Earnings of Economics Majors

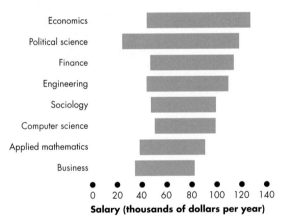

The bars show the range of earnings for eight majors in a sample of jobs monitored by the jobs survey firm PayScale. Economics graduates are the highest earners among the eight majors shown here.

Source of data: payscale.com

———————— MyLab Economics Animation ————————

Chapter 2 has a new section prompted by the ongoing concern about the rust-belt economy, its causes and cures, which describes and illustrates the changing patterns of production as an economy expands, and explains how technical change and economic growth first shrinks the share of agriculture as manufacturing expands and later shrinks the share of manufacturing as services expand.

Chapter 2 also has an expanded explanation and graphical derivation of the outward-bowed *PPF*.

Chapter 6 now explains the effects of taxes by emphasizing the tax wedge and its independence of the side of the market on which the law imposes a tax.

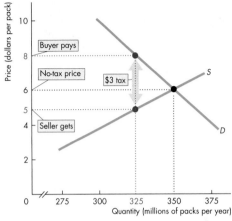

(c) Tax wedge

After extensive reviewing, we have removed the chapter on organizing production of the earlier editions and placed its explanation of the distinction between economic cost and profit and accounting cost and profit as the first section of the chapter on output and costs (now Chapter 10).

Chapter 17, Markets for Factors of Production, now has material on the gig economy and the sharing economy, using Uber and Airbnb as applications.

Economics in the News

The new *Economics in the News* features are listed at the back of the book. They are all chosen to address current issues likely to interest and motivate the student. An example is the one in Chapter 2 on expanding production possibilities of a B.C. First Nation.

ECONOMICS IN THE NEWS

Expanding Production Possibilities

B.C. First Nation Gives Nod to Proposed LNG Export Facility
The Canadian Press
March 27, 2017

A First Nation on Vancouver Island has approved a proposed liquefied natural gas export facility on its traditional territories.

Leaders of the Huu-ay-aht First Nation and the CEO of Vancouver-based Steelhead LNG held a joint news conference in Vancouver on Monday to announce what Chief Robert Dennis said was the First Nation's "official entry into the international business world."

Members of the small First Nation voted Saturday to approve development of the LNG facility at Sarita Bay, on the west coast of Vancouver Island ...

The company's plans could even include building a new pipeline linking Vancouver Island and the B.C. mainland ...

The company planned to make a final investment decision on Sarita Bay by 2019 or 2020, with first production targeted for 2024, he said. ...

John Jack, executive councillor with the Huu-ay-aht, said it's time the First Nation took its place within Canada and British Columbia.

"This is an example of a First Nation working with business and working with the people of B.C. and Canada in order to create value that fits both of our interests."

© The Canadian Press

ESSENCE OF THE STORY

- The Huu-ay-aht First Nation on Vancouver Island has approved a liquefied natural gas export facility on its traditional territories.
- Steelhead LNG will build and operate the facility.
- A new pipeline linking Vancouver Island and the B.C. mainland is a possible part of the plan.
- Production is targeted to start in 2024.

MyLab Economics Economics in the News

News-Based Problems and Applications

Just a sample of the topics covered in the 80 new news-based problems and applications include: Shrinking brick-and-mortar retail and expanding online shopping; Facebook and Google in the mobile ads market; U.S. tariffs on Canadian softwood lumber; data plans; tuition hikes; IKEA expanding in Edmonton; cap-and-trade auction; gig and sharing economy; and vinyl record stores in Toronto.

◆ Solving Teaching and Learning Challenges

To change the way students see the world: this is our goal in teaching economics, in writing this book, and in playing a major role in creating content for MyLab Economics.

Three facts about students are our guiding principles. First, they want to learn, but they are over-whelmed by the volume of claims on their time and energy. So, they must see the relevance to their lives and future careers of what they are being asked to learn. Second, students want to get it, and get it quickly. So, they must be presented with clear and succinct explanations. And third, students want to make sense of today's world and be better prepared for life after school. So, they must be shown how to apply the timeless principles of economics and its models to illuminate and provide a guide to understanding today's events and issues, and the future challenges they are likely to encounter.

The organization of this text and MyLab arise directly from these guiding principles. Each chapter begins with a clear statement of learning objectives that correspond to each chapter section.

The learning resources also arise directly from the three guiding principles, and we will describe them by placing them in five groups:

- Making economics real
- Learning the vocabulary
- Seeing the action and telling the story
- Learning interactively—learning by doing
- MyLab Economics

Making Economics Real

The student needs to see economics as a lens that sharpens the focus on real-world issues and events, and not as a series of logical exercises with no real purpose. *Economics in the News* and *At Issue* are designed to achieve this goal.

Each chapter opens with a student-friendly vignette that raises a question to motivate and focus the chapter. The chapter explains the principles, or model, that address the question and ends with an *Economics in the News* application that helps students to think like economists by connecting chapter tools and concepts to the world around them. All these news exercises are in MyLab with instant targeted feedback and auto-grading and constant uploading of new, current exercises.

In many chapters, an additional briefer *Economics in the News* (shown here) presents a short news clip, supplemented by data where needed, poses some questions, and walks through the answers.

ECONOMICS IN THE NEWS

The Market for Vanilla Bean

Price of Ice Cream Set to Spike
A poor harvest in Madagascar has exploded the price of vanilla bean, the flavouring in Canada's top ice cream.
Source: *The Toronto Star*, April 7, 2016

THE DATA

Year	Quantity of Vanilla Bean (billions of tonnes per year)	Price of Vanilla Bean (dollars per kilogram)
2015	7.6	70
2016	5.6	425

THE QUESTIONS
- What does the data table tell us?
- Why did the price of vanilla bean rise? Is it because demand changed or supply changed, and in which direction?

THE ANSWERS
- The data table tells us that during 2016, the quantity of vanilla bean produced increased and the price of vanilla bean increased sharply.
- An increase in demand brings an increase in the quantity and a rise in the price.
- A decrease in supply brings a decrease in the quantity and a rise in the price.
- Because the quantity of vanilla bean decreased and the price increased, there must have been a decrease in the supply of vanilla bean
- The supply of vanilla bean decreases if a poor harvest decreases production.
- The news clip says there was a poor harvest in Madagascar. This decrease in production brought a decrease in the supply of vanilla bean.
- The figure illustrates the market for vanilla bean in 2015 and 2016. The demand curve D shows the demand for vanilla bean.
- In 2015, the supply curve was S_{15}, the price was $70 per kilogram, and the quantity of vanilla bean traded was 7.6 billion tonnes.
- In 2016, the decreased production in Madagascar decreased the supply of vanilla bean to S_{16}.
- The price increased to $425 per kilogram and the quantity traded decreased to 5.6 billion tonnes.
- The higher price brought a decrease in the quantity of vanilla bean demanded, which is shown by the movement along the demand curve.

The Market for Vanilla Bean in 2015–2016

MyLab Economics Economics in the News

Six *At Issue* boxes, one of which is new, engage the student in debate and controversy. An *At Issue* box introduces an issue and then presents two opposing views. It leaves the matter unsettled so that students and the instructor can continue the argument in class and reach their own conclusions.

Economics in Action boxes make economics real by providing data and information that links models to real-world economic activity. Some of the issues covered in these boxes include the best affordable choice of recorded music; the low cost of making and the high cost of selling a pair of shoes; how Apple doesn't make the iPhone; opposing trends in air pollution and carbon concentration; price gouging; and taxing carbon emissions.

Interviews with leading economists, whose work correlates to what the student is learning, are the final component of making economics real. These interviews explore the education and research of prominent economists and their advice for those who want to continue studying the subject.

Learning the Vocabulary

Learning the vocabulary isn't exciting, but it is the vital first step to every discipline and it needs to be effective and quick. Highlighted key terms simplify this task. Each key term is defined in the sentence in which it is highlighted and appears in an end-of-chapter list and the end-of-book glossary (both with its page number); boldfaced in the index; and in MyLab Economics in a Flash Card tool and an auto-graded Key Terms Quiz with targeted student feedback.

Key Terms   MyLab Economics Key Terms Quiz

Change in demand, 62	Demand curve, 62	Quantity demanded, 61
Change in supply, 67	Equilibrium price, 70	Quantity supplied, 66
Change in the quantity demanded, 65	Equilibrium quantity, 70	Relative price, 60
	Inferior good, 64	Substitute, 63
Change in the quantity supplied, 68	Law of demand, 61	Supply, 66
Competitive market, 60	Law of supply, 66	Supply curve, 66
Complement, 63	Money price, 60	
Demand, 61	Normal good, 64	

Showing the Action and Telling the Story

Through the past nine editions, this book has set the standard of clarity in its diagrams; the tenth edition continues to uphold this tradition. Our goal is to show "where the economic action is." The diagrams in this book continue to generate an enormously positive response, which confirms our view that graphical analysis is the most powerful tool available for teaching and learning economics at the principles level.

Recognizing that some students find graphs hard to work with, we have developed the entire art program with the study and review needs of the student in mind.

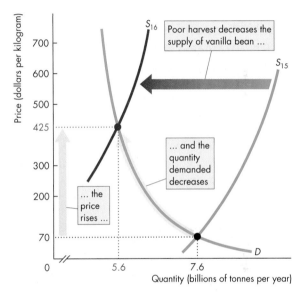

The Market for Vanilla Bean in 2015–2016

The diagrams feature

- Axes that measure and display concrete real-world data, and where possible and relevant, the most recent data
- Graphs paired with data tables from which curves are plotted
- Original curves consistently shown in blue
- Shifted curves, equilibrium points, and other important features highlighted in red
- Colour-blended arrows to indicate movement
- Diagrams labelled with boxed notes that tell the story
- Extended captions that make each diagram and its caption a self-contained object for study and review

Learning Interactively–Learning by Doing

At the end of every chapter section, a *Review Quiz* invites the student to rework the section with questions that cover the key ideas. A parallel set of questions in MyLab Study Plan enable the student to work the questions and get instant targeted feedback.

As part of the chapter review, the student has an opportunity to work a multi-part problem called *Worked Problem* that covers the core content of the chapter and consists of questions, solutions, key points, and a key figure. This feature increases the incentive for the student to learn-by-doing and review the chapter actively, rather than passively. The Worked Problems are available in MyLab Study Plan.

MyLab™ Economics

Reach Every Student with MyLab Economics

Pearson MyLab provides a rich menu of teaching and learning resources that support your course needs and serve the learning style of each individual student.

At the core of MyLab is the Study Plan, an online learning experience that continuously adapts to the student's individual performance. MyLab learning resources also include animations of textbook figures, student PowerPoint lecture notes, and Dynamic Study Modules.

Among MyLab's instructor tools are the Assignment Manager, which enables you to create homework, quiz, test, media, and experiment assignments; the Study Plan Manager, which lets you control chapter coverage; and the Gradebook, with which you can review and manage student results.

MyLab's weekly update of *Economics in the News* brings current issues to your classroom to motivate students, and exercises arising from these stories are available to be assigned and auto-graded.

Teach Your Course Your Way Your course is unique. So whether you'd like to build your own assignments, teach multiple sections, or set prerequisites, MyLab Economics gives you the flexibility to easily create *your* course to fit *your* needs.

Improve Student Results When you teach with MyLab, student performance improves. That's why instructors have chosen MyLab for over 15 years, touching the lives of over 50 million students.

Developing Employability Skills

The economic way of thinking is a foundational skill for citizenship and career. Every feature of the text helps the student develop this skill, repeatedly using its central ideas of tradeoff; opportunity cost; the margin; incentives; the gains from voluntary exchange; the forces of demand, supply, and equilibrium; the pursuit of economic rent; and the tension between self-interest and the social interest.

The new section of Chapter 1, "Economists in the Economy," identifies a further five general skills that are crucial for getting a job and developing a successful career. The table lists these skills and the features of this text that promote them.

CAREER SKILLS AND THE FEATURES THAT PROMOTE THEM

Skill	Feature
Critical thinking	Economics in the News
	At Issue
Analytical skills	The economic way of thinking
	Manipulation of models
	Application of models
	Graphical analysis
Math skills	Math appendices
Writing skills	Review Quiz and end-of-chapter problems and applications as short-answer written assignments
Oral communication skills	Economics in the News and At Issue as topics for classroom discussion and debate

Table of Contents Overview and Flexibility

You have preferences for how you want to teach your course, and we've organized this book to enable you to choose your teaching path. The chart on p. xii illustrates the book's flexibility. By following the arrows through the chart you can select the path that best fits your preference for course structure. Whether you want to teach a traditional course that blends theory and policy, or one that takes a fasttrack through either theory or policy issues, this text gives you the choice.

Instructor Teaching Resources

The program comes with the following teaching resources.

Supplements available to instructors at www.pearsonhighered.com/irc	Features of the Supplement
Instructor's Manual *Microeconomics* Instructor's Manual	• Chapter-by-chapter overviews • List of what's new in the tenth edition • Ready-to-use lecture notes
Solutions Manual *Microeconomics* Solutions Manual by Jeannie Shearer, University of Western Ontario	• Solutions to Review Quizzes • Solutions to the end-of-chapter Study Plan Problems and Applications • Solutions to the end-of-chapter Additional Problems and Applications

Test Bank New questions for the *Microeconomics* Test Bank by Jeannie Shearer, University of Western Ontario Jeannie reviewed all questions to ensure their clarity and consistency	• Nearly 5,000 multiple-choice, true/false, short-answer, and graphing questions with these annotations:
	  ▪ Difficulty level (1 for straight recall, 2 for some analysis, 3 for complex analysis)
	  ▪ Type (Multiple-choice, true/false, short-answer, essay)
	  ▪ Topic (the chapter section the question supports)

Computerized TestGen	• TestGen enables instructors to:
	  ▪ Customize, save, and generate classroom tests
	  ▪ Edit, add, or delete questions from the Test Item Files
	  ▪ Analyze test results
	  ▪ Organize a database of tests and student results

PowerPoints	• Slides include:
	  ▪ Lectures with the textbook figures and tables animated and speaking notes from the Instructor's Manual
	  ▪ Large-scale versions of all textbook figures and tables animated for instructors to incorporate into their own slide shows
	• A student version of the lectures with animated textbook figures and tables
	• Accessibility PowerPoints meet standards for students with disabilities. Features include, but are not limited to:
	  ▪ Keyboard and screen reader access
	  ▪ Alternative text for images
	  ▪ High colour contrast between the background and foreground

◆ Acknowledgments

We thank our current and former colleagues and friends at the University of Western Ontario who have taught us so much. They are Jim Davies, Jeremy Greenwood, Ig Horstmann, Peter Howitt, Greg Huffman, David Laidler, Phil Reny, Chris Robinson, John Whalley, and Ron Wonnacott.

We also thank Doug McTaggart and Christopher Findlay, coauthors of the Australian edition, and Melanie Powell and Kent Matthews, coauthors of the European edition. Suggestions arising from their adaptations of earlier editions have been helpful to us in preparing this edition.

We thank the several thousand students whom we have been privileged to teach. The instant response that comes from the look of puzzlement or enlightenment has taught us how to teach economics.

We thank the management team at Pearson Canada who have built a culture that brings out the best in its editors and authors. They are Marlene Olsavsky, General Manager Higher Education, and Anne Williams, Vice President, Editorial, Higher Education. It is a special joy to thank the outstanding editors, media specialists, and others at Pearson Canada who contributed to the concerted publishing effort that brought this edition to completion. They are Emily Dill, Content Manager; Avinash Chandra, Lead Project Manager; Leanne Rancourt, Developmental Editor; Nicole Mellow, Digital Content Manager; Joanne Tang, Permissions Project Manager; Susan Bindernagel, Copy Editor; and Leigh-Anne Graham, Marketing Manager.

Leanne Rancourt was our lifeline. She kept the production process on track, provided outstanding management, and gave our manuscript a most thorough proofread and accuracy check.

Anthony Leung designed the cover and package and yet again surpassed the challenge of ensuring that we meet the highest design standards.

We thank the many exceptional reviewers who have shared their insights through the various editions of this book. Their contribution has been invaluable.

We thank the people who work directly with us. Jeannie Shearer and Sharmistha Nag provided research assistance and created exercises for MyLab Economics. Richard Parkin created the electronic art files and offered many ideas that improved the figures in this book.

Classroom experience will test the value of this book. We would appreciate hearing from instructors and students about how we can continue to improve it in future editions.

Michael Parkin
mparkin@uwo.ca

Robin Bade
robin@econ100.com

◆ Reviewers

Syed Ahmed, Red Deer Community College
Ather H. Akbari, Saint Mary's University
Doug Allen, Simon Fraser University
Benjamin Amoah, University of Guelph
Torben Andersen, Red Deer College
Terri Anderson, Fanshawe College
Syed Ashan, Concordia University
Fred Aswani, McMaster University
Iris Au, University of Toronto, Scarborough
Keith Baxter, Bishop's University
Andy Baziliauskas, University of Winnipeg
Dick Beason, University of Alberta
Karl Bennett, University of Waterloo
Ronald Bodkin, University of Ottawa
Caroline Boivin, Concordia University
Paul Booth, University of Alberta
John Boyd, University of British Columbia
John Brander, University of New Brunswick
Larry Brown, Selkirk College
Sam Bucovetsky, York University
Bogdan Buduru, Concordia University
Lutz-Alexander Busch, University of Waterloo
Beverly J. Cameron, University of Manitoba
Norman Cameron, University of Manitoba
Emanuel Carvalho, University of Waterloo
Francois Casas, University of Toronto
Alan Tak Yan Chan, Atlantic Baptist University
Robert Cherneff, University of Victoria
Jason Childs, University of New Brunswick, Saint John
Saud Choudhry, Trent University
Louis Christofides, University of Guelph
Kam Hon Chu, Memorial University of Newfoundland
George Churchman, University of Manitoba
Avi J. Cohen, York University
Constantin Colonescu, Grant MacEwan University
Ryan A. Compton, University of Manitoba
Marilyn Cottrell, Brock University
Rosilyn Coulson, Douglas College
Brian Coulter, University College of the Fraser Valley
Stanya Cunningham, Concordia University College of Alberta
Douglas Curtis, Trent University
Garth Davies, Olds College
Ajit Dayanandan, University of Northern British Columbia
Carol Derksen, Red River College
David Desjardins, John Abbott College
Vaughan Dickson, University of New Brunswick (Fredericton)
Livio Di Matteo, Lakehead University
Mohammed Dore, Brock University
Torben Drewes, Trent University
Byron Eastman, Laurentian University
Fahira Eston, Humber College

Sigrid Ewender, Kwantlen Polytechnic University
Brian Ferguson, University of Guelph
Len Fitzpatrick, Carleton University
Peter Fortura, Algonquin College
Oliver Franke, Athabasca University
Bruno Fullone, George Brown College
Donald Garrie, Georgian College
Philippe Ghayad, Dawson College and Concordia University
David Gray, University of Ottawa
Sandra Hadersbeck, Okanagan College
Rod Hill, University of New Brunswick
Eric Kam, Ryerson University
Susan Kamp, University of Alberta
Cevat Burc Kayahan, University of Guelph
Peter Kennedy, Simon Fraser University
Harvey King, University of Regina
Patricia Koss, Concordia University
Robert Kunimoto, Mt. Royal University
David Johnson, Wilfrid Laurier University
Cliff Jutlah, York University, Glendon Campus
Michael G. Lanyi, University of Lethbridge
Eva Lau, University of Waterloo
Gordon Lee, University of Alberta
Byron Lew, Trent University
Anastasia M. Lintner, University of Guelph
Scott Lynch, Memorial University
Dan MacKay, SIAST
Leigh MacDonald, University of Western Ontario
Keith MacKinnon, York University
Mohammad Mahbobi, Thompson Rivers University
S. Manchouri, University of Alberta
Christian Marfels, Dalhousie University
Raimo Martalla, Malaspina University College
Perry Martens, University of Regina
Roberto Martínez-Espíneira, St. Francis Xavier University
Dennis McGuire, Okanagan University College
Rob Moir, University of New Brunswick, Saint John
Saeed Moshiri, University of Manitoba
Joseph Muldoon, Trent University
David Murrell, University of New Brunswick, Fredericton
Robin Neill, Carleton University
A. Gyasi Nimarko, Vanier College
Sonia Novkovic, Saint Mary's University
John O'Brien, Concordia University
Arne Paus-Jenssen, University of Saskatchewan
Andrea Podhorsky, York University
Derek Pyne, Memorial University of Newfoundland
Stephen Rakoczy, Humber College
Don Reddick, Kwantlen University College
June Riley, John Abbott College
E. Riser, Memorial University
Roberta Robb, Brock University
Nick Rowe, Carleton University

Michael Rushton, University of Regina

Balbir Sahni, Concordia University

Brian Scarfe, University of Regina

Marlyce Searcy, SIAST Palliser

Jim Sentance, University of Prince Edward Island

Lance Shandler, Kwantlen University College

Stan Shedd, University of Calgary

Chandan Shirvaikar, Red Deer College

Peter Sinclair, Wilfrid Laurier University

Ian Skaith, Fanshawe College

Scott Skjei, Acadia University

Judith Skuce, Georgian College

George Slasor, University of Toronto

Norman Smith, Georgian College

Bert Somers, John Abbott College

Lewis Soroka, Brock University

Glen Stirling, University of Western Ontario

Brennan Thompson, Ryerson University

Irene Trela, University of Western Ontario

Russell Uhler, University of British Columbia

Brian VanBlarcom, Acadia University

Marianne Vigneault, Bishop's University

Jane Waples, Memorial University of Newfoundland

Tony Ward, Brock University

Bruce Wilkinson, University of Alberta

Christopher Willmore, University of Victoria

Andrew Wong, Grant MacEwan University

Peter Wylie, University of British Columbia, Okanagan

Arthur Younger, Humber College Institute of Technology and Advanced Learning

Ayoub Yousefi, University of Western Ontario

Weiqiu Yu, University of New Brunswick, Fredericton

PARKIN ◆ BADE

MICROECONOMICS

CANADA IN THE GLOBAL ENVIRONMENT TENTH EDITION

1

WHAT IS ECONOMICS?

After studying this chapter, you will be able to:

- ◆ Define economics and distinguish between microeconomics and macroeconomics
- ◆ Explain the two big questions of economics
- ◆ Explain the key ideas that define the economic way of thinking
- ◆ Explain how economists go about their work as social scientists and policy advisers
- ◆ Describe the jobs available to the graduates of a major in economics

Is economics about money: How people make it and spend it? Is it about business, government, and jobs? Is it about why some people and some nations are rich and others poor? Economics is about all these things. But its core is the study of *choices* and their *consequences*.

Your life will be shaped by the choices that you make and the challenges that you face. To face those challenges and seize the opportunities they present, you must understand the powerful forces at play. The economics that you're about to learn will become your most reliable guide. This chapter gets you started by describing the questions that economists try to answer and looking at how economists think as they search for the answers.

1

◆ Definition of Economics

A fundamental fact dominates our lives: We want more than we can get. Our inability to get everything we want is called **scarcity**. Scarcity is universal. It confronts all living things. Even parrots face scarcity!

Not only do I want a cracker—we all want a cracker!

© The New Yorker Collection 1985
Frank Modell from cartoonbank.com. All Rights Reserved.

Think about the things that *you* want and the scarcity that *you* face. You want to go to a good school, college, or university. You want to live in a well-equipped, spacious, and comfortable home. You want the latest smartphone and the fastest Internet connection for your laptop or iPad. You want some sports and recreational gear—perhaps some new running shoes, or a new bike. You want much more time than is available to go to class, do your homework, play sports and games, read novels, go to the movies, listen to music, travel, and hang out with your friends. And you want to live a long and healthy life.

What you can afford to buy is limited by your income and by the prices you must pay. And your time is limited by the fact that your day has 24 hours.

You want some other things that only governments provide. You want to live in a safe neighbourhood in a peaceful and secure world, and enjoy the benefits of clean air, lakes, rivers, and oceans.

What governments can afford is limited by the taxes they collect. Taxes lower people's incomes and compete with the other things they want to buy.

What *everyone* can get—what *society* can get—is limited by the productive resources available. These resources are the gifts of nature, human labour and ingenuity, and all the previously produced tools and equipment.

Because we can't get everything we want, we must make *choices*. You can't afford *both* a laptop *and* an iPhone, so you must *choose* which one to buy. You can't spend tonight *both* studying for your next test *and* going to the movies, so again, you must *choose* which one to do. Governments can't spend a tax dollar on *both* national defence *and* environmental protection, so they must *choose* how to spend that dollar.

Your choices must somehow be made consistent with the choices of *others*. If you choose to buy a laptop, someone else must choose to sell it. Incentives reconcile choices. An **incentive** is a reward that encourages an action or a penalty that discourages one. Prices act as incentives. If the price of a laptop is too high, more will be offered for sale than people want to buy. And if the price is too low, fewer will be offered for sale than people want to buy. But there is a price at which choices to buy and sell are consistent.

> **Economics** is the social science that studies the *choices* that individuals, businesses, governments, and entire societies make as they cope with *scarcity* and the *incentives* that influence and reconcile those choices.

The subject has two parts:

- Microeconomics
- Macroeconomics

Microeconomics is the study of the choices that individuals and businesses make, the way these choices interact in markets, and the influence of governments. Some examples of microeconomic questions are: Why are people downloading more movies? How would a tax on e-commerce affect eBay?

Macroeconomics is the study of the performance of the national economy and the global economy. Some examples of macroeconomic questions are: Why does the Canadian unemployment rate fluctuate? Can the Bank of Canada make the unemployment rate fall by keeping interest rates low?

◆ REVIEW QUIZ

1 List some examples of the scarcity that you face.
2 Find examples of scarcity in today's headlines.
3 Find an example of the distinction between microeconomics and macroeconomics in today's headlines.

Work these questions in Study Plan 1.1 and get instant feedback.   MyLab Economics

◆ Two Big Economic Questions

Two big questions summarize the scope of economics:

- How do choices end up determining *what, how*, and *for whom* goods and services are produced?
- Do choices made in the pursuit of *self-interest* also promote the *social interest*?

What, How, and For Whom?

Goods and services are the objects that people value and produce to satisfy wants. *Goods* are physical objects such as cellphones and automobiles. *Services* are tasks performed for people such as cellphone service and auto-repair service.

What? *What* we produce varies across countries and changes over time. In Canada today, agriculture accounts for 2 percent of total production, manufactured goods for 28 percent, and services (retail and wholesale trade, healthcare, and education are the biggest ones) for 70 percent. In contrast, in China today, agriculture accounts for 8 percent of total production, manufactured goods for 41 percent, and services for 51 percent.

Figure 1.1 shows these numbers and also the percentages for China, which fall between those for the Canada and Ethiopia.

What determines these patterns of production? How do choices end up determining the quantities of cellphones, automobiles, cellphone service, auto-repair service, and the millions of other items that are produced in Canada and around the world?

How? *How* we produce is described by the technologies and resources that we use. The resources used to produce goods and services are called **factors of production**, which are grouped into four categories:

- Land
- Labour
- Capital
- Entrepreneurship

Land The "gifts of nature" that we use to produce goods and services are called **land**. In economics, *land* is what in everyday language we call *natural resources*. It includes land in the everyday sense

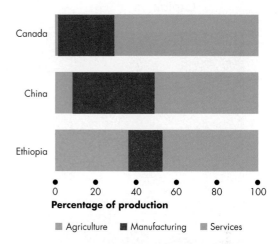

FIGURE 1.1 What Three Countries Produce

Percentage of production

▪ Agriculture ▪ Manufacturing ▪ Services

Agriculture and manufacturing are small percentages of production in rich countries such as Canada and large percentages of production in poorer countries such as Ethiopia. Most of what is produced in Canada is services.

Source of data: CIA Factbook 2016, Central Intelligence Agency.

MyLab Economics Animation

together with minerals, oil, gas, coal, water, air, forests, and fish.

Our land surface and water resources are renewable, and some of our mineral resources can be recycled. But the resources that we use to create energy are nonrenewable—they can be used only once.

Labour The work time and work effort that people devote to producing goods and services is called **labour**. Labour includes the physical and mental efforts of all the people who work on farms and construction sites and in factories, shops, and offices.

The *quality* of labour depends on **human capital**, which is the knowledge and skill that people obtain from education, on-the-job training, and work experience. You are building your own human capital right now as you work on your economics course, and your human capital will continue to grow as you gain work experience.

Human capital expands over time. Today, 95 percent of the adult population of Canada have completed high school and 25 percent have a college or university degree. Figure 1.2 shows these measures of human capital in Canada and its growth over the past 41 years.

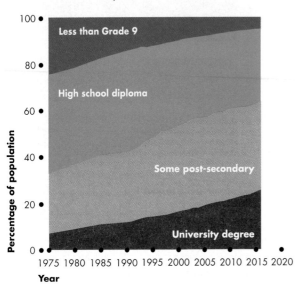

FIGURE 1.2 A Measure of Human Capital

In 2016, 25.3 percent of the adult population had a university degree. A further 38.4 percent had some post-secondary education, and 94.8 percent had completed high school.

Source of data: Statistics Canada.

MyLab Economics Animation

Capital The tools, instruments, machines, buildings, and other constructions that businesses use to produce goods and services are called **capital**.

In everyday language, we talk about money, stocks, and bonds as being "capital." These items are *financial capital*. Financial capital plays an important role in enabling businesses to borrow the funds that they use to buy physical capital. But financial capital is not used to produce goods and services and it is not a factor of production.

Entrepreneurship The human resource that organizes labour, land, and capital is called **entrepreneurship**. Entrepreneurs are the drivers of economic progress. They develop new ideas about what and how to produce, make business decisions, and bear the risks that arise from these decisions.

What determines how the factors of production are used to produce each good and service?

For Whom? *Who* consumes the goods and services that are produced depends on the incomes that people earn. People with large incomes can buy

a wide range of goods and services. People with small incomes have fewer options and can afford a smaller range of goods and services.

People earn their incomes by selling the services of the factors of production they own:

- Land earns **rent**.
- Labour earns **wages**.
- Capital earns **interest**.
- Entrepreneurship earns **profit**.

Which factor of production earns the most income? The answer is labour. Wages and fringe benefits are around 70 percent of total income, and the incomes from land, capital, and entrepreneurship share the rest. These shares have been remarkably constant over time.

Knowing how income is shared among the factors of production doesn't tell us how it is shared among individuals. And the distribution of income among individuals is extremely unequal. You know of some people who earn very large incomes: Dwayne "The Rock" Johnson (Hercules) earned $64.5 million in 2016; and Canadian Shea Weber of the Montreal Canadiens earned $16 million in 2017.

You know of even more people who earn very small incomes. Servers at Tim Hortons, grocery store cashiers, cleaners, and janitors all earn the provincial minimum wage.

You probably know about other persistent differences in incomes. Men, on average, earn more than women; whites earn more than minorities; university graduates earn more than high school graduates.

We can get a good sense of who consumes the goods and services produced by looking at the percentages of total income earned by different groups of people. The 20 percent of people with the lowest incomes earn about 5 percent of total income, while the richest 20 percent earn close to 50 percent of total income. So on average, people in the richest 20 percent earn more than 10 times the incomes of those in the poorest 20 percent. There is even huge inequality within the richest 20 percent, and the top 1 percent earns almost 15 percent of total income.

Why is the distribution of income so unequal?

Economics provides some answers to all these questions about *what, how*, and *for whom* goods and services are produced and much of the rest of this book will help you to understand those answers.

We're now going to look at the second big question of economics: Do choices made in the pursuit of self-interest also promote the social interest?

Do Choices Made in the Pursuit of Self-Interest also Promote the Social Interest?

Every day, you and 35.4 million other Canadians, along with 7.2 billion people in the rest of the world, make economic choices that result in *what, how*, and *for whom* goods and services are produced. These choices are made by people who are pursuing their self-interest.

Self-Interest You make a choice in your **self-interest** if you think that choice is the best one available for you. All the choices that people make about how to use their time and other resources are made in the pursuit of self-interest. When you allocate your time or your budget, you do what makes the most sense to you. You might think about how your choices affect other people and take into account how you feel about that, but it is how *you* feel that influences your choice. You order a home-delivery pizza because you're hungry, not because the delivery person needs a job. And when the pizza delivery person shows up at your door, he's not doing you a favour. He's pursuing *his* self-interest and hoping for a tip and another call next week.

The big question is: Is it possible that all the choices that each one of us makes in the pursuit of self-interest could end up achieving an outcome that is best for everyone?

Social Interest An outcome is in the **social interest** if it is best for society as a whole. It is easy to see how you decide what is in *your* self-interest. But how do we decide if something is in the social interest? To help you answer this question, imagine a scene like that in *Economics in the News* on p. 6.

Ted, an entrepreneur, creates a new business. He hires a thousand workers and pays them $20 an hour, $1 an hour more than they earned in their old jobs. Ted's business is extremely profitable and his own earnings increase by $1 million per week.

You can see that Ted's decision to create the business is in his self-interest—he gains $1 million a week. You can also see that for Ted's employees, their decisions to work for Ted are in their self-interest—they gain $1 an hour (say $40 a week). And the decisions of Ted's customers must be in their self-interest, otherwise they wouldn't buy from him. But is this outcome in the social interest?

The economist's answer is "Yes." It is in the social interest because it makes everyone better off. There are no losers.

Efficiency and the Social Interest Economists use the everyday word "efficient" to describe a situation that can't be improved upon. Resource use is **efficient** if it is *not* possible to make someone better off without making someone else worse off. If it *is* possible to make someone better off without making anyone worse off, society can be made better off and the situation is not efficient.

In the Ted story everyone is better off, so it improves efficiency and the outcome is in the social interest. But notice that it would also have been efficient if the workers and customers had gained nothing and Ted had gained even more than $1 million a week. But would that efficient outcome be in the social interest?

Many people have trouble seeing the outcome in which Ted is the only winner as being in the social interest. They say that the social interest requires Ted to share some of his gain either with his workers in higher wages or with his customers in lower prices, or with both groups.

Fair Shares and the Social Interest The idea that the social interest requires "fair shares" is a deeply held one. Think about what you regard as a fair share. To help you, imagine the following game.

I put $100 on the table and tell someone you don't know and who doesn't know you to *propose* a share of the money between the two of you. If you *accept* the proposed share, you each get the agreed shares. If you don't accept the proposed share, you both get nothing.

It would be efficient—you would both be better off—if the proposer offered to take $99 and leave you with $1 and you accepted that offer.

But would you accept the $1? If you are like most people, the idea that the other person gets 99 times as much as you is just too much to stomach. "No way," you say and the $100 disappears. That outcome is inefficient. You have both given up something.

When the game I've just described is played in a classroom experiment, about half of the players reject offers of below $30.

So fair shares matter. But what is *fair*? There isn't a crisp definition of fairness to match that of efficiency. Reasonable people have a variety of views about it. Almost everyone agrees that too much inequality is unfair. But how much is too much? And inequality of what: income, wealth, or the *opportunity* to work, earn an income, and accumulate wealth?

You will examine efficiency again in Chapter 2 and efficiency and fairness in Chapter 5.

Questions about the social interest are hard ones to answer and they generate discussion, debate, and disagreement. Four issues in today's world put some flesh on these questions. The issues are:

- Globalization
- Information-age monopolies
- Climate change
- Economic instability

Globalization The term *globalization* means the expansion of international trade, borrowing and lending, and investment.

When Nike produces sports shoes, people in Malaysia get work; and when China Airlines buys new regional jets, Canadians who work at Bombardier build them. While globalization brings expanded production and job opportunities for some workers, it destroys many Canadian jobs. Workers across the manufacturing industries must learn new skills or take service jobs, which often pay less, or retire earlier than previously planned.

Globalization is in the self-interest of those consumers who buy low-cost goods and services produced in other countries; and it is in the self-interest of the multinational firms that produce in low-cost regions and sell in high-price regions. But is globalization in the self-interest of the low-wage worker in Malaysia who sews your new running shoes and the displaced shoemaker in Toronto? Is it in the social interest?

◆ ECONOMICS IN THE NEWS

The Invisible Hand

From Brewer to Bio-Tech Entrepreneur

Kiran Mazumdar-Shaw trained to become a master brewer and learned about enzymes, the stuff from which bio-pharmaceuticals are made. Discovering it was impossible for a woman in India to become a master brewer, the 25-year-old Kiran decided to create a bio-pharmaceutical business.

Kiran's firm, Biocom, employed uneducated workers who loved their jobs and the living conditions made possible by their high wages. But when a labour union entered the scene and unionized the workers, a furious Kiran fired the workers, automated their jobs, and hired a smaller number of educated workers. Biocom continued to grow and today, Kiran's wealth exceeds $1 billion.

Kiran has become wealthy by developing and producing bio-pharmaceuticals that improve people's lives. But Kiran is sharing her wealth in creative ways. She has opened a cancer treatment centre to help thousands of patients who are too poor to pay and created a health insurance scheme.

Source: Ariel Levy, "Drug Test," *The New Yorker*, January 2, 2012.

THE QUESTIONS

- Whose decisions in the story were taken in self-interest?
- Whose decisions turned out to be in the social interest?
- Did any of the decisions harm the social interest?

THE ANSWERS

- All the decisions—Kiran's, the workers', the union's, and the firm's customers'—are taken in the pursuit of self-interest.
- Kiran's decisions serve the social interest: She creates jobs that benefit her workers and products that benefit her customers. And her charitable work brings yet further social benefits.
- The labour union's decision might have harmed the social interest because it destroyed the jobs of uneducated workers.

KIRAN MAZUMDAR-SHAW, FOUNDER AND CEO OF BIOCOM

Information-Age Monopolies The technological change of the past forty years has been called the *Information Revolution*. Bill Gates, a co-founder of Microsoft, held a privileged position in this revolution. For many years, Windows was the only available operating system for the PC. The PC and Mac competed, but the PC had a huge market share.

An absence of competition gave Microsoft the power to sell Windows at prices far above the cost of production. With lower prices, many more people would have been able to afford and buy a computer.

The information revolution has clearly served your self-interest: It has provided your cellphone, laptop, loads of handy applications, and the Internet. It has also served the self-interest of Bill Gates who has seen his wealth soar.

But did the information revolution best serve the social interest? Did Microsoft produce the best possible Windows operating system and sell it at a price that was in the social interest? Or was the quality too low and the price too high?

Climate Change Burning fossil fuels to generate electricity and to power airplanes, automobiles, and trucks pours a staggering 28 billion tonnes—4 tonnes per person—of carbon dioxide into the atmosphere each year. These carbon emissions, two-thirds of which come from the United States, China, the European Union, Russia, and India, bring global warming and climate change.

Every day, when you make self-interested choices to use electricity and gasoline, you leave your carbon footprint. You can lessen this footprint by walking, riding a bike, taking a cold shower, or planting a tree.

But can each one of us be relied upon to make decisions that affect the Earth's carbon-dioxide concentration in the social interest? Must governments change the incentives we face so that our self-interested choices are also in the social interest? How can governments change incentives? How can we

encourage the use of wind and solar power to replace the burning of fossil fuels that brings climate change?

Economic Instability In 2008, U.S. banks were in trouble. They had made loans that borrowers couldn't repay and they were holding securities the values of which had crashed.

Banks' choices to take deposits and make loans are made in self-interest, but does this lending and borrowing serve the social interest? Do banks lend too much in the pursuit of profit?

When U.S. banks got into trouble in 2008, the U.S. Federal Reserve (the Fed) bailed them out with big loans backed by taxpayer dollars. Did the Fed's bailout of troubled banks serve the social interest? Or might the Fed's rescue action encourage banks to repeat their dangerous lending in the future?

We've looked at four topics and asked many questions that illustrate the potential conflict between the pursuit of self-interest and the social interest. We've asked questions but not answered them because we've not yet explained the economic principles needed to do so. We answer these questions in future chapters.

◆ **REVIEW QUIZ**

1 Describe the broad facts about *what*, *how*, and *for whom* goods and services are produced.
2 Use headlines from the recent news to illustrate the potential for conflict between self-interest and the social interest.

Work these questions in Study Plan 1.2 and get instant feedback.　　MyLab Economics

AT **ISSUE**

The Protest Against Market Capitalism

Market capitalism is an economic system in which individuals own land and capital and are free to buy and sell land, capital, and goods and services in markets. Markets for goods and services, along with markets for land and capital, coordinate billions of self-interested choices, which determine what, how, and for whom goods and services are produced. A few people earn enormous incomes, many times the average income. There is no supreme planner guiding the use of scarce resources, and the outcome is unintended and unforeseeable.

Centrally planned socialism is an economic system in which the government owns all the land and capital, directs workers to jobs, and decides what, how, and for whom to produce. The Soviet Union, several Eastern European countries, and China have used this system in the past but have now abandoned it. Only Cuba and North Korea use this system today. A few bureaucrats in positions of great power receive huge incomes, many times that of an average person.

Our economy today is a **mixed economy**, which is market capitalism with government regulation.

The Protest

The protest against market capitalism takes many forms. Historically, **Karl Marx** and other communist and socialist thinkers wanted to replace it with *socialism* and *central planning*. Today, thousands of people who feel let down by the economic system want less market capitalism and more government regulation. The **Occupy Wall Street** movement, with its focus on the large incomes of the top 1 percent, is a visible example of today's protest. Protesters say:

- Big corporations (especially big banks) have too much power and influence on governments.

- Democratically elected governments can do a better job of allocating resources and distributing income than uncoordinated markets.

- More regulation in the social interest is needed—to serve "human need, not corporate greed."

- In a market, for every winner, there is a loser.

- Big corporations are the winners. Workers and unemployed people are the losers.

The Economist's Response

Economists agree that market capitalism isn't perfect. But they argue that it is the best system available and while some government intervention and regulation can help, government attempts to serve the social interest often end up harming it.

Adam Smith (see p. 57), who gave the first systematic account of how market capitalism works, says:

- The self-interest of big corporations is *maximum profit*.

- But an *invisible hand* leads production decisions made in pursuit of self-interest to *unintentionally* promote the social interest.

- Politicians are ill-equipped to regulate corporations or to intervene in markets, and those who think they can improve on the market outcome are most likely wrong.

- In a market, buyers get what they want for less than they would be willing to pay and sellers earn a profit. Both buyers and sellers gain. A market transaction is a "win-win" event.

An Occupy Wall Street protester

"It is not from the benevolence of the butcher, the brewer, or the baker that we expect our dinner, but from their regard to their own interest."
The Wealth of Nations, 1776

Adam Smith

◆ The Economic Way of Thinking

The questions that economics tries to answer tell us about the *scope of economics,* but they don't tell us how economists *think* and go about seeking answers to these questions. You're now going to see how economists go about their work.

We're going to look at six key ideas that define the *economic way of thinking.* These ideas are:

- A choice is a *tradeoff.*
- People make *rational choices* by comparing *benefits* and *costs.*
- *Benefit* is what you gain from something.
- *Cost* is what you *must give up* to get something.
- Most choices are *"how-much"* choices made at the *margin.*
- Choices respond to *incentives.*

A Choice Is a Tradeoff

Because we face scarcity, we must make choices. And when we make a choice, we select from the available alternatives. For example, you can spend Saturday night studying for your next test or having fun with your friends, but you can't do both of these activities at the same time. You must choose how much time to devote to each. Whatever choice you make, you could have chosen something else.

You can think about your choices as tradeoffs. A **tradeoff** is an exchange—giving up one thing to get something else. When you choose how to spend your Saturday night, you face a tradeoff between studying and hanging out with your friends.

Making a Rational Choice

Economists view the choices that people make as rational. A **rational choice** is one that compares costs and benefits and achieves the greatest benefit over cost for the person making the choice.

Only the wants of the person making a choice are relevant to determine its rationality. For example, you might like your coffee black and strong but your friend prefers his milky and sweet. So it is rational for you to choose espresso and for your friend to choose cappuccino.

The idea of rational choice provides an answer to the first question: *What* goods and services will be produced and in what quantities? The answer is those that people rationally choose to buy!

But how do people choose rationally? Why do more people choose an iPhone rather than a Black-Berry? Why don't CN and CPR build high-speed tracks so that VIA Rail can run Bombardier super-fast trains like those used in Europe? The answers turn on comparing benefits and costs.

Benefit: What You Gain

The **benefit** of something is the gain or pleasure that it brings and is determined by **preferences**—by what a person likes and dislikes and the intensity of those feelings. If you get a huge kick out of "Leagues of Legends," that video game brings you a large benefit. And if you have little interest in listening to Yo-Yo Ma playing a Vivaldi cello concerto, that activity brings you a small benefit.

Some benefits are large and easy to identify, such as the benefit that you get from being in school. A big piece of that benefit is the goods and services that you will be able to enjoy with the boost to your earning power when you graduate. Some benefits are small, such as the benefit you get from a slice of pizza.

Economists measure benefit as the most that a person is *willing to give up* to get something. You are willing to give up a lot to be in school. But you would give up only an iTunes download for a slice of pizza.

Cost: What You *Must* Give Up

The **opportunity cost** of something is the highest-valued alternative that must be given up to get it.

To make the idea of opportunity cost concrete, think about *your* opportunity cost of being in school. It has two components: the things you can't afford to buy and the things you can't do with your time.

Start with the things you can't afford to buy. You've spent all your income on tuition, residence fees, books, and a laptop. If you weren't in school, you would have spent this money on tickets to ball games and movies and all the other things that you enjoy. But that's only the start of your opportunity cost.

You've also given up the opportunity to get a job and earn an income. Suppose that the best job you could get if you weren't in school is working at CIBC as a teller earning $25,000 a year. Another part of your opportunity cost of being in school is all the things that you could buy with the extra $25,000 you would have.

As you well know, being a student eats up many hours in class time, doing homework assignments, preparing for tests, and so on. To do all these school activities, you must give up many hours of what would otherwise be leisure time spent with your friends.

So the opportunity cost of being in school is all the good things that you can't afford and don't have the spare time to enjoy. You might want to put a dollar value on that cost or you might just list all the items that make up the opportunity cost.

The examples of opportunity cost that we've just considered are all-or-nothing costs—you're either in school or not in school. Most situations are not like this one. They involve choosing *how much* of an activity to do.

How Much? Choosing at the Margin

You can allocate the next hour between studying and chatting online with your friends, but the choice is not all or nothing. You must decide how many minutes to allocate to each activity. To make this decision, you compare the benefit of a little bit more study time with its cost—you make your choice at the **margin**.

The benefit that arises from an increase in an activity is called **marginal benefit**. For example, your marginal benefit from one more night of study before a test is the boost it gives to your grade. Your marginal benefit doesn't include the grade you're already achieving without that extra night of work.

The *opportunity cost* of an *increase* in an activity is called **marginal cost**. For you, the marginal cost of studying one more night is the cost of not spending that night on your favourite leisure activity.

To make your decisions, you compare marginal benefit and marginal cost. If the marginal benefit from an extra night of study exceeds its marginal cost, you study the extra night. If the marginal cost exceeds the marginal benefit, you don't study the extra night.

Choices Respond to Incentives

Economists take human nature as given and view people as acting in their self-interest. All people—you, other consumers, producers, politicians, and public servants—pursue their self-interest.

Self-interested actions are not necessarily *selfish* actions. You might decide to use your resources in ways that bring pleasure to others as well as to yourself. But a self-interested act gets the most benefit for *you* based on *your* view about benefit.

The central idea of economics is that we can predict the self-interested choices that people make by looking at the *incentives* they face. People undertake those activities for which marginal benefit exceeds marginal cost; they reject options for which marginal cost exceeds marginal benefit.

For example, your economics instructor gives you a problem set and tells you these problems will be on the next test. Your marginal benefit from working these problems is large, so you diligently work them. In contrast, your math instructor gives you a problem set on a topic that she says will never be on a test. You get little marginal benefit from working these problems, so you decide to skip most of them.

Economists see incentives as the key to reconciling self-interest and social interest. When our choices are *not* in the social interest, it is because of the incentives we face. One of the challenges for economists is to figure out the incentives that result in self-interested choices being in the social interest.

Economists emphasize the crucial role that institutions play in influencing the incentives that people face as they pursue their self-interest. Laws that protect private property and markets that enable voluntary exchange are the fundamental institutions. You will learn as you progress with your study of economics that where these institutions exist, self-interest can indeed promote the social interest.

REVIEW QUIZ

1 Explain the idea of a tradeoff and think of three tradeoffs that you have made today.
2 Explain what economists mean by rational choice and think of three choices that you've made today that are rational.
3 Explain why opportunity cost is the best forgone alternative and provide examples of some opportunity costs that you have faced today.
4 Explain what it means to choose at the margin and illustrate with three choices at the margin that you have made today.
5 Explain why choices respond to incentives and think of three incentives to which you have responded today.

Work these questions in Study Plan 1.3 and get instant feedback.   MyLab Economics

◆ Economics as Social Science and Policy Tool

Economics is both a social science and a toolkit for advising on policy decisions.

Economist as Social Scientist

As social scientists, economists seek to discover how the economic world works. In pursuit of this goal, like all scientists, economists distinguish between positive and normative statements.

Positive Statements A *positive* statement is about what *is*. It says what is currently believed about the way the world operates. A positive statement might be right or wrong, but we can test it by checking it against the facts. "Our planet is warming because of the amount of coal that we're burning" is a positive statement. We can test whether it is right or wrong.

A central task of economists is to test positive statements about how the economic world works and to weed out those that are wrong. Economics first got off the ground in the late 1700s, so it is a young science compared with, for example, physics, and much remains to be discovered.

Normative Statements A *normative* statement is about what *ought to be*. It depends on values and cannot be tested. Policy goals are normative statements. For example, "We ought to cut our use of coal by 50 percent" is a normative policy statement. You may agree or disagree with it, but you can't test it. It doesn't assert a fact that can be checked.

Unscrambling Cause and Effect Economists are particularly interested in positive statements about cause and effect. Are computers getting cheaper because people are buying them in greater quantities? Or are people buying computers in greater quantities because they are getting cheaper? Or is some third factor causing both the price of a computer to fall and the quantity of computers bought to increase?

To answer such questions, economists create and test economic models. An **economic model** is a description of some aspect of the economic world that includes only those features that are needed for the purpose at hand. For example, an economic model of a cellphone network might include features such as the prices of calls, the number of cellphone users, and the volume of calls. But the model would ignore cellphone colours and ringtones.

A model is tested by comparing its predictions with the facts. But testing an economic model is difficult because we observe the outcomes of the simultaneous change of many factors. To cope with this problem, economists look for natural experiments (situations in the ordinary course of economic life in which the one factor of interest is different and other things are equal or similar); conduct statistical investigations to find correlations; and perform economic experiments by putting people in decision-making situations and varying the influence of one factor at a time to discover how they respond.

Economist as Policy Adviser

Economics is useful. It is a toolkit for advising governments and businesses and for making personal decisions. Some of the most famous economists work partly as policy advisers.

Many leading Canadian economists have advised governments and other organizations on a wide range of economic policy issues. Among them are David Laidler of the University of Western Ontario, Christopher Ragan of McGill University, and Angela Reddish of the University of British Columbia, all of whom have spent time advising the Bank of Canada and the Department of Finance.

All the policy questions on which economists provide advice involve a blend of the positive and the normative. Economics can't help with the normative part—the policy goal. But it can help to clarify the goal. And for a given goal, economics provides the tools for evaluating alternative solutions—comparing marginal benefits and marginal costs and finding the solution that makes the best use of the available resources.

◆ REVIEW QUIZ

1 Distinguish between a positive statement and a normative statement and provide examples.

2 What is a model? Can you think of a model that you might use in your everyday life?

3 How do economists try to disentangle cause and effect?

4 How is economics used as a policy tool?

Work these questions in Study Plan 1.4 and get instant feedback.   MyLab Economics

◆ Economists in the Economy

What are the jobs available to an economics major? Is the number of economics jobs expected to grow or shrink? How much do economics graduates earn? And what are the skills needed for an economics job?

Jobs for an Economics Major

A major in economics opens the door to the pursuit of a master's or Ph.D. and a career as an economist. Relatively few people take this path, but for those who do, the challenges are exciting and job satisfaction is high.

Economics majors work in a wide variety of jobs and situations. Some create and manage their own business, and others get jobs in private firms, government departments, think-tanks, and international organizations.

The economic way of thinking is a basic tool for running a successful business. Courtney Roofing Ltd. is an example. Jim Courtney started this business when he was a student at Western. He went on to graduate with an economics major in 1979, and today, Courtney Roofing is one of the London area's largest and most successful roofing firms.

The jobs of economics majors can generally be described as collecting and analyzing data on the production and use of resources, goods, and services; predicting future trends; and studying ways of using resources more efficiently.

Writing reports and giving talks are a big part of the job of an economist.

An economics major also opens the door to a range of jobs that have the word "analyst" in the title. Three of these jobs, that between them employ almost 1 million people, are market research analyst, financial analyst, and budget analyst.

A *market research analyst* works with data on buying patterns and tries to forecast the likely success of a product and the price that buyers are willing to pay for it.

A *financial analyst* studies trends and fluctuations in interest rates and stock and bond prices and tries to predict the cost of borrowing and the returns on investments.

A *budget analyst* keeps track of an organization's cash flow—its receipts and payments—and prepares budget plans that incorporate predictions of future cash flows.

Jim Courtney started his roofing business when he was an economics student at the University of Western Ontario.

Will Jobs for Economics Majors Grow?

The future is always uncertain and things rarely turn out as expected. But we can't avoid trying to peep into the future when we make choices that commit to a long-term plan. Economists at the U.S. Bureau of Labor Statistics (the BLS) have done their best to provide some forecasts for the U.S. economy.

The BLS forecasts that employment growth from 2014 to 2024 will be 7 percent—for every 100 jobs in 2014, there will be 107 in 2024.

Jobs for those with a Ph.D. in economics are forecasted to grow by 6 percent. This growth is a bit slower than for jobs on average because government jobs for economists are expected to shrink.

Budget analyst jobs are expected to grow by a slow 2 percent because this job is easy to replace with artificial intelligence. But jobs for financial analysts are expected to grow by 12 percent and for market research analysts by 19 percent.

Although these forecasts are for the U.S. economy, it is likely that the numbers in Canada will be similar. While there are no guarantees, these forecasts imply a bright future for people who choose to major in economics.

Earnings of Economics Majors

Earnings of economics majors vary a lot depending on the job and the level of qualifications. The Web resource payscale.com reports a pay range for its sample of economists from $44,441 to $127,500, with a median of $85,970.

A person who majors in economics and goes on to complete a Ph.D. and gets a job as an economist would expect to earn about $100,000 a year by mid-career. Economists working in finance, insurance, and government jobs earn more than the average.

Pay in "analyst" jobs are lower and range from an average of $62,000 a year for market research analysts to $80,000 a year for financial analysts.

These rates of pay put economics graduates at the top of the distribution, as you can see in Fig. 1.3. Graduates who major in political science, finance, engineering, applied math, and business earn less than economists in this sample of jobs.

Skills Needed for Economics Jobs

What are the skills that an employer looks for in a candidate for an economics-related job? Five skill requirments stand out. They are:

- Critical-thinking skills
- Analytical skills
- Math skills
- Writing skills
- Oral communication skills

Critical-Thinking Skills The ability to clarify and solve problems using logic and relevant evidence

Analytical Skills The use of economic ideas and tools to examine data, notice patterns, and reach a logical conclusion

Math Skills The ability to use mathematical and statistical tools to analyze data and reach valid conclusions

Writing Skills The ability to present ideas, conclusions, and reasons in succinct written reports appropriate for the target audience

Oral Communication Skills The ability to explain ideas, conclusions, and reasons to people with a limited background in economics

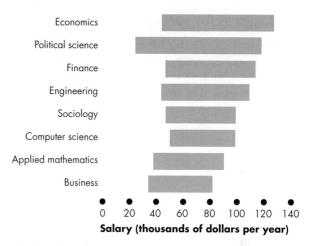

FIGURE 1.3 Earnings of Economics Majors

The bars show the range of earnings for eight majors in a sample of jobs monitored by the jobs survey firm PayScale. Economics graduates are the highest earners among the eight majors shown here.

Source of data: payscale.com

———— MyLab Economics Animation ————

You can see these skills at work (except the last one) in the forecasts of the BLS economists described earlier. These economists used their critical-thinking skills to focus on a manageable number of key features of jobs. They went on to gather relevant data on earnings and employment for a large number of jobs categories, analyzed the data using their math and economics tools, and predicted future jobs growth. They then presented their findings online at https://www.bls.gov/ooh. Round off this topic by taking a look at their work.

◆ REVIEW QUIZ

1 What types of jobs do economists do?
2 What is the range and median level of economists' pay?
3 What are the skills needed for an economics job?

Work these questions in Study Plan 1.5 and get instant feedback.   MyLab Economics

ECONOMICS IN THE NEWS

The Internet for Everyone

Mark Zuckerberg's Big Idea: The "Next 5 Billion"
Facebook founder Mark Zuckerberg wants to make it so that anyone, anywhere, can get online. To achieve this goal, he has created internet.org, "a global partnership between technology leaders, nonprofits, local communities, and experts who are working together to bring the Internet to the two-thirds of the world's population that don't have it."

Sources: CNN Money, August 21, 2013, and internet.org

THE DATA

- The figure shows that almost 80 percent of Americans and Canadians have Internet access compared to only 16 percent of Africans and 28 percent of Asians.

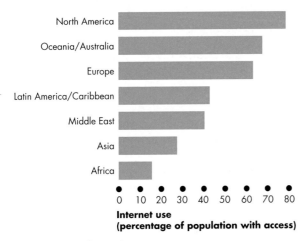

Internet use (percentage of population with access)

Internet Access by Region

- Of the 5 billion people who Mark Zuckerberg wants to have Internet access, 1 billion live in Africa and 2.8 billion live in Asia.
- To figure out what it would take for everyone to have Internet access, we must make an assumption about how many people share resources.
- If four people shared, it would cost about $285 billion for computers and $115 billion a year for Internet access for everyone to get online.
- Satisfying Mark Zuckerberg's want would cost the equivalent of 400 years of Facebook's 2012 profit, or 1,600 Boeing 787 Dreamliners, or 90 aircraft carriers, or 87 billion Big Macs.

THE QUESTIONS

- What is the fundamental economic problem and how does this news clip illustrate it?
- What are some of the things that might be forgone for more people to get online?
- Why don't more people make the tradeoffs needed to get online?
- Why might it be in Mark Zuckerberg's self-interest to get everyone online?
- Why might it not be in the social interest for everyone to get online?

In Africa, 4 in 5 people lack Internet access.

THE ANSWERS

- The fundamental economic problem is scarcity—the fact that wants exceed the resources available to satisfy them. The news clip illustrates scarcity because Mark Zuckerberg's want for everyone to get online *exceeds* the resources available to satisfy it.
- Some of the scarce resources that are used to produce airplanes, war ships, and Big Macs could be reallocated and used to produce more computers and Internet service.
- People don't make the tradeoffs needed to get online because for them the marginal cost of doing so would exceed the marginal benefit.
- It might be in Mark Zuckerberg's self-interest to get everyone online because that would increase the number of Facebook users and increase the firm's advertising revenues.
- It would not be in the social interest to get everyone online if the marginal cost of an Internet connection exceeded its marginal benefit.

SUMMARY

Key Points

Definition of Economics (p. 2)

- All economic questions arise from scarcity—from the fact that wants exceed the resources available to satisfy them.
- Economics is the social science that studies the choices that people make as they cope with scarcity.
- The subject divides into microeconomics and macroeconomics.

Working Problem 1 will give you a better understanding of the definition of economics.

Two Big Economic Questions (pp. 3–8)

- Two big questions summarize the scope of economics:

  1. How do choices end up determining *what, how,* and *for whom* goods and services are produced?
  2. When do choices made in the pursuit of *self-interest* also promote the *social interest?*

Working Problems 2 and 3 will give you a better understanding of the two big questions of economics.

The Economic Way of Thinking (pp. 9–10)

- Every choice is a tradeoff—exchanging more of something for less of something else.

- People make rational choices by comparing benefit and cost.
- Cost—*opportunity cost*—is what you must give up to get something.
- Most choices are "how much" choices made at the *margin* by comparing marginal benefit and marginal cost.
- Choices respond to incentives.

Working Problems 4 and 5 will give you a better understanding of the economic way of thinking.

Economics as Social Science and Policy Tool (p. 11)

- Economists distinguish between positive statements—what is—and normative statements—what ought to be.
- To explain the economic world, economists create and test economic models.
- Economics is a toolkit used to provide advice on government, business, and personal economic decisions.

Working Problem 6 will give you a better understanding of economics as social science and policy tool.

Economists in the Economy (pp. 12–14)

- Economics majors work in a wide range of jobs as economists and analysts.
- The job growth outlook for economics majors is good and pay is above average.

Key Terms

MyLab Economics Key Terms Quiz

Benefit, 9
Capital, 4
Economic model, 11
Economics, 2
Efficient, 5
Entrepreneurship, 4
Factors of production, 3
Goods and services, 3
Human capital, 3
Incentive, 2

Interest, 4
Labour, 3
Land, 3
Macroeconomics, 2
Margin, 10
Marginal benefit, 10
Marginal cost, 10
Microeconomics, 2
Opportunity cost, 9
Preferences, 9

Profit, 4
Rational choice, 9
Rent, 4
Scarcity, 2
Self-interest, 5
Social interest, 5
Tradeoff, 9
Wages, 4

STUDY PLAN PROBLEMS AND APPLICATIONS

MyLab Economics Work Problems 1 to 6 in Chapter 1 Study Plan and get instant feedback.

Definition of Economics (Study Plan 1.1)

1. Apple Inc. decides to make iTunes freely available in unlimited quantities.
   a. Does Apple's decision change the incentives that people face?
   b. Is Apple's decision an example of a microeconomic or a macroeconomic issue?

Two Big Economic Questions (Study Plan 1.2)

2. Which of the following pairs does not match?
   a. Labour and wages
   b. Land and rent
   c. Entrepreneurship and profit
   d. Capital and profit

3. Explain how the following news headlines concern self-interest and the social interest.
   a. Starbucks Expands in China
   b. McDonald's Moves into Online Ordering
   c. Food Must Be Labelled with Nutrition Data

The Economic Way of Thinking (Study Plan 1.3)

4. The night before an economics test, you decide to go to the movies instead of staying home and working your MyLab Study Plan. Your grade on the test was 50 percent, lower than your usual score of 70 percent.
   a. Did you face a tradeoff?
   b. What was the opportunity cost of your evening at the movies?

5. **Cost of Rio Olympics**
   Brazilian federal, state, and local governments spent R$2.8 billion and private sponsors spent R$4.2 billion on 17 new Olympic facilities, 10 of which will be used for sporting events after the Olympics.
   Source: *Financial Times*, August 6, 2016

   Was the opportunity cost of the Rio Olympics R$2.8 billion or R$7 billion? Explain your answer.

Economics as Social Science and Policy Tool (Study Plan 1.4)

6. Which of the following statements is positive, which is normative, and which can be tested?
   a. Canada should cut its imports.
   b. China is Canada's largest trading partner.
   c. If the price of gasoline rises, people will drive less and use less gasoline.

ADDITIONAL PROBLEMS AND APPLICATIONS

MyLab Economics Work these problems in Homework or Test if assigned by your instructor.

Definition of Economics

7. **Kanye West Offers Free Concert Tickets**
   Kayne West has teamed with Los Angeles inner-city schools to offer free passes for students!
   Source: consequenceofsound.net, November 27, 2016

   When Kayne West gave away tickets, what was free and what was scarce? Explain your answer.

Two Big Economic Questions

8. How does the creation of a successful movie influence *what, how*, and *for whom* goods and services are produced?

9. How does a successful movie illustrate self-interested choices that are also in the social interest?

The Economic Way of Thinking

10. Before starting in *Guardians of the Galaxy*, Chris Pratt had appeared in 11 movies that grossed an average of $7 million on the opening weekend. *Guardians of the Galaxy* grossed $94 million.
    a. How will the success of *Guardians of the Galaxy* influence the opportunity cost of hiring Chris Pratt?.
    b. How have the incentives for a movie producer to hire Chris Pratt changed?

11. What might be an incentive for you to take a class in summer school? List some of the benefits and costs involved in your decision. Would your choice be rational?

Economics as Social Science and Policy Tool

12. Look at today's *National Post*. What is the leading economic news story? Which big economic questions and tradeoffs does it discuss or imply?

13. Provide two microeconomic statements and two macroeconomic statements. Classify your statements as positive or normative. Explain why.

APPENDIX

Graphs in Economics

After studying this appendix, you will be able to:

◆ Make and interpret a scatter diagram

◆ Identify linear and nonlinear relationships and relationships that have a maximum and a minimum

◆ Define and calculate the slope of a line

◆ Graph relationships among more than two variables

◆ Graphing Data

A graph represents a quantity as a distance on a line. In Fig. A1.1, a distance on the horizontal line represents temperature, measured in degrees Celsius. A movement from left to right shows an increase in temperature. The point 0 represents zero degrees Celsius. To the right of 0, the temperature is positive. To the left of 0, the temperature is negative (as indicated by the minus sign). A distance on the vertical line represents height, measured in thousands of metres. The point 0 represents sea level. Points above 0 represent metres above sea level. Points below 0 represent metres below sea level (indicated by a minus sign).

In Fig. A1.1, the two scale lines are perpendicular to each other and are called *axes*. The vertical line is the *y*-axis, and the horizontal line is the *x*-axis. Each axis has a zero point, which is shared by the two axes and called the *origin*.

To make a two-variable graph, we need two pieces of information: the value of the variable *x* and the value of the variable *y*. For example, off the coast of British Columbia, the temperature is 10 degrees—the value of *x*. A fishing boat is located at 0 metres above sea level—the value of *y*. These two bits of information appear as point *A* in Fig. A1.1. A climber at the top of Mount McKinley on a cold day is 6,194 metres above sea level in a zero-degree gale. These two pieces of information appear as point *B*. On a warmer day, a climber might be at the peak of Mt. McKinley when the temperature is 10 degrees, at point *C*.

FIGURE A1.1   Making a Graph

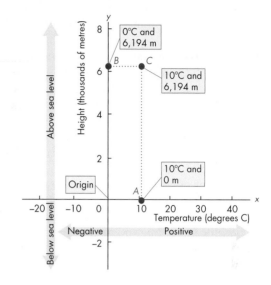

Graphs have axes that measure quantities as distances. Here, the horizontal axis (*x*-axis) measures temperature, and the vertical axis (*y*-axis) measures height. Point *A* represents a fishing boat at sea level (0 on the *y*-axis) on a day when the temperature is 10°C. Point *B* represents a climber at the top of Mt. McKinley, 6,194 metres above sea level, at a temperature of 0°C. Point *C* represents a climber at the top of Mt. McKinley, 6,194 metres above sea level, at a temperature of 10°C.

—————— MyLab Economics Animation ——————

We can draw two lines, called *coordinates*, from point *C*. One, called the *x*-coordinate, runs from *C* to the vertical axis. This line is called "the *x*-coordinate" because its length is the same as the value marked off on the *x*-axis. The other, called the *y*-coordinate, runs from *C* to the horizontal axis. This line is called "the *y*-coordinate" because its length is the same as the value marked off on the *y*-axis.

We describe a point on a graph by the values of its *x*-coordinate and its *y*-coordinate. For example, at point *C*, *x* is 10 degrees and *y* is 6,194 metres.

A graph like that in Fig. A1.1 can be made using any quantitative data on two variables. The graph can show just a few points, like Fig. A1.1, or many points. Before we look at graphs with many points, let's reinforce what you've just learned by looking at two graphs made with economic data.

Graphing Economic Data

Economists measure variables that describe *what, how,* and *for whom* goods and services are produced. These variables are quantities produced and consumed and their prices.

Figure A1.2 shows an example of an economics graph. This graph provides information about movies in 2016. The *x*-axis measures the quantity of movie tickets sold and the *y*-axis measures the average price of a ticket. Point *A* tells us what the quantity and price were. You can "read" this graph as telling you that in 2016, 1.3 billion movie tickets were sold at an average ticket price of $8.43.

The two graphs that you've just seen show you how to make a graph and how to read a data point on a graph, but they don't improve on the raw data. Graphs become interesting and revealing when they contain a number of data points because then you can visualize the data.

FIGURE A1.2   Making an Economics Graph

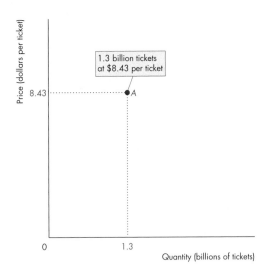

When you look at a graph, start by reading the axis labels. In this economics graph, the horizontal axis (*x*-axis) measures the quantity of movie tickets sold, and the vertical axis (*y*-axis) measures the average price of a ticket.

Once you are clear about what is being measured on the axes, look at the data graphed.

Here, there is just one point, *A*. It tells us the data for 2016. In that year, 1.3 billion tickets were sold at an average price of $8.43.

———— MyLab Economics Animation ————

Economists create graphs based on the principles in Figs. A1.1 and A1.2 to reveal, describe, and visualize the relationships among variables. We're now going to look at some examples. These graphs are called scatter diagrams.

Scatter Diagrams

A **scatter diagram** is a graph that plots the value of one variable against the value of another variable for a number of different values of each variable. Such a graph reveals whether a relationship exists between two variables and describes their relationship.

The table in Fig. A1.3 shows some data on two variables: the number of tickets sold at the box office and the worldwide box office revenue from the ticket sales for these movies.

What is the relationship between these two variables? Does a big production budget generate large ticket sales and box office revenue? Or does accurate forecasting of box office success lead to a big production budget? Or is there no connection between these two variables?

We can answer these questions by making a scatter diagram. We do so by graphing the data in the table. In the graph in Fig. A1.3, each point shows the production budget (the *x* variable) and the box office revenue (the *y* variable) of one of the movies. There are 10 movies, so there are 10 points "scattered" within the graph.

The point labelled *A* tells us that *Star Wars Episode VII: The Force Awakens* cost $306 million to produce and generated $2,059 million of box office revenue.

Star Wars was the second most costly movie to produce and brought in the second most revenue. Find the point in the graph for *Avatar*. Notice that it cost more to produce and brought in more revenue than *Star Wars*. These two points in the graph suggest that large box office sales and a big production budget are related. But look at the other eight points and a different picture emerges. There is no clear pattern formed by these data. If you want to predict a movie's box office success with any confidence, you need to know more than the movie's production budget.

Figure A1.4 shows two scatter diagrams of economic variables. Part (a) shows the relationship between income and expenditure, on average, from 2005 to 2015. Each point represents income and expenditure in a given year. For example, point *A* shows that in 2010, income was $40,000 and expenditure was $27,000. This graph shows that as income increases, so does expenditure, and the relationship is a close one.

FIGURE A1.3 A Scatter Diagram

Movie	Production budget	Worldwide box office
	(millions of dollars)	
Avatar	425	2,784
Star Wars Ep. VII: The Force Awakens	306	2,059
Pirates of the Caribbean: At World's End	300	963
Spectre	300	880
The Lone Ranger	275	260
John Carter	275	283
The Dark Knight Rises	275	1,084
Tangled	260	587
Spider-Man 3	258	891
Harry Potter and the Half-Blood Prince	250	935

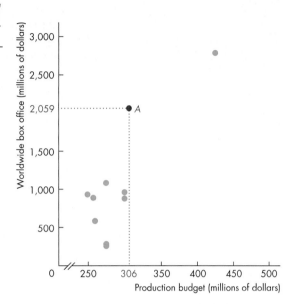

The table lists the production budget and worldwide box office revenue for 10 popular movies.

The scatter diagram reveals the relationship between these two variables. Each point shows the values of the variables for a specific movie. For example, point A shows the point for *Star Wars: The Force Awakens*, which cost $306 million to produce and brought in $2,059 million at the box office.

The pattern formed by the points shows no clear tendency for a larger production budget to bring a greater box office revenue.

Figure A1.4(b) shows a scatter diagram of inflation and unemployment in Canada from 2006 to 2016. Here, the points show no relationship between the two variables. For example, when unemployment was high, the inflation rate was high in 2011 and low in 2009.

You can see that a scatter diagram conveys a wealth of information, and it does so in much less space than we have used to describe only some of its features. But you do have to "read" the graph to obtain all this information.

FIGURE A1.4 Two Economic Scatter Diagrams

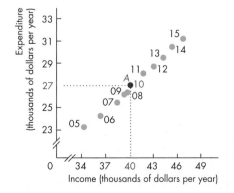

(a) Income and expenditure

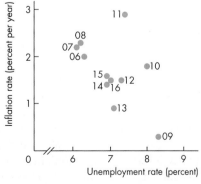

(b) Unemployment and inflation

The scatter diagram in part (a) shows the relationship between income and expenditure from 2005 to 2015. Point A shows that in 2010, income was $40,000 on the x-axis and expenditure was $27,000 on the y-axis. This graph shows that as income rises, so does expenditure, and the relationship is a close one.

The scatter diagram in part (b) shows a weak relationship between unemployment and inflation in Canada during most of the years.

Breaks in the Axes The graph in Fig. A1.4(a) has breaks in its axes, as shown by the small gaps. The breaks indicate that there are jumps from the origin, 0, to the first values recorded.

The breaks are used because the lowest value of income is $34,300 and the lowest value of expenditure exceeds $23,300. If we made this graph with no breaks in its axes, there would be a lot of empty space, the points would be crowded into the top right corner, and it would be difficult to see whether a relationship exists between these two variables. By breaking the axes, we are able to bring the relationship into view.

Putting a break in one or both axes is like using a zoom lens to bring the relationship into the centre of the graph and magnify it so that the relationship fills the graph.

Misleading Graphs Breaks can be used to highlight a relationship, but they can also be used to mislead—to make a graph that lies. The most common way of making a graph lie is to put a break in the axis and either to stretch or compress the scale. For example, suppose that in Fig. A1.4(a), the *y*-axis that measures expenditure ran from zero to $28,000 while the *x*-axis was the same as the one shown. The graph would now create the impression that despite a huge increase in income, expenditure had barely changed.

To avoid being misled, it is a good idea to get into the habit of always looking closely at the values and the labels on the axes of a graph before you start to interpret it.

Correlation and Causation A scatter diagram that shows a clear relationship between two variables, such as Fig. A1.4(a), tells us that the two variables have a high correlation. When a high correlation is present, we can predict the value of one variable from the value of the other variable. But correlation does not imply causation.

Sometimes a high correlation does arise from a causal relationship. It is likely that rising income causes rising expenditure (Fig. A1.4a). But a high correlation can mean that two variables have a common cause. For example, ice cream sales and pool drownings are correlated not because one causes the other, but because both are caused by hot weather.

You've now seen how we can use graphs in economics to show economic data and to reveal relationships. Next, we'll learn how economists use graphs to construct and display economic models.

Graphs Used in Economic Models

The graphs used in economics are not always designed to show real-world data. Often they are used to show general relationships among the variables in an economic model.

An *economic model* is a stripped-down, simplified description of an economy or of a component of an economy such as a business or a household. It consists of statements about economic behaviour that can be expressed as equations or as curves in a graph. Economists use models to explore the effects of different policies or other influences on the economy in ways that are similar to the use of model airplanes in wind tunnels and models of the climate.

You will encounter many different kinds of graphs in economic models, but there are some repeating patterns. Once you've learned to recognize these patterns, you will instantly understand the meaning of a graph. Here, we'll look at the different types of curves that are used in economic models, and we'll see some everyday examples of each type of curve. The patterns to look for in graphs are the four cases in which:

- Variables move in the same direction.
- Variables move in opposite directions.
- Variables have a maximum or a minimum.
- Variables are unrelated.

Let's look at these four cases.

Variables That Move in the Same Direction

Figure A1.5 shows graphs of the relationships between two variables that move up and down together. A relationship between two variables that move in the same direction is called a **positive relationship** or a **direct relationship**. A line that slopes upward shows such a relationship.

Figure A1.5 shows three types of relationships: one that has a straight line and two that have curved lines. All the lines in these three graphs are called curves. Any line on a graph—no matter whether it is straight or curved—is called a *curve*.

A relationship shown by a straight line is called a **linear relationship**. Figure A1.5(a) shows a linear relationship between the number of kilometres travelled

FIGURE A1.5   Positive (Direct) Relationships

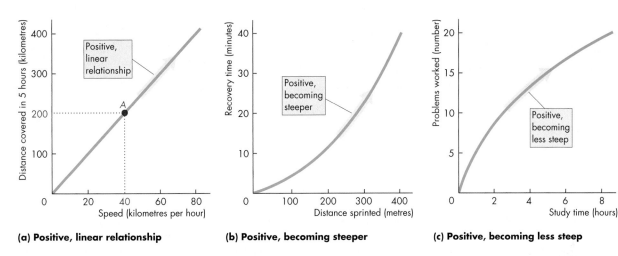

(a) Positive, linear relationship   **(b) Positive, becoming steeper**   **(c) Positive, becoming less steep**

Each part shows a positive (direct) relationship between two variables. That is, as the value of the variable measured on the *x*-axis increases, so does the value of the variable measured on the *y*-axis. Part (a) shows a linear positive relationship—as the two variables increase together, we move along a straight line.

Part (b) shows a positive relationship such that as the two variables increase together, we move along a curve that becomes steeper.

Part (c) shows a positive relationship such that as the two variables increase together, we move along a curve that becomes flatter.

MyLab Economics Animation

in 5 hours and speed. For example, point *A* shows that you will travel 200 kilometres in 5 hours if your speed is 40 kilometres an hour. If you double your speed to 80 kilometres an hour, you will travel 400 kilometres in 5 hours.

Figure A1.5(b) shows the relationship between distance sprinted and recovery time (the time it takes the heart rate to return to its normal resting rate). This relationship is an upward-sloping one that starts out quite flat but then becomes steeper as we move along the curve away from the origin. The reason this curve becomes steeper is that the additional recovery time needed from sprinting an additional 100 metres increases. It takes less than 5 minutes to recover from sprinting 100 metres but more than 10 minutes to recover from 200 metres.

Figure A1.5(c) shows the relationship between the number of problems worked by a student and the amount of study time. This relationship is an upward-sloping one that starts out quite steep and becomes flatter as we move along the curve away from the origin. Study time becomes less productive as the student spends more hours studying and becomes more tired.

Variables That Move in Opposite Directions

Figure A1.6 shows relationships between things that move in opposite directions. A relationship between variables that move in opposite directions is called a **negative relationship** or an **inverse relationship**.

Figure A1.6(a) shows the relationship between the hours spent playing squash and the hours spent playing tennis when the total time available is 5 hours. One extra hour spent playing tennis means one hour less spent playing squash and vice versa. This relationship is negative and linear.

Figure A1.6(b) shows the relationship between the cost per kilometre travelled and the length of a journey. The longer the journey, the lower is the cost per kilometre. But as the journey length increases, even though the cost per kilometre decreases, the fall in the cost per kilometre is smaller, the longer is the journey. This feature of the relationship is shown by the fact that the curve slopes downward, starting out steep at a short journey length and then becoming flatter as the journey length increases. This relationship arises because some of the costs are fixed, such as auto insurance, and the fixed costs are spread over a longer journey.

FIGURE A1.6 Negative (Inverse) Relationships

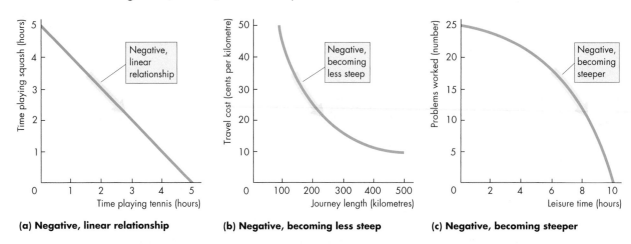

(a) Negative, linear relationship

(b) Negative, becoming less steep

(c) Negative, becoming steeper

Each part shows a negative (inverse) relationship between two variables. Part (a) shows a linear negative relationship. The total time spent playing tennis and squash is 5 hours. As the time spent playing tennis increases, the time spent playing squash decreases, and we move along a straight line.

Part (b) shows a negative relationship such that as the journey length increases, the travel cost decreases as we move along a curve that becomes less steep.

Part (c) shows a negative relationship such that as leisure time increases, the number of problems worked decreases as we move along a curve that becomes steeper.

MyLab Economics Animation

Figure A1.6(c) shows the relationship between the amount of leisure time and the number of problems worked by a student. Increasing leisure time produces an increasingly large reduction in the number of problems worked. This relationship is a negative one that starts out with a gentle slope at a small number of leisure hours and becomes steeper as the number of leisure hours increases. This relationship is a different view of the idea shown in Fig. A1.5(c).

Variables That Have a Maximum or a Minimum

Many relationships in economic models have a maximum or a minimum. For example, firms try to make the maximum possible profit and to produce at the lowest possible cost. Figure A1.7 shows relationships that have a maximum or a minimum.

Figure A1.7(a) shows the relationship between rainfall and wheat yield. When there is no rainfall, wheat will not grow, so the yield is zero. As the rainfall increases up to 10 days a month, the wheat yield increases. With 10 rainy days each month, the wheat

yield reaches its maximum at 2 tonnes per hectare (point *A*). Rain in excess of 10 days a month starts to lower the yield of wheat. If every day is rainy, the wheat suffers from a lack of sunshine and the yield decreases to zero. This relationship is one that starts out sloping upward, reaches a maximum, and then slopes downward.

Figure A1.7(b) shows the reverse case—a relationship that begins sloping downward, falls to a minimum, and then slopes upward. Most economic costs are like this relationship. An example is the relationship between the cost per kilometre and the speed of the car. At low speeds, the car is creeping in a traffic snarl-up. The number of kilometres per litre is low, so the gasoline cost per kilometre is high. At high speeds, the car is travelling faster than its efficient speed, using a large quantity of gasoline, and again the number of kilometres per litre is low and the gasoline cost per kilometre is high. At a speed of 100 kilometres an hour, the gasoline cost per kilometre is at its minimum (point *B*). This relationship is one that starts out sloping downward, reaches a minimum, and then slopes upward.

FIGURE A1.7   Maximum and Minimum Points

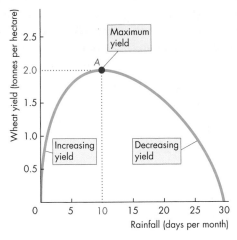

(a) Relationship with a maximum

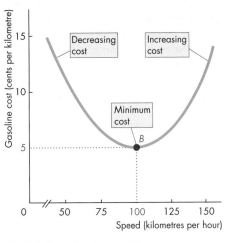

(b) Relationship with a minimum

Part (a) shows a relationship that has a maximum point, *A*. The curve slopes upward as it rises to its maximum point, is flat at its maximum, and then slopes downward.

Part (b) shows a relationship with a minimum point, *B*. The curve slopes downward as it falls to its minimum, is flat at its minimum, and then slopes upward.

Variables That Are Unrelated

There are many situations in which no matter what happens to the value of one variable, the other variable remains constant. Sometimes we want to show the independence between two variables in a graph, and Fig. A1.8 shows two ways of achieving this.

In describing the graphs in Fig. A1.5 through Fig. A1.7, we have talked about curves that slope upward or slope downward and curves that become less steep or steeper. Let's spend a little time discussing exactly what we mean by *slope* and how we measure the slope of a curve.

FIGURE A1.8   Variables That Are Unrelated

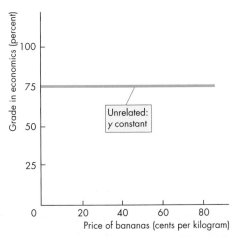

(a) Unrelated: *y* constant

(b) Unrelated: *x* constant

This figure shows how we can graph two variables that are unrelated. In part (a), a student's grade in economics is plotted at 75 percent on the *y*-axis regardless of the price of bananas on the *x*-axis. The curve is horizontal.

In part (b), the output of the vineyards of France on the *x*-axis does not vary with the rainfall in Ontario on the *y*-axis. The curve is vertical.

◆ The Slope of a Relationship

We can measure the influence of one variable on another by the slope of the relationship. The **slope** of a relationship is the change in the value of the variable measured on the y-axis divided by the change in the value of the variable measured on the x-axis. We use the Greek letter Δ (*delta*) to represent "change in." Thus Δy means the change in the value of the variable measured on the y-axis, and Δx means the change in the value of the variable measured on the x-axis. Therefore the slope of the relationship is

$$\text{Slope} = \frac{\Delta y}{\Delta x}.$$

If a large change in the variable measured on the y-axis (Δy) is associated with a small change in the variable measured on the x-axis (Δx), the slope is large and the curve is steep. If a small change in the variable measured on the y-axis (Δy) is associated with a large change in the variable measured on the x-axis (Δx), the slope is small and the curve is flat.

We can make the idea of slope clearer by doing some calculations.

The Slope of a Straight Line

The slope of a straight line is the same regardless of where on the line you calculate it. The slope of a straight line is constant. Let's calculate the slope of the positive relationship in Fig. A1.9.

FIGURE A1.9   The Slope of a Straight Line

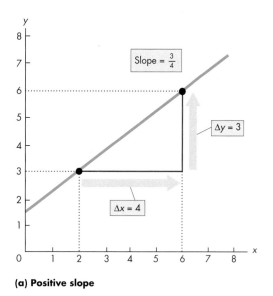

(a) Positive slope

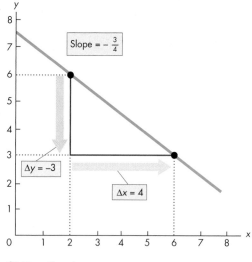

(b) Negative slope

To calculate the slope of a straight line, we divide the change in the value of the variable measured on the y-axis (Δy) by the change in the value of the variable measured on the x-axis (Δx) as we move along the line.

Part (a) shows the calculation of a positive slope. When x increases from 2 to 6, Δx equals 4. That change in

x brings about an increase in y from 3 to 6, so Δy equals 3. The slope ($\Delta y/\Delta x$) equals 3/4.

Part (b) shows the calculation of a negative slope. When x increases from 2 to 6, Δx equals 4. That increase in x brings about a decrease in y from 6 to 3, so Δy equals -3. The slope ($\Delta y/\Delta x$) equals $-3/4$.

In part (a), when x increases from 2 to 6, y increases from 3 to 6. The change in x is $+4$—that is, Δx is 4. The change in y is $+3$—that is, Δy is 3. The slope of that line is

$$\frac{\Delta y}{\Delta x} = \frac{3}{4}.$$

In part (b), when x increases from 2 to 6, y decreases from 6 to 3. The change in y is *minus* 3—that is, Δy is -3. The change in x is *plus* 4—that is, Δx is 4. The slope of the curve is

$$\frac{\Delta y}{\Delta x} = \frac{-3}{4}.$$

Notice that the two slopes have the same magnitude (3/4), but the slope of the line in part (a) is positive ($+3/+4 = 3/4$) while that in part (b) is negative ($-3/+4 = -3/4$). The slope of a positive relationship is positive; the slope of a negative relationship is negative.

The Slope of a Curved Line

The slope of a curved line is trickier. The slope of a curved line is not constant, so the slope depends on where on the curved line we calculate it. There are two ways to calculate the slope of a curved line: You can calculate the slope at a point, or you can calculate the slope across an arc of the curve. Let's look at the two alternatives.

Slope at a Point To calculate the slope at a point on a curve, you need to construct a straight line that has the same slope as the curve at the point in question. Figure A1.10 shows how this is done. Suppose you want to calculate the slope of the curve at point A. Place a ruler on the graph so that the ruler touches point A and no other point on the curve, then draw a straight line along the edge of the ruler. The straight red line is this line, and it is the tangent to the curve at point A. If the ruler touches the curve only at point A, then the slope of the curve at point A must be the same as the slope of the edge of the ruler. If the curve and the ruler do not have the same slope, the line along the edge of the ruler will cut the curve instead of just touching it.

Now that you have found a straight line with the same slope as the curve at point A, you can calculate the slope of the curve at point A by calculating the slope of the straight line. Along the straight

FIGURE A1.10   Slope at a Point

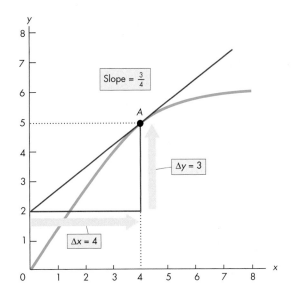

To calculate the slope of the curve at point A, draw the red line that just touches the curve at A—the tangent. The slope of this straight line is calculated by dividing the change in y by the change in x along the red line. When x increases from 0 to 4, Δx equals 4. That change in x is associated with an increase in y from 2 to 5, so Δy equals 3. The slope of the red line is 3/4, so the slope of the curve at point A is 3/4.

———— MyLab Economics Animation ————

line, as x increases from 0 to 4 (Δx is 4) y increases from 2 to 5 (Δy is 3). Therefore the slope of the straight line is

$$\frac{\Delta y}{\Delta x} = \frac{3}{4}.$$

So the slope of the curve at point A is 3/4.

Slope Across an Arc An arc of a curve is a piece of a curve. Figure A1.11 shows the same curve as in Fig. A1.10, but instead of calculating the slope at point A, we are now going to calculate the slope across the arc from point B to point C. You can see that the slope of the curve at point B is greater than at point C. When we calculate the slope across an arc, we are calculating the average slope between two points. As we move along the arc from B to C, x increases from 3 to 5 and y increases from 4.0 to 5.5. The change in x is 2 (Δx is 2), and the change in y is 1.5 (Δy is 1.5).

FIGURE A1.11 Slope Across an Arc

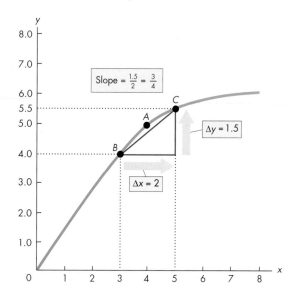

To calculate the average slope of the curve along the arc *BC*, draw a straight line from point *B* to point *C*. The slope of the line *BC* is calculated by dividing the change in *y* by the change in *x*. In moving from *B* to *C*, the increase in *x* is 2 (Δ*x* equals 2) and the change in *y* is 1.5 (Δ*y* equals 1.5). The slope of the line *BC* is 1.5 divided by 2, or 3/4. So the slope of the curve across the arc *BC* is 3/4.

———————————— MyLab Economics Animation ——

Therefore the slope is

$$\frac{\Delta y}{\Delta x} = \frac{1.5}{2} = \frac{3}{4}.$$

So the slope of the curve across the arc *BC* is 3/4.

This calculation gives us the slope of the curve between points *B* and *C*. The actual slope calculated is the slope of the straight line from *B* to *C*. This slope approximates the average slope of the curve along the arc *BC*. In this particular example, the slope across the arc *BC* is identical to the slope of the curve at point *A*, but the calculation of the slope of a curve does not always work out so neatly. You might have fun constructing some more examples and a few counter examples.

You now know how to make and interpret a graph. So far, we've limited our attention to graphs of two variables. We're now going to learn how to graph more than two variables.

◆ Graphing Relationships Among More Than Two Variables

We have seen that we can graph the relationship between two variables as a point formed by the *x*- and *y*-coordinates in a two-dimensional graph. You might be thinking that although a two-dimensional graph is informative, most of the things in which you are likely to be interested involve relationships among many variables, not just two. For example, the amount of ice cream consumed depends on the price of ice cream and the temperature. If ice cream is expensive and the temperature is low, people eat much less ice cream than when ice cream is inexpensive and the temperature is high. For any given price of ice cream, the quantity consumed varies with the temperature; and for any given temperature, the quantity of ice cream consumed varies with its price.

Figure A1.12 shows a relationship among three variables. The table shows the number of litres of ice cream consumed each day at two different temperatures and at a number of different prices of ice cream. How can we graph these numbers?

To graph a relationship that involves more than two variables, we use the *ceteris paribus* assumption.

Ceteris Paribus

Ceteris paribus (often shortened to *cet par*) means "if all other relevant things remain the same." To isolate the relationship of interest in a laboratory experiment, a scientist holds everything constant except for the variable whose effect is being studied. Economists use the same method to graph a relationship that has more than two variables.

Figure A1.12 shows an example. There, you can see what happens to the quantity of ice cream consumed when the price of ice cream varies but the temperature is held constant.

The curve labelled 21°C shows the relationship between ice cream consumption and the price of ice cream if the temperature remains at 21°C. The numbers used to plot that curve are those in the first two columns of the table. For example, if the temperature is 21°C, 10 litres of ice cream are consumed when the price is $2.75 a scoop and 18 litres are consumed when the price is $2.25 a scoop.

The curve labelled 32°C shows the relationship between ice cream consumption and the price of ice cream if the temperature remains at 32°C. The numbers used to plot that curve are those in the first

FIGURE A1.12   Graphing a Relationship Among Three Variables

Price	Ice cream consumption (litres per day)	
(dollars per scoop)	21°C	32°C
2.00	25	50
2.25	18	36
2.50	13	26
2.75	**10**	**20**
3.00	7	14
3.25	5	10
3.50	3	6

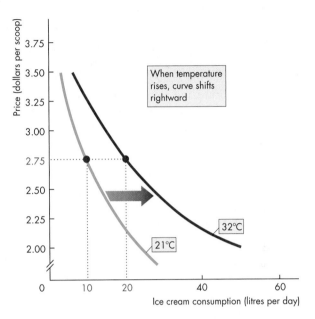

Ice cream consumption depends on its price and the temperature. The table tells us how many litres of ice cream are consumed each day at different prices and two different temperatures. For example, if the price is $2.75 a scoop and the temperature is 21°C, 10 litres of ice cream are consumed. But if the temperature is 32°C, 20 litres are consumed.

To graph a relationship among three variables, the value of one variable is held constant. The graph shows the relationship between price and consumption when the temperature is held constant. One curve holds the temperature at 21°C and the other holds it at 32°C.

A change in the price of ice cream brings a movement along one of the curves—along the blue curve at 21°C and along the red curve at 32°C.

When the temperature *rises* from 21°C to 32°C, the curve that shows the relationship between consumption and the price *shifts* rightward from the blue curve to the red curve.

MyLab Economics Animation

and third columns of the table. For example, if the temperature is 32°C, 20 litres are consumed when the price is $2.75 a scoop and 36 litres are consumed when the price is $2.25 a scoop.

When the price of ice cream changes but the temperature is constant, you can think of what happens in the graph as a movement along one of the curves. At 21°C there is a movement along the blue curve, and at 32°C there is a movement along the red curve.

When Other Things Change

The temperature is held constant along each of the curves in Fig. A1.12, but in reality the temperature changes. When that event occurs, you can think of

what happens in the graph as a shift of the curve. When the temperature rises from 21°C to 32°C, the curve that shows the relationship between ice cream consumption and the price of ice cream shifts rightward from the blue curve to the red curve.

You will encounter these ideas of movements along and shifts of curves at many points in your study of economics. Think carefully about what you've just learned and make up some examples (with assumed numbers) about other relationships.

With what you have learned about graphs, you can move forward with your study of economics. There are no graphs in this book that are more complicated than those that have been explained in this appendix.

MATHEMATICAL NOTE

Equations of Straight Lines

If a straight line in a graph describes the relationship between two variables, we call it a linear relationship. Figure 1 shows the *linear relationship* between a person's expenditure and income. This person spends $100 a week (by borrowing or spending previous savings) when income is zero. Out of each dollar earned, this person spends 50 cents (and saves 50 cents).

All linear relationships are described by the same general equation. We call the quantity that is measured on the horizontal axis (or x-axis) x, and we call the quantity that is measured on the vertical axis (or y-axis) y. In the case of Fig. 1, x is income and y is expenditure.

A Linear Equation

The equation that describes a straight-line relationship between x and y is

$$y = a + bx.$$

In this equation, a and b are fixed numbers and they are called *constants*. The values of x and y vary, so these numbers are called *variables*. Because the equation describes a straight line, the equation is called a *linear equation*.

The equation tells us that when the value of x is zero, the value of y is a. We call the constant a the y-axis intercept. The reason is that on the graph the straight line hits the y-axis at a value equal to a. Figure 1 illustrates the y-axis intercept.

For positive values of x, the value of y exceeds a. The constant b tells us by how much y increases above a as x increases. The constant b is the slope of the line.

Slope of the Line

As we explain in the appendix, the *slope* of a relationship is the change in the value of y divided by the change in the value of x. We use the Greek letter Δ (delta) to represent "change in." So Δy means the change in the value of the variable measured on the y-axis, and Δx means the change in the value of the variable measured on the x-axis. Therefore the slope of the relationship is

$$\text{Slope} = \frac{\Delta y}{\Delta x}.$$

To see why the slope is b, suppose that initially the value of x is x_1, or $200 in Fig. 2. The corresponding value of y is y_1, also $200 in Fig. 2. The equation of the line tells us that

$$y_1 = a + bx_1. \tag{1}$$

Now the value of x increases by Δx to $x_1 + \Delta x$ (or $400 in Fig. 2). And the value of y increases by Δy to $y_1 + \Delta y$ (or $300 in Fig. 2). The equation of the line now tells us that

$$y_1 + \Delta y = a + b(x_1 + \Delta x). \tag{2}$$

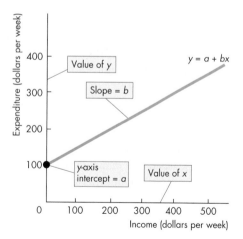

Figure 1 Linear Relationship

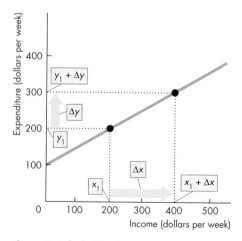

Figure 2 Calculating Slope

To calculate the slope of the line, subtract equation (1) from equation (2) to obtain

$$\Delta y = b\Delta x \qquad (3)$$

and now divide equation (3) by Δx to obtain

$$\Delta y / \Delta x = b.$$

So the slope of the line is b.

Position of the Line

The y-axis intercept determines the position of the line on the graph. Figure 3 illustrates the relationship between the y-axis intercept and the position of the line. In this graph, the y-axis measures saving and the x-axis measures income.

When the y-axis intercept, a, is positive, the line hits the y-axis at a positive value of y—as the blue line does. Its y-axis intercept is 100. When the y-axis intercept, a, is zero, the line hits the y-axis at the origin—as the purple line does. Its y-axis intercept is 0. When the y-axis intercept, a, is negative, the line hits the y-axis at a negative value of y—as the red line does. Its y-axis intercept is -100.

As the equations of the three lines show, the value of the y-axis intercept does not influence the slope of the line. All three lines have a slope equal to 0.5.

Positive Relationships

Figure 1 shows a positive relationship—the two variables x and y move in the same direction. All positive relationships have a slope that is positive. In the equation of the line, the constant b is positive. In this example, the y-axis intercept, a, is 100. The slope b equals $\Delta y / \Delta x$, which in Fig. 2 is 100/200 or 0.5. The equation of the line is

$$y = 100 + 0.5x.$$

Negative Relationships

Figure 4 shows a negative relationship—the two variables x and y move in the opposite direction. All negative relationships have a slope that is negative. In the equation of the line, the constant b is negative. In the example in Fig. 4, the y-axis intercept, a, is 30. The slope, b, equals $\Delta y / \Delta x$, which is $-20/2$ or -10. The equation of the line is

$$y = 30 + (-10)x$$

or

$$y = 30 - 10x.$$

Example

A straight line has a y-axis intercept of 50 and a slope of 2. What is the equation of this line?

The equation of a straight line is

$$y = a + bx$$

where a is the y-axis intercept and b is the slope. So the equation is

$$y = 50 + 2x.$$

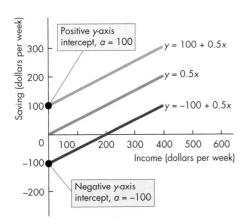

Figure 3 The y-Axis Intercept

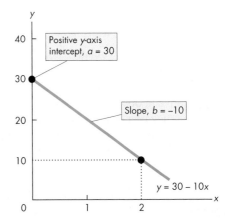

Figure 4 Negative Relationship

◆ REVIEW QUIZ

1 Explain how we "read" the two graphs in Figs. A1.1 and A1.2.

2 Explain what scatter diagrams show and why we use them.

3 Explain how we "read" the three scatter diagrams in Figs. A1.3 and A1.4.

4 Draw a graph to show the relationship between two variables that move in the same direction.

5 Draw a graph to show the relationship between two variables that move in opposite directions.

6 Draw a graph of two variables whose relationship shows (a) a maximum and (b) a minimum.

7 Which of the relationships in Questions 4 and 5 is a positive relationship and which is a negative relationship?

8 What are the two ways of calculating the slope of a curved line?

9 How do we graph a relationship among more than two variables?

10 Explain what change will bring a *movement along* a curve.

11 Explain what change will bring a *shift* of a curve.

Work these questions in Study Plan 1A and get instant feedback. MyLab Economics

◆ SUMMARY

Key Points

Graphing Data (pp. 17–20)

■ A graph is made by plotting the values of two variables x and y at a point that corresponds to their values measured along the x-axis and the y-axis.

■ A scatter diagram is a graph that plots the values of two variables for a number of different values of each.

■ A scatter diagram shows the relationship between the two variables. It shows whether they are positively related, negatively related, or unrelated.

Graphs Used in Economic Models (pp. 20–23)

■ Graphs are used to show relationships among variables in economic models.

■ Relationships can be positive (an upward-sloping curve), negative (a downward-sloping curve), positive and then negative (have a maximum point), negative and then positive (have a minimum point), or unrelated (a horizontal or vertical curve).

The Slope of a Relationship (pp. 24–26)

■ The slope of a relationship is calculated as the change in the value of the variable measured on the y-axis divided by the change in the value of the variable measured on the x-axis—that is, $\Delta y/\Delta x$.

■ A straight line has a constant slope.

■ A curved line has a varying slope. To calculate the slope of a curved line, we calculate the slope at a point or across an arc.

Graphing Relationships Among More Than Two Variables (pp. 26–27)

■ To graph a relationship among more than two variables, we hold constant the values of all the variables except two.

■ We then plot the value of one of the variables against the value of another.

■ A *cet par* change in the value of a variable on an axis of a graph brings a movement along the curve.

■ A change in the value of a variable held constant along the curve brings a shift of the curve.

Key Terms

MyLab Economics Key Terms Quiz

Ceteris paribus, 26

Direct relationship, 20

Inverse relationship, 21

Linear relationship, 20

Negative relationship, 21

Positive relationship, 20

Scatter diagram, 18

Slope, 24

STUDY PLAN PROBLEMS AND APPLICATIONS

MyLab Economics Work Problems 1 to 11 in Chapter 1A Study Plan and get instant feedback.

Use the following spreadsheet to work Problems 1 to 3. The spreadsheet provides the economic data: Column A is the year, column B is the inflation rate, column C is the interest rate, column D is the growth rate, and column E is the unemployment rate.

	A	B	C	D	E
1	2006	2.5	4.9	2.7	4.6
2	2007	4.1	4.5	1.8	4.6
3	2008	0.1	1.4	−0.3	5.8
4	2009	2.7	0.2	−2.8	9.3
5	2010	1.5	0.1	2.5	9.6
6	2011	3.0	0.1	1.6	8.9
7	2012	1.7	0.1	2.2	8.1
8	2013	1.5	0.1	1.7	7.4
9	2014	0.8	0.0	2.4	6.2
10	2015	0.7	0.1	2.6	5.3
11	2016	2.1	0.3	1.6	4.9

1. Draw a scatter diagram of the inflation rate and the interest rate. Describe the relationship.
2. Draw a scatter diagram of the growth rate and the unemployment rate. Describe the relationship.
3. Draw a scatter diagram of the interest rate and the unemployment rate. Describe the relationship.

Use the following news clip to work Problems 4 to 6.

Kong Tops the Box Office

Movie	Theatres (number)	Revenue (dollars per theatre)
Kong: Skull Island	3,846	$15,867
Logan	4,071	$9,362
Get Out	3,143	$6,600
The Shack	2,888	$3,465

Source: boxofficemojo.com,
Data for weekend of February 10–12, 2017

4. Draw a graph of the relationship between the revenue per theatre on the *y*-axis and the number of theatres on the *x*-axis. Describe the relationship.
5. Calculate the slope of the relationship in Problem 4 between 3,846 and 4,071 theatres.
6. Calculate the slope of the relationship in Problem 4 between 4,071 and 3,143 theatres.

7. Calculate the slope of the following relationship.

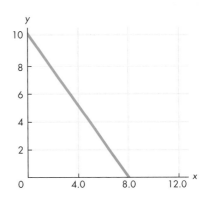

Use the following relationship to work Problems 8 and 9.

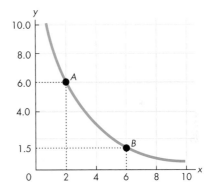

8. Calculate the slope of the relationship at point *A* and at point *B*.
9. Calculate the slope across the arc *AB*.

Use the following table to work Problems 10 and 11. The table gives the price of a balloon ride, the temperature, and the number of rides a day.

Price (dollars per ride)	Balloon rides (number per day)		
	10°C	20°C	30°C
5	32	40	50
10	27	32	40
15	18	27	32

10. Draw a graph to show the relationship between the price and the number of rides when the temperature is 20°C. Describe this relationship.
11. What happens in the graph in Problem 10 if the temperature rises to 30°C?

ADDITIONAL PROBLEMS AND APPLICATIONS

Use the following spreadsheet to work Problems 12 to 14. The spreadsheet provides data on oil and gasoline: Column A is the year, column B is the price of oil (dollars per barrel), column C is the price of gasoline (cents per litre), column D is oil production, and column E is the quantity of gasoline refined (both in millions of barrels per day).

	A	B	C	D	E
1	2006	66	262	5.1	15.6
2	2007	72	284	5.1	15.4
3	2008	100	330	5.0	15.3
4	2009	62	241	5.4	14.8
5	2010	79	284	5.5	15.2
6	2011	95	358	5.6	15.1
7	2012	94	368	6.5	15.5
8	2013	98	358	7.5	15.2
9	2014	93	344	8.8	15.5
10	2015	49	252	9.4	16.6
11	2016	45	225	8.9	16.4

12. Draw a scatter diagram of the price of oil and the quantity of oil produced. Describe the relationship.

13. Draw a scatter diagram of the price of gasoline and the quantity of gasoline refined. Describe the relationship.

14. Draw a scatter diagram of the quantity of oil produced and the quantity of gasoline refined. Describe the relationship.

Use the following data to work Problems 15 to 17. Draw a graph that shows the relationship between the two variables x and y:

x	0	1	2	3	4	5
y	25	24	22	18	12	0

15. a. Is the relationship positive or negative?
    b. Does the slope of the relationship become steeper or flatter as the value of x increases?
    c. Think of some economic relationships that might be similar to this one.

16. Calculate the slope of the relationship between x and y when x equals 3.

17. Calculate the slope of the relationship across the arc as x increases from 4 to 5.

18. Calculate the slope of the curve in the figure in the next column at point A.

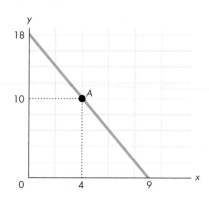

Use the following relationship to work Problems 19 and 20.

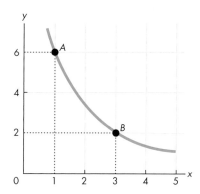

19. Calculate the slope at point A and at point B.

20. Calculate the slope across the arc AB.

Use the following table to work Problems 21 to 23. The table gives data about umbrellas: price, the number purchased, and rainfall in millimetres (mm).

Price (dollars per umbrella)	Umbrellas (number purchased per day)		
	0 mm	200 mm	400 mm
20	4	7	8
30	2	4	7
40	1	2	4

21. Draw a graph to show the relationship between the price and the number of umbrellas purchased, holding the amount of rainfall constant at 200 mm. Describe this relationship.

22. What happens in the graph in Problem 21 if the price rises and rainfall is constant?

23. What happens in the graph in Problem 21 if the rainfall increases from 200 mm to 400 mm?

2

THE ECONOMIC PROBLEM

After studying this chapter, you will be able to:

◆ Define the production possibilities frontier and use it to calculate opportunity cost

◆ Distinguish between production possibilities and preferences and describe an efficient allocation of resources

◆ Explain how specialization and trade expand production possibilities

◆ Explain how current production choices expand future production possibilities, change what we produce, and destroy and create jobs

◆ Describe the economic institutions that coordinate decisions

Canada has vast oil and natural gas resources and we produce much more energy than we consume. We are an energy-exporting nation. Should we produce and export even more oil and gas? How do we know when we are using our energy and other resources efficiently?

In this chapter, you study an economic model that answers questions about the efficiency of production and trade.

At the end of the chapter, in *Economics in the News*, we'll apply what you learn to explain why it is smart to export some of our oil and gas, and why it might not be smart to increase our gas exports.

◆ Production Possibilities and Opportunity Cost

Every working day, in mines, factories, shops, and offices and on farms and construction sites across Canada, 18 million people produce a vast variety of goods and services valued at $60 billion. But the quantities of goods and services that we can produce are limited by our available resources and by technology. And if we want to increase our production of one good, we must decrease our production of something else—we face a tradeoff. You are now going to study the limits to production.

The **production possibilities frontier** (*PPF*) is the boundary between those combinations of goods and services that can be produced and those that cannot. To illustrate the *PPF*, we look at a *model economy* in which the quantities produced of only two goods change, while the quantities produced of all the other goods and services remain the same.

Let's look at the production possibilities frontier for cola and pizza, which represent *any* pair of goods or services.

Production Possibilities Frontier

The *production possibilities frontier* for cola and pizza shows the limits to the production of these two goods, given the total resources and technology available to produce them. Figure 2.1 shows this production possibilities frontier. The table lists combinations of the quantities of pizza and cola that can be produced in a month and the figure graphs these combinations. The *x*-axis shows the quantity of pizzas produced, and the *y*-axis shows the quantity of cola produced.

The *PPF* illustrates *scarcity* because the points outside the frontier are *unattainable*. These points describe wants that can't be satisfied.

We can produce at any point *inside* the *PPF* or *on* the *PPF*. These points are *attainable*. For example, we can produce 4 million pizzas and 5 million cans of cola. Figure 2.1 shows this combination as point *E* in the graph and as possibility *E* in the table.

Moving along the *PPF* from point *E* to point *D* (possibility *D* in the table) we produce more cola and less pizza: 9 million cans of cola and 3 million pizzas. Or moving in the opposite direction from point *E* to point *F* (possibility *F* in the table), we produce more pizza and less cola: 5 million pizzas and no cola.

FIGURE 2.1   Production Possibilities Frontier

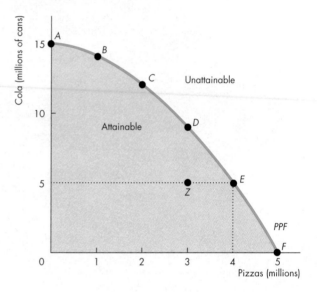

Possibility	Pizzas (millions)		Cola (millions of cans)
A	0	and	15
B	1	and	14
C	2	and	12
D	3	and	9
E	4	and	5
F	5	and	0

The table lists six production possibilities for cola and pizzas. Row *A* tells us that if we produce no pizzas, the maximum quantity of cola we can produce is 15 million cans. Points *A*, *B*, *C*, *D*, *E*, and *F* in the figure represent the rows of the table. The curve passing through these points is the production possibilities frontier (*PPF*).

The *PPF* separates the attainable from the unattainable. Production is possible at any point *inside* the orange area or *on* the frontier. Points outside the frontier are unattainable. Points inside the frontier, such as point *Z*, are inefficient because resources are wasted or misallocated. At such points, it is possible to use the available resources to produce more of either or both goods.

⎯ MyLab Economics Animation and Draw Graph ⎯

Production Efficiency

We achieve **production efficiency** if we produce goods and services at the lowest possible cost. This outcome occurs at all the points *on* the *PPF*. At points *inside* the *PPF*, production is inefficient because we are giving up more than necessary of one good to produce a given quantity of the other good.

For example, at point *Z* in Fig. 2.1, we produce 3 million pizzas and 5 million cans of cola, but we have enough resources to produce 3 million pizzas and 9 million cans of cola. Our pizzas cost more cola than necessary. We can get them for a lower cost. Only when we produce *on* the *PPF* do we incur the lowest possible cost of production.

Production inside the *PPF* is *inefficient* because resources are either *unused* or *misallocated* or both.

Resources are *unused* when they are idle but could be working. For example, we might leave some of the factories idle or some workers unemployed.

Resources are *misallocated* when they are assigned to tasks for which they are not the best match. For example, we might assign skilled pizza chefs to work in a cola factory and skilled cola workers to cook pizza in a pizzeria. We could get more pizzas *and* more cola if we reassigned these workers to the tasks that more closely match their skills.

Tradeoff Along the *PPF*

A choice *along* the *PPF* involves a *tradeoff*. Tradeoffs like that between cola and pizza arise in every imaginable real-world situation in which a choice must be made. At any given time, we have a fixed amount of labour, land, capital, and entrepreneurship and a given state of technology. We can employ these resources and technology to produce goods and services, but we are limited in what we can produce.

When doctors want to spend more on cancer research, they face a tradeoff: more medical research for less of some other things. When Parliament wants to spend more on education, it faces a tradeoff: more education for less national defence or border security. When an environmental group argues for less logging, it is suggesting a tradeoff: greater conservation of endangered wildlife for less paper. When you want a higher grade on your next test, you face a tradeoff: spend more time studying and less leisure or sleep time.

All the tradeoffs you've just considered involve a cost—an opportunity cost.

Opportunity Cost

The **opportunity cost** of an action is the highest-valued alternative forgone. The *PPF* makes this idea precise and enables us to calculate opportunity cost. Along the *PPF*, there are only two goods, so there is only one alternative forgone: some quantity of the other good. To produce more pizzas we must produce less cola. The opportunity cost of producing an additional pizza is the cola we *must* forgo. Similarly, the opportunity cost of producing an additional can of cola is the quantity of pizza we must forgo.

In Fig. 2.1, if we move from point *C* to point *D*, we produce an additional 1 million pizzas but 3 million fewer cans of cola. The additional 1 million pizzas *cost* 3 million cans of cola. Or 1 pizza costs 3 cans of cola. Similarly, if we move from *D* to *C*, we produce an additional 3 million cans of cola but 1 million fewer pizzas. The additional 3 million cans of cola *cost* 1 million pizzas. Or 1 can of cola costs 1/3 of a pizza.

Opportunity Cost Is a Ratio Opportunity cost is a ratio. It is the decrease in the quantity produced of one good divided by the increase in the quantity produced of another good as we move along the production possibilities frontier.

Because opportunity cost is a ratio, the opportunity cost of producing an additional can of cola is equal to the *inverse* of the opportunity cost of producing an additional pizza. Check this proposition by returning to the calculations we've just done. In the move from *C* to *D*, the opportunity cost of a pizza is 3 cans of cola. In the move from *D* to *C*, the opportunity cost of a can of cola is 1/3 of a pizza. So the opportunity cost of pizza is the inverse of the opportunity cost of cola.

Increasing Opportunity Cost The opportunity cost of a pizza increases as the quantity of pizzas produced increases. The outward-bowed shape of the *PPF* reflects increasing opportunity cost. When we produce a large quantity of cola and a small quantity of pizza—between points *A* and *B* in Fig. 2.1—the frontier has a gentle slope. An increase in the quantity of pizzas costs a small decrease in the quantity of cola—the opportunity cost of a pizza is a small quantity of cola.

When we produce a large quantity of pizzas and a small quantity of cola—between points *E* and *F* in Fig. 2.1—the frontier is steep. A given increase in the quantity of pizzas *costs* a large decrease in the quantity of cola, so the opportunity cost of a pizza is a large quantity of cola.

ECONOMICS IN THE NEWS

Opportunity Cost of Kale

Kale Popularity Puts Pressure on Seed Supply

With kale's surging popularity, kale farmers are taking pre-
cautions to avoid wasting seeds. Kale sales are up more
than 30 percent and the price has gone up 80 percent
over the past three years.

Source: *CBS News*, January 18, 2016

THE QUESTIONS

■ How does the *PPF* illustrate (1) the limits to kale production; (2) the tradeoff we must make to increase
kale production; and (3) the effect of increased kale
consumption on the cost of producing kale?

THE ANSWERS

■ The figure shows the global *PPF* for kale and other
goods and services. Point *A* on the *PPF* tells us that if
4 million tonnes of kale are produced, a maximum of
96 units of other goods and services can be produced.

■ The movement along the *PPF* from *A* to *B* shows the
tradeoff we must make to increase kale production.

■ The slope of the *PPF* measures the opportunity cost
of producing kale. If kale production increases from
zero to 4 million tonnes, the production of other
goods and services decreases from 100 units to
96 units. The opportunity cost of producing 1 tonne
of kale is 1 unit of other goods and services.

■ But if kale production increases from 4 million tonnes

to 8 million tonnes, the production of other goods
and services decreases from 96 units to 80 units. The
opportunity cost of producing 1 tonne of kale is now
4 units of other goods and services.

■ As resources are moved into producing kale, labour,
land, and capital less suited to the task of kale production are used and the cost of the additional kale produced increases.

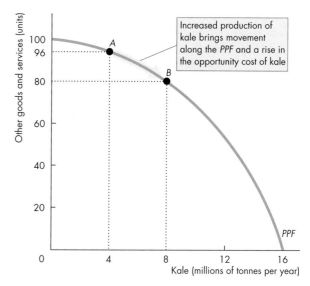

PPF for Kale and Other Goods and Services

The *PPF* is bowed outward because resources are
not all equally productive in all activities. People with
many years of experience working for PepsiCo are good
at producing cola but not very good at making pizzas.
So if we move some of these people from PepsiCo to
Domino's, we get a small increase in the quantity of
pizzas but a large decrease in the quantity of cola.

Similarly, people who have spent years working at
Domino's are good at producing pizzas, but they have
no idea how to produce cola. So if we move some people from Domino's to PepsiCo, we get a small increase
in the quantity of cola but a large decrease in the quantity of pizzas. The more we produce of either good, the
less productive are the additional resources we use and
the larger is the opportunity cost of a unit of that good.

How do we choose among the points on the *PPF*?
How do we know which point is the best?

MyLab Economics Economics in the News

REVIEW QUIZ

1 How does the production possibilities frontier
illustrate scarcity?

2 How does the production possibilities frontier
illustrate production efficiency?

3 How does the production possibilities frontier
show that every choice involves a tradeoff?

4 How does the production possibilities frontier
illustrate opportunity cost?

5 Why is opportunity cost a ratio?

6 Why does the *PPF* bow outward and what
does that imply about the relationship between
opportunity cost and the quantity produced?

Work these questions in Study Plan 2.1 and
get instant feedback.
MyLab Economics

◆ Using Resources Efficiently

We achieve *production efficiency* at every point on the *PPF*, but which of these points is best? The answer is the point on the *PPF* at which goods and services are produced in the quantities that provide the greatest possible benefit. When goods and services are produced at the lowest possible cost and in the quantities that provide the greatest possible benefit, we have achieved **allocative efficiency**.

The questions that we raised when we reviewed the four big issues in Chapter 1 are questions about allocative efficiency. To answer such questions, we must measure and compare costs and benefits.

The *PPF* and Marginal Cost

The **marginal cost** of a good is the opportunity cost of producing one more unit of it. We calculate marginal cost from the slope of the *PPF*. As the quantity of pizzas produced increases, the *PPF* gets steeper and the marginal cost of a pizza increases. Figure 2.2 illustrates the calculation of the marginal cost of a pizza.

Begin by finding the opportunity cost of pizza in blocks of 1 million pizzas. The cost of the first million pizzas is 1 million cans of cola; the cost of the second million pizzas is 2 million cans of cola; the cost of the third million pizzas is 3 million cans of cola, and so on. The bars in part (a) illustrate these calculations.

The bars in part (b) show the cost of an average pizza in each of the 1 million pizza blocks. Focus on the third million pizzas—the move from *C* to *D* in part (a). Over this range, because 1 million pizzas cost 3 million cans of cola, one of these pizzas, on average, costs 3 cans of cola—the height of the bar in part (b).

Next, find the opportunity cost of each additional pizza—the marginal cost of a pizza. The marginal cost of a pizza increases as the quantity of pizzas produced increases. The marginal cost at point *C* is less than it is at point *D*. On average over the range from *C* to *D*, the marginal cost of a pizza is 3 cans of cola. But it exactly equals 3 cans of cola only in the middle of the range between *C* and *D*.

The red dot in part (b) indicates that the marginal cost of a pizza is 3 cans of cola when 2.5 million pizzas are produced. Each black dot in part (b) is interpreted in the same way. The red curve that passes through these dots, labelled *MC*, is the marginal cost curve. It shows the marginal cost of a pizza at each quantity of pizzas as we move along the *PPF*.

FIGURE 2.2   The *PPF* and Marginal Cost

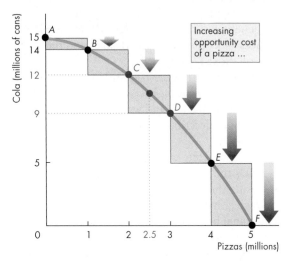

(a) *PPF* **and opportunity cost**

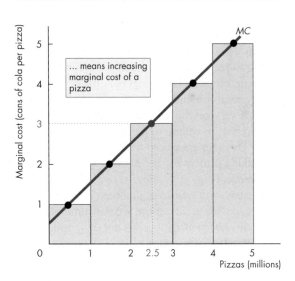

(b) Marginal cost

Marginal cost is calculated from the slope of the *PPF*. As the quantity of pizzas produced increases, the *PPF* gets steeper and the marginal cost of a pizza increases. The bars in part (a) show the opportunity cost of pizza in blocks of 1 million pizzas. The bars in part (b) show the cost of an average pizza in each of these 1 million blocks. The red curve, *MC*, shows the marginal cost of a pizza at each point along the *PPF*. This curve passes through the centre of each of the bars in part (b).

—————— MyLab Economics Animation ——————

Preferences and Marginal Benefit

The **marginal benefit** from a good or service is the benefit received from consuming one more unit of it. This benefit is subjective. It depends on people's **preferences**—people's likes and dislikes and the intensity of those feelings.

Marginal benefit and *preferences* stand in sharp contrast to *marginal cost* and *production possibilities*. Preferences describe what people like and want and the production possibilities describe the limits or constraints on what is feasible.

We need a concrete way of illustrating preferences that parallels the way we illustrate the limits to production using the *PPF*.

The device that we use to illustrate preferences is the **marginal benefit curve**, which is a curve that shows the relationship between the marginal benefit from a good and the quantity consumed of that good. Note that the *marginal benefit curve* is *unrelated* to the *PPF* and cannot be derived from it.

We measure the marginal benefit from a good or service by the most that people are *willing to pay* for an additional unit of it. The idea is that you are willing to pay less for a good than it is worth to you but you are not willing to pay more: The most you are willing to pay for something is its marginal benefit.

It is a general principle that the more we have of any good or service, the smaller is its marginal benefit and the less we are willing to pay for an additional unit of it. This tendency is so widespread and strong that we call it a principle—the *principle of decreasing marginal benefit*.

The basic reason why marginal benefit decreases is that we like variety. The more we consume of any one good or service, the more we tire of it and would prefer to switch to something else.

Think about your willingness to pay for a pizza. If pizza is hard to come by and you can buy only a few slices a year, you might be willing to pay a high price to get an additional slice. But if pizza is all you've eaten for the past few days, you are willing to pay almost nothing for another slice.

You've learned to think about cost as opportunity cost, not as a dollar cost. You can think about marginal benefit and willingness to pay in the same way. The marginal benefit, measured by what you are willing to pay for something, is the quantity of other goods and services that you are willing to forgo. Let's continue with the example of cola and pizza and illustrate preferences this way.

FIGURE 2.3 Preferences and the Marginal Benefit Curve

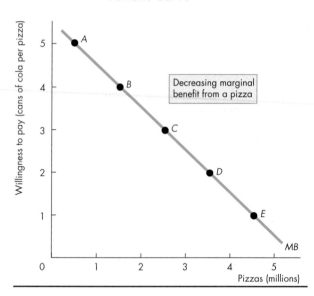

Decreasing marginal benefit from a pizza

Possibility	Pizzas (millions)	Willingness to pay (cans of cola per pizza)
A	0.5	5
B	1.5	4
C	2.5	3
D	3.5	2
E	4.5	1

The smaller the quantity of pizzas available, the more cola people are willing to give up for an additional pizza. With 0.5 million pizzas available, people are willing to pay 5 cans of cola per pizza. But with 4.5 million pizzas, people are willing to pay only 1 can of cola per pizza. Willingness to pay measures marginal benefit. A universal feature of people's preferences is that marginal benefit decreases.

MyLab Economics Animation

Figure 2.3 illustrates preferences as the willingness to pay for pizza in terms of cola. In row *A*, with 0.5 million pizzas available, people are willing to pay 5 cans of cola per pizza. As the quantity of pizzas increases, the amount that people are willing to pay for a pizza falls. With 4.5 million pizzas available, people are willing to pay only 1 can of cola per pizza.

Let's now use the concepts of marginal cost and marginal benefit to describe allocative efficiency.

FIGURE 2.4 Efficient Use of Resources

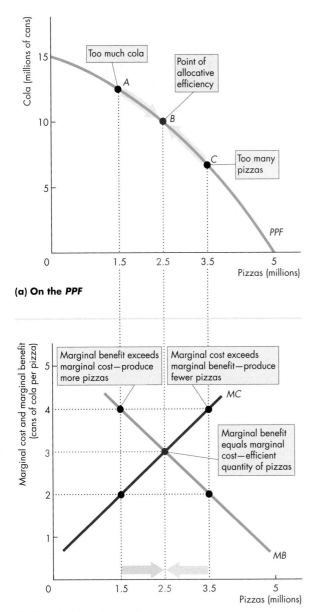

(a) On the PPF

(b) Marginal benefit equals marginal cost

The greater the quantity of pizzas produced, the smaller is the marginal benefit (MB) from pizza—the less cola people are willing to give up to get an additional pizza. But the greater the quantity of pizzas produced, the greater is the marginal cost (MC) of a pizza—the more cola people must give up to get an additional pizza. When marginal benefit equals marginal cost, resources are being used efficiently.

MyLab Economics Animation

Allocative Efficiency

At *any* point on the *PPF*, we cannot produce more of one good without giving up some other good. At the *best* point on the *PPF*, we cannot produce more of one good without giving up some other good that provides greater benefit. We are producing at the point of allocative efficiency—the point on the *PPF* that we prefer above all other points.

Suppose in Fig. 2.4 we produce 1.5 million pizzas. In part (b), the marginal cost of a pizza is 2 cans of cola and the marginal benefit from a pizza is 4 cans of cola. Because someone values an additional pizza more highly than it costs to produce, we can get more value from our resources by moving some of them out of producing cola and into producing pizza.

Now suppose we produce 3.5 million pizzas. The marginal cost of producing a pizza is now 4 cans of cola, but the marginal benefit from a pizza is only 2 cans of cola. Because the additional pizza costs more than anyone thinks it is worth, we can get more value from our resources by moving some of them away from producing pizza and into producing cola.

Suppose we produce 2.5 million pizzas. Marginal cost and marginal benefit are now equal at 3 cans of cola. This allocation of resources between pizzas and cola is efficient. If more pizzas are produced, the forgone cola is worth more than the additional pizzas. If fewer pizzas are produced, the forgone pizzas are worth more than the additional cola.

◆ REVIEW QUIZ

1 What is marginal cost? How is it measured?
2 What is marginal benefit? How is it measured?
3 How does the marginal benefit from a good change as the quantity produced of that good increases?
4 What is allocative efficiency and how does it relate to the production possibilities frontier?
5 What conditions must be satisfied if resources are used efficiently?

Work these questions in Study Plan 2.2 and get instant feedback. MyLab Economics

You now understand the limits to production and the conditions under which resources are used efficiently. Your next task is to to see how both buyer and seller gain from specialization and trade.

◆ Gains from Trade

People can produce for themselves all the goods and services that they consume, or they can produce one good or a few goods and trade with others. Producing only one good or a few goods is called *specialization*. We are going to learn how people gain by specializing in the production of the good in which they have a *comparative advantage* and trading with others.

Comparative Advantage and Absolute Advantage

A person has a **comparative advantage** in an activity if that person can perform the activity at a lower opportunity cost than anyone else. Differences in opportunity costs arise from differences in individual abilities and from differences in the characteristics of other resources.

No one excels at everything. One person is an outstanding pitcher but a poor catcher; another person is a brilliant lawyer but a poor teacher. In almost all human endeavours, what one person does easily, someone else finds difficult. The same applies to land and capital. One plot of land is fertile but has no mineral deposits; another plot of land has outstanding views but is infertile. One machine has great precision but is difficult to operate; another is fast but often breaks down.

Although no one excels at everything, some people excel and can outperform others in a large number of activities—perhaps even in all activities. A person who is more productive than others has an **absolute advantage**.

Absolute advantage involves comparing productivities—production per hour—whereas comparative advantage involves comparing opportunity costs.

A person who has an absolute advantage does not have a *comparative* advantage in every activity. John Grisham is a better lawyer and a better author of fast-paced thrillers than most people. He has an absolute advantage in these two activities. But compared to others, he is a better writer than lawyer, so his *comparative* advantage is in writing.

Because ability and resources vary from one person to another, people have different opportunity costs of producing various goods. These differences in opportunity cost are the source of comparative advantage.

Let's explore the idea of comparative advantage by looking at two smoothie bars: one operated by Liz and the other operated by Joe.

Joe's Smoothie Bar Joe produces smoothies and salads in a small, low-tech bar. He has only one blender, and it's a slow, old machine that keeps stopping. Even if Joe uses all his resources to produce smoothies, he can produce only 6 an hour—see Table 2.1. But Joe is good at making salads, and if he uses all his resources in this activity, he can produce 30 salads an hour.

Joe's ability to make smoothies and salads is the same regardless of how he splits an hour between the two tasks. He can make a salad in 2 minutes or a smoothie in 10 minutes. For each additional smoothie Joe produces, he must decrease his production of salads by 5. And for each additional salad he produces, he must decrease his production of smoothies by 1/5 of a smoothie. So

> Joe's opportunity cost of producing 1 smoothie is 5 salads,

and

> Joe's opportunity cost of producing 1 salad is 1/5 of a smoothie.

Joe's customers buy smoothies and salads in equal quantities. So Joe spends 50 minutes of each hour making smoothies and 10 minutes of each hour making salads. With this division of his time, Joe produces 5 smoothies and 5 salads an hour.

Figure 2.5(a) illustrates the production possibilities at Joe's smoothie bar—Joe's *PPF*.

Joe's *PPF* is linear (not outward bowed) because his ability to produce salads and smoothies is the same no matter how he divides his time between the two activities. Joe's opportunity cost of a smoothie is constant—it is the same at all quantities of smoothies produced.

TABLE 2.1 Joe's Production Possibilities

Item	Minutes to produce 1	Quantity per hour
Smoothies	10	6
Salads	2	30

Liz's Smoothie Bar Liz also produces smoothies and salads but in a high-tech bar that is much more productive than Joe's. Liz can turn out either a smoothie or a salad every 2 minutes—see Table 2.2.

If Liz spends all her time making smoothies, she can produce 30 an hour. And if she spends all her time making salads, she can also produce 30 an hour.

Liz's ability to make smoothies and salads, like Joe's, is the same regardless of how she divides her time between the two tasks. She can make a salad in 2 minutes or a smoothie in 2 minutes. For each additional smoothie Liz produces, she must decrease her production of salads by 1. And for each additional salad she produces, she must decrease her production of smoothies by 1. So

> Liz's opportunity cost of producing 1 smoothie is 1 salad,

and

> Liz's opportunity cost of producing 1 salad is 1 smoothie.

TABLE 2.2   Liz's Production Possibilities

Item	Minutes to produce 1	Quantity per hour
Smoothies	2	30
Salads	2	30

Liz's customers buy smoothies and salads in equal quantities, so she splits her time equally between the two items and produces 15 smoothies and 15 salads an hour.

Figure 2.5(b) illustrates the production possibilities at Liz's smoothie bar—Liz's *PPF*.

Like Joe's, Liz's *PPF* is linear because her ability to produce salads and smoothies is the same no matter how she divides her time between the two activities. Liz's opportunity cost of a smoothie is 1 salad at all quantities of smoothies produced.

FIGURE 2.5   The Production Possibilities Frontiers

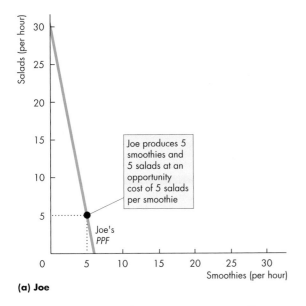

(a) Joe

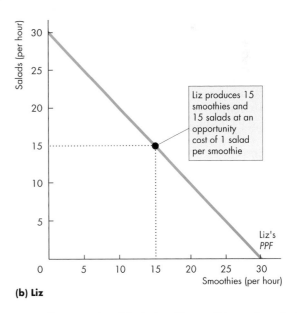

(b) Liz

Joe can produce 30 salads per hour, 1 every 2 minutes, if he produces no smoothies. Or, he can produce 6 smoothies per hour, 1 every 10 minutes, if he produces no salads. Joe's customers buy equal quantities of salads and smoothies, so Joe produces 5 of each. His opportunity cost of a smoothie is 5 salads.

Liz can produce 30 salads or 30 smoothies per hour, 1 of either item every 2 minutes. Liz's customers buy equal quantities of salads and smoothies, so she produces 15 of each. Liz's opportunity cost of a smoothie is 1 salad.

Joe's Comparative Advantage In which of the two activities does Joe have a comparative advantage? To answer this question, first recall the definition of comparative advantage. A person has a comparative advantage when that person's opportunity cost of producing a good is lower than another person's opportunity cost of producing that same good.

Joe's opportunity cost of producing a salad is only 1/5 of a smoothie, while Liz's opportunity cost of producing a salad is 1 smoothie. So Joe has a comparative advantage in producing salads.

Liz's Comparative Advantage If Joe has a comparative advantage in producing salads, Liz must have a comparative advantage in producing smoothies. Check the numbers. For Joe, a smoothie costs 5 salads, and for Liz, a smoothie costs only 1 salad. So Liz has a comparative advantage in making smoothies.

Achieving the Gains from Trade

Liz and Joe run into each other one evening in a singles bar. After a few minutes of getting acquainted, Liz tells Joe about her amazing smoothie business. Her only problem, she tells Joe, is that she would like to produce more because potential customers leave when her lines get too long.

Joe doesn't want to risk spoiling a potential relationship by telling Liz about his own struggling business, but he takes the risk. Joe explains to Liz that he spends 50 minutes of every hour making 5 smoothies and 10 minutes making 5 salads. Liz's eyes pop. "Have I got a deal for you!" she exclaims.

Liz's Proposal Here's the deal that Liz sketches on a paper napkin:

1. We'll both specialize in producing the good in which we have a comparative advantage.

2. Joe will stop making smoothies and allocate all his time to producing salads.

3. Liz will stop making salads and allocate all her time to producing smoothies.

4. Together we will produce 30 smoothies and 30 salads—see Table 2.3(b).

5. We will then trade. Joe will get smoothies from Liz, and Liz will get salads from Joe.

6. We must agree on a price at which to trade.

Agreeing on a Price Liz is buying salads from Joe, and Joe is buying smoothies from Liz. Normally, in

TABLE 2.3 Liz and Joe Gain from Trade

(a) Initially	Liz	Joe
Smoothies	15	5
Salads	15	5
(b) After specialization	**Liz**	**Joe**
Smoothies	30	0
Salads	0	30
(c) Trade	**Liz**	**Joe**
Smoothies	sell 10	buy 10
Salads	buy 20	sell 20
(d) After trade	**Liz**	**Joe**
Smoothies	20	10
Salads	20	10
(e) Gains from trade	**Liz**	**Joe**
Smoothies	+5	+5
Salads	+5	+5

a situation like this one, the trading partners will bargain about the price, with each person trying for the lowest price at which to buy and the highest price at which to sell.

But Liz and Joe like each other and quickly agree on a price that ends up sharing the gains from the new arrangement equally.

The price is not expressed in dollars but in salads per smoothie. They agree on a price of 2 salads per smoothie. For Liz, that is a good deal because she can produce a smoothie at a cost of 1 salad and sell it to Joe for 2 salads. It is also a good deal for Joe because he can produce a salad at a cost of 1/5 of a smoothie and sell it to Liz for 1/2 a smoothie.

Liz explains that any price above 1 salad per smoothie is good for her and any price below 5 salads per smoothie is good for Joe, so a price of 2 salads per smoothie lets them both gain, as she now describes.

At the proposed price of 2 salads per smoothie, Liz offers to sell Joe 10 smoothies in exchange for 20 salads. Equivalently, Joe sells Liz 20 salads in exchange for 10 smoothies—see Table 2.3(c).

FIGURE 2.6 The Gains from Trade

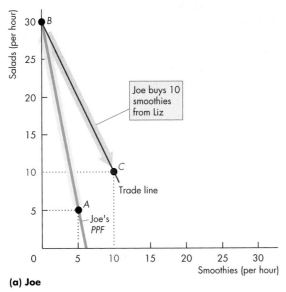

(a) Joe

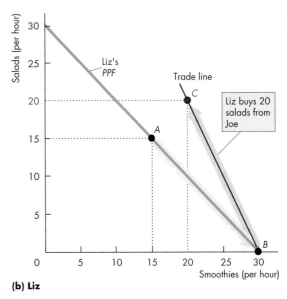

(b) Liz

Initially, Joe produces at point *A* on his *PPF* in part (a), and Liz produces at point *A* on her *PPF* in part (b). Joe's opportunity cost of producing a salad is less than Liz's, so Joe has a comparative advantage in producing salads. Liz's opportunity cost of producing a smoothie is less than Joe's, so Liz has a comparative advantage in producing smoothies.

If Joe specializes in making salads, he produces 30 salads and no smoothies at point *B* on his *PPF*. If Liz specializes in

making smoothies, she produces 30 smoothies and no salads at point *B* on her *PPF*. They exchange salads for smoothies along the red "Trade line." Liz buys salads from Joe for less than her opportunity cost of producing them. Joe buys smoothies from Liz for less than his opportunity cost of producing them. Each goes to point *C*—a point outside his or her *PPF*. With specialization and trade, Joe and Liz gain 5 smoothies and 5 salads each with no extra resources.

MyLab Economics Animation and Draw Graph

After this trade, Joe has 10 salads—the 30 salads he produces minus the 20 he sells to Liz. He also has the 10 smoothies that he buys from Liz. So Joe now has increased the quantities of smoothies and salads that he can sell to his customers—see Table 2.3(d).

Liz has 20 smoothies—the 30 she produces minus the 10 she sells to Joe. She also has the 20 salads that she buys from Joe. Liz has increased the quantities of smoothies and salads that she can sell to her customers—see Table 2.3(d). Both Liz and Joe gain 5 smoothies and 5 salads an hour—see Table 2.3(e).

Illustrating Liz's Idea To illustrate her idea, Liz grabs a fresh napkin and draws the graphs in Fig. 2.6. First, she sketches Joe's *PPF* in part (a) and shows the point at which he is producing before they meet. Recall that he is producing 5 smoothies and 5 salads an hour at point *A*.

She then sketches her own *PPF* in part (b), and marks the point *A* at which she is producing 15 smoothies and 15 salads an hour.

She then shows what happens when they each specialize in producing the good in which they have a comparative advantage. Joe specializes in producing salads and produces 30 salads and no smoothies at point *B* on his *PPF*. Liz specializes in producing smoothies and produces 30 smoothies and no salads at point *B* on her *PPF*.

They then trade smoothies and salads at a price of 2 salads per smoothie or 1/2 a smoothie per salad. The red "Trade line" that Liz draws on each part of the figure illustrates the tradeoff that each faces at the proposed price.

Liz now shows Joe the amazing outcome of her idea. After specializing and trading, Joe gets 10 smoothies and 10 salads at point *C*—a gain of 5 smoothies and 5 salads. He moves to a point *outside* his *PPF*. And Liz gets 20 smoothies and 20 salads at point *C*—also a gain of 5 smoothies and 5 salads— and moves to a point *outside* her *PPF*.

Despite Liz being more productive than Joe, both gain from specializing at producing the good in which they have a comparative advantage and trading.

The Liz–Joe Economy and Its *PPF*

With specialization and trade, Liz and Joe get outside their individual *PPF*s. But think about Liz and Joe as representing an entire economy. You know that it isn't possible to produce outside the economy's *PPF*. So, what's going on?

The answer is that although Liz and Joe get outside their individual *PPF*s with specialization, they produce on the economy's *PPF*.

Figure 2.7 illustrates the construction of the economy's *PPF*.

If both Liz and Joe produce only salads, the economy produces 60 salads per hour at point *A* in Fig. 2.7. Liz produces the first 30 at a cost of 1 salad per smoothie.

When Liz is using all her resources to produce smoothies, the economy is at point *B*. At this point, both are specializing in the good for which they have a comparative advantage.

If the economy is to produce more than 30 smoothies, Joe must join Liz in producing some. But the 31st smoothie, produced by Joe, costs 5 salads. If all its resources are used to produce smoothies, the economy produces 36 per hour at point *C*.

Outward-Bowed *PPF* The outward-kinked curve, *PPF*, is the Liz–Joe economy's production possibilities frontier. Despite Liz and Joe having constant opportunity costs—linear *PPF*s—along the economy's *PPF* opportunity cost is increasing. For the economy with only two people, the economy's *PPF* is kinked rather than bowed outward. But applying the same ideas that you've seen in the Liz–Joe economy to an economy with millions of people, the *PPF* is outward bowed.

Efficiency and Inefficiency When Liz and Joe specialize, they produce efficiently on the economy's *PPF*. They can also produce efficiently at any other point along their economy *PPF*. But without specialization and trade, they produce at an inefficient point inside the economy's *PPF*. You can see this fact in Fig. 2.7. If Liz and Joe produce their own smoothies and salads, they produce at point *D* inside the economy *PPF*. All the economy's resources are fully employed at point *D*, but they are misallocated.

FIGURE 2.7   The Liz–Joe Economy *PPF*

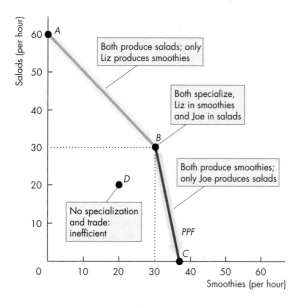

When the economy produces more than 30 salads per hour, both Liz and Joe produce salads but only Liz produces smoothies. When the economy produces more than 30 smoothies per hour, both Liz and Joe produce smoothies but only Joe produces salads.

When Liz and Joe specialize in their comparative advantage, the economy produces 30 salads and 30 smoothies at an efficient point on the economy's *PPF*.

Without specialization and trade, Liz and Joe produce at an inefficient point inside the economy's *PPF*.

—— MyLab Economics Animation and Draw Graph ——

REVIEW QUIZ

1 What gives a person a comparative advantage?
2 Distinguish between comparative advantage and absolute advantage.
3 Why do people specialize and trade?
4 What are the gains from specialization and trade?
5 What is the source of the gains from trade?
6 Why do specialization and the gains from trade make the economy's *PPF* bow outward?
7 Why is not specializing and reaping the gains from trade inefficient?

Work these questions in Study Plan 2.3 and get instant feedback.   MyLab Economics

◆ Economic Growth

During the past 30 years, production per person in Canada has doubled. The expansion of production possibilities is called **economic growth**. Economic growth increases our *standard of living,* but it doesn't overcome scarcity and avoid opportunity cost. To make our economy grow, we face a tradeoff—the faster we make production grow, the greater is the opportunity cost of economic growth.

The Cost of Economic Growth

Economic growth comes from technological change and capital accumulation. **Technological change** is the development of new goods and of better ways of producing goods and services. **Capital accumulation** is the growth of capital resources, including *human capital*.

Technological change and capital accumulation have vastly expanded our production possibilities. We can produce automobiles that provide us with more transportation than was available when we had only horses and carriages. We can produce satellites that provide global communications on a much larger scale than that available with the earlier cable technology. But if we use our resources to develop new technologies and produce capital, we must decrease our production of consumption goods and services. New technologies and new capital have an opportunity cost. Let's look at this opportunity cost.

Instead of studying the *PPF* of pizzas and cola, we'll hold the quantity of cola produced constant and examine the *PPF* for pizzas and pizza ovens. Figure 2.8 shows this *PPF* as the blue curve PPF_0. If we devote no resources to producing pizza ovens, we produce at point *A*. If we produce 3 million pizzas, we can produce 6 pizza ovens at point *B*. If we produce no pizza, we can produce 10 ovens at point *C*.

The amount by which our production possibilities expand depends on the resources we devote to technological change and capital accumulation. If we devote no resources to this activity (point *A*), our *PPF* remains the blue curve PPF_0 in Fig. 2.8. If we cut the current pizza production and produce 6 ovens (point *B*), then in the future, we'll have more capital and our *PPF* will rotate outward to the position shown by the red curve PPF_1.

By allocating fewer resources to producing pizza and more resources to producing ovens, the greater is the expansion of our future production possibilities.

FIGURE 2.8   Economic Growth

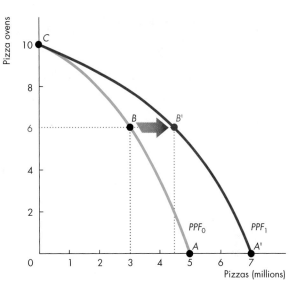

PPF_0 shows the limits to the production of pizzas and pizza ovens, with the production of all other goods and services remaining the same. If we devote no resources to producing pizza ovens and produce 5 million pizzas, our production possibilities will remain the same at PPF_0. But if we decrease pizza production to 3 million and produce 6 ovens, at point *B*, our production possibilities expand. After one period, the *PPF* rotates outward to PPF_1 and we can produce at point *B'*, a point outside the original PPF_0. We can rotate the *PPF* outward, but we cannot avoid opportunity cost. The opportunity cost of producing more pizzas in the future is fewer pizzas today.

—— MyLab Economics Animation and Draw Graph ——

Economic growth brings enormous benefits in the form of increased consumption in the future, but economic growth is not free and it doesn't abolish scarcity.

In Fig. 2.8, to make economic growth happen, we must use some resources to produce new capital (ovens), which leaves fewer resources to produce pizzas. To move to *B'* in the future, we must move from *A* to *B* today. The opportunity cost of producing more pizzas in the future is fewer pizzas today. Also, on the new *PPF*, we still face a tradeoff and opportunity cost.

The ideas about economic growth that we have explored in the setting of the pizza industry also apply to nations. Hong Kong and Canada provide a striking case study.

ECONOMICS IN ACTION

Hong Kong Overtakes Canada

In 1966, the production possibilities per person in Canada were more than three times those in Hong Kong (see the figure). Canada devotes one-fifth of its resources to accumulating capital, and in 1966, Canada was at point *A* on its *PPF*. Hong Kong devotes one-third of its resources to accumulating capital, and in 1966, Hong Kong was at point *A* on its *PPF*.

Since 1966, both economies have experienced economic growth, but because Hong Kong devotes a bigger fraction of its resources to accumulating capital, its production possibilities have expanded more quickly.

By 2016, production possibilities per person in Hong Kong had *overtaken* those in Canada. If Hong Kong continues to devote more resources to accumulating capital (at point *B* on its 2016 *PPF*) than Canada does, Hong Kong will continue to grow more rapidly than Canada. But if Hong Kong decreases its capital accumulation (moving to point *D* on its 2016 *PPF*), then its rate of economic growth will slow.

Hong Kong is typical of the fast-growing Asian economies, which include Taiwan, Thailand, South Korea, China, and India. Production possibilities

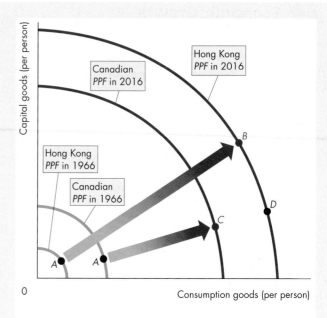

Economic Growth in Canada and Hong Kong

expand in these countries by between 5 percent and almost 10 percent a year.

If such high economic growth rates are maintained, these other Asian countries will continue to catch up with and eventually overtake Canada, as Hong Kong has done.

A Nation's Economic Growth

The experiences of Canada and Hong Kong make a striking example of the effects of our choices about consumption and capital accumulation on the rate of economic growth.

If an economy devotes all its factors of production to producing consumption goods and services and none to advancing technology and accumulating capital, its production possibilities in the future will be the same as they are today.

To expand production possibilities in the future, a nation or an economy must devote fewer resources to producing current consumption goods and services and allocate some resources to accumulating capital and developing new technologies. As production possibilities expand, consumption in the future can increase. The decrease in today's consumption is the opportunity cost of tomorrow's increase in consumption.

When production possibilities expand, the pattern of what is produced changes. Let's see how and why.

Changes in What We Produce

You saw in Chapter 1 that there are large differences in what is produced in a poor country like Ethiopia, and a middle-income country like China, and a rich country like Canada. Economic growth brings these changes, and the model that you've learned about in this chapter enables you to understand the differences in the patterns of production.

In a low-income country, just producing enough food is a high priority, and the marginal benefit from food is high. So in Ethiopia, agriculture accounts for a large percent of total production (36 percent).

As a country invests in capital and uses more advanced technologies, its production possibilities expand. The country can easily satisfy the want for food, so most of the increase in production is in industry (manufactured goods). In China, where production per person is 7 times that of Ethiopia, agriculture shrinks to 9 percent of total production and industry expands to 41 percent.

FIGURE 2.9   How Economic Growth Changes What We Produce

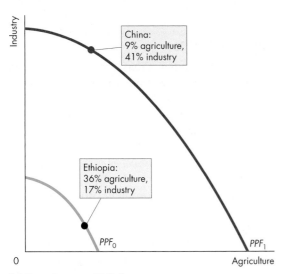

(a) From low to middle income

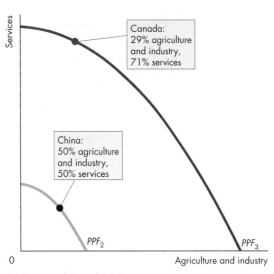

(b) From middle to high income

Ethiopia, a low-income country, has production possibilities per person on PPF_0. More than one-third of its production, 36 percent, is from agriculture and 17 percent from industry.

Investment in capital and more productive technology expands production possibilities to the middle-income level in China on PPF_1. Industry increases to 41 percent of production and agriculture shrinks to 9 percent.

In part (b), at China's level of production on PPF_2, production is divided equally between services and a combination of agriculture and industry.

When investment in capital and more productive technology expands production possibilities to the high-income level in Canada on PPF_3, most of the increase is in production of services, which increases to 80 percent.

MyLab Economics Animation and Draw Graph

If China invests even more in capital and advanced robot technologies, production possibilities will expand to Canada's level, which today is 4 times (per person) its level in China. Manufacturing is reaping most of the advances in technology, which means that industrial production is increasing, but the industrial labour force is shrinking. Labour released from industrial jobs, in turn, expands production possibilities in the services sector. It is the production of services that expands the most. The share of agriculture shrinks to 19 percent, and services expand to 80 percent.

Figure 2.9 illustrates the contrasts between Ethiopia and China in part (a) and China and Canada in part (b).

If the pace of industrial jobs loss and service jobs creation is rapid, as it has been in Canada over the past 40 years, serious problems arise for those workers whose jobs disappear. Many of these workers lack the skills needed for the new jobs, and they must be trained in new skills. Because most of the new jobs are in different places from those in which jobs are lost, people must relocate to get a new job. Job

training and relocating are costly and time-consuming activities, so a large number of people avoid those costs and remain unemployed, which places the economy inside its *PPF*.

REVIEW QUIZ

1   What generates economic growth?
2   How does economic growth influence the production possibilities frontier?
3   What is the opportunity cost of economic growth?
4   Explain why Hong Kong has experienced faster economic growth than Canada.
5   Does economic growth overcome scarcity?
6   How does economic growth change the patterns of production?
7   Why does economic growth destroy and create jobs?

Work these questions in Study Plan 2.4 and get instant feedback.   MyLab Economics

◆ Economic Coordination

For 7 billion people to specialize and produce millions of different goods and services, individual choices must somehow be coordinated. Two competing coordination systems have been used: central economic planning and markets (see *At Issue*, p. 8).

Central economic planning works badly because economic planners don't know people's production possibilities and preferences, so production ends up *inside* the *PPF* and the wrong things are produced.

Decentralized coordination works best, but to do so it needs four complementary social institutions. They are:

- Firms
- Markets
- Property rights
- Money

Firms

A **firm** is an economic unit that hires factors of production and organizes them to produce and sell goods and services.

Firms coordinate a huge amount of economic activity. For example, Loblaws buys or rents large buildings, equips them with storage shelves and checkout lanes, and hires labour. Loblaws directs the labour and decides what goods to buy and sell.

But Galen Weston would not have become one of the wealthiest people in Canada if Loblaws produced everything that it sells. He became rich by specializing in providing retail services and buying from other firms that specialize in producing goods (just as Liz and Joe did). This trade needs markets.

Markets

In ordinary speech, the word *market* means a place where people buy and sell goods such as fish, meat, fruits, and vegetables.

In economics, a **market** is any arrangement that enables buyers and sellers to get information and to do business with each other. An example is the world oil market, which is not a place but a network of producers, consumers, wholesalers, and brokers who buy and sell oil. In the world oil market, decision makers make deals by using the Internet. Enterprising individuals and firms, each pursuing their own self-interest, have profited by making markets—by

standing ready to buy or sell items in which they specialize. But markets can work only when property rights exist.

Property Rights

The social arrangements that govern the ownership, use, and disposal of anything that people value are called **property rights**. *Real property* includes land and buildings—the things we call property in ordinary speech—and durable goods such as plant and equipment. *Financial property* includes stocks and bonds and money in the bank. *Intellectual property* is the intangible product of creative effort. This type of property includes books, music, computer programs, and inventions of all kinds and is protected by copyrights and patents.

Where property rights are enforced, people have the incentive to specialize and produce the goods and services in which they have a comparative advantage. Where people can steal the production of others, resources are devoted not to production but to protecting possessions.

Money

Money is any commodity or token that is generally acceptable as a means of payment. Liz and Joe don't need money. They can exchange salads and smoothies. In principle, trade in markets can exchange any item for any other item. But you can perhaps imagine how complicated life would be if we exchanged goods for other goods. The "invention" of money makes trading in markets much more efficient.

Circular Flows Through Markets

Trading in markets for goods and services and factors of production creates a circular flow of expenditures and incomes. Figure 2.10 shows the circular flows. Households specialize and choose the quantities of labour, land, capital, and entrepreneurial services to sell or rent to firms. Firms choose the quantities of factors of production to hire. These (red) flows go through the *factor markets*. Households choose the quantities of goods and services to buy, and firms choose the quantities to produce. These (red) flows go through the *goods markets*. Households receive incomes and make expenditures on goods and services (the green flows).

How do markets coordinate all these decisions?

FIGURE 2.10 Circular Flows in the Market Economy

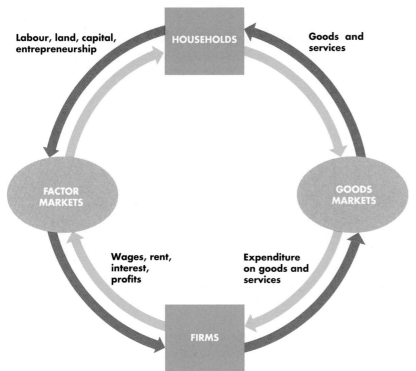

Households and firms make economic choices and markets coordinate these choices.

Households choose the quantities of labour, land, capital, and entrepreneurial services to sell or rent to firms in exchange for wages, rent, interest, and profits. Households also choose how to spend their incomes on the various types of goods and services available.

Firms choose the quantities of factors of production to hire and the quantities of goods and services to produce.

Goods markets and factor markets coordinate these choices of households and firms.

The counterclockwise red flows are real flows—the flow of factors of production from households to firms and the flow of goods and services from firms to households.

The clockwise green flows are the payments for the red flows. They are the flow of incomes from firms to households and the flow of expenditure on goods and services from households to firms.

MyLab Economics Animation

Coordinating Decisions

Markets coordinate decisions through price adjustments. Suppose that some people who want to buy hamburgers are not able to do so. To make buying and selling plans the same, either more hamburgers must be offered for sale or buyers must scale down their appetites (or both). A rise in the price of a hamburger produces this outcome. It encourages producers to offer more hamburgers for sale and encourages some people to change their lunch plans. When the price is right, buying plans and selling plans match.

Alternatively, suppose that more hamburgers are available than people want to buy. In this case, more hamburgers must be bought or fewer hamburgers must be offered for sale (or both). A fall in the price of a hamburger achieves this outcome. It encourages people to buy more hamburgers and it encourages firms to produce a smaller quantity of hamburgers.

◆ REVIEW QUIZ

1 Why are social institutions such as firms, markets, property rights, and money necessary?
2 What are the main functions of markets?
3 What are the flows in the market economy that go from firms to households and the flows from households to firms?

Work these questions in Study Plan 2.5 and get instant feedback. MyLab Economics

◆ You have now begun to see how economists approach economic questions. You can see all around you the lessons you've learned in this chapter. *Economics in the News* on pp. 50–51 provides an opportunity to apply the *PPF* model to deepen your understanding of why Canada produces more liquified natural gas (LNG) than it consumes and exports the rest.

Expanding Production Possibilities

B.C. First Nation Gives Nod to Proposed LNG Export Facility

The Canadian Press
March 27, 2017

A First Nation on Vancouver Island has approved a proposed liquefied natural gas export facility on its traditional territories.

Leaders of the Huu-ay-aht First Nation and the CEO of Vancouver-based Steelhead LNG held a joint news conference in Vancouver on Monday to announce what Chief Robert Dennis said was the First Nation's "official entry into the international business world."

Members of the small First Nation voted Saturday to approve development of the LNG facility at Sarita Bay, on the west coast of Vancouver Island …

The company's plans could even include building a new pipeline linking Vancouver Island and the B.C. mainland …

The company planned to make a final investment decision on Sarita Bay by 2019 or 2020, with first production targeted for 2024, he said. …

John Jack, executive councillor with the Huu-ay-aht, said it's time the First Nation took its place within Canada and British Columbia.

"This is an example of a First Nation working with business and working with the people of B.C. and Canada in order to create value that fits both of our interests."

© The Canadian Press

ESSENCE OF THE STORY

- The Huu-ay-aht First Nation on Vancouver Island has approved a liquefied natural gas export facility on its traditional territories.

- Steelhead LNG will build and operate the facility.

- A new pipeline linking Vancouver Island and the B.C. mainland is a possible part of the plan.

- Production is targeted to start in 2024.

ECONOMIC ANALYSIS

- Steelhead LNG is one of Canada's hundreds of liquefied natural gas (LNG) producers.

- In 2017, Canada produced 426 million cubic metres of LNG per day, consumed 256 million, and exported 170 million.

- We can use the ideas you have learned in this chapter to explain Canada's LNG production, consumption, and exports as well as the effects of the deal reported in the news article.

- Figure 1 shows how building new LNG production and export facilities changes Canada's production possibilities.

- The blue curve PPF_0 shows what our production possibilities would be without the new facilities.

- The investment in new facilities expands our production possibilities and the PPF becomes the red PPF_{2017}. At each quantity of other goods and services (measured on the y-axis), Canada can produce more LNG (measured on the x-axis).

- Figure 2 shows the point on PPF_{2017} at which Canada produced in 2017. It produced 426 million cubic metres of LNG and 30 units of other goods and services a day at point A.

- The slope of the PPF at point A measures the opportunity cost of producing LNG—the units of other goods and services that must be forgone to get another million cubic metres of LNG per day.

- Canada can sell LNG to other countries and the terms on which that trade occurs is shown by the red "Trade line." This line is like that for trade between Joe and Liz in Fig. 2.6.

- In 2017, Canada consumed 256 million cubic metres of LNG a day at point B, and exported 170 million cubic metres a day, as shown by the blue arrow.

- Canada's consumption at point B is outside its PPF, which means that by exporting LNG, Canadians consume more other goods and services than could have been produced in Canada.

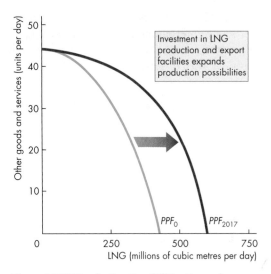

Figure 1 LNG Production Possibilities Expand

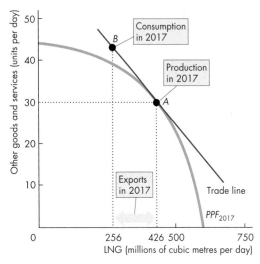

Figure 2 Production, Exports, and Consumption of LNG in 2017

WORKED PROBLEM

MyLab Economics Work this problem in Chapter 2 Study Plan.

Leisure Island has 50 hours of labour a day that it can use to produce entertainment and good food. The table shows the maximum quantity of each good that it can produce with different quantities of labour.

Labour (hours)	Entertainment (shows per week)		Good food (meals per week)
0	0	or	0
10	2	or	5
20	4	or	9
30	6	or	12
40	8	or	14
50	10	or	15

Questions

1. Can Leisure Island produce 4 shows and 14 meals a week?

2. If Leisure Island produces 4 shows and 9 meals a week, is production efficient?

3. If Leisure Island produces 8 shows and 5 meals a week, do the people of Leisure Island face a tradeoff?

4. Suppose that Leisure Island produces 4 shows and 12 meals a week. Calculate the opportunity cost of producing 2 additional shows a week.

Solutions

1. To produce 4 shows it would use 20 hours and to produce 14 meals it would use 40 hours, so to produce 4 shows and 14 meals a week, Leisure Island would use 60 hours of labour. Leisure Island has only 50 hours of labour available, so it cannot produce 4 shows and 14 meals a week.

Key Point: Production is *unattainable* if it uses more resources than are available.

2. When Leisure Island produces 4 shows it uses 20 hours of labour and when it produces 9 meals it uses 20 hours. In total, it uses 40 hours, which is *less than* the 50 hours of labour available. So Leisure Island's production is not efficient.

Key Point: Production is *efficient* only if the economy uses all its resources.

3. When Leisure Island produces 8 shows and 5 meals, it uses 50 hours of labour. Leisure Island is using all its resources, so to produce more of either good it would face a tradeoff.

Key Point: An economy faces a *tradeoff* only when it uses all the available resources.

4. When Leisure Island produces 4 shows and 12 meals a week, it uses 50 hours of labour. To produce 2 additional shows a week, Leisure Island faces a tradeoff and incurs an opportunity cost.

To produce 2 additional shows a week, Leisure Island moves 10 hours of labour from good food production, which decreases the quantity of meals from 12 to 9 a week—a decrease of 3 meals. That is, to get 2 additional shows a week Leisure Island *must give up* 3 meals a week. The opportunity cost of the 2 additional shows is 3 meals a week.

Key Point: When an economy is using all its resources and it decides to increase production of one good, it incurs an opportunity cost equal to the quantity of the good that it *must* forgo.

Key Figure

Each row of the following table sets out the combination of shows and meals that Leisure Island can produce in a week when it uses 50 hours of labour.

	Entertainment (shows per week)		Good food (meals per week)
A	0	and	15
B	2	and	14
C	4	and	12
D	6	and	9
E	8	and	5
F	10	and	0

Points *A* through *F* plot these combinations of shows and meals. The blue curve through these points is Leisure Island's *PPF*. Point *X* (4 shows and 14 meals in Question 1) is unattainable; Point *Y* (4 shows and 9 meals in Question 2) is inefficient. Point *E* (8 shows and 5 meals in Question 3) is on the *PPF* and the arrow illustrates the tradeoff and from it you can calculate the opportunity cost of 2 extra shows a week.

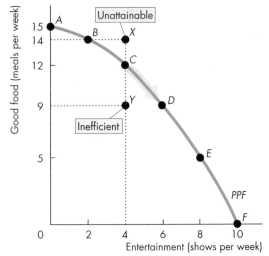

MyLab Economics Interactive Animation

SUMMARY

Key Points

Production Possibilities and Opportunity Cost (pp. 34–36)

- The production possibilities frontier is the boundary between production levels that are attainable and those that are unattainable when all the available resources are used to their limits.
- Production efficiency occurs at points on the production possibilities frontier.
- Along the production possibilities frontier, the opportunity cost of producing more of one good is the amount of the other good that must be given up.
- The opportunity cost of all goods increases as the production of the good increases.

Working Problems 1 to 3 will give you a better understanding of production possibilities and opportunity cost.

Using Resources Efficiently (pp. 37–39)

- Allocative efficiency occurs when goods and services are produced at the least possible cost and in the quantities that bring the greatest possible benefit.
- The marginal cost of a good is the opportunity cost of producing one more unit of it.
- The marginal benefit from a good is the benefit received from consuming one more unit of it and is measured by the willingness to pay for it.
- The marginal benefit of a good decreases as the amount of the good available increases.
- Resources are used efficiently when the marginal cost of each good is equal to its marginal benefit.

Working Problems 4 to 6 will give you a better understanding of the efficient use of resources.

Gains from Trade (pp. 40–44)

- A person has a comparative advantage in producing a good if that person can produce the good at a lower opportunity cost than everyone else.
- People gain by specializing in the activity in which they have a comparative advantage and trading with others.

Working Problems 7 and 8 will give you a better understanding of the gains from trade.

Economic Growth (pp. 45–47)

- Economic growth, which is the expansion of production possibilities, results from capital accumulation and technological change.
- The opportunity cost of economic growth is forgone current consumption.
- The benefit of economic growth is increased future consumption.

Working Problem 9 will give you a better understanding of economic growth.

Economic Coordination (pp. 48–49)

- Firms coordinate a large amount of economic activity, but there is a limit to the efficient size of a firm.
- Markets coordinate the economic choices of people and firms.
- Markets can work efficiently only when property rights exist.
- Money makes trading in markets more efficient.

Working Problem 10 will give you a better understanding of economic coordination.

Key Terms

MyLab Economics Key Terms Quiz

Absolute advantage, 40
Allocative efficiency, 37
Capital accumulation, 45
Comparative advantage, 40
Economic growth, 45
Firm, 48

Marginal benefit, 38
Marginal benefit curve, 38
Marginal cost, 37
Market, 48
Money, 48
Opportunity cost, 35

Preferences, 38
Production efficiency, 35
Production possibilities frontier, 34
Property rights, 48
Technological change, 45

STUDY PLAN PROBLEMS AND APPLICATIONS

MyLab Economics Work Problems 1 to 10 in Chapter 2 Study Plan and get instant feedback.

Production Possibilities and Opportunity Cost
(Study Plan 2.1)

Use the following data to work Problems 1 to 3.

Brazil produces ethanol from sugar, and the land used to grow sugar can be used to grow food crops. The table sets out Brazil's production possibilities for ethanol and food crops.

Ethanol (barrels per day)		Food crops (tonnes per day)
70	and	0
64	and	1
54	and	2
40	and	3
22	and	4
0	and	5

1. a. Draw a graph of Brazil's *PPF* and explain how your graph illustrates scarcity.

   b. If Brazil produces 40 barrels of ethanol a day, how much food must it produce to achieve production efficiency?

   c. Why does Brazil face a tradeoff on its *PPF*?

2. a. If Brazil increases ethanol production from 40 barrels per day to 54 barrels a day, what is the opportunity cost of the additional ethanol?

   b. If Brazil increases food production from 2 tonnes per day to 3 tonnes per day, what is the opportunity cost of the additional food?

   c. What is the relationship between your answers to parts (a) and (b)?

3. Does Brazil face an increasing opportunity cost of ethanol? What feature of Brazil's *PPF* illustrates increasing opportunity cost?

Using Resources Efficiently (Study Plan 2.2)

Use the table above to work Problems 4 and 5.

4. Define marginal cost and calculate Brazil's marginal cost of producing a tonne of food when the quantity produced is 2.5 tonnes per day.

5. Define marginal benefit. Explain how it is measured and why the data in the table do not enable you to calculate Brazil's marginal benefit from food.

6. Distinguish between *production efficiency* and *allocative efficiency*. Explain why many production possibilities achieve production efficiency but only one achieves allocative efficiency.

Gains from Trade (Study Plan 2.3)

Use the following data to work Problems 7 and 8.

In an hour, Sue can produce 40 caps or 4 jackets and Tessa can produce 80 caps or 4 jackets.

7. a. Calculate Sue's opportunity cost of producing a cap.

   b. Calculate Tessa's opportunity cost of producing a cap.

   c. Who has a comparative advantage in producing caps?

   d. If Sue and Tessa specialize in producing the good in which they have a comparative advantage and then trade 1 jacket for 15 caps, who gains from the specialization and trade?

8. Suppose that Tessa buys a new machine that enables her to make 20 jackets an hour. (She can still make only 80 caps per hour.)

   a. Who now has a comparative advantage in producing jackets?

   b. Can Sue and Tessa still gain from trade?

   c. Would Sue and Tessa still be willing to trade 1 jacket for 15 caps? Explain your answer.

Economic Growth (Study Plan 2.4)

9. A farm grows wheat and produces pork. The marginal cost of producing each of these products increases as more of it is produced.

   a. Make a graph that illustrates the farm's *PPF*.

   b. The farm adopts a new technology that allows it to use fewer resources to fatten pigs. On your graph, sketch the impact of the new technology on the farm's *PPF*.

   c. With the farm using the new technology in part (b), has the opportunity cost of producing a tonne of wheat changed? Explain and illustrate your answer.

   d. Is the farm more efficient with the new technology than it was with the old one? Why?

Economic Coordination (Study Plan 2.5)

10. For 50 years, Cuba has had a centrally planned economy in which the government makes the big decisions on how resources will be allocated.

    a. Why would you expect Cuba's production possibilities (per person) to be smaller than those of Canada?

    b. What are the social institutions that Cuba might lack that help Canada to achieve allocative efficiency?

ADDITIONAL PROBLEMS AND APPLICATIONS

MyLab Economics Work these problems in Homework or Test if assigned by your instructor.

Production Possibilities and Opportunity Cost

Use the following table to work Problems 11 and 12.
Suppose that Yucatan's production possibilities are:

Food (kilograms per month)		Sunscreen (litres per month)
300	and	0
200	and	50
100	and	100
0	and	150

11. a. Draw a graph of Yucatan's *PPF* and explain how your graph illustrates a tradeoff.
    b. If Yucatan produces 150 kilograms of food per month, how much sunscreen must it produce if it achieves production efficiency?
    c. What is Yucatan's opportunity cost of producing (i) 1 kilogram of food and (ii) 1 litre of sunscreen?
    d. What is the relationship between your answers to part (c)?
12. What feature of a *PPF* illustrates increasing opportunity cost? Explain why Yucatan's opportunity cost does or does not increase.

Using Resources Efficiently

13. In Problem 11, what is the marginal cost of 1 kilogram of food in Yucatan when the quantity produced is 150 kilograms per day? What is special about the marginal cost of food in Yucatan?
14. The table describes the preferences in Yucatan.

Sunscreen (litres per month)	Willingness to pay (kilograms of food per litre)
25	3
75	2
125	1

    a. What is the marginal benefit from sunscreen and how is it measured?
    b. Using the table in Problem 11, what does Yucatan produce to achieve allocative efficiency?
15. **Macy's, Kmart, JCPenney: More Retailers Closing Brick-and-Mortar Stores**
    As more people choose online shopping over brick-and-mortar stores, Macy's, Kmart, JCPenney and others are closing stores.
    Source: *Springfield News-Sun*, March 24, 2017
    a. Draw the *PPF* curves for brick-and mortar retailers and online retailers before and after the Internet became available.

    b. Draw the marginal cost and marginal benefit curves for brick-and-mortar retailers and online retailers before and after the Internet became available.
    c. Explain how changes in production possibilities, preferences or both have changed the way in which goods are retailed.

Use the following news clip to work Problems 16 and 17.

Gates Doubles Down on Malaria Eradication

The End Malaria Council, convened by Bill Gates and Ray Chambers, seeks to mobilize resources to prevent and treat malaria. The current level of financing is too low to end malaria. Bruno Moonen, deputy director for malaria at the Gates Foundation, says that more resources, more leadership, and new technologies are needed to eradicate malaria in the current generation.

Source: Catherine Cheney, *Devex*, January 20, 2017

16. Is Bruno Moonen talking about *production efficiency* or *allocative efficiency* or both?
17. Make a graph with the percentage of malaria cases eliminated on the *x*-axis and the marginal cost and marginal benefit of driving down malaria cases on the *y*-axis. On your graph:
    (i) Draw a marginal cost curve and a marginal benefit curve that are consistent with Bruno Moonen's opinion.
    (ii) Identify the quantity of malaria eradicated that achieves allocative efficiency.

Gains from Trade

Use the following data to work Problems 18 and 19.

Kim can produce 40 pies or 400 cakes an hour. Liam can produce 100 pies or 200 cakes an hour.

18. a. Calculate Kim's opportunity cost of a pie and Liam's opportunity cost of a pie.
    b. If each spends 30 minutes of each hour producing pies and 30 minutes producing cakes, how many pies and cakes does each produce?
    c. Who has a comparative advantage in producing (i) pies and (ii) cakes?
19. a. Draw a graph of Kim's *PPF* and Liam's *PPF* and show the point at which each produces when each spends 30 minutes of each hour producing pies and 30 minutes producing cakes.

b. On your graph, show what Kim produces and what Liam produces when they specialize.

c. When they specialize and trade, what are the total gains from trade?

d. If Kim and Liam share the total gains equally, what trade takes place between them?

20. Tony and Patty produce skis and snowboards. The tables show their production possibilities. Each week, Tony produces 5 snowboards and 40 skis; Patty produces 10 snowboards and 5 skis.

Tony's Production Possibilities

Snowboards (units per week)		Skis (units per week)
25	and	0
20	and	10
15	and	20
10	and	30
5	and	40
0	and	50

Patty's Production Possibilities

Snowboards (units per week)		Skis (units per week)
20	and	0
10	and	5
0	and	10

a. Who has a comparative advantage in producing (i) snowboards and (ii) skis?

b. If Tony and Patty specialize and trade 1 snowboard for 1 ski, what are the gains from trade?

Economic Growth

21. Capital accumulation and technological change bring economic growth: Production that was unattainable yesterday becomes attainable today; production that is unattainable today will become attainable tomorrow. Why doesn't economic growth bring an end to scarcity?

Use the following data to work Problems 22 and 23.

SpaceX Plans to Send Two People Around the Moon

SpaceX CEO Elon Musk announced that SpaceX plans to send two citizens on a one-week, 350,000-mile trip around the moon in 2018.

Source: *The Verge*, February 27, 2017

22. What is the opportunity cost of creating the technology for trips around the moon?

23. Sketch SpaceX's *PPF* for trips around the moon and other goods and services and its planned production in 2018.

Economic Coordination

24. On a graph of the circular flows in the market economy, indicate the real and money flows in which the following items belong:

a. You buy an iPad from the Apple Store.

b. Apple Inc. pays the designers of the iPad.

c. Apple Inc. decides to expand and rents an adjacent building.

d. You buy a new e-book from Amazon.

e. Apple Inc. hires a student as an intern during the summer.

Economics in the News

25. After you have studied *Economics in the News* on pp. 50–51, answer the following questions.

a. How does investing in LNG production and export facilities change Canada's *PPF*?

b. How do technological advances in the production of other goods and services change Canada's *PPF*?

c. How will the deal between Huu-ay-aht First Nation and Steelhead LNG change Canada's opportunity cost of exporting LNG?

d. When technological advances in the production of other goods and services occur, how does the opportunity cost of producing LNG change? Does it increase or decrease?

26. **YouTube Launches Live TV in the U.S.**

Google has launched YouTube TV, a $35-a-month service that carries live streaming from all the major broadcast and sports networks as well as some cable networks and local sports and news channels. Users will be able to record an unlimited amount of content and multiple shows simultaneously, without using up any data space on mobile devices.

Source: *Mediatel*, March 1, 2017

a. How has live streaming changed the production possibilities of video entertainment and other goods and services?

b. Sketch a *PPF* for video entertainment and other goods and services before live streaming.

c. Show how the arrival of inexpensive live streaming has changed the *PPF*.

d. Sketch a marginal benefit curve and marginal cost curve for video entertainment before and after live streaming.

e. Explain how the efficient quantity of video entertainment has changed.

Your Economic Revolution

UNDERSTANDING THE SCOPE OF ECONOMICS

Three periods in human history stand out as ones of economic revolution. The first, the *Agricultural Revolution,* occurred 10,000 years ago. In what is today Iraq, people learned to domesticate animals and plant crops. People stopped roaming in search of food and settled in villages, towns, and cities where they specialized in the activities in which they had a comparative advantage and developed markets in which to exchange their products. Wealth increased enormously.

Economics was born during the *Industrial Revolution,* which began in England during the 1760s. For the first time, people began to apply science and create new technologies for the manufacture of textiles and iron, to create steam engines, and to boost the output of farms.

You are studying economics at a time that future historians will call the *Information Revolution.* Over the entire world, people are embracing new information technologies and prospering on an unprecedented scale.

During all three economic revolutions, many have prospered but others have been left behind. It is the range of human progress that poses the greatest question for economics and the one that Adam Smith addressed in the first work of economic science: What causes the differences in wealth among nations?

Many people had written about economics before **Adam Smith***, but he made economics a science. Born in 1723 in Kirkcaldy, a small fishing town near Edinburgh, Scotland, Smith was the only child of the town's customs officer. Lured from his professorship (he was a full professor at 28) by a wealthy Scottish duke who gave him a pension of £300 a year—10 times the average income at that time—Smith devoted 10 years to writing his masterpiece:* An Inquiry into the Nature and Causes of the Wealth of Nations, *published in 1776.*

Why, Adam Smith asked, are some nations wealthy while others are poor? He was pondering these questions at the height of the Industrial Revolution, and he answered by emphasizing the power of the division of labour and free markets in raising labour productivity.

To illustrate his argument, Adam Smith described two pin factories. In the first, one person, using the hand tools available in the 1770s, could make 20 pins a day. In the other, by using those same hand tools but breaking the process into a number of individually small operations in which people specialize—by the division of labour—10 people could make a staggering 48,000 pins a day. One draws out the wire,

Every individual who intends only his own gain is led by an invisible hand to promote an end (the public good) which was no part of his intention.

ADAM SMITH
The Wealth of Nations

another straightens it, a third cuts it, a fourth points it, a fifth grinds it. Three specialists make the head, and a fourth attaches it. Finally, the pin is polished and packaged.

But a large market is needed to support the division of labour: One factory employing 10 workers would need to sell more than 15 million pins a year to stay in business!

ESTHER DUFLO is the Abdul Latif Jameel Professor of Poverty Alleviation and Development Economics at the Massachusetts Institute of Technology. Among her many honours are the 2010 John Bates Clark Medal for the best economist under 40 and the Financial Times and Goldman Sachs Business Book of the Year Award in 2011 for her book (with Abhijit Banerjee) *Poor Economics: A Radical Rethinking of the Way to Fight Global Poverty*. Professor Duflo's research seeks to advance our understanding of the economic choices of the extremely poor by conducting massive real-world experiments.

Professor Duflo was an undergraduate student of history and economics at École Normale Supérieure and completed a master's degree at DELTA in Paris before moving to the United States. She earned her Ph.D. in economics at MIT in 1999.

Michael Parkin and Robin Bade talked with her about her work, which advances our understanding of the economic choices and condition of the very poor.

Professor Duflo, what's the story about how you became an economist and in particular the architect of experiments designed to understand the economic choices of the very poor?

When I was a kid, I was exposed to many stories and images of poor children: through my mother's engagement as a doctor in a small NGO dealing with child victims of war and through books and stories about children living all around the world.

I remember asking myself how I could justify my luck of being born where I was. I had a very exaggerated idea of what it was to be poor, but this idea caused sufficient discomfort that I knew I had to do something about it, if I could. Quite by accident, I discovered that economics was the way in which I could actually be useful: While spending a year in Russia teaching French and studying history, I realized that academic economists have the ability to intervene in the world while keeping enough sanity to analyze it. I thought this would be ideal for me and I have never regretted it. I have the best job in the world.

> … imagine living on under a dollar a day after your rent is paid in Seattle or Denver. Not easy!

The very poor who you study are people who live on $1 a day or $2 a day. … Is $1 a day a true measure that includes everything these poor people consume?

For defining the poverty line, we don't include the cost of housing. The poor also get free goods, sometimes of bad quality (education, healthcare) and the value of those is also not included. Other than that, yes, it is everything.

Moreover, you have to realize this is everything, taking into account the fact that life is much cheaper in many poor countries because salaries are lower, so anything that is made and consumed locally (e.g., a haircut) is cheaper.

For example, in India, the purchasing power of a dollar (in terms of the real goods you can buy) is about 3 times what it is in the United States. So the poverty line we use for India is 33 cents per day, not a dollar.

All told, you really have to imagine living on under a dollar a day after your rent is paid in Seattle or Denver. Not easy!

*Read the full interview with Esther Duflo in MyLab Economics.

DEMAND AND SUPPLY

After studying this chapter, you will be able to:

◆ Describe a competitive market and think about a price as an opportunity cost

◆ Explain the influences on demand

◆ Explain the influences on supply

◆ Explain how demand and supply determine prices and quantities bought and sold

◆ Use the demand and supply model to make predictions about changes in prices and quantities

As more of us get breakfast on the go, we're drinking more smoothies and energy drinks and less orange juice. What is happening to the price of orange juice and the quantity of oranges harvested? The demand and supply model answers this question.

This model that you're about to study is the main tool of economics. It explains how prices are determined and how they guide the use of resources to influence *what*, *how*, and *for whom* goods and services are produced.

Economics in the News at the end of the chapter answers the questions about orange juice.

◆ Markets and Prices

When you need a new pair of running shoes, want a bagel and a latte, plan to upgrade your smartphone, or need to fly home for Thanksgiving, you must find a place where people sell those items or offer those services. The place in which you find them is a *market*. You learned in Chapter 2 (p. 48) that a market is any arrangement that enables buyers and sellers to get information and to do business with each other.

A market has two sides: buyers and sellers. There are markets for *goods* such as apples and hiking boots, for *services* such as haircuts and tennis lessons, for *factors of production* such as computer programmers and earthmovers, and for other manufactured *inputs* such as memory chips and auto parts. There are also markets for money such as Japanese yen and for financial securities such as Yahoo! stock. Only our imagination limits what can be traded in markets.

Some markets are physical places where buyers and sellers meet and where an auctioneer or a broker helps to determine the prices. Examples of this type of market are live car and house auctions and the wholesale fish, meat, and produce markets.

Some markets are groups of people spread around the world who never meet and know little about each other but are connected through the Internet or by telephone and fax. Examples are the e-commerce markets and the currency markets.

But most markets are unorganized collections of buyers and sellers. You do most of your trading in this type of market. An example is the market for basketball shoes. The buyers in this $3 billion-a-year market are the 45 million Canadians and Americans who play basketball (or who want to make a fashion statement). The sellers are the tens of thousands of retail sports equipment and footwear stores. Each buyer can visit several different stores, and each seller knows that the buyer has a choice of stores.

Markets vary in the intensity of competition that buyers and sellers face. In this chapter, we're going to study a **competitive market**—a market that has many buyers and many sellers, so no single buyer or seller can influence the price.

Producers offer items for sale only if the price is high enough to cover their opportunity cost. And consumers respond to changing opportunity cost by seeking cheaper alternatives to expensive items.

We are going to study how people respond to *prices* and the forces that determine prices. But to pursue these tasks, we need to understand the relationship between a price and an opportunity cost.

In everyday life, the *price* of an object is the number of dollars that must be given up in exchange for it. Economists refer to this price as the **money price**.

The *opportunity cost* of an action is the highest-valued alternative forgone. If, when you buy a cup of coffee, the highest-valued thing you forgo is some gum, then the opportunity cost of the coffee is the *quantity* of gum forgone. We can calculate the quantity of gum forgone from the money prices of the coffee and the gum.

If the money price of coffee is $1 a cup and the money price of gum is 50¢ a pack, then the opportunity cost of one cup of coffee is two packs of gum. To calculate this opportunity cost, we divide the price of a cup of coffee by the price of a pack of gum and find the *ratio* of one price to the other. The ratio of one price to another is called a **relative price**, and a *relative price is an opportunity cost.*

We can express the relative price of coffee in terms of gum or any other good. The normal way of expressing a relative price is in terms of a "basket" of all goods and services. To calculate this relative price, we divide the money price of a good by the money price of a "basket" of all goods (called a *price index*). The resulting relative price tells us the opportunity cost of the good in terms of how much of the "basket" we must give up to buy it.

The demand and supply model that we are about to study determines *relative prices,* and the word "price" means *relative* price. When we predict that a price will fall, we do not mean that its *money* price will fall—although it might. We mean that its *relative* price will fall. That is, its price will fall *relative* to the average price of other goods and services.

◆ REVIEW QUIZ

1 What is the distinction between a money price and a relative price?
2 Explain why a relative price is an opportunity cost.
3 Think of examples of goods whose relative price has risen or fallen by a large amount.

Work these questions in Study Plan 3.1 and get instant feedback.   MyLab Economics

Let's begin our study of demand and supply, starting with demand.

◆ Demand

If you demand something, then you:

1. Want it.
2. Can afford it.
3. Plan to buy it.

Wants are the unlimited desires or wishes that people have for goods and services. How many times have you thought that you would like something "if only you could afford it" or "if it weren't so expensive"? Scarcity guarantees that many—perhaps most—of our wants will never be satisfied. Demand reflects a decision about which wants to satisfy.

The **quantity demanded** of a good or service is the amount that consumers plan to buy during a given time period at a particular price. The quantity demanded is not necessarily the same as the quantity actually bought. Sometimes the quantity demanded exceeds the amount of goods available, so the quantity bought is less than the quantity demanded.

The quantity demanded is measured as an amount per unit of time. For example, suppose that you buy one cup of coffee a day. The quantity of coffee that you demand can be expressed as 1 cup per day, 7 cups per week, or 365 cups per year.

Many factors influence buying plans, and one of them is the price. We look first at the relationship between the quantity demanded of a good and its price. To study this relationship, we keep all other influences on buying plans the same and we ask: How, other things remaining the same, does the quantity demanded of a good change as its price changes?

The law of demand provides the answer.

The Law of Demand

The **law of demand** states:

> Other things remaining the same, the higher the price of a good, the smaller is the quantity demanded; and the lower the price of a good, the greater is the quantity demanded.

Why does a higher price reduce the quantity demanded? For two reasons:

- Substitution effect
- Income effect

Substitution Effect When the price of a good rises, other things remaining the same, its *relative* price— its opportunity cost—rises. Although each good is unique, it has *substitutes*—other goods that can be used in its place. As the opportunity cost of a good rises, the incentive to economize on its use and switch to a substitute becomes stronger.

Income Effect When a price rises, other things remaining the same, the price rises *relative* to income. Faced with a higher price and an unchanged income, people cannot afford to buy all the things they previously bought. They must decrease the quantities demanded of at least some goods and services. Normally, the good whose price has increased will be one of the goods that people buy less of.

To see the substitution effect and the income effect at work, think about the effects of a change in the price of an energy bar. Several different goods are substitutes for an energy bar. For example, an energy drink could be consumed instead of an energy bar.

Suppose that an energy bar initially sells for $3 and then its price falls to $1.50. People now substitute energy bars for energy drinks—the substitution effect. And with a budget that now has some slack from the lower price of an energy bar, people buy even more energy bars—the income effect. The quantity of energy bars demanded increases for these two reasons.

Now suppose that an energy bar initially sells for $3 and then the price doubles to $6. People now buy fewer energy bars and more energy drinks—the substitution effect. And faced with a tighter budget, people buy even fewer energy bars—the income effect. The quantity of energy bars demanded decreases for these two reasons.

Demand Curve and Demand Schedule

You are now about to study one of the two most used curves in economics: the demand curve. You are also going to encounter one of the most critical distinctions: the distinction between *demand* and *quantity demanded*.

The term **demand** refers to the entire relationship between the price of a good and the quantity demanded of that good. Demand is illustrated by the demand curve and the demand schedule. The term *quantity demanded* refers to a point on a demand curve—the quantity demanded at a particular price.

Figure 3.1 shows the demand curve for energy bars. A **demand curve** shows the relationship between the quantity demanded of a good and its price when all other influences on consumers' planned purchases remain the same.

The table in Fig. 3.1 is the demand schedule for energy bars. A *demand schedule* lists the quantities demanded at each price when all the other influences on consumers' planned purchases remain the same. For example, if the price of a bar is 50¢, the quantity demanded is 22 million a week. If the price is $2.50, the quantity demanded is 5 million a week. The other rows of the table show the quantities demanded at prices of $1.00, $1.50, and $2.00.

We graph the demand schedule as a demand curve with the quantity demanded on the *x*-axis and the price on the *y*-axis. The points on the demand curve labelled *A* through *E* correspond to the rows of the demand schedule. For example, point *A* on the graph shows a quantity demanded of 22 million energy bars a week at a price of 50¢ a bar.

Willingness and Ability to Pay Another way of looking at the demand curve is as a willingness-and-ability-to-pay curve. The willingness and ability to pay is a measure of *marginal benefit.*

If a small quantity is available, the highest price that someone is willing and able to pay for one more unit is high. But as the quantity available increases, the marginal benefit of each additional unit falls and the highest price that someone is willing and able to pay also falls along the demand curve.

In Fig. 3.1, if only 5 million energy bars are available each week, the highest price that someone is willing to pay for the 5 millionth bar is $2.50. But if 22 million energy bars are available each week, someone is willing to pay 50¢ for the last bar bought.

A Change in Demand

When any factor that influences buying plans changes, other than the price of the good, there is a **change in demand**. Figure 3.2 illustrates an increase in demand. When demand increases, the demand curve shifts rightward and the quantity demanded at each price is greater. For example, at $2.50 a bar, the quantity demanded on the original (blue) demand curve is 5 million energy bars a week. On the new (red) demand curve, at $2.50 a bar, the quantity demanded is 15 million bars a week. Look closely at the numbers in the table and check that the quantity demanded at each price is greater.

FIGURE 3.1 The Demand Curve

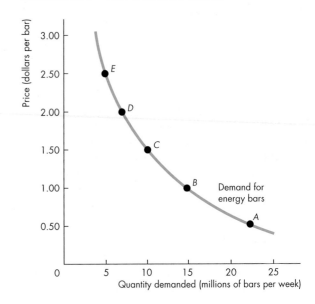

	Price (dollars per bar)	Quantity demanded (millions of bars per week)
A	0.50	22
B	1.00	15
C	1.50	10
D	2.00	7
E	2.50	5

The table shows a demand schedule for energy bars. At a price of 50¢ a bar, 22 million bars a week are demanded; at a price of $1.50 a bar, 10 million bars a week are demanded. The demand curve shows the relationship between quantity demanded and price, other things remaining the same. The demand curve slopes downward: As the price falls, the quantity demanded increases.

The demand curve can be read in two ways. For a given price, the demand curve tells us the quantity that people plan to buy. For example, at a price of $1.50 a bar, people plan to buy 10 million bars a week. For a given quantity, the demand curve tells us the maximum price that consumers are willing and able to pay for the last bar available. For example, the maximum price that consumers will pay for the 15 millionth bar is $1.00.

MyLab Economics Animation

FIGURE 3.2   An Increase in Demand

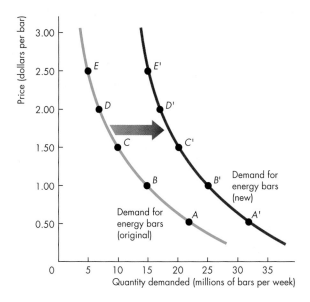

Original demand schedule		New demand schedule	
Original income		New higher income	
Price (dollars per bar)	Quantity demanded (millions of bars per week)	Price (dollars per bar)	Quantity demanded (millions of bars per week)
A 0.50	22	A' 0.50	32
B 1.00	15	B' 1.00	25
C 1.50	10	C' 1.50	20
D 2.00	7	D' 2.00	17
E 2.50	5	E' 2.50	15

A change in any influence on buying plans other than the price of the good itself results in a new demand schedule and a shift of the demand curve. A change in income changes the demand for energy bars. At a price of $1.50 a bar, 10 million bars a week are demanded at the original income (row C of the table) and 20 million bars a week are demanded at the new higher income (row C'). A rise in income increases the demand for energy bars. The demand curve shifts *rightward*, as shown by the shift arrow and the resulting red curve.

Six main factors bring changes in demand. They are changes in:

- The prices of related goods
- Expected future prices
- Income
- Expected future income and credit
- Population
- Preferences

Prices of Related Goods The quantity of energy bars that consumers plan to buy depends in part on the prices of substitutes for energy bars. A **substitute** is a good that can be used in place of another good. For example, a bus ride is a substitute for a train ride; a hamburger is a substitute for a hot dog; and an energy drink is a substitute for an energy bar. If the price of a substitute for an energy bar rises, people buy less of the substitute and more energy bars. For example, if the price of an energy drink rises, people buy fewer energy drinks and more energy bars. The demand for energy bars increases.

The quantity of energy bars that people plan to buy also depends on the prices of complements with energy bars. A **complement** is a good that is used in conjunction with another good. Hamburgers and fries are complements, and so are energy bars and exercise. If the price of an hour at the gym falls, people buy more gym time *and more* energy bars.

Expected Future Prices If the expected future price of a good rises and if the good can be stored, the opportunity cost of obtaining the good for future use is lower today than it will be in the future when people expect the price to be higher. So people retime their purchases—they substitute over time. They buy more of the good now before its price is expected to rise (and less afterward), so the demand for the good today increases.

For example, suppose that a Florida frost damages the season's orange crop. You expect the price of orange juice to rise, so you fill your freezer with enough frozen juice to get you through the next six months. Your current demand for frozen orange juice has increased, and your future demand has decreased.

Similarly, if the expected future price of a good falls, the opportunity cost of buying the good today is high relative to what it is expected to be in the future. So again, people retime their purchases. They buy less of the good now before its price is expected to fall, so the demand for the good decreases today and increases in the future.

Computer prices are constantly falling, and this fact poses a dilemma. Will you buy a new computer now, in time for the start of the school year, or will you wait until the price has fallen some more? Because people expect computer prices to keep falling, the current demand for computers is less (and the future demand is greater) than it otherwise would be.

Income Consumers' income influences demand. When income increases, consumers buy more of most goods; and when income decreases, consumers buy less of most goods. Although an increase in income leads to an increase in the demand for *most* goods, it does not lead to an increase in the demand for *all* goods. A **normal good** is one for which demand increases as income increases. An **inferior good** is one for which demand decreases as income increases. As incomes increase, the demand for air travel (a normal good) increases and the demand for long-distance bus trips (an inferior good) decreases.

Expected Future Income and Credit When expected future income increases or credit becomes easier to get, demand for a good might increase now. For example, a salesperson gets the news that she will receive a big bonus at the end of the year, so she goes into debt and buys a new car right now, rather than waiting until she receives the bonus.

Population Demand also depends on the size and the age structure of the population. The larger the population, the greater is the demand for all goods and services; the smaller the population, the smaller is the demand for all goods and services.

For example, the demand for parking spaces, running shoes, movies, or just about anything that you can imagine is much greater in the Greater Toronto Area (population 6 million) than it is in Thunder Bay, Ontario (population 146,000).

Also, the larger the proportion of the population in an age group, the greater is the demand for the goods and services used by that group. For example, in 2010, there were 2.3 million 20- to 24-year-olds in Canada compared with 2.1 million in 2000. As a result, the demand for university places in 2010 was greater than in 2000. During this period, the number of Canadians aged 90 years more than doubled and the demand for nursing home services increased.

TABLE 3.1 The Demand for Energy Bars

The Law of Demand

The quantity of energy bars demanded

Decreases if:	Increases if:
■ The price of an energy bar rises	■ The price of an energy bar falls

Changes in Demand

The demand for energy bars

Decreases if:	Increases if:
■ The price of a substitute falls	■ The price of a substitute rises
■ The price of a complement rises	■ The price of a complement falls
■ The expected future price of an energy bar falls	■ The expected future price of an energy bar rises
■ Income falls*	■ Income rises*
■ Expected future income falls or credit becomes harder to get*	■ Expected future income rises or credit becomes easier to get*
■ The population decreases	■ The population increases

*An energy bar is a normal good.

Preferences Demand depends on preferences. *Preferences* determine the value that people place on each good and service. Preferences depend on such things as the weather, information, and fashion. For example, greater health and fitness awareness has shifted preferences in favour of energy bars, so the demand for energy bars has increased.

Table 3.1 summarizes the influences on demand and the direction of those influences.

A Change in the Quantity Demanded Versus a Change in Demand

Changes in the influences on buying plans bring either a change in the quantity demanded or a change in demand. Equivalently, they bring either a movement along the demand curve or a shift of the demand curve. The distinction between a change in the quantity demanded and a change in demand is the same as that between a movement along the demand curve and a shift of the demand curve.

A point on the demand curve shows the quantity demanded at a given price, so a movement along the demand curve shows a **change in the quantity demanded**. The entire demand curve shows demand, so a shift of the demand curve shows a *change in demand*. Figure 3.3 illustrates these distinctions.

Movement Along the Demand Curve If the price of the good changes but no other influence on buying plans changes, we illustrate the effect as a movement along the demand curve.

A fall in the price of a good increases the quantity demanded of it. In Fig. 3.3, we illustrate the effect of a fall in price as a movement down along the demand curve D_0.

A rise in the price of a good decreases the quantity demanded of it. In Fig. 3.3, we illustrate the effect of a rise in price as a movement up along the demand curve D_0.

A Shift of the Demand Curve If the price of a good remains constant but some other influence on buying plans changes, there is a change in demand for that good. We illustrate a change in demand as a shift of the demand curve. For example, if more people work out at the gym, consumers buy more energy bars regardless of the price of a bar. That is what a rightward shift of the demand curve shows—more energy bars are demanded at each price.

In Fig. 3.3, there is a *change in demand* and the demand curve shifts when any influence on buying plans changes, other than the price of the good. Demand *increases* and the demand curve *shifts rightward* (to the red demand curve D_1) if the price of a substitute rises, the price of a complement falls, the expected future price of the good rises, income increases (for a normal good), expected future income or credit increases, or the population increases. Demand *decreases* and the demand curve *shifts leftward* (to the red demand curve D_2) if the price of a substitute falls, the price of a complement rises, the expected future price of the good falls, income decreases (for a normal good), expected future income or credit decreases, or the population decreases. (For an inferior good, the effects of changes in income are in the opposite direction to those described above.)

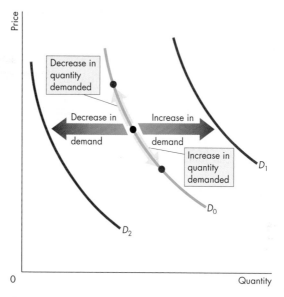

FIGURE 3.3 A Change in the Quantity Demanded Versus a Change in Demand

When the price of the good changes, there is a movement along the demand curve and *a change in the quantity demanded*, shown by the blue arrows on demand curve D_0. When any other influence on buying plans changes, there is a shift of the demand curve and a *change in demand*. An increase in demand shifts the demand curve rightward (from D_0 to D_1). A decrease in demand shifts the demand curve leftward (from D_0 to D_2).

—— MyLab Economics Animation and Draw Graph ——

◆ REVIEW QUIZ

1 Define the quantity demanded of a good or service.
2 What is the law of demand and how do we illustrate it?
3 What does the demand curve tell us about the price that consumers are willing to pay?
4 List all the influences on buying plans that change demand, and for each influence, say whether it increases or decreases demand.
5 Why does demand not change when the price of a good changes with no change in the other influences on buying plans?

Work these questions in Study Plan 3.2 and get instant feedback.   MyLab Economics

◆ Supply

If a firm supplies a good or service, the firm:

1. Has the resources and technology to produce it.
2. Can profit from producing it.
3. Plans to produce it and sell it.

A supply is more than just having the *resources* and the *technology* to produce something. *Resources and technology* are the constraints that limit what is possible.

Many useful things can be produced, but they are not produced unless it is profitable to do so. Supply reflects a decision about which technologically feasible items to produce.

The **quantity supplied** of a good or service is the amount that producers plan to sell during a given time period at a particular price. The quantity supplied is not necessarily the same amount as the quantity actually sold. Sometimes the quantity supplied is greater than the quantity demanded, so the quantity sold is less than the quantity supplied.

Like the quantity demanded, the quantity supplied is measured as an amount per unit of time. For example, suppose that GM produces 1,000 cars a day. The quantity of cars supplied by GM can be expressed as 1,000 a day, 7,000 a week, or 365,000 a year. Without the time dimension, we cannot tell whether a particular quantity is large or small.

Many factors influence selling plans, and again one of them is the price of the good. We look first at the relationship between the quantity supplied of a good and its price. Just as we did when we studied demand, to isolate the relationship between the quantity supplied of a good and its price, we keep all other influences on selling plans the same and ask: How does the quantity supplied of a good change as its price changes when other things remain the same?

The law of supply provides the answer.

The Law of Supply

The **law of supply** states:

> Other things remaining the same, the higher the price of a good, the greater is the quantity supplied; and the lower the price of a good, the smaller is the quantity supplied.

Why does a higher price increase the quantity supplied? It is because *marginal cost increases.* As the quantity produced of any good increases, the marginal cost of producing the good increases. (See Chapter 2, p. 37, to review marginal cost.)

It is never worth producing a good if the price received for the good does not at least cover the marginal cost of producing it. When the price of a good rises, other things remaining the same, producers are willing to incur a higher marginal cost, so they increase production. The higher price brings forth an increase in the quantity supplied.

Let's now illustrate the law of supply with a supply curve and a supply schedule.

Supply Curve and Supply Schedule

You are now going to study the second of the two most used curves in economics: the supply curve. You're also going to learn about the critical distinction between *supply* and *quantity supplied*.

The term **supply** refers to the entire relationship between the price of a good and the quantity supplied of it. Supply is illustrated by the supply curve and the supply schedule. The term *quantity supplied* refers to a point on a supply curve—the quantity supplied at a particular price.

Figure 3.4 shows the supply curve of energy bars. A **supply curve** shows the relationship between the quantity supplied of a good and its price when all other influences on producers' planned sales remain the same. The supply curve is a graph of a supply schedule.

The table in Fig. 3.4 sets out the supply schedule for energy bars. A *supply schedule* lists the quantities supplied at each price when all the other influences on producers' planned sales remain the same. For example, if the price of an energy bar is 50¢, the quantity supplied is zero—in row *A* of the table. If the price of an energy bar is $1.00, the quantity supplied is 6 million energy bars a week—in row *B*. The other rows of the table show the quantities supplied at prices of $1.50, $2.00, and $2.50.

To make a supply curve, we graph the quantity supplied on the *x*-axis and the price on the *y*-axis. The points on the supply curve labelled *A* through *E* correspond to the rows of the supply schedule. For example, point *A* on the graph shows a quantity supplied of zero at a price of 50¢ an energy bar. Point *E* shows a quantity supplied of 15 million bars at $2.50 an energy bar.

FIGURE 3.4   The Supply Curve

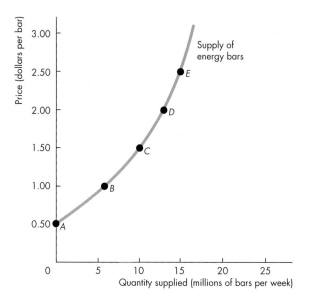

	Price (dollars per bar)	Quantity supplied (millions of bars per week)
A	0.50	0
B	1.00	6
C	1.50	10
D	2.00	13
E	2.50	15

The table shows the supply schedule of energy bars. For example, at a price of $1.00, 6 million bars a week are supplied; at a price of $2.50, 15 million bars a week are supplied. The supply curve shows the relationship between the quantity supplied and the price, other things remaining the same. The supply curve slopes upward: As the price of a good increases, the quantity supplied increases.

A supply curve can be read in two ways. For a given price, the supply curve tells us the quantity that producers plan to sell at that price. For example, at a price of $1.50 a bar, producers are planning to sell 10 million bars a week. For a given quantity, the supply curve tells us the minimum price at which producers are willing to sell one more bar. For example, if 15 million bars are produced each week, the lowest price at which a producer is willing to sell the 15 millionth bar is $2.50.

———— MyLab Economics Animation ————

Minimum Supply Price The supply curve can be interpreted as a minimum-supply-price curve—a curve that shows the lowest price at which someone is willing to sell. This lowest price is the *marginal cost.*

If a small quantity is produced, the lowest price at which someone is willing to sell one more unit is low. But as the quantity produced increases, the marginal cost of each additional unit rises, so the lowest price at which someone is willing to sell an additional unit rises along the supply curve.

In Fig. 3.4, if 15 million bars are produced each week, the lowest price at which someone is willing to sell the 15 millionth bar is $2.50. But if 10 million bars are produced each week, someone is willing to accept $1.50 for the last bar produced.

A Change in Supply

When any factor that influences selling plans other than the price of the good changes, there is a **change in supply**. Six main factors bring changes in supply. They are changes in:

- The prices of factors of production
- The prices of related goods produced
- Expected future prices
- The number of suppliers
- Technology
- The state of nature

Prices of Factors of Production The prices of the factors of production used to produce a good influence its supply. To see this influence, think about the supply curve as a minimum-supply-price curve. If the price of a factor of production rises, the lowest price that a producer is willing to accept for that good rises, so supply decreases. For example, during 2008, as the price of jet fuel increased, the supply of air travel decreased. Similarly, a rise in the minimum wage decreases the supply of hamburgers.

Prices of Related Goods Produced The prices of related goods that firms produce influence supply. For example, if the price of an energy drink rises, firms switch production from sugary drinks to energy drinks. The supply of sugary drinks decreases. Energy drinks and sugary drinks are *substitutes in production*—goods that can be produced by using the same resources. If the price of beef rises, the supply of cowhide increases. Beef and cowhide are *complements in production*—goods that must be produced together.

Expected Future Prices If the expected future price of a good rises, the return from selling the good in the future increases and is higher than it is today. So supply decreases today and increases in the future.

The Number of Suppliers The larger the number of firms that produce a good, the greater is the supply of the good. As new firms enter an industry, the supply in that industry increases. As firms leave an industry, the supply in that industry decreases.

Technology The term "technology" is used broadly to mean the way that factors of production are used to produce a good. A technology change occurs when a new method is discovered that lowers the cost of producing a good. For example, new methods used in the factories that produce computer chips have lowered the cost and increased the supply of chips.

The State of Nature The state of nature includes all the natural forces that influence production. It includes the state of the weather and, more broadly, the natural environment. Good weather can increase the supply of many agricultural products and bad weather can decrease their supply. Extreme natural events such as earthquakes, tornadoes, and hurricanes can also influence supply.

Figure 3.5 illustrates an increase in supply. When supply increases, the supply curve shifts rightward and the quantity supplied at each price is larger. For example, at $1.00 per bar, on the original (blue) supply curve, the quantity supplied is 6 million bars a week. On the new (red) supply curve, the quantity supplied is 15 million bars a week. Look closely at the numbers in the table in Fig. 3.5 and check that the quantity supplied is larger at each price.

Table 3.2 summarizes the influences on supply and the directions of those influences.

A Change in the Quantity Supplied Versus a Change in Supply

Changes in the influences on selling plans bring either a change in the quantity supplied or a change in supply. Equivalently, they bring either a movement along the supply curve or a shift of the supply curve.

A point on the supply curve shows the quantity supplied at a given price. A movement along the supply curve shows a **change in the quantity supplied**. The entire supply curve shows supply. A shift of the supply curve shows a *change in supply*.

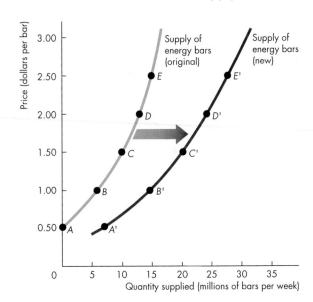

FIGURE 3.5   An Increase in Supply

Original supply schedule Old technology		New supply schedule New technology		
	Price (dollars per bar)	Quantity supplied (millions of bars per week)	Price (dollars per bar)	Quantity supplied (millions of bars per week)
A 0.50	0	A'	0.50	7
B 1.00	6	B'	1.00	15
C 1.50	10	C'	1.50	20
D 2.00	13	D'	2.00	25
E 2.50	15	E'	2.50	27

A change in any influence on selling plans other than the price of the good itself results in a new supply schedule and a shift of the supply curve. For example, a new, cost-saving technology for producing energy bars changes the supply of energy bars. At a price of $1.50 a bar, 10 million bars a week are supplied when producers use the old technology (row C of the table) and 20 million energy bars a week are supplied when producers use the new technology (row C'). An advance in technology *increases* the supply of energy bars. The supply curve shifts *rightward*, as shown by the shift arrow and the resulting red curve.

MyLab Economics Animation

Figure 3.6 illustrates and summarizes these distinctions. If the price of the good changes and other things remain the same, there is a *change in the quantity supplied* of that good. If the price of the good falls, the quantity supplied decreases and there is a movement down along the supply curve S_0. If the price of the good rises, the quantity supplied increases and there is a movement up along the supply curve S_0. When any other influence on selling plans changes, the supply curve shifts and there is a *change in supply*. If supply increases, the supply curve shifts rightward to S_1. If supply decreases, the supply curve shifts leftward to S_2.

TABLE 3.2 The Supply of Energy Bars

The Law of Supply

The quantity of energy bars supplied

Decreases if:	Increases if:
■ The price of an energy bar falls	■ The price of an energy bar rises

---

Changes in Supply

The supply of energy bars

Decreases if:	Increases if:
■ The price of a factor of production used to produce energy bars rises	■ The price of a factor of production used to produce energy bars falls
■ The price of a substitute in production rises	■ The price of a substitute in production falls
■ The price of a complement in production falls	■ The price of a complement in production rises
■ The expected future price of an energy bar rises	■ The expected future price of an energy bar falls
■ The number of suppliers of bars decreases	■ The number of suppliers of bars increases
■ A technology change decreases energy bar production	■ A technology change increases energy bar production
■ A natural event decreases energy bar production	■ A natural event increases energy bar production

---

FIGURE 3.6 A Change in the Quantity Supplied Versus a Change in Supply

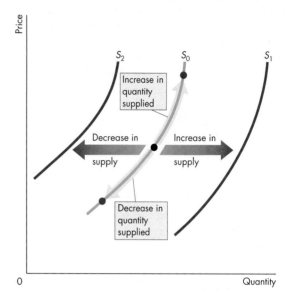

When the price of the good changes, there is a movement along the supply curve and a *change in the quantity supplied*, shown by the blue arrows along the supply curve S_0. When any other influence on selling plans changes, there is a shift of the supply curve and a *change in supply*. An increase in supply shifts the supply curve rightward (from S_0 to S_1), and a decrease in supply shifts the supply curve leftward (from S_0 to S_2).

—— MyLab Economics Animation and Draw Graph ——

REVIEW QUIZ

1 Define the quantity supplied of a good or service.
2 What is the law of supply and how do we illustrate it?
3 What does the supply curve tell us about the producer's minimum supply price?
4 List all the influences on selling plans, and for each influence, say whether it changes supply.
5 What happens to the quantity of smartphones supplied and the supply of smartphones if the price of a smartphone falls?

Work these questions in Study Plan 3.3 and get instant feedback.　　　　MyLab Economics

Now we're going to combine demand and supply and see how prices and quantities are determined.

◆ Market Equilibrium

We have seen that when the price of a good rises, the quantity demanded *decreases* and the quantity supplied *increases*. We are now going to see how the price adjusts to coordinate buying plans and selling plans and achieve an equilibrium in the market.

An *equilibrium* is a situation in which opposing forces balance each other. Equilibrium in a market occurs when the price balances buying plans and selling plans. The **equilibrium price** is the price at which the quantity demanded equals the quantity supplied. The **equilibrium quantity** is the quantity bought and sold at the equilibrium price. A market moves toward its equilibrium because:

■ Price regulates buying and selling plans.
■ Price adjusts when plans don't match.

Price as a Regulator

The price of a good regulates the quantities demanded and supplied. If the price is too high, the quantity supplied exceeds the quantity demanded. If the price is too low, the quantity demanded exceeds the quantity supplied. There is one price at which the quantity demanded equals the quantity supplied. Let's work out what that price is.

Figure 3.7 shows the market for energy bars. The table shows the demand schedule (from Fig. 3.1) and the supply schedule (from Fig. 3.4). If the price is 50¢ a bar, the quantity demanded is 22 million bars a week but no bars are supplied. There is a shortage of 22 million bars a week. The final column of the table shows this shortage. At a price of $1.00 a bar, there is still a shortage but only of 9 million bars a week.

If the price is $2.50 a bar, the quantity supplied is 15 million bars a week but the quantity demanded is only 5 million bars. There is a surplus of 10 million bars a week.

The one price at which there is neither a shortage nor a surplus is $1.50 a bar. At that price, the quantity demanded equals the quantity supplied: 10 million bars a week. The equilibrium price is $1.50 a bar, and the equilibrium quantity is 10 million bars a week.

Figure 3.7 shows that the demand curve and the supply curve intersect at the equilibrium price of $1.50 a bar. At each price *above* $1.50 a bar, there is a surplus of bars. For example, at $2.00 a bar, the surplus is

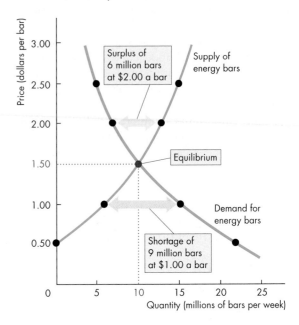

FIGURE 3.7 Equilibrium

Price (dollars per bar)	Quantity demanded	Quantity supplied	Shortage (−) or surplus (+)
	(millions of bars per week)		
0.50	22	0	−22
1.00	15	6	−9
1.50	**10**	**10**	**0**
2.00	7	13	+6
2.50	5	15	+10

The table lists the quantity demanded and the quantity supplied as well as the shortage or surplus of bars at each price. If the price is $1.00 a bar, 15 million bars a week are demanded and 6 million bars are supplied. There is a shortage of 9 million bars a week, and the price rises.

If the price is $2.00 a bar, 7 million bars a week are demanded and 13 million bars are supplied. There is a surplus of 6 million bars a week, and the price falls.

If the price is $1.50 a bar, 10 million bars a week are demanded and 10 million bars are supplied. There is neither a shortage nor a surplus, and the price does not change. The price at which the quantity demanded equals the quantity supplied is the equilibrium price, and 10 million bars a week is the equilibrium quantity.

—— MyLab Economics Animation and Draw Graph ——

6 million bars a week, as shown by the blue arrow. At each price *below* $1.50 a bar, there is a shortage of bars. For example, at $1.00 a bar, the shortage is 9 million bars a week, as shown by the red arrow.

Price Adjustments

You've seen that if the price is below equilibrium there is a shortage, and that if the price is above equilibrium there is a surplus. But can we count on the price to change and eliminate a shortage or a surplus? We can, because such price changes are beneficial to both buyers and sellers. Let's see why the price changes when there is a shortage or a surplus.

A Shortage Forces the Price Up Suppose that the price of an energy bar is $1. Consumers plan to buy 15 million bars a week, and producers plan to sell 6 million bars a week. Consumers can't force producers to sell more than they plan, so the quantity that is actually offered for sale is 6 million bars a week. In this situation, powerful forces operate to increase the price and move it toward the equilibrium price. Some producers, noticing lines of unsatisfied consumers, raise the price. Some producers increase their output. As producers push the price up, the price rises toward its equilibrium. The rising price reduces the shortage because it decreases the quantity demanded and increases the quantity supplied. When the price has increased to the point at which there is no longer a shortage, the forces moving the price stop operating and the price comes to rest at its equilibrium.

A Surplus Forces the Price Down Suppose the price of a bar is $2. Producers plan to sell 13 million bars a week, and consumers plan to buy 7 million bars a week. Producers cannot force consumers to buy more than they plan, so the quantity that is actually bought is 7 million bars a week. In this situation, powerful forces operate to lower the price and move it toward the equilibrium price. Some producers, unable to sell the quantities of energy bars they planned to sell, cut their prices. In addition, some producers scale back production. As producers cut the price, the price falls toward its equilibrium. The falling price decreases the surplus because it increases the quantity demanded and decreases the quantity supplied. When the price has fallen to the point at which there is no longer a surplus, the forces moving the price stop operating and the price comes to rest at its equilibrium.

The Best Deal Available for Buyers and Sellers

When the price is below equilibrium, it is forced upward. Why don't buyers resist the increase and refuse to buy at the higher price? The answer is because they value the good more highly than its current price and they can't satisfy their demand at the current price. In some markets—for example, the markets that operate on eBay—the buyers might even be the ones who force the price up by offering to pay a higher price.

When the price is above equilibrium, it is bid downward. Why don't sellers resist this decrease and refuse to sell at the lower price? The answer is because their minimum supply price is below the current price and they cannot sell all they would like to at the current price. Sellers willingly lower the price to gain market share.

At the price at which the quantity demanded and the quantity supplied are equal, neither buyers nor sellers can do business at a better price. Buyers pay the highest price they are willing to pay for the last unit bought, and sellers receive the lowest price at which they are willing to supply the last unit sold.

When people freely make offers to buy and sell and when demanders try to buy at the lowest possible price and suppliers try to sell at the highest possible price, the price at which trade takes place is the equilibrium price—the price at which the quantity demanded equals the quantity supplied. The price coordinates the plans of buyers and sellers, and no one has an incentive to change it.

◆ REVIEW QUIZ

1 What is the equilibrium price of a good or service?
2 Over what range of prices does a shortage arise? What happens to the price when there is a shortage?
3 Over what range of prices does a surplus arise? What happens to the price when there is a surplus?
4 Why is the price at which the quantity demanded equals the quantity supplied the equilibrium price?
5 Why is the equilibrium price the best deal available for both buyers and sellers?

Work these questions in Study Plan 3.4 and get instant feedback.   MyLab Economics

Predicting Changes in Price and Quantity

The demand and supply model that we have just studied provides us with a powerful way of analyzing influences on prices and the quantities bought and sold. According to the model, a change in price stems from a change in demand, a change in supply, or a change in both demand and supply. Let's look first at the effects of a change in demand.

An Increase in Demand

If more people join health clubs, the demand for energy bars increases. The table in Fig. 3.8 shows the original and new demand schedules for energy bars as well as the supply schedule of energy bars.

The increase in demand creates a shortage at the original price, and to eliminate the shortage the price must rise.

Figure 3.8 shows what happens. The figure shows the original demand for and supply of energy bars. The original equilibrium price is $1.50 an energy bar, and the equilibrium quantity is 10 million energy bars a week. When demand increases, the demand curve shifts rightward. The equilibrium price rises to $2.50 an energy bar, and the quantity supplied increases to 15 million energy bars a week, as highlighted in the figure. There is an *increase in the quantity supplied* but *no change in supply*—a movement along, but no shift of, the supply curve.

A Decrease in Demand

We can reverse this change in demand. Start at a price of $2.50 a bar with 15 million energy bars a week being bought and sold, and then work out what happens if demand decreases to its original level. Such a decrease in demand might arise if people switch to energy drinks (a substitute for energy bars). The decrease in demand shifts the demand curve leftward. The equilibrium price falls to $1.50 a bar, the quantity supplied decreases, and the equilibrium quantity decreases to 10 million bars a week.

We can now make our first two predictions:

1. When demand increases, the price rises and the quantity increases.
2. When demand decreases, the price falls and the quantity decreases.

FIGURE 3.8   The Effects of a Change in Demand

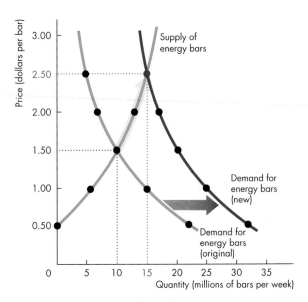

Price (dollars per bar)	Quantity demanded (millions of bars per week)		Quantity supplied (millions of bars per week)
	Original	New	
0.50	22	32	0
1.00	15	25	6
1.50	**10**	20	**10**
2.00	7	17	13
2.50	5	**15**	**15**

Initially, the demand for energy bars is the blue demand curve. The equilibrium price is $1.50 a bar, and the equilibrium quantity is 10 million bars a week. When more health-conscious people do more exercise, the demand for energy bars increases and the demand curve shifts rightward to become the red curve.

At $1.50 a bar, there is now a shortage of 10 million bars a week. The price of a bar rises to a new equilibrium of $2.50. As the price rises to $2.50, the quantity supplied increases—shown by the blue arrow on the supply curve—to the new equilibrium quantity of 15 million bars a week. Following an increase in demand, the quantity supplied increases but supply does not change—the supply curve does not shift.

—— MyLab Economics Animation and Draw Graph ——

ECONOMICS IN THE NEWS

The Markets for Chocolate and Cocoa

World's Sweet Tooth Heats Up Cocoa

With rising incomes in China and other fast-growing economies, the consumption of chocolate and the cocoa from which it is made is soaring. And the price of cocoa is soaring too.

Source: *The Wall Street Journal*, February 3, 2014

THE DATA

Year	Quantity of Cocoa (millions of tonnes per year)	Price of Cocoa (dollars per tonne)
2010	4	1,500
2014	5	3,000

THE QUESTIONS

- What does the data table tell us?
- Why did the price of cocoa increase? Is it because the demand for cocoa changed or the supply changed, and in which direction?

THE ANSWERS

- The data table tells us that from 2010 to 2014, both the quantity of cocoa produced and the price of cocoa increased.
- An increase in demand brings an increase in the quantity and a rise in the price.
- An increase in supply brings an increase in the quantity and a fall in the price.
- Because both the quantity of cocoa and the price of cocoa increased, there must have been in increase in the demand for cocoa.
- The demand for cocoa increases if cocoa is a normal good and incomes increase.
- Cocoa is a normal good and the news clip says that incomes are rising fast in China and some other countries. These increases in income have brought an increase in the demand for cocoa.
- The figure illustrates the market for cocoa in 2010 and 2014. The supply curve *S* shows the supply of cocoa.

- In 2010, the demand curve was D_{2010}, the price was $1,500 per tonne, and the quantity of cocoa traded was 4 million tonnes.
- By 2014, the higher incomes in China and other countries had increased the demand for cocoa to D_{2014}. The price rose to $3,000 per tonne and the quantity traded increased to 5 million tonnes.
- The higher price brought an increase in the quantity of cocoa supplied, which is shown by the movement upward along the supply curve.

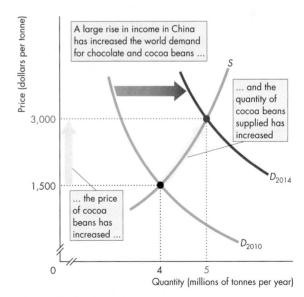

The Market for Cocoa Beans

An Increase in Supply

When Nestlé (the producer of PowerBar) and other energy bar producers switch to a new cost-saving technology, the supply of energy bars increases. Figure 3.9 shows the new supply schedule (the same one that was shown in Fig. 3.5). What are the new equilibrium price and quantity? The price falls to $1.00 a bar, and the quantity increases to 15 million bars a week. You can see why by looking at the quantities demanded and supplied at the old price of $1.50 a bar. The new quantity supplied at that price is 20 million bars a week, and there is a surplus. The price falls. Only when the price is $1.00 a bar does the quantity supplied equal the quantity demanded.

Figure 3.9 illustrates the effect of an increase in supply. It shows the demand curve for energy bars and the original and new supply curves. The initial equilibrium price is $1.50 a bar, and the equilibrium quantity is 10 million bars a week. When supply increases, the supply curve shifts rightward. The equilibrium price falls to $1.00 a bar, and the quantity demanded increases to 15 million bars a week, highlighted in the figure. There is an *increase in the quantity demanded* but *no change in demand*—a movement along, but no shift of, the demand curve.

A Decrease in Supply

Start out at a price of $1.00 a bar with 15 million bars a week being bought and sold. Then suppose that the cost of labour or raw materials rises and the supply of energy bars decreases. The decrease in supply shifts the supply curve leftward. The equilibrium price rises to $1.50 a bar, the quantity demanded decreases, and the equilibrium quantity decreases to 10 million bars a week.

We can now make two more predictions:

1. When supply increases, the price falls and the quantity increases.
2. When supply decreases, the price rises and the quantity decreases.

You've now seen what happens to the price and the quantity when either demand or supply changes while the other one remains unchanged. In real markets, both demand and supply can change together. When this happens, to predict the changes in price and quantity, we must combine the effects that you've just seen. That is your final task in this chapter.

FIGURE 3.9   The Effects of a Change in Supply

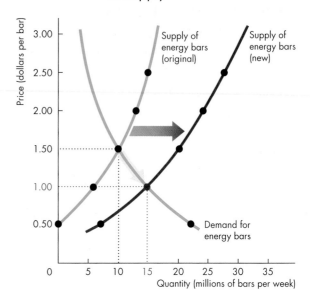

Price (dollars per bar)	Quantity demanded (millions of bars per week)	Quantity supplied (millions of bars per week)	
		Original	New
0.50	22	0	7
1.00	**15**	6	**15**
1.50	**10**	**10**	20
2.00	7	13	25
2.50	5	15	27

Initially, the supply of energy bars is shown by the blue supply curve. The equilibrium price is $1.50 a bar, and the equilibrium quantity is 10 million bars a week. When the new cost-saving technology is adopted, the supply of energy bars increases and the supply curve shifts rightward to become the red curve.

At $1.50 a bar, there is now a surplus of 10 million bars a week. The price of an energy bar falls to a new equilibrium of $1.00 a bar. As the price falls to $1.00, the quantity demanded increases—shown by the blue arrow on the demand curve—to the new equilibrium quantity of 15 million bars a week. Following an increase in supply, the quantity demanded increases but demand does not change—the demand curve does not shift.

—— MyLab Economics Animation and Draw Graph ——

◆ ECONOMICS IN THE NEWS

The Market for Vanilla Bean

Price of Ice Cream Set to Spike

A poor harvest in Madagascar has exploded the price of vanilla bean, the flavouring in Canada's top ice cream.

Source: *The Toronto Star*, April 7, 2016

THE DATA

Year	Quantity of Vanilla Bean (billions of tonnes per year)	Price of Vanilla Bean (dollars per kilogram)
2015	7.6	70
2016	5.6	425

THE QUESTIONS

- What does the data table tell us?
- Why did the price of vanilla bean rise? Is it because demand changed or supply changed, and in which direction?

THE ANSWERS

- The data table tells us that during 2016, the quantity of vanilla bean produced increased and the price of vanilla bean increased sharply.
- An increase in demand brings an increase in the quantity and a rise in the price.
- A decrease in supply brings a decrease in the quantity and a rise in the price.
- Because the quantity of vanilla bean decreased and the price increased, there must have been a decrease in the supply of vanilla bean
- The supply of vanilla bean decreases if a poor harvest decreases production.
- The news clip says there was a poor harvest in Madagascar. This decrease in production brought a decrease in the supply of vanilla bean.
- The figure illustrates the market for vanilla bean in 2015 and 2016. The demand curve D shows the demand for vanilla bean.
- In 2015, the supply curve was S_{15}, the price was $70 per kilogram, and the quantity of vanilla bean traded was 7.6 billion tonnes.

- In 2016, the decreased production in Madagasscar decreased the supply of vanilla bean to S_{16}.
- The price increased to $425 per kilogram and the quantity traded decreased to 5.6 billion tonnes.
- The higher price brought a decrease in the quantity of vanilla bean demanded, which is shown by the movement along the demand curve.

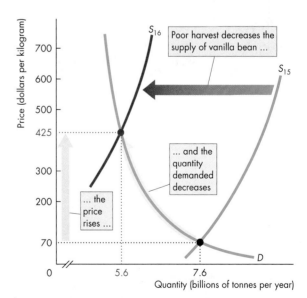

The Market for Vanilla Bean in 2015–2016

Changes in Both Demand and Supply

You now know how a change in demand or a change in supply changes the equilibrium price and quantity. But sometimes, events occur that change both demand and supply. When both demand and supply change, we find the resulting change in the equilibrium price and equilibrium quantity by combining the separate cases you've just studied.

Four cases need to be considered. Both demand and supply increase or decrease, or either demand or supply increases and the other decreases.

Demand and Supply Change in the Same Direction

When demand and supply change in the *same* direction, the equilibrium quantity changes in that same direction, but to predict whether the price rises or falls, we need to know the magnitudes of the changes in demand and supply.

If demand increases by more than supply increases, the price rises. But if supply increases by more than demand increases, the price falls.

Figure 3.10(a) shows the case when both demand and supply increase and by the same amount. The equilibrium quantity increases. But because the increase in demand equals the increase in supply, neither a shortage nor a surplus arises so the price doesn't change. A bigger increase in demand would have created a shortage and a rise in the price; a bigger increase in supply would have created a surplus and a fall in the price.

Figure 3.10(b) shows the case when both demand and supply decrease by the same amount. Here the equilibrium quantity decreases and again the price might either rise or fall.

Demand and Supply Change in Opposite Directions

When demand and supply change in *opposite* directions, we can predict how the price changes, but we need to know the magnitudes of the changes in demand and supply to say whether the equilibrium quantity increases or decreases.

If demand changes by more than supply, the equilibrium quantity changes in the same direction as the change in demand. But if supply changes by more than demand, the equilibrium quantity changes in the same direction as the change in supply.

FIGURE 3.10 The Effects of Changes in Demand and Supply in the Same Direction

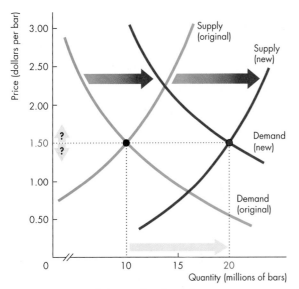

(a) Increase in both demand and supply

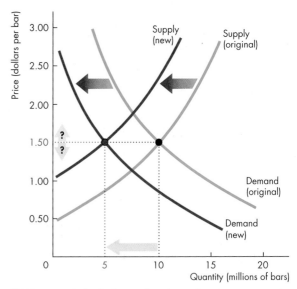

(b) Decrease in both demand and supply

An increase in demand shifts the demand curve rightward to become the red new demand curve and an increase in supply shifts the supply curve rightward to become the red new supply curve. The price might rise or fall, but the quantity increases.

A decrease in demand shifts the demand curve leftward to become the red new demand curve and a decrease in supply shifts the supply curve leftward to become the red new supply curve. The price might rise or fall, but the quantity decreases.

MyLab Economics Animation

FIGURE 3.11   The Effects of Changes in Demand and Supply in Opposite Directions

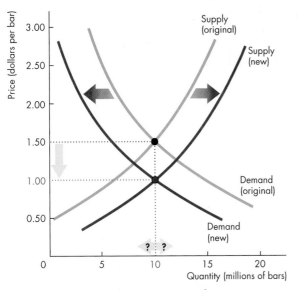

(a) Decrease in demand; increase in supply

A decrease in demand shifts the demand curve leftward to become the red new demand curve and an increase in supply shifts the supply curve rightward to become the red new supply curve. The price falls, but the quantity might increase or decrease.

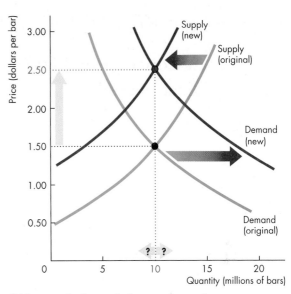

(b) Increase in demand; decrease in supply

An increase in demand shifts the demand curve rightward to become the red new demand curve and a decrease in supply shifts the supply curve leftward to become the red new supply curve. The price rises, but the quantity might increase or decrease.

MyLab Economics Animation

Figure 3.11(a) illustrates what happens when demand decreases and supply increases by the *same* amount. At the initial price, there is a surplus, so the price falls. A decrease in demand decreases the quantity and an increase in supply increases the quantity, so when these changes occur together, we can't say what happens to the quantity unless we know the magnitudes of the changes.

Figure 3.11(b) illustrates what happens when demand increases and supply decreases by the same amount. In this case, at the initial price, there is a shortage, so the price rises. An increase in demand increases the quantity and a decrease in supply decreases the quantity, so again, when these changes occur together, we can't say what happens to the quantity unless we know the magnitudes of the changes in demand and supply.

For all the cases in Figures 3.10 and 3.11 where you "can't say" what happens to price or quantity, draw some examples that go in each direction.

◆ REVIEW QUIZ

What is the effect on the price and quantity of smartphones if:

1   The price of a music-streaming subscription falls or the price of a wireless plan rises? (Draw the diagrams!)

2   More firms produce smartphones or electronics workers' wages rise? (Draw the diagrams!)

3   Any two of the events in questions 1 and 2 occur together? (Draw the diagrams!)

Work these questions in Study Plan 3.5 and get instant feedback.   MyLab Economics

◆ To complete your study of demand and supply, take a look at *Economics in the News* on pp. 78–79, which explains what has happened in the market for frozen concentrated orange juice. Try to get into the habit of using the demand and supply model to understand the changes in prices in your everyday life.

Demand and Supply:
The Market for Orange Juice

The Frozen Concentrated Orange-Juice Market Has Virtually Disappeared

The Wall Street Journal
August 28, 2016

The once-thriving market for frozen orange-juice concentrate is getting squeezed. …

Americans drank less orange juice in 2015 than in any year since Nielsen began collecting data in 2002, as more exotic beverages like tropical smoothies and energy drinks take market share and fewer Americans sit down for breakfast.

When they do drink orange juice, they aren't drinking it from concentrate.

Frozen concentrated orange juice was invented in Florida in the 1940s, primarily as a way to provide juice for the military, readily storable, and easy to ship. But frozen juice has been losing favor for years.

Not-from-concentrate orange juice surpassed the concentrated orange-juice market in the 1980s. Now, the 1.4 million gallons of frozen concentrate that Americans drink each month pales in comparison to the 19.1 million gallons of fresh juice consumed each month, Nielsen said.

Louis Dreyfus Co. is scaling back the one citrus facility in Florida that is devoted entirely to concentrated orange juice. The commodities giant is laying off 59 of the plant's 94 workers as it sells the operation that packs frozen concentrated orange juice into cans for retail.

There are now seven orange-juice processors left in Florida, down from the four dozen that once called the state home. …

A bacterial disease, citrus greening, … has slashed the orange crop in half in recent years. … Diseased trees are plucked out and replaced by new ones, which also catch the disease.

ESSENCE OF THE STORY

- Americans are drinking less frozen concentrated orange juice and more tropical smoothies, energy drinks, and not-from-concentrate orange juice.

- Today, Americans drink 1.4 million gallons of frozen concentrate each month compared to 19.1 million gallons of fresh juice consumed each month.

- Florida producers of concentrated orange juice are cutting production and laying off workers and dozens have gone out of business.

- In recent years, a bacterial disease, citrus greening, has halved the orange crop.

ECONOMIC ANALYSIS

- The quantity of frozen concentrated orange juice produced has been falling, and in 2016, the quantity produced was less than half that of 2008.

- Figure 1 shows the falling and fluctuating quantity produced.

- Figure 1 also shows the price of frozen concentrated orange juice, which has also trended downward.

- Look carefully at Fig. 1 and notice that from 2012 to 2014, the price and quantity moved in the same direction—they both fell; and from 2014 to 2015, the price and quantity moved in opposite directions—the quantity continued to fall but the price rose.

- The demand and supply model can be put to work to explain these changes in price and quantity.

- Figure 2 explains what occurred from 2012 to 2014.

- In 2012, the supply of frozen concentrated orange juice was S_0 and the demand was D_0. The price was $2.40 per can and the equilibrium quantity was 149 million boxes of cans of orange juice.

- By 2014, with unchanged supply, changing preferences decreased demand to D_1. The price fell to $2.14 per can and the equilibrium quantity decreased to 105 million boxes of cans.

- Figure 3 explains what happened in 2015.

- The bacterial disease citrus greening decreased the orange crop, which decreased the supply of frozen concentrated orange juice from S_0 to S_1. With demand unchanged at D_1, the price increased to $2.31 a can and the equilibrium quantity decreased to 97 million boxes.

- So, the demand and supply model explains the fall in the quantity of orange juice in 2014 as resulting from a decrease in demand, which brought a fall in price and a decrease in the quantity supplied.

- The demand and supply model also explains the fall in the quantity of orange juice in 2015 as resulting from a decrease in supply, which brought a rise in price and a decrease in the quantity demanded.

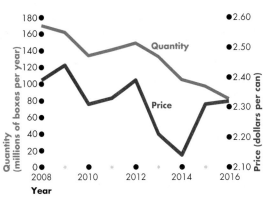

Figure 1 Quantity and Price of Orange Juice

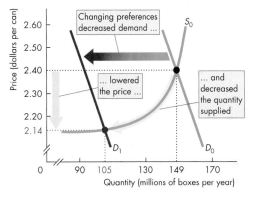

Figure 2 The Decreasing Demand for Orange Juice

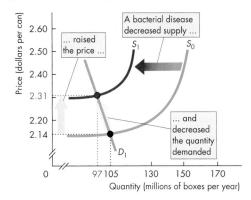

Figure 3 The Decrease in the Supply of Orange Juice

MATHEMATICAL NOTE

Demand, Supply, and Equilibrium

Demand Curve

The law of demand says that as the price of a good or service falls, the quantity demanded of that good or service increases. We can illustrate the law of demand by drawing a graph of the demand curve or writing down an equation. When the demand curve is a straight line, the following equation describes it:

$$P = a - bQ_D,$$

where P is the price and Q_D is the quantity demanded. The a and b are positive constants.

The demand equation tells us three things:

1. The price at which no one is willing to buy the good (Q_D is zero). That is, if the price is a, then the quantity demanded is zero. You can see the price a in Fig. 1. It is the price at which the demand curve hits the y-axis—what we call the demand curve's "y-intercept."

2. As the price falls, the quantity demanded increases. If Q_D is a positive number, then the price P must be less than a. As Q_D gets larger, the price P becomes smaller. That is, as the quantity increases, the maximum price that buyers are willing to pay for the last unit of the good falls.

3. The constant b tells us how fast the maximum price that someone is willing to pay for the good falls as the quantity increases. That is, the constant b tells us about the steepness of the demand curve. The equation tells us that the slope of the demand curve is $-b$.

Supply Curve

The law of supply says that as the price of a good or service rises, the quantity supplied of that good or service increases. We can illustrate the law of supply by drawing a graph of the supply curve or writing down an equation. When the supply curve is a straight line, the following equation describes it:

$$P = c + dQ_S,$$

where P is the price and Q_S is the quantity supplied. The c and d are positive constants.

The supply equation tells us three things:

1. The price at which sellers are not willing to supply the good (Q_S is zero). That is, if the price is c, then no one is willing to sell the good. You can see the price c in Fig. 2. It is the price at which the supply curve hits the y-axis—what we call the supply curve's "y-intercept."

2. As the price rises, the quantity supplied increases. If Q_S is a positive number, then the price P must be greater than c. As Q_S increases, the price P becomes larger. That is, as the quantity increases, the minimum price that sellers are willing to accept for the last unit rises.

3. The constant d tells us how fast the minimum price at which someone is willing to sell the good rises as the quantity increases. That is, the constant d tells us about the steepness of the supply curve. The equation tells us that the slope of the supply curve is d.

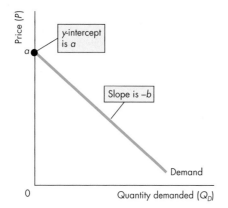

Figure 1 Demand Curve

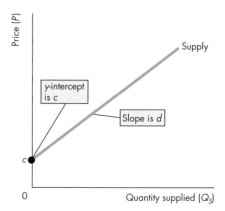

Figure 2 Supply Curve

Market Equilibrium

Demand and supply determine market equilibrium. Figure 3 shows the equilibrium price ($P*$) and equilibrium quantity ($Q*$) at the intersection of the demand curve and the supply curve.

We can use the equations to find the equilibrium price and equilibrium quantity. The price of a good adjusts until the quantity demanded Q_D equals the quantity supplied Q_S. So at the equilibrium price ($P*$) and equilibrium quantity ($Q*$),

$$Q_D = Q_S = Q*.$$

To find the equilibrium price and equilibrium quantity, substitute $Q*$ for Q_D in the demand equation and $Q*$ for Q_S in the supply equation. Then the price is the equilibrium price ($P*$), which gives

$$P* = a - bQ*$$

$$P* = c + dQ*.$$

Notice that

$$a - bQ* = c + dQ*.$$

Now solve for $Q*$:

$$a - c = bQ* + dQ*$$

$$a - c = (b + d)Q*$$

$$Q* = \frac{a - c}{b + d}.$$

To find the equilibrium price $P*$, substitute for $Q*$ in either the demand equation or the supply equation.

Using the demand equation, we have

$$P* = a - b\left(\frac{a - c}{b + d}\right)$$

$$P* = \frac{a(b + d) - b(a - c)}{b + d}$$

$$P* = \frac{ad + bc}{b + d}.$$

Alternatively, using the supply equation, we have

$$P* = c + d\left(\frac{a - c}{b + d}\right)$$

$$P* = \frac{c(b + d) + d(a - c)}{b + d}$$

$$P* = \frac{ad + bc}{b + d}.$$

An Example

The demand for ice-cream cones is

$$P = 800 - 2Q_D.$$

The supply of ice-cream cones is

$$P = 200 + 1Q_S.$$

The price of a cone is expressed in cents, and the quantities are expressed in cones per day.

To find the equilibrium price ($P*$) and equilibrium quantity ($Q*$), substitute $Q*$ for Q_D and Q_S and $P*$ for P. That is,

$$P* = 800 - 2Q*$$

$$P* = 200 + 1Q*.$$

Now solve for $Q*$:

$$800 - 2Q* = 200 + 1Q*$$

$$600 = 3Q*$$

$$Q* = 200.$$

And

$$P* = 800 - 2(200)$$

$$= 400.$$

The equilibrium price is $4 a cone, and the equilibrium quantity is 200 cones per day.

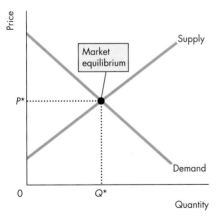

Figure 3 Market Equilibrium

◆ **WORKED PROBLEM**

MyLab Economics Work this problem in Chapter 3 Study Plan.

The table sets out the demand and supply schedules for roses on a normal weekend.

Price (dollars per rose)	Quantity demanded	Quantity supplied
	(roses per week)	
6.00	150	60
7.00	100	100
8.00	70	130
9.00	50	150

Questions

1. If the price of a rose is $6, describe the situation in the rose market. Explain how the price adjusts.

2. If the price of a rose is $9, describe the situation in the rose market. Explain how the price adjusts.

3. What is the market equilibrium?

4. Rose sellers know that Mother's Day is next weekend and they expect the price to be higher, so they withhold 60 roses from the market this weekend. What is the price this weekend?

5. On Mother's Day, demand increases by 160 roses. What is the price of a rose on Mother's Day?

Solutions

1. At $6 a rose, the quantity demanded is 150 and the quantity supplied is 60. The quantity demanded exceeds the quantity supplied and there is a *shortage* of 90 roses. With people lining up and a shortage, the price rises above $6 a rose.

Key Point: When a shortage exists, the price rises.

2. At $9 a rose, the quantity demanded is 50 and the quantity supplied is 180. The quantity supplied exceeds the quantity demanded and there is a *surplus* of 130 roses. With slow sales of roses and a surplus, the price falls to below $9 a rose.

Key Point: When a surplus exists, the price falls.

3. Market equilibrium occurs at the price at which the quantity demanded *equals* the quantity supplied. That price is $7 a rose. The market equilibrium is a price of $7 a rose and 100 roses a week are bought and sold, Point *A* on the figure.

Key Point: At market equilibrium, there is no shortage or surplus.

4. Sellers expect a higher price next weekend, so they decrease the supply this weekend by 60 roses at each price. Create the new table:

Price (dollars per rose)	Quantity demanded	Quantity supplied
	(roses per week)	
6.00	150	0
7.00	**100**	**40**
8.00	70	70
9.00	50	90

At $7 a rose, there was a shortage of 60 roses, so the price rises to $8 a rose at which the quantity demanded equals the quantity supplied (Point *B*).

Key Point: When supply decreases, the price rises.

5. Demand increases by 160 roses. Sellers plan to increase the normal supply by the 60 roses withheld last weekend. Create the new table:

Price (dollars per rose)	Quantity demanded	Quantity supplied
	(roses per week)	
6.00	310	120
7.00	**260**	**160**
8.00	230	190
9.00	210	210

At $7 a rose, there is a shortage of 100 roses, so the price rises. It rises until at $9 a rose, the quantity demanded equals the quantity supplied. The price on Mother's Day is $9 a rose (Point *C*).

Key Point: When demand increases by more than supply, the price rises.

Key Figure

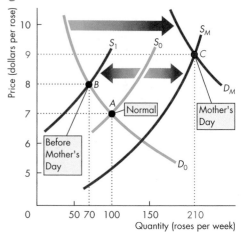

MyLab Economics Interactive Animation

SUMMARY

Key Points

Markets and Prices (p. 60)

- A competitive market is one that has so many buyers and sellers that no single buyer or seller can influence the price.
- Opportunity cost is a relative price.
- Demand and supply determine relative prices.

Working Problem 1 will give you a better understanding of markets and prices.

Demand (pp. 61–65)

- Demand is the relationship between the quantity demanded of a good and its price when all other influences on buying plans remain the same.
- The higher the price of a good, other things remaining the same, the smaller is the quantity demanded—the law of demand.
- Demand depends on the prices of related goods (substitutes and complements), expected future prices, income, expected future income and credit, the population, and preferences.

Working Problems 2 to 4 will give you a better understanding of demand.

Supply (pp. 66–69)

- Supply is the relationship between the quantity supplied of a good and its price when all other influences on selling plans remain the same.
- The higher the price of a good, other things remaining the same, the greater is the quantity supplied—the law of supply.

- Supply depends on the prices of factors of production used to produce a good, the prices of related goods produced, expected future prices, the number of suppliers, technology, and the state of nature.

Working Problems 5 and 6 will give you a better understanding of supply.

Market Equilibrium (pp. 70–71)

- At the equilibrium price, the quantity demanded equals the quantity supplied.
- At any price above the equilibrium price, there is a surplus and the price falls.
- At any price below the equilibrium price, there is a shortage and the price rises.

Working Problem 7 will give you a better understanding of market equilibrium.

Predicting Changes in Price and Quantity (pp. 72–77)

- An increase in demand brings a rise in the price and an increase in the quantity supplied. A decrease in demand brings a fall in the price and a decrease in the quantity supplied.
- An increase in supply brings a fall in the price and an increase in the quantity demanded. A decrease in supply brings a rise in the price and a decrease in the quantity demanded.
- An increase in demand and an increase in supply bring an increased quantity but an uncertain price change. An increase in demand and a decrease in supply bring a higher price but an uncertain change in quantity.

Working Problems 8 to 10 will give you a better understanding of predicting changes in price and quantity.

Key Terms

Change in demand, 62
Change in supply, 67
Change in the quantity demanded, 65
Change in the quantity supplied, 68
Competitive market, 60
Complement, 63
Demand, 61

Demand curve, 62
Equilibrium price, 70
Equilibrium quantity, 70
Inferior good, 64
Law of demand, 61
Law of supply, 66
Money price, 60
Normal good, 64

MyLab Economics Key Terms Quiz

Quantity demanded, 61
Quantity supplied, 66
Relative price, 60
Substitute, 63
Supply, 66
Supply curve, 66

STUDY PLAN PROBLEMS AND APPLICATIONS

MyLab Economics Work Problems 1 to 10 in Chapter 3 Study Plan and get instant feedback.

Markets and Prices (Study Plan 3.1)

1. In April 2014, the money price of a litre of milk was $2.01 and the money price of a litre of gasoline was $1.30. Calculate the real price of a litre of gasoline in terms of milk.

Demand (Study Plan 3.2)

2. The price of food increased during the past year.
   a. Explain why the law of demand applies to food just as it does to other goods and services.
   b. Explain how the substitution effect influences food purchases when the price of food rises and other things remain the same.
   c. Explain how the income effect influences food purchases and provide some examples of the income effect.

3. Which of the following goods are likely substitutes and which are likely complements? (You may use an item more than once.)

   coal, oil, natural gas, wheat, corn, pasta, pizza, sausage, skateboard, roller blades, video game, laptop, iPad, smartphone, text message, email

4. As the average income in China continues to increase, explain how the following would change:
   a. The demand for beef
   b. The demand for rice

Supply (Study Plan 3.3)

5. In 2016, the price of corn fell and some corn farmers switched from growing corn in 2017 to growing soybeans.
   a. Does this fact illustrate the law of demand or the law of supply? Explain your answer.
   b. Why would a corn farmer grow soybeans?

6. Dairies make low-fat milk from full-cream milk, and in the process they produce cream, which is made into ice cream. The following events occur one at a time:
   (i)   The wage rate of dairy workers rises.
   (ii) The price of cream rises.
   (iii) The price of low-fat milk rises.
   (iv) With a drought forecasted, dairies raise their expected price of low-fat milk next year.
   (v)   New technology lowers the cost of producing ice cream.

   Explain the effect of each event on the supply of low-fat milk.

Market Equilibrium (Study Plan 3.4)

7. The demand and supply schedules for gum are:

Price (cents per pack)	Quantity demanded	Quantity supplied
	(millions of packs a week)	
20	180	60
40	140	100
60	100	140
80	60	180

   a. Suppose that the price of gum is 70¢ a pack. Describe the situation in the gum market and explain how the price adjusts.
   b. Suppose that the price of gum is 30¢ a pack. Describe the situation in the gum market and explain how the price adjusts.

Predicting Changes in Price and Quantity (Study Plan 3.5)

8. The following events occur one at a time:
   (i)   The price of crude oil rises.
   (ii) The price of a car rises.
   (iii) All speed limits on highways are abolished.
   (iv) Robots cut car production costs.

   Explain the effect of each of these events on the market for gasoline.

9. In Problem 7, a fire destroys some factories that produce gum and the quantity of gum supplied decreases by 40 million packs a week at each price.
   a. Explain what happens in the market for gum and draw a graph to illustrate the changes.
   b. Suppose that at the same time as the fire, the teenage population increases and the quantity of gum demanded increases by 40 million packs a week at each price. What is the new market equilibrium? Illustrate these changes on your graph.

10. **Singing the Blues: March Frost Destroys Blueberry Crop**
    Chris and Rhonda Luther had big plans for their small blueberry farm, but freezing temperatures killed these plans, reducing their usual output by about 95 percent. The freeze cut total production by 80 percent.

    Source: *Red and Black*, March 25, 2017

    Draw a graph to show the market for blueberries before and after the freeze in March.

ADDITIONAL PROBLEMS AND APPLICATIONS

MyLab Economics You can work these problems in Homework or Test if assigned by your instructor.

Markets and Prices

11. What features of the world market for crude oil make it a competitive market?

12. The money price of a textbook is $90 and the money price of the Wii game *Super Mario Galaxy* is $45.

    a. What is the opportunity cost of a textbook in terms of the Wii game?

    b. What is the relative price of the Wii game in terms of textbooks?

Demand

13. The price of gasoline has increased during the past year.

    a. Explain why the law of demand applies to gasoline just as it does to all other goods and services.

    b. Explain how the substitution effect influences gasoline purchases and provide some examples of substitutions that people might make when the price of gasoline rises and other things remain the same.

    c. Explain how the income effect influences gasoline purchases and provide some examples of the income effects that might occur when the price of gasoline rises and other things remain the same.

14. Think about the demand for the three game consoles: Xbox One, PlayStation 4, and Wii U. Explain the effect of each of the following events on the demand for Xbox One games and the quantity of Xbox One games demanded, other things remaining the same. The events are:

    a. The price of an Xbox One falls.

    b. The prices of a PlayStation 4 and a Wii U fall.

    c. The number of people writing and producing Xbox One games increases.

    d. Consumers' incomes increase.

    e. Programmers who write code for Xbox One games become more costly to hire.

    f. The expected future price of an Xbox One game falls.

    g. A new game console that is a close substitute for Xbox One comes onto the market.

Supply

15. Classify the following pairs of goods and services as substitutes in production, complements in production, or neither.

    a. Bottled water and health club memberships

    b. French fries and baked potatoes

    c. Leather boots and leather shoes

    d. Hybrids and SUVs

    e. Diet Coke and regular Coke

16. When a timber mill makes logs from trees it also produces sawdust, which is used to make plywood.

    a. Explain how a rise in the price of sawdust influences the supply of logs.

    b. Explain how a rise in the price of sawdust influences the supply of plywood.

17. **New Maple Syrup Sap Method**
    With the new way to tap maple trees, farmers could produce 10 times as much maple syrup per acre.
    Source: cbc.ca, February 5, 2014

    Will the new method change the supply of maple syrup or the quantity supplied of maple syrup, other things remaining the same? Explain.

Market Equilibrium

Use the following figure to work Problems 18 and 19.

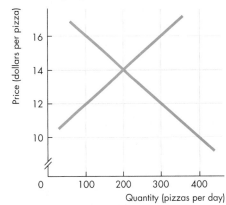

18. a. Label the curves. Which curve shows the willingness to pay for a pizza?

    b. If the price of a pizza is $16, is there a shortage or a surplus and does the price rise or fall?

c. Sellers want to receive the highest possible price, so why would they be willing to accept less than $16 a pizza?

19. a. If the price of a pizza is $12, is there a shortage or a surplus and does the price rise or fall?

b. Buyers want to pay the lowest possible price, so why would they be willing to pay more than $12 for a pizza?

20. The demand and supply schedules for potato chips are:

Price (cents per bag)	Quantity demanded	Quantity supplied
	(millions of bags per week)	
50	160	130
60	150	140
70	140	150
80	130	160
90	120	170
100	110	180

a. Draw a graph of the potato chip market and mark in the equilibrium price and quantity.

b. If the price is 60¢ a bag, is there a shortage or a surplus, and how does the price adjust?

Predicting Changes in Price and Quantity

21. In Problem 20, a new dip increases the quantity of potato chips that people want to buy by 30 million bags per week at each price.

a. Does the demand for chips change? Does the supply of chips change? Describe the change.

b. How do the equilibrium price and equilibrium quantity of chips change?

22. In Problem 20, if a virus destroys potato crops and the quantity of potato chips produced decreases by 40 million bags a week at each price, how does the supply of chips change?

23. If the virus in Problem 22 hits just as the new dip in Problem 21 comes onto the market, how do the equilibrium price and equilibrium quantity of chips change?

24. **U.S. Craft Beer Bolsters U.K. Hop Production**

U.K. hop farmers stepped up production in response to a rapid growth of U.S. craft beer production. U.S. craft beer makers prefer the subtle taste of U.K. hop varieties.

Source: BBC, October 3, 2014

a. Describe the changes in the market for U.S. craft beer.

b. Explain whether the increase in U.K. hop production is a change in supply or a change in the quantity supplied.

c. What could be the impact on the price of U.K. hops if U.S. farmers switched to U.K. hop varieties?

25. **Vietnamese Farmers Switch to Pepper as Coffee Prices Fall**

The high pepper price and falling coffee price has made Vietnamese farmers replace coffee plants with pepper plants. Analysts fear farmers have used diseased pepper plants which could fail.

Source: *VietNam News*, May 28, 2016

a. Explain how the market for Vietnamese coffee will change as farmers switch to pepper.

b. If pepper plants fail, what would happen to the price of pepper?

26. **Watch Out for Rising Dry-Cleaning Bills**

The price of dry-cleaning solvent doubled and more than 4,000 dry cleaners disappeared as consumers cut back. The price of hangers used by dry cleaners is now expected to double.

Source: CNN Money, June 4, 2012

a. Explain the effect of rising solvent prices on the market for dry cleaning.

b. Explain the effect of consumers becoming more budget conscious along with the rising price of solvent on the price of dry cleaning.

c. If the price of hangers does rise this year, do you expect additional dry cleaners to disappear? Explain why or why not.

Economics in the News

27. After you have studied *Economics in the News* on pp. 78–79, answer the following questions.

a. Would you classify frozen concentrated orange juice as a normal good or an inferior good? Why?

b. What would happen to the price of orange juice if citrus greening wiped out the Florida orange crop?

c. What are some of the substitutes for orange juice and what would happen to the demand, supply, price, and quantity in the markets for each of these items if citrus greening became more severe?

d. What are some of the complements of orange juice and what would happen to the demand, supply, price, and quantity in the markets for each of these items if citrus greening became more severe?

4

ELASTICITY

After studying this chapter, you will be able to:

◆ Define, calculate, and explain the factors that influence the price elasticity of demand

◆ Define, calculate, and explain the factors that influence the income elasticity of demand and the cross elasticity of demand

◆ Define, calculate, and explain the factors that influence the elasticity of supply

Concerned about an obesity crisis, an increasing number of cities and countries are trying to cut the consumption of sugar-sweetened drinks by imposing a tax on them. How does a tax on sugary drinks influence the quantity of these drinks consumed?

To answer this and similar questions, we use the tool that you study in this chapter: elasticity.

At the end of the chapter, in *Economics in the News*, we use the concept of elasticity to answer the question about the market for sugary drinks. But we begin by explaining elasticity in another familiar setting: the market for pizza.

◆ Price Elasticity of Demand

You know that when supply decreases, the equilibrium price rises and the equilibrium quantity decreases. But does the price rise by a large amount and the quantity decrease by a little? Or does the price barely rise and the quantity decrease by a large amount?

The answer depends on the responsiveness of the quantity demanded of a good to a change in its price. If the quantity demanded is not very responsive to a change in the price, the price rises a lot and the equilibrium quantity doesn't change much. If the quantity demanded *is* very responsive to a change in the price, the price barely rises and the equilibrium quantity changes a lot.

You might think about the responsiveness of the quantity demanded of a good to a change in its price in terms of the slope of the demand curve. If the demand curve is steep, the quantity demanded of the good isn't very responsive to a change in the price. If the demand curve is almost flat, the quantity demanded *is* very responsive to a change in the price.

But the slope of a demand curve depends on the units in which we measure the price and the quantity—we can make the curve steep or almost flat just by changing the units in which we measure the price and the quantity. Also we often want to compare the demand for different goods and services, and their quantities are measured in unrelated units. For example, a pizza producer might want to compare the demand for pizza with the demand for soft drinks. Which quantity demanded is more responsive to a price change? This question can't be answered by comparing the slopes of two demand curves. The units of measurement of pizza and soft drinks are unrelated. But the question *can* be answered with a measure of responsiveness that is *independent* of units of measurement. Elasticity is such a measure.

The **price elasticity of demand** is a units-free measure of the responsiveness of the quantity demanded of a good to a change in its price when all other influences on buying plans remain the same.

Calculating Price Elasticity of Demand

We calculate the *price elasticity of demand* by using the formula:

$$\text{Price elasticity of demand} = \frac{\text{Percentage change in quantity demanded}}{\text{Percentage change in price}}.$$

To calculate the price elasticity of demand for pizza, we need to know the quantity demanded of pizza at two different prices, when all other influences on buying plans remain the same.

Figure 4.1 zooms in on a section of the demand curve for pizza and shows how the quantity demanded responds to a small change in price. Initially, the price is $20.50 a pizza and 9 pizzas an hour are demanded—the original point. The price then falls to $19.50 a pizza, and the quantity demanded increases to 11 pizzas an hour—the new point. When the price falls by $1 a pizza, the quantity demanded increases by 2 pizzas an hour.

To calculate the price elasticity of demand, we express the change in price as a percentage of the *average price* and the change in the quantity demanded as a percentage of the *average quantity*. By using the average price and average quantity, we calculate the elasticity at a point on the demand curve midway between the original point and the new point.

The original price is $20.50 and the new price is $19.50, so the price change is $1 and the average price is $20 a pizza. Call the percentage change in the price $\%\Delta P$, then

$$\%\Delta P = \Delta P/P_{ave} \times 100 = (\$1/\$20) \times 100 = 5\%.$$

The original quantity demanded is 9 pizzas and the new quantity demanded is 11 pizzas, so the quantity change is 2 pizzas and the average quantity demanded is 10 pizzas. Call the percentage change in the quantity demanded $\%\Delta Q$, then

$$\%\Delta Q = \Delta Q/Q_{ave} \times 100 = (2/10) \times 100 = 20\%.$$

The price elasticity of demand equals the percentage change in the quantity demanded (20 percent) divided by the percentage change in price (5 percent) and is 4. That is,

$$\begin{aligned}\text{Price elasticity of demand} &= \frac{\%\Delta Q}{\%\Delta P} \\ &= \frac{20\%}{5\%} = 4.\end{aligned}$$

Average Price and Quantity Notice that we use the *average* price and *average* quantity. We do this because it gives the most precise measurement of elasticity—at the *midpoint* between the original price and the new price. If the price falls from $20.50 to $19.50, the $1 price change is 4.9 percent of $20.50. The 2 pizza change in quantity is 22.2 percent of 9 pizzas, the original quantity. So if we use

FIGURE 4.1   Calculating the Elasticity
of Demand

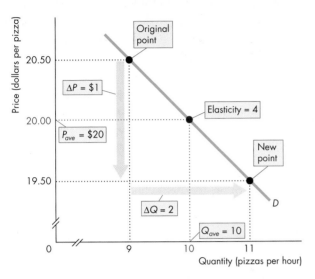

The elasticity of demand is calculated by using the formula:*

$$\text{Price elasticity of demand} = \frac{\text{Percentage change in quantity demanded}}{\text{Percentage change in price}}$$

$$= \frac{\%\Delta Q}{\%\Delta P}$$

$$= \frac{\%\Delta Q / Q_{ave}}{\%\Delta P / P_{ave}}$$

$$= \frac{2/10}{1/20} = 4.$$

This calculation measures the elasticity at an average price of $20 a pizza and an average quantity of 10 pizzas an hour.

*In the formula, the Greek letter delta (Δ) stands for "change in" and %Δ stands for "percentage change in."

_____ MyLab Economics Animation and Draw Graph _____

these numbers, the price elasticity of demand is 22.2 divided by 4.9, which equals 4.5. But if the price rises from $19.50 to $20.50, the $1 price change is 5.1 percent of $19.50. The 2 pizza change in quantity is 18.2 percent of 11 pizzas, the original quantity. So if we use these numbers, the price elasticity of demand is 18.2 divided by 5.1, which equals 3.6.

By using percentages of the *average* price and *average* quantity, we get the *same value* for the elasticity regardless of whether the price falls from $20.50 to $19.50 or rises from $19.50 to $20.50.

Percentages and Proportions Elasticity is the ratio of two percentage changes, so when we divide one percentage change by another, the 100s cancel. A percentage change is a *proportionate* change multiplied by 100. The proportionate change in price is $\Delta P / P_{ave}$, and the proportionate change in quantity demanded is $\Delta Q / Q_{ave}$. So if we divide $\Delta Q / Q_{ave}$ by $\Delta P / P_{ave}$ we get the same answer as we get by using percentage changes.

A Units-Free Measure Now that you've calculated a price elasticity of demand, you can see why it is a *units-free measure*. Elasticity is a units-free measure because the percentage change in each variable is independent of the units in which it is measured. So the ratio of the two percentages is a number without units.

Minus Sign and Elasticity When the price of a good *rises*, the quantity demanded *decreases*. Because a *positive* change in price brings a *negative* change in the quantity demanded, the price elasticity of demand is a negative number. But it is the magnitude, or *absolute value*, of the price elasticity of demand that tells us how responsive the quantity demanded is. So to compare price elasticities of demand, we use the *magnitude* of the elasticity and ignore the minus sign.

Inelastic and Elastic Demand

If the quantity demanded remains constant when the price changes, then the price elasticity of demand is zero and the good is said to have a **perfectly inelastic demand**. One good that has a very low price elasticity of demand (perhaps zero over some price range) is insulin. Insulin is of such importance to some diabetics that if the price rises or falls, they do not change the quantity they buy.

If the percentage change in the quantity demanded equals the percentage change in the price, then the price elasticity equals 1 and the good is said to have a **unit elastic demand**.

Between perfectly inelastic demand and unit elastic demand is a general case in which *the percentage change in the quantity demanded is less than the percentage change in the price*. In this case, the price elasticity of demand is between zero and 1 and the good is said to have an **inelastic demand**. Food and shelter are examples of goods with inelastic demand.

If the quantity demanded changes by an infinitely large percentage in response to a tiny price change, then the price elasticity of demand is infinity and the good is said to have a **perfectly elastic demand**. An example of a good that has a very high elasticity of demand (almost infinite) is a soft drink from two campus machines located side by side. If the two machines offer the same soft drinks for the same price, some people buy from one machine and some from the other. But if one machine's price is higher than the other's, by even a small amount, no one buys from the machine with the higher price. Drinks from the two machines are perfect substitutes. The demand for a good that has a perfect substitute is perfectly elastic.

Between unit elastic demand and perfectly elastic demand is another general case in which *the percentage change in the quantity demanded exceeds the percentage change in price*. In this case, the price elasticity of demand is greater than 1 and the good is said to have an **elastic demand**. Automobiles and furniture are examples of goods that have elastic demand.

Figure 4.2 shows three demand curves that cover the entire range of possible elasticities of demand that you've just reviewed. In Fig. 4.2(a), the quantity demanded is constant regardless of the price, so this demand is perfectly inelastic. In Fig. 4.2(b), the percentage change in the quantity demanded equals the percentage change in price, so this demand is unit elastic. In Fig. 4.2(c), the price is constant regardless of the quantity demanded, so this figure illustrates a perfectly elastic demand.

You now know the distinction between elastic and inelastic demand. But what determines whether the demand for a good is elastic or inelastic?

The Factors That Influence the Elasticity of Demand

The elasticity of demand for a good depends on:

- The closeness of substitutes
- The proportion of income spent on the good
- The time elapsed since the price change

Closeness of Substitutes The closer the substitutes for a good, the more elastic is the demand for it. Oil as fuel or raw material for chemicals has no close substitutes, so the demand for oil is inelastic. Plastics are close substitutes for metals, so the demand for metals is elastic.

The degree of substitutability depends on how narrowly (or broadly) we define a good. For example, a smartphone has no close substitutes, but an Apple iPhone is a close substitute for a Samsung Galaxy. So the elasticity of demand for smartphones is lower than the elasticity of demand for an iPhone or a Galaxy.

In everyday language we call goods such as food and shelter *necessities* and goods such as exotic vacations *luxuries*. A necessity has poor substitutes, so it generally has an inelastic demand. A luxury usually has many substitutes, one of which is not buying it. So a luxury generally has an elastic demand.

Proportion of Income Spent on the Good Other things remaining the same, the greater the proportion of income spent on a good, the more elastic (or less inelastic) is the demand for it.

FIGURE 4.2 Inelastic and Elastic Demand

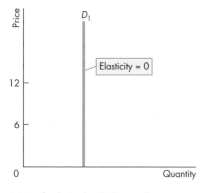

(a) Perfectly inelastic demand

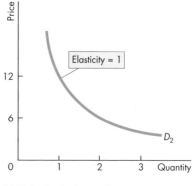

(b) Unit elastic demand

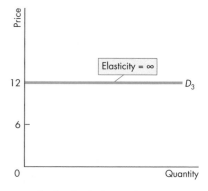

(c) Perfectly elastic demand

Each demand illustrated here has a constant elasticity. The demand curve in part (a) illustrates the demand for a good that has a zero elasticity of demand. The demand curve in part (b) illustrates the demand for a good with a unit elasticity of demand. And the demand curve in part (c) illustrates the demand for a good with an infinite elasticity of demand.

Think about your own elasticity of demand for chewing gum and housing. If the price of gum rises, you consume almost as much as before. Your demand for gum is inelastic. If apartment rents rise, you look for someone to share with. Your demand for housing is not as inelastic as your demand for gum. Why the difference? Housing takes a big chunk of your budget, and gum takes only a little. You barely notice the higher price of gum, while the higher rent puts your budget under severe strain.

Time Elapsed Since Price Change The longer the time that has elapsed since a price change, the more elastic is demand. When the price of oil increased by 400 percent during the 1970s, people barely changed the quantity of oil and gasoline they bought. But gradually, as more efficient auto and airplane engines were developed, the quantity bought decreased. The demand for oil became more elastic as more time elapsed following the huge price hike.

Elasticity Along a Linear Demand Curve

Elasticity of demand is not the same as slope. And a good way to see this fact is by studying a demand curve that has a constant slope but a varying elasticity.

The demand curve in Fig. 4.3 is linear, which means that it has a constant slope. Along this demand curve, a $5 rise in the price brings a decrease of 10 pizzas an hour.

But the price elasticity of demand is not constant along this demand curve. To see why, let's calculate some elasticities.

At the midpoint of the demand curve, the price is $12.50 and the quantity is 25 pizzas per hour. If the price rises from $10 to $15 a pizza, the quantity demanded decreases from 30 to 20 pizzas an hour and the average price and average quantity are at the midpoint of the demand curve. So

$$\text{Price elasticity of demand} = \frac{10/25}{5/12.50}$$

$$= 1.$$

That is, at the midpoint of a linear demand curve, the price elasticity of demand is 1.

At prices *above* the midpoint, the price elasticity of demand is greater than 1: Demand is elastic. To see that demand is elastic, let's calculate the elasticity when the price rises from $15 to $25 a pizza. You can see that quantity demanded decreases from 20 to zero pizzas an hour. The average price is $20 a pizza, and

FIGURE 4.3   Elasticity Along a Linear Demand Curve

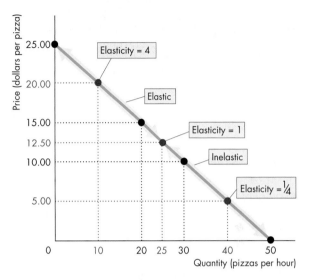

On a linear demand curve, demand is unit elastic at the midpoint (elasticity is 1), elastic above the midpoint, and inelastic below the midpoint.

—— MyLab Economics Animation and Draw Graph ——

the average quantity is 10 pizzas. Putting these numbers into the elasticity formula:

$$\text{Price elasticity of demand} = \frac{\Delta Q/Q_{ave}}{\Delta P/P_{ave}}$$

$$= \frac{20/10}{10/20}$$

$$= 4.$$

That is, the price elasticity of demand at an average price of $20 a pizza is 4.

At prices *below* the midpoint, the price elasticity of demand is less than 1: Demand is inelastic. For example, if the price rises from zero to $10 a pizza, the quantity demanded decreases from 50 to 30 pizzas an hour. The average price is now $5 and the average quantity is 40 pizzas an hour. So

$$\text{Price elasticity of demand} = \frac{20/40}{10/5}$$

$$= 1/4.$$

That is, the price elasticity of demand at an average price of $5 a pizza is 1/4.

Total Revenue and Elasticity

The **total revenue** from the sale of a good equals the price of the good multiplied by the quantity sold. When a price changes, total revenue also changes. But a cut in the price does not always decrease total revenue. The change in total revenue depends on the elasticity of demand in the following way:

- If demand is elastic, a 1 percent price cut increases the quantity sold by more than 1 percent and total revenue increases.
- If demand is inelastic, a 1 percent price cut increases the quantity sold by less than 1 percent and total revenue decreases.
- If demand is unit elastic, a 1 percent price cut increases the quantity sold by 1 percent and total revenue does not change.

In Fig. 4.4(a), over the price range $25 to $12.50 a pizza, demand is elastic. At a price of $12.50 a pizza, demand is unit elastic. Over the price range from $12.50 a pizza to zero, demand is inelastic.

Figure 4.4(b) shows total revenue. At a price of $25, the quantity sold is zero, so total revenue is zero. At a price of zero, the quantity demanded is 50 pizzas an hour and total revenue is again zero. A price cut in the elastic range brings an increase in total revenue—the percentage increase in the quantity demanded is greater than the percentage decrease in price. A price cut in the inelastic range brings a decrease in total revenue—the percentage increase in the quantity demanded is less than the percentage decrease in price. At unit elasticity, total revenue is at a maximum.

Figure 4.4 shows how we can use this relationship between elasticity and total revenue to estimate elasticity using the total revenue test. The **total revenue test** is a method of estimating the price elasticity of demand by observing the change in total revenue that results from a change in the price, when all other influences on the quantity sold remain the same.

- If a price cut increases total revenue, demand is elastic.
- If a price cut decreases total revenue, demand is inelastic.
- If a price cut leaves total revenue unchanged, demand is unit elastic.

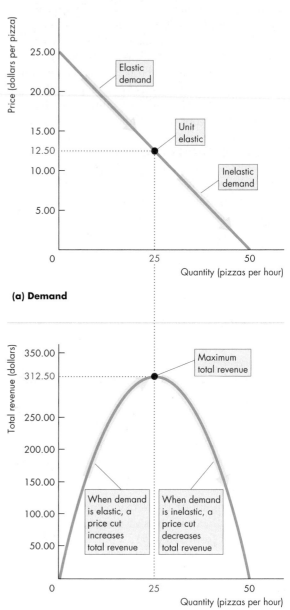

FIGURE 4.4 Elasticity and Total Revenue

(a) Demand

(b) Total revenue

When demand is elastic, in the price range from $25 to $12.50, a decrease in price (part a) brings an increase in total revenue (part b). When demand is inelastic, in the price range from $12.50 to zero, a decrease in price (part a) brings a decrease in total revenue (part b). When demand is unit elastic, at a price of $12.50 (part a), total revenue is at a maximum (part b).

MyLab Economics Animation

ECONOMICS IN ACTION

Elastic and Inelastic Demand

The real-world price elasticities of demand in the table range from 1.52 for metals, the item with the most elastic demand in the table, to 0.05 for oil, the item with the most inelastic demand in the table. The demand for food is also inelastic.

Oil and food, which have poor substitutes and inelastic demand, might be classified as necessities. Furniture and motor vehicles, which have good substitutes and elastic demand, might be classified as luxuries.

Price Elasticities of Demand

Good or Service	Elasticity
Elastic Demand	
Metals	1.52
Electrical engineering products	1.39
Mechanical engineering products	1.30
Furniture	1.26
Motor vehicles	1.14
Instrument engineering products	1.10
Transportation services	1.03
Inelastic Demand	
Gas, electricity, and water	0.92
Chemicals	0.89
Clothing	0.64
Banking and insurance services	0.56
Housing services	0.55
Agricultural and fish products	0.42
Books, magazines, and newspapers	0.34
Food	0.12
Cigarettes	0.11
Soft drinks	0.05
Oil	0.05

Sources of data: Ahsan Mansur and John Whalley, "Numerical Specification of Applied General Equilibrium Models: Estimation, Calibration, and Data," in *Applied General Equilibrium Analysis*, eds. Herbert E. Scarf and John B. Shoven (New York: Cambridge University Press, 1984), 109; Henri Theil, ChingFan Chung, and James L. Seale, Jr., *Advances in Econometrics, Supplement I, 1989, International Evidence on Consumption Patterns* (Greenwich, Conn.: JAI Press Inc., 1989); Emilio Pagoulatos and Robert Sorensen, "What Determines the Elasticity of Industry Demand," *International Journal of Industrial Organization*, 1986; and Geoffrey Heal, Columbia University, Web site.

Price Elasticities of Demand for Food

The price elasticity of demand for food in the United States is estimated to be 0.12. This elasticity is an average over all types of food. The demand for most food items is inelastic, but there is a wide range of elasticities, as the figure below shows for a range of fruits, vegetables, and meats.

The demand for grapes and the demand for beef are elastic. The demand for oranges is unit elastic. These food items, especially grapes and beef, have many good substitutes. Florida winter tomatoes have closer substitutes than tomatoes in general, so the demand for the Florida winter variety is more elastic (less inelastic) than the demand for tomatoes.

Carrots and cabbage, on which we spend a very small proportion of income, have an almost zero elastic demand.

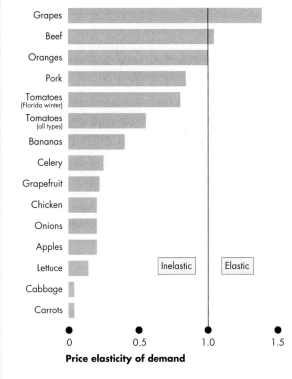

Price Elasticities of Demand for Food

Sources of data: Kuo S. Huang, *U.S. demand for food: A complete system of price and income effects*, U.S. Dept. of Agriculture, Economic Research Service, Washington, DC, 1985; J. Scott Shonkwiler and Robert D. Emerson, "Imports and the Supply of Winter Tomatoes: An Application of Rational Expectations," *American Journal of Agricultural Economics*, Vol. 64, No. 4 (Nov., 1982), pp. 634–641; and Kuo S. Huang, "A Further Look at Flexibilities and Elasticities," *American Journal of Agricultural Economics*, Vol. 76, No. 2 (May, 1994), pp. 313–317.

ECONOMICS IN THE NEWS

The Elasticity of Demand for Peanut Butter

Peanut Butter Prices to Rise 30 to 40 Percent

Scott Karns, president and CEO of Karns Foods, said "People are still going to need it for their family. It's still an extremely economical item." Patty Nolan, who is on a fixed income, said "I love peanut butter so I'm using a little less so I don't go through it."

Source: *The Patriot-News*, November 2, 2011

THE DATA

Year	Quantity (millions of tonnes per year)	Price (dollars per kilogram)
2011	350	4.00
2012	300	5.60

THE QUESTIONS

- Does the news clip imply that the demand for peanut butter is elastic or inelastic?
- If the data are two points on the demand curve for peanut butter, what is the price elasticity of demand?

THE ANSWERS

- The two remarks in the news clip suggest that the quantity of peanut butter demanded will decrease when the price rises, but not by much. The demand for peanut butter is inelastic.

- The data table says the price of peanut butter increased by $1.60 with an average price of $4.80, so the price increased by 33.3 percent. The quantity demanded decreased by 50 million tonnes with an average quantity of 325 million tonnes, so the quantity demanded decreased by 15.4 percent. The price elasticity of demand is 15.4 percent divided by 33.3 percent, which equals 0.46.

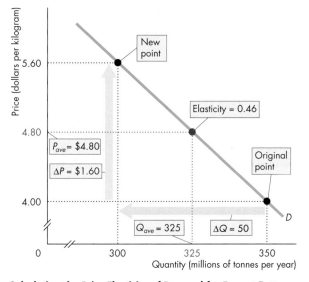

Calculating the Price Elasticity of Demand for Peanut Butter

MyLab Economics Economics in the News

Your Expenditure and Your Elasticity

When the price of a good changes, the change in your expenditure on the good depends on *your* elasticity of demand.

- If your demand for the good is elastic, a 1 percent price cut increases the quantity you buy by more than 1 percent and your expenditure on the item increases.

- If your demand for the good is inelastic, a 1 percent price cut increases the quantity you buy by less than 1 percent and your expenditure on the item decreases.

- If your demand for the good is unit elastic, a 1 percent price cut increases the quantity you buy by 1 percent and your expenditure on the item does not change.

So if you spend more on an item when its price falls, your demand for that item is elastic; if you spend the same amount, your demand is unit elastic; and if you spend less, your demand is inelastic.

REVIEW QUIZ

1 Why do we need a units-free measure of the responsiveness of the quantity demanded of a good or service to a change in its price?
2 Define the price elasticity of demand and show how it is calculated.
3 What makes the demand for some goods elastic and the demand for other goods inelastic?
4 Why is the demand for a luxury generally more elastic (or less inelastic) than the demand for a necessity?
5 What is the total revenue test?

Work these questions in Study Plan 4.1 and get instant feedback.   MyLab Economics

You've now completed your study of the *price* elasticity of demand. Two other elasticity concepts tell us about the effects of other influences on demand. Let's look at these other elasticities of demand.

◆ More Elasticities of Demand

Suppose the economy is expanding and people are enjoying rising incomes. You know that a change in income changes demand. So this increased prosperity brings an increase in the demand for most types of goods and services. By how much will a rise in income increase the demand for pizza? This question is answered by the income elasticity of demand.

Income Elasticity of Demand

The **income elasticity of demand** is a measure of the responsiveness of the demand for a good or service to a change in income, other things remaining the same. It tells us by how much a demand curve shifts at a given price.

The income elasticity of demand is calculated by using the formula:

$$\text{Income elasticity of demand} = \frac{\text{Percentage change in quantity demanded}}{\text{Percentage change in income}}.$$

Income elasticities of demand can be positive or negative and they fall into three interesting ranges:

- Positive and greater than 1 (*normal* good, income elastic)
- Positive and less than 1 (*normal* good, income inelastic)
- Negative (*inferior* good)

Income Elastic Demand Suppose that the price of pizza is constant and 9 pizzas an hour are bought. Then incomes rise from $975 to $1,025 a week. No other influence on buying plans changes and the quantity of pizzas sold increases to 11 an hour.

The change in the quantity demanded is 2 pizzas. The average quantity is 10 pizzas, so the quantity demanded increases by 20 percent. The change in income is $50 and the average income is $1,000, so incomes increase by 5 percent. The income elasticity of demand for pizza is

$$\frac{20\%}{5\%} = 4.$$

The demand for pizza is income elastic. The percentage increase in the quantity of pizza demanded exceeds the percentage increase in income.

Necessities and Luxuries

The demand for a necessity such as food or clothing is income inelastic, while the demand for a luxury such as airline and foreign travel is income elastic. But what is a necessity and what is a luxury depends on the level of income. For people with a low income, food and clothing can be luxuries. So the level of income has a big effect on income elasticities of demand.

The figure shows this effect on the income elasticity of demand for food in 10 countries. In countries with low incomes, such as Tanzania and India, the income elasticity of demand for food is high. In countries with high incomes, such as Canada, the income elasticity of demand for food is low. That is, as income increases, the income elasticity of demand for food decreases. Low-income consumers spend a larger percentage of any increase in income on food than do high-income consumers.

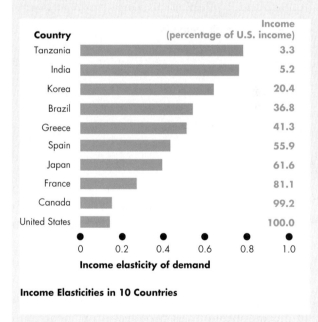

Income Elasticities in 10 Countries

Income Inelastic Demand If the income elasticity of demand is positive but less than 1, demand is income inelastic. The percentage increase in the quantity demanded is positive but less than the percentage increase in income.

Whether demand is income elastic or income inelastic has an important implication for the percentage of income spent on a good. If the demand for a good is *income elastic,* the percentage

ECONOMICS IN ACTION
Income Elastic and Inelastic Demand

The table shows some real-world income elasticities of demand and confirms that a necessity such as food or clothing is income inelastic, while the demand for a luxury such as airline travel is income elastic.

Some Real-World Income Elasticities of Demand

Income Elastic Demand

Airline travel	5.82
Movies	3.41
Foreign travel	3.08
Electricity	1.94
Restaurant meals	1.61
Local buses and trains	1.38
Haircuts	1.36
Automobiles	1.07

Income Inelastic Demand

Tobacco	0.86
Alcoholic drinks	0.62
Furniture	0.53
Clothing	0.51
Newspapers and magazines	0.38
Telephone	0.32
Food	0.14

Sources of data: H.S. Houthakker and Lester D. Taylor, *Consumer Demand in the United States* (Cambridge, Mass.: Harvard University Press, 1970); and Henri Theil, Ching-Fan Chung, and James L. Seale, Jr., *Advances in Econometrics, Supplement 1, 1989, International Evidence on Consumption Patterns* (Greenwich, Conn.: JAI Press, Inc., 1989).

of income spent on that good *increases* as income increases. And if the demand for a good is *income inelastic,* the percentage of income spent on that good *decreases* as income increases.

Inferior Goods If the income elasticity of demand is negative, the good is an *inferior* good. The quantity demanded of an inferior good and the amount spent on it *decrease* when income increases. Goods in this category include small motorcycles, potatoes, and rice. Low-income consumers buy these goods and spend a large percentage of their incomes on them.

Cross Elasticity of Demand

The burger shop next to your pizzeria has just raised the price of its burger. You know that pizzas and burgers are substitutes. You also know that when the price of a substitute for pizza *rises,* the demand for pizza *increases.* But how big is the influence of the price of burgers on the demand for pizza?

You know, too, that pizza and soft drinks are complements. And you know that if the price of a complement of pizza *rises,* the demand for pizza *decreases.* So you wonder, by how much will a rise in the price of a soft drink decrease the demand for your pizza?

To answer this question, you need to know about the cross elasticity of demand for pizza. Let's examine this elasticity measure.

We measure the influence of a change in the price of a substitute or complement by using the concept of the cross elasticity of demand. **Cross elasticity of demand** is a measure of the responsiveness of the demand for a good to a change in the price of a substitute or complement, other things remaining the same.

We calculate the *cross elasticity of demand* by using the formula:

$$\text{Cross elasticity of demand} = \frac{\text{Percentage change in quantity demanded}}{\text{Percentage change in price of a substitute or complement}}.$$

The cross elasticity of demand can be positive or negative. If the cross elasticity of demand is *positive,* demand and the price of the other good change in the *same* direction, so the two goods are *substitutes.* If the cross elasticity of demand is *negative,* demand and the price of the other good change in *opposite* directions, so the two goods are *complements.*

Substitutes Suppose that the price of pizza is constant and people buy 9 pizzas an hour. Then the price of a burger rises from $1.50 to $2.50. No other influence on buying plans changes and the quantity of pizzas bought increases to 11 an hour.

The change in the quantity demanded at the current price is +2 pizzas—the new quantity, 11 pizzas, minus the original quantity, 9 pizzas. The average quantity is 10 pizzas. So the quantity of pizzas demanded increases by 20 percent. That is,

$$\Delta Q / Q_{ave} \times 100 = (+2/10) \times 100 = +20\%.$$

The change in the price of a burger, a substitute for pizza, is +$1—the new price, $2.50, minus the original price, $1.50. The average price is $2 a burger. So the price of a burger rises by 50 percent. That is,

$$\Delta P/P_{ave} \times 100 = (+\$1/\$2) \times 100 = +50\%.$$

So the cross elasticity of demand for pizza with respect to the price of a burger is:

$$\frac{+20\%}{+50\%} = 0.4.$$

Figure 4.5 illustrates the cross elasticity of demand. Because pizza and burgers are substitutes, when the price of a burger rises, the demand for pizza increases. The demand curve for pizza shifts rightward from D_0 to D_1. Because a *rise* in the price of a burger brings an *increase* in the demand for pizza, the cross elasticity of demand for pizza with respect to the price of a burger is *positive*. Both the price and the quantity change in the same direction.

Complements Now suppose that the price of pizza is constant and 11 pizzas an hour are bought. Then the price of a soft drink rises from $1.50 to $2.50. No other influence on buying plans changes and the quantity of pizzas bought falls to 9 an hour.

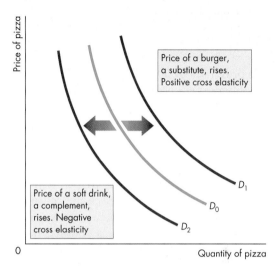

FIGURE 4.5   Cross Elasticity of Demand

A burger is a *substitute* for pizza. When the price of a burger rises, the demand for pizza increases and the demand curve for pizza shifts rightward from D_0 to D_1. The cross elasticity of demand is *positive*.

A soft drink is a *complement* of pizza. When the price of a soft drink rises, the demand for pizza decreases and the demand curve for pizza shifts leftward from D_0 to D_2. The cross elasticity of demand is *negative*.

— MyLab Economics Animation and Draw Graph —

ECONOMICS IN THE NEWS

More Peanut Butter Demand Elasticities

Markets for Peanut Butter and Related Goods
Professor Timothy Mathews teaches economics at Kennesaw State University, Georgia, the nation's number one peanut-producing state. The data table below shows his guesses about some demand elasticities for peanut butter.

Source: Timothy Mathews

THE DATA

Income elasticity	−0.31
Cross elasticity peanut butter and grape jelly	−0.27
Cross elasticity peanut butter and cheese	+0.18

THE QUESTIONS

- What do the data provided tell us about the demand for peanut butter? Is it a normal good?

- Is grape jelly a substitute for or a complement of peanut butter? Is cheese a substitute for or a complement of peanut butter?

THE ANSWERS

- The income elasticity of demand for peanut butter is *negative*, which means that peanut butter is an *inferior good*. People buy less peanut butter as income rises.

- The cross elasticity of demand for peanut butter with respect to the price of grape jelly is *negative*, which means that peanut butter and grape jelly are *complements*.

- The cross elasticity of demand for peanut butter with respect to the price of cheese is *positive*, which means that peanut butter and cheese are *substitutes*.

— MyLab Economics Economics in the News —

The change in the quantity demanded is the opposite of what we've just calculated: The quantity of pizzas demanded decreases by 20 percent (-20%).

The change in the price of a soft drink, a rise of $1 from $1.50 to $2.50, is the same as the change in the price of a burger that we've just calculated. That is, the price rises by 50 percent ($+50\%$).

So the cross elasticity of demand for pizza with respect to the price of a soft drink is

$$\frac{-20\%}{+50\%} = -0.4.$$

Because pizza and soft drinks are complements, when the price of a soft drink rises, the demand for pizza decreases.

In Fig. 4.5, when the price of soft drinks rises the demand curve for pizza shifts leftward from D_0 to D_2. Because a *rise* in the price of a soft drink brings a *decrease* in the demand for pizza, the cross elasticity of demand for pizza with respect to the price of a soft drink is *negative*. The price and quantity change in *opposite* directions.

The magnitude of the cross elasticity of demand determines how far the demand curve shifts. The larger the cross elasticity (absolute value), the greater is the change in demand and the larger is the shift in the demand curve.

If two items are close substitutes, such as two brands of spring water, the cross elasticity is large. If two items are close complements, such as movies and popcorn, the cross elasticity is large.

If two items are somewhat unrelated to each other, such as newspapers and orange juice, the cross elasticity is small—perhaps even zero.

REVIEW QUIZ

1 What does the income elasticity of demand measure?
2 What does the sign (positive/negative) of the income elasticity tell us about a good?
3 What does the cross elasticity of demand measure?
4 What does the sign (positive/negative) of the cross elasticity of demand tell us about the relationship between two goods?

Work these questions in Study Plan 4.2 and get instant feedback.   MyLab Economics

◆ Elasticity of Supply

You know that when demand increases, the equilibrium price rises and the equilibrium quantity increases. But does the price rise by a large amount and the quantity increase by a little? Or does the price barely rise and the quantity increase by a large amount?

The answer depends on the responsiveness of the quantity supplied to a change in the price. If the quantity supplied is not very responsive to price, then an increase in demand brings a large rise in the price and a small increase in the equilibrium quantity. If the quantity supplied is highly responsive to price, then an increase in demand brings a small rise in the price and a large increase in the equilibrium quantity.

The problems that arise from using the slope of the supply curve to indicate responsiveness are the same as those we considered when discussing the responsiveness of the quantity demanded, so we use a units-free measure—the elasticity of supply.

Calculating the Elasticity of Supply

The **elasticity of supply** measures the responsiveness of the quantity supplied to a change in the price of a good when all other influences on selling plans remain the same. It is calculated by using the formula:

$$\text{Elasticity of supply} = \frac{\text{Percentage change in quantity supplied}}{\text{Percentage change in price}}.$$

We use the same method that you learned when you studied the elasticity of demand. (Refer back to p. 88 to check this method.)

Elastic and Inelastic Supply If the elasticity of supply is greater than 1, we say that supply is elastic; and if the elasticity of supply is less than 1, we say that supply is inelastic.

Suppose that when the price rises from $20 to $21, the quantity supplied increases from 10 to 20 pizzas per hour. The price rise is $1 and the average price is $20.50, so the price rises by 4.9 percent of the average price. The quantity increases from 10 to 20 pizzas an hour, so the increase is 10 pizzas, the average quantity is 15 pizzas, and the quantity increases by 67 percent. The elasticity of supply is equal to 67 percent divided by 4.9 percent, which equals 13.67. Because the elasticity of supply exceeds 1 (in this case by a lot), supply is elastic.

In contrast, suppose that when the price rises from $20 to $30, the quantity of pizza supplied increases from 10 to 13 per hour. The price rise is $10 and the average price is $25, so the price rises by 40 percent of the average price. The quantity increases from 10 to 13 pizzas an hour, so the increase is 3 pizzas, the average quantity is 11.5 pizzas an hour, and the quantity increases by 26 percent. The elasticity of supply is equal to 26 percent divided by 40 percent, which equals 0.65. Now, because the elasticity of supply is less than 1, supply is inelastic.

Figure 4.6 shows the range of elasticities of supply. If the quantity supplied is fixed regardless of the price, the supply curve is vertical and the elasticity of supply is zero. Supply is perfectly inelastic. This case is shown in Fig. 4.6(a). A special intermediate case occurs when the percentage change in price equals the percentage change in quantity. Supply is then unit elastic. This case is shown in Fig. 4.6(b). No matter how steep the supply curve is, if it is linear and passes through the origin, supply is unit elastic. If there is a price at which sellers are willing to offer any quantity for sale, the supply curve is horizontal and the elasticity of supply is infinite. Supply is perfectly elastic. This case is shown in Fig. 4.6(c).

The Factors That Influence the Elasticity of Supply

The elasticity of supply of a good depends on:

- Resource substitution possibilities
- Time frame for the supply decision

Resource Substitution Possibilities Some goods and services can be produced only by using unique or rare productive resources. These items have a low, perhaps even a zero, elasticity of supply. Other goods and services can be produced by using commonly available resources that could be allocated to a wide variety of alternative tasks. Such items have a high elasticity of supply.

A Van Gogh painting is an example of a good with a vertical supply curve and a zero elasticity of supply. At the other extreme, wheat can be grown on land that is almost equally good for growing corn, so it is just as easy to grow wheat as corn. The opportunity cost of wheat in terms of forgone corn is almost constant. As a result, the supply curve of wheat is almost horizontal and its elasticity of supply is very large. Similarly, when a good is produced in many different countries (for example, sugar and beef), the supply of the good is highly elastic.

The supply of most goods and services lies between these two extremes. The quantity produced

---

FIGURE 4.6   Inelastic and Elastic Supply

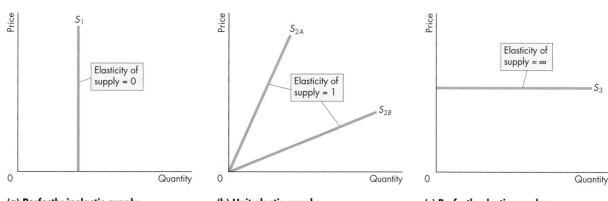

(a) Perfectly inelastic supply   **(b) Unit elastic supply**   **(c) Perfectly elastic supply**

Each supply illustrated here has a constant elasticity. The supply curve in part (a) illustrates the supply of a good that has a zero elasticity of supply. Each supply curve in part (b) illustrates the supply of a good with a unit elasticity of supply. All linear supply curves that pass through the origin illustrate supplies that are unit elastic. The supply curve in part (c) illustrates the supply of a good with an infinite elasticity of supply.

can be increased but only by incurring a higher cost. If a higher price is offered, the quantity supplied increases. Such goods and services have an elasticity of supply between zero and infinity.

Time Frame for the Supply Decision To study the influence of the amount of time elapsed since a price change, we distinguish three time frames of supply:

- Momentary supply
- Short-run supply
- Long-run supply

Momentary Supply When the price of a good changes, the immediate response of the quantity supplied is determined by the *momentary supply* of that good.

Some goods, such as fruits and vegetables, have a perfectly inelastic momentary supply—a vertical supply curve. The quantities supplied depend on crop-planting decisions made earlier. In the case of oranges, for example, planting decisions have to be made many years in advance of the crop being available. Momentary supply is perfectly inelastic because, on a given day, no matter what the price of oranges, producers cannot change their output. They have picked, packed, and shipped their crop to market, and the quantity available for that day is fixed.

In contrast, some goods have a perfectly elastic momentary supply. Long-distance phone calls are an example. When many people simultaneously make a call, there is a big surge in the demand for telephone cables, computer switching, and satellite time. The quantity supplied increases, but the price remains constant. Long-distance carriers monitor fluctuations in demand and reroute calls to ensure that the quantity supplied equals the quantity demanded without changing the price.

Short-Run Supply The response of the quantity supplied to a price change when only *some* of the possible adjustments to production can be made is determined by *short-run supply*. Most goods have an inelastic short-run supply. To increase output in the short run, firms must work their labour force overtime and perhaps hire additional workers. To decrease their output in the short run, firms either lay off workers or reduce their hours of work. With the passage of time, firms can make more adjustments, perhaps training additional workers or buying additional tools and other equipment.

For the orange grower, if the price of oranges falls, some pickers can be laid off and oranges left on the trees to rot. Or if the price of oranges rises, the grower can use more fertilizer and improved irrigation to increase the yield of the existing trees.

But an orange grower can't change the number of trees producing oranges in the short run.

Long-Run Supply The response of the quantity supplied to a price change after *all* the technologically possible ways of adjusting supply have been exploited is determined by *long-run supply*. For most goods and services, long-run supply is elastic and perhaps perfectly elastic.

For the orange grower, the long run is the time it takes new tree plantings to grow to full maturity—about 15 years. In some cases, the long-run adjustment occurs only after a completely new production plant has been built and workers have been trained to operate it—typically a process that might take several years.

REVIEW QUIZ

1 Why do we need a units-free measure of the responsiveness of the quantity supplied of a good or service to a change in its price?
2 Define the elasticity of supply and show how it is calculated.
3 What are the main influences on the elasticity of supply that make the supply of some goods elastic and the supply of other goods inelastic?
4 Provide examples of goods or services whose elasticities of supply are (a) zero, (b) greater than zero but less than infinity, and (c) infinity.
5 How does the time frame over which a supply decision is made influence the elasticity of supply? Explain your answer.

Work these questions in Study Plan 4.3 and get instant feedback.   MyLab Economics

◆ You have now learned about the elasticities of demand and supply. Table 4.1 summarizes all the elasticities that you've met in this chapter. In the next chapter, we study the efficiency of competitive markets. But first study *Economics in the News* on pp. 102–103, which puts the elasticity of demand at work and looks at the effect of a tax on sugary drinks.

TABLE 4.1   A Compact Glossary of Elasticities

Price Elasticities of Demand

A relationship is described as	When its magnitude is	Which means that
Perfectly elastic	Infinity	The smallest possible increase in price causes an infinitely large decrease in the quantity demanded*
Elastic	Less than infinity but greater than 1	The percentage decrease in the quantity demanded exceeds the percentage increase in price
Unit elastic	1	The percentage decrease in the quantity demanded equals the percentage increase in price
Inelastic	Less than 1 but greater than zero	The percentage decrease in the quantity demanded is less than the percentage increase in price
Perfectly inelastic	Zero	The quantity demanded is the same at all prices

Income Elasticities of Demand

A relationship is described as	When its value is	Which means that
Income elastic (normal good)	Greater than 1	The percentage increase in the quantity demanded is greater than the percentage increase in income*
Income inelastic (normal good)	Less than 1 but greater than zero	The percentage increase in the quantity demanded is greater than zero but less than the percentage increase in income
Negative (inferior good)	Less than zero	When income increases, quantity demanded decreases

Cross Elasticities of Demand

A relationship is described as	When its value is	Which means that
Close substitutes	Large	The smallest possible increase in the price of one good causes an infinitely large increase in the quantity demanded* of the other good
Substitutes	Positive	If the price of one good increases, the quantity demanded of the other good also increases
Unrelated goods	Zero	If the price of one good increases, the quantity demanded of the other good remains the same
Complements	Negative	If the price of one good increases, the quantity demanded of the other good decreases

Elasticities of Supply

A relationship is described as	When its magnitude is	Which means that
Perfectly elastic	Infinity	The smallest possible increase in price causes an infinitely large increase in the quantity supplied*
Elastic	Less than infinity but greater than 1	The percentage increase in the quantity supplied exceeds the percentage increase in the price
Unit elastic	1	The percentage increase in the quantity supplied equals the percentage increase in the price
Inelastic	Greater than zero but less than 1	The percentage increase in the quantity supplied is less than the percentage increase in the price
Perfectly inelastic	Zero	The quantity supplied is the same at all prices

*In each description, the directions of change may be reversed. For example, in the perfectly elastic demand case, the smallest possible *decrease* in price causes an infinitely large *increase* in the quantity demanded.

The Elasticity of Demand for Sugar-Sweetened Drinks

Berkeley Sees a Big Drop in Soda Consumption after Penny-per-Ounce "Soda Tax"

Los Angeles Times
August 23, 2016

After Berkeley instituted a penny-per-ounce tax on sugar-sweetened beverages, consumption of the high-calorie drinks fell by 21% in the city's low-income neighborhoods. …

Instead of swilling as much Coke, Gatorade, Red Bull, and Hawaiian Punch, the Berkeley residents boosted their water consumption by 63%. In the neighboring cities, low-income residents drank only 19% more water during the study period. …

About two dozen states have considered excise taxes on sugar-sweetened beverages, as have cities such as Baltimore, Chicago, Philadelphia, San Francisco, and Washington, D.C., according to the Rudd Center for Food Policy and Obesity at the University of Connecticut. But Berkeley was the first jurisdiction to pass one. …

Three months after [the tax] … went into effect, 47% of the penny-per-ounce tax had been passed along to consumers in the form of higher prices for sugar-sweetened beverages, [and for] sodas, 69% of the tax was incorporated into the price. …

More than one in five Berkeley residents told the survey-takers that the tax had caused them to change their drinking habits. Among these 124 people, 82% said they consumed sugary drinks less frequently, and 40% said they had reduced their portion sizes.

The researchers didn't translate these reductions into calories saved or pounds shed, so the policy's effect on waistlines remains unknown. Nor could the team say for sure that the tax itself—and not the health messages that were discussed during the election campaign—was causing residents to shift from sugary drinks to water.

From Karen Kaplan, "Berkeley sees a big drop in soda consumption after penny-per-ounce soda tax," August 23, 2016. *Los Angeles Times*. Reprinted with permission.

ESSENCE OF THE STORY

- Berkeley imposed a penny-per-ounce tax on sugar-sweetened drinks.

- The price of these drinks increased by 47% of the penny-per-ounce tax, and by 69% of the tax for sodas.

- Consumption of sugar-sweetened drinks fell by 21% in the city's low-income neighbourhoods.

- Berkeley's low-income residents drank 63% more water.

- It is not possible to say whether the tax or health messages caused the shift from sugary drinks to water.

ECONOMIC ANALYSIS

- When Berkeley imposed a tax on sugar-sweetened drinks, the price of these drinks increased.

- The tax is 1¢ per ounce, and on sodas, the price increased by 69 percent of the tax.

- So the price of a 20-ounce drink increased by 14¢ (69 percent of 20¢ tax) from the pre-tax price of $1.75 to $1.89.

- After the tax was imposed, the quantity of sugar-sweetened drinks consumed decreased by 21 percent.

- A rise in the price of sugar-sweetened drinks decreases the quantity demanded of those drinks.

- The amount by which the quantity demanded decreases depends on the price rise and on the price elasticity of demand for sugar-sweetened drinks.

- Assuming that demand didn't change, we can estimate the price elasticity of demand for sugar-sweetened drinks using the data in the news article and information on the price before the tax was imposed.

- Figure 1 summarizes this elasticity calculation. The price increased by 14¢ and the average price was $1.82. The quantity demanded decreased by 21 and the average quantity was 89.5 (both percentages of the original quantity).

- Using these numbers in the elasticity formula, the price elasticity of demand is (21/89.5) ÷ (0.14/1.82), which equals 3.05. A price rise of 1 percent brings a decrease in the quantity demanded of 3.05 percent.

- This estimate of the price elasticity of demand for sugar-sweetened drinks is higher than most other estimates, which suggests that some of the decrease in consumption occurred because demand decreased—the demand curve shifted leftward.

- Figure 2 illustrates this interpretation of the data using an estimate of the price elasticity of demand for sugar-sweetened drinks of 1.37. This estimate comes from a careful statistical study that controls for all the other possible influences on buying plans.

- Before the tax and health publicity, the demand for sugar-sweetened drinks was D_0. The tax-induced price rise decreased the quantity demanded along this demand curve, as shown by the blue arrow.

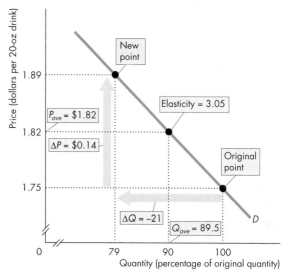

Figure 1 Assuming No Change in Demand

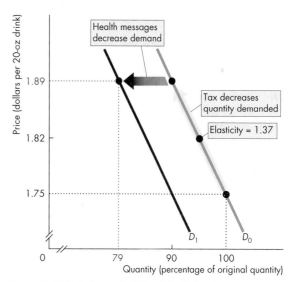

Figure 2 With Independent Elasticity Estimate

- But the health publicity, which came at the same time as the tax, decreased the demand for sugar-sweetened drinks and shifted the demand curve from D_0 to D_1.

- If the elasticity of demand for sugar-sweetened drinks is 1.37, the tax brought one half of the decrease in consumption and the health message brought the other half.

WORKED PROBLEM

MyLab Economics Work this problem in Chapter 4 Study Plan.

A rise in the price of a smoothie from $2 to $3 results in a fall in the quantity of smoothies demanded from 220 million to 180 million a day; and at today's price of a muffin, $1.50, the quantity of muffins demanded increases from 80 million to 100 million a day.

Questions

1. Calculate the percentage change in the price of a smoothie and the percentage change in the quantity demanded of smoothies.
2. Calculate the price elasticity of demand for smoothies.
3. Is the demand for smoothies elastic or inelastic?
4. Calculate the cross elasticity of demand for muffins with respect to the price of a smoothie.

Solutions

1. The price of a smoothie rises by $1 and the quantity demanded falls by 40 million a day.

   To calculate the percentage changes in the price and quantity demanded use the average price and average quantity. The figure illustrates the calculations.

   The average price of a smoothie is $2.50, so the percentage change in the price was ($1/$2.50) × 100, or 40 percent.

   The average quantity of smoothies is 200 million, so the percentage change in the quantity demanded was (40 million/200 million) × 100, or 20 percent.

   Key Point: When working with elasticity, the percentage change in the price and quantity is the percentage of the average price and average quantity.

2. The price elasticity of demand is the ratio of the percentage change in the quantity to the percentage change in price.

   The price elasticity of demand for smoothies equals 20 percent divided by 40 percent, which equals 0.5.

   Key Point: The price elasticity calculated is the price elasticity of demand at the price midway between the original and the new prices. That is, it calculates the elasticity at the average price.

3. The price elasticity of demand for smoothies is *less than* 1, so the demand is inelastic.

   Key Point: When the percentage change in the quantity is *less than* the percentage change in the price, demand is inelastic and the price elasticity of demand is less than 1.

4. To calculate the cross elasticity of demand for muffins with respect to the price of a smoothie divide the percentage change in the quantity of muffins demanded by the percentage change in the price of a smoothie.

   When the price of a smoothie rises by 40 percent, the quantity of muffins demanded increases from 80 million to 100 million, a change of 20 million.

   The average quantity of muffins is 90 million, so the percentage change in the quantity of muffins is (20 million/90 million) × 100, which equals 22.2 percent.

   The cross elasticity of demand for muffins with respect to the price of a smoothie equals 22.2 percent/40 percent, which equals 0.55.

   The cross elasticity of demand for muffins with respect to the price of a smoothie is *positive*, which means that muffins and smoothies are substitutes—just as you thought!

Key Point: The cross elasticity of demand is positive for substitutes and negative for complements.

Key Figure

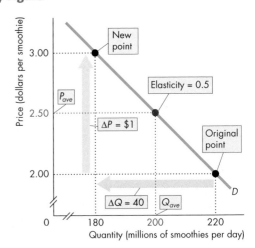

MyLab Economics Interactive Animation

SUMMARY

Key Points

Price Elasticity of Demand (pp. 88–94)

- Elasticity is a measure of the responsiveness of the quantity demanded of a good to a change in its price, other things remaining the same.
- Price elasticity of demand equals the percentage change in the quantity demanded divided by the percentage change in the price.
- The larger the magnitude of the price elasticity of demand, the greater is the responsiveness of the quantity demanded to a given price change.
- If demand is elastic, a cut in price leads to an increase in total revenue. If demand is unit elastic, a cut in price leaves total revenue unchanged. And if demand is inelastic, a cut in price leads to a decrease in total revenue.
- Price elasticity of demand depends on how easily one good serves as a substitute for another, the proportion of income spent on the good, and the length of time elapsed since the price change.

Working Problems 1 to 5 will give you a better understanding of the price elasticity of demand.

More Elasticities of Demand (pp. 95–98)

- Income elasticity of demand measures the responsiveness of demand to a change in income, other things remaining the same. For a normal good, the income elasticity of demand is positive. For an inferior good, the income elasticity of demand is negative.
- When the income elasticity of demand is greater than 1 (income elastic), the percentage of income spent on the good increases as income increases.
- When the income elasticity of demand is less than 1 (income inelastic or inferior), the percentage of income spent on the good decreases as income increases.
- Cross elasticity of demand measures the responsiveness of the demand for one good to a change in the price of a substitute or a complement, other things remaining the same.
- The cross elasticity of demand with respect to the price of a substitute is positive. The cross elasticity of demand with respect to the price of a complement is negative.

Working Problems 6 to 8 will give you a better understanding of cross and income elasticities of demand.

Elasticity of Supply (pp. 98–101)

- Elasticity of supply measures the responsiveness of the quantity supplied of a good to a change in its price, other things remaining the same.
- The elasticity of supply is usually positive and ranges between zero (vertical supply curve) and infinity (horizontal supply curve).
- Supply decisions have three time frames: momentary, short run, and long run.
- Momentary supply refers to the response of the quantity supplied to a price change at the instant that the price changes.
- Short-run supply refers to the response of the quantity supplied to a price change after some of the technologically feasible adjustments in production have been made.
- Long-run supply refers to the response of the quantity supplied to a price change when all the technologically feasible adjustments in production have been made.

Working Problem 9 will give you a better understanding of the elasticity of supply.

Key Terms

MyLab Economics Key Terms Quiz

Cross elasticity of demand, 96
Elastic demand, 90
Elasticity of supply, 98
Income elasticity of demand, 95

Inelastic demand, 89
Perfectly elastic demand, 89
Perfectly inelastic demand, 89
Price elasticity of demand, 88

Total revenue, 92
Total revenue test, 92
Unit elastic demand, 89

STUDY PLAN PROBLEMS AND APPLICATIONS

MyLab Economics Work Problems 1 to 9 in Chapter 4 Study Plan and get instant feedback.

Price Elasticity of Demand (Study Plan 4.1)

1. Rain spoils the strawberry crop, the price rises from $4 to $6 a box, and the quantity demanded decreases from 1,000 to 600 boxes a week.
   a. Calculate the price elasticity of demand over this price range.
   b. Describe the demand for strawberries.

2. If the quantity of dental services demanded increases by 10 percent when the price of dental services falls by 10 percent, is the demand for dental services inelastic, elastic, or unit elastic?

3. The demand schedule for hotel rooms is:

Price (dollars per room per night)	Quantity demanded (millions of rooms per night)
200	100
250	80
400	50
500	40
800	25

   a. What happens to total revenue when the price falls from $400 to $250 a room per night and from $250 to $200 a room per night?
   b. Is the demand for hotel rooms elastic, inelastic, or unit elastic?

4. The figure shows the demand for pens.

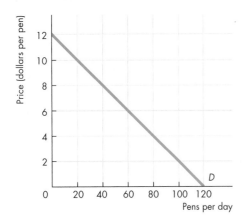

   Calculate the elasticity of demand when the price rises from $4 to $6 a pen. Over what price range is the demand for pens elastic?

5. In 2015, an outbreak of Avian Flu (bird flu) decreased the quantity of eggs produced by

18 percent. A shortage of eggs was avoided by a rise in their wholesale price from $1.34 to $2.40 per dozen.
   a. If the demand for eggs didn't change, what is your estimate of the price elasticity of demand for eggs?
   b. Thinking about the influences on the price elasticity of demand, why would you expect the demand for eggs to be inelastic?

More Elasticities of Demand (Study Plan 4.2)

6. When Judy's income increased from $130 to $170 a week, she increased her demand for concert tickets by 15 percent and decreased her demand for bus rides by 10 percent. Calculate Judy's income elasticity of demand for (a) concert tickets and (b) bus rides.

7. If a 12 percent rise in the price of orange juice decreases the quantity of orange juice demanded by 22 percent and increases the quantity of apple juice demanded by 14 percent, calculate the:
   a. Price elasticity of demand for orange juice.
   b. Cross elasticity of demand for apple juice with respect to the price of orange juice.

8. If a rise in the price of sushi from 98¢ to $1.02 a piece decreases the quantity of soy sauce demanded from 101 units to 99 units an hour and decreases the quantity of sushi demanded by 1 percent an hour, calculate the:
   a. Price elasticity of demand for sushi.
   b. Cross elasticity of demand for soy sauce with respect to the price of sushi.

Elasticity of Supply (Study Plan 4.3)

9. The table sets out the supply schedule of jeans.

Price (dollars per pair)	Quantity supplied (millions of pairs per year)
120	24
125	28
130	32
135	36

   a. Calculate the elasticity of supply when the price rises from $125 to $135 a pair.
   b. Calculate the elasticity of supply when the average price is $125 a pair.
   c. Is the supply of jeans elastic, inelastic, or unit elastic?

ADDITIONAL PROBLEMS AND APPLICATIONS

MyLab Economics You can work these problems in Homework or Test if assigned by your instructor.

Price Elasticity of Demand

10. With higher fuel costs, airlines raised their average fare from 75¢ to $1.25 per passenger kilometre and the number of passenger kilometres decreased from 2.5 million a day to 1.5 million a day.
    a. What is the price elasticity of demand for air travel over this price range?
    b. Describe the demand for air travel.

11. The figure shows the demand for DVD rentals.

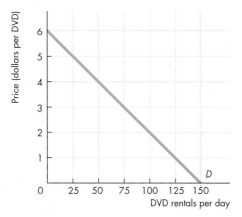

    a. Calculate the elasticity of demand when the price of a DVD rental rises from $3 to $5.
    b. At what price is the elasticity of demand for DVD rentals equal to 1?

Use the following table to work Problems 12 to 14. The demand schedule for computer chips is:

Price (dollars per chip)	Quantity demanded (millions of chips per year)
200	50
250	45
300	40
350	35
400	30

12. a. What happens to total revenue if the price falls from $400 to $350 a chip and from $350 to $300 a chip?
    b. At what price is total revenue at a maximum?

13. At an average price of $350, is the demand for chips elastic, inelastic, or unit elastic? Use the total revenue test to answer this question.

14. At $250 a chip, is the demand for chips elastic or inelastic? Use the total revenue test to answer this question.

15. Your price elasticity of demand for bananas is 4. If the price of bananas rises by 5 percent, what is:
    a. The percentage change in the quantity of bananas you buy?
    b. The change in your expenditure on bananas?

16. **Border Crossings into B.C. Up 15 Percent**
    Cheap gasoline brought 964,000 American visitors through border crossings in B.C. during the first four months of 2016, a 15 percent increase from the previous year.
    Source: *Vancouver Sun*, July 9, 2016

    The U.S. Energy Information Administration reports the average price of gasoline was $2.83 a gallon in July 2015 and $2.22 a gallon in July 2016.
    a. List and explain the elasticities of demand that are implicitly referred to in the news clip.
    b. Estimate a price elasticity of demand for B.C. border crossings.

More Elasticities of Demand

Use this information to work Problems 17 and 18.

Ride-Hailing Could Lead to More Road Congestion
An American study says ride-hailing companies Uber and Lyft, now arriving in Canada, bolster public transit by extending its reach from the first to the last mile. Another view is that they undermine public transit by providing a lower-cost service that worsens congestion.
Source: *Vancouver Sun*, March 10, 2017

17. Are Uber rides and transit rides complements or substitutes? Explain your answer.

18. If Uber bolsters public transit more than it undermines it, is the cross elasticity of demand for Uber rides with respect to the price of public transit rides positive or negative? Explain your answer.

19. When Alex's income was $3,000, he bought 4 bagels and 12 donuts a month. Now his income is $5,000 and he buys 8 bagels and 6 donuts a month. Calculate Alex's income elasticity of demand for (a) bagels and (b) donuts.

20. **Pet Care Is a True Recession-Proof Industry**
    Two out of three Americans own a pet—almost half own a dog and a third a cat—and pet

ownership is projected to grow. Households have spent more on pets every year through recessions and booms, growing from $17 billion in 1994 to near $63 billion in 2016. People are clearly willing to pay pet expenses even in hard times, and there's no reason to expect that to change in the next recession.

Source: *Business Insider*, January 28, 2017

a. What does this news clip imply about the income elasticity of demand for pet food and and pet care products?

b. Would the income elasticity of demand for pet food and pet care products be greater or less than 1? Explain.

21. If a 5 percent fall in the price of chocolate sauce increases the quantity demanded of chocolate sauce by 10 percent and increases the quantity of ice cream demanded by 15 percent, calculate the:

a. Price elasticity of demand for chocolate sauce.

b. Cross elasticity of demand for ice cream with respect to the price of chocolate sauce.

Elasticity of Supply

22. The table sets out the supply schedule of long-distance phone calls.

Price (cents per minute)	Quantity supplied (millions of minutes per day)
10	200
20	400
30	600
40	800

Calculate the elasticity of supply when:

a. The price falls from 40¢ to 30¢ a minute.

b. The average price is 20¢ a minute.

23. **Coal Production and Coal Price Down**

U.S. coal production in 2016 is down 17 percent from that of 2015. Almost all coal use in the United States is for electricity generation and the price of coal for power plants fell from $2.27 per million Btu in 2015 to $2.17 per million Btu in 2016.

Source: *Hellenic Shipping News*, January 10, 2017

Calculate the price elasticity of supply of coal assuming no change in the supply of coal. Is the supply of coal elastic or inelastic?

Economics in the News

24. After you have studied *Economics in the News* on pp. 102–103, answer the following questions.

a. Use the information in the news article to estimate the cross elasticity of demand for water with respect to the price of sugar-sweetened drinks.

b. How does the total revenue test work for a rise in price? What do you predict happened to total revenue from sugar-sweetened drinks when the tax was imposed on them? Why?

c. Would you expect the elasticity of demand for Coke, or Gatorade, or Red Bull, or Hawaiian Punch to be the same as the elasticity of demand for sugar-sweetened drinks? Explain why or why not.

25. **Comcast Is Planning a Netflix Rival**

Comcast plans to compete with Netflix and CBS by offering an online video service featuring hit shows from its NBC Universal TV networks.

Source: Bloomberg, April 11, 2017

a. How will Comcast's entry into the online video service market influence the demand for Netflix's service?

b. Given your answer to part (a), explain why Netflix might lower its price.

c. What can you say about the effect of Comcast's entry on the price elasticity of demand for Netflix online movie viewing?

26. **Saudi Arabia Oil Revenues Shrink**

As the price of oil fell from $99 a barrel in September 2014 to $53 a barrel by September 2015, Saudi Arabia's oil revenues fell by 23 percent, compared with its 2014 oil revenues of 444.5 billion riyals.

Source: News.markets, December 29, 2015

a. How can you use the information in the news clip to determine whether the demand for Saudi Arabian oil is elastic or inelastic?

b. How can you use the information in the news clip to estimate the magnitude of the price elasticity of demand for Saudi Arabian oil?

c. Does the news article tell us whether the supply of Saudi Arabian oil is elastic or inelastic? Explain.

5 EFFICIENCY AND EQUITY

After studying this chapter, you will be able to:

◆ Describe the alternative methods of allocating scarce resources

◆ Explain the connection between demand and marginal benefit and define consumer surplus; and explain the connection between supply and marginal cost and define producer surplus

◆ Explain the conditions under which markets are efficient and inefficient

◆ Explain the main ideas about fairness and evaluate claims that markets result in unfair outcomes

Every day, millions of people make self-interested choices to drive to work rather than take the bus or train. The outcome of these choices is gridlock and a lot of lost time. Are we using our highways and our time efficiently?

One way of eliminating traffic jams is to make people pay for road use—to make all the highways toll roads. Rich people can easily pay a toll, but poor people can't afford to pay. Would tolls be fair?

We'll answer these questions about highway use in *Economics in the News* at the end of the chapter. But first, we examine the efficiency and fairness of alternative ways of allocating scarce resources.

Resource Allocation Methods

If resources were abundant, and not scarce, we would not need to allocate them among alternative uses. But resources *are* scarce: They must be allocated somehow. Our goal is to discover how resources might be allocated efficiently and fairly. So what are the alternative methods of allocating scarce resources?

Eight alternative methods that might be used are:

- Market price
- Command
- Majority rule
- Contest
- First-come, first-served
- Lottery
- Personal characteristics
- Force

Let's briefly examine each method.

Market Price

When a market price allocates a scarce resource, the people who are willing and able to pay that price get the resource. Two kinds of people decide not to pay the market price: those who can afford to pay but choose not to buy and those who are too poor and simply can't afford to buy.

For many goods and services, distinguishing between those who choose not to buy and those who can't afford to buy doesn't matter. But for a few items, it does matter. For example, poor people can't afford to pay school fees and doctors' fees. Because poor people can't afford items that most people consider to be essential, these items are usually allocated by one of the other methods.

Command

A **command system** allocates resources by the order (command) of someone in authority. In the Canadian economy, the command system is used extensively inside firms and government departments. For example, if you have a job, most likely someone tells you what to do. Your labour is allocated to specific tasks by a command.

A command system works well in organizations in which the lines of authority and responsibility are clear and it is easy to monitor the activities being performed. But a command system works badly when the range of activities to be monitored is large and when it is easy for people to fool those in authority. North Korea uses a command system and it works so badly that it even fails to deliver an adequate supply of food.

Majority Rule

Majority rule allocates resources in the way that a majority of voters choose. Societies use majority rule to elect representative governments that make some of the biggest decisions. For example, majority rule decides the tax rates that end up allocating scarce resources between private use and public use. And majority rule decides how tax dollars are allocated among competing uses such as education and healthcare.

Majority rule works well when the decisions being made affect large numbers of people and self-interest must be suppressed to use resources most effectively.

Contest

A contest allocates resources to a winner (or a group of winners). Sporting events use this method. Milos Raonic competes with other tennis professionals, and the winner gets the biggest payoff. But contests are more general than those in a sports arena, though we don't normally call them contests. For example, Bill Gates won a contest to provide the world's personal computer operating system.

Contests do a good job when the efforts of the "players" are hard to monitor and reward directly. When a manager offers everyone in the company the opportunity to win a big prize, people are motivated to work hard and try to become the winner. Only a few people end up with a big prize, but many people work harder in the process of trying to win. The total output produced by the workers is much greater than it would be without the contest.

First-Come, First-Served

A first-come, first-served method allocates resources to those who are first in line. Many casual restaurants won't accept reservations. They use first-come, first-served to allocate their scarce tables. Highway space is allocated in this way too: The first to arrive at the on-ramp gets the road space. If too many vehicles enter the highway, the speed slows and people wait in line for some space to become available.

First-come, first-served works best when, as in the above examples, a scarce resource can serve just one user at a time in a sequence. By serving the user who arrives first, this method minimizes the time spent waiting for the resource to become free.

Lottery

Lotteries allocate resources to those who pick the winning number, draw the lucky cards, or come up lucky on some other gaming system. State lotteries and casinos reallocate millions of dollars worth of goods and services every year.

But lotteries are more widespread than jackpots and roulette wheels in casinos. They are used to allocate landing slots to airlines at some airports, places in the New York and Boston marathons, and have been used to allocate fishing rights and the electromagnetic spectrum used by wireless service providers.

Lotteries work best when there is no effective way to distinguish among potential users of a scarce resource.

Personal Characteristics

When resources are allocated on the basis of personal characteristics, people with the "right" characteristics get the resources. Some of the resources that matter most to you are allocated in this way. For example, you will choose a marriage partner on the basis of personal characteristics. But this method can also be used in unacceptable ways. Allocating the best jobs to white, Anglo-Saxon males and discriminating against visible minorities and women is an example.

Force

Force plays a crucial role, for both good and ill, in allocating scarce resources. Let's start with the ill.

War, the use of military force by one nation against another, has played an enormous role historically in allocating resources. The economic supremacy of European settlers in the Americas and Australia owes much to the use of this method.

Theft, taking the property of others without their consent, also plays a large role. Both large-scale organized crime and small-scale petty crime collectively allocate billions of dollars worth of resources annually.

But force plays a crucial positive role in allocating resources. It provides the state with an effective method of transferring wealth from the rich to the poor, and it provides the legal framework in which voluntary exchange in markets takes place.

A legal system is the foundation on which our market economy functions. Without courts to enforce contracts, it would not be possible to do business. But the courts could not enforce contracts without the ability to apply force if necessary. The state provides the ultimate force that enables the courts to do their work.

More broadly, the force of the state is essential to uphold the principle of the rule of law. This principle is the bedrock of civilized economic (and social and political) life. With the rule of law upheld, people can go about their daily economic lives with the assurance that their property will be protected—that they can sue for violations against their property (and be sued if they violate the property of others).

Free from the burden of protecting their property and confident in the knowledge that those with whom they trade will honour their agreements, people can get on with focusing on the activity in which they have a comparative advantage and trading for mutual gain.

◆ REVIEW QUIZ

1 Why do we need methods of allocating scarce resources?
2 Describe the alternative methods of allocating scarce resources.
3 Provide an example of each allocation method that illustrates when it works well.
4 Provide an example of each allocation method that illustrates when it works badly.

Work these questions in Study Plan 5.1 and get instant feedback.   MyLab Economics

In the next sections, we're going to see how a market can achieve an efficient use of resources, examine the obstacles to efficiency, and see how sometimes an alternative method might improve on the market. After looking at efficiency, we'll turn our attention to the more difficult issue of fairness.

Benefit, Cost, and Surplus

Resources are allocated efficiently and in the *social interest* when they are used in the ways that people value most highly. You saw in Chapter 2 that this outcome occurs when the quantities produced are at the point on the *PPF* at which marginal benefit equals marginal cost (see pp. 37–39). We're now going to see whether competitive markets produce the efficient quantities.

We begin on the demand side of a market.

Demand, Willingness to Pay, and Value

In everyday life, we talk about "getting value for money." When we use this expression, we are distinguishing between *value* and *price*. Value is what we get, and price is what we pay.

The value of one more unit of a good or service is its marginal benefit. We measure marginal benefit by the maximum price that is willingly paid for another unit of the good or service. But willingness to pay determines demand. *A demand curve is a marginal benefit curve.*

In Fig. 5.1(a), Lisa is willing to pay $1 for the 30th slice of pizza and $1 is her marginal benefit from that slice. In Fig. 5.1(b), Nick is willing to pay $1 for the 10th slice of pizza and $1 is his marginal benefit from that slice. But at what quantity is the market willing to pay $1 for the marginal slice? The answer is provided by the *market demand curve*.

Individual Demand and Market Demand

The relationship between the price of a good and the quantity demanded by one person is called *individual demand*. And the relationship between the price of a good and the quantity demanded by all buyers is called *market demand*.

> The market demand curve is the horizontal sum of the individual demand curves and is formed by adding the quantities demanded by all the individuals at each price.

Figure 5.1(c) illustrates the market demand for pizza if Lisa and Nick are the only people in the market. Lisa's demand curve in part (a) and Nick's demand curve in part (b) sum horizontally to the market demand curve in part (c).

FIGURE 5.1 Individual Demand, Market Demand, and Marginal Social Benefit

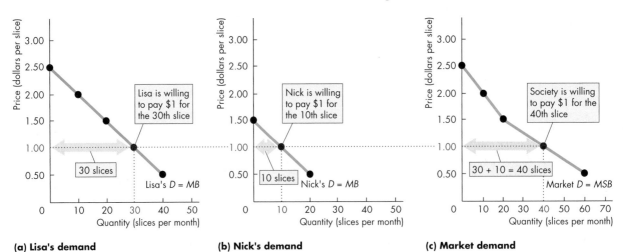

(a) Lisa's demand   **(b) Nick's demand**   **(c) Market demand**

At a price of $1 a slice, the quantity demanded by Lisa is 30 slices and the quantity demanded by Nick is 10 slices, so the quantity demanded by the market is 40 slices. Lisa's demand curve in part (a) and Nick's demand curve in part (b) sum horizontally to the market demand curve in part (c). The market demand curve is the marginal social benefit (*MSB*) curve.

MyLab Economics Animation

At a price of $1 a slice, Lisa demands 30 slices and Nick demands 10 slices, so the market quantity demanded at $1 a slice is 40 slices.

For Lisa and Nick, their demand curves are their marginal benefit curves. For society, the market demand curve is the marginal benefit curve. We call the marginal benefit to the entire society *marginal social benefit*. So the market demand curve is also the *marginal social benefit (MSB) curve*.

Consumer Surplus

We don't always have to pay as much as we are willing to pay. We get a bargain. When people buy something for less than it is worth to them, they receive a consumer surplus. **Consumer surplus** is the excess of the benefit received from a good over the amount paid for it. We can calculate consumer surplus as the marginal benefit (or value) of a good minus its price, summed over the quantity bought.

Figure 5.2(a) shows Lisa's consumer surplus from pizza when the price is $1 a slice. At this price, she buys 30 slices a month because the 30th slice is worth exactly $1 to her. But Lisa is willing to pay $2 for the 10th slice, so her marginal benefit from this slice is

$1 more than she pays for it—she receives a surplus of $1 on the 10th slice.

Lisa's consumer surplus is the sum of the surpluses on *all of the slices she buys*. This sum is the area of the green triangle—the area below the demand curve and above the market price line. The area of this triangle is equal to its base (30 slices) multiplied by its height ($1.50) divided by 2, which is $22.50. The area of the blue rectangle in Fig. 5.2(a) shows what Lisa pays for 30 slices of pizza.

Figure 5.2(b) shows Nick's consumer surplus, and part (c) shows the consumer surplus for the market. The consumer surplus for the market is the sum of the consumer surpluses of Lisa and Nick.

All goods and services have decreasing marginal benefit, so people receive more benefit from their consumption than the amount they pay.

Supply and Marginal Cost

Your next task is to see how market supply reflects marginal cost. The connection between supply and cost closely parallels the related ideas about demand and benefit that you've just studied. Firms are in business to make a profit. To do so, they must sell

FIGURE 5.2   Demand and Consumer Surplus

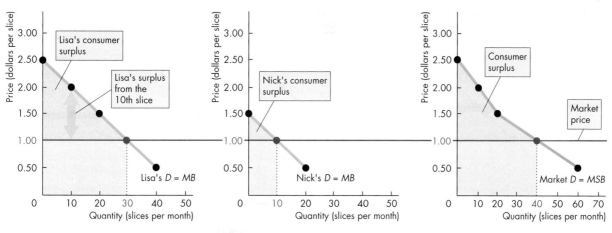

(a) Lisa's consumer surplus   **(b) Nick's consumer surplus**   **(c) Market consumer surplus**

Lisa is willing to pay $2 for her 10th slice of pizza in part (a). At a market price of $1 a slice, Lisa receives a surplus of $1 on the 10th slice. The green triangle shows her consumer surplus on the 30 slices she buys at $1 a slice. The

green triangle in part (b) shows Nick's consumer surplus on the 10 slices that he buys at $1 a slice. The green area in part (c) shows the consumer surplus for the market. The blue rectangles show the amounts spent on pizza.

their output for a price that exceeds the cost of production. Let's investigate the relationship between cost and price.

Supply, Cost, and Minimum Supply-Price

Firms make a profit when they receive more from the sale of a good or service than the cost of producing it. Just as consumers distinguish between value and price, so producers distinguish between *cost* and *price*. Cost is what a firm gives up when it produces a good or service, and price is what a firm receives when it sells the good or service.

The cost of producing one more unit of a good or service is its marginal cost. Marginal cost is the minimum price that producers must receive to induce them to offer one more unit of a good or service for sale. But the minimum supply-price determines supply. *A supply curve is a marginal cost curve.*

In Fig. 5.3(a), Maria is willing to produce the 100th pizza for $15, her marginal cost of that pizza. In Fig. 5.3(b), Max is willing to produce the 50th pizza for $15, his marginal cost.

What quantity is this market willing to produce for $15 a pizza? The answer is provided by the *market supply curve.*

Individual Supply and Market Supply

The relationship between the price of a good and the quantity supplied by one producer is called *individual supply*. And the relationship between the price of a good and the quantity supplied by all producers is called *market supply*.

> The market supply curve is the horizontal sum of the individual supply curves and is formed by adding the quantities supplied by all the producers at each price.

Figure 5.3(c) illustrates the market supply of pizzas if Maria and Max are the only producers. Maria's supply curve in part (a) and Max's supply curve in part (b) sum horizontally to the market supply curve in part (c).

At a price of $15 a pizza, Maria supplies 100 pizzas and Max supplies 50 pizzas, so the quantity supplied by the market at $15 a pizza is 150 pizzas.

For Maria and Max, their supply curves are their marginal cost curves. For society, the market supply curve is its marginal cost curve. We call society's marginal cost the *marginal social cost*. So the market supply curve is also the *marginal social cost (MSC) curve.*

FIGURE 5.3 Individual Supply, Market Supply, and Marginal Social Cost

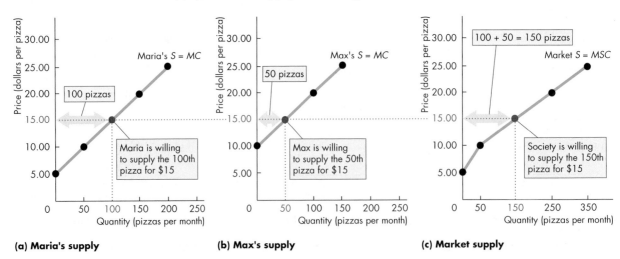

(a) Maria's supply **(b) Max's supply** **(c) Market supply**

At a price of $15 a pizza, the quantity supplied by Maria is 100 pizzas and the quantity supplied by Max is 50 pizzas, so the quantity supplied by the market is 150 pizzas. Maria's supply curve in part (a) and Max's supply curve in part (b) sum horizontally to the market supply curve in part (c). The market supply curve is the marginal social cost (MSC) curve.

Producer Surplus

When price exceeds marginal cost, the firm receives a producer surplus. **Producer surplus** is the excess of the amount received from the sale of a good or service over the cost of producing it. We calculate producer surplus as the price received minus the marginal cost (or minimum supply-price), summed over the quantity sold.

Figure 5.4(a) shows Maria's producer surplus from pizza when the price is $15 a pizza. At this price, she sells 100 pizzas a month because the 100th pizza costs her $15 to produce. But Maria is willing to produce the 50th pizza for her marginal cost, which is $10, so she receives a surplus of $5 on this pizza.

Maria's producer surplus is the sum of the surpluses on the pizzas she sells. This sum is the area of the blue triangle—the area below the market price and above the supply curve. The area of this triangle is equal to its base (100) multiplied by its height ($10) divided by 2, which is $500.

The red area below the supply curve in Fig. 5.4(a) shows what it costs Maria to produce 100 pizzas.

The area of the blue triangle in Fig. 5.4(b) shows Max's producer surplus, and the blue area in Fig. 5.4(c) shows the producer surplus for the market. The

producer surplus for the market is the sum of the producer surpluses of Maria and Max.

◆ **REVIEW QUIZ**

1 What is the relationship between the marginal benefit, value, and demand?

2 What is the relationship between individual demand and market demand?

3 What is consumer surplus? How is it measured?

4 What is the relationship between the marginal cost, minimum supply-price, and supply?

5 What is the relationship between individual supply and market supply?

6 What is producer surplus? How is it measured?

Work these questions in Study Plan 5.2 and get instant feedback.   MyLab Economics

Consumer surplus and producer surplus can be used to measure the efficiency of a market. Let's see how we can use these concepts to study the efficiency of a competitive market.

FIGURE 5.4   Supply and Producer Surplus

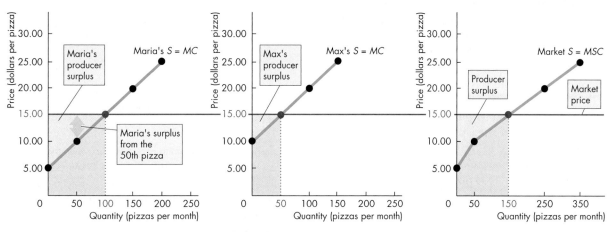

(a) Maria's producer surplus   **(b) Max's producer surplus**   **(c) Market producer surplus**

Maria is willing to produce the 50th pizza for $10 in part (a). At a market price of $15 a pizza, Maria gets a surplus of $5 on the 50th pizza. The blue triangle shows her producer surplus on the 100 pizzas she sells at $15 each.

The blue triangle in part (b) shows Max's producer surplus on the 50 pizzas that he sells at $15 each. The blue area in part (c) shows producer surplus for the market. The red areas show the cost of producing the pizzas sold.

Is the Competitive Market Efficient?

Figure 5.5(a) shows the market for pizza. The market forces that you studied in Chapter 3 (pp. 70–71) pull the pizza market to its equilibrium price of $15 a pizza and equilibrium quantity of 10,000 pizzas a day. Buyers enjoy a consumer surplus (green area) and sellers enjoy a producer surplus (blue area), but is this competitive equilibrium efficient?

Efficiency of Competitive Equilibrium

You've seen that the market demand curve for a good or service tells us the marginal social benefit from it. You've also seen that the market supply curve of a good or service tells us the marginal social cost of producing it.

Equilibrium in a competitive market occurs when the quantity demanded equals the quantity supplied at the intersection of the demand curve and the supply curve. At this intersection point, marginal social benefit on the demand curve equals marginal social cost on the supply curve. This equality is the condition for allocative efficiency. So in equilibrium, a competitive market achieves allocative efficiency.

Figure 5.5 illustrates the efficiency of competitive equilibrium. The demand curve and the supply curve intersect in part (a) and marginal social benefit equals marginal social cost in part (b).

If production is less than 10,000 pizzas a day, the marginal pizza is valued more highly than it costs to produce. If production exceeds 10,000 pizzas a day, the marginal pizza costs more to produce than the value that consumers place on it. Only when 10,000 pizzas a day are produced is the marginal pizza worth exactly what it costs.

The competitive market pushes the quantity of pizzas produced to its efficient level of 10,000 a day. If production is less than 10,000 pizzas a day, a shortage raises the price, which increases production. If production exceeds 10,000 pizzas a day, a surplus of pizzas lowers the price, which decreases production. So a competitive pizza market is efficient.

Figure 5.5(a) also shows the consumer surplus and producer surplus. The sum of consumer surplus and producer surplus is called **total surplus**. When the efficient quantity is produced, total surplus is maximized. Buyers and sellers acting in their self-interest end up promoting the social interest.

FIGURE 5.5 An Efficient Market for Pizza

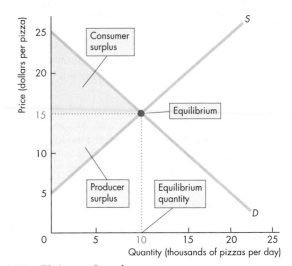

(a) Equilibrium and surpluses

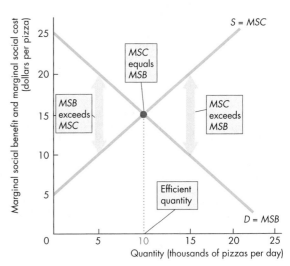

(b) Efficiency

Competitive equilibrium in part (a) occurs when the quantity demanded equals the quantity supplied. Resources are used efficiently in part (b) when marginal social benefit, MSB, equals marginal social cost, MSC. Total surplus, which is the sum of consumer surplus (the green triangle) and producer surplus (the blue triangle), is maximized.

The efficient quantity in part (b) is the same as the equilibrium quantity in part (a). The competitive pizza market produces the efficient quantity of pizzas.

MyLab Economics Animation and Draw Graph

ECONOMICS IN ACTION

Seeing the Invisible Hand

Adam Smith said that a seller in a competitive market is "led by *an invisible hand* to promote an end which was no part of his intention" (see p. 8). Smith believed that the invisible hand sends resources to the uses in which they have the highest value.

You can't *see* the invisible hand, but you can imagine it, and you can see its consequences in the cartoon and in today's world.

Umbrella for Sale The cold drinks vendor has cold drinks and shade and he has a marginal cost and a minimum supply-price of each. The reader on the park bench has a marginal benefit and willingness to pay for each. The reader's marginal benefit from shade exceeds the vendor's marginal cost; but the vendor's marginal cost of a cold drink exceeds the reader's marginal benefit. They trade the umbrella. The vendor gets a producer surplus from selling the shade for more than its marginal cost, and the reader gets a consumer surplus from buying the shade for less than its marginal benefit. Both are better off and the umbrella has moved to a higher-valued use.

The Invisible Hand at Work Today Many of the markets in which you trade work like that in the cartoon to achieve an efficient allocation of resources.

When you order a pizza for home delivery, you make a choice about how scarce resources will be used. You make your choice in your self-interest. The pizza cook and the person who delivers your pizza also make their choices in their self-interest.

The pizza market coordinates these choices. You buy the quantity of pizza that makes the price you pay equal to your marginal benefit. And the pizza producer sells the quantity at which the price equals his marginal cost. Total surplus is maximized in an efficient pizza market.

Market Failure

Markets are not always efficient, and when a market is inefficient, we call the outcome **market failure**. In a market failure, either too little (underproduction) or too much (overproduction) of an item is produced.

Underproduction In Fig. 5.6(a), the quantity of pizzas produced is 5,000 a day. At this quantity, consumers are willing to pay $20 for a pizza that costs only $10 to produce. The quantity produced is inefficient—there is underproduction—and total surplus is smaller than its maximum possible level.

We measure the scale of inefficiency by **deadweight loss**, which is the decrease in total surplus that results from an inefficient level of production. The grey triangle in Fig. 5.6(a) shows the deadweight loss.

Overproduction In Fig. 5.6(b), the quantity of pizzas produced is 15,000 a day. At this quantity, consumers are willing to pay only $10 for a pizza that costs $20 to produce. By producing the 15,000th pizza, $10 of resources are wasted. Again, the grey triangle shows the deadweight loss, which reduces the total surplus to less than its maximum.

Inefficient production creates a deadweight loss that is borne by the entire society: It is a social loss.

Sources of Market Failure

Obstacles to efficiency that bring market failure are:

- Price and quantity regulations
- Taxes and subsidies
- Externalities
- Public goods and common resources
- Monopoly
- High transactions costs

Price and Quantity Regulations A *price regulation*, either a price cap or a price floor, blocks the price adjustments that balance the quantity demanded and the quantity supplied and lead to underproduction. A *quantity regulation* that limits the amount that a farm or a firm is permitted to produce also leads to underproduction.

Taxes and Subsidies *Taxes* increase the prices paid by buyers, lower the prices received by sellers, and lead to underproduction. *Subsidies*, which are payments by the government to producers, decrease the prices paid by buyers, increase the prices received by sellers, and lead to overproduction.

FIGURE 5.6 Underproduction and Overproduction

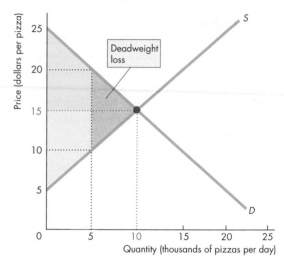

(a) Underproduction

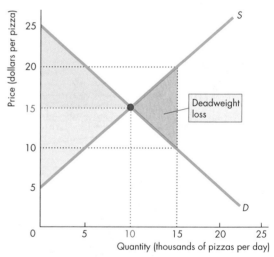

(b) Overproduction

If 5,000 pizzas a day are produced, in part (a), total surplus (the sum of the green and blue areas) is smaller than its maximum by the amount of the deadweight loss (the grey triangle). At all quantities below 10,000 pizzas a day, the benefit from one more pizza exceeds its cost.

If 15,000 pizzas a day are produced, in part (b), total surplus is also smaller than its maximum by the amount of the deadweight loss. At all quantities in excess of 10,000 pizzas a day, the cost of one more pizza exceeds its benefit.

MyLab Economics Animation and Draw Graph

Externalities An *externality* is a cost or a benefit that affects someone other than the seller or the buyer. An *external cost* arises when an electric utility burns coal and emits carbon dioxide. The utility doesn't consider the cost of climate change when it decides how much power to produce. The result is overproduction. An *external benefit* arises when an apartment owner installs a smoke detector and decreases her neighbour's fire risk. She doesn't consider the benefit to her neighbour when she decides how many detectors to install. The result is underproduction.

Public Goods and Common Resources A *public good* is a good or service from which everyone benefits and no one can be excluded. National defence is an example. A competitive market would underproduce national defence because everyone would try to free ride on everyone else.

A *common resource* is owned by no one but is available to be used by everyone. Atlantic salmon is an example. It is in everyone's self-interest to ignore the costs they impose on others when they decide how much of a common resource to use: It is overused.

Monopoly A *monopoly* is a firm that is the sole provider of a good or service. Local water supply and cable television are supplied by firms that are monopolies. The monopoly's self-interest is to maximize its profit, and because it has no competitors, it produces too little and charges too high a price: It underproduces.

High Transactions Costs When you buy your first house, you will also buy the services of an agent and a lawyer to do the transaction. Economists call the costs of the services that enable a market to bring buyers and sellers together **transactions costs**. It is costly to operate *any* market, but some markets are so costly to operate that they simply don't. For example, there's no market in time slots on a local tennis court. Instead, the court uses first-come, first-served: You hang around until the court becomes vacant and "pay" with your waiting time. When transactions costs are high, the market might underproduce.

You now know the conditions under which resource allocation is efficient. You've seen how a competitive market can be efficient, and you've seen some obstacles to efficiency. Can alternative allocation methods improve on the market?

Alternatives to the Market

When a market is inefficient, can one of the alternative nonmarket methods that we described at the beginning of this chapter do a better job? Sometimes it can.

Often, majority rule might be used in an attempt to improve the allocation of resources. But majority rule has its own shortcomings. A group that pursues the self-interest of its members can become the majority. For example, a price or quantity regulation that creates inefficiency is almost always the result of a self-interested group becoming the majority and imposing costs on the minority. Also, with majority rule, votes must be translated into actions by bureaucrats who have their own agendas based on their self-interest.

Managers in firms issue commands and avoid the transactions costs that they would incur if they went to a market every time they needed a job done.

First-come, first-served works best in some situations. Think about the scene at a busy ATM. Instead of waiting in line people might trade places at a "market" price. But someone would need to ensure that trades were honoured. At a busy ATM, first-come, first-served is the most efficient arrangement.

There is no one efficient mechanism that allocates all resources efficiently. But markets, when supplemented by other mechanisms such as majority rule, command systems, and first-come, first-served, do an amazingly good job.

REVIEW QUIZ

1 Do competitive markets use resources efficiently? Explain why or why not.
2 What is deadweight loss and under what conditions does it occur?
3 What are the obstacles to achieving an efficient allocation of resources in the market economy?

Work these questions in Study Plan 5.3 and get instant feedback.   MyLab Economics

Is an efficient allocation of resources also a fair allocation? Does the competitive market provide people with fair incomes for their work? Do people always pay a fair price for the things they buy? Don't we need the government to step into some competitive markets to prevent the price from rising too high or falling too low? Let's now study these questions.

◆ Is the Competitive Market Fair?

When a natural disaster strikes, such as a severe winter storm or a hurricane, the prices of many essential items jump. The reason prices jump is that the demand and willingness to pay for these items has increased, but the supply has not changed. So the higher prices achieve an efficient allocation of scarce resources. News reports of these price hikes almost never talk about efficiency. Instead, they talk about equity or fairness. The claim that is often made is that it is unfair for profit-seeking dealers to cheat the victims of natural disaster.

Similarly, when low-skilled people work for a wage that is below what most would regard as a "living wage," the media and politicians talk of employers taking unfair advantage of their workers.

How do we decide whether something is fair or unfair? You know when you *think* something is unfair, but how do you *know*? What are the *principles* of fairness?

Philosophers have tried for centuries to answer this question. Economists have offered their answers too. But before we look at the proposed answers, you should know that there is no universally agreed upon answer.

Economists agree about efficiency. That is, they agree that it makes sense to make the economic pie as large as possible and to produce it at the lowest possible cost. But they do not agree about equity. That is, they do not agree about what are fair shares of the economic pie for all the people who make it. The reason is that ideas about fairness are not exclusively economic ideas. They touch on politics, ethics, and religion. Nevertheless, economists have thought about these issues and have a contribution to make. Let's examine the views of economists on this topic.

To think about fairness, think of economic life as a game—a serious game. All ideas about fairness can be divided into two broad groups. They are:

- It's not fair if the *result* isn't fair.
- It's not fair if the *rules* aren't fair.

It's Not Fair if the *Result* Isn't Fair

The earliest efforts to establish a principle of fairness were based on the view that the result is what matters. The general idea was that it is unfair if people's incomes are too unequal. For example, it is unfair

that a bank president earns millions of dollars a year while a bank teller earns only thousands of dollars. It is unfair that a store owner makes a larger profit and her customers pay higher prices in the aftermath of a winter storm.

During the nineteenth century, economists thought they had made an incredible discovery: Efficiency requires equality of incomes. To make the economic pie as large as possible, it must be cut into equal pieces, one for each person. This idea turns out to be wrong. But there is a lesson in the reason that it is wrong, so this idea is worth a closer look.

Utilitarianism The nineteenth-century idea that only equality brings efficiency is called *utilitarianism*. **Utilitarianism** is a principle that states that we should strive to achieve "the greatest happiness for the greatest number." The people who developed this idea were known as utilitarians. They included eminent thinkers such as Jeremy Bentham and John Stuart Mill.

Utilitarians argued that to achieve "the greatest happiness for the greatest number," income must be transferred from the rich to the poor up to the point of complete equality—to the point at which there are no rich and no poor.

They reasoned in the following way: First, everyone has the same basic wants and a similar capacity to enjoy life. Second, the greater a person's income, the smaller is the marginal benefit of a dollar. The millionth dollar spent by a rich person brings a smaller marginal benefit to that person than the marginal benefit that the thousandth dollar spent brings to a poorer person. So by transferring a dollar from the millionaire to the poorer person, more is gained than is lost. The two people added together are better off.

Figure 5.7 illustrates this utilitarian idea. Tom and Jerry have the same marginal benefit curve, *MB*. (Marginal benefit is measured on the same scale of 1 to 3 for both Tom and Jerry.) Tom is at point *A*. He earns $5,000 a year, and his marginal benefit from a dollar is 3 units. Jerry is at point *B*. He earns $45,000 a year, and his marginal benefit from a dollar is 1 unit. If a dollar is transferred from Jerry to Tom, Jerry loses 1 unit of marginal benefit and Tom gains 3 units. So together, Tom and Jerry are better off—they are sharing the economic pie more efficiently. If a second dollar is transferred, the same thing happens: Tom gains more than Jerry loses. And the same is true for every dollar transferred until they both reach point *C*. At point *C*, Tom and Jerry have $25,000

FIGURE 5.7 Utilitarian Fairness

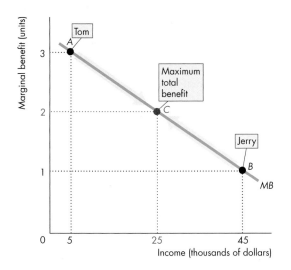

Tom earns $5,000 and has 3 units of marginal benefit at point *A*. Jerry earns $45,000 and has 1 unit of marginal benefit at point *B*. If income is transferred from Jerry to Tom, Jerry's loss is less than Tom's gain. Only when each of them has $25,000 and 2 units of marginal benefit (at point *C*) can the sum of their total benefit increase no further.

MyLab Economics Animation

each and a marginal benefit of 2 units. Now they are sharing the economic pie in the most efficient way. It brings the greatest happiness to Tom and Jerry.

The Big Tradeoff One big problem with the utilitarian ideal of complete equality is that it ignores the costs of making income transfers. Recognizing the costs of making income transfers leads to what is called the **big tradeoff**, which is a tradeoff between efficiency and fairness.

The big tradeoff is based on the following facts. Income can be transferred from people with high incomes to people with low incomes only by taxing the high incomes. Taxing people's income from employment makes them work less. It results in the quantity of labour being less than the efficient quantity. Taxing people's income from capital makes them save less. It results in the quantity of capital being less than the efficient quantity. With smaller quantities of both labour and capital, the quantity of goods and services produced is less than the efficient quantity. The economic pie shrinks.

The tradeoff is between the size of the economic pie and the degree of equality with which it is shared. The greater the amount of income redistribution through income taxes, the greater is the inefficiency—the smaller is the economic pie.

There is a second source of inefficiency. A dollar taken from a rich person does not end up as a dollar in the hands of a poorer person. Some of the dollar is spent on administration of the tax and transfer system. The cost of the tax-collecting agency, Canada Revenue Agency (CRA), and the welfare-administering agencies, such as Employment and Social Development Canada, must be paid with some of the taxes collected. Also, taxpayers hire accountants, auditors, and lawyers to help them ensure that they pay the correct amount of taxes. These activities use skilled labour and capital resources that could otherwise be used to produce goods and services that people value.

When all these costs are taken into account, taking a dollar from a rich person does not give a dollar to a poor person. It is possible that with high taxes, people with low incomes might end up being worse off. Suppose, for example, that highly taxed entrepreneurs decide to work less hard and shut down some of their businesses. Low-income workers get fired and must seek other, perhaps even lower-paid, work.

Today, because of the big tradeoff, no one says that fairness requires complete equality of incomes.

Make the Poorest as Well Off as Possible A new solution to the big-tradeoff problem was proposed by philosopher John Rawls in a classic book entitled *A Theory of Justice*, published in 1971. Rawls says that, taking all the costs of income transfers into account, the fair distribution of the economic pie is the one that makes the poorest person as well off as possible. The incomes of rich people should be taxed, and after paying the costs of administering the tax and transfer system, what is left should be transferred to the poor. But the taxes must not be so high that they make the economic pie shrink to the point at which the poorest person ends up with a smaller piece. A bigger share of a smaller pie can be less than a smaller share of a bigger pie. The goal is to make the piece enjoyed by the poorest person as big as possible. Most likely, this piece will not be an equal share.

The "fair results" idea requires a change in the results after the game is over. Some economists say that these changes are themselves unfair and propose a different way of thinking about fairness.

It's Not Fair if the *Rules* Aren't Fair

The idea that it's not fair if the rules aren't fair is based on a fundamental principle that seems to be hardwired into the human brain: the symmetry principle. The **symmetry principle** is the requirement that people in similar situations be treated similarly. It is the moral principle that lies at the centre of all the big religions and that says, in some form or other, "Behave toward other people in the way you expect them to behave toward you."

In economic life, this principle translates into *equality of opportunity*. But equality of opportunity to do what? This question is answered by the philosopher Robert Nozick in a book entitled *Anarchy, State, and Utopia*, published in 1974.

Nozick argues that the idea of fairness as an outcome or result cannot work and that fairness must be based on the fairness of the rules. He suggests that fairness obeys two rules:

1. The state must enforce laws that establish and protect private property.
2. Private property may be transferred from one person to another only by voluntary exchange.

The first rule says that everything that is valuable must be owned by individuals and that the state must ensure that theft is prevented. The second rule says that the only legitimate way a person can acquire property is to buy it in exchange for something else that the person owns. If these rules, which are the only fair rules, are followed, then the result is fair. It doesn't matter how unequally the economic pie is shared, provided that the pie is made by people, each one of whom voluntarily provides services in exchange for the share of the pie offered in compensation.

These rules satisfy the symmetry principle. If these rules are not followed, the symmetry principle is broken. You can see these facts by imagining a world in which the laws are not followed.

First, suppose that some resources or goods are not owned. They are common property. Then everyone is free to participate in a grab to use them. The strongest will prevail. But when the strongest prevails, the strongest effectively *owns* the resources or goods in question and prevents others from enjoying them.

Second, suppose that we do not insist on voluntary exchange for transferring ownership of resources from one person to another. The alternative is *involuntary* transfer. In simple language, the alternative is theft.

Both of these situations violate the symmetry principle. Only the strong acquire what they want. The weak end up with only the resources and goods that the strong don't want.

In a majority-rule political system, the strong are those in the majority or those with enough resources to influence opinion and achieve a majority.

In contrast, if the two rules of fairness are followed, everyone, strong and weak, is treated in a similar way. All individuals are free to use their resources and human skills to create things that are valued by themselves and others and to exchange the fruits of their efforts with all others. This set of arrangements is the only one that obeys the symmetry principle.

Fair Rules and Efficiency If private property rights are enforced and if voluntary exchange takes place in a competitive market with none of the obstacles described above (pp. 118–119), resources will be allocated efficiently.

According to the Nozick fair-rules view, no matter how unequal is the resulting distribution of income and wealth, it will be fair.

It would be better if everyone were as well off as those with the highest incomes, but scarcity prevents that outcome and the best attainable outcome is the efficient one.

Case Study: A Generator Shortage in a Natural Disaster

Hurricane Katrina shut down electricity supplies over a wide area and increased the demand for portable generators. What is the fair way to allocate the available generators?

If the market price is used, the outcome is efficient. Sellers *and buyers* are better off and no one is worse off. But people who own generators make a larger profit and the generators go to those who want them most and can afford them. Is that fair?

On the Nozick rules view, the outcome is fair. On the fair outcome view, the outcome might be considered unfair. But what are the alternatives? They are command; majority rule; contest; first-come, first-served; lottery; personal characteristics; and force. Except by chance, none of these methods delivers an allocation of generators that is either fair or efficient. It is unfair in the rules view because the distribution involves involuntary transfers of resources among citizens. It is unfair in the results view because the poorest don't end up being made as well off as possible.

◆ AT **ISSUE**

Price Gouging

Price gouging is the practice of offering to sell an essential item following a natural disaster at a price much higher than its normal price.

When floods wiped out the Calgary Stampede and inundated the city in the summer of 2013, bags of ice, bottled water, and fruit were all in short supply. Stores with items for sale were getting exceptionally high prices. One store offered ice for $20 a bag. Another sold bottled water but not at the normal price. Angry shoppers took to social media to denounce price gougers and call for boycotts of their stores.

In Favour of a Law Against Price Gouging

Supporters of laws against price gouging say:

- It unfairly exploits vulnerable, needy buyers.
- It unfairly rewards unscrupulous sellers.
- In situations of extraordinary shortage, prices should be regulated to prevent these abuses and scarce resources should be allocated by one of the nonmarket mechanisms such as majority vote or equal shares for all.

The Economist's Response

Economists say that preventing a voluntary market transaction leads to inefficiency—it makes some people worse off without making anyone better off.

- In the figure below, when the supply of ice is much less than normal, the equilibrium price rises from $2 to $20 per bag.
- Calling the price rise "gouging" and blocking it with a law prevents additional units from being made available and creates a deadweight loss.

Should the price that a seller of ice may charge be regulated?

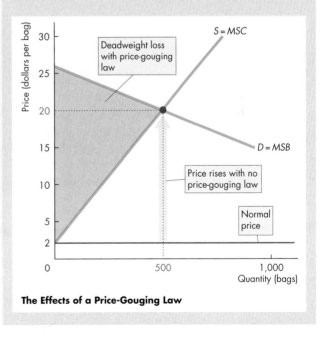

The Effects of a Price-Gouging Law

◆ REVIEW QUIZ

1. What are the two big approaches to thinking about fairness?
2. What is the utilitarian idea of fairness and what is wrong with it?
3. Explain the big tradeoff. What idea of fairness has been developed to deal with it?
4. What is the idea of fairness based on fair rules?

Work these questions in Study Plan 5.4 and get instant feedback.   MyLab Economics

◆ You've now studied efficiency and equity (fairness), the two biggest issues that run through the whole of economics. *Economics in the News* on pp. 124–125 looks at an example of an *inefficiency* in our economy today. At many points throughout this book—and in your life—you will return to and use the ideas you've learned in this chapter. We start to apply these ideas in the next chapter where we study some sources of *in*efficiency and *un*fairness.

Making Traffic Flow Efficiently

Toronto Dominates List of Worst Traffic Jams Across Canada

The Canadian Press
January 11, 2017

A new report suggests Canada's worst traffic bottlenecks are serious enough to compare with those in New York and Los Angeles.

The report commissioned by the Canadian Automobile Association (CAA) found that the most consistently congested stretch of highway in the country, a portion of Hwy. 401 running through central Toronto, is the ninth-most-clogged artery in Canada and the United States.

A bottleneck in Montreal, considered the third-worst in Canada according to the new research, compares with congestion levels in Boston. …

Vancouver rounded out the top 10 with two particularly busy stretches of road. Two more Vancouver roadways, along with one in Quebec City, completed the top 20. …

The research showed that a commute along the busiest stretch of Toronto highways can add an average of 36 minutes to a 60-minute commute, resulting in an annual total of 3.2 million driver-hours in delays on that route.

The study estimated the country's worst bottlenecks result in 11.5 million hours worth of delays and waste about 22 million litres of fuel per year. …

Former Vancouver chief city planner Brent Toderian said there's value in assessing high-traffic areas, but said most research of this kind is based on the assumption that driving is the best way to travel. …

Toderian said … price-based tools, such as tolls, are the most effective ways to keep traffic in check.

© The Canadian Press

ESSENCE OF THE STORY

- A report commissioned by the Canadian Automobile Association (CAA) says a section of Hwy 401 through Toronto is the most congested road in Canada and the ninth most congested in North America.

- Highways in Montreal, Vancouver, and Quebec City are in the top 20 most congested.

- The busiest stretch of Toronto highway more than doubles commute times and costs 3.2 million driver-hours in delays.

- The worst bottlenecks result in 11.5 million hours of delays and 22 million litres of wasted fuel per year.

- Brent Toderian says price-based tools, such as tolls, are the most effective ways to keep traffic in check.

ECONOMIC ANALYSIS

- To see how a price-based tool advocated by Brent Toderian works, we'll look at an economic model of a highway.

- The model highway has the marginal social cost curve *MSC* in the figures. It can carry only 10,000 vehicles per hour with no congestion.

- At the peak time, the demand curve and marginal benefit curve is $D_p = MSB_p$.

- Figure 1 illustrates inefficient road use. At the peak demand time, at a zero price, 40,000 vehicles per hour enter the road. The marginal social cost is $6 per vehicle-hour and there is a deadweight loss (of time and gasoline) shown by the grey triangle.

- Figure 2 illustrates efficient road use at the peak period. Imposing a congestion charge of $3 per vehicle-hour brings an equilibrium at 25,000 vehicles per hour, which is the efficient quantity. Total surplus, the sum of consumer surplus (green) plus producer surplus (blue), is maximized.

- To achieve an efficient outcome, congestion charges would be paid by all road users, regardless of whether they are rich or poor, but they don't have to leave the poor worse off.

- Revenue raised from the congestion charges can be redistributed to low-income households if there is a fairness problem.

- So long as road users pay the marginal social cost of their decision, road use is efficient.

- San Francisco has introduced a system of congestion pricing on a section of I-80 that imposes a time-varying charge when a vehicle enters an on-ramp.

While traffic grinds to a halt on many Canadian highways, Electronic Road Pricing (ERP) keeps vehicles moving in Singapore.

- Singapore has the world's most sophisticated congestion pricing with the price displayed on electronic signs above the road (see photo). The price rises as congestion increases and falls as congestion eases.

- Advances in information technology make congestion pricing an attractive tool for achieving an efficient use of the road transportation system.

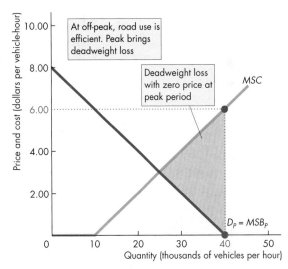

Figure 1 Inefficient Rush-Hour Road Use

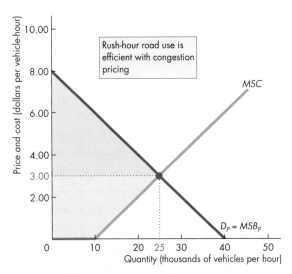

Figure 2 Efficient Rush-Hour Road Use

125

WORKED PROBLEM

MyLab Economics Work this problem in Chapter 5 Study Plan.

The figure illustrates the market for sunscreen.

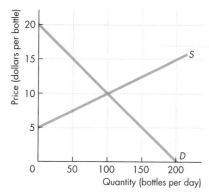

Questions

1. At the market equilibrium, calculate:
   (a) consumer surplus and (b) producer surplus.
2. Is the market for sunscreen efficient? Why?
3. What is deadweight loss? Calculate it if factories produce only 50 bottles of sunscreen.

Solutions

1 (a) Consumer surplus is the excess of the benefit received over the amount buyers paid for it. The demand curve tells us the benefit, so consumer surplus equals the area under the demand curve above the market price, summed over the quantity bought. The price paid is $10 a bottle, the quantity bought is 100 bottles, so consumer surplus equals the area of the green triangle in the figure below.

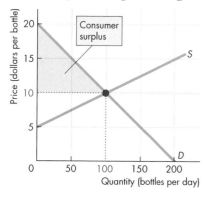

Area of the triangle = (Base × Height) ÷ 2. The base is the quantity bought (100 bottles) and the height is the maximum price ($20 a bottle) *minus* the market price ($10 a bottle). Consumer surplus equals 100 × ($20 − $10) ÷ 2, which is $500.

Key Point: Consumer surplus equals the area under the demand curve above the market price.

1 (b) Producer surplus is the excess of the amount received by sellers over the cost of production. The supply curve tells us the cost of producing the good, so producer surplus is equal to the area under the market price above the supply curve, summed over the quantity sold and is equal to the area of the blue triangle in the following figure.

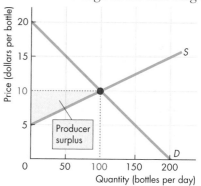

In this triangle, the base is 100 bottles and the height is ($10 − $5), so producer surplus equals 100 × ($10 − $5) ÷ 2, or $250.

Key Point: Producer surplus equals the area under the market price above the supply curve.

2. Total surplus (consumer surplus plus producer surplus) is a maximum, so the market is efficient.

Key Point: A competitive market is always efficient.

3. When factories produce *less* than the efficient quantity (100 bottles), some total surplus is lost. This loss is called the deadweight loss and it is equal to the area of the grey triangle in the figure below. The base is ($15 − $7.50), the height is the quantity not produced (50 bottles), so deadweight loss equals ($15 − $7.50) × 50 ÷ 2, which is $187.50.

Key Point: Underproduction creates a deadweight loss.

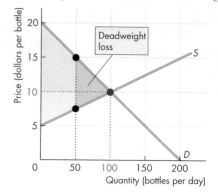

MyLab Economics Interactive Animation

Key Points

Resource Allocation Methods (pp. 110–111)

- Because resources are scarce, some mechanism must allocate them.
- The alternative allocation methods are market price; command; majority rule; contest; first-come, first-served; lottery; personal characteristics; and force.

Working Study Plan Problem 1 will give you a better understanding of resource allocation methods.

Benefit, Cost, and Surplus (pp. 112–115)

- The maximum price willingly paid is marginal benefit, so a demand curve is also a marginal benefit curve.
- The market demand curve is the horizontal sum of the individual demand curves and is the marginal social benefit curve.
- Value is what people are *willing* to pay; price is what people *must* pay.
- Consumer surplus is the excess of the benefit received from a good or service over the amount paid for it.
- The minimum supply-price is marginal cost, so a supply curve is also a marginal cost curve.
- The market supply curve is the horizontal sum of the individual supply curves and is the marginal social cost curve.
- Cost is what producers pay; price is what producers receive.

- Producer surplus is the excess of the amount received from the sale of a good or service over the cost of producing it.

Working Study Plan Problems 2 to 7 will give you a better understanding of benefit, cost, and surplus.

Is the Competitive Market Efficient? (pp. 116–119)

- In a competitive equilibrium, marginal social benefit equals marginal social cost and resource allocation is efficient.
- Buyers and sellers acting in their self-interest end up promoting the social interest.
- Total surplus, consumer surplus plus producer surplus, is maximized.
- Producing less than or more than the efficient quantity creates deadweight loss.
- Price and quantity regulations; taxes and subsidies; externalities; public goods and common resources; monopoly; and high transactions costs can lead to market failure.

Working Study Plan Problem 8 will give you a better understanding of the efficiency of competitive markets.

Is the Competitive Market Fair? (pp. 120–123)

- Ideas about fairness can be divided into two groups: fair *results* and fair *rules*.
- Fair-results ideas require income transfers from the rich to the poor.
- Fair-rules ideas require property rights and voluntary exchange.

Working Study Plan Problems 9 and 10 will give you a better understanding of the fairness of competitive markets.

Key Terms

Big tradeoff, 121
Command system, 110
Consumer surplus, 113
Deadweight loss, 118

Market failure, 118
Producer surplus, 115
Symmetry principle, 122
Total surplus, 116

Transactions costs, 119
Utilitarianism, 120

STUDY PLAN PROBLEMS AND APPLICATIONS

MyLab Economics Work Problems 1 to 10 in Chapter 5 Study Plan and get instant feedback.

Resource Allocation Methods (Study Plan 5.1)

1. At West, a restaurant in Vancouver, reservations are essential. At Cibo, a restaurant in downtown Vancouver, reservations are recommended. At Vij's, a restaurant near the University of British Columbia, reservations are not accepted.

   Describe the method of allocating scarce table resources at these three restaurants. Why do you think restaurants don't use the market price to allocate their tables?

Benefit, Cost, and Surplus (Study Plan 5.2)

Use the following table to work Problems 2 to 4. The table gives the demand schedules for train travel for the only buyers in the market: Ann, Beth, and Cy.

Price (dollars per kilometre)	Quantity demanded (kilometres)		
	Ann	Beth	Cy
3	30	25	20
4	25	20	15
5	20	15	10
6	15	10	5
7	10	5	0
8	5	0	0
9	0	0	0

2. a. Construct the market demand schedule.
   b. What is the maximum price that each traveller is willing to pay to travel 20 kilometres? Why?
3. a. What is the marginal social benefit when the total distance travelled is 60 kilometres?
   b. When the total distance travelled is 60 kilometres, how many kilometres does each travel and what is their marginal private benefit?
4. What is each traveller's consumer surplus when the price is $4 a kilometre? What is the market consumer surplus when the price is $4 a kilometre?

Use the following data to work Problems 5 to 7.

The table in the next column gives the supply schedules of the only sellers of hot air balloon rides: Xavier, Yasmin, and Zack.

5. a. Construct the market supply schedule.
   b. What are the minimum prices that Xavier, Yasmin, and Zack are willing to accept to supply 20 rides? Why?

Price (dollars per ride)	Quantity supplied (rides per week)		
	Xavier	Yasmin	Zack
100	30	25	20
90	25	20	15
80	20	15	10
70	15	10	5
60	10	5	0
50	5	0	0
40	0	0	0

6. a. What is the marginal social cost when the total number of rides is 30?
   b. What is the marginal cost for each supplier when the total number of rides is 30 and how many rides does each seller supply?
7. When the price is $70 a ride, what is each seller's producer surplus? What is the market producer surplus?

Is the Competitive Market Efficient? (Study Plan 5.3)

8. The figure shows the competitive market for smartphones.

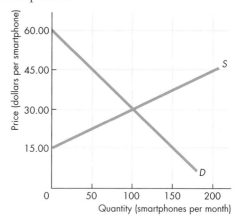

   a. What is the market equilibrium?
   b. Shade in the consumer surplus and label it.
   c. Shade in the producer surplus and label it.
   d. Calculate total surplus.
   e. Is the market for smartphones efficient?

Is the Competitive Market Fair? (Study Plan 5.4)

9. Explain why the allocation method used by each restaurant in Problem 1 is fair or not fair.
10. In the Worked Problem (p. 126), how can the 50 bottles available be allocated to beach-goers? Would the possible methods be fair or unfair?

ADDITIONAL PROBLEMS AND APPLICATIONS

Resource Allocation Methods

11. At the Stratford Festival Theatre no reservations are accepted on the day of the performance; at matinees reservations are accepted; at opening night performances reservations are essential. Describe the method of allocating seats in these three performances. Why do you think the Stratford Festival Theatre has different reservation policies?

Benefit, Cost, and Surplus

Use the following table to work Problems 12 to 15. The table gives the supply schedules for jet-ski rides by the only suppliers: Rick, Sam, and Tom.

Price (dollars per ride)	Quantity supplied (rides per day)		
	Rick	Sam	Tom
10.00	0	0	0
12.50	5	0	0
15.00	10	5	0
17.50	15	10	5
20.00	20	15	10

12. What is each owner's minimum supply-price of 10 rides a day?
13. Which owner has the largest producer surplus when the price of a ride is $17.50? Explain.
14. What is the marginal social cost of 45 rides a day?
15. Construct the market supply schedule of rides.
16. The table below gives the demand and supply schedules for sandwiches.

Price (dollars per sandwich)	Quantity demanded	Quantity supplied
	(sandwiches per hour)	
0	300	0
1	250	50
2	200	100
3	150	150
4	100	200
5	50	250
6	0	300

a. What is the maximum price that a consumer is willing to pay for the 200th sandwich?

b. What is the minimum price that a producer is willing to accept for the 200th sandwich?

c. If 200 sandwiches a day are available, what is the total surplus?

17. **Home Heating Bills Surge Amid Record Cold**

If there's one thing that can set home heating costs soaring, it's a long, frigid blast from one of the coldest winters in 20 years, and people are going to use 10 to 12 percent more natural gas this year than they have normally.

Source: CBC News, March 3, 2014

a. How is the price of natural gas determined?

b. When demand increases, explain the process by which the market adjusts.

c. On a graph, show the effect of the increase in demand on consumer surplus and producer surplus.

Is the Competitive Market Efficient?

18. Use the data in the table in Problem 16.

a. If the sandwich market is efficient, what is the consumer surplus, what is the producer surplus, and what is the total surplus?

b. If the demand for sandwiches increases and sandwich makers produce the efficient quantity, what happens to producer surplus and deadweight loss?

Use the following news clip to work Problems 19 to 21.

Music's Value in the Internet Age

The price of streaming services has been $10 a month or zero. Amazon and Pandora Media are poised to change the streaming scene. Pandora is a streaming Internet radio service, and its new $5 version will be more like Spotify and Apple Music, which let users create their own playlists. Amazon, which offers limited on-demand music for $99 a year, is expected to expand its catalog and offer it for $10 a month or $5 a month for customers who use the Echo, Amazon's voice-activated speaker system.

Source: *The New York Times*, September 11, 2016

Assume that the marginal social cost of streaming is zero. (This assumption means that the cost of operating a streaming service doesn't change if more people stream more songs.)

19. a. Draw a graph of the market for streaming music with a price of $10 a month. On your graph, show consumer surplus and producer surplus.

b. With a price of $10 a month, is the market efficient or inefficient? If it is inefficient, show the deadweight loss on your graph.

20. If the $5 price described in the news clip were adopted, how would consumer surplus, producer surplus, and the deadweight loss change?

21. a. If the $5 price described in the news clip were adopted, would the market be efficient or inefficient? Explain.

   b. Is the $5 price described in the news clip a competitive market price? Explain.

22. Only 1 percent of the world supply of water is fit for human consumption. Some places have more water than they can use; some could use much more than they have. The 1 percent available would be sufficient if only it were in the right place.

   a. What is the major problem in achieving an efficient use of the world's water?

   b. If there were a global market in water, like there is in oil, how do you think the market would be organized?

   c. Would a free world market in water achieve an efficient use of the world's water resources? Explain why or why not.

Is the Competitive Market Fair?

23. Use the information in Problem 22. Would a free world market in water achieve a fair use of the world's water resources? Explain why or why not and be clear about the concept of fairness that you are using.

24. The winner of the men's and women's tennis singles at the Canadian Open is paid twice as much as the runner-up, but it takes two players to have a singles final. Is the compensation arrangement fair?

25. **Thousands of Gouging Complaints after Hurricane Matthew**

   After Hurricane Matthew, more than 2,000 Florida consumers complained of price gouging to the State Attorney General. Two examples: a hotel room normally $65 a night cost $150, and a $1 bottle of water was $5. In a declared state of emergency, "unconscionable prices" are prohibited.

   Source: News-press.com, October 7, 2016

   a. Are the two examples in the news clip examples of price gouging or of competitive

markets doing their job of allocating scarce resources? Explain.

   b. Are the two examples of price increases in the news clip fair?

   c. Is it fair to prohibit "unconscionable prices"?

Economics in the News

26. After you have studied *Economics in the News* on pp. 124–125, answer the following questions.

   a. What is the method used to allocate highway space in Canada and what is the method used in Singapore?

   b. Who benefits from the Canadian method of highway resource allocation? Explain your answer using the ideas of marginal social benefit, marginal social cost, consumer surplus, and producer surplus.

   c. Who benefits from the Singaporean method of highway resource allocation? Explain your answer using the ideas of marginal social benefit, marginal social cost, consumer surplus, and producer surplus.

   d. If road use were rationed by limiting drivers with even-date birthdays to drive only on even days (and odd-date birthdays to drive only on odd days), would highway use be more efficient? Explain your answer.

27. **Water Rate Hikes Have Farmers Steaming**

   Most residents of Ventura County, California, pay $3.10 per 100 cubic feet of water. Agricultural water users pay $1.79 per 100 cubic feet. Water officials propose to increase these prices to $4.24 for residential users and to $4.92 for agricultural users by 2020. Water district officials say these price increases are fair.

   Source: *Moorpark Acorn*, January 13, 2017

   a. Do you think that the allocation of water between agricultural and residential users is likely to be efficient? Explain your answer.

   b. If agricultural users paid a higher price, would the allocation of resources be more efficient?

   c. If agricultural users paid a higher price, what would happen to consumer surplus and producer surplus from water?

   d. Is the difference in price paid by agricultural and residential users fair?

6

GOVERNMENT ACTIONS IN MARKETS

After studying this chapter, you will be able to:

◆ Explain how a rent ceiling creates a housing shortage

◆ Explain how a minimum wage law creates unemployment

◆ Explain the effects of a tax

◆ Explain the effects of production quotas and subsidies

◆ Explain how markets for illegal goods work

In Toronto, where food servers and grocery clerks earn the minimum wage of $11.25 an hour, a budget one-bedroom apartment rents for $1,000 a month. For the lowest paid, that leaves $500 a month for food, clothing, and other necessities. What can governments do to help these people?

This chapter explains the effects of a minimum wage and rent ceiling, and *Economics in the News* at the end of the chapter looks at a movement that seeks an Ontario minimum wage of $15 an hour. The chapter also explains the effects of taxes, production quotas and subsidies, and laws that make trading in some things illegal.

◆ A Housing Market with a Rent Ceiling

We spend more of our income on housing than on any other good or service, so it isn't surprising that rents can be a political issue. When rents are high, or when they jump by a large amount, renters might lobby the government for limits on rents.

A government regulation that makes it illegal to charge a price higher than a specified level is called a **price ceiling** or **price cap**.

The effects of a price ceiling on a market depend crucially on whether the ceiling is imposed at a level that is above or below the equilibrium price.

A price ceiling set *above the equilibrium price* has no effect. The reason is that the price ceiling does not constrain the market forces. The force of the law and the market forces are not in conflict. But a price ceiling *below the equilibrium price* has powerful effects on a market. The reason is that the price ceiling attempts to prevent the price from regulating the quantities demanded and supplied. The force of the law and the market forces are in conflict.

When a price ceiling is applied to a housing market, it is called a **rent ceiling**. A rent ceiling set below the equilibrium rent creates:

- A housing shortage
- Increased search activity
- A black market

A Housing Shortage

At the equilibrium price, the quantity demanded equals the quantity supplied. In a housing market, when the rent is at the equilibrium level, the quantity of housing supplied equals the quantity of housing demanded and there is neither a shortage nor a surplus of housing.

But at a rent set below the equilibrium rent, the quantity of housing demanded exceeds the quantity of housing supplied—there is a shortage. So if a rent ceiling is set below the equilibrium rent, there will be a shortage of housing.

When there is a shortage, the quantity available is the quantity supplied, and somehow this quantity must be allocated among the frustrated demanders. One way in which this allocation occurs is through increased search activity.

Increased Search Activity

The time spent looking for someone with whom to do business is called **search activity**. We spend some time in search activity almost every time we make a purchase. When you're shopping for the latest hot new cellphone, and you know four stores that stock it, how do you find which store has the best deal? You spend a few minutes on the Internet, checking out the various prices. In some markets, such as the housing market, people spend a lot of time checking the alternatives available before making a choice.

When a price is regulated and there is a shortage, search activity increases. In the case of a rent-controlled housing market, frustrated would-be renters scan the newspapers, not only for housing ads but also for death notices! Any information about newly available housing is useful, and apartment seekers race to be first on the scene when news of a possible supplier breaks.

The *opportunity cost* of a good is equal not only to its price but also to the value of the search time spent finding the good. So the opportunity cost of housing is equal to the rent (a regulated price) plus the time and other resources spent searching for the restricted quantity available. Search activity is costly. It uses time and other resources, such as phone calls, automobiles, and gasoline, that could have been used in other productive ways.

A rent ceiling controls only the rent portion of the cost of housing. The cost of increased search activity might end up making the full cost of housing *higher* than it would be without a rent ceiling.

A Black Market

A rent ceiling also encourages illegal trading in a **black market**, an illegal market in which the equilibrium price exceeds the price ceiling. Black markets occur in rent-controlled housing and many other markets. For example, scalpers run black markets in tickets for big sporting events and rock concerts.

When a rent ceiling is in force, frustrated renters and landlords constantly seek ways of increasing rents. One common way is for a new tenant to pay a high price for worthless fittings, such as charging $2,000 for threadbare drapes. Another is for the tenant to pay an exorbitant price for new locks and keys—called "key money."

The level of a black market rent depends on how tightly the rent ceiling is enforced. With loose enforcement, the black market rent is close to the unregulated rent. But with strict enforcement, the black market rent is equal to the maximum price that a renter is willing to pay.

Figure 6.1 illustrates the effects of a rent ceiling. The demand curve for housing is *D* and the supply curve is *S*. A rent ceiling is imposed at $800 a month. Rents that exceed $800 a month are in the grey-shaded illegal region in the figure. You can see that the equilibrium rent, where the demand and supply curves intersect, is in the illegal region.

At a rent of $800 a month, the quantity of housing supplied is 60,000 units and the quantity demanded is 100,000 units. So with a rent of $800 a month, there is a shortage of 40,000 units of housing.

To rent the 60,000th unit, someone is willing to pay $1,200 a month. They might pay this amount by incurring search costs that bring the total cost of housing to $1,200 a month, or they might pay a black market price of $1,200 a month. Either way, they end up incurring a cost that exceeds what the equilibrium rent would be in an unregulated market.

Inefficiency of a Rent Ceiling

A rent ceiling set below the equilibrium rent results in an inefficient underproduction of housing services. The *marginal social benefit* of housing exceeds its *marginal social cost* and a deadweight loss shrinks the producer surplus and consumer surplus (Chapter 5, pp. 116–118).

Figure 6.2 shows this inefficiency. The rent ceiling ($800 per month) is below the equilibrium rent ($1,000 per month) and the quantity of housing supplied (60,000 units) is less than the efficient quantity (80,000 units).

Because the quantity of housing supplied (the quantity available) is less than the efficient quantity, a deadweight loss is created. The grey triangle illustrates this deadweight loss. Producer surplus shrinks to the blue triangle and consumer surplus shrinks to the green triangle. The red rectangle represents the potential loss from increased search activity. This loss is borne by consumers, and the full loss from the rent ceiling is the sum of the deadweight loss and the increased cost of search.

FIGURE 6.1   A Rent Ceiling

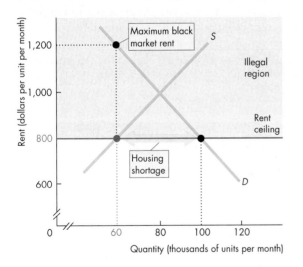

A rent above the rent ceiling of $800 a month is illegal (in the grey-shaded illegal region). At a rent of $800 a month, the quantity of housing supplied is 60,000 units. Frustrated renters spend time searching for housing and they make deals with landlords in a black market. Someone is willing to pay $1,200 a month for the 60,000th unit.

FIGURE 6.2   The Inefficiency of a Rent Ceiling

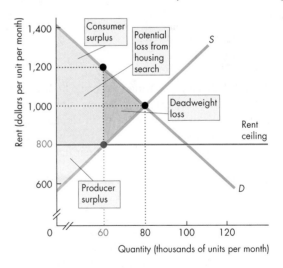

Without a rent ceiling, the market produces an efficient 80,000 units of housing at a rent of $1,000 a month. A rent ceiling of $800 a month decreases the quantity of housing supplied to 60,000 units. Producer surplus and consumer surplus shrink and a deadweight loss arises. The red rectangle represents the cost of resources used in increased search activity. The full loss from the rent ceiling equals the sum of the red rectangle and grey triangle.

Are Rent Ceilings Fair?

Rent ceilings might be inefficient, but don't they achieve a fairer allocation of scarce housing? Let's explore this question.

Chapter 5 (pp. 120–122) reviews two key ideas about fairness. According to the *fair-rules* view, anything that blocks voluntary exchange is unfair, so rent ceilings are unfair. But according to the *fair-result* view, a fair outcome is one that benefits the less well off. So according to this view, the fairest outcome is the one that allocates scarce housing to the poorest. To see whether rent ceilings help to achieve a fairer outcome in this sense, we need to consider how the market allocates scarce housing resources in the face of a rent ceiling.

Blocking rent adjustments doesn't eliminate scarcity. Rather, because it decreases the quantity of housing available, it creates an even bigger challenge for the housing market. Somehow, the market must ration a smaller quantity of housing and allocate that housing among the people who demand it.

When the rent is not permitted to allocate scarce housing, what other mechanisms are available, and are *they* fair? Some possible mechanisms are:

- A lottery
- First-come, first-served
- Discrimination

A lottery allocates housing to those who are lucky, not to those who are poor. First-come, first-served (a method used to allocate housing in England after World War II) allocates housing to those who have the greatest foresight and who get their names on a list first, not to the poorest. Discrimination allocates scarce housing based on the views and self-interest of the owner of the housing. In the case of public housing, what counts is the self-interest of the bureaucracy that administers the allocation.

In principle, self-interested owners and bureaucrats could allocate housing to satisfy some criterion of fairness, but that isn't the usual outcome. Discrimination based on friendship, family ties, and criteria such as race, ethnicity, or sex is more likely to enter the equation. We might make such discrimination illegal, but we cannot prevent it from occurring.

It is hard, then, to make a case for rent ceilings on the basis of fairness. When rent adjustments are blocked, other methods of allocating scarce housing resources operate that do not produce a fair outcome.

ECONOMICS IN ACTION

Rent Control Winners: The Rich and Famous

New York, San Francisco, London, and Paris, four of the world's great cities, have rent ceilings in some part of their housing markets. Winnipeg has rent ceilings, and Toronto had them until the late 1990s. Other Canadian cities, including Calgary, Edmonton, and Vancouver, do not have rent ceilings.

To see the effects of rent ceilings in practice we can compare the housing markets in cities with ceilings with those without ceilings. We learn two main lessons from such a comparison.

First, rent ceilings definitely create a housing shortage. Second, they do lower the rents for some but raise them for others.

A survey* conducted in the United States in 1997 showed that the rents of housing units *actually available for rent* were 2.5 times the average of all rents in New York but equal to the average rent in Philadelphia. The winners from rent ceilings are the families that have lived in a city for a long time. In New York, these families include some rich and famous ones. The voting power of the winners keeps the rent ceilings in place. Mobile newcomers are the losers in a city with rent ceilings.

The bottom line is that, in principle and in practice, rent ceilings are inefficient and unfair.

*William Tucker, "How Rent Control Drives Out Affordable Housing," Cato Policy Analysis No. 274, May 21, 1997, Cato Institute.

◆ REVIEW QUIZ

1 What is a rent ceiling and what are its effects if it is set above the equilibrium rent?
2 What are the effects of a rent ceiling that is set below the equilibrium rent?
3 How are scarce housing resources allocated when a rent ceiling is in place?
4 Why does a rent ceiling create an inefficient and unfair outcome in the housing market?

Work these questions in Study Plan 6.1 and get instant feedback.   MyLab Economics

You now know how a price ceiling (rent ceiling) works. Next, we'll learn about the effects of a price floor by studying a minimum wage in a labour market.

◆ A Labour Market with a Minimum Wage

For each one of us, the labour market is the market that influences the jobs we get and the wages we earn. Firms decide how much labour to demand, and the lower the wage rate, the greater is the quantity of labour demanded. Households decide how much labour to supply, and the higher the wage rate, the greater is the quantity of labour supplied. The wage rate adjusts to make the quantity of labour demanded equal to the quantity supplied.

When wage rates are low, or when they fail to keep up with rising prices, labour unions might turn to governments and lobby for a higher wage rate.

A government regulation that makes it illegal to charge a price lower than a specified level is called a **price floor**.

The effects of a price floor on a market depend crucially on whether the floor is imposed at a level that is above or below the equilibrium price.

A price floor set *below the equilibrium price* has no effect. The reason is that the price floor does not constrain the market forces. The force of the law and the market forces are not in conflict. But a price floor set *above the equilibrium price* has powerful effects on a market. The reason is that the price floor attempts to prevent the price from regulating the quantities demanded and supplied. The force of the law and the market forces are in conflict.

When a price floor is applied to a labour market, it is called a **minimum wage**. A minimum wage imposed at a level that is above the equilibrium wage creates unemployment. Let's look at the effects of a minimum wage.

Minimum Wage Brings Unemployment

At the market equilibrium price, the quantity demanded equals the quantity supplied. In a labour market, when the wage rate is at the equilibrium level, the quantity of labour supplied equals the quantity of labour demanded: There is neither a shortage of labour nor a surplus of labour.

But at a wage rate above the equilibrium wage, the quantity of labour supplied exceeds the quantity of labour demanded—there is a surplus of labour. So when a minimum wage is set above the equilibrium wage, there is a surplus of labour. The demand for labour determines the level of employment, and the surplus of labour is unemployed.

FIGURE 6.3   Minimum Wage and Unemployment

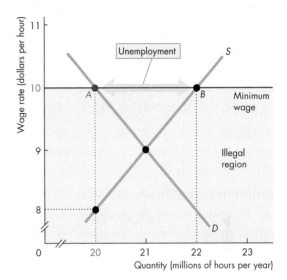

The minimum wage rate is set at $10 an hour. Any wage rate below $10 an hour is illegal (in the grey-shaded illegal region). At the minimum wage of $10 an hour, 20 million hours are hired but 22 million hours are available. Unemployment—*AB*—of 2 million hours a year is created. With only 20 million hours demanded, someone is willing to supply the 20 millionth hour for $8.

———— MyLab Economics Animation and Draw Graph ————

Figure 6.3 illustrates the effect of the minimum wage on unemployment. The demand for labour curve is *D* and the supply of labour curve is *S*. The horizontal red line shows the minimum wage set at $10 an hour. A wage rate below this level is illegal, in the grey-shaded illegal region of the figure. At the minimum wage rate, 20 million hours of labour are demanded (point *A*) and 22 million hours of labour are supplied (point *B*), so 2 million hours of available labour are unemployed.

With only 20 million hours demanded, someone is willing to supply that 20 millionth hour for $8. Frustrated unemployed workers spend time and other resources searching for hard-to-find jobs.

Is the Minimum Wage Fair?

The minimum wage is unfair on both views of fairness: It delivers an unfair *result* and imposes an unfair *rule*.

The *result* is unfair because only those people who have jobs and keep them benefit from the minimum wage. The unemployed end up worse off than they would be with no minimum wage. Some of those who search for jobs and find them end up worse off because of the increased cost of job search they incur. Also, those who search and find jobs aren't always the least well off. When the wage rate doesn't allocate labour, other mechanisms determine who finds a job. One such mechanism is discrimination, which is yet another source of unfairness.

The minimum wage imposes an unfair *rule* because it blocks voluntary exchange. Firms are willing to hire more labour and people are willing to work more, but they are not permitted by the minimum wage law to do so.

Inefficiency of a Minimum Wage

In the labour market, the supply curve measures the marginal social cost of labour to workers. This cost is leisure forgone. The demand curve measures the marginal social benefit from labour. This benefit is the value of the goods and services produced. An unregulated labour market allocates the economy's scarce labour resources to the jobs in which they are valued most highly. The market is efficient.

The minimum wage frustrates the market mechanism and results in unemployment and increased job search. At the quantity of labour employed, the marginal social benefit of labour exceeds its marginal social cost and a deadweight loss shrinks the firms' surplus and the workers' surplus.

Figure 6.4 shows this inefficiency. The minimum wage ($10 an hour) is above the equilibrium wage ($9 an hour) and the quantity of labour demanded and employed (20 million hours) is less than the efficient quantity (21 million hours).

Because the quantity of labour employed is less than the efficient quantity, a deadweight loss arises. The grey triangle illustrates this deadweight loss. The firms' surplus shrinks to the blue triangle and the workers' surplus shrinks to the green triangle. The red rectangle shows the potential loss from increased job search, which is borne by workers. The full loss from the minimum wage is the sum of the deadweight loss and the increased cost of job search.

AT **ISSUE**

Does the Minimum Wage Cause Unemployment?

Minimum wage rates in Canada are set by the provincial governments, and in October 2017 they ranged from a low of $10.72 an hour in Saskatchewan to a high of $13.60 an hour in Alberta.

Does the minimum wage result in unemployment, and if so, how much unemployment does it create?

No, It Doesn't

David Card of the University of California at Berkeley and Alan Krueger of Princeton University say:

- An increase in the minimum wage *increases teenage employment* and *decreases unemployment.*
- Their study of minimum wages in California, New Jersey, and Texas found that the employment rate of low-income workers increased following an increase in the minimum wage.
- A higher wage *increases* employment by making workers more conscientious and productive as well as less likely to quit, which lowers unproductive labour turnover.
- A higher wage rate also encourages managers to seek ways to increase labour productivity.

Yes, It Does

Michele Campolieti and Morley Gunderson of the University of Toronto and Tony Fang of the University of Northern British Columbia* say:

- A 10 percent rise in the minimum wage decreases employment by between 3 percent and 5 percent.
- They studied employment data for thousands of individuals whose wage rates were higher than the old minimum but lower than the new minimum.
- They observed how employment changed when the minimum wage changed compared to a control group in the same wage range but in provinces where the minimum wage didn't change.
- Dozens of other studies for 20 countries agree that the minimum wage kills jobs.

*Michele Campolieti, Tony Fang, and Morley Gunderson, "Minimum Wage Impacts on Youth Employment Transitions, 1993-1999," *Canadian Journal of Economics*, Vol. 38, No. 1, February 2005, pp. 81–104.

FIGURE 6.4 The Inefficiency of a Minimum Wage

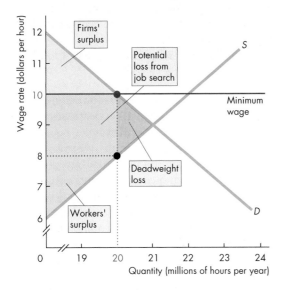

A minimum wage decreases employment. Firms' surplus (blue area) and workers' surplus (green area) shrink and a deadweight loss (grey area) arises. Job search increases and the red area shows the loss from this activity.

MyLab Economics Animation

REVIEW QUIZ

1 What is a minimum wage and what are its effects if it is set above the equilibrium wage?

2 What are the effects of a minimum wage set below the equilibrium wage?

3 Explain how scarce jobs are allocated when a minimum wage is in place.

4 Explain why a minimum wage creates an inefficient allocation of labour resources.

5 Explain why a minimum wage is unfair.

Work these questions in Study Plan 6.2 and get instant feedback. MyLab Economics

Next we're going to study a more widespread government action in markets: taxes. We'll see how taxes change prices and quantities. You will discover the surprising fact that while the government can impose a tax, it can't decide who will pay the tax! You will also see that a tax creates a deadweight loss.

 Taxes

Everything you earn and almost everything you buy is taxed. Income taxes and social security taxes are deducted from your earnings, and sales taxes such as the GST and HST are added to the bill when you buy something. Employers also pay social security taxes such as the Employment Insurance tax for their workers, and producers of tobacco products, alcoholic drinks, and gasoline pay a tax every time they sell something.

Who *really* pays these taxes? Because the income tax and social security taxes are deducted from your pay, and the sales tax is added to the prices that you pay, isn't it obvious that *you* pay these taxes? And isn't it equally obvious that your employer pays the employer's contribution to the Employment Insurance tax and that tobacco producers pay the tax on cigarettes?

You're going to discover that it isn't obvious who *really* pays a tax and that lawmakers don't make that decision.

When a transaction is taxed, there are two prices: the price that includes the tax and the price that excludes the tax. Buyers respond to the price that includes the tax while sellers respond to the price that excludes the tax.

You're about to discover that a tax is like a wedge between the price buyers pay and the price sellers receive, and that the elasticities of demand and supply determine who pays the tax, not the side of the market on which the government imposes the tax.

We begin with a definition of tax incidence.

Tax Incidence

Tax incidence is the division of the burden of a tax between buyers and sellers. When the government imposes a tax on the sale of a good (or services and factors of production—land, labour, and capital) the price paid by buyers might rise by the full amount of the tax, by a lesser amount, or not at all. If the price paid by buyers rises by the full amount of the tax, then the burden of the tax falls entirely on buyers— the buyers pay the tax. If the price paid by buyers rises by a lesser amount than the tax, then the burden of the tax falls partly on buyers and partly on sellers. And if the price paid by buyers doesn't change at all, then the burden of the tax falls entirely on sellers.

Tax incidence does not depend on the tax law. The law might impose a tax on sellers or on buyers, but the outcome is the same in either case. To see why, let's look at a tax on cigarettes.

Equivalence of a Tax on Buyers and Sellers

In April 2017, the Ontario tax on cigarettes was $3.30 a pack. To reduce the amount of smoking, is it better to hit cigarette producers with the tax when they manufacture cigarettes, or to make smokers pay the tax when they buy cigarettes?

You're going to see that the effect of the tax is the same, regardless of the side of the market on which the tax is imposed. We begin by describing the market for cigarettes with no tax.

The Market with No Tax In Fig. 6.5(a), the demand curve is *D* and the supply curve is *S*. With no tax, the equilibrium price is $6 per pack and 350 million packs a year are bought and sold.

A Tax on Sellers A tax on sellers is like a rise in their cost, so it decreases supply. To determine the position of the new supply curve, we add the tax to the minimum price that sellers are willing to accept for each quantity offered for sale. You can see that with no tax, sellers are willing to offer 350 million packs a year for $6 a pack. So with a $3 tax, sellers will offer 350 million packs a year only if the price is $9 a pack. The supply curve shifts to the red curve labelled *S + tax on sellers*.

Equilibrium occurs where the new supply curve intersects the demand curve at 325 million packs a year. The price paid by buyers rises by $2 to $8 a pack. And the price received by sellers falls by $1 to $5 a pack. So buyers pay $2 of the tax on a pack and sellers pay the other $1.

Suppose that instead of taxing sellers, Ontario taxes cigarette buyers $3 a pack.

A Tax on Buyers A tax on buyers lowers the amount they are willing to pay sellers, so it decreases demand and shifts the demand curve leftward. To determine the position of this new demand curve, we subtract the tax from the maximum price that buyers are willing to pay for each quantity bought. You can see, in Fig. 6.5(b), that with no tax, buyers are willing to buy 350 million packs a year for $6 a pack. So with a $3 tax, they are willing to buy 350 million packs a year only if the price including the tax is $6 a pack, which means that they're willing to pay sellers only $3 a pack. The demand curve shifts to become the red curve labelled *D – tax on buyers*.

Equilibrium occurs where the new demand curve intersects the supply curve at a quantity of 325 million packs a year. Sellers receive $5 a pack and buyers pay $8 a pack.

FIGURE 6.5 A Tax on Sellers or Buyers Is the Same Tax Wedge

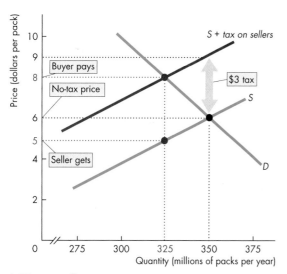

(a) Tax on sellers

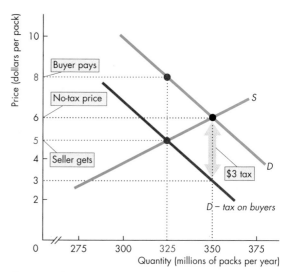

(b) Tax on buyers

With no tax, 350 million packs a year are bought and sold at $6 a pack.

In part (a), a $3 tax on sellers shifts the supply curve from *S* to *S + tax on sellers*. The equilibrium quantity decreases

to 325 million packs a year, the price buyers pay rises to $8 a pack, and the price sellers receive falls to $5 a pack.

In part (b), a $3 tax on buyers shifts the demand curve to *D – tax on buyers*. The equilibrium quantity decreases

A Tax as a Wedge You can see that the tax on buyers in Fig. 6.5(b) has the same effects as the tax on sellers in Fig. 6.5(a). In both cases, the equilibrium quantity decreases to 325 million packs a year, the price buyers pay rises to $8 a pack, and the price sellers receive falls to $5 a pack. Buyers pay $2 of the $3 tax, and sellers pay the other $1 of the tax.

In Fig. 6.5(c), the tax is like a wedge driven between the price the buyer pays and the price the seller gets. With a tax, the equilibrium quantity is no longer at the intersection of the demand and supply curves but at the quantity where the vertical gap between the curves equals the size of the tax.

Taxes and Efficiency

Because a tax drives a wedge between the price buyers pay and the price sellers receive, it results in inefficient underproduction. The price buyers pay is also the buyers' willingness to pay, which measures marginal social benefit. The price sellers receive is also the sellers' minimum supply-price, which equals marginal social cost.

A tax makes marginal social benefit exceed marginal social cost, shrinks the producer surplus and consumer surplus, and creates a deadweight loss.

Figure 6.6 shows the inefficiency of a tax on tablet computers. The demand curve, *D*, shows marginal social benefit, and the supply curve, *S*, shows marginal social cost. With no tax, the equilibrium price is $600 per tablet and the market produces the efficient quantity of 5 million tablets a week.

A $200 tax drives a $200 wedge between the price buyers pay and the price sellers receive. In this example, the price buyers pay rises by $100 per tablet and the price sellers receive falls by $100—they share the tax burden equally.

The equilibrium quantity decreases to 3 million tablets a week. Both consumer surplus and producer surplus shrink. Part of each surplus goes to the government in tax revenue—the purple area; part becomes a deadweight loss—the grey area.

In the cigarette tax example, buyers pay twice the amount of tax paid by sellers. In the tablet computer example, the tax burden is shared equally. Why are they different? The division of the burden of a tax between buyers and sellers depends on the elasticities of demand and supply. As you will now see, in special cases, either buyers or sellers pay the entire tax and, in special cases, a tax creates no deadweight loss. We begin by seeing how the elasticity of demand influences tax incidence and inefficiency.

FIGURE 6.6 Taxes and Efficiency

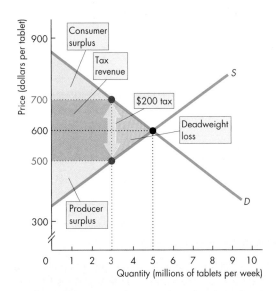

(c) Tax wedge

to 325 million packs a year, the price buyers pay rises to $8 a pack, and the price sellers receive falls to $5 a pack.

In part (c), the $3 tax drives a wedge between the price buyers pay and sellers receive.

A tax shrinks consumer surplus and producer surplus. Part of the loss of total surplus goes to the government as tax revenue and part becomes a deadweight loss.

Tax Incidence and Elasticity of Demand

To see how the elasticity of demand influences the division of the tax between buyers and sellers, we'll look at two extreme cases:

- Perfectly inelastic demand—buyers pay.
- Perfectly elastic demand—sellers pay.

Perfectly Inelastic Demand Figure 6.7(a) shows the market for insulin, a vital daily medication for those with diabetes. Demand is perfectly inelastic at 100,000 doses a day, regardless of the price, as shown by the vertical demand curve *D*. That is, a diabetic would sacrifice all other goods and services rather than not consume the insulin dose that provides good health. The supply curve of insulin is *S*. With no tax, the price is $2 a dose and the quantity is 100,000 doses a day.

If insulin is taxed at 20¢ a dose, the price buyers pay rises by that amount to $2.20 a dose. The quantity does not change, and the price drug companies receive doesn't change, so buyers pay the 20¢ tax.

Because the equilibrium quantity doesn't change, there is no underproduction and no deadweight loss from the tax when demand is perfectly inelastic.

Perfectly Elastic Demand Figure 6.7(b) shows the market for pink marker pens. Demand is perfectly elastic at $1 a pen, as shown by the horizontal demand curve *D*. If pink pens are less expensive than other colours, everyone uses pink. If pink pens are more expensive than other colours, no one uses pink. The supply curve is *S*. With no tax, the price of a pink pen is $1 and the quantity is 4,000 pens a week.

Suppose that the government imposes a tax of 10¢ a pen on pink marker pens but not on other colours. The price buyers pay remains at $1 a pen, but the price sellers receive falls by the full amount of the tax.

The new equilibrium quantity, 1,000 pink pens a week, is the quantity supplied at 90¢ ($1 minus 10¢) per pen. So, sellers pay the tax.

Because the equilibrium quantity decreases, there is underproduction and deadweight loss. Deadweight loss arises when demand is not perfectly inelastic and is largest when demand is perfectly elastic.

We've seen that when demand is perfectly inelastic, buyers pay the entire tax and when demand is perfectly elastic, sellers pay the entire tax. In the usual case, the tax is split between buyers and sellers. But the division depends on the elasticity of demand: The more inelastic the demand, the larger is the amount of the tax paid by buyers.

FIGURE 6.7　Tax and the Elasticity of Demand

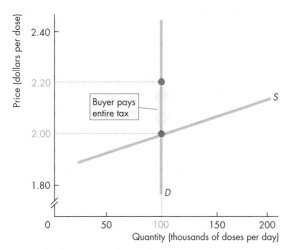

(a) Perfectly inelastic demand

In this market for insulin, demand is perfectly inelastic. With no tax, the price is $2 a dose and the quantity is 100,000 doses a day. With a 20¢ tax, buyers pay $2.20 a dose, sellers receive $2 a dose and sell 100,000 doses a day. Buyers pay the entire tax.

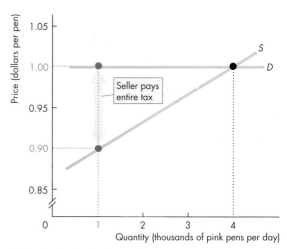

(b) Perfectly elastic demand

In this market for pink pens in part (b), demand is perfectly elastic. With no tax, the price is $1 a pen and the quantity is 4,000 pens a week. With a 10¢ tax, buyers continue to pay $1 a pen, sellers receive 90¢ a pen, and the quantity sold decreases to 1,000 a week. Sellers pay the entire tax.

Tax Incidence and Elasticity of Supply

To see how the elasticity of supply influences the division of the tax between buyers and sellers, we'll look again at two extreme cases:

- Perfectly inelastic supply—sellers pay.
- Perfectly elastic supply—buyers pay.

Perfectly Inelastic Supply Figure 6.8(a) shows the market for water from a mineral spring that flows at a constant rate that can't be controlled. Supply is perfectly inelastic at 100,000 bottles a week, as shown by the supply curve *S*. The demand curve for the water from this spring is *D*. With no tax, the price is 50¢ a bottle and the quantity is 100,000 bottles.

Suppose this spring water is taxed at 5¢ a bottle. The supply curve does not change because the spring owners still produce 100,000 bottles a week, even though the price they receive falls. But buyers are willing to buy the 100,000 bottles only if the price is 50¢ a bottle, so the price remains at 50¢ a bottle. The tax lowers the price sellers receive to 45¢ a bottle, and sellers pay the entire tax.

Because the equilibrium quantity doesn't change, there is no underproduction and deadweight loss arising from a tax when supply is perfectly inelastic.

Perfectly Elastic Supply Figure 6.8(b) shows the market for sand from which computer-chip makers extract silicon. Supply of this sand is perfectly elastic at a price of 10¢ a kilogram, as shown by the supply curve *S*. The demand curve for sand is *D*. With no tax, the price is 10¢ a kilogram and 5,000 kilograms a week are bought.

Suppose that the government imposes a sand tax of 2¢ a kilogram. The price sellers receive remains at 10¢ a kilogram, but the price buyers pay rises by the full amount of the tax. The new equilibrium quantity, 3,000 kilograms a week, is the quantity demanded at 12¢ (10¢ plus 2¢) per kilogram. So, buyers pay the tax.

Because the equilibrium quantity decreases, there is underproduction and a deadweight loss arises. A deadweight loss arises from a tax when supply is *not* perfectly inelastic and is largest when supply is perfectly elastic.

We've seen that when supply is perfectly inelastic, sellers pay the entire tax; when supply is perfectly elastic, buyers pay the entire tax. In the usual case, supply is neither perfectly inelastic nor perfectly elastic and the tax is split between buyers and sellers. But how the tax is split depends on the elasticity of supply: The more elastic the supply, the larger is the amount of the tax paid by buyers.

FIGURE 6.8 Tax and the Elasticity of Supply

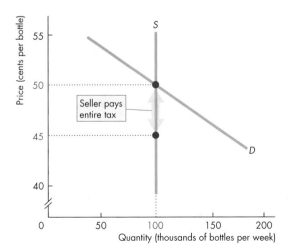

(a) Perfectly inelastic supply

In part (a) the supply of water from a mineral spring is perfectly inelastic. With no tax, the price is 50¢ a bottle. With a tax of 5¢ a bottle, the buyer continues to pay 50¢ a bottle and buy the same quantity, but the price received by sellers decreases to 45¢ a bottle. Sellers pay the entire tax.

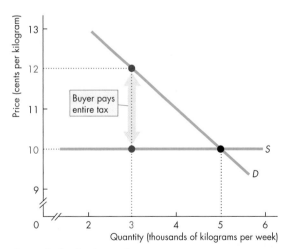

(b) Perfectly elastic supply

In part (b), the supply of sand is perfectly elastic. With no tax, the price is 10¢ a kilogram. A tax of 2¢ a kilogram raises the price buyers pay to 12¢ a kilogram and decreases the quantity they buy. Sellers continue to receive 10¢ a kilogram. So, buyers pay the entire tax.

Taxes and Fairness

We've examined the incidence and the efficiency of taxes. But when political leaders debate tax issues, it is fairness, not incidence and efficiency, that gets the most attention. The NDP complain that tax cuts are unfair because they give the benefits of lower taxes to the rich. Conservatives counter that it is fair that the rich get most of the tax cuts because they pay most of the taxes. No easy answers are available to the questions about the fairness of taxes.

Economists have proposed two conflicting principles of fairness to apply to a tax system:

- The benefits principle
- The ability-to-pay principle

The Benefits Principle The *benefits principle* is the proposition that people should pay taxes equal to the benefits they receive from the services provided by government. This arrangement is fair because it means that those who benefit most pay the most taxes. It makes tax payments and the consumption of government-provided services similar to private consumption expenditures.

The benefits principle can justify high fuel taxes to pay for highways, high taxes on alcoholic beverages and tobacco products to pay for public health-care services, and high rates of income tax on high incomes to pay for the benefits from law and order and from living in a secure environment, from which the rich might benefit more than the poor.

The Ability-to-Pay Principle The *ability-to-pay principle* is the proposition that people should pay taxes according to how easily they can bear the burden of the tax. A rich person can more easily bear the burden than a poor person can, so the ability-to-pay principle can reinforce the benefits principle to justify high rates of income tax on high incomes.

The Big Tradeoff

Questions about the fairness of taxes conflict with efficiency questions and create the *big tradeoff* that you met in Chapter 5. The taxes that generate the greatest deadweight loss are those on the income from capital. But most capital is owned by a relatively small number of people who have the greatest ability to pay taxes. So a conflict arises between efficiency and fairness. Designing a tax system that is efficient and fair is an unsolved problem.

ECONOMICS IN ACTION

Workers and Consumers Pay the Most Tax

The elasticity of the supply of labour is low and the elasticity of demand for labour is high, so workers pay most of the income taxes. The elasticities of demand for alcohol, tobacco, and gasoline are low and the elasticities of supply of these items are high, so consumers (buyers) pay more of the taxes on goods and services than producers (sellers) pay.

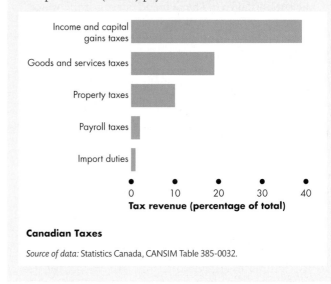

Canadian Taxes

Source of data: Statistics Canada, CANSIM Table 385-0032.

◆ REVIEW QUIZ

1 How does the elasticity of demand influence the incidence of a tax, the tax revenue, and the deadweight loss?
2 How does the elasticity of supply influence the incidence of a tax, the quantity bought, the tax revenue, and the deadweight loss?
3 Why is a tax inefficient?
4 When would a tax be efficient?
5 What are the two principles of fairness that are applied to tax systems?

Work these questions in Study Plan 6.3 and get instant feedback.   MyLab Economics

---

Your next task is to study production quotas and subsidies, tools that are used to influence the markets for farm products.

Production Quotas and Subsidies

An early or late frost, a hot dry summer, and a wet spring present just a few of the challenges that fill the lives of farmers with uncertainty and sometimes with economic hardship. Fluctuations in the weather bring fluctuations in farm output and prices and sometimes leave farmers with low incomes. To help farmers avoid low prices and low incomes, governments intervene in the markets for farm products.

Price floors that work a bit like the minimum wage that you've already studied might be used. But as you've seen, this type of government action creates a surplus and is inefficient. These same conclusions apply to the effects of a price floor for farm products.

Governments often use two other methods of intervention in the markets for farm products:

- Production quotas
- Subsidies

Production Quotas

In the markets for milk, eggs, and poultry (among others), governments have, from time to time, imposed production quotas. A **production quota** is an upper limit to the quantity of a good that may be produced in a specified period. To discover the effects of a production quota, let's look at what a production quota does to the market for milk.

Suppose that the dairy farmers want to limit total production of milk to get a higher price. They persuade the government to introduce a production quota on milk.

The effect of the production quota depends on whether it is set below or above the equilibrium quantity. If the government introduced a production quota above the equilibrium quantity, nothing would change because dairy farmers would already be producing less than the quota. But a production quota set *below the equilibrium quantity* has big effects, which are:

- A decrease in supply
- A rise in price
- A decrease in marginal cost
- Inefficient underproduction
- An incentive to cheat and overproduce

Figure 6.9 illustrates these effects.

FIGURE 6.9   The Effects of a
Production Quota

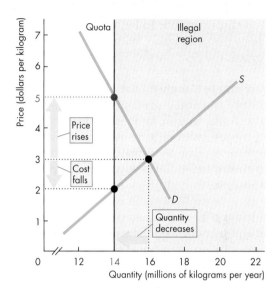

With no quota, farmers produce 16 million kilograms of milk (powder) a year and the price is $3 a kilogram. A production quota of 14 million kilograms a year restricts total production to that amount. The quantity produced decreases to 14 million kilograms a year, the price rises to $5 a kilogram, and the farmers' marginal cost falls to $2 a kilogram. Because marginal social cost (on the supply curve) is less than marginal social benefit (on the demand curve), a deadweight loss arises from the underproduction.

_____ MyLab Economics Animation _____

A Decrease in Supply A production quota on milk decreases the supply of milk. Each grower is assigned a production limit that is less than the amount that would be produced—and supplied—without the quota. The total of the growers' limits equals the quota, and any production in excess of the quota is illegal.

The quantity supplied becomes the amount permitted by the production quota, and this quantity is fixed. The supply of milk becomes perfectly inelastic at the quantity permitted under the quota.

In Fig. 6.9, with no quota, growers would produce 16 million kilograms of milk (powder) a year—the market equilibrium quantity. With a production quota set at 14 million kilograms a year, the grey-shaded area shows the illegal region. As in the case of price ceilings and price floors, market forces and political forces are in conflict in this illegal region.

The vertical red line labelled "Quota" becomes the supply curve of milk at prices above $2 a kilogram.

A Rise in Price The production quota raises the price of milk. When the government sets a production quota, it leaves market forces free to determine the price. Because the quota decreases the supply of milk, it raises the price. In Fig. 6.9, with no quota, the price is $3 a kilogram. With a quota of 14 million kilograms, the price rises to $5 a kilogram.

A Decrease in Marginal Cost The production quota lowers the marginal cost of producing milk. Marginal cost decreases because farmers produce less and stop using the resources with the highest marginal cost. Dairy farmers slide down their supply (and marginal cost) curves. In Fig. 6.9, marginal cost decreases to $2 a kilogram.

Inefficiency The production quota results in inefficient underproduction. Marginal social benefit at the quantity produced is equal to the market price, which has increased. Marginal social cost at the quantity produced has decreased and is less than the market price. So marginal social benefit exceeds marginal social cost and a deadweight loss arises.

An Incentive to Cheat and Overproduce The production quota creates an incentive for farmers to cheat and produce more than their individual production limit. With the quota, the price exceeds marginal cost, so the farmer can get a larger profit by producing one more unit. Of course, if all farmers produce more than their assigned limit, the production quota becomes ineffective, and the price falls to the equilibrium (no quota) price.

To make the production quota effective, farmers must set up a monitoring system to ensure that no one cheats and overproduces. But it is costly to set up and operate a monitoring system and it is difficult to detect and punish producers who violate their quotas.

Because of the difficulty of operating a quota, producers often lobby governments to establish a quota and provide the monitoring and punishment systems that make it work.

Subsidies

In Canada, the European Union, and the United States, the producers of many farm products, including grain, meat, milk, and eggs, receive government subsidies. A **subsidy** is a payment made by the government to a producer.

The effects of a subsidy are similar to the effects of a tax but they go in the opposite direction. These effects are:

- An increase in supply
- A fall in price and increase in quantity produced
- An increase in marginal cost
- Payments by government to farmers
- Inefficient overproduction

Figure 6.10 illustrates the effects of a subsidy to grain farmers.

An Increase in Supply In Fig. 6.10, with no subsidy, the demand curve D and the supply curve S determine the price of grain at $40 a tonne and the quantity of grain at 40 million tonnes a year.

Suppose that the government introduces a subsidy of $20 a tonne to grain farmers. A subsidy is like a negative tax. A tax is equivalent to an increase in cost, so a subsidy is equivalent to a decrease in cost. The subsidy brings an increase in supply.

To determine the position of the new supply curve, we subtract the subsidy from the farmers' minimum supply-price. In Fig. 6.10, with no subsidy, farmers are willing to offer 40 million tonnes a year at a price of $40 a tonne. With a subsidy of $20 a tonne, they will offer 40 million tonnes a year if the price is as low as $20 a tonne. The supply curve shifts to the red curve labelled $S - subsidy$.

A Fall in Price and Increase in Quantity Produced The subsidy lowers the price of grain and increases the quantity produced. In Fig. 6.10, equilibrium occurs where the new supply curve intersects the demand curve at a price of $30 a tonne and a quantity of 60 million tonnes a year.

An Increase in Marginal Cost The subsidy lowers the price paid by consumers but increases the marginal cost of growing grain. Marginal cost increases because farmers grow more grain, which means that they must begin to use some resources that are less ideal for growing grain. Farmers slide up their supply (and marginal cost) curves. In Fig. 6.10, marginal cost increases to $50 a tonne.

Payments by Government to Farmers The government pays a subsidy to farmers on each tonne of grain produced. In this example, farmers increase production to 60 million tonnes a year and receive a

FIGURE 6.10 The Effects of a Subsidy

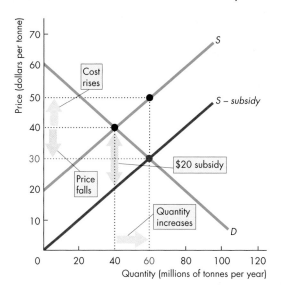

With no subsidy, farmers produce 40 million tonnes a year at $40 a tonne. A subsidy of $20 a tonne shifts the supply curve rightward to *S – subsidy*. The equilibrium quantity increases to 60 million tonnes a year, the price falls to $30 a tonne, and the price plus the subsidy received by farmers rises to $50 a tonne. In the new equilibrium, marginal social cost (on the supply curve) exceeds marginal social benefit (on the demand curve) and the subsidy results in inefficient overproduction.

—————————— MyLab Economics Animation ——————————

subsidy of $20 a tonne. So farmers receive payments from the government that total $1,200 million a year.

Inefficient Overproduction The subsidy results in inefficient overproduction. At the quantity produced with the subsidy, marginal social benefit is equal to the market price, which has fallen. Marginal social cost has increased and it exceeds the market price. Because marginal social cost exceeds marginal social benefit, the increased production brings inefficiency.

Subsidies spill over to the rest of the world. Because a subsidy lowers the domestic market price, subsidized farmers will offer some of their output for sale on the world market. The increase in supply on the world market lowers the price in the rest of the world. Faced with lower prices, farmers in other countries decrease production and receive smaller revenues.

ECONOMICS IN ACTION

Rich High-Cost Farmers the Winners

Farm subsidies are a major obstacle to achieving an efficient use of resources in the global markets for farm products and are a source of tension between rich and developing nations.

Canada, the United States, and the European Union pay their farmers subsidies, which create inefficient overproduction of food in these rich economies.

One international study concluded that Canadians would be better off if they imported all their food rather than produce any themselves!

At the same time, Canadian, U.S., and European subsidies make it more difficult for farmers in the developing nations of Africa, Asia, and Central and South America to compete in global food markets. Farmers in these countries can often produce at a lower opportunity cost than Canadian, U.S., and European farmers.

Two rich countries, Australia and New Zealand, have stopped subsidizing farmers. The result has been an improvement in the efficiency of farming in these countries. New Zealand is so efficient at producing lamb and dairy products that it has been called the Saudi Arabia of milk (an analogy to Saudi Arabia's huge oil reserve and production).

International opposition to farm subsidies is strong. Opposition to farm subsidies inside Canada, the European Union, and the United States is growing, but it isn't as strong as the pro-farm lobby, so don't expect an early end to these subsidies.

◆ **REVIEW QUIZ**

1 Summarize the effects of a production quota on the market price and the quantity produced.
2 Explain why a production quota is inefficient.
3 Explain why a voluntary production quota is difficult to operate.
4 Summarize the effects of a subsidy on the market price and the quantity produced.
5 Explain why a subsidy is inefficient.

Work these questions in Study Plan 6.4 and get instant feedback.   MyLab Economics

————————————————————————————————

Governments intervene in some markets by making it illegal to trade in a good. Let's now see how these markets work.

Markets for Illegal Goods

The markets for many goods and services are regulated, and buying and selling some goods is illegal. Examples of such goods are drugs such as cocaine, heroin, and methamphetamine.

Despite the fact that these drugs are illegal, trade in them is a multibillion-dollar business. This trade can be understood by using the same economic model and principles that explain trade in legal goods. To study the market for illegal goods, we're first going to examine the prices and quantities that would prevail if these goods were not illegal. Next, we'll see how prohibition works. Then we'll see how a tax might be used to limit the consumption of these goods.

A Free Market for a Drug

Figure 6.11 shows the market for a drug. The demand curve, D, shows that, other things remaining the same, the lower the price of the drug, the larger is the quantity of the drug demanded. The supply curve, S, shows that, other things remaining the same, the lower the price of the drug, the smaller is the quantity supplied. If the drug were not illegal, the quantity bought and sold would be Q_C and the price would be P_C.

A Market for an Illegal Drug

When a good is illegal, the cost of trading in the good increases. By how much the cost increases and who bears the cost depend on the penalties for violating the law and the degree to which the law is enforced. The larger the penalties and the better the policing, the higher are the costs. Penalties might be imposed on sellers, buyers, or both.

Penalties on Sellers Drug dealers in Canada face large penalties if their activities are detected. For example, a person found in possession of cocaine, heroin, or methamphetamine for the purpose of trafficking would receive a jail term of two years. This penalty is part of the cost of supplying illegal drugs, and it brings a decrease in supply—a leftward shift in the supply curve. To determine the new supply curve, we add the cost of breaking the law to the minimum price that drug dealers are willing to accept.

In Fig. 6.11, the cost of breaking the law by selling drugs (CBL) is added to the minimum price that dealers will accept and the supply curve shifts

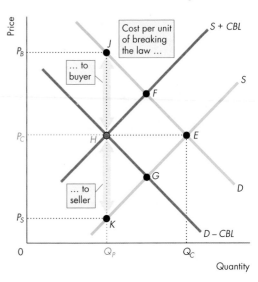

FIGURE 6.11   Market for an Illegal Good

The demand curve for drugs is D, and the supply curve is S. If drugs are not illegal, the quantity bought and sold is Q_C at a price of P_C—point E. If selling drugs is illegal, the cost of breaking the law by selling drugs (CBL) is added to the minimum supply-price and supply decreases to $S + CBL$. The market moves to point F. If buying drugs is illegal, the cost of breaking the law is subtracted from the maximum price that buyers are willing to pay, and demand decreases to $D - CBL$. The market moves to point G. With both buying and selling illegal, the supply curve and the demand curve shift and the market moves to point H. The market price remains at P_C, but the market price plus the penalty for buying rises—point J—and the market price minus the penalty for selling falls—point K.

MyLab Economics Animation

leftward to $S + CBL$. If penalties were imposed only on sellers, the market equilibrium would move from point E to point F.

Penalties on Buyers In Canada, it is illegal to *possess* drugs such as cocaine, heroin, or methamphetamine. Possession of cocaine can bring a prison term of 6 months and a fine of $1,000. Possession of heroin can bring a prison term of 7 years. Penalties fall on buyers, and the cost of breaking the law must be subtracted from the value of the good to determine the maximum price buyers are willing to pay for the drugs. Demand decreases, and the demand curve shifts leftward. In Fig. 6.11, the demand curve shifts to $D - CBL$. If penalties were imposed only on buyers, the market equilibrium would move from point E to point G.

Penalties on Both Sellers and Buyers

If penalties are imposed on both sellers *and* buyers, both supply and demand decrease and both the supply curve and the demand curve shift. In Fig. 6.11, the costs of breaking the law are the same for both buyers and sellers, so both curves shift leftward by the same amount. The market equilibrium moves to point H. The market price remains at the competitive market price P_C, but the quantity bought decreases to Q_P. Buyers pay P_C plus the cost of breaking the law, which equals P_B. Sellers receive P_C minus the cost of breaking the law, which equals P_S.

The larger the penalties and the greater the degree of law enforcement, the larger is the decrease in demand and/or supply. If the penalties are heavier on sellers, the supply curve shifts farther than the demand curve and the market price rises above P_C. If the penalties are heavier on buyers, the demand curve shifts farther than the supply curve and the market price falls below P_C. In the United States, the penalties on sellers are larger than those on buyers, so the quantity of drugs traded decreases and the market price increases compared with a free market.

With high-enough penalties and effective law enforcement, it is possible to decrease demand and/or supply to the point at which the quantity bought is zero. But in reality, such an outcome is unusual. It does not happen in Canada in the case of illegal drugs. The key reason is the high cost of law enforcement and insufficient resources for the police to achieve effective enforcement. Because of this situation, Canada is now proposing that marijuana be legalized and sold openly but also taxed at a high rate in the same way that legal drugs such as alcohol are taxed. How would such an arrangement work?

Legalizing and Taxing Drugs

From your study of the effects of taxes, it is easy to see that the quantity bought of a drug could decrease if the drug were legalized and taxed. Imposing a sufficiently high tax could decrease the supply, raise the price, and achieve the same decrease in the quantity bought as does a prohibition on drugs. The government would collect a large tax revenue. A C.D. Howe Institute study says the legalized sale of marijuana could bring tax revenues of $675 million in 2018.

Illegal Trading to Evade the Tax

It is likely that an extremely high tax rate would be needed to cut the quantity of drugs bought to the level prevailing with a prohibition. It is also likely that many drug dealers and consumers would try to cover up their activities to evade the tax. If they did act in this way, they would face the cost of breaking the law—the tax law. If the penalty for tax law violation is as severe and as effectively policed as drug-dealing laws, the analysis we've already conducted applies also to this case. The quantity of drugs bought would depend on the penalties for law breaking and on the way in which the penalties are assigned to buyers and sellers.

Taxes Versus Prohibition: Some Pros and Cons

Which is more effective: prohibition or taxes? In favour of taxes and against prohibition is the fact that the tax revenue can be used to make law enforcement more effective. It can also be used to run a more effective education campaign against illegal drug use. In favour of prohibition and against taxes is the fact that prohibition sends a signal that might influence preferences, decreasing the demand for illegal drugs. Also, some people intensely dislike the idea of the government profiting from trade in harmful substances.

◆ REVIEW QUIZ

1 How does the imposition of a penalty for selling an illegal drug influence demand, supply, price, and the quantity of the drug consumed?
2 How does the imposition of a penalty for possessing an illegal drug influence demand, supply, price, and the quantity of the drug consumed?
3 How does the imposition of a penalty for selling *or* possessing an illegal drug influence demand, supply, price, and the quantity of the drug consumed?
4 Is there any case for legalizing drugs?

Work these questions in Study Plan 6.5 and get instant feedback.   MyLab Economics

---

◆ You now know how to use the demand and supply model to predict prices, to study government actions in markets, and to study the sources and costs of inefficiency. In *Economics in the News* on pp. 148–149, you will see how to apply what you've learned by looking at the effects of the minimum wage rate in the market for low-skilled labour.

Push to Raise the Minimum Wage

Campaigners Push Liberals for $15 Minimum Wage in Ontario

CBC News
January 19, 2017

Labour groups are optimistic Premier Kathleen Wynne and her provincial Liberals will … commit to raising Ontario's minimum wage to $15 an hour.

The campaigners are hoping to persuade the Liberals with evidence that a higher minimum wage will be both politically popular and make life more comfortable for people struggling to get by.

"This government has committed to a social justice agenda, to a decent work agenda," said Pam Frache, provincial co-ordinator of the group Fight for $15 & Fairness. "Ontarians have high expectations that this government is going to do the right thing."

Ontario's current minimum wage is $11.40 an hour, after a 15-cent increase last fall. The minimum wage now rises yearly in line with the rate of inflation, following a Wynne campaign promise in the 2014 election. …

Frache pushes back against arguments that a higher minimum wage would hurt business in Ontario.

"Most small businesses will tell you the most important thing they need is customers and if workers don't have money to spend, they can't participate in the economy," Frache said in an interview Wednesday.

Figures from Statistics Canada show that 9.2 per cent of Ontario's workforce—some 540,000 people—earn minimum wage. The campaigners estimate that nearly 1.5 million workers in the province earn less than $15 an hour.

The Liberals are publicly non-committal about adopting the $15 target in time for the June 2018 election. …

ESSENCE OF THE STORY

- Labour groups want the Ontario government to raise the province's minimum wage to $15 an hour.

- Ontario's current minimum wage is $11.40 an hour and it rises yearly in line with the inflation rate.

- Pam Frache of Fight for $15 & Fairness says a higher minimum wage would not hurt business in Ontario.

- Currently, 0.5 million Ontario workers earn the minimum wage.

- An estimated 1.5 million Ontario workers earn less than $15 an hour.

ECONOMIC ANALYSIS

- The news article reports that an Ontario labour organization wants the provincial minimum wage rate raised to $15 per hour.

- The Ontario minimum wage was $11.40 an hour in 2017 and linked to the cost of living.

- Supporters of the increase believe that employment would not be adversely affected, and argue that the higher minimum wage would be good for business because workers would have more to spend.

- The alternative and standard view is that a higher minimum wage set above the market equilibrium wage rate would decrease the quantity of labour demanded and increase the unemployment rate.

- The figures illustrate these two views about the effect of a higher minimum wage rate.

- Figure 1 illustrates a market for low-skilled labour in which the minimum wage rate equals the market equilibrium wage rate.

- The demand for labour is D_0 and the supply of labour is S_0, so the equilibrium wage rate is $15 an hour, which is also the minimum wage rate.

- Because the equilibrium wage rate equals the minimum wage rate, the quantity of labour demanded equals the quantity of labour supplied and the minimum wage rate has no effect on the market outcome.

- Figure 2 illustrates a market for low-skilled labour in which the equilibrium wage rate is below the minimum wage rate.

- The demand for labour is D_1 and the supply of labour is S_1, so the equilibrium wage rate is $14 an hour.

- The minimum wage rate is $15 an hour, and the quantity of labour employed equals the quantity demanded at the minimum wage rate.

- The quantity of labour demanded and employed is 1.4 million workers (an assumed quantity).

- At the equilibrium wage rate, the quantity of labour supplied is 1.6 million workers (also an assumed quantity), so 200,000 workers are unemployed.

- With the equilibrium wage rate less than the minimum wage rate, the quantity of labour demanded is less than the quantity of labour supplied and the minimum wage rate brings an increase in unemployment.

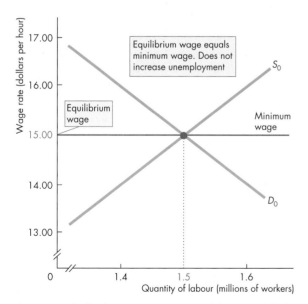

Figure 1 Fight for $15 & Fairness View of the Low-Skilled Labour Market

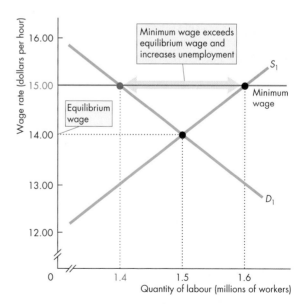

Figure 2 Alternative View of the Low-Skilled Labour Market

WORKED PROBLEM

MyLab Economics Work this problem in Chapter 6 Study Plan.

The table gives the demand and supply schedules for tickets to a concert in the park.

Price (dollars per ticket)	Quantity demanded	Quantity supplied
	(tickets per concert)	
5	600	200
6	500	300
7	400	400
8	300	500
9	200	600
10	100	700

Questions

1. If there is no tax on concert tickets, what is the price of a ticket and how many tickets are bought?

If a sales tax of $2 a ticket is levied on sellers of concert tickets:

2. What is the price a concert-goer pays for a ticket and how many tickets are bought?

3. Who pays the tax and what is the government's tax revenue?

4. Is the market for concert tickets efficient? Explain.

Solutions

1. With no sales tax on concert tickets, the price of a ticket is the market equilibrium price, which is $7 a ticket. At $7 a ticket, the quantity of tickets bought is 400 per concert.

2. With a sales tax of $2 a ticket levied on sellers of concert tickets, the supply of tickets decreases. It decreases because at any ticket price paid by buyers, concert organizers will receive $2 less per ticket.

   For example, concert organizers are willing to supply 700 tickets per concert if they receive $10 a ticket. But with a tax of $2 a ticket, concert organizers will receive only $8 a ticket after paying the government the $2 tax per ticket. So concert organizers will not be willing to supply 700 tickets at the after-tax price of $8 a ticket. The table above tells us that concert organizers are willing to supply only 500 tickets per concert when they receive $8 a ticket.

   We need to create the new supply schedule. We have already found one point on the new supply schedule: At a market price of $10 a ticket, concert organizers are willing to supply 500 tickets.

   The table in the next column shows the new supply schedule.

Price (dollars per ticket)	Quantity demanded	New quantity supplied
	(tickets per concert)	
6	500	
7	400	200
8	**300**	**300**
9	200	400
10	100	500

Check that you can explain why at a market price of $7 a ticket, concert organizers are willing to supply 400 tickets when tickets are not taxed but only 200 tickets when tickets are taxed $2 per ticket.

With the $2 tax, concert-goers pay $8 a ticket and buy 300 tickets.

Key Point: A sales tax raises the market price and the quantity bought decreases.

3. If a sales tax of $2 a ticket is levied on concert tickets, the price concert-goers pay rises from $7 a ticket to $8 a ticket. So concert-goers pay $1 of the $2 tax. The other $1 of tax is paid by concert organizers.

   The government's tax revenue is $2 × 300, or $600.

Key Point: Some of the tax is paid by buyers and some by sellers.

4. With no tax, 400 tickets bought per concert is the efficient outcome. With the tax, the ticket price rises and the quantity bought decreases to 300 per concert. The outcome is inefficient and a deadweight loss arises.

Key Point: A sales tax that decreases the quantity sold is inefficient and creates a deadweight loss.

Key Figure

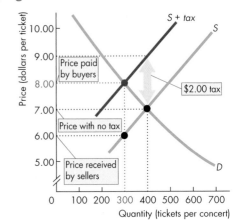

MyLab Economics Interactive Animation

SUMMARY

Key Points

A Housing Market with a Rent Ceiling (pp. 132–134)

- A rent ceiling that is set above the equilibrium rent has no effect.
- A rent ceiling that is set below the equilibrium rent creates a housing shortage, increased search activity, and a black market.
- A rent ceiling that is set below the equilibrium rent is inefficient and unfair.

Working Problems 1 and 2 will give you a better understanding of a housing market with a rent ceiling.

A Labour Market with a Minimum Wage (pp. 135–137)

- A minimum wage set below the equilibrium wage rate has no effect.
- A minimum wage set above the equilibrium wage rate creates unemployment and increases the amount of time people spend searching for a job.
- A minimum wage set above the equilibrium wage rate is inefficient, unfair, and hits low-skilled young people hardest.

Working Problems 3 and 4 will give you a better understanding of a labour market with a minimum wage.

Taxes (pp. 137–142)

- A tax raises the price paid by buyers, but usually by less than the tax.
- The elasticity of demand and the elasticity of supply determine the share of a tax paid by buyers and sellers.

- The less elastic the demand or the more elastic the supply, the larger is the share of the tax paid by buyers.
- If demand is perfectly elastic or supply is perfectly inelastic, sellers pay the entire tax. And if demand is perfectly inelastic or supply is perfectly elastic, buyers pay the entire tax.

Working Problem 5 will give you a better understanding of taxes.

Production Quotas and Subsidies (pp. 143–145)

- A production quota leads to inefficient underproduction, which raises the price.
- A subsidy is like a negative tax. It lowers the price, increases the cost of production, and leads to inefficient overproduction.

Working Problems 6 and 7 will give you a better understanding of production quotas and subsidies.

Markets for Illegal Goods (pp. 146–147)

- Penalties on sellers increase the cost of selling the good and decrease the supply of the good.
- Penalties on buyers decrease their willingness to pay and decrease the demand for the good.
- Penalties on buyers and sellers decrease the quantity of the good, raise the price buyers pay, and lower the price sellers receive.
- Legalizing and taxing can achieve the same outcome as penalties on buyers and sellers.

Working Problem 8 will give you a better understanding of markets for illegal goods.

Key Terms

MyLab Economics Key Terms Quiz

Black market, 132
Minimum wage, 135
Price cap, 132
Price ceiling, 132

Price floor, 135
Production quota, 143
Rent ceiling, 132
Search activity, 132

Subsidy, 144
Tax incidence, 137

STUDY PLAN PROBLEMS AND APPLICATIONS

MyLab Economics Work Problems 1 to 8 in Chapter 6 Study Plan and get instant feedback.

A Housing Market with a Rent Ceiling (Study Plan 6.1)

Use the following graph of the market for rental housing in Townsville to work Problems 1 and 2.

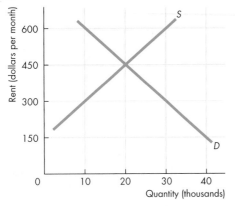

1. a. What are the equilibrium rent and the quantity of housing rented?

    b. If a rent ceiling is set at $600 a month, what is the rent paid? What is the shortage of housing?

2. If the rent ceiling is $300 a month, what is the quantity rented, the shortage of housing, and the maximum price that someone is willing to pay for the last unit of housing available?

A Labour Market with a Minimum Wage (Study Plan 6.2)

Use the following data on the demand and supply schedules of teenage labour to work Problems 3 and 4.

Wage rate (dollars per hour)	Quantity demanded	Quantity supplied
	(hours per month)	
6	2,500	1,500
7	2,000	2,000
8	1,500	2,500
9	1,000	3,000

3. Calculate the equilibrium wage rate, the hours worked, and the quantity of unemployment.

4. The minimum wage for teenagers is $8 an hour.

    a. How many hours are unemployed?

    b. If the demand for teenage labour increases by 500 hours a month, what is the wage rate and how many hours are unemployed?

Taxes (Study Plan 6.3)

5. The table in the next column sets out the demand and supply schedules for chocolate brownies.

Price (cents per brownie)	Quantity demanded	Quantity supplied
	(millions per day)	
50	5	3
60	4	4
70	3	5
80	2	6

    a. If sellers are taxed 20¢ a brownie, what is the price and who pays the tax?

    b. If buyers are taxed 20¢ a brownie, what is the price and who pays the tax?

Production Quotas and Subsidies (Study Plan 6.4)

Use the following data to work Problems 6 and 7. The demand and supply schedules for rice are:

Price (dollars per box)	Quantity demanded	Quantity supplied
	(boxes per week)	
1.20	3,000	1,500
1.30	2,750	2,000
1.40	2,500	2,500
1.50	2,250	3,000
1.60	2,000	3,500

Calculate the price, the marginal cost of rice, and the quantity produced if the government:

6. Sets a production quota of 2,000 boxes a week.

7. Introduces a subsidy of $0.30 a box.

Markets for Illegal Goods (Study Plan 6.5)

8. The figure shows the market for an illegal good.

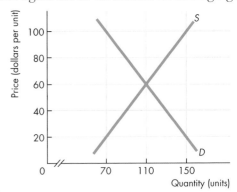

Calculate the market price and the quantity bought if a penalty of $20 a unit is imposed on:

    a. Sellers only or buyers only.

    b. Both sellers and buyers.

ADDITIONAL PROBLEMS AND APPLICATIONS

MyLab Economics You can work these problems in Homework or Test if assigned by your instructor.

A Housing Market with a Rent Ceiling

Use the following table to work Problems 9 and 10. The table sets out the demand and supply schedules for college meals.

Price (dollars per meal)	Quantity demanded	Quantity supplied
	(meals per week)	
4	3,000	1,500
5	2,750	2,000
6	2,500	2,500
7	2,250	3,000
8	2,000	3,500

9. a. What is the market equilibrium?

   b. If the college put a price ceiling on meals at $7 a meal, what is the price students pay for a meal? How many meals do they buy?

10. If the college put a price ceiling on meals at $4 a meal, what is the quantity bought, the shortage of meals, and the maximum price that someone is willing to pay for the last meal available?

A Labour Market with a Minimum Wage

Use the following news clip to work Problems 11 and 12.

E.U. Minimum Wage

Bulgaria has the lowest minimum wage in the European Union (E.U.), but its level has doubled. The minimum wage in Greece has fallen.

> Source: Euronews, February 10, 2017

Assume that in both countries, the minimum wage is above the equilibrium wage.

11. What is the effect of the changes in the minimum wage on the quantity of labour employed in Bulgaria and in Greece?

12. Explain the effect of the change in the minimum wage on the workers' surplus, the firms' surplus, and the efficiency of the market for low-skilled workers in Bulgaria and in Greece.

Taxes

13. The government wants to discourage the consumption of sugary drinks and proposes introducing a 20 percent tax on them. A survey shows that the demand for sugary drinks is perfectly elastic and people are equally happy to stop consuming those drinks and switch to healthier alternatives. Producers of sugary drinks complain and say they will increase their prices by 20 percent. Explain, and illustrate with a graph, why sugary drinks producers are wrong.

14. The demand and supply schedules for tulips are:

Price (dollars per bunch)	Quantity demanded	Quantity supplied
	(bunches per week)	
10	100	40
12	90	60
14	80	80
16	70	100
18	60	120

   a. If tulips are not taxed, what is the price and how many bunches are bought?

   b. If tulips are taxed $6 a bunch, what are the price and quantity bought? Who pays the tax?

15. **New Brunswick Government to Boost Taxes on Tobacco**

   The New Brunswick tax on cigarettes will jump to $6.25 for a 25-cigarette pack—without HST. A regular pack of cigarettes now costs up to $13. Jeff Elliott, a seller of cigarettes and a smoker said, "I enjoy smoking so I'll pay whatever the difference is I guess." Smokers told CBC that they were unlikely to quit despite taxes going up.

   > Source: *CBC News*, February 1, 2017

   a. How will the New Brunswick market for cigarettes respond to the tax increase?

   b. What do the statements about smokers' responses to the cigarette tax imply about the elasticity of demand for cigarettes?

   c. Why does a rise in the cigarette tax bring an increase in tax revenue?

Production Quotas and Subsidies

Use the following news clip to work Problems 16 to 18.

Farmers Get Biggest Subsidy Check in Decade

In 2016, 25 percent of an estimated $55 billion farm profit will come from government. Since 2012, global corn and soybean output has increased faster than demand and prices have tumbled. The subsidies law of 2014 ties subsidies to prices—low prices trigger high subsidies.

> Source: *Bloomberg*, April 12, 2016

16. a. Why are U.S. soybean farmers subsidized?

    b. Explain how a subsidy paid to soybean farmers affects the price of soybean and the marginal cost of producing it.

17. Explain how a subsidy paid to soybean farmers affects the consumer surplus and the producer surplus from soybean. Does the subsidy make the soybean market more efficient or less efficient? Explain.

18. In the market for corn, explain why the corn price has fallen and explain how an increased subsidy influences the price and quantity of corn.

Use the following figure, which shows the market for tomatoes, to work Problems 19 and 20.

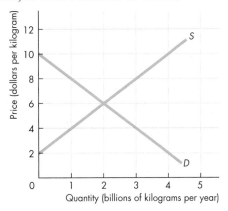

19. If the government subsidizes growers at $4 a kilogram, what is the quantity produced, the quantity demanded, and the subsidy paid to growers?

20. If the government subsidizes tomato growers at $4 a kilogram, who gains and who loses from the subsidy? What is the deadweight loss? Could the subsidy be regarded as being fair?

Markets for Illegal Goods

21. The table gives the demand and supply schedules for an illegal drug.

Price (dollars per unit)	Quantity demanded	Quantity supplied
	(units per day)	
50	500	300
60	400	400
70	300	500
80	200	600
90	100	700

    a. What is the price and how many units are bought if there is no penalty on drugs?

    b. If the penalty on sellers is $20 a unit, what are the price and quantity consumed?

    c. If the penalty on buyers is $20 a unit, what are the price and quantity consumed?

Economics in the News

22. Study *Economics in the News* on pp. 148–149, and note that the Ontario minimum wage is linked to the cost of the things that people buy. Then answer the following questions.

    a. How would you expect the demand for and supply of low-skilled labour to have changed in 2017?

    b. How would you expect the equilibrium wage rate of low-skilled labour to have changed in 2017?

    c. How would you expect a $15 minimum wage to change employment and unemployment in 2018?

    d. Draw a graph to illustrate your answers to parts (a), (b), and (c).

23. **Pot Legalization Brings Fears of Social Costs**

    A C.D. Howe Institute study says the legalized sale of marijuana could bring tax revenues of $675 million in 2018. But if governments get too greedy, consumers will go to the black market as they do for cigarettes. There are deepening concerns about the increased use of pot when it is legalized.

    Source: *The Gazette*, Montreal, April 13, 2017

    Assume that the marginal cost of producing a gram of marijuana (legal or illegal) is a constant $5 and that legal marijuana bears a tax of $2 per gram.

    a. Draw a graph of the market for marijuana, assuming that there are no penalties on either buyers or sellers for breaking the law.

    b. How does the tax of $2 change the market outcome? Show the effects in your graph.

    c. With no penalty on buyers, if a penalty for breaking the law is imposed on sellers at more than $2 per gram, how does the market work and what is the equilibrium price?

    d. With no penalty on sellers, if a penalty of more than $2 per gram is imposed on buyers for breaking the law, how does the market work? What is the equilibrium price?

    e. What is the marginal benefit of an illegal gram of marijuana in the situations described in parts (c) and (d)?

    f. Can legalizing and taxing marijuana achieve the same quantity of marijuana use as occurs if marijuana is illegal?

7

GLOBAL MARKETS IN ACTION

After studying this chapter, you will be able to:

◆ Explain how markets work with international trade

◆ Identify the gains from international trade and its winners and losers

◆ Explain the effects of international trade barriers

◆ Explain and evaluate arguments used to justify restricting international trade

iPhones, Wii games, and Nike shoes are just three of the items that you might buy that are not produced in Canada. Why don't we produce phones, games, and shoes in Canada? Isn't the globalization of production killing good Canadian jobs?

You will find the answers in this chapter. You will see that global trade is a win-win deal and also why governments restrict trade.

In *Economics in the News* at the end of the chapter, you'll see why Donald Trump's ideas about NAFTA and tariffs would end up costing Americans as well as Canadians and Mexicans. But first, we study the gains from international trade.

How Global Markets Work

Because we trade with people in other countries, the goods and services that we can buy and consume are not limited by what we can produce. The goods and services that we buy from other countries are our **imports**, and the goods and services that we sell to people in other countries are our **exports**.

International Trade Today

Global trade today is enormous. In 2016, global exports and imports were $21 trillion, which is one-third of the value of global production. The United States is the world's largest international trader and accounts for 10 percent of world exports and 12 percent of world imports. Germany and China, which rank 2 and 3 behind the United States, lag by a large margin.

In 2016, total Canadian exports were $629 billion, which is 31 percent of the value of Canadian production. Total Canadian imports were $677 billion, which is about 33 percent of total expenditure in Canada.

We trade both goods and services. In 2016, exports of services were about 17 percent of total exports and imports of services were about 19 percent of total imports.

What Drives International Trade?

Comparative advantage is the fundamental force that drives international trade. Comparative advantage (see Chapter 2, p. 40) is a situation in which a person can perform an activity or produce a good or service at a lower opportunity cost than anyone else. This same idea applies to nations. We can define *national comparative advantage* as a situation in which a nation can perform an activity or produce a good or service at a lower opportunity cost than any other nation.

The opportunity cost of producing a T-shirt is lower in China than in Canada, so China has a comparative advantage in producing T-shirts. The opportunity cost of producing a regional jet is lower in Canada than in China, so Canada has a comparative advantage in producing regional jets.

You saw in Chapter 2 how Liz and Joe reap gains from trade by specializing in the production of the good at which they have a comparative advantage and then trading with each other. Both are better off.

This same principle applies to trade among nations. Because China has a comparative advantage

ECONOMICS IN ACTION

We Trade Metals for Consumer Goods

The figure shows Canada's four largest exports and imports by value. Motor vehicles and parts are our biggest exports and second biggest imports. Consumer goods are our biggest imports. We export ores, oil, and lumber and import machinery and equipment.

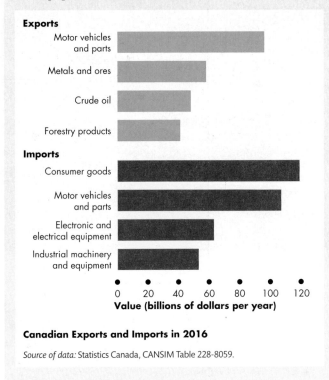

Canadian Exports and Imports in 2016

Source of data: Statistics Canada, CANSIM Table 228-8059.

at producing T-shirts and Canada has a comparative advantage at producing regional jets, the people of both countries can gain from specialization and trade. China can buy regional jets from Canada at a lower opportunity cost than that at which Chinese firms can produce them. And Canadians can buy T-shirts from China at a lower opportunity cost than that at which Canadian firms can produce them. Also, through international trade, Chinese producers can get higher prices for their T-shirts and Canadian firms can sell regional jets for a higher price. Both countries gain from international trade.

Let's now illustrate the gains from trade that we've just described by studying demand and supply in the global markets for T-shirts and regional jets.

Why Canada Imports T-Shirts

Canada imports T-shirts because the rest of the world has a comparative advantage in producing T-shirts. Figure 7.1 illustrates how this comparative advantage generates international trade and how trade affects the price of a T-shirt and the quantities produced and bought.

The demand curve D_C and the supply curve S_C show the demand and supply in the Canadian domestic market only. The demand curve tells us the quantity of T-shirts that Canadians are willing to buy at various prices. The supply curve tells us the quantity of T-shirts that Canadian garment makers are willing to sell at various prices—that is, the quantity supplied at each price when all T-shirts sold in Canada are produced in Canada.

Figure 7.1(a) shows what the Canadian T-shirt market would be like with no international trade.

The price of a shirt would be $8 and 4 million shirts a year would be produced by Canadian garment makers and bought by Canadian consumers.

Figure 7.1(b) shows the market for T-shirts with international trade. Now the price of a T-shirt is determined in the world market, not the Canadian domestic market. The world price of a T-shirt is less than $8, which means that the rest of the world has a comparative advantage in producing T-shirts. The world price line shows the world price at $5 a shirt.

The Canadian demand curve, D_C, tells us that at $5 a shirt, Canadians buy 6 million shirts a year. The Canadian supply curve, S_C, tells us that at $5 a shirt, Canadian garment makers produce 2 million T-shirts a year. To buy 6 million T-shirts when only 2 million are produced in Canada, we must import T-shirts from the rest of the world. The quantity of T-shirts imported is 4 million a year.

FIGURE 7.1   A Market with Imports

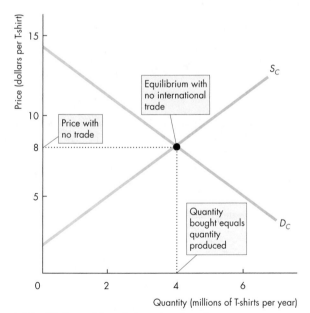

(a) Equilibrium with no international trade

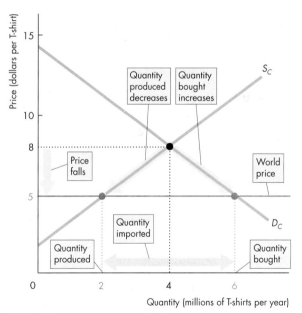

(b) Equilibrium in a market with imports

Part (a) shows the Canadian market for T-shirts with no international trade. The Canadian domestic demand curve D_C and Canadian domestic supply curve S_C determine the price of a T-shirt at $8 and the quantity of T-shirts produced and bought in Canada at 4 million a year.

Part (b) shows the Canadian market for T-shirts with international trade. World demand for and world supply of

T-shirts determine the world price of a T-shirt, which is $5. The price in the Canadian market falls to $5 a shirt. Canadian purchases of T-shirts increase to 6 million a year, and Canadian production of T-shirts decreases to 2 million a year. Canada imports 4 million T-shirts a year.

Why Canada Exports Regional Jets

Figure 7.2 illustrates international trade in regional jets. The demand curve D_C and the supply curve S_C show the demand and supply in the Canadian domestic market only. The demand curve tells us the quantity of regional jets that Canadian airlines are willing to buy at various prices. The supply curve tells us the quantity of regional jets that Canadian aircraft makers are willing to sell at various prices.

Figure 7.2(a) shows what the Canadian regional jet market would be like with no international trade. The price of a regional jet would be $100 million and 40 airplanes a year would be produced by Bombardier and bought by Canadian airlines.

Figure 7.2(b) shows the Canadian airplane market with international trade. Now the price of a regional jet is determined in the world market and the world price of a regional jet is higher than $100 million, which means that Canada has a comparative advantage

in producing regional jets. The world price line shows the world price at $150 million.

The Canadian demand curve, D_C, tells us that at $150 million each, Canadian airlines buy 20 regional jets a year. The Canadian supply curve, S_C, tells us that at $150 million each, Bombardier produces 70 regional jets a year. The quantity produced in Canada (70 a year) minus the quantity purchased by Canadian airlines (20 a year) is the quantity exported, which is 50 regional jets a year.

◆ REVIEW QUIZ

1 Describe the situation in the market for a good or service that Canada imports.
2 Describe the situation in the market for a good or service that Canada exports.

Work these questions in Study Plan 7.1 and get instant feedback. MyLab Economics

---

FIGURE 7.2 A Market with Exports

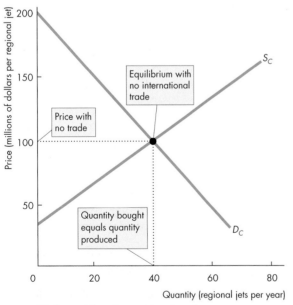

(a) Equilibrium without international trade

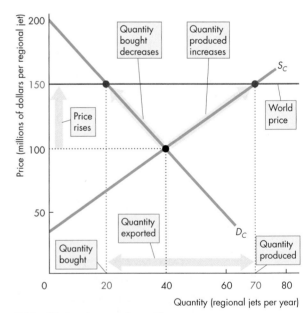

(b) Equilibrium in a market with exports

In part (a), the Canadian market with no international trade, the domestic demand curve D_C and the domestic supply curve S_C determine the price of a regional jet in Canada at $100 million and 40 regional jets are produced and bought each year.

In part (b), the Canadian market with international trade, world demand and world supply determine the world price of a regional jet at $150 million. The price in Canada rises. Canadian production increases to 70 a year, Canadian purchases decrease to 20 a year, and Canada exports 50 regional jets a year.

Winners, Losers, and the Net Gain from Trade

In Chapter 1 (see p. 6), we asked whether globalization is in the self-interest of the low-wage worker in Malaysia who sews your new running shoes and the displaced shoemaker in Toronto. Is globalization in the social interest? We're now going to answer these questions. You will learn why producers complain about cheap foreign imports, but consumers of imports never complain.

Gains and Losses from Imports

We measure the gains and losses from imports by examining their effect on consumer surplus, producer surplus, and total surplus. In the importing country the winners are those whose surplus increases and the losers are those whose surplus decreases.

Figure 7.3(a) shows what consumer surplus and producer surplus would be with no international trade in T-shirts. Domestic demand, D_C, and domestic supply, S_C, determine the price and quantity. The green area shows consumer surplus and the blue area shows producer surplus. Total surplus is the sum of consumer surplus and producer surplus.

Figure 7.3(b) shows how these surpluses change when the Canadian market opens to imports. The price in Canada falls to the world price. The quantity bought increases to the quantity demanded at the world price and consumer surplus expands from A to the larger green area $A + B + D$. The quantity produced in Canada decreases to the quantity supplied at the world price and producer surplus shrinks to the smaller blue area C.

Part of the gain in consumer surplus, the area B, is a loss of producer surplus—a redistribution of total surplus. But the other part of the increase in consumer surplus, the area D, is a net gain. This increase in total surplus results from the lower price and increased purchases and is the gain from imports.

FIGURE 7.3   Gains and Losses in a Market with Imports

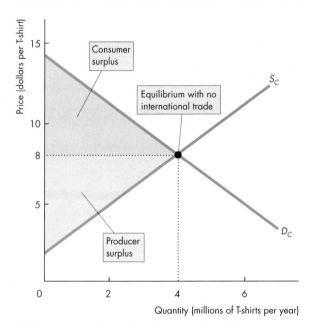

(a) Consumer surplus and producer surplus with no international trade

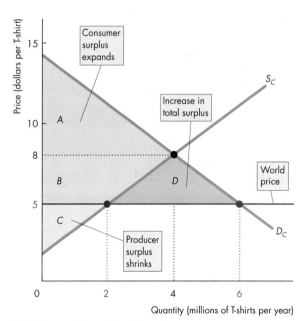

(b) Gains and losses from imports

In part (a), with no international trade, the green area shows the consumer surplus and the blue area shows the producer surplus.

In part (b), with international trade, the price falls to the world price of $5 a shirt. Consumer surplus expands from area A to the area $A + B + D$. Producer surplus shrinks to area C. Area B is a transfer of surplus from producers to consumers. Area D is an increase in total surplus—the gain from imports.

Gains and Losses from Exports

We measure the gains and losses from exports just like we measured those from imports, by their effect on consumer surplus, producer surplus, and total surplus.

Figure 7.4(a) shows the situation with no international trade. Domestic demand, D_C, and domestic supply, S_C, determine the price and quantity, the consumer surplus, and the producer surplus.

Figure 7.4(b) shows how the consumer surplus and producer surplus change when the good is exported. The price rises to the world price. The quantity bought decreases to the quantity demanded at the world price and the consumer surplus shrinks to the green area A. The quantity produced increases to the quantity supplied at the world price and the producer surplus expands to the blue area $B + C + D$.

Part of the gain in producer surplus, the area B, is a loss in consumer surplus—a redistribution of the total surplus. But the other part of the increase in producer surplus, the area D, is a net gain. This increase in total surplus results from the higher price and increased production and is the gain from exports.

Gains for All

You've seen that both imports and exports bring gains. Because one country's exports are other countries' imports, international trade brings gain for all countries. International trade is a win-win game.

FIGURE 7.4 Gains and Losses in a Market with Exports

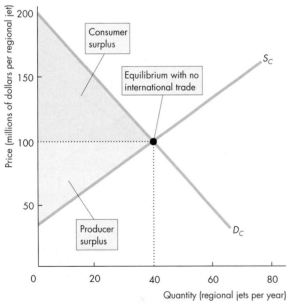

(a) Consumer surplus and producer surplus with no international trade

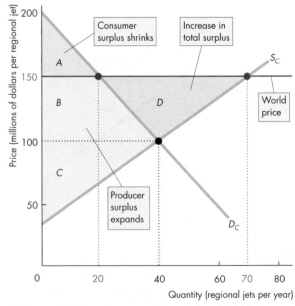

(b) Gains and losses from exports

In part (a), the Canadian market with no international trade, the green area shows the consumer surplus and the blue area shows the producer surplus. In part (b), the Canadian market with international trade, the price rises to the world price. Consumer surplus shrinks to area A. Producer surplus expands from area C to the area $B + C + D$. Area B is a transfer of surplus from consumers to producers. Area D is an increase in total surplus—the gain from exports.

◆ International Trade Restrictions

Governments use four sets of tools to influence international trade and protect domestic industries from foreign competition. They are:

- Tariffs
- Import quotas
- Other import barriers
- Export subsidies

Tariffs

A **tariff** is a tax on a good that is imposed by the importing country when an imported good crosses its international boundary. For example, the government of India imposes a 100 percent tariff on wine imported from Ontario. So when an Indian imports a $10 bottle of Ontario wine, he pays the Indian government a $10 import duty.

Tariffs raise revenue for governments and serve the self-interest of people who earn their incomes in import-competing industries. But as you will see, restrictions on free international trade decrease the gains from trade and are not in the social interest.

The Effects of a Tariff To see the effects of a tariff, let's return to the example in which Canada imports T-shirts. With free trade, the T-shirts are imported and sold at the world price. Then, under pressure from Canadian garment makers, the government imposes a tariff on imported T-shirts. Buyers of T-shirts must now pay the world price plus the tariff. Several consequences follow and Fig. 7.5 illustrates them.

Figure 7.5(a) shows the situation with free international trade. Canada produces 2 million T-shirts a year and imports 4 million a year at the world price of $5 a shirt. Figure 7.5(b) shows what happens when the Canadian government imposes a tariff of $2 per T-shirt.

FIGURE 7.5   The Effects of a Tariff

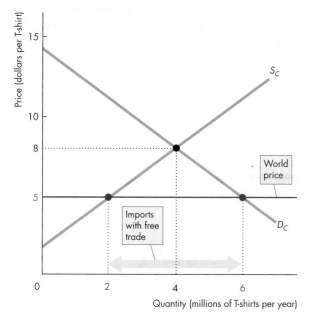

(a) Free trade

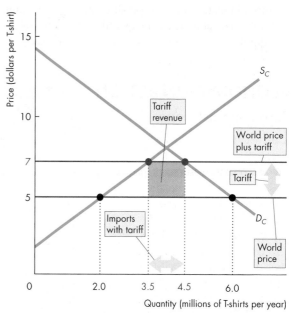

(b) Market with tariff

The world price of a T-shirt is $5. With free trade in part (a), Canadians buy 6 million T-shirts a year. Canadian garment makers produce 2 million T-shirts a year and Canada imports 4 million a year.

With a tariff of $2 per T-shirt in part (b), the price in

Canada rises to $7 a T-shirt. Canadian production increases, Canadian purchases decrease, and the quantity imported decreases. The Canadian government collects a tariff revenue of $2 on each T-shirt imported, which is shown by the purple rectangle.

MyLab Economics Animation

The following changes occur in the market for T-shirts in Canada:

- The price of a T-shirt rises by $2.
- The quantity of T-shirts bought decreases.
- The quantity of T-shirts produced in Canada increases.
- The quantity of T-shirts imported into Canada decreases.
- The Canadian government collects a tariff revenue.

Rise in Price of a T-Shirt To buy a T-shirt, Canadians must pay the world price plus the tariff, so the price of a T-shirt rises by the $2 tariff to $7. Figure 7.5(b) shows the new domestic price line, which lies $2 above the world price line. The price rises by the full amount of the tariff. The buyer pays the entire tariff because supply from the rest of the world is perfectly elastic (see Chapter 6, p. 141).

Decrease in Purchases The higher price of a T-shirt brings a decrease in the quantity demanded along the demand curve. Figure 7.5(b) shows the decrease from 6 million T-shirts a year at $5 a shirt to 4.5 million a year at $7 a shirt.

Increase in Domestic Production The higher price of a T-shirt stimulates domestic production, and Canadain garment makers increase the quantity supplied along the supply curve. Figure 7.5(b) shows the increase from 2 million T-shirts at $5 a shirt to 3.5 million a year at $7 a shirt.

Decrease in Imports T-shirt imports decrease from 4 million to 1 million a year. Both the decrease in Canadian purchases and the increase in Canadian production contribute to the 3 milion decrease in Canadian imports.

Tariff Revenue The government's tariff revenue is $2 million—$2 per shirt on 1 million imported shirts—shown by the purple rectangle.

Winners, Losers, and the Social Loss from a Tariff A tariff on an imported good creates winners and losers and a social loss. When the Canadian government imposes a tariff on an imported good:

- Canadian consumers of the good lose.
- Canadian producers of the good gain.
- Canadian consumers lose more than Canadian producers gain.
- Society loses: a deadweight loss arises.

Canadian Consumers of the Good Lose Because the price of a T-shirt in Canada rises, the quantity of T-shirts demanded decreases. The combination of a higher price and smaller quantity bought decreases consumer surplus—the loss to Canadian consumers that arises from a tariff.

ECONOMICS IN ACTION

Tariffs Almost Gone

Canadian tariffs were in place before Confederation. They increased sharply in the 1870s and remained high until the 1930s. In 1947, the **General Agreement on Tariffs and Trade (GATT)** was established to reduce international tariffs. Since then, tariffs have fallen in a series of negotiating rounds, the most significant of which are identified in the figure. Tariffs are now as low as they have ever been, but import quotas and other trade barriers persist.

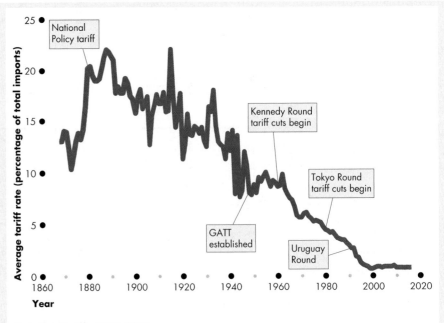

Canadian Tariffs: 1867–2016

Sources of data: Statistics Canada, *Historical Statistics of Canada*, Catalogue 11-516, July 1999, and CANSIM Tables 380-0002 and 380-0034.

Canadian Producers of the Good Gain Because the price of an imported T-shirt rises by the amount of the tariff, Canadian T-shirt producers are now able to sell their T-shirts for the world price plus the tariff, so the quantity of T-shirts supplied by Canadian producers increases. The combination of a higher price and larger quantity produced increases producer surplus—the gain to Canadian producers from the tariff.

Canadian Consumers Lose More Than Canadian Producers Gain As the Canadian price rises, some consumer surplus is transferred to producers. But the loss of consumer surplus exceeds this gain in producer surplus because some of the gains from free trade are lost. Figure 7.6 shows the sources of the lost consumer surplus.

Figure 7.6(a) shows the consumer surplus and producer surplus with free international trade in T-shirts. Figure 7.6(b) shows the consumer surplus and producer surplus with a $2 tariff on imported T-shirts. By comparing Fig. 7.6(b) with Fig. 7.6(a), you can see how a tariff changes these surpluses.

Consumer surplus—the green area—shrinks for four reasons. First, the higher price transfers surplus from consumers to producers. The blue area B represents this loss (and gain of producer surplus). Second, domestic producers have higher costs than foreign producers. The supply curve S_C shows the higher cost of production, and the grey area C shows this loss of consumer surplus. Third, some of the consumer surplus is transferred to the government as tariff revenue. The purple area D shows this loss (and gain of government revenue). Fourth, Canadians buy fewer imported T-shirts, so some consumer surplus is lost because imports decrease. The grey area E shows this loss. The loss of consumer surplus exceeds the gain in producer surplus by the area $C + D + E$.

Society Loses: A Deadweight Loss Arises Some of the loss of consumer surplus is transferred to producers and some is transferred to the government and spent on government programs that people value. But the increase in production cost and the loss from decreased imports is transferred to no one: It is a social loss—a deadweight loss. The grey areas labelled C and E represent this deadweight loss. Total surplus decreases by the area $C + E$.

FIGURE 7.6   The Winners and Losers from a Tariff

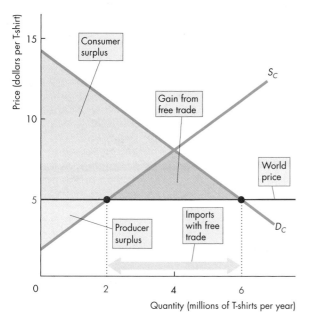

(a) Free trade

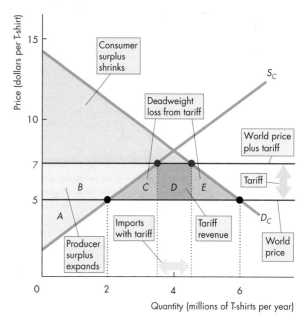

(b) Market with tariff

The world price of a T-shirt is $5. In part (a), with free trade, Canada imports 4 million T-shirts. The gain from free trade makes the sum of consumer surplus and producer surplus as large as possible.

In part (b), a tariff of $2 per T-shirt raises the price of a T-shirt in Canada to $7. The quantity imported decreases.

Consumer surplus shrinks by the area $B + C + D + E$. Producer surplus expands by area B. The government's tariff revenue equals the area D, and the tariff creates a deadweight loss equal to the area $C + E$.

Import Quotas

We now look at the second tool for restricting trade: import quotas. An **import quota** is a restriction that limits the quantity of a good that may be imported in a given period.

Most countries impose import quotas on a wide range of items. Canada imposes them on food products such as meat, eggs, and dairy and manufactured goods such as textiles and steel.

Import quotas enable the government to satisfy the self-interest of the people who earn their incomes in the import-competing industries. But you will discover that, like a tariff, an import quota decreases the gains from trade and is not in the social interest.

The Effects of an Import Quota The effects of an import quota are similar to those of a tariff. The price rises, the quantity bought decreases, and the quantity produced in Canada increases. Figure 7.7 illustrates the effects.

Figure 7.7(a) shows the situation with free international trade. Figure 7.7(b) shows what happens with an import quota of 1 million T-shirts a year. The Canadian supply curve of T-shirts becomes the domestic supply curve, S_C, plus the quantity that the import quota permits. So the supply curve becomes $S_C + quota$. The price of a T-shirt rises to $7, the quantity of T-shirts bought in Canada decreases to 4.5 million a year, the quantity of T-shirts produced in Canada increases to 3.5 million a year, and the quantity of T-shirts imported into Canada decreases to the quota quantity of 1 million a year. All the effects of this quota are identical to the effects of a $2 per shirt tariff, as you can check in Fig. 7.5(b).

Winners, Losers, and the Social Loss from an Import Quota An import quota creates winners and losers that are similar to those of a tariff but with an interesting difference.

FIGURE 7.7 The Effects of an Import Quota

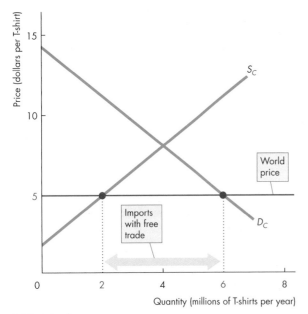

(a) Free trade

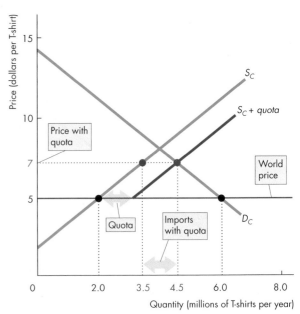

(b) Market with import quota

With free trade, in part (a), Canadians buy 6 million T-shirts at the world price. Canada produces 2 million T-shirts and imports 4 million a year. With an import quota of 1 million T-shirts a year, in part (b), the supply of T-shirts in Canada

is shown by the curve $S_C + quota$. The price in Canada rises to $7 a T-shirt. Canadian production increases, Canadian purchases decrease, and the quantity of T-shirts imported decreases.

When the government imposes an import quota:

- Canadian consumers of the good lose.
- Canadian producers of the good gain.
- Importers of the good gain.
- Society loses: a deadweight loss arises.

Figure 7.8 shows these gains and losses from a quota. By comparing Fig. 7.8(b) with a quota and Fig. 7.8(a) with free trade, you can see how an import quota of 1 million T-shirts a year changes the consumer and producer surpluses.

Consumer surplus—the green area—shrinks. This decrease is the loss to consumers from the import quota. The decrease in consumer surplus is made up of four parts. First, some of the consumer surplus is transferred to producers. The blue area B represents this loss of consumer surplus (and gain of producer surplus). Second, part of the consumer surplus is lost because the domestic cost of production is

higher than the world price. The grey area C represents this loss. Third, part of the consumer surplus is transferred to importers who buy T-shirts for $5 (the world price) and sell them for $7 (the Canadian domestic price). The two blue areas D represent this loss of consumer surplus and profit for importers. Fourth, part of the consumer surplus is lost because imports decrease. The grey area E represents this loss.

The loss of consumer surplus from the higher cost of production and the decrease in imports is a social loss—a deadweight loss. The grey areas labelled C and E represent this deadweight loss. Total surplus decreases by the area $C + E$.

You can now see the one difference between a quota and a tariff. A tariff brings in revenue for the government while a quota brings a profit for the importers. All the other effects are the same, provided the quota is set at the same quantity of imports that results from the tariff.

FIGURE 7.8   The Winners and Losers from an Import Quota

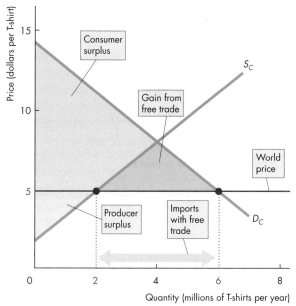

(a) Free trade

The world price of a T-shirt is $5. In part (a), with free trade, Canada produces 2 million T-shirts a year and imports 4 million T-shirts. The gain from free trade makes the sum of consumer surplus and producer surplus as large as possible.

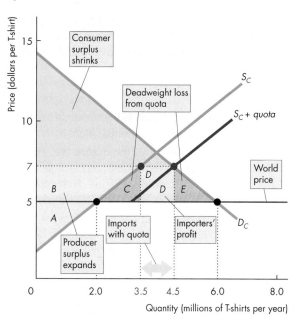

(b) Market with import quota

In part (b), the import quota raises the price of a T-shirt to $7. The quantity imported decreases. Consumer surplus shrinks by the area $B + C + D + E$. Producer surplus expands by area B. Importers' profit is the two areas D, and the quota creates a deadweight loss equal to the area $C + E$.

ECONOMICS IN THE NEWS

The U.S.–Canada Lumber Dispute

20% Tariff on Canadian Softwood-Lumber Imports
The Trump administration wants to put a 20% tariff on Canadian softwood lumber that is used to build single-family homes. The U.S. International Trade Commission will need to find that U.S. loggers have been injured by low Canadian prices.

Source: *The Wall Street Journal,* April 24, 2017

SOME FACTS

Canada is one of the world's largest lumber producers and it has been exporting lumber to the United States since the 1800s. Most U.S. forests are privately owned and leased to lumber producers at market prices. Canadian forests are state owned and leased to lumber producers at low prices set by law. U.S. producers say Canadian producers receive a subsidy and are "dumping"—selling lumber on the U.S. market at a price lower than the cost of production or the selling price in Canada.

THE PROBLEM

Explain how U.S. lumber mills would gain from a tariff on imported lumber. Would everyone in the United States be better off? Illustrate your explanation and answer with a graph.

THE SOLUTION

- A tariff imposed on U.S. imports of lumber increases the price of lumber in the United States.
- The higher price decreases the quantity of lumber demanded in the United States, increases the quantity supplied by U.S. producers, and decreases U.S. imports of lumber.
- U.S. producers of lumber enjoy a greater producer surplus but, faced with a higher price, the consumers of lumber are worse of. And the gain to producers is less than the loss to consumers—a deadweight loss arises.
- The figure illustrates the U.S. market for lumber. The demand curve is D_{US} and the supply curve is S_{US}.
- With a Canadian and world price *PW* of $120 per cubic metre, Canada has a comparative advantage in producing lumber.
- At the world price *PW*, the United States produces 100 billion cubic metres a year, uses 150 billion, and imports 50 billion. The figure shows this quantity of U.S. imports.

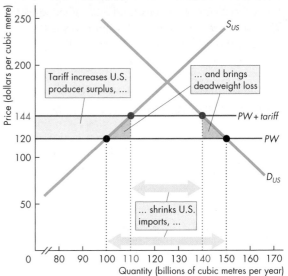

U.S. Market for Softwood Lumber

- If the United States imposes a 20 percent tariff, the price in the United States rises to $144 on the line *PW + tariff.*
- U.S. production increases to 110 billion cubic metres, the quantity bought decreases to 140 billion, and imports decrease to 30 billion.
- At the higher price and increased production, U.S. producer surplus increases by the blue area. But U.S. consumer surplus shrinks and a deadweight loss shown by the two grey triangles is created.
- The fact that the tariff is a response to Canada's alleged subsidy and dumping does not make the tariff efficient. Free trade in lumber, even if subsidized, brings a gain for U.S. consumers that exceeds the loss to U.S. producers.

Other Import Barriers

Two sets of policies that influence imports are:

- Health, safety, and regulation barriers
- Voluntary export restraints

Health, Safety, and Regulation Barriers Thousands of detailed health, safety, and other regulations restrict international trade. For example, Canadian food imports are examined by the Canadian Food Inspection Agency, which is "mandated to safeguard Canada's food supply and the plants and animals upon which safe and high-quality food depends." The discovery of BSE (mad cow disease) in just one cow in 2003 was enough to close down international trade in Canadian beef. The European Union bans imports of most genetically modified foods, such as Canadian-produced soybeans. Although regulations of the type we've just described are not designed to limit international trade, they have that effect.

Voluntary Export Restraints A *voluntary export restraint* is like a quota allocated to a foreign exporter of a good. This type of trade barrier isn't common. It was initially used during the 1980s when Japan voluntarily limited its exports of car parts to the United States.

Export Subsidies

A *subsidy* is a payment by the government to a producer. You studied the effects of a subsidy on the quantity produced and the price of a subsidized farm product in Chapter 6, pp. 144–145.

An *export subsidy* is a payment by the government to the producer of an exported good. Export subsidies are illegal under a number of international agreements, including the North American Free Trade Agreement (NAFTA), and the rules of the World Trade Organization (WTO).

Although export subsidies are illegal, the subsidies that the Canadian, U.S., and E.U. governments pay to farmers end up increasing domestic production, some of which gets exported. These exports of subsidized farm products make it harder for producers in other countries, notably in Africa and Central and South America, to compete in global markets. Export subsidies bring gains to domestic producers, but they result in inefficient underproduction in the rest of the world and create a deadweight loss.

ECONOMICS IN ACTION
Self-Interest Beats the Social Interest

The **World Trade Organization (WTO)** is an international body established by the world's major trading nations for the purpose of supervising international trade and lowering the barriers to trade.

In 2001, at a meeting of trade ministers from all the WTO member-countries held in Doha, Qatar, an agreement was made to begin negotiations to lower tariff barriers and quotas that restrict international trade in farm products and services. These negotiations are called the **Doha Development Agenda** or the **Doha Round**.

In the period since 2001, thousands of hours of conferences from Cancún in 2003 to Bali in 2013 and ongoing meetings at WTO headquarters in Geneva, costing millions of taxpayers' dollars, have made disappointing progress.

Rich nations, led by the United States, the European Union, and Japan, want greater access to the markets of developing nations in exchange for allowing those nations greater access to the markets of the rich world, especially those for farm products.

Developing nations, led by Brazil, China, India, and South Africa, want access to the markets of farm products of the rich world, but they also want to protect their infant industries.

With two incompatible positions, these negotiations are stalled and show no signs of a breakthrough. The self-interests of rich nations and developing nations are preventing the achievement of the social interest.

◆ REVIEW QUIZ

1 What are the tools that a country can use to restrict international trade?
2 Explain the effects of a tariff on domestic production, the quantity bought, and the price.
3 Explain who gains and who loses from a tariff and why the losses exceed the gains.
4 Explain the effects of an import quota on domestic production, consumption, and price.
5 Explain who gains and who loses from an import quota and why the losses exceed the gains.

Work these questions in Study Plan 7.3 and get instant feedback.   MyLab Economics

◆ The Case Against Protection

You've just seen that free trade promotes prosperity and protection is inefficient. Yet trade is restricted with tariffs, quotas, and other barriers. Why? Seven arguments for trade restrictions are that protecting domestic industries from foreign competition:

- Helps an infant industry grow.
- Counteracts dumping.
- Saves domestic jobs.
- Allows us to compete with cheap foreign labour.
- Penalizes lax environmental standards.
- Prevents rich countries from exploiting developing countries.
- Reduces offshore outsourcing that sends good Canadian jobs to other countries.

Helps an Infant Industry Grow

Comparative advantages change with on-the-job experience—*learning-by-doing*. When a new industry or a new product is born—an *infant industry*—it is not as productive as it will become with experience. It is argued that such an industry should be protected from international competition until it can stand alone and compete.

It is true that learning-by-doing can change comparative advantage, but this fact doesn't justify protecting an infant industry. Firms anticipate and benefit from learning-by-doing without protection from foreign competition.

When Research In Motion started to build its smartphone, BlackBerry, productivity was at first low. But after a period of learning-by-doing, huge productivity gains followed. Research In Motion didn't need a tariff to achieve these productivity gains.

Counteracts Dumping

Dumping occurs when a foreign firm sells its exports at a lower price than its cost of production. Dumping might be used by a firm that wants to gain a global monopoly. In this case, the foreign firm sells its output at a price below its cost to drive domestic firms out of business. When the domestic firms have gone, the foreign firm takes advantage of its monopoly position and charges a higher price for its product.

Dumping is illegal under the rules of the World Trade Organization and is usually regarded as a justification for temporary tariffs, which are called *countervailing duties*.

But it is virtually impossible to detect dumping because it is hard to determine a firm's costs. As a result, the test for dumping is whether a firm's export price is below its domestic price. But this test is weak because it is rational for a firm to charge a low price in a market in which the quantity demanded is highly sensitive to price and a higher price in a market in which demand is less price sensitive.

Saves Domestic Jobs

First, free trade destroy some jobs, but it also creates other jobs. It brings about a global rationalization of labour and allocates labour resources to their highest-valued activities. International trade in textiles has cost tens of thousands of jobs in Canada as textile mills and other factories closed. But tens of thousands of jobs have been created in other countries as textile mills opened. And tens of thousands of Canadian workers have better-paying jobs than as textile workers because Canadian export industries have expanded and created new jobs. More jobs have been created than destroyed.

Although protection can save particular jobs, it does so at a high cost. For example, until 2005, U.S. textile jobs were protected by an international agreement called the Multifibre Arrangement. The U.S. International Trade Commission (ITC) has estimated that, because of import quotas, 72,000 jobs existed in the textile industry that would otherwise have disappeared and that the annual clothing expenditure in the United States was $15.9 billion ($160 per family) higher than it would have been with free trade. Equivalently, the ITC estimated that each textile job saved cost $221,000 a year.

Imports don't only destroy jobs. They create jobs for retailers that sell imported goods and for firms that service those goods. Imports also create jobs by creating income in the rest of the world, some of which is spent on Canadian-made goods and services.

Allows Us to Compete with Cheap Foreign Labour

With the removal of tariffs on trade between Canada, the United States, and Mexico, people said we would hear a "giant sucking sound" as jobs rushed to Mexico. That didn't happen. Why?

It didn't happen because low-wage labour is low-productivity labour. If a Canadian autoworker earns

$40 an hour and produces 20 units of output an hour, the average labour cost of a unit of output is $2. If a Mexican autoworker earns $4 an hour and produces 1 unit of output an hour, the average labour cost of a unit of output is $4. Other things remaining the same, the higher a worker's productivity, the higher is the worker's wage rate. High-wage workers have high productivity; low-wage workers have low productivity.

It is *comparative advantage*, not wage differences, that drive international trade and that enable us to compete with Mexico and Mexico to compete with us.

Penalizes Lax Environmental Standards

Another argument for protection is that it provides an incentive to poor countries to raise their environmental standards—free trade with the richer and "greener" countries is a reward for improved environmental standards.

This argument for protection is weak. First, a poor country cannot afford to be as concerned about its environmental standard as a rich country can. Today, some of the worst pollution of air and water is found in China, Mexico, and Eastern Europe. But only a few decades ago, London and Los Angeles topped the pollution league chart. The best hope for cleaner air in Beijing and Mexico City is rapid income growth, which free trade promotes. As incomes grow, emerging countries have the *means* to match their desires to improve their environment. Second, a poor country may have a comparative advantage at doing "dirty" work, which helps it to raise its income and at the same time enables the global economy to achieve higher environmental standards than would otherwise be possible.

Prevents Rich Countries from Exploiting Developing Countries

Another argument for protection is that international trade must be restricted to prevent the people of the rich industrial world from exploiting the poorer people of the developing countries and forcing them to work for slave wages.

Child labour and near-slave labour are serious problems. But by trading with poor countries, we increase the demand for the goods that these countries produce and increase the demand for their labour. When the demand for labour in developing countries increases, the wage rate rises. So, rather than exploiting people in developing countries, trade can improve their opportunities and increase their incomes.

Reduces Offshore Outsourcing that Sends Good Canadian Jobs to Other Countries

Offshore outsourcing—buying goods, components, or services from firms in other countries—brings gains from trade identical to those of any other type of trade. We could easily change the names of the items traded from T-shirts and regional jets (the examples in the previous sections of this chapter) to banking services and call-centre services (or any other pair of services). A Canadian bank might export banking services to Indian firms, and Indians might provide call-centre services to Canadian firms. This type of trade would benefit both Canadians and Indians, provided Canada has a comparative advantage in banking services and India has a comparative advantage in call-centre services.

Despite the gain from specialization and trade that offshore outsourcing brings, many people believe that it also brings costs that eat up the gains. Why?

A major reason is that it seems to send good Canadian jobs to other countries. It is true that some manufacturing and service jobs are going overseas. But others are expanding at home. Canada imports call-centre services, but it exports education, healthcare, legal, financial, and a host of other types of services. The number of jobs in these sectors is expanding and will continue to expand.

The exact number of jobs that have moved to lower-cost offshore locations is not known, and estimates vary. But even the highest estimate is small compared to the normal rate of job creation and labour turnover.

Gains from trade do not bring gains for every single person. Canadians, on average, gain from offshore outsourcing, but some people lose. The losers are those who have invested in the human capital to do a specific job that has now gone offshore.

Unemployment benefits provide short-term temporary relief for these displaced workers. But the long-term solution requires retraining and the acquisition of new skills.

Beyond bringing short-term relief through unemployment benefits, government has a larger role to play. By providing education and training, it can enable the labour force of the twenty-first century to engage in the ongoing learning and sometimes rapid retooling that jobs we can't foresee today will demand.

Schools, colleges, and universities will expand and become better at doing their job of producing a more highly educated and flexible labour force.

AT **ISSUE**

Is Offshore Outsourcing Bad or Good for Canada?

The Royal Bank of Canada, Bell Canada, and the Hudson Bay Company engage in offshore outsourcing. They buy services from firms in other countries. Buying goods and components has been going on for centuries, but buying *services* such as customer support call-centre services is new and is made possible by the development of low-cost telephone and Internet service.

Should this type of offshore outsourcing be discouraged and penalized with taxes and regulations?

Bad

- Whenever a major company announces job cuts and a decision to send some jobs abroad, there is an outcry from not only the affected workers but also the broader community. It seems clear: Offshore outsourcing is bad for Canadians.

- Surveys of opinion find that around 70 percent of people in advanced economies such as Canada think outsourcing hurts jobs and incomes at home and only a small minority think it helps.

Have these Indian call-centre workers destroyed Canadian jobs? Or does their work benefit Canadian workers?

Good

- Economist N. Gregory Mankiw speaking about the U.S. situation, but relevant to all countries, says, "I think outsourcing … is probably a plus for the economy in the long run."

- Mankiw goes on to say that it doesn't matter whether "items produced abroad come on planes, ships, or over fibre-optic cables … the economics is basically the same."

- What Greg Mankiw is saying is that the economic analysis of the gains from international trade—exactly the same as what you have studied on pp. 156–160—applies to all types of international trade.

- Offshore outsourcing, like all other forms of international trade, is a source of gains for all.

Avoiding Trade Wars

We have reviewed the arguments commonly heard in favour of protection and the counterarguments against it. But one counterargument to protection that is general and quite overwhelming is that protection invites retaliation and can trigger a trade war.

A trade war is a contest in which when one country raises its import tariffs, other countries retaliate with increases of their own, which trigger yet further increases from the first country.

A trade war occurred during the Great Depression of the 1930s when the United States introduced the Smoot-Hawley tariff. Country after country retaliated with its own tariff, and in a short period, world trade had almost disappeared. The costs to all countries were large and led to a renewed international resolve to avoid such self-defeating moves in the future. The costs are also the impetus behind current attempts to liberate trade.

Why Is International Trade Restricted?

Why, despite all the arguments against protection, is trade restricted? There are two key reasons:

- Tariff revenue
- Rent seeking

Tariff Revenue Government revenue is costly to collect. In developed countries such as Canada, a well-organized tax collection system is in place that can generate billions of dollars of income tax and sales tax revenues.

But governments in developing countries have a difficult time collecting taxes from their citizens. Much economic activity takes place in an informal economy with few financial records. The one area in which economic transactions are well recorded is international trade. So tariffs on international trade are a convenient source of revenue in these countries.

Rent Seeking   Rent seeking is the major reason why international trade is restricted. **Rent seeking** is lobbying for special treatment by the government to create economic profit or to divert consumer surplus or producer surplus away from others. Free trade increases consumption possibilities *on average*, but not everyone shares in the gain and some people even lose. Free trade brings benefits to some and imposes costs on others, with total benefits exceeding total costs. The uneven distribution of costs and benefits is the principal obstacle to achieving more liberal international trade.

Returning to the example of trade in T-shirts and airplanes, the benefits from free trade accrue to all the producers of airplanes and to those producers of T-shirts that do not bear the costs of adjusting to a smaller garment industry. These costs are transition costs, not permanent costs. The costs of moving to free trade are borne by the garment producers and their employees who must become producers of other goods and services in which Canada has a comparative advantage.

The number of winners from free trade is large, but because the gains are spread thinly over a large number of people, the gain per person is small. The winners could organize and become a political force lobbying for free trade. But political activity is costly. It uses time and other scarce resources and the gains per person are too small to make the cost of political activity worth bearing.

In contrast, the number of losers from free trade is small, but the loss per person is large. Because the loss per person is large, the people who lose *are* willing to incur considerable expense to lobby against free trade.

Both the winners and losers weigh benefits and costs. Those who gain from free trade weigh the benefits it brings against the cost of achieving it. Those who lose from free trade and gain from protection weigh the benefit of protection against the cost of maintaining it. The protectionists undertake a larger quantity of political lobbying than the free traders.

Compensating Losers

If, in total, the gains from free international trade exceed the losses, why don't those who gain compensate those who lose so that everyone is in favour of free trade?

Some compensation does take place. When Canada entered the North American Free Trade Agreement (NAFTA) with the United States and Mexico, the United States set up a $56 million fund to support and retrain workers who lost their jobs as a result of the new trade agreement. During NAFTA's first six months, only 5,000 workers applied for benefits under this scheme.

The losers from international trade are also compensated indirectly through the normal unemployment compensation arrangements. But only limited attempts are made to compensate those who lose.

The main reason full compensation is not attempted is that the costs of identifying all the losers and estimating the value of their losses would be enormous. Also, it would never be clear whether a person who has fallen on hard times is suffering because of free trade or for other reasons that might be largely under her or his control. Furthermore, some people who look like losers at one point in time might, in fact, end up gaining. The young autoworker who loses his job in Windsor and gets a job on Alberta's oil patch might resent the loss of work and the need to move. But a year later, looking back on events, he counts himself fortunate.

Because we do not, in general, compensate the losers from free international trade, protectionism is a popular and permanent feature of our national economic and political life.

◆ REVIEW QUIZ

1 What are the infant industry and dumping arguments for protection? Are they correct?

2 Can protection save jobs and the environment and prevent workers in developing countries from being exploited?

3 What is offshore outsourcing? Who benefits from it and who loses?

4 What are the main reasons for imposing a tariff?

5 Do the winners from free trade win the political argument? Why or why not?

Work these questions in Study Plan 7.4 and get instant feedback.   MyLab Economics

---

◆ We end this chapter on global markets in action with *Economics in the News* on pp. 172–173, where we apply what you've learned by looking at why Donald Trump's ideas about trade protection are wrong.

The Cost of a Tariff

A 20% Mexico Tariff Would Pay for the Wall. But It Would Hurt Americans

Shortly after President Donald Trump took office, his now former press secretary Sean Spicer gave a news conference aboard Air Force One in which he talked about the U.S. imposing an import tariff as a way of making Mexico pay for Trump's proposed border wall.

"When you look at the plan that's taking shape right now, using comprehensive tax reforms as a means to tax imports from countries that we have a trade deficit from like Mexico—if you tax that $50 billion at 20% of imports, which is, by the way, a practice that 160 other countries do right now (our country's policy is to tax exports and to let imports flow freely in, which is ridiculous), but by doing it that way, we could do $10 billion a year and easily pay for the wall just through that mechanism alone."

A tariff on Mexican imports would raise the prices faced by U.S. consumers. The *Washington Post* did some calculations, providing pre- and post-tariff pricing for some common Mexican imports:

Item	Price	Price + Tax
An avocado	$3.00	$3.60
Papermate pen refills	$5.54	$6.65
Six pack of Tecate beer	$6.00	$7.20
LG refrigerator	$1,600	$1,920
Ford Fiesta	$21,435	$25,722

In response to the idea shared by Spicer, Senator Lindsey Graham (R-South Carolina) employed one of the president's favourite communication methods by tweeting: "Simply put, any policy proposal which drives up costs of Corona, tequila, or margaritas is a big-time bad idea. Mucho Sad."

Sources: Based on Gillespie, Patrick, "A 20% Mexico Tariff Would Pay for the Wall. But It Would Hurt Americans." CNN Money, January 26, 2017; Bump, Philip, "Americans Might Need to Buy 25 Billion Avocados so Mexico Could Pay for the Wall." *Washington Post*, January 26, 2017; Sean Spicer on C-SPAN video; Lindsey Graham on Twitter.

ESSENCE OF THE STORY

- The Trump administration floated the idea of paying for a border wall with the revenue from a 20% tariff on imports from Mexico.

- A 20% tariff would raise enough revenue to pay for a border wall.

- American consumers, not Mexico, would be paying for the wall.

- Americans would bear the cost of the tariff by paying higher prices for cars, refrigerators, avocados, beer, and many other products imported from Mexico.

MyLab Economics Economics in the News

ECONOMIC ANALYSIS

- You might think a border wall is a bad idea, or you might think it is a good idea. This news article is not taking sides on that question, nor is this analysis.

- The questions addressed are would a 20 percent tariff on imports from Mexico bring in enough revenue to pay for a wall, and who would end up paying?

- The article says the tariff would generate enough revenue, and Americans, not Mexicans, would pay.

- The article is correct about who would pay, but it makes a mistake in its revenue calculation.

- To see why, we'll look at the U.S. market for just one of the items we import from Mexico—avocados.

- In Fig. 1, the demand curve D_{US} shows the demand for avocados in the United States, and the supply curve S_{US} shows the supply of avocados produced in the United States.

- The world price of avocados is $1,750 a ton, shown by the line PW. The United States can import avocados at this price, so this is the price in the United States.

- With free trade, the United States produces 200,000 tons of avocados a year, imports 600,000 tons, and consumes 800,000 tons. The green area shows the gain in consumer surplus from this free trade.

- Figure 2 shows what happens when a 20 percent tariff is imposed on avocados. The U.S. demand curve and the U.S. supply curve don't change. But the United States is no longer able to buy avocados from Mexico for $1,750 a ton.

- The U.S. price now rises by 20 percent to $2,100 per ton. At that price, the quantity of avocados demanded decreases to 555,000 tons, the quantity supplied by U.S. growers increases to 240,000 tons, and imports decrease to 315,000 tons. (These quantities are based on realistic assumptions about the elasticities of demand and supply of avocados.)

- U.S. avocado producers' surplus increases (the blue area), but U.S. consumers take a hit. They lose consumer surplus.

- Some of the lost consumer surplus is deadweight loss (the two grey triangles) and some is tariff revenue (the purple rectangle).

- The tariff revenue is not 20 percent of the value of imports with free trade. It is 20 percent of a lower value of imports that result from the 20 percent higher price.

- So, a tariff to pay for a wall would mean American consumers pay for the wall; and a 20 percent tariff might not generate enough revenue to pay for a wall.

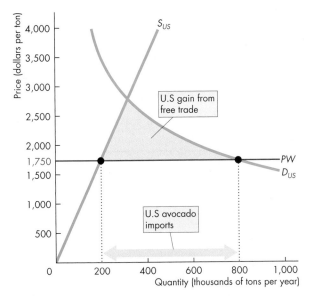

Figure 1 U.S. Avocado Market with Free Trade

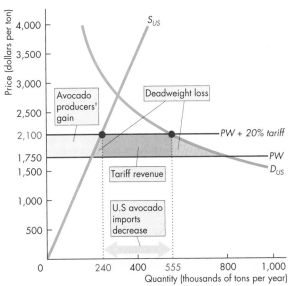

Figure 2 U.S. Avocado Market with 20% Tariff

WORKED PROBLEM

MyLab Economics Work this problem in Chapter 7 Study Plan.

The table shows the Canadian demand schedule for honey and the supply schedule of honey by Canadian producers. The world price of honey is $8 a jar.

Price (dollars per jar)	Quantity demanded	Quantity supplied
	(millions of jars per year)	
5	10	0
6	8	3
7	6	6
8	4	9
9	2	12
10	0	15

Questions

1. With no international trade, what is the price of honey and the quantity bought and sold in Canada? Does Canada have a comparative advantage in producing honey? With free international trade, does Canada export or import honey?

2. With free international trade, what is the Canadian price of honey, the quantity bought by Canadians, the quantity produced in Canada, and the quantity of honey exported or imported?

3. Does Canada gain from international trade in honey? Do all Canadians gain? If not, who loses and do the gains exceed the losses?

Solutions

1. With no international trade, the price of honey is that at which the quantity demanded equals the quantity supplied. The table shows that this price is $7 a jar at which the equilibrium quantity is 6 million jars a year.

   The price of honey in Canada is less than the world price, which means that the opportunity cost of producing a jar of honey in Canada is *less* than the opportunity cost of producing it in the rest of the world. So Canadian producers have a comparative advantage in producing honey, and with free international trade, Canada exports honey.

Key Point: Comparative advantage is determined by comparing the opportunity cost of producing the good in Canada and the world price.

2. With free international trade, the price of honey in Canada rises to the world price of $8 a jar. Canadians cut their consumption of honey to 4 million jars a year while Canadian honey producers expand

production to 9 million jars a year. Canada exports 5 million jars of honey a year. The figure shows the quantities bought and produced in Canada and the quantity exported.

Key Point: As the domestic price rises to the world price, the quantity demanded decreases and the quantity supplied increases, and the difference is exported.

3. With free international trade, Canada gains from exporting honey because the higher world price and the larger quantity of honey produced increase Canada's total surplus from honey.

   Consumers lose because the price of honey rises and they buy less honey. Consumer surplus from honey decreases. But the higher price and the larger quantity produced increase producer surplus from honey. Canada gains because the increase in producer surplus is greater than the loss in consumer surplus.

   The figure shows that, with no trade, consumer surplus equals area $A + B$ and producer surplus equals area C. With free international trade, consumer surplus shrinks to area A, producer surplus expands to area $B + C + D$, and total surplus (the gains from trade in honey) increases by area D.

Key Point: Free trade increases the total surplus, but for an exporting country some consumer surplus is transferred to producers of the exported good.

Key Figure

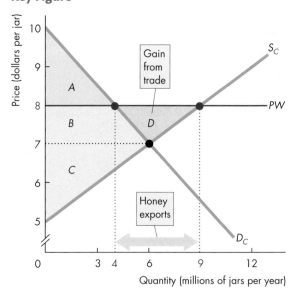

MyLab Economics Interactive Graph

SUMMARY

Key Points

How Global Markets Work (pp. 156–158)

- Comparative advantage drives international trade.
- If the world price of a good is lower than the domestic price, the rest of the world has a comparative advantage in producing that good and the domestic country gains by producing less, consuming more, and importing the good.
- If the world price of a good is higher than the domestic price, the domestic country has a comparative advantage in producing that good and gains by producing more, consuming less, and exporting the good.

Working Problems 1 to 3 will give you a better understanding of how global markets work.

Winners, Losers, and the Net Gain from Trade (pp. 159–160)

- Compared to a no-trade situation, in a market with imports, consumer surplus is larger, producer surplus is smaller, and total surplus is larger with free international trade.
- Compared to a no-trade situation, in a market with exports, consumer surplus is smaller, producer surplus is larger, and total surplus is larger with free international trade.

Working Problem 4 will give you a better understanding of winners, losers, and the net gains from trade.

International Trade Restrictions (pp. 161–167)

- Countries restrict international trade by imposing tariffs, import quotas, and other import barriers.
- Trade restrictions raise the domestic price of imported goods, lower the quantity imported, decrease consumer surplus, increase producer surplus, and create a deadweight loss.

Working Problems 5 to 10 will give you a better understanding of international trade restrictions.

The Case Against Protection (pp. 168–171)

- Arguments that protection helps an infant industry to grow and counteracts dumping are weak.
- Arguments that protection saves jobs, allows us to compete with cheap foreign labour, is needed to penalize lax environmental standards, and prevents exploitation of developing countries are flawed.
- Offshore outsourcing is just a new way of reaping gains from trade and does not justify protection.
- Trade restrictions are popular because protection brings a small loss per person to a large number of people and a large gain per person to a small number of people. Those who gain have a stronger political voice than those who lose and it is too costly to identify and compensate losers.

Working Problem 11 will give you a better understanding of the case against protection.

Key Terms

MyLab Economics Key Terms Quiz

Dumping, 168

Exports, 156

Import quota, 164

Imports, 156

Offshore outsourcing, 169

Rent seeking, 171

Tariff, 161

STUDY PLAN PROBLEMS AND APPLICATIONS

MyLab Economics Work Problems 1 to 11 in Chapter 7 Study Plan and get instant feedback.

How Global Markets Work (Study Plan 7.1)

Use the following data to work Problems 1 to 3.
Wholesalers buy and sell roses in containers that hold 120 stems. The table provides information about the wholesale market for roses in North America. The demand schedule is the wholesalers' demand and the supply schedule is the North American rose growers' supply.

Price (dollars per container)	Quantity demanded	Quantity supplied
	(millions of containers per year)	
100	15	0
125	12	2
150	9	4
175	6	6
200	3	8
225	0	10

Wholesalers can buy roses at auction in Aalsmeer, Holland, for $125 per container.

1. a. With no international trade, what would be the price of a container of roses and how many containers of roses a year would be bought and sold in North America?

    b. At the price in your answer to part (a), does North America or the rest of the world have a comparative advantage in producing roses?

2. If North American wholesalers buy roses at the lowest possible price, how many do they buy from North American growers and how many do they import?

3. Draw a graph to illustrate the North American wholesale market for roses. Show the equilibrium in that market with no international trade and the equilibrium with free trade. Mark the quantity of roses grown in North America, the quantity imported, and the total quantity bought.

Winners, Losers, and the Net Gain from Trade
(Study Plan 7.2)

4. Use the data on the market for roses in Problem 1 to work this problem.

    a. Explain who gains and who loses from free international trade in roses compared to a situation in which North Americans buy only roses grown locally.

    b. Draw a graph to illustrate the gains and losses from free trade.

    c. Calculate the gain from international trade.

International Trade Restrictions (Study Plan 7.3)

Use the information on the North American wholesale market for roses in Problem 1 to work Problems 5 to 10.

5. If a tariff of $25 per container is imposed on imports of roses, explain how the price of roses, the quantity of roses bought, the quantity produced in North America, and the quantity imported change.

6. Who gains and who loses from this tariff?

7. Draw a graph of the North American market for roses to illustrate the gains and losses from the tariff. On the graph identify the gains and losses, the tariff revenue, and the deadweight loss created.

8. If an import quota of 5 million containers is imposed on roses, what happens to the price of roses, the quantity of roses bought, the quantity produced in North America, and the quantity imported?

9. Who gains and who loses from this quota?

10. Draw a graph to illustrate the gains and losses from the import quota. On the graph identify the gains and losses, the importers' profit, and the deadweight loss.

The Case Against Protection (Study Plan 7.4)

11. **Cheese Makers Brace for European Imports**
    The Canada-European Union Comprehensive Economic and Trade Agreement (CETA) becomes effective July 2017. It will increase Canada's European cheese import quota by 17,700 tonnes. The change could cost Canadian producers $230-million a year up to 400 jobs lost.
    Source: *The Globe and Mail*, April 15, 2017

    a. What does the news clip imply about the comparative advantage of producing cheese in the European Union and Canada?

    b. Are any of the arguments for protection valid reasons for a cheese import quota?

ADDITIONAL PROBLEMS AND APPLICATIONS

MyLab Economics You can work these problems in Homework or Test if assigned by your instructor.

How Global Markets Work

12. Suppose that the world price of eggs is $1 a dozen, Canada does not trade internationally, and the equilibrium price of eggs in Canada is $3 a dozen. Canada then begins to trade internationally.

    a. How does the price of eggs in Canada change?

    b. Do Canadians buy more or fewer eggs?

    c. Do Canadian egg farmers produce more or fewer eggs?

    d. Does Canada export or import eggs and why?

    e. Would employment in the Canadian egg industry change? If so, how?

13. Suppose that the world price of steel is $100 a tonne, India does not trade internationally, and the equilibrium price of steel in India is $60 a tonne. India then begins to trade internationally.

    a. How does the price of steel in India change?

    b. How does the quantity of steel produced in India change?

    c. How does the quantity of steel bought by India change?

    d. Does India export or import steel and why?

14. A semiconductor is a key component in your laptop, smartphone, and iPad. The table provides information about the market for semiconductors in Canada.

Price (dollars per unit)	Quantity demanded	Quantity supplied
	(billions of units per year)	
10	25	0
12	20	20
14	15	40
16	10	60
18	5	80
20	0	100

    Producers of semiconductors can get $18 a unit on the world market.

    a. With no international trade, what would be the price of a semiconductor and how many semiconductors a year would be bought and sold in Canada?

    b. Does Canada have a comparative advantage in producing semiconductors?

15. **Food Versus Fuel**

    Biofuels (mainly ethanol) make up 10 percent of auto fuel in the United States and 5 percent in Canada, and the mandated shares have risen. Farmers are smiling because taxpayers subsidize the fuel. Using ethanol makes food prices higher than they should be.

    Source: *The Globe and Mail*, October 28, 2016

    a. What is the effect on the world price of corn of the increased use of corn to produce ethanol in Canada and the United States?

    b. How does the change in the world price of corn affect the quantity of corn produced and consumed in a corn-exporting nation?

    c. How does the change in the world price of corn affect the quantity of corn produced and consumed in a corn-importing nation?

Winners, Losers, and the Net Gain from Trade

16. Draw a graph of the market for corn in the corn-exporting nation in Problem 15(b) to show the changes in consumer surplus and producer surplus that arise.

Use the following news clip to work Problems 17 and 18.

Beef Exporters Re-Focus on South Korea

South Korea recently lifted its temporary mad cow disease ban on Canadian beef and veal imports. Canadian beef exporters predict that with the free trade, beef exports to South Korea might exceed $50 million a year.

Source: *The Vancouver Sun*, January 11, 2016

17. Explain how South Korea's temporary import ban on Canadian beef affected beef producers and consumers in South Korea. Draw a graph of the South Korean market for beef to show how this ban changed Korean consumer surplus and producer surplus from beef.

18. Assuming that South Korea is the only importer of Canadian beef, explain how South Korea's ban on beef imports affected beef producers and consumers in Canada. Draw a graph of the market for beef in Canada to show how this ban changes Canadian consumer surplus and producer surplus from beef.

International Trade Restrictions

Use the following information to work Problems 19 to 21.

Before 1995, trade between Canada and Mexico was subject to tariffs. In 1995, Mexico joined NAFTA and all Canadian and Mexican tariffs have gradually been removed.

19. Explain how the price that Canadian consumers pay for goods from Mexico and the quantity of Canadian imports from Mexico have changed. Who are the winners and who are the losers from this free trade?

20. Explain how the quantity of Canadian exports to Mexico and the Canadian government's tariff revenue from trade with Mexico have changed.

21. Suppose that this year, tomato growers in Ontario lobby the Canadian government to impose an import quota on Mexican tomatoes. Explain who in Canada would gain and who would lose from such a quota.

Use the following information to work Problems 22 and 23.

Suppose that in response to huge job losses in the Canadian textile industry, the Government of Canada imposes a 100 percent tariff on imports of textiles from China.

22. Explain how the tariff on textiles will change the price that Canadians pay for textiles, the quantity of textiles imported, and the quantity of textiles produced in Canada.

23. Explain how the Canadian and Chinese gains from trade will change. Who in Canada will lose and who will gain?

Use the following information to work Problems 24 and 25.

With free trade between Australia and Canada, Australia would export beef to Canada. But Canada imposes an import quota on Australian beef.

24. Explain how this quota influences the price that Canadians pay for beef, the quantity of beef produced in Canada, and the Canadian and the Australian gains from trade.

25. Explain who in Canada gains from the quota on beef imports and who loses.

The Case Against Protection

26. **The Cost of Bringing Home American Jobs**
    Donald Trump says he'll bring home jobs lost to China and Mexico. It is possible but costly.

American consumers would face higher prices and those on low incomes would suffer most because they spend a high share of their income on clothes, shoes, and toys—things that are made at low cost and imported.

Source: CNNMoney, April 14, 2016

a. What are the arguments for bringing jobs back to America? Explain why these arguments are faulty.

b. Is there any merit in bringing jobs back?

Economics in the News

27. After you have studied *Economics in the News* on pp. 172–173, answer the following questions.

a. What was the value of U.S. imports from Mexico in 2015 and why would the value of imports fall if a 20 percent tariff were imposed on them?

b. How do the elasticities of demand and supply influence the revenue that a tariff generates?

c. Who in the United States would benefit and who would lose from a 20 percent tariff on imports from Mexico?

d. Illustrate your answer to part (c) with an appropriate graphical analysis.

28. **NAFTA: What Canada Could Gain from Renegotiation**
    NAFTA is light on trade in services. But it is services that have dominated Canada's export growth in the past decade. If U.S. President Donald Trump makes good on his election pledge to renegotiate NAFTA, reducing barriers to trading digitally delivered goods and services should be Canada's priority.

Source: *The Globe and Mail,* January 28, 2017

a. What is NAFTA? What is its aim?

b. In the market for e-commerce—delivering services digitally—explain how barriers to free trade influence the quantity of these services produced, consumed, and traded. Illustrate your answer with an appropriate graphical analysis.

c. Show on your graph the changes in consumer surplus and producer surplus that result from free trade in digitally delivered services.

d. Explain why U.S. producers of e-commerce services would be expected to oppose free trade in these services with Canada.

The Amazing Market

UNDERSTANDING HOW MARKETS WORK

The five chapters that you've just studied explain how markets work. The market is an amazing instrument. It enables people who have never met and who know nothing about each other to interact and do business. It also enables us to allocate our scarce resources to the uses that we value most highly. Markets can be very simple or highly organized. Markets are ancient and they are modern.

A simple and ancient market is one that the American historian Daniel J. Boorstin describes in *The Discoverers* (p. 161). In the late fourteenth century,

> *The Muslim caravans that went southward from Morocco across the Atlas Mountains arrived after twenty days at the shores of the Senegal River. There the Moroccan traders laid out separate piles of salt, of beads from Ceutan coral, and cheap manufactured goods. Then they retreated out of sight. The local tribesmen, who lived in the strip mines where they dug their gold, came to the shore and put a heap of gold beside each pile of Moroccan goods. Then they, in turn, went out of view, leaving the Moroccan traders either to take the gold offered for a particular pile or to reduce the pile of their merchandise to suit the offered price in gold. Once again the Moroccan traders withdrew, and the process went on. By this system of commercial etiquette, the Moroccans collected their gold.*

Auctions on eBay and government auction of the airwaves that wireless service providers use are organized and modern markets. Susan Athey, whom you will meet on the following page, is a world-renowned expert on the design of auctions.

Everything and anything that can be exchanged is traded in markets to the benefit of both buyers and sellers.

Alfred Marshall *(1842–1924) grew up in an England that was being transformed by the railroad and by the expansion of manufacturing. Mary Paley was one of Marshall's students at Cambridge, and when Alfred and Mary married in 1877, celibacy rules barred Alfred from continuing to teach at Cambridge. By 1884, with more liberal rules, the Marshalls returned to Cambridge, where Alfred became Professor of Political Economy.*

Many economists had a hand in refining the demand and supply model, but the first thorough and complete statement of the model as we know it today was set out by Alfred Marshall, with the help of Mary Paley Marshall. Published in 1890, this monumental treatise, The Principles of Economics, *became the textbook on economics on both sides of the Atlantic for almost half a century.*

"The forces to be dealt with are … so numerous, that it is best to take a few at a time. … Thus we begin by isolating the primary relations of supply, demand, and price."

ALFRED MARSHALL
The Principles of Economics

SUSAN ATHEY is Professor of Economics at Harvard University. Born in 1970, she completed high school in three years, wrapped up three majors—in economics, mathematics, and computer science—at Duke University at 20, completed her Ph.D. at Stanford University at 24, and was voted tenure at MIT and Stanford at 29. After teaching at MIT for six years and Stanford for five years, she moved to Harvard in 2006. Among her many honours and awards, the most prestigious is the John Bates Clark Medal given to the best economist under 40. She is the first woman to receive this award.

Professor Athey's research is broad both in scope and style. A government that wants to auction natural resources will turn to her fundamental discoveries (and possibly consult with her) before deciding how to organize the auction. An economist who wants to test a theory using a large data set will use her work on statistics and econometrics.

Michael Parkin and Robin Bade talked with Susan Athey about her research, what economists have learned about designing markets, and her advice to students.

Professor Athey, what sparked your interest in economics?

I was studying mathematics and computer science, but I felt that the subjects were not as relevant as I would like. I discovered economics through a research project with a professor who was working on auctions. I had a summer job working for a firm that sold computers to the government through auctions. Eventually my professor, Bob Marshall, wrote two articles on the topic and testified before Congress to help reform the system for government procurement of computers. That really inspired me and showed me the power of economic ideas to change the world and to make things work more efficiently.

What is the connection between an auction and the supply and demand model?

The basic laws of supply and demand can be seen in evidence in an auction market like eBay. The more sellers that are selling similar products, the lower the prices they can expect to achieve. Similarly the more buyers there are demanding those objects, the higher the prices the sellers can achieve.

An important thing for an auction marketplace is to attract a good balance of buyers and sellers so that both the buyers and the sellers find it more profitable to transact in that marketplace rather than using some other mechanism. From a seller's perspective, the more bidders there are on the platform, the greater the demand and the higher the prices. And from the buyer's perspective, the more sellers there are on the platform, the greater the supply and the lower the prices.

> **The basic laws of supply and demand can be seen in evidence in an auction market like eBay.**

Can we think of an auction as a mechanism for finding the equilibrium price and quantity?

Exactly. We can think of the whole collection of auctions on eBay as being a mechanism to discover a market-clearing price, and individual items might sell a little higher or a little lower but overall we believe that the prices on eBay auctions will represent equilibrium prices.

*Read the full interview with Susan Athey in MyLab Economics.

8

UTILITY AND DEMAND

After studying this chapter, you will be able to:

◆ Explain the limits to consumption and describe preferences using the concept of utility

◆ Explain the marginal utility theory of consumer choice

◆ Use marginal utility theory to predict the effects of changes in prices and incomes and to explain the paradox of value

◆ Describe some new ways of explaining consumer choices

You enjoy streaming music and movies to your digital devices. What determines our choices about the quantity of data we use?

You know that diamonds are expensive and water is cheap. Doesn't that seem odd? Why do we place a higher value on useless diamonds than on essential-to-life water?

The theory of consumer choice that you're going to study in this chapter answers questions like the ones we've just posed. *Economics in the News* at the end of the chapter applies what you learn to explaining how your cellular data plan influences the amount of data you stream or download.

◆ Consumption Choices

The choices that you make as a buyer of goods and services—your consumption choices—are influenced by many factors. We can summarize them under two broad headings:

- Consumption possibilities
- Preferences

Consumption Possibilities

Your consumption possibilities are all the things that you can afford to buy. You can afford many different combinations of goods and services, but they are all limited by your income and by the prices that you must pay. For example, you might decide to spend a big part of your income on a gym membership and personal trainer and little on movies and music, or you might spend lots on movies and music and use the free gym at school.

The easiest way to describe consumption possibilities is to consider a model consumer who buys only two items. That's what we'll do now. We'll study the consumption possibilities of Lisa, who buys only movies and cola.

A Consumer's Budget Line Consumption possibilities are limited by Lisa's income and by the prices of movies and cola. When Lisa spends all her income, she reaches the limits to her consumption possibilities. We describe this limit with a **budget line**, which marks the boundary between those combinations of goods and services that a household can afford to buy and those that it cannot afford.

Figure 8.1 illustrates Lisa's consumption possibilities of movies and cola and her budget line. Lisa has an income of $40 a month, the price of a movie is $8, and the price of cola is $4 a case. Rows *A* through *F* in the table show six possible ways of allocating $40 to these two goods. For example, in row *A* Lisa buys 10 cases of cola and sees no movies; in row *F* she sees 5 movies and buys no cola; and in row *C* she sees 2 movies and buys 6 cases of cola.

Points *A* through *F* in the graph illustrate the possibilities presented in the table, and the line passing through these points is Lisa's budget line.

The budget line constrains the consumer's choices: It marks the boundary between what is affordable and unaffordable. Lisa can afford all the points on the budget line and inside it. Points outside the line are unaffordable.

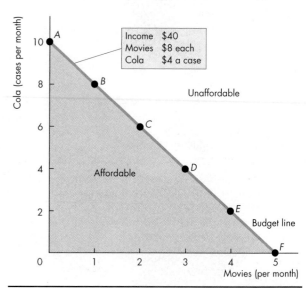

FIGURE 8.1 Lisa's Budget Line

Income $40
Movies $8 each
Cola $4 a case

Possibility	Movies		Cola	
	Quantity	Expenditure (dollars)	Cases	Expenditure (dollars)
A	0	0	10	40
B	1	8	8	32
C	**2**	**16**	**6**	**24**
D	3	24	4	16
E	4	32	2	8
F	5	40	0	0

The graph and the table show six possible ways in which Lisa can allocate $40 to movies and cola. In row *C* and at point *C*, she sees 2 movies and buys 6 cases of cola. The line *AF* is Lisa's budget line and is a boundary between what she can afford and what she cannot afford. Her choices must lie along the line *AF* or inside the orange area.

——— MyLab Economics Animation and Draw Graph ———

Changes in Consumption Possibilities Consumption possibilities change when income or prices change. A rise in income shifts the budget line outward but leaves its slope unchanged. A change in a price changes the slope of the line.* Our goal is to predict the effects of such changes on consumption choices. To do so, we must determine the choice a consumer makes. The budget line shows what is possible; preferences determine which possibility is chosen. We'll now describe a consumer's preferences.

---

*Chapter 9 explains an alternative model of consumer choice, and pp. 207–208 provides some detail on how changes in income and prices change the budget line.

Preferences

Lisa's income and the prices that she faces limit her consumption choices, but she still has lots of choice. The choice that she makes depends on her **preferences**—a description of her likes and dislikes.

You saw one way that economists use to describe preferences in Chapter 2 (p. 38), the concept of *marginal benefit* and the *marginal benefit curve*. But you also saw in Chapter 5 (p. 112) that a marginal benefit curve is also a demand curve. The goal of a theory of consumer choice is to derive the demand curve from a deeper account of how consumers make their buying plans. That is, we want to *explain what determines demand and marginal benefit.*

To achieve this goal, we need a deeper way of describing preferences. One approach to this problem uses the idea of utility, and defines **utility** as the benefit or satisfaction that a person gets from the consumption of goods and services. We distinguish two utility concepts:

- Total utility
- Marginal utility

Total Utility The total benefit that a person gets from the consumption of all the different goods and services is called **total utility**. Total utility depends on the level of consumption—more consumption generally gives more total utility.

To illustrate the concept of total utility, think about Lisa's choices. We tell Lisa that we want to measure her utility from movies and cola. We can use any scale that we wish to measure her total utility and we give her two starting points: (1) We will call the total utility from no movies and no cola zero utility; and (2) We will call the total utility she gets from seeing 1 movie a month 50 units.

We then ask Lisa to tell us, using the same scale, how much she would like 2 movies, and more, up to 10 movies a month. We also ask her to tell us, on the same scale, how much she would like 1 case of cola a month, 2 cases, and more, up to 10 cases a month.

In Table 8.1, the columns headed "Total utility" show Lisa's answers. Looking at those numbers, you can say a lot about how much Lisa likes cola and movies. She says that 1 case of cola gives her 75 units of utility—50 percent more than the utility that she gets from seeing 1 movie. You can also see that her total utility from cola climbs more slowly than does her total utility from movies. This difference turns on the second utility concept: *marginal utility.*

TABLE 8.1 Lisa's Utility from Movies and Cola

Movies			Cola		
Quantity (per month)	Total utility	Marginal utility	Cases (per month)	Total utility	Marginal utility
0	0		0	0	
		 50			 75
1	50		1	75	
		 40			 48
2	90		2	123	
		 32			 36
3	122		3	159	
		 28			 24
4	150		4	183	
		 26			 22
5	176		5	205	
		 24			 20
6	200		6	225	
		 22			 13
7	222		7	238	
		 20			 10
8	242		8	248	
		 17			 7
9	259		9	255	
		 16			 5
10	275		10	260	

Marginal Utility We define **marginal utility** as the *change* in total utility that results from a one-unit increase in the quantity of a good consumed.

In Table 8.1, the columns headed "Marginal utility" show Lisa's marginal utility from movies and cola. You can see that if Lisa increases the cola she buys from 1 to 2 cases a month, her total utility from cola increases from 75 units to 123 units. For Lisa, the marginal utility from the second case each month is 48 units (123 − 75).

The marginal utility numbers appear midway between the quantities of cola because it is the *change* in the quantity she buys from 1 to 2 cases that produces the marginal utility of 48 units.

Marginal utility is *positive,* but it *diminishes* as the quantity of a good consumed increases.

Positive Marginal Utility The things that people enjoy and want more of have a positive marginal utility. Some objects and activities can generate negative marginal utility and lower total utility. Two examples are hard labour and polluted air. But all the goods and services that people value and that we are thinking about here have positive marginal utility: Total utility increases as the quantity consumed increases.

Diminishing Marginal Utility As Lisa sees more movies, her total utility from movies increases but her marginal utility from movies decreases. Similarly, as she

FIGURE 8.2 Total Utility and Marginal Utility

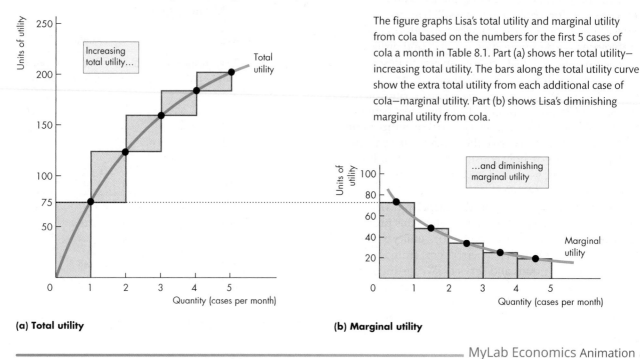

The figure graphs Lisa's total utility and marginal utility from cola based on the numbers for the first 5 cases of cola a month in Table 8.1. Part (a) shows her total utility—increasing total utility. The bars along the total utility curve show the extra total utility from each additional case of cola—marginal utility. Part (b) shows Lisa's diminishing marginal utility from cola.

(a) Total utility

(b) Marginal utility

MyLab Economics Animation

consumes more cola, her total utility from cola increases but her marginal utility from cola decreases.

The tendency for marginal utility to decrease as the consumption of a good increases is so general and universal that we give it the status of a *principle*—the principle of **diminishing marginal utility**.

You can see Lisa's diminishing marginal utility by calculating a few numbers. Her marginal utility from cola decreases from 75 units from the first case to 48 units from the second case and to 36 units from the third. Her marginal utility from movies decreases from 50 units for the first movie to 40 units for the second and 32 units for the third. Lisa's marginal utility diminishes as she buys more of each good.

Your Diminishing Marginal Utility You've been studying all day and into the evening, and you've been too busy finishing an assignment to shop for cola. A friend drops by with a can of cola. The utility you get from that cola is the marginal utility from your first cola of the day—from *one* can. On another day you've been on a cola binge. You've been working on an assignment, but you've guzzled 10 cans of cola while doing so, and are now totally wired. You are happy enough to have one more can, but the enjoyment that you get from it is not very large. It is the marginal utility from the *eleventh* can in a day.

Graphing Lisa's Utility Schedules Figure 8.2(a) illustrates Lisa's total utility from cola. The more cola Lisa consumes in a month, the more total utility she gets. Her total utility curve slopes upward.

Figure 8.2(b) illustrates Lisa's marginal utility from cola. It is a graph of the marginal utility numbers in Table 8.1. This graph shows Lisa's diminishing marginal utility from cola. Her marginal utility curve slopes downward as she consumes more cola.

We've described Lisa's consumption possibilities and preferences. Your next task is to see how Lisa chooses what to consume.

REVIEW QUIZ

1 Explain how a consumer's income and the prices of goods limit consumption possibilities.
2 What is utility and how do we use the concept of utility to describe a consumer's preferences?
3 What is the distinction between total utility and marginal utility?
4 What is the key assumption about marginal utility?

Work these questions in Study Plan 8.1 and get instant feedback. MyLab Economics

Utility-Maximizing Choice

Consumers want to get the most utility possible from their limited resources. They make the choice that maximizes utility. To discover this choice, we combine the constraint imposed by the budget and the consumer's preferences and find the point on the budget line that gives the consumer the maximum attainable utility. Let's find Lisa's utility-maximizing choice.

A Spreadsheet Solution

Lisa's most direct way of finding the quantities of movies and cola that maximize her utility is to make a table in a spreadsheet with the information and calculations shown in Table 8.2. Let's see what that table tells us.

Find the Just-Affordable Combinations Table 8.2 shows the combinations of movies and cola that Lisa can afford and that exhaust her $40 income. For example, in row *A*, Lisa buys only cola and at $4 a case she can buy 10 cases. In row *B*, Lisa sees 1 movie and buys 8 cases of cola. She spends $8 on the movie. At $4 a case, she spends $32 on cola and can buy 8 cases. The combination in row *B* just exhausts her $40. The combinations shown in the table are the same as those plotted on her budget line in Fig. 8.1.

We noted that the budget line shows that Lisa can also afford any combination *inside* the budget line. The quantities in those combinations would be smaller than the ones shown in Table 8.2, and they do not exhaust her $40. But smaller quantities don't maximize her utility. Why? The marginal utilities of movies and cola are positive, so the more of each that Lisa buys, the more total utility she gets.

Find the Total Utility for Each Just-Affordable Combination Table 8.2 shows the total utility that Lisa gets from the just-affordable quantities of movies and cola. The second and third columns show the numbers for movies and the fifth and sixth columns show those for cola. The centre column adds the total utility from movies to the total utility from cola. This number, the total utility from movies *and* cola, is what Lisa wants to maximize.

In row *A* of the table, Lisa's choice is to see no movies and to buy 10 cases of cola. She gets no utility from movies and 260 units of utility from cola, so her total utility from movies and cola (the centre column) is 260 units.

TABLE 8.2   Lisa's Utility-Maximizing Choice

	Movies $8		Total utility from movies and cola	Cola $4	
	Quantity (per month)	Total utility		Total utility	Cases (per month)
A	0	0	260	260	10
B	1	50	298	248	8
C	**2**	**90**	**315**	**225**	**6**
D	3	122	305	183	4
E	4	150	273	123	2
F	5	176	176	0	0

In row *C* of the table, Lisa sees 2 movies and buys 6 cases of cola. She gets 90 units of utility from movies and 225 units of utility from cola. Her total utility from movies and cola is 315 units. This combination of movies and cola maximizes Lisa's total utility. That is, given the prices of movies and cola, Lisa's best choice when she has $40 to spend is to see 2 movies and buy 6 cases of cola.

If Lisa sees 1 movie, she can buy 8 cases of cola, but she gets only 298 units of total utility—17 units less than the maximum attainable. If she sees 3 movies, she can buy only 4 cases of cola. She gets 305 units of total utility—10 units less than the maximum attainable.

Consumer Equilibrium We've just described Lisa's consumer equilibrium. A **consumer equilibrium** is a situation in which a consumer has allocated all of his or her available income in the way that maximizes his or her total utility, given the prices of goods and services. Lisa's consumer equilibrium is 2 movies and 6 cases of cola.

To find Lisa's consumer equilibrium, we did something that an economist might do but that a consumer is not likely to do: We measured her total utility from all the affordable combinations of movies and cola and then, by inspection of the numbers, selected the combination that gives the highest total utility. There is a more natural way of finding a consumer's equilibrium—a way that uses the idea that choices are made at the margin, as you first met in Chapter 1. Let's look at this approach.

Choosing at the Margin

When you go shopping you don't do utility calculations. But you do decide how to allocate your budget, and you do so in a way that you think is best for you. If you could make yourself better off by spending a few more dollars on an extra unit of one item and the same number of dollars less on something else, you would make that change. So, when you've allocated your budget in the best possible way, you can't make yourself better off by spending more on one item and less on others.

Marginal Utility per Dollar Economists interpret your best possible choice by using the idea of marginal utility per dollar. *Marginal utility* is the increase in total utility that results from consuming *one more unit* of a good. **Marginal utility per dollar** is the *marginal utility* from a good that results from spending *one more dollar* on it.

The distinction between these two marginal concepts is clearest for a good that is infinitely divisible, such as gasoline. You can buy gasoline by the smallest fraction of a litre and literally choose to spend one more or one less dollar at the pump. The increase in total utility that results from spending one more dollar at the pump is the marginal utility per dollar from gasoline. When you buy a movie ticket or a case of cola, you must spend your dollars in bigger lumps. So to buy our marginal movie ticket or case of cola, you must pay the price of one unit and your total utility increases by the marginal utility from that item. So in this caae, to calculate the marginal utility per dollar from movies (or from cola), we must divide marginal utility from the good by its price.

Call the marginal utility from movies MU_M and the price of a movie P_M. Then the *marginal utility per dollar from movies* is equal to:

$$MU_M/P_M.$$

Call the marginal utility from cola MU_C and the price of a case of cola P_C. Then the *marginal utility per dollar from cola* is equal to:

$$MU_C/P_C.$$

By comparing the marginal utility per dollar from all the goods that a person buys, we can determine whether the budget has been allocated in the way that maximizes total utility.

Let's see how we use the marginal utility per dollar to define a utility-maximizing rule.

Utility-Maximizing Rule A consumer's total utility is maximized by following the rule:

- Spend all the available income.
- Equalize the marginal utility per dollar for all goods.

Spend All the Available Income Because more consumption brings more utility, only those choices that exhaust income can maximize utility. For Lisa, combinations of movies and cola that leave her with money to spend don't give her as much total utility as those that exhaust her $40 per month income.

Equalize the Marginal Utility per Dollar The basic idea behind this rule is to move dollars from good B to good A if doing so increases the utility from good A by more than it decreases the utility from good B. Such a utility-increasing move is possible if the marginal utility per dollar from good A *exceeds* that from good B.

But buying more of good A decreases its marginal utility. And buying less of good B increases its marginal utility. So by moving dollars from good B to good A, total utility rises, and the gap between the marginal utilities per dollar gets smaller.

As long as the gap exists—as long as the marginal utility per dollar from good A exceeds that from good B—total utility can be increased by spending more on A and less on B. But when enough dollars have been moved from B to A to make the two marginal utilities per dollar equal, total utility cannot be increased further. Total utility is maximized.

Lisa's Marginal Calculation Let's apply the basic idea to Lisa. To calculate Lisa's marginal utility per dollar, we divide her marginal utility numbers for each quantity of each good by the price of the good. The table in Fig. 8.3 shows these calculations for Lisa, and the graph illustrates the situation on Lisa's budget line. The rows of the table are three of her affordable combinations of movies and cola.

Too Much Cola and Too Few Movies In row B, Lisa sees 1 movie a month and consumes 8 cases of cola a month. Her marginal utility from seeing 1 movie a month is 50 units. Because the price of a movie is $8, Lisa's marginal utility per dollar from movies is 50 units divided by $8, or 6.25 units of utility per dollar.

Lisa's marginal utility from cola when she consumes 8 cases of cola a month is 10 units. Because the price of cola is $4 a case, Lisa's marginal utility per dollar from cola is 10 units divided by $4, or 2.50 units of utility per dollar.

When Lisa sees 1 movie and consumes 8 cases of cola a month, her marginal utility per dollar from cola is *less than* her marginal utility per dollar from movies. That is,

$$MU_C/P_C < MU_M/P_M.$$

If Lisa spent an extra dollar on movies and a dollar less on cola, her total utility would increase. She would get 6.25 units from the extra dollar spent on movies and lose 2.50 units from the dollar less spent on cola. Her total utility would increase by 3.75 units (6.25 − 2.50).

Too Little Cola and Too Many Movies In row *D*, Lisa sees 3 movies a month and consumes 4 cases of cola. Her marginal utility from seeing the third movie a month is 32 units. At a price of $8 a movie, Lisa's marginal utility per dollar from movies is 32 units divided by $8, or 4 units of utility per dollar.

Lisa's marginal utility from cola when she buys 4 cases a month is 24 units. At a price of $4 a case, Lisa's marginal utility per dollar from cola is 24 units divided by $4, or 6 units of utility per dollar.

When Lisa sees 3 movies and consumes 4 cases of cola a month, her marginal utility per dollar from cola *exceeds* her marginal utility per dollar from movies. That is,

$$MU_C/P_C > MU_M/P_M.$$

If Lisa spent an extra dollar on cola and a dollar less on movies, her total utility would increase. She would get 6 units from the extra dollar spent on cola and she would lose 4 units from the dollar less spent on movies. Her total utility would increase by 2 units (6 − 4).

Utility-Maximizing Movies and Cola In Fig. 8.3, if Lisa moves from row *B* to row *C,* she increases the movies she sees from 1 to 2 a month and decreases the cola she consumes from 8 to 6 cases a month. Her marginal utility per dollar from movies falls to 5 and her marginal utility per dollar from cola rises to 5.

Similarly, if Lisa moves from row *D* to row *C,* she decreases the movies she sees from 3 to 2 a month and increases the cola she consumes from 4 to 6 cases a month. Her marginal utility per dollar from movies rises to 5 and her marginal utility per dollar from cola falls to 5.

When Lisa sees 2 movies and consumes 6 cases of cola a month, her marginal utility per dollar from

cola *equals* her marginal utility per dollar from movies. That is,

$$MU_C/P_C = MU_M/P_M.$$

Lisa can't move from this allocation of her budget without making herself worse off.

FIGURE 8.3 Equalizing Marginal Utilities per Dollar

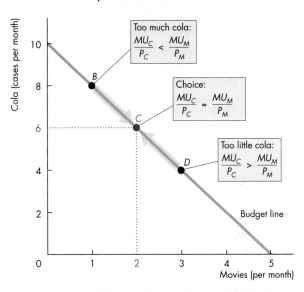

The graph shows Lisa's budget line and identifies three points on it. The rows of the table describe these points.

At point *B* (row *B*), with 1 movie and 8 cases of cola, Lisa's marginal utility per dollar from cola is less than that from movies: Buy less cola and see more movies.

At point *D* (row *D*), with 3 movies and 4 cases of cola, Lisa's marginal utility per dollar from cola is greater than that from movies: Buy more cola and see fewer movies.

At point *C* (row *C*), with 2 movies and 6 cases of cola, Lisa's marginal utility per dollar from cola is equal to that from movies: Lisa's utility is maximized.

	Movies ($8 each)			Cola ($4 per case)		
	Quantity	Marginal utility	Marginal utility per dollar	Cases	Marginal utility	Marginal utility per dollar
B	1	50	6.25	8	10	2.50
C	2	40	**5.00**	6	20	**5.00**
D	3	32	4.00	4	24	6.00

———MyLab Economics Animation and Draw Graph———

The Power of Marginal Analysis

The method we've just used to find Lisa's utility-maximizing choice of movies and cola is an example of the power of marginal analysis. Lisa doesn't need a computer and a spreadsheet program to maximize utility. She can achieve this goal by comparing the marginal gain from having more of one good with the marginal loss from having less of another good.

The rule that Lisa follows is simple: If the marginal utility per dollar from movies exceeds the marginal utility per dollar from cola, see more movies and buy less cola; if the marginal utility per dollar from cola exceeds the marginal utility per dollar from movies, buy more cola and see fewer movies.

More generally, if the marginal gain from an action exceeds the marginal loss, take the action. You will meet this principle time and again in your study of economics, and you will find yourself using it when you make your own economic choices, especially when you must make big decisions.

Revealing Preferences

When we introduced the idea of utility, we arbitrarily chose 50 units as Lisa's total utility from 1 movie, and we pretended that we asked Lisa to tell us how many units of utility she got from different quantities of cola and movies.

You're now about to discover that we don't need to ask Lisa to tell us her preferences. We can figure them out for ourselves by observing what she buys at various prices.

Also, the units in which we measure Lisa's preferences don't matter. Any arbitrary units will work. In this respect, utility is like temperature. Predictions about the freezing point of water don't depend on the temperature scale; and predictions about a household's consumption choice don't depend on the units of utility.

Lisa's Preferences In maximizing total utility by making the marginal utility per dollar equal for all goods, the units in which utility is measured do not matter.

You've seen that when Lisa maximizes her total utility, her marginal utility per dollar from cola, MU_C/P_C, equals her marginal utility per dollar from movies, MU_M/P_M. That is,

$$MU_C/P_C = MU_M/P_M.$$

Multiply both sides of this equation by the price of cola, P_C, to obtain

$$MU_C = MU_M \times (P_C/P_M).$$

This equation says that the marginal utility from cola, MU_C, is equal to the marginal utility from movies, MU_M, multiplied by the ratio of the price of cola, P_C, to the price of a movie, P_M.

The ratio P_C/P_M is the relative price of cola in terms of movies: It is the number of movies that must be forgone to get 1 case of cola, which is the opportunity cost of a case of cola. (See Chapter 2, p. 35, and Chapter 3, p. 60.)

For Lisa, when $P_M = \$8$ and $P_C = \$4$ we observe that in a month she goes to the movies twice and buys 6 cases of cola. So we know that her MU_C from 6 cases of cola equals her MU_M from 2 movies multiplied by \$4/\$8 or 0.5. That is, for Lisa, the marginal utility from 6 cases of cola equals one-half of the marginal utility from 2 movies.

If we observe the choices that Lisa makes at more prices, we can find more rows in her utility schedule. By her choices, Lisa reveals her preferences.

Units of Utility Don't Matter Lisa's marginal utility from 6 cases of cola is one-half of her marginal utility from 2 movies. So if the marginal utility from the second movie is 40 units, then the marginal utility from the sixth case of cola is 20 units. But if we call the marginal utility from the second movie 50 units, then the marginal utility from the sixth case of cola is 25 units. The units of utility are arbitrary.

◆ REVIEW QUIZ

1 Why does a consumer spend the entire budget?
2 What is the marginal utility per dollar and how is it calculated?
3 What two conditions are met when a consumer is maximizing utility?
4 Explain why equalizing the marginal utility per dollar for all goods maximizes utility.

Work these questions in Study Plan 8.2 and get instant feedback.   MyLab Economics

---

You now understand the marginal utility theory of consumer choices. Your next task is to see what the theory predicts.

Predictions of Marginal Utility Theory

We're now going to use marginal utility theory to make some predictions. You will see that marginal utility theory predicts the law of demand. The theory also predicts that a fall in the price of a substitute of a good decreases the demand for the good and that for a normal good, a rise in income increases demand. All these effects, which in Chapter 3 we simply assumed, are predictions of marginal utility theory.

To derive these predictions, we will study the effects of three events:

- A fall in the price of a movie
- A rise in the price of cola
- A rise in income

A Fall in the Price of a Movie

With the price of a movie at $8 and the price of cola at $4, Lisa is maximizing utility by seeing 2 movies and buying 6 cases of cola each month. Then, with no change in her $40 income and no change in the price of cola, the price of a movie falls from $8 to $4. How does Lisa change her buying plans?

Finding the New Quantities of Movies and Cola You can find the effect of a fall in the price of a movie on the quantities of movies and cola that Lisa buys in a three-step calculation:

1. Determine the just-affordable combinations of movies and cola at the new prices.
2. Calculate the new marginal utilities per dollar from the good whose price has changed.
3. Determine the quantities of movies and cola that make their marginal utilities per dollar equal.

Affordable Combinations The lower price of a movie means that Lisa can afford more movies or more cola. Table 8.3 shows her new affordable combinations. In row *A*, if she continues to see 2 movies a month, she can now afford 8 cases of cola; and in row *B*, if she continues to buy 6 cases of cola, she can now afford 4 movies. Lisa can afford any of the combinations shown in the rows of Table 8.3.

The next step is to find her new marginal utilities per dollar from movies.

New Marginal Utilities per Dollar from Movies A person's preferences don't change just because a price has changed. With no change in her preferences, Lisa's marginal utilities in Table 8.3 are the same as those in Table 8.1. But because the price of a movie has changed, the marginal utility *per dollar* from movies changes. In fact, with a halving of the price of a movie from $8 to $4, the marginal utility per dollar from movies has doubled.

The numbers in Table 8.3 show Lisa's new marginal utility per dollar from movies for each quantity of movies. The table also shows Lisa's marginal utility per dollar from cola for each quantity.

Equalizing the Marginal Utilities per Dollar You can see that if Lisa continues to see 2 movies a month and buy 6 cases of cola, her marginal utility per dollar from movies (row *A*) is 10 units and her marginal utility per dollar from cola (row *B*) is 5 units. Lisa is buying too much cola and too few movies. If she spends a dollar more on movies and a dollar less on cola, her total utility increases by 5 units (10 − 5).

If Lisa continues to buy 6 cases of cola and increases the number of movies to 4 (row *B*), her

TABLE 8.3 How a Change in the Price of Movies Affects Lisa's Choices

		Movies ($4 each)			Cola ($4 per case)		
	Quantity	Marginal utility	Marginal utility per dollar	Cases	Marginal utility	Marginal utility per dollar
	0	0		10	5	1.25
	1	50	12.50	9	7	1.75
A	2	40	**10.00**	8	10	2.50
	3	32	8.00	7	13	3.25
B	4	28	7.00	**6**	20	**5.00**
	5	26	6.50	5	22	5.50
C	6	24	**6.00**	4	24	**6.00**
	7	22	5.50	3	36	9.00
	8	20	5.00	2	48	12.00
	9	17	4.25	1	75	18.75
	10	16	4.00	0	0	

marginal utility per dollar from movies falls to 7 units, but her marginal utility per dollar from cola is 5 units. Lisa is still buying too much cola and seeing too few movies. If she spends a dollar more on movies and a dollar less on cola, her total utility increases by 2 units (7 − 5).

But if Lisa sees 6 movies and buys 4 cases of cola a month (row *C*), her marginal utility per dollar from movies (6 units) equals her marginal utility per dollar from cola and she is maximizing utility. If Lisa moves from this allocation of her budget in either direction, her total utility decreases.

Lisa's increased purchases of movies results from a substitution effect—she substitutes the now lower-priced movies for cola—and an income effect—she can afford more movies.

A Change in the Quantity Demanded Lisa's increase in the quantity of movies that she sees is a change in the quantity demanded. It is the change in the quantity of movies that she plans to see each month when the price of a movie changes and all other influences on buying plans remain the same. We illustrate a change in the quantity demanded by a movement along a demand curve.

Figure 8.4(a) shows Lisa's demand curve for movies. When the price of a movie is $8, Lisa sees 2 movies a month. When the price of a movie falls to $4, she sees 6 movies a month. Lisa moves downward along her demand curve for movies.

The demand curve traces the quantities that maximize utility at each price, with all other influences remaining the same. You can also see that utility-maximizing choices generate a downward-sloping demand curve. Utility maximization with diminishing marginal utility implies the law of demand.

A Change in Demand The decrease in the quantity of cola that Lisa buys at a given price of cola is the change in the quantity of cola that she plans to buy at that price when the price of a movie changes. It is a change in her demand for cola. We illustrate a change in demand by a shift of a demand curve.

Figure 8.4(b) shows Lisa's demand curve for cola. The price of cola is fixed at $4 a case. When the price of a movie is $8, Lisa buys 6 cases of cola on demand curve D_0. When the price of a movie falls to $4, Lisa buys 4 cases of cola on demand curve D_1. The fall in the price of a movie decreases Lisa's demand for cola. Her demand curve for cola shifts leftward. For Lisa, cola and movies are substitutes.

FIGURE 8.4 A Fall in the Price of a Movie

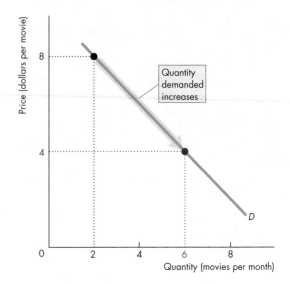

(a) Demand for movies

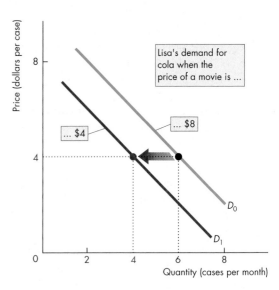

(b) Demand for cola

When the price of a movie falls and the price of cola remains the same, the quantity of movies demanded by Lisa increases, and in part (a), Lisa moves along her demand curve for movies. Also, when the price of a movie falls, Lisa's demand for cola decreases, and in part (b), her demand curve for cola shifts leftward. For Lisa, cola and movies are substitutes.

MyLab Economics Animation

A Rise in the Price of Cola

Now suppose that with the price of a movie at $4, the price of cola rises from $4 to $8 a case. How does this price change influence Lisa's buying plans? We find the answer by repeating the three-step calculation with the new price of cola.

Table 8.4 shows Lisa's new affordable combinations. In row *A*, if she continues to buy 4 cases of cola a month she can afford to see only 2 movies; and in row *B*, if she continues to see 6 movies a month, she can afford only 2 cases of cola.

Table 8.4 show Lisa's marginal utility per dollar from cola for each quantity of cola when the price is $8 a case. The table also shows Lisa's marginal utility per dollar from movies for each quantity.

If Lisa continues to buy 4 cases of cola (row *A*), her marginal utility per dollar from cola is 3 units. But she must cut the movies she sees to 2, which increases her marginal utility per dollar from movies to 10 units. Lisa is buying too much cola and seeing too few movies. If she spends a dollar less on cola and a dollar more on movies, her utility increases by 7 units (10 − 3).

But if Lisa sees 6 movies a month and cuts her cola to 2 cases (row *B*), her marginal utility per dollar from movies (6 units) equals her marginal utility per dollar from cola. She is maximizing utility.

Lisa's decreased purchases of cola results from an income effect—she can afford fewer cases and she buys fewer cases. But she continues to buy the same quantity of movies.

Lisa's Demand for Cola Now that we've calculated the effect of a change in the price of cola on Lisa's buying plans when income and the price of movies remain the same, we have found two points on her demand curve for cola: When the price of cola is $4 a case, Lisa buys 4 cases a month; and when the price of cola is $8 a case, she buys 2 cases a month.

Figure 8.5 shows these points on Lisa's demand curve for cola. It also shows the change in the quantity of cola demanded when the price of cola rises and all other influences on Lisa's buying plans remain the same.

In this example, Lisa continues to buy the same quantity of movies, but this outcome does not always occur. It is a consequence of Lisa's preferences. With different marginal utilities, she might have decreased or increased the quantity of movies that she sees when the price of cola changes.

You've seen that marginal utility theory predicts the law of demand—the way in which the quantity demanded of a good changes when its price changes. Next, we'll see how marginal utility theory predicts the effect of a change in income on demand.

TABLE 8.4 How a Change in the Price of Cola Affects Lisa's Choices

	Movies ($4 each)			Cola ($8 per case)		
	Quantity	Marginal utility	Marginal utility per dollar	Cases	Marginal utility	Marginal utility per dollar
	0	0		5	22	2.75
A	2	40	10.00	**4**	24	**3.00**
	4	28	7.00	3	36	4.50
B	**6**	24	**6.00**	**2**	48	**6.00**
	8	20	5.00	1	75	9.38
	10	16	4.00	0	0	

FIGURE 8.5 A Rise in the Price of Cola

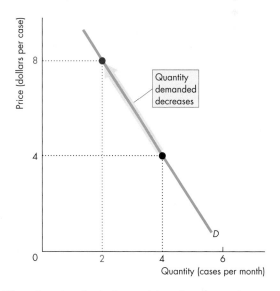

When the price of cola rises and the price of a movie and Lisa's income remain the same, the quantity of cola demanded by Lisa decreases. Lisa moves along her demand curve for cola.

A Rise in Income

Suppose that Lisa's income increases from $40 to $56 a month and that the price of a movie is $4 and the price of cola is $4 a case. With these prices and with an income of $40 a month, Lisa sees 6 movies and buys 4 cases of cola a month (Table 8.3). How does the increase in Lisa's income from $40 to $56 change her buying plans?

Table 8.5 shows the calculations needed to answer this question. If Lisa continues to see 6 movies a month, she can now afford to buy 8 cases of cola (row *A*); if she continues to buy 4 cases of cola, she can now afford to see 10 movies (row *C*).

In row *A*, Lisa's marginal utility per dollar from movies is greater than her marginal utility per dollar from cola. She is buying too much cola and too few movies. In row *C*, Lisa's marginal utility per dollar from movies is less than her marginal utility per dollar from cola. She is buying too little cola and too many movies. But in row *B*, when Lisa sees 8 movies a month and buys 6 cases of cola, her marginal utility per dollar from movies equals that from cola. She is maximizing utility.

Figure 8.6 shows the effects of the rise in Lisa's income on her demand curves for movies and cola. The price of each good is $4. When Lisa's income

TABLE 8.5   Lisa's Choices with an Income of $56 a Month

Movies ($4 each)			Cola ($4 per case)		
Quantity	Marginal utility	Marginal utility per dollar	Cases	Marginal utility	Marginal utility per dollar
4	28	7.00	10	5	1.25
5	26	6.50	9	7	1.75
A 6	24	**6.00**	8	10	2.50
7	22	5.50	7	13	3.25
B 8	20	**5.00**	**6**	20	**5.00**
9	17	4.25	5	22	5.50
C 10	16	4.00	**4**	24	**6.00**

rises to $56 a month, she sees 2 more movies and buys 2 more cases of cola. Her demand curves for both movies and cola shift rightward—her demand for both movies and cola increases. With a larger income, the consumer always buys more of a *normal* good. For Lisa, movies and cola are normal goods.

FIGURE 8.6   The Effects of a Rise in Income

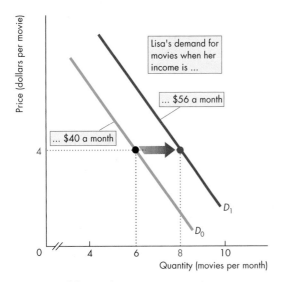

(a) Demand for movies

When Lisa's income increases, her demand for movies and her demand for cola increase. Lisa's demand curves for movies, in

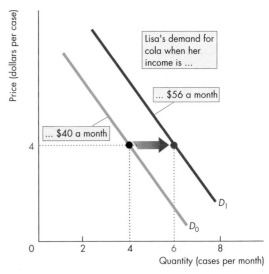

(b) Demand for cola

part (a), and for cola, in part (b), shift rightward. For Lisa, movies and cola are normal goods.

The Paradox of Value

The price of water is low and the price of a diamond is high, but water is essential to life while diamonds are used mostly for decoration. How can valuable water be so cheap while a relatively useless diamond is so expensive? This so-called *paradox of value* has puzzled philosophers for centuries. Not until the theory of marginal utility had been developed could anyone give a satisfactory answer.

The Paradox Resolved The paradox is resolved by distinguishing between *total* utility and *marginal* utility. The total utility that we get from water is enormous. But remember, the more we consume of something, the smaller is its marginal utility.

We use so much water that its marginal utility—the benefit we get from one more glass of water or another 30 seconds in the shower—diminishes to a small value.

Diamonds, on the other hand, have a small total utility relative to water, but because we buy few diamonds, they have a high marginal utility.

When a household has maximized its total utility, it has allocated its income in the way that makes the marginal utility per dollar equal for all goods. That is, the marginal utility from a good divided by the price of the good is equal for all goods.

This equality of marginal utilities per dollar holds true for diamonds and water: Diamonds have a high price and a high marginal utility. Water has a low price and a low marginal utility. When the high marginal utility from diamonds is divided by the high price of a diamond, the result is a number that equals the low marginal utility from water divided by the low price of water. The marginal utility per dollar is the same for diamonds and water.

Value and Consumer Surplus Another way to think about the paradox of value and illustrate how it is resolved uses *consumer surplus*. Figure 8.7 explains the paradox of value by using this idea. The supply of water in part (a) is perfectly elastic at price P_W, so the quantity of water consumed is Q_W and the large green area shows the consumer surplus from water. The supply of diamonds in part (b) is perfectly inelastic at the quantity Q_D, so the price of a diamond is P_D and the small green area shows the consumer surplus from diamonds. Water is cheap, but brings a large consumer surplus; diamonds are expensive, but bring a small consumer surplus.

FIGURE 8.7   The Paradox of Value

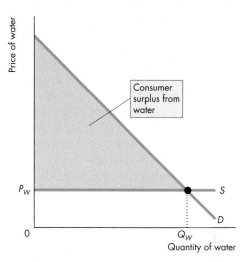

(a) Water

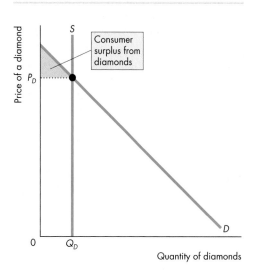

(b) Diamonds

Part (a) shows the demand for and supply of water. Supply is perfectly elastic at the price P_W. At this price, the quantity of water consumed is Q_W and the large green triangle shows consumer surplus. Part (b) shows the demand for and supply of diamonds. Supply is perfectly inelastic at the quantity Q_D. At this quantity, the price of a diamond is P_D and the small green triangle shows consumer surplus. Water is valuable—has a large consumer surplus—but cheap. Diamonds are less valuable than water—have a smaller consumer surplus—but are expensive.

—— MyLab Economics Animation and Draw Graph ——

Temperature: An Analogy

Utility is similar to temperature—both are abstract concepts. You can't *observe* temperature. You can observe water turning to steam if it is hot enough or turning to ice if it is cold enough. You can also construct an instrument—a thermometer—that can help you to predict when such changes will occur. We call the scale on the thermometer *temperature* and we call the units of temperature *degrees*. But like the units of utility, these degree units are arbitrary. We can use Celsius units or Fahrenheit units or some other units.

The concept of utility helps us to make predictions about consumption choices in much the same way that the concept of temperature helps us to make predictions about physical phenomena.

Admittedly, marginal utility theory does not enable us to predict how buying plans change with the same precision that a thermometer enables us to predict when water will turn to ice or steam. But the theory provides important insights into buying plans and has some powerful implications. It helps us to understand why people buy more of a good or service when its price falls and why people buy more of most goods when their incomes increase. It also resolves the paradox of value.

We're going to end this chapter by looking at some new ways of studying individual economic choices and consumer behaviour.

REVIEW QUIZ

1 When the price of a good falls and the prices of other goods and a consumer's income remain the same, explain what happens to the consumption of the good whose price has fallen and to the consumption of other goods.

2 Elaborate on your answer to the previous question by using demand curves. For which good does demand change and for which good does the quantity demanded change?

3 If a consumer's income increases and if all goods are normal goods, explain how the quantity bought of each good changes.

4 What is the paradox of value and how is the paradox resolved?

5 What are the similarities between utility and temperature?

Work these questions in Study Plan 8.3 and get instant feedback.   MyLab Economics

ECONOMICS IN ACTION

Maximizing Utility from Recorded Music

In 2016, Americans spent $7.7 billion on recorded music, down from $14 billion in 2001. But the combined quantity of discs and downloads bought didn't fall. It was almost the same in 2016 as it had been in 2001, at 1 billion units.

The amount spent on recorded music fell because the mix of formats bought changed dramatically. In 2001, we bought 900 million CDs; in 2016, we bought only 99 million CDs and downloaded 850 million music files. At its peak in 2012, we downloaded 1.6 billion music files. Figure 1 shows the history of the changing formats of recorded music since 1973.

The biggest change in recent years is streaming. Starting with 9 percent of the revenue in 2011, streaming had grown to 51 percent of revenue in 2016.

The music that we buy isn't just one good—it is several goods. Singles and albums are different goods; streams, downloads, and physical discs are different goods.

We get utility from the singles and albums that we buy, and the more songs and albums we have, the more utility we get. But our marginal utility from songs and albums decreases as the quantity that we own increases.

We also get utility from convenience. A song that we can buy with a mouse click and play with the touch of a screen is more convenient both to buy and to use than a song on a CD. The convenience of songs streamed or downloaded over the Internet means that, song for song, we get more utility from a digital song than we get from a song on a physical CD.

But albums are still played at home on a CD player. So, for some people, a physical CD is a more convenient medium for delivering an album. Album for album, people on average get more utility from a physical CD than from a digital album.

When we decide how many singles and albums to stream, download, or buy on CD, we compare the marginal utility per dollar from each type of music in each format. We make the marginal utility per dollar from each type of music in each format equal.

The market for single downloads created consumer surplus. We can get an indication of the size of this surplus by estimating the demand for singles. Figure 2 illustrates this demand. One point on the demand curve is the 2001 price and quantity—100 million singles were bought at an average price of $5.00. Another point on the demand curve is that for 2012—1,400 million singles downloaded at $1.20 each.

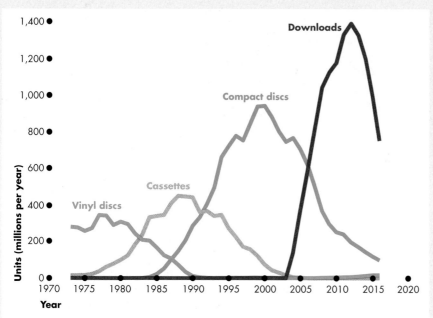

Figure 1 **Changing Formats of Recorded Music**

In the 1970s, recorded music came on vinyl discs. Cassettes gradually replaced vinyl, then compact discs (CDs) gradually replaced cassettes, and today, digital files downloaded to computers and mobile devices replaced physical CDs. And now, downloads are in decline as streaming takes off. (We don't know the quantity of files streamed.)

Source of data: The Recording Industry Association of America.

If the demand curve has not shifted and is linear (assumed here), we can calculate the consumer surplus in 2012, shown as the green area of Fig. 2. Consumer surplus was ($5.30 − $1.20) × 1,400/2, or $2.9 billion. The amount spent on downloads in 2012 was $1.7 billion ($1.20 × 1,400 million).

The market for music streaming has also created consumer surplus. Figure 3 illustrates this surplus using the same demand curve. Streaming is paid for with an up-front subscription, so the price of an additional streamed single is zero and the quantity demanded is where the demand curve hits the *x*-axis. Consumer surplus was $5.30 × 1,800/2, or $4.8 billion, minus the amount spent on streaming subscriptions, which in 2016 was $2.6 billion, so consumer surplus was $2.2 billion. Apple, Spotify, and other suppliers of streaming have taken some of the consumer surplus that downloaders used to enjoy!

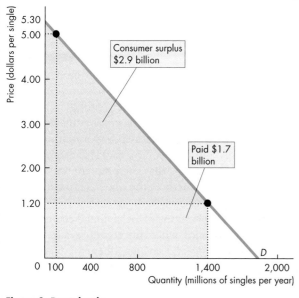

Figure 2 **Downloads**

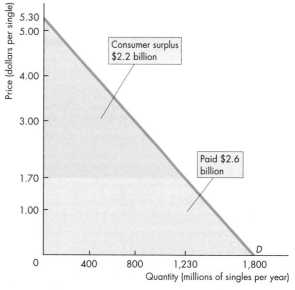

Figure 3 **Streaming**

◆ New Ways of Explaining Consumer Choices

When William Stanley Jevons developed marginal utility theory in the 1860s, he would have loved to look inside people's brains and "see" their utility. But he believed that the human brain was the ultimate black box that could never be observed directly. For Jevons, and for most economists today, the purpose of marginal utility theory is to explain our *actions*, not what goes on inside our brains.

Economics has developed over the past 150 years with little help from and paying little attention to advances being made in psychology. Both economics and psychology seek to explain human behaviour, but they have developed different ways of attacking the challenge.

A few researchers *have* paid attention to the potential payoff from exploring economic problems by using the tools of psychology. These researchers, some economists and some psychologists, think that marginal utility theory is based on a view of how people make choices that attributes too much to reason and rationality. They propose an alternative approach based on the methods of psychology.

Other researchers, some economists and some neuroscientists, are using new tools to look inside the human brain and open up Jevons' "black box."

This section provides a very brief introduction to these new and exciting areas of economics. We'll explore the two related research agendas:

- Behavioural economics
- Neuroeconomics

Behavioural Economics

Behavioural economics studies the ways in which limits on the human brain's ability to compute and implement rational decisions influences economic behaviour—both the decisions that people make and the consequences of those decisions for the way markets work.

Behavioural economics starts with observed behaviour. It looks for anomalies—choices that do not seem to be rational. It then tries to account for the anomalies by using ideas developed by psychologists that emphasize features of the human brain that limit rational choice.

In behavioural economics, instead of being rational utility maximizers, people are assumed to have three impediments that prevent rational choice: bounded rationality, bounded willpower, and bounded self-interest.

Bounded Rationality Bounded rationality is rationality that is limited by the computing power of the human brain. We can't always work out the rational choice.

For Lisa, choosing between movies and cola, it seems unlikely that she would have much trouble figuring out what to buy. But toss Lisa some uncertainty and the task becomes harder. She's read the reviews of *Iron Man 3* on Fandango, but does she really want to see that movie? How much marginal utility will it give her? Faced with uncertainty, people might use rules of thumb, listen to the views of others, and make decisions based on gut instinct rather than on rational calculation.

Bounded Willpower Bounded willpower is the less-than-perfect willpower that prevents us from making a decision that we know, at the time of implementing the decision, we will later regret.

Lisa might be feeling particularly thirsty when she passes a cola vending machine. Under Lisa's rational utility-maximizing plan, she buys her cola at the discount store, where she gets it for the lowest possible price. Lisa has already bought her cola for this month, but it is at home. Spending $1 on a can now means giving up a movie later this month.

Lisa's rational choice is to ignore the temporary thirst and stick to her plan. But she might not possess the willpower to do so—sometimes she will and sometimes she won't.

Bounded Self-Interest Bounded self-interest is the limited self-interest that results in sometimes suppressing our own interests to help others.

A hurricane hits the Florida coast and Lisa, feeling sorry for the victims, donates $10 to a fundraiser. She now has only $30 to spend on movies and cola this month. The quantities that she buys are not, according to her utility schedule, the ones that maximize her utility.

The main applications of behavioural economics are in two areas: finance, where uncertainty is a key factor in decision making, and savings, where the future is a key factor. But one behaviour observed by behavioural economists is more general and might affect your choices. It is called the endowment effect.

The Endowment Effect The endowment effect is the tendency for people to value something more highly simply because they own it. If you have allocated your income to maximize utility, then the price you would be willing to accept to give up something that you own (for example, your coffee mug) should be the same as the price you are willing to pay for an identical one.

In experiments, students seem to display the endowment effect: The price they are willing to pay for a coffee mug that is identical to the one they own is less than the price they would be willing to accept to give up the coffee mug that they own. Behavioural economists say that this behaviour contradicts marginal utility theory.

Neuroeconomics

Neuroeconomics is the study of the activity of the human brain when a person makes an economic decision. The discipline uses the observational tools and ideas of neuroscience to obtain a better understanding of economic decisions.

Neuroeconomics is an experimental discipline. In an experiment, a person makes an economic decision and the electrical or chemical activity of the person's brain is observed and recorded using the same type of equipment that neurosurgeons use to diagnose brain disorders.

The observations provide information about which regions of the brain are active at different points in the process of making an economic decision.

Observations show that some economic decisions generate activity in the area of the brain (called the prefrontal cortex) where we store memories, analyze data, and anticipate the consequences of our actions. If people make rational utility-maximizing decisions, it is in this region of the brain that the decision occurs.

But observations also show that some economic decisions generate activity in the region of the brain (called the hippocampus) where we store memories of anxiety and fear. Decisions that are influenced by activity in this part of the brain might not be rational and be driven by fear or panic.

Neuroeconomists are also able to observe the amount of a brain hormone (called dopamine), the quantity of which increases in response to pleasurable events and decreases in response to disappointing events. These observations might one day enable neuroeconomists to actually measure utility and shine a bright light inside what was once believed to be the ultimate black box.

Controversy

The new ways of studying consumer choice that we've briefly described here are being used more widely to study business decisions and decisions in financial markets, and this type of research is surely going to become more popular.

But behavioural economics and neuroeconomics generate controversy. Most economists hold the view of Jevons that the goal of economics is to explain the decisions that we observe people making and not to explain what goes on inside people's heads.

Most economists would prefer to probe apparent anomalies more deeply and figure out why they are not anomalies after all.

Economists also point to the power of marginal utility theory and its ability to explain consumer choice and demand as well as resolve the paradox of value.

REVIEW QUIZ

1 Define behavioural economics.
2 What are the three limitations on human rationality that behavioural economics emphasizes?
3 Define neuroeconomics.
4 What do behavioural economics and neuroeconomics seek to achieve?

Work these questions in Study Plan 8.4 and get instant feedback.   MyLab Economics

◆ You have now completed your study of the marginal utility theory and learned some new ideas about how people make economic choices. You can see marginal utility theory in action once again in *Economics in the News* on pp. 198–199, where it is used to compare Canadian cellphone data plans with the new unlimited data deals that U.S. wireless service providers now offer.

Consumer Choice with Unlimited Data

R.I.P. Data Plans

CBC News

March 7, 2017

The United States is in the midst of an unlimited data revolution. Its five largest cellular providers — AT&T, Verizon, Sprint, T-Mobile, and U.S. Cellular — all now offer phone plans with unlimited wireless data.

Prices range from $50 to $90 U.S. a month, and there are some caveats. For example, you might not get high-definition video streaming. Also, data speeds can slow down after burning through 22 to 28 GB — still, that's a lot of data.

Meanwhile, in Canada no major provider offers a true unlimited deal. That's something that frustrates many Canadians, who have a growing appetite for it.

"At this point in 2017, now, we should totally have unlimited data plans," says Toronto cellphone customer Simon Connolly.

He pays $85 a month for a plan with 5 GB, and uses his data for everything from communicating to banking. . . .

None of the big three in Canada — Bell, Rogers, and Telus — offer unlimited wireless data plans. . . .

CBC News asked the major players why they don't offer unlimited wireless plans.

Bell said that its customers already have plenty of options including plans with "generous" amounts of data. The company also said that the usage-based approach is needed to pay for the "tremendous costs" required to build high-speed broadband networks in Canada and manage the surge in mobile data use. As for Rogers, "It just isn't feasible to offer unlimited plans," said spokesperson Andrew Garas in an email to CBC News. He added that the company offers customers tools to manage and monitor their data use. . . .

© CBC Licensing

ESSENCE OF THE STORY

- The five largest U.S. cellular providers offer phone plans with unlimited wireless data.

- Prices range from $50 to $90 U.S. a month— equivalent to $70 to $125 Canadian.

- Data speeds can slow after using 22 GB to 28 GB.

- No Canadian provider offers unlimited data.

- A Toronto cellphone customer pays $85 Canadian a month for a plan with 5 GB of data.

ECONOMIC ANALYSIS

- Which cellular user gets the better deal, an American with unlimited wireless data, or a Canadian who pays for the data used?

- We can answer this question by comparing the situation facing a U.S. cellular user with that of a Canadian user described in the news article.

- A U.S. cellular user can get unlimited wireless data for a price that ranges between $50 and $90 U.S. a month—between $70 and $125 in Canadian.

- We will assume that an average U.S user pays $95 Canadian a month—for high speed unlimited wireless data.

- The news article tells us that a Canadian pays $85 for 5 gigabytes (GB) a month.

- Canadian cellular data plans start at about $60 for 1 GB, and increase for more GB.

- For $95 a month, a typical Canadian cellular plan provides 6 GB of data.

- You can now see that which cellphone user gets the better deal depends on the amount of data used. Below 6 GB per month, a Canadian pays less for cellular data than an American pays; at 6 GB, both pay the same; and above 6 GB, an American pays less.

- But what determines the amount of wireless data that a person uses?

- The answer is the person's utility schedule.

- For an American with unlimited wireless data, the quantity of data used is that at which marginal utility is zero. That is the quantity that maximizes total utility.

- For a Canadian who pays about $7 per GB per month, the quantity of data used is that at which the marginal utility per dollar from data equals the marginal utility per dollar from other goods and services.

- A Canadian with a marginal utility per dollar from data equal to the marginal utility per dollar from other goods and services at 5 GB per month gets a better deal than an American whose marginal utility per dollar from data is zero at 5 GB. The Canadian pays $85 and the American pays $95.

- But a Canadian with a marginal utility per dollar from data equal to the marginal utility per dollar from other goods and services at (say) 10 GB per month gets a worse deal than an American whose marginal utility per dollar from data is zero at 10 GB. The Canadian pays around $115 but the American still pays $95.

- Figure 1 illustrates these outcomes and comparisons. The figure shows the budget line for an American, BL_{US}, and the budget line for a Canadian, BL_{CAN}, where each has a monthly budget of $400 to spend on data and other goods and services.

- The American budget line shows that any amount of data can be used with 305 units of other goods and services costing $305.

- The Canadian budget line shows that as data use increases, other goods and services decrease.

- The Canadian in the news article uses 5 GB, the point at which the marginal utility per dollar (MU_D/P_D) from data equals the marginal utility per dollar (MU_O/P_O) from other goods and services.

- An American who uses 10 GB of data when the marginal utility from data (MU_D) equals zero at that quantity gets the better deal.

- An American and a Canadian get equal deals if their utility-maximizing choice is 6 GB per month.

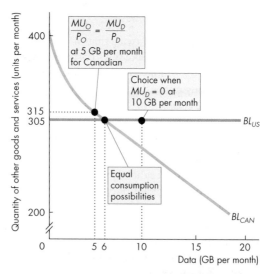

Figure 1 Cellphone Data Plan Budget Lines

WORKED PROBLEM

MyLab Economics Work this problem in Chapter 8 Study Plan.

Jake has a budget of $10 per week to spend on song downloads and cookies. The table shows his marginal utility from each good.

Quantity per week	Marginal utility from a song	Marginal utility from a cookie
1	14	20
2	12	16
3	11	12
4	10	8
5	9	4
6	8	3
7	7	2
8	6	1

Questions

1. If the price of a song is $1 and the price of a cookie is $2, what are the quantities of songs and cookies in the table that exhaust Jake's budget?

2. How does Jake allocate his $10 between songs and cookies?

3. If the price of a song rises to $2 and the price of a cookie remains at $2, does Jake buy fewer songs and cookies, or only fewer songs?

Solutions

1. The price of a cookie is twice that of a song, so each additional cookie Jake buys costs him 2 fewer songs—the opportunity cost of a cookie is 2 songs. So Jake can buy either 8 songs and 1 cookie, or 6 songs and 2 cookies, or 4 songs and 3 cookies, or 2 songs and 4 cookies.

   Key Point: To exhaust the budget, all income is spent.

2. To find the quantities of songs and cookies that Jake buys, use the fact that to maximize utility, he must make the marginal utility per dollar the same for the two goods.

   Make a table in which each row is an affordable combination and that shows the marginal utility for each good. Then calculate the marginal utility per dollar for each row.

   The table in the next column shows the calculations. Check the calculation on row B, with 4 songs and 3 cookies. The marginal utility of a song is 10 units and because the price of a song is $1, the marginal utility per dollar is also 10 units.

	Songs ($1 each)			Cookies ($2 each)		
	Quantity	Marginal utility	Marginal utility per dollar	Quantity	Marginal utility	Marginal utility per dollar
A	2	12	12	4	8	4
B	4	10	10	3	12	6
C	6	8	8	2	16	8
D	8	6	6	1	20	10

The marginal utility of a cookie is 12 units, and because the price of a cookie is $2, the marginal utility per dollar is 6 units.

Because the marginal utility per dollar from 4 songs *exceeds* that from 3 cookies, Jake can increase his total utility by buying more songs and fewer cookies.

In the highlighted row C, the marginal utilities per dollar are equal and total utility is maximized. So Jake buys 6 songs and 2 cookies to maximize utility.

Key Point: Total utility is maximized when the marginal utility per dollar is the same for all goods.

3. If the price of a song rises to $2, the affordable combinations shrink. Jake can now afford combinations of quantities that total 5. The table shows the new combinations that exhaust Jake's budget. It also shows the marginal utility per dollar for each possibility.

	Songs ($2 each)			Cookies ($2 each)		
	Quantity	Marginal utility	Marginal utility per dollar	Quantity	Marginal utility	Marginal utility per dollar
A	1	14	14	4	8	4
B	2	12	6	3	12	6
C	3	11	5.5	2	16	8
D	4	10	5	1	20	10

To maximize his utility, Jake now buys only 2 songs and increases his consumption of cookies to 3 per week in row B.

Key Point: When the price of a good rises, the utility-maximizing quantity of that good decreases, but the quantity of other goods bought might increase or decrease.

◆ SUMMARY

Key Points

Consumption Choices (pp. 182–184)

- A household's consumption choices are determined by its consumption possibilities and preferences.
- A budget line defines a household's consumption possibilities.
- A household's preferences can be described by a utility schedule that lists the total utility and marginal utility derived from various quantities of goods and services consumed.
- The principle of diminishing marginal utility is that the marginal utility from a good or service decreases as consumption of the good or service increases.

Working Problems 1 to 5 will give you a better understanding of consumption choices.

Utility-Maximizing Choice (pp. 185–188)

- A consumer's objective is to maximize total utility.
- Total utility is maximized when all the available income is spent and when the marginal utility per dollar from all goods is equal.
- If the marginal utility per dollar from good *A* exceeds that from good *B*, total utility increases if the quantity of good *A* purchased increases and the quantity of good *B* purchased decreases.

Working Problems 6 to 8 will give you a better understanding of a consumer's utility-maximizing choice.

Predictions of Marginal Utility Theory (pp. 189–195)

- Marginal utility theory predicts the law of demand. That is, other things remaining the same, the higher the price of a good, the smaller is the quantity demanded of that good.
- Marginal utility theory also predicts that, other things remaining the same, an increase in the consumer's income increases the demand for a normal good.
- Marginal utility theory resolves the paradox of value.
- Total value is *total* utility or consumer surplus. But price is related to *marginal* utility.
- Water, which we consume in large amounts, has a high total utility and a large consumer surplus, but the price of water is low and the marginal utility from water is low.
- Diamonds, which we buy in small quantities, have a low total utility and a small consumer surplus, but the price of a diamond is high and the marginal utility from diamonds is high.

Working Problems 9 to 13 will give you a better understanding of the predictions of marginal utility theory.

New Ways of Explaining Consumer Choices (pp. 196–197)

- Behavioural economics studies limits on the ability of the human brain to compute and implement rational decisions.
- Bounded rationality, bounded willpower, and bounded self-interest are believed to explain some choices.
- Neuroeconomics uses the ideas and tools of neuroscience to study the effects of economic events and choices inside the human brain.

Working Problems 14 and 15 will give you a better understanding of the new ways of explaining consumer choices.

Key Terms

MyLab Economics Key Terms Quiz

Behavioural economics, 196

Budget line, 182

Consumer equilibrium, 185

Diminishing marginal utility, 184

Marginal utility, 183

Marginal utility per dollar, 186

Neuroeconomics, 197

Preferences, 183

Total utility, 183

Utility, 183

STUDY PLAN PROBLEMS AND APPLICATIONS

MyLab Economics   Work Problems 1 to 15 in Chapter 8 Study Plan and get instant feedback.

Consumption Choices (Study Plan 8.1)

Jerry has $12 a week to spend on yogurt and berries. The price of yogurt is $2, and berries are $4 a box.

1. List the combinations of yogurt and berries that Jerry can afford. Draw a graph of his budget line with the quantity of berries plotted on the x-axis.

2. How do Jerry's consumption possibilities change if, other things remaining the same, (i) the price of berries falls and (ii) Jerry's income increases?

Use the following data to work Problems 3 to 5.

Max has $35 a day to spend on windsurfing and snorkelling and he can spend as much time as he likes doing them. The price of renting equipment for windsurfing is $10 an hour and for snorkelling is $5 an hour. The table shows the total utility Max gets from each activity.

Hours per day	Total utility from windsurfing	Total utility from snorkelling
1	120	40
2	220	76
3	300	106
4	360	128
5	396	140
6	412	150
7	422	158

3. Calculate Max's marginal utility from windsurfing at each number of hours per day. Does Max's marginal utility from windsurfing obey the principle of diminishing marginal utility?

4. Calculate Max's marginal utility from snorkelling at each number of hours per day. Does Max's marginal utility from snorkelling obey the principle of diminishing marginal utility?

5. Which does Max enjoy more: his 6th hour of windsurfing or his 6th hour of snorkelling?

Utility-Maximizing Choice (Study Plan 8.2)

Use the data in Problem 3 to work Problems 6 to 8.

6. Make a table of the combinations of hours spent windsurfing and snorkelling that Max can afford.

7. Add two columns to your table in Problem 6 and list Max's marginal utility per dollar from windsurfing and from snorkelling.

8. a. To maximize his utility, how many hours a day does Max spend on each activity?

b. If Max spent a dollar more on windsurfing and a dollar less on snorkelling than in part (a), how would his total utility change?

c. If Max spent a dollar less on windsurfing and a dollar more on snorkelling than in part (a), how would his total utility change?

Predictions of Marginal Utility Theory (Study Plan 8.3)

Use the data in Problem 3 to work Problems 9 to 13.

9. If the price of renting windsurfing equipment is cut to $5 an hour, how many hours a day does Max spend on each activity?

10. Draw Max's demand curve for rented windsurfing equipment. Over the price range $5 to $10 an hour, is Max's demand elastic or inelastic?

11. How does Max's demand for snorkelling equipment change when the price of windsurfing equipment falls? What is Max's cross elasticity of demand for snorkelling with respect to the price of windsurfing? Are windsurfing and snorkelling substitutes or complements for Max?

12. If Max's income increases from $35 to $55 a day, how does his demand for windsurfing equipment change? Is windsurfing a normal good? Explain.

13. If Max's income increases from $35 to $55 a day, how does his demand for snorkelling equipment change? Is snorkelling a normal good? Explain.

New Ways of Explaining Consumer Choices (Study Plan 8.4)

Use the news clip to work Problems 14 and 15.

A Great Deal and a Great Way to Enjoy a Game!

The Pittsburgh Pirates offer all the hot dogs, hamburgers, nachos, salads, popcorn, peanuts, ice cream, and soda you can handle for a fixed price at every home game.

Source: Pittsburgh Pirates website

14. What conflict might exist between utility maximization and eating "all you can handle"? What feature of the marginal utility from ballpark food enables the Pirates to make this offer?

15. How can over-eating at a ball game be reconciled with marginal utility theory? Which ideas of behavioural economics are consistent with over-eating at a ball game?

ADDITIONAL PROBLEMS AND APPLICATIONS

MyLab Economics You can work these problems in Homework or Test if assigned by your instructor.

Consumption Choices

16. Tim buys 2 pizzas and sees 1 movie a week when he has $16 to spend, a movie ticket is $8, and a pizza is $4. Draw Tim's budget line. If the price of a movie ticket falls to $4, describe how Tim's consumption possibilities change.

17. Cindy has $70 a month to spend, and she can spend as much time as she likes playing golf and tennis. The price of an hour of golf is $10, and the price of an hour of tennis is $5. The table shows Cindy's marginal utility from each sport.

Hours per month	Marginal utility from golf	Marginal utility from tennis
1	80	40
2	60	36
3	40	30
4	30	10
5	20	5
6	10	2
7	6	1

Make a table that shows Cindy's affordable combinations of hours playing golf and tennis. If Cindy increases her expenditure to $100, describe how her consumption possibilities change.

Utility-Maximizing Choice

Use the information in Problem 17 to work Problems 18 to 24.

18. a. How many hours of golf and how many hours of tennis does Cindy play to maximize her utility?

    b. Compared to part (a), if Cindy spent a dollar more on golf and a dollar less on tennis, by how much would her total utility change?

    c. Compared to part (a), if Cindy spent a dollar less on golf and a dollar more on tennis, by how much would her total utility change?

19. Explain why, if Cindy equalized the marginal utility per hour of golf and tennis, she would *not* maximize her utility.

Predictions of Marginal Utility Theory

Cindy's tennis club raises its price of an hour of tennis from $5 to $10, other things remaining the same.

20. a. List the combinations of hours spent playing golf and tennis that Cindy can now afford and her marginal utility per dollar from golf and from tennis.

    b. How many hours does Cindy now spend playing golf and how many hours does she spend playing tennis?

21. Use the information in Problem 20 to draw Cindy's demand curve for tennis. Over the price range of $5 to $10 an hour of tennis, is Cindy's demand for tennis elastic or inelastic?

22. Explain how Cindy's demand for golf changed when the price of an hour of tennis increased from $5 to $10 in Problem 20. What is Cindy's cross elasticity of demand for golf with respect to the price of tennis? Are tennis and golf substitutes or complements for Cindy?

23. Cindy loses her math tutoring job and the amount she has to spend on golf and tennis falls from $70 to $35 a month. With the price of an hour of golf at $10 and of tennis at $5, calculate the change in the hours she spends playing golf. For Cindy, is golf a normal good or an inferior good? Is tennis a normal good or an inferior good?

24. Cindy takes a Club Med vacation, the cost of which includes unlimited sports activities. With no extra charge for golf and tennis, Cindy allocates a total of 4 hours a day to these activities.

    a. How many hours does Cindy play golf and how many hours does she play tennis?

    b. What is Cindy's marginal utility from golf and from tennis?

    c. Why does Cindy equalize the marginal utilities rather than the marginal utility per dollar from golf and from tennis?

25. Jim has made his best affordable choice of muffins and coffee. He spends all of his income on 10 muffins at $1 each and 20 cups of coffee at $2 each. Now the price of a muffin rises to $1.50 and the price of coffee falls to $1.75 a cup.

    a. Can Jim still buy 10 muffins and 20 coffees?

b. If Jim changes the quantities he buys, will he buy more or fewer muffins and more or less coffee? Expain your answer.

26. Ben spends $50 a year on 2 bunches of flowers and $50 a year on 10,000 litres of tap water. Ben is maximizing utility and his marginal utility from water is 0.5 unit per litre.

a. Are flowers or water more valuable to Ben?

b. Explain how Ben's expenditure on flowers and water illustrates the paradox of value.

New Ways of Explaining Consumer Choices

Use the following news clip to work Problems 27 to 29.

Putting a Price on Human Life

Researchers at Stanford and the University of Pennsylvania estimated that a healthy human life is worth about $129,000. Using Medicare records on treatment costs for kidney dialysis as a benchmark, the authors tried to pinpoint the threshold beyond which ensuring another "quality" year of life was no longer financially worthwhile. The study comes amid debate over whether Medicare should start rationing healthcare on the basis of cost effectiveness.

Source: *Time*, June 9, 2008

27. Why might Medicare ration healthcare according to treatment that is "financially worthwhile" as opposed to providing as much treatment as is needed by a patient, regardless of costs?

28. What conflict might exist between a person's valuation of his or her own life and the rest of society's valuation of that person's life?

29. How does the potential conflict between self-interest and the social interest complicate setting a financial threshold for Medicare treatments?

Economics in the News

30. After you have studied *Economics in the News* (pp. 198–199), answer the following questions.

a. If the price of an unlimited data plan increased,

(i) How would the number of people who buy the service change?

(ii) How would the quantity of data used change for someone who keeps buying blocks of data?

b. If the price per GB of a Canadian data plan increased,

(i) How would the number of people who buy a 1 GB plan change?

(ii) How would the quantity of data used by the average person change?

31. **Companies Are Racing to Add Value to Water**

Svalbardi, a water sourced from Norwegian icebergs that are up to 4,000 years old, sells for $99 a bottle. From extreme luxury to the ordinary, the market for bottled water is growing quickly as people switch from soft drinks and alcohol to healthier alternatives. Market researchers report that consumption of bottled water overtook that of sugary soft drinks in America in 2016.

Source: *The Economist*, March 25, 2017

a. Assuming that the price of an ordinary bottle of water is $1, what can we infer about the marginal utility of a bottle of ordinary water and the marginal utility of a bottle of Svalbardi for a person who buys 1 bottle of Svalbardi and 100 bottles of ordinary water per year?

b. Why might the marginal utility from a bottle of Svalbardi decrease more rapidly than the marginal utility from ordinary bottled water?

32. **Money Can Buy Happiness, But Only to a Point**

They say money can't buy happiness. Of course, they're wrong. Research by economist David Clingingsmith at the Weatherhead School of Management shows that household income is positively related to emotional well-being and a person's evaluation of their own quality of life. For people who earn less than $200,000 a year, getting a pay rise improves their emotional well-being. Above $200,000 the effects tail off.

Source: CNBC, December 14, 2015

Based on the research reported in the news clip,

a. How does an increase in income for people who earn less than $200,000 a year influence total utility?

b. How does an increase in income for people who earn less than $200,000 a year influence marginal utility?

POSSIBILITIES, PREFERENCES, AND CHOICES

After studying this chapter, you will be able to:

◆ Describe a household's budget line and show how it changes when prices or income change

◆ Use indifference curves to map preferences and explain the principle of diminishing marginal rate of substitution

◆ Predict the effects of changes in prices and income on consumption choices

Video streaming has revolutionized the way we watch movies, yet we're still going to movie theatres in similar numbers. Why? Why hasn't Netflix replaced the movie theatre?

Most Canadian students complete a 4-year degree in 4 years, but only 40 percent of American students do, and this percentage has been falling. Why does it take Americans longer to get a degree?

In this chapter, you're going to study a model that answers these questions. You will see why streaming hasn't replaced movie theatres and why an increasing percentage of U.S. college students take longer than their Canadian cousins to complete a degree.

◆ Consumption Possibilities

Consumption choices are limited by income and by prices. A household has a given amount of income to spend and cannot influence the prices of the goods and services it buys. A household's **budget line** describes the limits to its consumption choices.

Let's look at Lisa's budget line.* Lisa has an income of $40 a month to spend. She buys two goods: movies and cola. The price of a movie is $8, and the price of cola is $4 a case.

Figure 9.1 shows alternative combinations of movies and cola that Lisa can afford. In row *A*, she sees no movies and buys 10 cases of cola. In row *F*, she sees 5 movies and buys no cola. Both of these combinations of movies and cola exhaust the $40 available. Check that the combination of movies and cola in each of the other rows also exhausts Lisa's $40 of income. The numbers in the table and the points *A* through *F* in the graph describe Lisa's consumption possibilities.

Divisible and Indivisible Goods Some goods— called divisible goods—can be bought in any quantity desired. Examples are gasoline and electricity. We can best understand household choice if we suppose that all goods and services are divisible. For example, Lisa can see half a movie a month on average by seeing one movie every two months. When we think of goods as being divisible, the consumption possibilities are not only the points *A* through *F* shown in Fig. 9.1, but also all the intermediate points that form the line running from *A* to *F*. This line is Lisa's budget line.

Affordable and Unaffordable Quantities Lisa's budget line is a constraint on her choices. It marks the boundary between what is affordable and what is unaffordable. She can afford any point on the line and inside it. She cannot afford any point outside the line. The constraint on her consumption depends on the prices and her income, and the constraint changes when the price of a good or her income changes. To see how, we use a budget equation.

---

*If you have studied Chapter 8 on marginal utility theory, you have already met Lisa. This tale of her thirst for cola and zeal for movies will sound familiar to you—up to a point. In this chapter, we're going to explore her budget line in more detail and use a different method for representing preferences—one that does not require the idea of utility.

FIGURE 9.1 The Budget Line

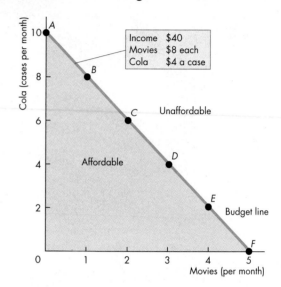

Consumption possibility	Movies (per month)	Cola (cases per month)
A	0	10
B	1	8
C	2	6
D	3	4
E	4	2
F	5	0

Lisa's budget line shows the boundary between what she can and cannot afford. The rows of the table list Lisa's affordable combinations of movies and cola when her income is $40, the price of cola is $4 a case, and the price of a movie is $8. For example, row *A* tells us that Lisa spends all of her $40 income when she buys 10 cases of cola and sees no movies. The figure graphs Lisa's budget line. Points *A* through *F* in the graph represent the rows of the table. For divisible goods, the budget line is the continuous line *AF*. To calculate the equation for Lisa's budget line, start with expenditure equal to income:

$$\$4Q_C + \$8Q_M = \$40.$$

Divide by $4 to obtain

$$Q_C + 2Q_M = 10.$$

Subtract $2Q_M$ from both sides to obtain

$$Q_C = 10 - 2Q_M.$$

MyLab Economics Animation

Budget Equation

We can describe the budget line by using a *budget equation*. The budget equation starts with the fact that

$$\text{Expenditure} = \text{Income}.$$

Expenditure is equal to the sum of the price of each good multiplied by the quantity bought. For Lisa,

$$\text{Expenditure} = (\text{Price of cola} \times \text{Quantity of cola})$$
$$+ (\text{Price of a movie} \times \text{Quantity of movies}).$$

Call the price of cola P_C, the quantity of cola Q_C, the price of a movie P_M, the quantity of movies Q_M, and income Y. We can now write Lisa's budget equation as

$$P_C Q_C + P_M Q_M = Y.$$

Or, using the prices Lisa faces, $4 a case of cola and $8 a movie, and Lisa's income, $40, we get

$$\$4 Q_C + \$8 Q_M = \$40.$$

Lisa can choose any quantities of cola (Q_C) and movies (Q_M) that satisfy this equation. To find the relationship between these quantities, divide both sides of the equation by the price of cola (P_C) to get

$$Q_C + (P_M/P_C) \times QM = Y/P_C$$

Now subtract the term $(P_M/P_C) \times Q_M$ from both sides of this equation to get

$$Q_C = Y/P_C - (P_M/P_C) \times Q_M$$

For Lisa, income (Y) is $40, the price of a movie (P_M) is $8, and the price of cola (P_C) is $4 a case. So Lisa must choose the quantities of movies and cola to satisfy the equation

$$Q_C = \$40/\$4 - (\$8/\$4)Q_M$$

or

$$Q_C = 10 - 2Q_M.$$

To interpret the equation, look at the budget line in Fig. 9.1 and check that the equation delivers that budget line. First, set Q_M equal to zero. The budget equation tells us that Q_C, the quantity of cola, is Y/P_C, which is 10 cases. This combination of Q_M and Q_C is the one shown in row A of the table in Fig. 9.1. Next set Q_M equal to 5. Q_C now equals zero (row F of the table). Check that you can derive the other rows.

The budget equation contains two variables chosen by the household (Q_M and Q_C) and two variables that the household takes as given (Y/P_C and P_M/P_C). Let's look more closely at these variables.

Real Income A household's **real income** is its income expressed as a quantity of goods that the household can afford to buy. Expressed in terms of cola, Lisa's real income is Y/P_C. This quantity of cola is the maximum quantity that she can buy. It is equal to her money income divided by the price of cola. Lisa's money income is $40 and the price of cola is $4 a case, so her real income in terms of cola is 10 cases, which is shown in Fig. 9.1 as the point at which the budget line intersects the y-axis.

Relative Price A **relative price** is the price of one good divided by the price of another good. In Lisa's budget equation, the variable P_M/P_C is the relative price of a movie in terms of cola. For Lisa, P_M is $8 a movie and P_C is $4 a case, so P_M/P_C is equal to 2 cases of cola per movie. That is, to see 1 movie, Lisa must give up 2 cases of cola.

You've just calculated Lisa's opportunity cost of seeing a movie. Recall that the opportunity cost of an action is the best alternative forgone. For Lisa to see 1 more movie a month, she must forgo 2 cases of cola. You've also calculated Lisa's opportunity cost of cola. For Lisa to buy 2 more cases of cola a month, she must forgo seeing 1 movie. So her opportunity cost of 2 cases of cola is 1 movie.

The relative price of a movie in terms of cola is the magnitude of the slope of Lisa's budget line. To calculate the slope of the budget line, recall the formula for slope (see the Chapter 1 Appendix): Slope equals the change in the variable measured on the y-axis divided by the change in the variable measured on the x-axis as we move along the line. In Lisa's case (Fig. 9.1), the variable measured on the y-axis is the quantity of cola and the variable measured on the x-axis is the quantity of movies. Along Lisa's budget line, as cola decreases from 10 to 0 cases, movies increase from 0 to 5. So the magnitude of the slope of the budget line is 10 cases divided by 5 movies, or 2 cases of cola per movie. The magnitude of this slope is exactly the same as the relative price we've just calculated. It is also the opportunity cost of a movie.

A Change in Prices When prices change, so does the budget line. The lower the price of the good measured on the x-axis, other things remaining the same, the flatter is the budget line. For example, if the price of a movie falls from $8 to $4, real income

FIGURE 9.2   Changes in Prices and Income

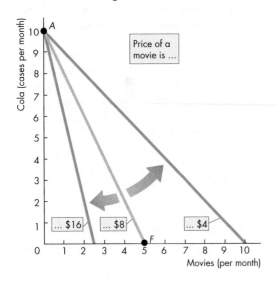

(a) A change in price

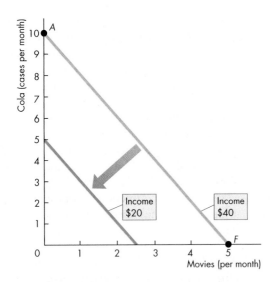

(b) A change in income

In part (a), the price of a movie changes. A fall in the price from $8 to $4 rotates the budget line outward and makes it flatter. A rise in the price from $8 to $16 rotates the budget line inward and makes it steeper.

In part (b), income falls from $40 to $20 while the prices of movies and cola remain the same. The budget line shifts leftward, but its slope does not change.

—— MyLab Economics Animation and Draw Graph ——

in terms of cola does not change, but the relative price of a movie falls. The budget line rotates outward and becomes flatter, as Fig. 9.2(a) illustrates. The higher the price of the good measured on the *x*-axis, other things remaining the same, the steeper is the budget line. For example, if the price of a movie rises from $8 to $16, the relative price of a movie increases. The budget line rotates inward and becomes steeper, as Fig. 9.2(a) illustrates.

A Change in Income A change in money income changes real income but does not change the relative price. The budget line shifts, but its slope does not change. An increase in money income increases real income and shifts the budget line rightward. A decrease in money income decreases real income and shifts the budget line leftward.

Figure 9.2(b) shows the effect of a change in money income on Lisa's budget line. The initial budget line when Lisa's income is $40 is the same as in Fig. 9.1. The new budget line shows how much Lisa can buy if her income falls to $20 a month. The two budget lines have the same slope because the relative price is the same. The new budget line is closer to the origin because Lisa's real income has decreased.

◆ REVIEW QUIZ

1 What does a household's budget line show?
2 How does the relative price and a household's real income influence its budget line?
3 If a household has an income of $40 and buys only bus rides at $2 each and magazines at $4 each, what is the equation of the household's budget line?
4 If the price of one good changes, what happens to the relative price and the slope of the household's budget line?
5 If a household's money income changes and prices do not change, what happens to the household's real income and budget line?

Work these questions in Study Plan 9.1 and get instant feedback.   MyLab Economics

We've studied the limits to what a household can consume. Let's now learn how we can describe preferences and make a map that contains a lot of information about a household's preferences.

Preferences and Indifference Curves

You are going to discover a very cool idea: that of drawing a map of a person's preferences. A preference map is based on the intuitively appealing idea that people can sort all the possible combinations of goods into three groups: preferred, not preferred, and indifferent. To make this idea more concrete, let's ask Lisa to tell us how she ranks various combinations of movies and cola.

Figure 9.3 shows part of Lisa's answer. She tells us that she currently sees 2 movies and buys 6 cases of cola a month at point C. She then lists all the combinations of movies and cola that she says are just as acceptable to her as her current situation. When we plot these combinations of movies and cola, we get the green curve in Fig. 9.3(a). This curve is the key element in a preference map and is called an indifference curve.

An **indifference curve** is a line that shows combinations of goods among which a consumer is *indifferent*. The indifference curve in Fig. 9.3(a) tells us that Lisa is just as happy to see 2 movies and buy 6 cases of cola a month at point C as she is to have the combination of movies and cola at point G or at any other point along the curve.

Lisa also says that she prefers all the combinations of movies and cola above the indifference curve in Fig. 9.3(a)—the yellow area—to those on the indifference curve. And she prefers any combination on the indifference curve to any combination in the grey area below the indifference curve.

The indifference curve in Fig. 9.3(a) is just one of a whole family of such curves. This indifference curve appears again in Fig. 9.3(b), labelled I_1. The curves labelled I_0 and I_2 are two other indifference curves. Lisa prefers any point on indifference curve I_2 to any point on indifference curve I_1, and she prefers any point on I_1 to any point on I_0. We refer to I_2 as being a higher indifference curve than I_1 and I_1 as being higher than I_0.

A preference map is a series of indifference curves that resemble the contour lines on a map. By looking at the shape of the contour lines on a map, we can draw conclusions about the terrain. Similarly, by looking at the shape of the indifference curves, we can draw conclusions about a person's preferences.

Let's learn how to "read" a preference map.

FIGURE 9.3 A Preference Map

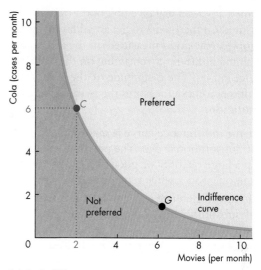

(a) An indifference curve

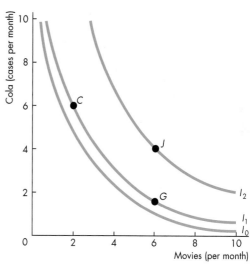

(b) Lisa's preference map

Part (a) shows one of Lisa's indifference curves. She is indifferent between point C (with 2 movies and 6 cases of cola) and all other points on the green indifference curve, such as G. She prefers points above the indifference curve (in the yellow area) to points on it, and she prefers points on the indifference curve to points below it (in the grey area). Part (b) shows three of the indifference curves—I_0, I_1, and I_2—in Lisa's preference map. She prefers point J to point C or G, and she prefers all the points on I_2 to those on I_1.

Marginal Rate of Substitution

The **marginal rate of substitution** (*MRS*) is the rate at which a person will give up good y (the good measured on the y-axis) to get an additional unit of good x (the good measured on the x-axis) while remaining indifferent (remaining on the same indifference curve). The magnitude of the slope of an indifference curve measures the marginal rate of substitution.

- If the indifference curve is *steep*, the marginal rate of substitution is *high*. The person is willing to give up a large quantity of good y to get an additional unit of good x while remaining indifferent.
- If the indifference curve is *flat*, the marginal rate of substitution is *low*. The person is willing to give up a small amount of good y to get an additional unit of good x while remaining indifferent.

Figure 9.4 shows you how to calculate the marginal rate of substitution.

At point C on indifference curve I_1, Lisa buys 6 cases of cola and sees 2 movies. Her marginal rate of substitution is the magnitude of the slope of the indifference curve at point C. To measure this magnitude, place a straight line against, or tangent to, the indifference curve at point C. Along that line, as the quantity of cola decreases by 10 cases, the number of movies increases by 5—or 2 cases per movie. At point C, Lisa is willing to give up cola for movies at the rate of 2 cases per movie—a marginal rate of substitution of 2.

At point G on indifference curve I_1, Lisa buys 1.5 cases of cola and sees 6 movies. Her marginal rate of substitution is measured by the slope of the indifference curve at point G. That slope is the same as the slope of the tangent to the indifference curve at point G. Now, as the quantity of cola decreases by 4.5 cases, the number of movies increases by 9—or 1/2 case per movie. At point G, Lisa is willing to give up cola for movies at the rate of 1/2 case per movie—a marginal rate of substitution of 1/2.

As Lisa sees more movies and buys less cola, her marginal rate of substitution diminishes. Diminishing marginal rate of substitution is the key assumption about preferences. A **diminishing marginal rate of substitution** is a general tendency for a person to be willing to give up less of good y to get one more unit of good x, while at the same time remaining indifferent as the quantity of x increases. In Lisa's case, she is less willing to give up cola to see one more movie as the number of movies she sees increases.

FIGURE 9.4 The Marginal Rate of Substitution

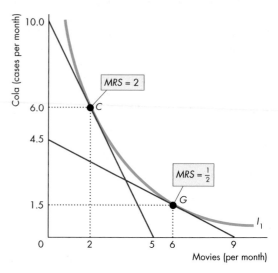

The magnitude of the slope of an indifference curve is called the marginal rate of substitution (*MRS*). The red line at point C tells us that Lisa is willing to give up 10 cases of cola to see 5 movies. Her marginal rate of substitution at point C is 10 divided by 5, which equals 2. The red line at point G tells us that Lisa is willing to give up 4.5 cases of cola to see 9 movies. Her marginal rate of substitution at point G is 4.5 divided by 9, which equals 1/2.

———MyLab Economics Animation and Draw Graph———

Your Diminishing Marginal Rate of Substitution Think about your own diminishing marginal rate of substitution. Imagine that in a week, you drink 10 cases of cola and see no movies. Most likely, you are willing to give up a lot of cola so that you can see just 1 movie. But now imagine that in a week, you buy 1 case of cola and see 6 movies. Most likely, you will now not be willing to give up much cola to see a seventh movie. As a general rule, the greater the number of movies you see, the smaller is the quantity of cola you are willing to give up to see one additional movie.

The shape of a person's indifference curves incorporates the principle of the diminishing marginal rate of substitution because the curves are bowed toward the origin. The tightness of the bend of an indifference curve tells us how willing a person is to substitute one good for another while remaining indifferent. Let's look at some examples that make this point clear.

Degree of Substitutability

Most of us would not regard movies and cola as being *close* substitutes, but they are substitutes. No matter how much you love cola, some increase in the number of movies you see will compensate you for being deprived of a can of cola. Similarly, no matter how much you love going to the movies, some number of cans of cola will compensate you for being deprived of seeing one movie. A person's indifference curves for movies and cola might look something like those for most ordinary goods and services shown in Fig. 9.5(a).

Close Substitutes Some goods substitute so easily for each other that most of us do not even notice which we are consuming. The different brands of marker pens and pencils are examples. Most people don't care which brand of these items they use or where they buy them. A marker pen from the campus bookstore is just as good as one from the local grocery store. You would be willing to forgo a pen from the campus store if you could get one more pen from

the local grocery store. When two goods are perfect substitutes, their indifference curves are straight lines that slope downward, as Fig. 9.5(b) illustrates. The marginal rate of substitution is constant.

Complements Some goods do not substitute for each other at all. Instead, they are complements. The complements in Fig. 9.5(c) are left and right running shoes. Indifference curves of perfect complements are L-shaped. One left running shoe and one right running shoe are as good as one left shoe and two right shoes. Having two of each is preferred to having one of each, but having two of one and one of the other is no better than having one of each.

The extreme cases of perfect substitutes and perfect complements shown here don't often happen in reality, but they do illustrate that the shape of the indifference curve shows the degree of substitutability between two goods. The closer the two goods are to perfect substitutes, the closer the marginal rate of substitution is to being constant (a straight line), rather than diminishing (a curved line). Indifference

---

FIGURE 9.5 The Degree of Substitutability

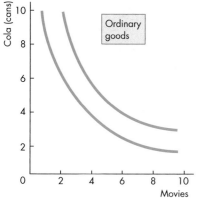

(a) Ordinary goods

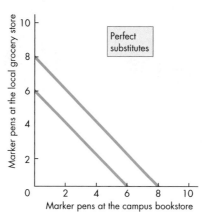

(b) Perfect substitutes

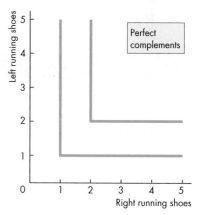

(c) Perfect complements

The shape of the indifference curves reveals the degree of substitutability between two goods. Part (a) shows the indifference curves for two ordinary goods: movies and cola. To drink less cola and remain indifferent, one must see more movies. The number of movies that compensates for a reduction in cola increases as less cola is consumed. Part (b) shows the indifference curves for two perfect substitutes. For the consumer to

remain indifferent, one fewer marker pen from the local grocery store must be replaced by one extra marker pen from the campus bookstore. Part (c) shows two perfect complements—goods that cannot be substituted for each other at all. Having two left running shoes with one right running shoe is no better than having one of each. But having two of each is preferred to having one of each.

"With the pork I'd recommend an Alsatian white or a Coke."

© The New Yorker Collection 1988
Robert Weber from cartoonbank.com. All Rights Reserved.

curves for poor substitutes are tightly curved and lie between the shapes of those shown in Figs. 9.5(a) and 9.5(c).

As you can see in the cartoon, according to the waiter's preferences, Coke and Alsatian white wine are perfect substitutes and each is a complement of pork. We hope the customers agree with him.

REVIEW QUIZ

1 What is an indifference curve and how does a preference map show preferences?
2 Why does an indifference curve slope downward and why is it bowed toward the origin?
3 What do we call the magnitude of the slope of an indifference curve?
4 What is the key assumption about a consumer's marginal rate of substitution?

Work these questions in Study Plan 9.2 and get instant feedback.   MyLab Economics

The two components of the model of household choice are now in place: the budget line and the preference map. We will now use these components to work out a household's choice and to predict how choices change when prices and income change.

◆ Predicting Consumer Choices

We are now going to predict the quantities of movies and cola that Lisa chooses to buy. We're also going to see how these quantities change when a price changes or when Lisa's income changes. Finally, we're going to see how the *substitution effect* and the *income effect*, two ideas that you met in Chapter 3 (see p. 61), guarantee that for a normal good, the demand curve slopes downward.

Best Affordable Choice

When Lisa makes her best affordable choice of movies and cola, she spends all her income and is on her highest attainable indifference curve. Figure 9.6 illustrates this choice: The budget line is from Fig. 9.1 and the indifference curves are from Fig. 9.3(b). Lisa's best affordable choice is 2 movies and 6 cases of cola at point *C*—the *best affordable point*.

FIGURE 9.6   The Best Affordable Choice

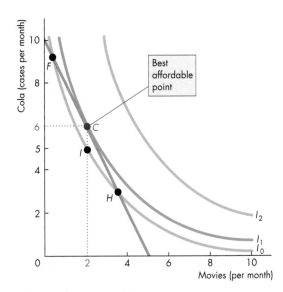

Lisa's best affordable choice is at point *C*, the point on her budget line and on her highest attainable indifference curve. At point *C*, Lisa's marginal rate of substitution between movies and cola (the magnitude of the slope of the indifference curve I_1) equals the relative price of movies and cola (the slope of the budget line).

—— MyLab Economics Animation and Draw Graph ——

On the Budget Line The best affordable point is on the budget line. For every point inside the budget line, such as point I, there are points on the budget line that Lisa prefers. For example, she prefers all the points on the budget line between F and H to point I, so she chooses a point on the budget line.

On the Highest Attainable Indifference Curve Every point on the budget line lies on an indifference curve. For example, points F and H lie on the indifference curve I_0. By moving along her budget line from either F or H toward C, Lisa reaches points on ever-higher indifference curves that she prefers to points F or H. When Lisa gets to point C, she is on the highest attainable indifference curve.

Marginal Rate of Substitution Equals Relative Price At point C, Lisa's marginal rate of substitution between movies and cola (the magnitude of the slope of the indifference curve) is equal to the relative price of movies and cola (the magnitude of the slope of the budget line). Lisa's willingness to pay for a movie equals her opportunity cost of a movie.

Let's now see how Lisa's choices change when a price changes.

A Change in Price

The effect of a change in the price of a good on the quantity of the good consumed is called the **price effect**. We will use Fig. 9.7(a) to work out the price effect of a fall in the price of a movie. We start with the price of a movie at $8, the price of cola at $4 a case, and Lisa's income at $40 a month. In this situation, she buys 6 cases of cola and sees 2 movies a month at point C.

Now suppose that the price of a movie falls to $4. With a lower price of a movie, the budget line rotates outward and becomes flatter. The new budget line is the darker orange one in Fig. 9.7(a). For a refresher on how a price change affects the budget line, check back to Fig. 9.2(a).

Lisa's best affordable point is now point J, where she sees 6 movies and drinks 4 cases of cola. Lisa drinks less cola and watches more movies now that movies are cheaper. She cuts her cola purchases from 6 to 4 cases and increases the number of movies she sees from 2 to 6 a month. When the price of a movie falls and the price of cola and her income remain constant, Lisa substitutes movies for cola.

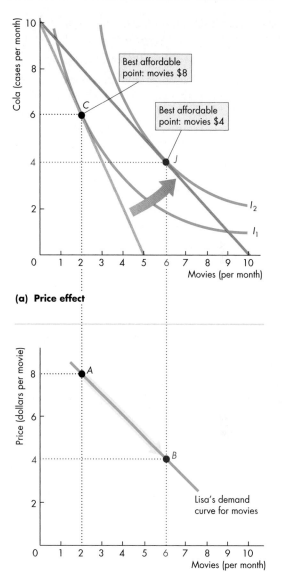

FIGURE 9.7 Price Effect and Demand Curve

(a) Price effect

(b) Demand curve

Initially, Lisa's best affordable point is C in part (a). If the price of a movie falls from $8 to $4, Lisa's best affordable point is J. The move from C to J is the price effect.

At a price of $8 a movie, Lisa sees 2 movies a month, at point A in part (b). At a price of $4 a movie, she sees 6 movies a month, at point B. Lisa's demand curve for movies traces out her best affordable quantity of movies as the price of a movie varies.

————— MyLab Economics Animation —————

ECONOMICS IN ACTION

Best Affordable Choice of Movies, DVD Rentals, and Streaming

Between 2005 and 2017, movie viewing increased but movie box-office numbers didn't change much. Why?

The answer is that changes in technology have changed the budget line and changed the best affordable choice. Let's look at the recent history of the markets for DVD rentals and movie streaming.

Back in 2005, there was no video streaming and home movies were delivered on rented DVDs. Blockbuster was the main player and the price of a DVD rental was around $4 a night. Redbox entered the market and the price of a DVD rental tumbled to $1 a night.

The next change was video streaming. In 2011, Netflix started offering unlimited streaming subscriptions for the price of one movie ticket—$7.99 a month. For existing subscribers, Netflix maintained this price to 2017.

The figure shows the effects of these changes on a student's budget line and the student's best affordable choice. The student has a budget of $48 a month to allocate to movies. The price of a movie ticket was unchanged at $8. The price of a DVD rental in 2005 was $4, so the student's budget line was the one labelled 2005. The student's best affordable point was 2 rentals and 5 movie tickets a month.

In 2010, the price of a DVD rental had fallen to $1 a night and with the price of a movie ticket remaining at $8, the budget line rotated outward. The student's best affordable point became 8 rentals and 5 movie tickets a month.

In 2017, a one-month Netflix subscription cost $8, so the student can now buy 5 movie tickets a month (spending $40) and watch an unlimited number of streamed movies.

The student's best affordable point is 18 streamed movies and 5 trips to the movie theatre. Indifference curve I_2 has a marginal rate of substitution of zero at 18 streamed movies and then slopes upward. The student would be willing to stream an additional movie a month but only if compensated with more other goods and services.

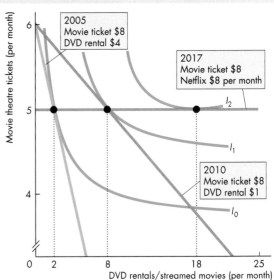

Best Affordable Movies, DVD Rentals, and Streaming

The Demand Curve In Chapter 3, we asserted that the demand curve slopes downward. We can now derive a demand curve from a consumer's budget line and indifference curves. By doing so, we can see that the law of demand and the downward-sloping demand curve are consequences of a consumer's choosing her or his best affordable combination of goods.

To derive Lisa's demand curve for movies, lower the price of a movie and find her best affordable point at different prices. We've just done this for two movie prices in Fig. 9.7(a). Figure 9.7(b) highlights these two prices and two points that lie on Lisa's demand curve for movies. When the price of a movie is $8, Lisa sees 2 movies a month at point A. When the price falls to $4, she increases the number of movies she sees to 6 a month at point B. The demand curve is made up of these two points plus all the other points that tell us Lisa's best affordable quantity of movies at each movie price, with the price of cola and Lisa's income remaining the same. As you can see, Lisa's demand curve for movies slopes downward—the lower the price of a movie, the more movies she sees. This is the law of demand.

Next, let's see how Lisa changes her purchases of movies and cola when her income changes.

A Change in Income

The effect of a change in income on buying plans is called the **income effect**. Let's work out the income effect by examining how buying plans change when income changes and prices remain constant. Figure 9.8 shows the income effect when Lisa's income falls. With an income of $40, the price of a movie at $4, and the price of cola at $4 a case, Lisa's best affordable point is J—she buys 6 movies and 4 cases of cola. If her income falls to $28, her best affordable point is K—she sees 4 movies and buys 3 cases of cola. When Lisa's income falls, she buys less of both goods. Movies and cola are normal goods.

The Demand Curve and the Income Effect A change in income leads to a shift in the demand curve, as shown in Fig. 9.8(b). With an income of $40, Lisa's demand curve for movies is D_0, the same as in Fig. 9.7(b). But when her income falls to $28, she plans to see fewer movies at each price, so her demand curve shifts leftward to D_1.

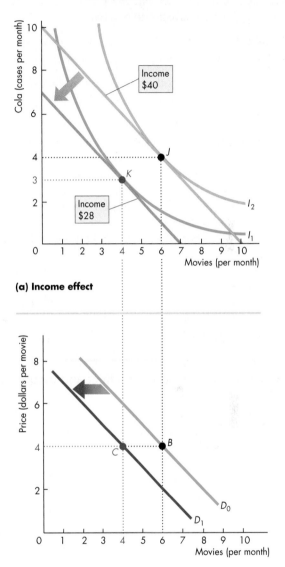

FIGURE 9.8 Income Effect and Change in Demand

(a) Income effect

(b) Demand curve for movies

A change in income shifts the budget line, changes the best affordable point, and changes demand.

In part (a), when Lisa's income decreases from $40 to $28, she sees fewer movies and buys less cola.

In part (b), when Lisa's income is $40, her demand curve for movies is D_0. When Lisa's income falls to $28, her demand curve for movies shifts leftward to D_1. For Lisa, going to the movies is a normal good. Her demand for movies decreases because she now sees fewer movies at each price.

———— MyLab Economics Animation ————

Substitution Effect and Income Effect

For a normal good, a fall in its price *always* increases the quantity bought. We can prove this assertion by dividing the price effect into two parts:

- Substitution effect
- Income effect

Figure 9.9(a) shows the price effect, and Figs. 9.9(b) and 9.9(c) show the two parts into which we separate the price effect.

Substitution Effect The **substitution effect** is the effect of a change in price on the quantity bought when the consumer (hypothetically) remains indifferent between the original situation and the new one. To work out Lisa's substitution effect when the price of a movie falls, we must lower her income by enough to keep her on the same indifference curve as before.

Figure 9.9(a) shows the price effect of a fall in the price of a movie from $8 to $4. The number of movies increases from 2 to 6 a month. When the price falls, suppose (hypothetically) that we cut Lisa's income to $28. What's special about $28? It is

the income that is just enough, at the new price of a movie, to keep Lisa's best affordable point on the same indifference curve (I_1) as her original point C. Lisa's budget line is now the medium orange line in Fig. 9.9(b). With the lower price of a movie and a smaller income, Lisa's best affordable point is K. The move from C to K along indifference curve I_1 is the substitution effect of the price change. The substitution effect of the fall in the price of a movie is an increase in the quantity of movies from 2 to 4. The direction of the substitution effect never varies: When the relative price of a good falls, the consumer substitutes more of that good for the other good.

Income Effect To calculate the substitution effect, we gave Lisa a $12 pay cut. To calculate the income effect, we give Lisa back her $12. The $12 increase in income shifts Lisa's budget line outward, as shown in Fig. 9.9(c). The slope of the budget line does not change because both prices remain the same. This change in Lisa's budget line is similar to the one illustrated in Fig. 9.8. As Lisa's budget line shifts outward, her consumption possibilities expand and her best

FIGURE 9.9 Substitution Effect and Income Effect

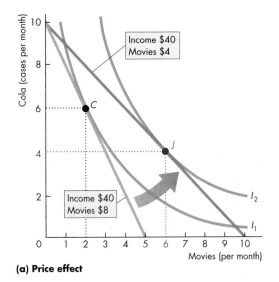

(a) Price effect

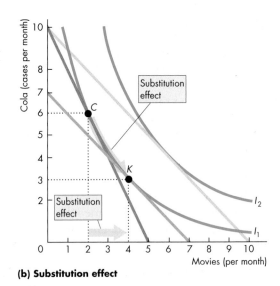

(b) Substitution effect

When the price of a movie falls from $8 to $4, Lisa moves from point C to point J in part (a). The price effect is an increase in the number of movies from 2 to 6 a month. This price effect is separated into a substitution effect in part (b) and an income effect in part (c).

To isolate the substitution effect, we confront Lisa with the new price but keep her on her original indifference curve, I_1. The substitution effect is the move from C to K along indifference curve I_1—an increase from 2 to 4 movies a month.

affordable point becomes *J* on indifference curve I_2. The move from *K* to *J* is the income effect of the price change.

As Lisa's income increases, she sees more movies. For Lisa, a movie is a normal good. For a normal good, the income effect *reinforces* the substitution effect. Because the two effects work in the same direction, we can be sure that the demand curve slopes downward. But some goods are inferior goods. What can we say about the demand for an inferior good?

Inferior Goods Recall that an *inferior good* is a good for which *demand decreases* when *income increases*. For an inferior good, the income effect is negative, which means that a lower price does not inevitably lead to an increase in the quantity demanded. The substitution effect of a fall in the price increases the quantity demanded, but the negative income effect works in the opposite direction and offsets the substitution effect to some degree. The key question is to what degree.

If the negative income effect *equals* the positive substitution effect, a fall in price leaves the quantity bought the same. When a fall in price leaves the

quantity demanded unchanged, the demand curve is vertical and demand is perfectly inelastic.

If the negative income effect *is smaller than* the positive substitution effect, a fall in price increases the quantity bought and the demand curve still slopes downward like that for a normal good. But the demand for an inferior good might be less elastic than that for a normal good.

If the negative income effect *exceeds* the positive substitution effect, a fall in the price *decreases* the quantity bought and the demand curve *slopes upward*. This case does not appear to occur in the real world.

You can apply the indifference curve model that you've studied in this chapter to explain the changes in the way we buy recorded music, see movies, and make all our other consumption choices. We allocate our budgets to make our best affordable choices. Changes in prices and incomes change our best affordable choices and change consumption patterns.

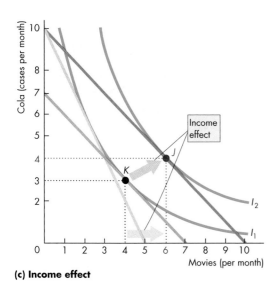

(c) Income effect

To isolate the income effect, we confront Lisa with the new price of movies but increase her income so that she can move from the original indifference curve, I_1, to the new one, I_2. The income effect is the move from *K* to *J*—an increase from 4 to 6 movies a month.

MyLab Economics Animation and Draw Graph

REVIEW QUIZ

1 When a consumer chooses the combination of goods and services to buy, what is she or he trying to achieve?

2 Explain the conditions that are met when a consumer has found the best affordable combination of goods to buy. (Use the terms *budget line*, *marginal rate of substitution*, and *relative price* in your explanation.)

3 If the price of a normal good falls, what happens to the quantity demanded of that good?

4 Into what two effects can we divide the effect of a price change?

5 For a normal good, does the income effect reinforce the substitution effect or does it partly offset the substitution effect?

Work these questions in Study Plan 9.3 and get instant feedback.   MyLab Economics

◆ *Economics in the News* on pp. 218–219 applies the theory of household choice to explain how students choose the amount of time to take to earn a four-year degree.

In the chapters that follow, we study the choices that firms make in their pursuit of profit and how those choices determine the supply of goods and services and the demand for productive resources.

Student Budget and Choice

Despite Protest, U of Windsor Hikes Tuition

CBC News

April 25, 2017

Despite their protest, students will be paying higher tuition fees at the University of Windsor after the school's board of governors approved another hike Tuesday. ...

Most undergraduate programs will see a three percent increase, while business and law programs will see jumps of five percent or higher. ...

School president Alan Wildeman said the board implemented a standard increase that is in line with other post-secondary institutions in Canada. ...

© CBC Licensing

Many Georgia Students Feel Overburdened by Rising College Costs

Jessica Hembree, a University of Georgia student, wants to become a doctor. But she took last semester off school in order to work and save money for her next semester of classes. For other students, changing majors puts them behind and they need an extra year or two to make up the required classes. Still others just aren't ready to buckle down and do the required work and waste a year or two.

But that extra time at college is costly. For students at the University of Georgia, tuition in 2017–2018 is $11,646. Back in 2002, that same year of classes at UGA cost $3,616. Somewhere around 55 percent of students at UGA graduate with debt that averages close to $27,000—roughly in the middle range of average debt across all states.

Sources: Based on Eric Stirgus, "Many Georgia Students Feel Overburdened by Rising College Costs," *Atlanta Journal-Constitution*, April 24, 2017; University of Georgia tuition schedules; Lendedu; ValuePenguin; Liberty Street Economics, "Staying in College Longer Than Four Years Costs More Than You Might Think," September 3, 2014.

ESSENCE OF THE STORY

- The University of Windsor has increased tuition in line with other Canadian universities.

- In the United States, tuition has almost doubled over the past 10 years.

- Students in both countries complain about tuition.

- Some U.S. students, like Jessica Hembree, take time out of school to spread the cost over more years.

MyLab Economics Economics in the News

ECONOMIC ANALYSIS

- Canadian university students protest tuition hikes, but they get a much better deal than students in the United States.

- Also, while a large and increasing percentage of U.S. students are taking more than 4 years to complete a 4-year degree, most Canadian students finish on time.

- The model of consumer choice that you've studied in this chapter enables you to explain the different choices of Canadian and American students.

- All students have a limited budget for tuition and other goods and services and must choose among the alternative combinations of tuition and other things that they can afford.

- Figure 1 shows two students' budget lines for degree courses and other goods and services: one Canadian and the other U.S. in 2017. Courses per year measure the quantity of instruction consumed, and dollar units measure the quantity of other goods and services consumed.

- Think of the quantity of courses as an average per year. A normal full-time load is 5 courses per year. A part-time load is 3 or fewer courses per year. A student who takes 6 years to complete a degree takes an average of 3⅓ courses per year.

- The students in Fig. 1 have an annual budget for tuition and other goods and services of $26,000 per year.

- The Canadian budget line tells us that a student can do a degree in 4 years by taking 5 courses per year and consuming $18,000 worth of other goods and services. The $18,000 is the $26,000 budget minus full-time tuition of $8,000 per year.

- The Canadian budget line also tells us the quantities of other goods and services that can be consumed at different levels of part-time tuition. The budget line has a kink because below 4 courses a year, tuition is per course but 4 and 5 courses cost the same full-time tuition.

- The U.S budget line is steeper than the Canadian budget line because U.S. tuition is higher.

- The U.S budget line tells us that students who take a full 5-course load can consume only $11,000 worth of other goods and services per year. The $11,000 is the $26,000 budget minus full-time tuition of $15,000 per year. The other points on the U.S. budget line represent combinations of full time, part time, and periods off school.

- Figure 2 shows a student's indifference curves for courses and other goods and services.

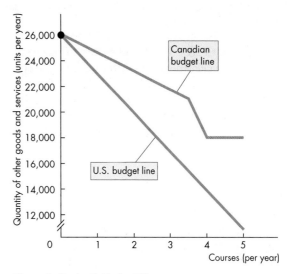

Figure 1 Student's Budget Line

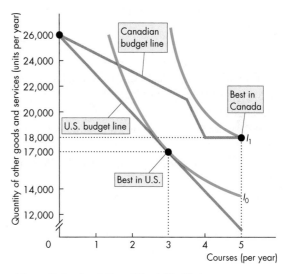

Figure 2 Student's Best Affordable Choices

- The best affordable choice in Canada is to take 5 courses per year and consume $18,000 worth of other goods and services on indifference curve I_2.

- The best affordable choice in the United States is to take 3 courses a year on indifference curve I_1, taking longer to complete a degree.

- Completing a U.S. degree in 4 years by taking 5 courses a year puts the student on the lower indifference curve I_0, which is not the best affordable point.

WORKED PROBLEM

MyLab Economics Work this problem in Chapter 9 Study Plan.

Wendy drinks 10 sugary drinks and 4 smoothies a week. Smoothies are $5 each and sugary drinks were $2 each. This week, things are different: The government has slapped a tax on sugary drinks and their price has doubled to $4. But it's not all bad news for Wendy. The government has also revised the income tax, so Wendy's drinks budget has increased. She can now just afford to buy her usual 10 sugary drinks and 4 smoothies a week.

Questions

1. What was Wendy's drinks budget last week and what is it this week?
2. What was Wendy's opportunity cost of a sugary drink last week and what is it this week?
3. Does Wendy buy 10 sugary drinks and 4 smoothies this week? Explain.
4. Is Wendy better off this week than last week? Explain.

Solutions

1. To find Wendy's drinks budget, use the fact that Income (available for drinks) = Expenditure.
   Expenditure = (Price of a sugary drink × Quantity of sugary drinks) + (Price of a smoothie × Quantity of smoothies).
   Last week, her income was ($2 × 10) + ($5 × 4) = $40.
   This week, her income is ($4 × 10) + ($5 × 4) = $60.

Key Point: Income limits expenditure and expenditure equals price multiplied by quantity, summed over the goods consumed.

2. Wendy's opportunity cost of a sugary drink is the number of smoothies she must forgo to get 1 sugary drink. Wendy's opportunity cost equals the relative price of a sugary drink, which is the price of a sugary drink divided by the price of a smoothie.
   Last week, Wendy's opportunity cost of a sugary drink was $2 ÷ $5 = 2/5 or 0.4 smoothies.
   This week, it is $4 ÷ $5 = 4/5 or 0.8 smoothies.

Key Point: A relative price is an opportunity cost.

3. Wendy does not buy 10 sugary drinks and 4 smoothies this week because it is not her best affordable choice.

At her best affordable choice, Wendy's marginal rate of substitution (*MRS*) between sugary drinks and smoothies is equal to the relative price of sugary drinks and smoothies.

Last week, when she chose 10 sugary drinks and 4 smoothies, her *MRS* was 0.4, equal to last week's relative price of 0.4 smoothies per sugary drink. This week, the relative price is 0.8 smoothies per sugary drink, so Wendy changes her choice to make her *MRS* equal 0.8.

To increase her *MRS* from 0.4 to 0.8, Wendy buys fewer sugary drinks and more smoothies. We know how she changes her choice but not the new quantities she buys. To get the quantities, we would need to know Wendy's preferences as described by her indifference curves.

Key Point: When the relative price of a good rises, the consumer buys less of that good to make the *MRS* increase to equal the higher relative price.

4. Wendy is better off! She can still buy her last week's choice but, at that choice, she is not at her best affordable point. So by buying more smoothies, she moves along her budget line to a higher indifference curve at which *MRS* equals 0.8.

Key Point: When both income and the relative price of a good change so that the old choice is still available, the consumer's best affordable choice changes.

Key Figure

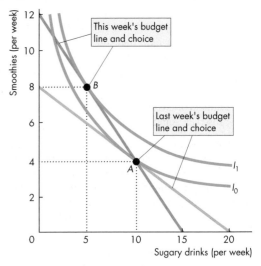

MyLab Economics Interactive Animation

SUMMARY

Key Points

Consumption Possibilities (pp. 206–208)

- The budget line is the boundary between what a household can and cannot afford, given its income and the prices of goods.
- The point at which the budget line intersects the y-axis is the household's real income in terms of the good measured on that axis.
- The magnitude of the slope of the budget line is the relative price of the good measured on the x-axis in terms of the good measured on the y-axis.
- A change in the price of one good changes the slope of the budget line. A change in income shifts the budget line but does not change its slope.

Working Problems 1 to 5 will give you a better understanding of consumption possibilities.

Preferences and Indifference Curves (pp. 209–212)

- A consumer's preferences can be represented by indifference curves. The consumer is indifferent among all the combinations of goods that lie on an indifference curve.
- A consumer prefers any point above an indifference curve to any point on it and prefers any point on an indifference curve to any point below it.
- The magnitude of the slope of an indifference curve is called the marginal rate of substitution.
- The marginal rate of substitution diminishes as consumption of the good measured on the y-axis

decreases and consumption of the good measured on the x-axis increases.

Working Problems 6 and 7 will give you a better understanding of preferences and indifference curves.

Predicting Consumer Choices (pp. 212–217)

- A household consumes at its best affordable point. This point is on the budget line and on the highest attainable indifference curve and has a marginal rate of substitution equal to relative price.
- The effect of a price change (the price effect) can be divided into a substitution effect and an income effect.
- The substitution effect is the effect of a change in price on the quantity bought when the consumer (hypothetically) remains indifferent between the original choice and the new choice.
- The substitution effect always results in an increase in consumption of the good whose relative price has fallen.
- The income effect is the effect of a change in income on consumption.
- For a normal good, the income effect reinforces the substitution effect. For an inferior good, the income effect works in the opposite direction to the substitution effect.

Working Problems 8 to 11 will give you a better understanding of predicting consumer choices.

Key Terms

MyLab Economics Key Terms Quiz

Budget line, 206
Diminishing marginal rate of
    substitution, 210
Income effect, 215

Indifference curve, 209
Marginal rate of substitution, 210
Price effect, 213
Real income, 207

Relative price, 207
Substitution effect, 216

STUDY PLAN PROBLEMS AND APPLICATIONS

MyLab Economics Work Problems 1 to 11 in Chapter 9 Study Plan and get instant feedback.

Consumption Possibilities (Study Plan 9.1)

Use the following data to work Problems 1 and 2.

Sara's income is $12 a week. The price of popcorn is $3 a bag, and the price of a smoothie is $3.

1. Calculate Sara's real income in terms of smoothies. Calculate her real income in terms of popcorn. What is the relative price of smoothies in terms of popcorn? What is the opportunity cost of a smoothie?

2. Calculate the equation for Sara's budget line (with bags of popcorn on the left side). Draw a graph of Sara's budget line with the quantity of smoothies on the x-axis. What is the slope of Sara's budget line? What determines its value?

Use the following data to work Problems 3 and 4.

Sara's income falls from $12 to $9 a week, while the price of popcorn is unchanged at $3 a bag and the price of a smoothie is unchanged at $3.

3. What is the effect of the fall in Sara's income on her real income in terms of (a) smoothies and (b) popcorn?

4. What is the effect of the fall in Sara's income on the relative price of a smoothie in terms of popcorn? What is the slope of Sara's new budget line if it is drawn with smoothies on the x-axis?

5. Sara's income is $12 a week. The price of popcorn rises from $3 to $6 a bag, and the price of a smoothie is unchanged at $3. Explain how Sara's budget line changes with smoothies on the x-axis.

Preferences and Indifference Curves (Study Plan 9.2)

6. Draw figures that show your indifference curves for the following pairs of goods:
   ▪ Right gloves and left gloves
   ▪ Coca-Cola and Pepsi
   ▪ Desktop computers and laptop computers
   ▪ Strawberries and ice cream

   For each pair, are the goods perfect substitutes, perfect complements, substitutes, complements, or unrelated?

7. Discuss the shape of the indifference curve for each of the following pairs of goods:
   ▪ Orange juice and smoothies
   ▪ Baseballs and baseball bats
   ▪ Left running shoes and right running shoes
   ▪ Eyeglasses and contact lenses

Explain the relationship between the shape of the indifference curve and the marginal rate of substitution as the quantities of the two goods change.

Predicting Consumer Choices (Study Plan 9.3)

Use the following data to work Problems 8 and 9.

Pam has made her best affordable choice of cookies and granola bars. She spends all of her weekly income on 30 cookies at $1 each and 5 granola bars at $2 each. Next week, she expects the price of a cookie to fall to 50¢ and the price of a granola bar to rise to $5.

8. a. Will Pam be able to buy and want to buy 30 cookies and 5 granola bars next week?

   b. Which situation does Pam prefer: cookies at $1 and granola bars at $2, or cookies at 50¢ and granola bars at $5?

9. a. If Pam changes how she spends her weekly income, will she buy more or fewer cookies and more or fewer granola bars?

   b. When the prices change next week, will there be an income effect, a substitution effect, or both at work?

Use the following news clip to work Problems 10 and 11.

Hamptons Glamour Finds a Humbler Home

Lucy Martin collected and sold vintage clothing in the wealthy Hamptons, but in the recession of 2008, her sales fell. She eventually moved her shop to Tannersville, N.Y., where her expenses are 70 percent less than they were in the Hamptons.

Source: *The New York Times*, December 22, 2016

10. a. According to the news clip, is vintage clothing a normal good or an inferior good? If the price of vintage clothing falls and income remains the same, explain how the quantity of vintage clothing bought changes.

    b. Describe the substitution effect and the income effect that occur.

11. Draw a graph of a person's indifference curves for vintage clothing and other goods. Then draw two budget lines to show the effect of a fall in income on the quantity of vintage clothing purchased.

ADDITIONAL PROBLEMS AND APPLICATIONS

MyLab Economics You can work these problems in Homework or Test if assigned by your instructor.

Consumption Possibilities

Use the following data to work Problems 12 to 15.

Marc has a budget of $20 a month to spend on root beer and DVDs. The price of root beer is $5 a bottle, and the price of a DVD is $10.

12. What is the relative price of root beer in terms of DVDs? What is the opportunity cost of a bottle of root beer?

13. Calculate Marc's real income in terms of root beer. Calculate his real income in terms of DVDs.

14. Calculate the equation for Marc's budget line (with the quantity of root beer on the left side).

15. Draw a graph of Marc's budget line with the quantity of DVDs on the *x*-axis. What is the slope of Marc's budget line? What determines its value?

Use the following data to work Problems 16 to 19.

Amy has $20 a week to spend on coffee and cake. The price of coffee is $4 a cup, and the price of cake is $2 a slice.

16. Calculate Amy's real income in terms of cake. Calculate the relative price of cake in terms of coffee.

17. Calculate the equation for Amy's budget line (with cups of coffee on the left side).

18. If Amy's income increases to $24 a week and the prices of coffee and cake remain unchanged, describe the change in her budget line.

19. If the price of cake doubles while the price of coffee remains at $4 a cup and Amy's income remains at $20, describe the change in her budget line.

Use the following news clip to work Problems 20 and 21.

More 'Staycations' Expected This Year

More Canadians and U.S. visitors are expected to drive to Canada's major tourism destinations prompted by low gas prices. Parks Canada forecasts that visits will by up by 7 percent.

Source: *Financial Post*, June 7, 2016

20. a. Sketch a budget line for a household that spends its income on only two goods:

gasoline and restaurant meals. Identify the combinations of gasoline and restaurant meals that are affordable and those that are unaffordable.

   b. Sketch a second budget line to show how a fall in the price of gasoline changes the affordable and unaffordable combinations of gasoline and restaurant meals. Describe how the household's consumption possibilities change.

21. How does a fall in the price of gasoline change the relative price of a restaurant meal? How does a fall in the price of gasoline change real income in terms of restaurant meals?

Preferences and Indifference Curves

Use the following information to work Problems 22 and 23.

Rashid buys only books and CDs, and the figure shows his preference map.

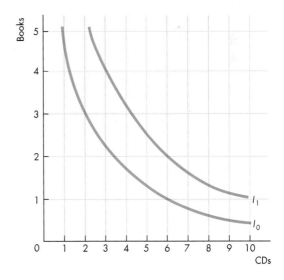

22. a. If Rashid chooses 3 books and 2 CDs, what is his marginal rate of substitution?

   b. If Rashid chooses 2 books and 6 CDs, what is his marginal rate of substitution?

23. Do Rashid's indifference curves display diminishing marginal rate of substitution? Explain why or why not.

24. **You May Be Paid More (or Less) Than You Think**

    It's so hard to put a price on happiness, isn't it? But if you've ever had to choose between a job you like and a better-paying one that you like less, you probably wished some economist would tell you how much job satisfaction is worth. Trust in management is by far the biggest component to consider. Say you get a new boss and your trust in management goes up a bit (say, up 1 point on a 10-point scale). That's like getting a 36-percent pay raise. In other words, that increased level of trust will boost your level of overall satisfaction in life by about the same amount as a 36-percent raise would.

    Source: CNN, March 29, 2006

    a. Measure trust in management on a 10-point scale, measure pay on the same 10-point scale, and think of them as two goods. Sketch an indifference curve (with trust on the *x*-axis) that is consistent with the news clip.

    b. What is the marginal rate of substitution between trust in management and pay according to this news clip?

    c. What does the news clip imply about the principle of diminishing marginal rate of substitution? Is that implication likely to be correct?

Predicting Consumer Choices

Use the following data to work Problems 25 and 26. Jim has made his best affordable choice of muffins and coffee. He spends all of his income on 10 muffins at $1 each and 20 cups of coffee at $2 each. Now the price of a muffin rises to $1.50 and the price of coffee falls to $1.75 a cup.

25. a. Will Jim now be able and want to buy 10 muffins and 20 coffees?

    b. Which situation does Jim prefer: muffins at $1 and coffee at $2 a cup, or muffins at $1.50 and coffee at $1.75 a cup?

26. a. If Jim changes the quantities that he buys, will he buy more or fewer muffins and more or less coffee? Explain your answer.

    b. When the prices change, will there be an income effect, a substitution effect, or both at work? Explain your answer.

Use the following data to work Problems 27 to 29. Sara's income is $12 a week. The price of popcorn is $3 a bag, and the price of cola is $1.50 a can. The figure shows Sara's preference map for popcorn and cola.

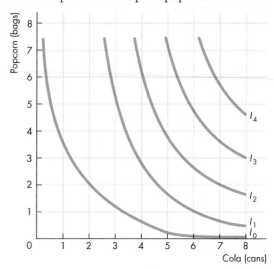

27. What quantities of popcorn and cola does Sara buy? What is Sara's marginal rate of substitution at the point at which she consumes?

28. Suppose that the price of cola rises from $1.50 to $3.00 a can while the price of popcorn and Sara's income remain the same. What quantities of cola and popcorn does Sara now buy? What are two points on Sara's demand curve for cola? Draw Sara's demand curve.

29. Suppose that the price of cola rises from $1.50 to $3.00 a can while the price of popcorn and Sara's income remain the same.

    a. What is the substitution effect of this price change, and what is the income effect of the price change?

    b. Is cola a normal good or an inferior good? Explain.

Economics in the News

30. After you have studied *Economics in the News* on pp. 218–219, answer the following questions.

    a. In Fig. 2, draw a budget line if Canadian students faced the U.S. level of tuition but had a high enough income to be on indifference curve I_2.

    b. Show the substitution effect and the income effect of the tuition difference.

Making the Most of Life

UNDERSTANDING HOUSEHOLDS' CHOICES

The powerful forces of demand and supply shape the fortunes of families, businesses, nations, and empires in the same unrelenting way that the tides and winds shape rocks and coastlines. You saw in Chapters 3 through 7 how these forces raise and lower prices, increase and decrease quantities bought and sold, cause revenues to fluctuate, and send resources to their most valuable uses.

These powerful forces begin quietly and privately with the choices that each one of us makes. Chapters 8 and 9 probe these individual choices, offering two alternative approaches to explaining both consumption plans and the allocation of time. These explanations of consumption plans can also explain "non-economic" choices, such as whether to marry and how many children to have. In a sense, there are no non-economic choices. If there is scarcity, there must be choice, and economics studies all choices.

The earliest economists (Adam Smith and his contemporaries) did not have a very deep understanding of households' choices. It was not until the nineteenth century that progress was made in this area when Jeremy Bentham (below) introduced the concept of utility and applied it to the study of human choices. Today, Steven Levitt, whom you will meet on the following page, is one of the most influential students of human behaviour.

Jeremy Bentham *(1748–1832), who lived in London, was the son and grandson of lawyers and was himself trained as a barrister. But Bentham rejected the opportunity to maintain the family tradition and, instead, spent his life as a writer, activist, and Member of Parliament in the pursuit of rational laws that would bring the greatest happiness to the greatest number of people.*

Bentham, whose embalmed body is preserved to this day in a glass cabinet in the University of London, was the first person to use the concept of utility to explain human choices. But in Bentham's day, the distinction between explaining and prescribing was not a sharp one, and Bentham was ready to use his ideas to tell people how they ought to behave. He was one of the first to propose pensions for the retired, guaranteed employment, minimum wages, and social benefits such as free education and free medical care.

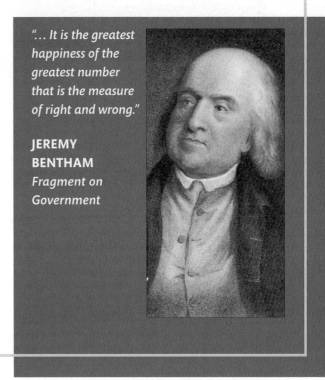

"… It is the greatest happiness of the greatest number that is the measure of right and wrong."

JEREMY BENTHAM
Fragment on Government

I think of economics as being primarily about a way of looking at the world and a set of tools for thinking clearly.

STEVEN D. LEVITT is William B. Ogden Distinguished Service Professor of Economics at the University of Chicago. Born in Minneapolis, he was an undergraduate at Harvard and a graduate student at MIT. Among his many honours, he was recently awarded the John Bates Clark Medal, given to the best economist under 40.

Professor Levitt has studied an astonishingly wide range of human choices and their outcomes. He has examined the effects of policing on crime, shown that real estate agents get a higher price when they sell their own homes than when they sell other people's, devised a test to detect cheating teachers, and studied the choices of drug dealers and gang members. Much of this research has been popularized in *Freakonomics* (Steven D. Levitt and Stephen J. Dubner, HarperCollins, 2005). What unifies this apparently diverse body of research is the use of natural experiments. Professor Levitt has an incredible ability to find just the right set of events and the data the events have generated to enable him to isolate the effect he's looking for.

Michael Parkin and Robin Bade talked with Steven Levitt about his work and what economists have discovered about how people respond to incentives.

Why did you become an economist?

As a freshman in college, I took introductory economics. All the ideas made perfect sense to me—it was the way I naturally thought. My friends were befuddled. I thought, "This is the field for me!"

The idea of rational choice made at the margin lies at the heart of economics. Would you say that your work generally supports that idea or challenges it? Can you provide some examples?

I don't like the word "rational" in this context. I think economists model agents as being rational just for convenience. What really matters is whether people respond to incentives. My work very much supports the idea that humans in all types of circumstances respond strongly to incentives. I've seen it with drug dealers, auto thieves, sumo wrestlers, real estate agents, and elementary school teachers, just to name a few examples.

Drug dealers, for instance, want to make money, but they also want to avoid being arrested or even killed. In the data we have on drug sellers, we see that when the drug trade is more lucrative, dealers are willing to take greater risks of arrest to carve out a share of the market. ... Sumo wrestlers, on the other hand, care mostly about their official ranking. Sometimes matches occur where one wrestler has more to lose or gain than the other wrestler. We find that sumo wrestlers make corrupt deals to make sure the wrestler who wins is the one who needs to win.

Why is an economist interested in crime and cheating?

I think of economics as being primarily about a way of looking at the world and a set of tools for thinking clearly. The topics you apply these tools to are unlimited. That is why I think economics has been so powerful. If you understand economics and use the tools wisely, you will be a better business person, doctor, public servant, parent.

*Read the full interview with Steven Levitt in MyLab Economics.

10

OUTPUT AND COSTS

After studying this chapter, you will be able to:

◆ Explain and distinguish between the economic and accounting measures of a firm's cost of production and profit

◆ Explain and illustrate a firm's short-run product curves

◆ Explain and derive a firm's short-run cost curves

◆ Explain and derive a firm's long-run average cost curve

Behind the scenes of an IKEA furniture store, many economic decisions have been made that affect the cost of serving its customers. IKEA has decided how many people to employ and how many and what size of stores to build. How does a firm like IKEA make these decisions?

We are going to answer this question in this chapter. And in *Economics in the News* at the end of the chapter, we'll look at a decision by IKEA to expand its Edmonton store. But first, we'll study the costs of a simpler, smaller firm, Campus Sweaters, a (fictional) producer of knitwear.

◆ Economic Cost and Profit

The 2 million firms in Canada differ in size and in the scope of what they do, but they all perform the same basic economic functions. Each **firm** is an institution that hires factors of production and organizes those factors to produce and sell goods and services. Our goal is to predict firms' behaviour. To do so, we need to know a firm's goal and the constraints it faces. We start with the goal.

The Firm's Goal

When economists ask entrepreneurs what they are trying to achieve, they get many different answers. Some talk about making a high-quality product, others about business growth, others about market share, others about the job satisfaction of their workforce, and an increasing number today talk about social and environmental responsibility. All of these goals are pursued by firms, but they are not the fundamental goal: They are the means to that goal.

A firm's goal is to maximize profit. A firm that does not seek to maximize profit is either eliminated or taken over by a firm that does seek that goal.

What is the profit that a firm seeks to maximize? To answer this question, we'll look at Campus Sweaters, Inc., a small producer of knitted sweaters owned and operated by Cindy.

Accounting Profit

In 2017, Campus Sweaters received $400,000 for the sweaters it sold and paid out $80,000 for wool, $20,000 for utilities, $120,000 for wages, $5,000 for the lease of a computer, and $5,000 in interest on a bank loan. These expenses total $230,000, so Campus Sweaters had a cash surplus of $170,000.

To measure the profit of Campus Sweaters, Cindy's accountant subtracted $20,000 for the depreciation of buildings and knitting machines from the $170,000 cash surplus. *Depreciation* is the fall in the value of a firm's capital. To calculate depreciation, accountants use Canada Revenue Agency rules, which are based on standards established by the accounting profession. Using these rules, Cindy's accountant calculated that Campus Sweaters made a profit of $150,000 in 2017.

Economic Accounting

Accountants measure a firm's profit to ensure that the firm pays the correct amount of income tax and to show its investors how their funds are being used.

Economists measure a firm's profit to enable them to predict the firm's decisions, and the goal of these decisions is to maximize *economic profit*. **Economic profit** is equal to total revenue minus total cost, with total cost measured as the *opportunity cost of production*.

A Firm's Opportunity Cost of Production

The *opportunity cost* of any action is the highest-valued alternative forgone. The *opportunity cost of production* is the value of the best alternative use of the resources that a firm uses in production.

A firm's opportunity cost of production is the value of real alternatives forgone. We express opportunity cost in money units so that we can compare and add up the value of the alternatives forgone.

A firm's opportunity cost of production is the sum of the cost of using resources:

- Bought in the market
- Owned by the firm
- Supplied by the firm's owner

Resources Bought in the Market A firm incurs an opportunity cost when it buys resources in the market. The amount spent on these resources is an opportunity cost of production because the firm could have bought different resources to produce some other good or service. For Campus Sweaters, the resources bought in the market are wool, utilities, labour, a leased computer, and a bank loan. The $230,000 spent on these items in 2017 could have been spent on something else, so it is an opportunity cost of producing sweaters.

Resources Owned by the Firm A firm incurs an opportunity cost when it uses its own capital. The cost of using capital owned by the firm is an opportunity cost of production because the firm could sell the capital that it owns and rent capital from another firm. When a firm uses its own capital, it implicitly rents it from itself. In this case, the firm's opportunity cost of using the capital it owns is called the **implicit rental rate** of capital. The implicit rental rate of capital has two components: economic depreciation and forgone interest.

Economic Depreciation Accountants measure *depreciation*, the fall in the value of a firm's capital, using formulas that are unrelated to the change in the market value of capital. **Economic depreciation** is the fall in the *market value* of a firm's capital over a given period. It equals the market price of the capital at the beginning of the period minus the market price of the capital at the end of the period.

Suppose that Campus Sweaters could have sold its buildings and knitting machines on January 1, 2017, for $400,000 and that it can sell the same capital on December 31, 2017, for $375,000. The firm's economic depreciation during 2017 is $25,000 ($400,000 − $375,000). This forgone $25,000 is an opportunity cost of production.

Forgone Interest The funds used to buy capital could have been used for some other purpose, and in their next best use, they would have earned interest. This forgone interest is an opportunity cost of production.

Suppose that Campus Sweaters used $300,000 of its own funds to buy capital. If the firm invested its $300,000 in bonds instead of a knitting factory (and rented the capital it needs to produce sweaters), it would have earned $15,000 a year in interest. This forgone interest is an opportunity cost of production.

Resources Supplied by the Firm's Owner A firm's owner might supply *both* entrepreneurship and labour.

Entrepreneurship The factor of production that organizes a firm and makes its decisions might be supplied by the firm's owner or by a hired entrepreneur. The return to entrepreneurship is profit, and the profit that an entrepreneur earns *on average* is called **normal profit**. Normal profit is the cost of entrepreneurship and is an opportunity cost of production.

If Cindy supplies entrepreneurial services herself, and if the normal profit she can earn on these services is $45,000 a year, this amount is an opportunity cost of production at Campus Sweaters.

Owner's Labour Services *In addition* to supplying entrepreneurship, the owner of a firm might supply labour but not take a wage. The opportunity cost of the owner's labour is the wage income forgone by not taking the best alternative job.

If Cindy supplies labour to Campus Sweaters, and if the wage she can earn on this labour at another firm is $55,000 a year, this amount of wages forgone is an opportunity cost of production at Campus Sweaters.

Economic Accounting: A Summary

Table 10.1 summarizes the economic accounting. Campus Sweaters' total revenue is $400,000; its opportunity cost of production is $370,000; and its economic profit is $30,000.

Cindy's personal income is the $30,000 of economic profit plus the $100,000 that she earns by supplying resources to Campus Sweaters.

Decisions

To achieve the objective of maximum economic profit, a firm must make five decisions:

1. What to produce and in what quantities
2. How to produce
3. How to organize and compensate its managers and workers
4. How to market and price its products
5. What to produce itself and buy from others

In all these decisions, a firm's actions are limited by the constraints that it faces. Your next task is to learn about these constraints.

TABLE 10.1   Economic Accounting

Item		Amount
Total Revenue		**$400,000**
Cost of Resources Bought in Market		
Wool	$80,000	
Utilities	20,000	
Wages	120,000	
Computer lease	5,000	
Bank interest	5,000	$230,000
Cost of Resources Owned by Firm		
Economic depreciation	$25,000	
Forgone interest	15,000	$40,000
Cost of Resources Supplied by Owner		
Cindy's normal profit	$45,000	
Cindy's forgone wages	55,000	$100,000
Opportunity Cost of Production		**$370,000**
Economic Profit		**$30,000**

Decision Time Frames

People who operate firms make many decisions, and all of their decisions are aimed at achieving one over-riding goal: maximum attainable profit. But not all decisions are equally critical. Some decisions are big ones. Once made, they are costly (or impossible) to reverse. If such a decision turns out to be incorrect, it might lead to the failure of the firm. Other decisions are small. They are easily changed. If one of these decisions turns out to be incorrect, the firm can change its actions and survive.

The biggest decision that an entrepreneur makes is in what industry to establish a firm. For most entrepreneurs, their background knowledge and interests drive this decision. But the decision also depends on profit prospects—on the expectation that total revenue will exceed total cost.

Cindy has decided to set up Campus Sweaters. But she has not decided the quantity to produce, the factors of production to hire, or the price to charge for sweaters.

Decisions about the quantity to produce and the price to charge depend on the type of market in which the firm operates, but decisions about *how* to produce a given output do not. *All* types of firms in *all* types of markets make similar decisions about how to produce.

The actions that a firm can take to influence the relationship between output and cost depend on how soon the firm wants to act. A firm that plans to change its output rate tomorrow has fewer options than one that plans to change its output rate six months or six years in the future.

To study the relationship between a firm's output decision and its costs, we distinguish between two decision time frames:

- The short run
- The long run

The Short Run The **short run** is a time frame in which the quantity of at least one factor of production is fixed. For most firms, capital, land, and entrepreneurship are fixed factors of production and labour is the variable factor of production. We call the fixed factors of production the firm's *plant*. In the short run, a firm's plant is fixed.

For Campus Sweaters, the fixed plant is its factory building and its knitting machines. For an electric power utility, the fixed plant is its buildings, generators, computers, and control systems.

To increase output in the short run, a firm must increase the quantity of a variable factor of production, which is usually labour. So to produce more output, Campus Sweaters must hire more labour and operate its knitting machines for more hours a day. Similarly, an electric power utility must hire more labour and operate its generators for more hours a day.

Short-run decisions are easily reversed. The firm can increase or decrease its output in the short run by changing the amount of labour it hires.

The Long Run The **long run** is a time frame in which the quantities of *all* factors of production can be varied. That is, the long run is a period in which the firm can change its *plant*.

To increase output in the long run, a firm can change its plant as well as the quantity of labour it hires. Campus Sweaters can decide whether to install more knitting machines, use a new type of machine, reorganize its management, or hire more labour. Long-run decisions are *not* easily reversed. Once a plant decision is made, the firm usually must live with it for some time. To emphasize this fact, we call the past expenditure on a plant that has no resale value a **sunk cost**. A sunk cost is irrelevant to the firm's current decisions. The only costs that influence its current decisions are the short-run cost of changing its labour inputs and the long-run cost of changing its plant.

REVIEW QUIZ

1 What is a firm's fundamental goal and what happens if the firm doesn't pursue this goal?
2 Why do accountants and economists calculate a firm's costs and profit in different ways?
3 What are the items that make opportunity cost differ from the accountant's measure of cost?
4 Why is normal profit an opportunity cost?
5 Distinguish between short run and long run.
6 Why is a sunk cost irrelevant to a firm's current decisions?

Work these questions in Study Plan 10.1 and get instant feedback. MyLab Economics

We're going to study costs in the short run and the long run. We begin with the short run and describe a firm's technology constraint.

◆ Short-Run Technology Constraint

To increase output in the short run, a firm must increase the quantity of labour employed. We describe the relationship between output and the quantity of labour employed by using three related concepts:

1. Total product
2. Marginal product
3. Average product

These product concepts can be illustrated either by product schedules or by product curves. Let's look first at the product schedules.

Product Schedules

Table 10.2 shows some data that describe Campus Sweaters' total product, marginal product, and average product. The numbers tell us how the quantity of sweaters produced increases as Campus Sweaters employs more workers. The numbers also tell us about the productivity of the labour that Campus Sweaters employs.

Focus first on the columns headed "Labour" and "Total product." **Total product** is the maximum output that a given quantity of labour can produce. You can see from the numbers in these columns that as Campus Sweaters employs more labour, total product increases. For example, when 1 worker is employed, total product is 4 sweaters a day, and when 2 workers are employed, total product is 10 sweaters a day. Each increase in employment increases total product.

The **marginal product** of labour is the increase in total product that results from a one-unit increase in the quantity of labour employed, with all other inputs remaining the same. For example, in Table 10.2, when Campus Sweaters increases employment from 2 to 3 workers and does not change its capital, the marginal product of the third worker is 3 sweaters—total product increases from 10 to 13 sweaters.

Average product tells how productive workers are on average. The **average product** of labour is equal to total product divided by the quantity of labour employed. For example, in Table 10.2, the average product of 3 workers is 4.33 sweaters per worker—13 sweaters a day divided by 3 workers.

TABLE 10.2   Total Product, Marginal Product, and Average Product

	Labour (workers per day)	Total product (sweaters per day)	Marginal product (sweaters per additional worker)	Average product (sweaters per worker)
A	0	0		
			4	
B	1	4		4.00
			6	
C	2	10		5.00
			3	
D	3	13		4.33
			2	
E	4	15		3.75
			1	
F	5	16		3.20

Total product is the total amount produced. Marginal product is the change in total product that results from a one-unit increase in labour. For example, when labour increases from 2 to 3 workers a day (row C to row D), total product increases from 10 to 13 sweaters a day. The marginal product of going from 2 to 3 workers is 3 sweaters. Average product is total product divided by the quantity of labour employed. For example, the average product of 3 workers is 4.33 sweaters per worker (13 sweaters a day divided by 3 workers).

If you look closely at the numbers in Table 10.2, you can see some patterns. As Campus Sweaters hires more labour, marginal product increases initially, and then begins to decrease. For example, marginal product increases from 4 sweaters a day for the first worker to 6 sweaters a day for the second worker and then decreases to 3 sweaters a day for the third worker. Average product also increases at first and then decreases. You can see the relationships between the quantity of labour hired and the three product concepts more clearly by looking at the product curves.

Product Curves

The product curves are graphs of the relationships between employment and the three product concepts you've just studied. They show how total product, marginal product, and average product change as employment changes. They also show the relationships among the three concepts. Let's look at the product curves.

Total Product Curve

Figure 10.1 shows Campus Sweaters' total product curve, *TP*, which is a graph of the total product schedule. Points *A* through *F* correspond to rows *A* through *F* in Table 10.2. To graph the entire total product curve, we vary labour by hours rather than whole days.

Notice the shape of the total product curve. As employment increases from zero to 1 worker a day, the curve becomes steeper. Then, as employment increases to 3, 4, and 5 workers a day, the curve becomes less steep.

The total product curve is similar to the *production possibilities frontier* (explained in Chapter 2). It separates the attainable output levels from those that are unattainable. All the points that lie above the curve are unattainable. Points that lie below the curve, in the orange area, are attainable, but they are inefficient—they use more labour than is necessary to produce a given output. Only the points *on* the total product curve are technologically efficient.

FIGURE 10.1 Total Product Curve

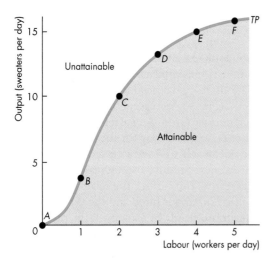

The total product curve, *TP*, is based on the data in Table 10.2. The total product curve shows how the quantity of sweaters produced changes as the quantity of labour employed changes. For example, 2 workers can produce 10 sweaters a day (point *C*). Points *A* through *F* on the curve correspond to the rows of Table 10.2. The total product curve separates attainable outputs from unattainable outputs. Points below the *TP* curve are inefficient.

MyLab Economics Animation

Marginal Product Curve

Figure 10.2 shows Campus Sweaters' marginal product of labour. Part (a) reproduces the total product curve from Fig. 10.1 and part (b) shows the marginal product curve, *MP*.

In part (a), the orange bars illustrate the marginal product of labour. The height of a bar measures marginal product. Marginal product is also measured by the slope of the total product curve. Recall that the slope of a curve is the change in the value of the variable measured on the *y*-axis—output—divided by the change in the variable measured on the *x*-axis—labour—as we move along the curve. A one-unit increase in labour, from 2 to 3 workers, increases output from 10 to 13 sweaters, so the slope from point *C* to point *D* is 3 sweaters per additional worker, the same as the marginal product we've just calculated.

Again varying the amount of labour in the smallest units possible, we can draw the marginal product curve shown in Fig. 10.2(b). The *height* of this curve measures the *slope* of the total product curve at a point. Part (a) shows that an increase in employment from 2 to 3 workers increases output from 10 to 13 sweaters (an increase of 3). The increase in output of 3 sweaters appears on the *y*-axis of part (b) as the marginal product of going from 2 to 3 workers. We plot that marginal product at the midpoint between 2 and 3 workers. Notice that the marginal product shown in Fig. 10.2(b) reaches a peak at 1.5 workers, and at that point, marginal product is 6 sweaters per additional worker. The peak occurs at 1.5 workers because the total product curve is steepest when employment increases from 1 worker to 2 workers.

The total product and marginal product curves differ across firms and types of goods. GM's product curves are different from those of Hydro One's, whose curves in turn are different from those of Campus Sweaters. But the shapes of the product curves are similar because almost every production process has two features:

- Increasing marginal returns initially
- Diminishing marginal returns eventually

Increasing Marginal Returns Increasing marginal returns occur when the marginal product of an additional worker exceeds the marginal product of the previous worker. Increasing marginal returns arise from increased specialization and division of labour in the production process.

FIGURE 10.2 Total Product and Marginal Product

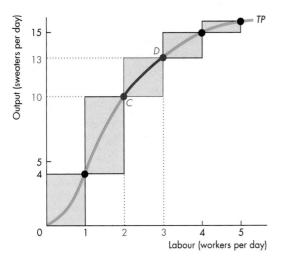

(a) Total product

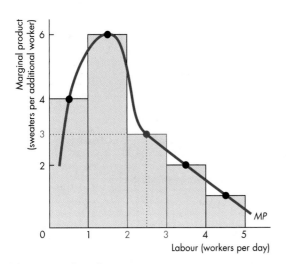

(b) Marginal product

Marginal product is illustrated by the orange bars. For example, when labour increases from 2 to 3 workers a day, marginal product is the orange bar whose height is 3 sweaters. (Marginal product is shown midway between the quantities of labour to emphasize that marginal product results from *changing* the quantity of labour.) The steeper the slope of the total product curve (*TP*) in part (a), the larger is marginal product (*MP*) in part (b). Marginal product increases to a maximum (in this example when 1.5 workers a day are employed) and then declines—diminishing marginal product.

MyLab Economics Animation

For example, if Campus Sweaters employs one worker, that person must learn all the aspects of sweater production: running the knitting machines, fixing breakdowns, packaging and mailing sweaters, buying and checking the type and colour of the wool. All these tasks must be performed by that one person.

If Campus Sweaters hires a second person, the two workers can specialize in different parts of the production process and can produce more than twice as much as one worker. The marginal product of the second worker is greater than the marginal product of the first worker. Marginal returns are increasing.

Diminishing Marginal Returns Most production processes experience increasing marginal returns initially, but all production processes eventually reach a point of *diminishing* marginal returns. **Diminishing marginal returns** occur when the marginal product of an additional worker is less than the marginal product of the previous worker.

Diminishing marginal returns arise from the fact that more and more workers are using the same capital and working in the same space. As more workers are added, there is less and less for the additional workers to do that is productive. For example, if Campus Sweaters hires a third worker, output increases but not by as much as it did when it hired the second worker. In this case, after two workers are hired, all the gains from specialization and the division of labour have been exhausted. By hiring a third worker, the factory produces more sweaters, but the equipment is being operated closer to its limits. There are even times when the third worker has nothing to do because the machines are running without the need for further attention. Hiring more and more workers continues to increase output but by successively smaller amounts. Marginal returns are diminishing. This phenomenon is such a pervasive one that it is called a "law"—the law of diminishing returns. The **law of diminishing returns** states that

> As a firm uses more of a variable factor of production with a given quantity of the fixed factor of production, the marginal product of the variable factor eventually diminishes.

You are going to return to the law of diminishing returns when we study a firm's costs, but before we do that, let's look at the average product of labour and the average product curve.

Average Product Curve

Figure 10.3 illustrates Campus Sweaters' average product of labour and shows the relationship between average product and marginal product. Points *B* through *F* on the average product curve *AP* correspond to those same rows in Table 10.2. Average product increases from 1 to 2 workers (its maximum value at point *C*) but then decreases as yet more workers are employed.

Notice also that average product is largest when average product and marginal product are equal. That is, the marginal product curve cuts the average product curve at the point of maximum average product. For the number of workers at which marginal product exceeds average product, average product is *increasing*. For the number of workers at which marginal product is less than average product, average product is *decreasing*.

The relationship between the average product and marginal product is a general feature of the relationship between the average and marginal values of any variable—even your grades.

FIGURE 10.3   Average Product

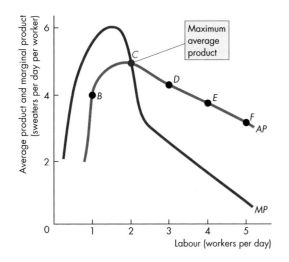

The figure shows the average product of labour and the connection between average product and marginal product. With 1 worker, marginal product exceeds average product, so average product is increasing. With 2 workers, marginal product equals average product, so average product is at its maximum. With more than 2 workers, marginal product is less than average product, so average product is decreasing.

———— MyLab Economics Animation ————

ECONOMICS IN ACTION

How to Pull Up Your Average

Do you want to pull up your average grade? Then make sure that your grade on your next test is better than your current average! Your next test is your marginal test. If your marginal grade exceeds your average grade (like the Economics grade in the figure), your average will rise. If your marginal grade equals your average grade (like the English grade in the figure), your average won't change. If your marginal grade is below your average grade (like the History grade in the figure), your average will fall.

The relationship between your marginal grade and average grade is exactly the same as that between marginal product and average product.

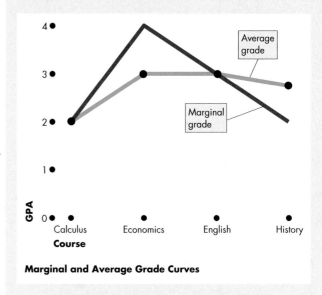

Marginal and Average Grade Curves

◆ REVIEW QUIZ

1   Explain how the marginal product and average product of labour change as the labour employed increases (a) initially and (b) eventually.
2   What is the law of diminishing returns? Why does marginal product eventually diminish?
3   Explain the relationship between marginal product and average product.

Work these questions in Study Plan 10.2 and get instant feedback.   MyLab Economics

Campus Sweaters' product curves influence its costs, as you are now going to see.

◆ Short-Run Cost

To produce more output in the short run, a firm must employ more labour, which means that it must increase its costs. We describe the relationship between output and cost by using three cost concepts:

- Total cost
- Marginal cost
- Average cost

Total Cost

A firm's **total cost** (TC) is the cost of *all* the factors of production it uses. We separate total cost into total *fixed* cost and total *variable* cost.

Total fixed cost (TFC) is the cost of the firm's fixed factors. For Campus Sweaters, total fixed cost includes the cost of renting knitting machines and *normal profit*, which is the opportunity cost of Cindy's entrepreneurship (see p. 229). The quantities of fixed factors don't change as output changes, so total fixed cost is the same at all outputs.

Total variable cost (TVC) is the cost of the firm's variable factors. For Campus Sweaters, labour is the variable factor, so this component of cost is its wage bill. Total variable cost changes as output changes.

Total cost is the sum of total fixed cost and total variable cost. That is,

$$TC = TFC + TVC.$$

The table in Fig. 10.4 shows total costs. Campus Sweaters rents one knitting machine for $25 a day, so its TFC is $25. To produce sweaters, the firm hires labour, which costs $25 a day. TVC is the number of workers multiplied by $25. For example, to produce 13 sweaters a day, in row D, the firm hires 3 workers and TVC is $75. TC is the sum of TFC and TVC, so to produce 13 sweaters a day, TC is $100. Check the calculations in the other rows of the table.

Figure 10.4 shows Campus Sweaters' total cost curves, which graph total cost against output. The green TFC curve is horizontal because total fixed cost ($25 a day) does not change when output changes. The purple TVC curve and the blue TC curve both slope upward because to increase output, more labour must be employed, which increases total variable cost. Total fixed cost equals the vertical distance between the TVC and TC curves.

Let's now look at a firm's marginal cost.

FIGURE 10.4   Total Cost Curves

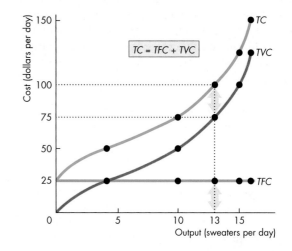

Labour (workers per day)	Output (sweaters per day)	Total fixed cost (TFC)	Total variable cost (TVC)	Total cost (TC)
		(dollars per day)		
A	0	0	25	0	25
B	1	4	25	25	50
C	2	10	25	50	75
D	**3**	**13**	**25**	**75**	**100**
E	4	15	25	100	125
F	5	16	25	125	150

Campus Sweaters rents a knitting machine for $25 a day, so this cost is the firm's total fixed cost. The firm hires workers at a wage rate of $25 a day, and this cost is its total variable cost. For example, in row D, Campus Sweaters employs 3 workers and its total variable cost is 3 × $25, which equals $75. Total cost is the sum of total fixed cost and total variable cost. For example, when Campus Sweaters employs 3 workers, total cost is $100—total fixed cost of $25 plus total variable cost of $75.

The graph shows Campus Sweaters' total cost curves. Total fixed cost is constant—the TFC curve is a horizontal line. Total variable cost increases as output increases, so the TVC curve and the TC curve increase as output increases. The vertical distance between the TC curve and the TVC curve equals total fixed cost, as illustrated by the two arrows.

MyLab Economics Animation

Marginal Cost

Figure 10.4 shows that total variable cost and total cost increase at a decreasing rate at small outputs but eventually, as output increases, total variable cost and total cost increase at an increasing rate. To understand this pattern in the change in total cost as output increases, we need to use the concept of *marginal cost*.

A firm's **marginal cost** is the increase in total cost that results from a one-unit increase in output. We calculate marginal cost as the increase in total cost divided by the increase in output. The table in Fig. 10.5 shows this calculation. When, for example, output increases from 10 sweaters to 13 sweaters, total cost increases from $75 to $100. The change in output is 3 sweaters, and the change in total cost is $25. The marginal cost of one of those 3 sweaters is ($25 ÷ 3), which equals $8.33.

Figure 10.5 graphs the marginal cost data in the table as the red marginal cost curve, *MC*. This curve is U-shaped because when Campus Sweaters hires a second worker, marginal cost decreases, but when it hires a third, a fourth, and a fifth worker, marginal cost successively increases.

At small outputs, marginal cost decreases as output increases because of greater specialization and the division of labour. But as output increases further, marginal cost eventually increases because of the *law of diminishing returns*. The law of diminishing returns means that the output produced by each additional worker is successively smaller. To produce an additional unit of output, ever more workers are required, and the cost of producing the additional unit of output—marginal cost—must eventually increase.

Marginal cost tells us how total cost changes as output increases. The final cost concept tells us what it costs, on average, to produce a unit of output. Let's now look at Campus Sweaters' average costs.

Average Cost

There are three average costs of production:

1. Average fixed cost
2. Average variable cost
3. Average total cost

Average fixed cost (*AFC*) is total fixed cost per unit of output. **Average variable cost** (*AVC*) is total variable cost per unit of output. **Average total cost** (*ATC*) is total cost per unit of output. The average cost concepts are calculated from the total cost concepts as follows:

$$TC = TFC + TVC.$$

Divide each total cost term by the quantity produced, Q, to get

$$\frac{TC}{Q} = \frac{TFC}{Q} + \frac{TVC}{Q},$$

or

$$ATC = AFC + AVC.$$

The table in Fig. 10.5 shows the calculation of average total cost. For example, in row C, output is 10 sweaters. Average fixed cost is ($25 ÷ 10), which equals $2.50; average variable cost is ($50 ÷ 10), which equals $5.00; and average total cost is ($75 ÷ 10), which equals $7.50. Note that average total cost is equal to average fixed cost ($2.50) plus average variable cost ($5.00).

Figure 10.5 shows the average cost curves. The green average fixed cost curve (*AFC*) slopes downward. As output increases, the same constant total fixed cost is spread over a larger output. The blue average total cost curve (*ATC*) and the purple average variable cost curve (*AVC*) are U-shaped. The vertical distance between the average total cost and average variable cost curves is equal to average fixed cost—as indicated by the two arrows. That distance shrinks as output increases because average fixed cost declines with increasing output.

Marginal Cost and Average Cost

The marginal cost curve (*MC*) intersects the average variable cost curve and the average total cost curve *at their minimum points*. When marginal cost is less than average cost, average cost is decreasing, and when marginal cost exceeds average cost, average cost is increasing. This relationship holds for both the *ATC* curve and the *AVC* curve. It is another example of the relationship that you saw in Fig. 10.3 between average product and marginal product and in your average and marginal grades.

Why the Average Total Cost Curve Is U-Shaped

Average total cost is the sum of average fixed cost and average variable cost, so the shape of the *ATC* curve

FIGURE 10.5   Marginal Cost and Average Costs

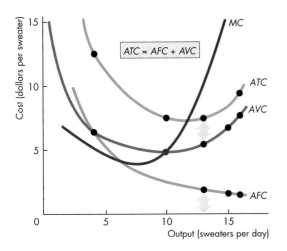

Marginal cost is calculated as the change in total cost divided by the change in output. When output increases from 4 to 10 sweaters, an increase of 6 sweaters, total cost increases by $25. Marginal cost is $25 ÷ 6, which is $4.17.

Each average cost concept is calculated by dividing the related total cost by output. When 10 sweaters are produced, *AFC* is $2.50 ($25 ÷ 10), *AVC* is $5.00 ($50 ÷ 10), and *ATC* is $7.50 ($75 ÷ 10).

The graph shows that the *MC* curve is U-shaped and intersects the *AVC* curve and the *ATC* curve at their minimum points. The average fixed cost curve (*AFC*) is downward sloping. The *ATC* curve and *AVC* curve are U-shaped. The vertical distance between the *ATC* curve and the *AVC* curve is equal to average fixed cost, as illustrated by the two arrows.

	Labour (workers per day)	Output (sweaters per day)	Total fixed cost (TFC)	Total variable cost (TVC)	Total cost (TC)	Marginal cost (MC) (dollars per additional sweater)	Average fixed cost (AFC)	Average variable cost (AVC)	Average total cost (ATC)
			(dollars per day)				(dollars per sweater)		
A	0	0	25	0	25		—	—	—
						.... 6.25			
B	1	4	25	25	50		6.25	6.25	12.50
						.... 4.17			
C	2	10	25	50	75		2.50	5.00	7.50
						.... 8.33			
D	3	13	25	75	100		1.92	5.77	7.69
						.... 12.50			
E	4	15	25	100	125		1.67	6.67	8.33
						.... 25.00			
F	5	16	25	125	150		1.56	7.81	9.38

MyLab Economics Animation and Draw Graph

combines the shapes of the *AFC* and *AVC* curves. The U shape of the *ATC* curve arises from the influence of two opposing forces:

1. Spreading total fixed cost over a larger output
2. Eventually diminishing returns

When the firm increases its output, its total fixed cost is spread over a larger output and so its average fixed cost decreases—its *AFC* curve slopes downward.

Diminishing returns means that as output increases, ever-larger amounts of labour are needed to produce an additional unit of output. So as output increases, average variable cost decreases initially but eventually increases, and the *AVC* curve slopes upward. The *AVC* curve is U-shaped.

The shape of the *ATC* curve combines these two effects. Initially, as output increases, both average fixed cost and average variable cost decrease, so average total cost decreases. The *ATC* curve slopes downward.

But as output increases further and diminishing returns set in, average variable cost starts to increase. With average fixed cost decreasing more quickly than average variable cost is increasing, the *ATC* curve continues to slope downward. Eventually, average variable cost starts to increase more quickly than average fixed cost decreases, so average total cost starts to increase. The *ATC* curve slopes upward.

Cost Curves and Product Curves

The technology that a firm uses determines its costs. A firm's cost curves come directly from its product curves. You've used this link in the tables in which we have calculated total cost from the total product schedule and information about the prices of the factors of production. We're now going to get a clearer view of the link between the product curves and the cost curves. We'll look first at the link between total cost and total product and then at the links between the average and marginal product and cost curves.

Total Product and Total Variable Cost Figure 10.6 shows the links between the firm's total product curve, *TP*, and its total *variable* cost curve, *TVC*. The graph is a bit unusual in two ways. First, it measures two variables on the *x*-axis—labour and variable cost. Second, it graphs the *TVC* curve but with variable cost on the *x*-axis and output on the *y*-axis. The graph can show labour and cost on the *x*-axis because variable cost is proportional to labour. One worker costs $25 a day. Graphing output against labour gives the *TP* curve, and graphing variable cost against output gives the *TVC* curve.

FIGURE 10.6 Total Product and Total Variable Cost

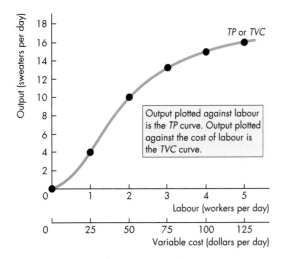

Output plotted against labour is the *TP* curve. Output plotted against the cost of labour is the *TVC* curve.

The figure shows the total product curve, *TP*, as a graph of output (sweaters per day) plotted against labour (workers per day). It also shows the total variable cost curve, *TVC*, as a graph of total variable cost (dollars per day) against output. The only difference between the *TVC* curve here and that in Fig. 10.4 is that we've switched the *x*-axis and *y*-axis.

Checkout Cost Curves

Self-Checkout Tops List of Retail Technology Wishes
IT professionals are looking forward to the expansion of self-checkout technology in retail stores in the coming year.

Source: *Business Wire*, May 24, 2017

DATA AND ASSUMPTIONS

A grocery store paid $20,000 to install 5 worker-operated checkout lines. With a life of 9 years and operating for 10 hours a day, these machines have an *implicit rental rate* of $1.00 an hour. Checkout clerks can be hired for $10 an hour. The total product schedule (checkouts per hour) for this store is:

Checkout clerks	1	2	3	4	5
Checkouts per hour	12	22	30	36	40

Another grocery store has converted to all self-checkout. It paid $100,000 to install a 5-line self-operated system. With a 5-year life and operating for 10 hours a day, the system has an *implicit rental rate* of $7.00 an hour. It hires checkout assistants to help customers at $10 an hour—the same wage as paid to checkout clerks. The total product schedule for this store is:

Checkout assistants	1	1	1	2
Checkouts per hour	12	22	30	36

That is, one checkout assistant can help shoppers check out up to a rate of 30 an hour and a second assistant can boost output to 36 an hour. (Shoppers using self-checkout aren't as quick as clerks, so the fastest rate at which this store can check out customers is 36 an hour.)

THE PROBLEM

- Which checkout system has the lower average total cost (*ATC*)? Which system has the lower marginal cost (*MC*)? Sketch the *ATC* and *MC* curves for the two systems.

THE SOLUTION

- Start with the worker-operated checkout system. Fixed cost is $1.00 per hour and variable cost is $10.00 per clerk. So the total cost schedule is:

Checkout clerks	1	2	3	4	5
Checkouts per hour	12	22	30	36	40
Total cost (*TC*) per hour	11	21	31	41	51

- Calculate MC as the change in TC divided by the change in output (change in number of checkouts) and calculate ATC as TC divided by output to get:

Checkouts per hour	12	22	30	36	40
Marginal cost (MC)	0.83	1.00	1.25	1.67	2.50
Average total cost (ATC)	0.92	0.95	1.03	1.14	1.28

- Figure 1 graphs the MC and ATC values at each output rate.

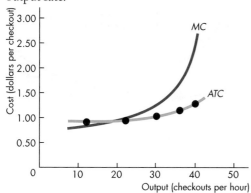

Figure 1 Operator Checkout

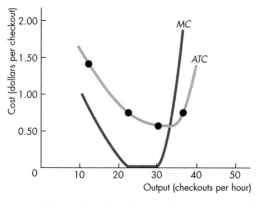

Figure 2 Self-Checkout

- Now do similar calculations for the self-checkout system. Fixed cost is $7.00 per hour and variable cost is $10.00 per clerk hour. So the total cost schedule is:

Checkout assistants	1	1	1	2
Checkouts per hour	12	22	30	36
Total cost (TC) per hour	17	17	17	27

- Calculate MC and ATC in the same way as before to get:

Checkouts per hour	12	22	30	36
Marginal cost (MC)	0.83	0	0	1.67
Average total cost (ATC)	1.42	0.77	0.57	0.75

- Figure 2 graphs the MC and ATC values at each output rate.
- Figure 3 compares the ATC of the two systems. You can see that the self-checkout system has higher ATC at low output rates and lower ATC at high output rates. The reason is that self-checkout has a higher fixed cost and lower variable cost than the worker-operated system.

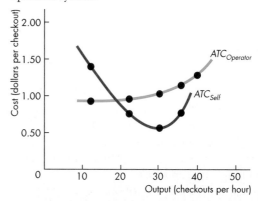

Figure 3 ATC Compared

Average and Marginal Product and Cost Figure 10.7 shows the links between the firm's average and marginal product curves and its average and marginal cost curves. The upper graph shows the average product curve, *AP*, and the marginal product curve, *MP*—like those in Fig. 10.3. The lower graph shows the average variable cost curve, *AVC*, and the marginal cost curve, *MC*—like those in Fig. 10.5.

As labour increases up to 1.5 workers a day (upper graph), output increases to 6.5 sweaters a day (lower graph). Marginal product and average product rise and marginal cost and average variable cost fall. At the point of maximum marginal product, marginal cost is at a minimum.

As the firm increases its labour from 1.5 workers to 2 workers a day (upper graph), output increases from 6.5 sweaters to 10 sweaters a day (lower graph). Marginal product falls and marginal cost rises, but average product continues to rise and average variable cost continues to fall. At the point of maximum average product, average variable cost is at a minimum. As labour increases further, output increases. Average product diminishes and average variable cost increases.

Shifts in the Cost Curves

The position of a firm's short-run cost curves depends on two factors:

- Technology
- Prices of factors of production

Technology A technological change that increases productivity increases the marginal product and average product of labour. With a better technology, the same factors of production can produce more output, so the technological advance lowers the costs of production and shifts the cost curves downward.

For example, advances in robot production techniques have increased productivity in the automobile industry. As a result, the product curves of Ford, GM, and Chrysler have shifted upward and their cost curves have shifted downward. But the relationships between their product curves and cost curves have not changed. The curves are still linked in the way shown in Figs. 10.6 and 10.7.

Often, as in the case of robots producing cars, a technological advance results in a firm using

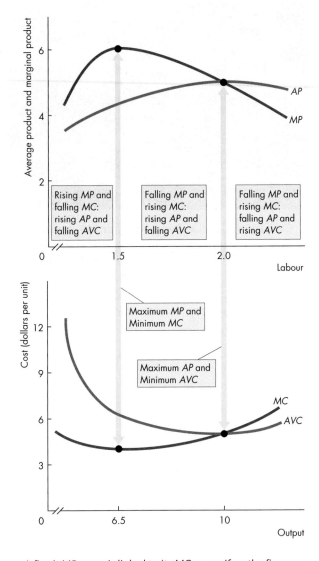

FIGURE 10.7 Average and Marginal Product Curves and Cost Curves

A firm's *MP* curve is linked to its *MC* curve. If, as the firm increases its labour from 0 to 1.5 workers a day, marginal product rises, the firm's marginal cost falls. When marginal product is at a maximum, the firm's marginal cost is at a minimum. If, as the firm hires more labour, marginal product diminishes, the firm's marginal cost rises.

A firm's *AP* curve is linked to its *AVC* curve. If, as the firm increases its labour to 2 workers a day, average product rises, the firm's average variable cost falls. When average product is at a maximum, the firm's average variable cost is at a minimum. If, as the firm hires more labour, average product diminishes, the firm's average variable cost rises.

MyLab Economics Animation

TABLE 10.3   A Compact Glossary of Costs

Term	Symbol	Definition	Equation
Fixed cost		Cost that is independent of the output level; cost of a fixed factor of production	
Variable cost		Cost that varies with the output level; cost of a variable factor of production	
Total fixed cost	TFC	Cost of the fixed factors of production	
Total variable cost	TVC	Cost of the variable factors of production	
Total cost	TC	Cost of all factors of production	$TC = TFC + TVC$
Output (total product)	TP	Total quantity produced (output Q)	
Marginal cost	MC	Change in total cost resulting from a one-unit increase in total product	$MC = \Delta TC \div \Delta Q$
Average fixed cost	AFC	Total fixed cost per unit of output	$AFC = TFC \div Q$
Average variable cost	AVC	Total variable cost per unit of output	$AVC = TVC \div Q$
Average total cost	ATC	Total cost per unit of output	$ATC = AFC + AVC$

more capital, a fixed factor, and less labour, a variable factor. Another example is the use of ATMs by banks to dispense cash. ATMs, which are fixed capital, have replaced tellers, which are variable labour. Such a technological change decreases total cost but increases fixed costs and decreases variable cost. This change in the mix of fixed cost and variable cost means that at small outputs, average total cost might increase, while at large outputs, average total cost decreases.

Prices of Factors of Production An increase in the price of a factor of production increases the firm's costs and shifts its cost curves. How the curves shift depends on which factor price changes.

An increase in rent or some other component of *fixed* cost shifts the *TFC* and *AFC* curves upward and shifts the *TC* curve upward but leaves the *AVC* and *TVC* curves and the *MC* curve unchanged. For example, if the interest expense paid by a trucking company increases, the fixed cost of transportation services increases.

An increase in wages, gasoline, or another component of *variable* cost shifts the *TVC* and *AVC* curves upward and shifts the *MC* curve upward but leaves

the *AFC* and *TFC* curves unchanged. For example, if truck drivers' wages or the price of gasoline increases, the variable cost and marginal cost of transportation services increase.

You've now completed your study of short-run costs. All the concepts that you've met are summarized in a compact glossary in Table 10.3.

◆ **REVIEW QUIZ**

1 What relationships do a firm's short-run cost curves show?
2 How does marginal cost change as output increases (a) initially and (b) eventually?
3 What does the law of diminishing returns imply for the shape of the marginal cost curve?
4 What is the shape of the *AFC* curve and why does it have this shape?
5 What are the shapes of the *AVC* curve and the *ATC* curve and why do they have these shapes?

Work these questions in Study Plan 10.3 and get instant feedback   MyLab Economics

◆ Long-Run Cost

We are now going to study the firm's long-run costs. In the long run, a firm can vary both the quantity of labour and the quantity of capital, so in the long run, all the firm's costs are variable.

The behaviour of long-run cost depends on the firm's *production function*, which is the relationship between the maximum output attainable and the quantities of both labour and capital.

The Production Function

Table 10.4 shows Campus Sweaters' production function. The table lists total product schedules for four different quantities of capital. The quantity of capital identifies the plant size. The numbers for plant 1 are for a factory with 1 knitting machine—the case we've just studied. The other three plants have 2, 3, and 4 machines. If Campus Sweaters uses plant 2 with 2 knitting machines, the various amounts of labour can produce the outputs shown in the second column of the table. The other two columns show the outputs of yet larger quantities of capital. Each column of the table could be graphed as a total product curve for each plant.

Diminishing Returns Diminishing returns occur with each of the four plant sizes as the quantity of labour increases. You can check that fact by calculating the marginal product of labour in each of the plants with 2, 3, and 4 machines. With each plant size, as the firm increases the quantity of labour employed, the marginal product of labour (eventually) diminishes.

Diminishing Marginal Product of Capital Diminishing returns also occur with each quantity of labour as the quantity of capital increases. You can check that fact by calculating the marginal product of capital at a given quantity of labour. The *marginal product of capital* is the change in total product divided by the change in capital when the quantity of labour is constant—equivalently, the change in output resulting from a one-unit increase in the quantity of capital. For example, if Campus Sweaters has 3 workers and increases its capital from 1 machine to 2 machines, output increases from 13 to 18 sweaters a day. The marginal product of the second machine is 5 sweaters a day. If Campus Sweaters continues to employ 3 workers

TABLE 10.4 The Production Function

Labour (workers per day)	Output (sweaters per day)			
	Plant 1	Plant 2	Plant 3	Plant 4
1	4	10	13	15
2	10	15	18	20
3	13	18	22	24
4	15	20	24	26
5	16	21	25	27
Knitting machines (number)	**1**	**2**	**3**	**4**

The table shows the total product data for four quantities of capital (plant sizes). The greater the plant size, the larger is the output produced by any given quantity of labour. For a given plant size, as more labour is employed, the marginal product of labour diminishes. For a given quantity of labour, the marginal product of capital diminishes as the quantity of capital used increases.

and increases the number of machines from 2 to 3, output increases from 18 to 22 sweaters a day. The marginal product of the third machine is 4 sweaters a day, down from 5 sweaters a day for the second machine.

Let's now see what the production function implies for long-run costs.

Short-Run Cost and Long-Run Cost

As before, Campus Sweaters can hire workers for $25 a day and rent knitting machines for $25 a day. Using these factor prices and the data in Table 10.4, we can calculate the average total cost and graph the ATC curves for factories with 1, 2, 3, and 4 knitting machines. We've already studied the costs of a factory with 1 machine in Figs. 10.4 and 10.5. In Fig. 10.8, the average total cost curve for that case is ATC_1. Figure 10.8 also shows the average total cost curve for a factory with 2 machines, ATC_2; with 3 machines, ATC_3; and with 4 machines, ATC_4.

You can see, in Fig. 10.8, that the plant size has a big effect on the firm's average total cost.

FIGURE 10.8   Short-Run Costs of Four Different Plants

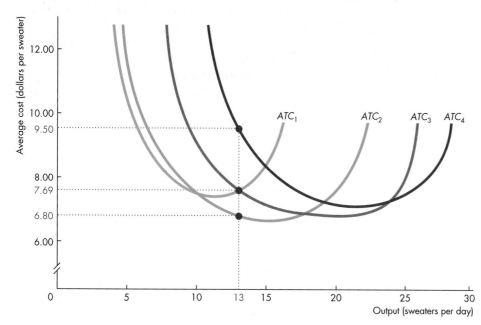

The figure shows short-run average total cost curves for four different quantities of capital at Campus Sweaters. The firm can produce 13 sweaters a day with 1 knitting machine on ATC_1 or with 3 knitting machines on ATC_3 for an average cost of $7.69 a sweater. The firm can produce 13 sweaters a day by using 2 machines on ATC_2 for $6.80 a sweater or by using 4 machines on ATC_4 for $9.50 a sweater.

If the firm produces 13 sweaters a day, the least-cost method of production, *the long-run method*, is with 2 machines on ATC_2.

In Fig. 10.8, two things stand out:

1. Each short-run ATC curve is U-shaped.
2. For each short-run ATC curve, the larger the plant, the greater is the output at which average total cost is at a minimum.

Each short-run ATC curve is U-shaped because, as the quantity of labour increases, its marginal product initially increases and then diminishes. This pattern in the marginal product of labour, which we examined in some detail for the plant with 1 knitting machine on pp. 232–233, occurs at all plant sizes.

The minimum average total cost for a larger plant occurs at a greater output than it does for a smaller plant because the larger plant has a higher total fixed cost and therefore, for any given output, a higher average fixed cost.

Which short-run ATC curve a firm operates on depends on the plant it has. In the long run, the firm can choose its plant and the plant it chooses is the one that enables it to produce its planned output at the lowest average total cost.

To see why, suppose that Campus Sweaters plans to produce 13 sweaters a day. In Fig. 10.8, with 1 machine, the average total cost curve is ATC_1 and

the average total cost of 13 sweaters a day is $7.69 a sweater. With 2 machines, on ATC_2, average total cost is $6.80 a sweater. With 3 machines, on ATC_3, average total cost is $7.69 a sweater, the same as with 1 machine. Finally, with 4 machines, on ATC_4, average total cost is $9.50 a sweater.

The economically efficient plant for producing a given output is the one that has the lowest average total cost. For Campus Sweaters, the economically efficient plant to use to produce 13 sweaters a day is the one with 2 machines.

In the long run, Cindy chooses the plant that minimizes average total cost. When a firm is producing a given output at the least possible cost, it is operating on its *long-run average cost curve*.

The **long-run average cost curve** is the relationship between the lowest attainable average total cost and output when the firm can change both the plant it uses and the quantity of labour it employs.

The long-run average cost curve is a planning curve. It tells the firm the plant and the quantity of labour to use at each output to minimize average cost. Once the firm chooses a plant, the firm operates on the short-run cost curves that apply to that plant.

The Long-Run Average Cost Curve

Figure 10.9 shows how a long-run average cost curve is derived. The long-run average cost curve $LRAC$ consists of pieces of the four short-run ATC curves. For outputs up to 10 sweaters a day, average total cost is the lowest on ATC_1. For outputs between 10 and 18 sweaters a day, average total cost is the lowest on ATC_2. For outputs between 18 and 24 sweaters a day, average total cost is the lowest on ATC_3. And for outputs in excess of 24 sweaters a day, average total cost is the lowest on ATC_4. The piece of each ATC curve with the lowest average total cost is highlighted in dark blue in Fig. 10.9. This dark blue scallop-shaped curve made up of the pieces of the four ATC curves is the $LRAC$ curve.

Economies and Diseconomies of Scale

Economies of scale are features of a firm's technology that make average total cost *fall* as output increases. When economies of scale are present, the $LRAC$ curve slopes downward. In Fig. 10.9, Campus Sweaters has economies of scale for outputs up to 15 sweaters a day.

Greater specialization of both labour and capital is the main source of economies of scale. For example,

if GM produces 100 cars a week, each worker must perform many different tasks and the capital must be general-purpose machines and tools. But if GM produces 10,000 cars a week, each worker specializes in a small number of tasks, uses task-specific tools, and becomes highly proficient.

Diseconomies of scale are features of a firm's technology that make average total cost *rise* as output increases. When diseconomies of scale are present, the $LRAC$ curve slopes upward. In Fig. 10.9, Campus Sweaters experiences diseconomies of scale at outputs greater than 15 sweaters a day.

The challenge of managing a large enterprise is the main source of diseconomies of scale.

Constant returns to scale are features of a firm's technology that keep average total cost constant as output increases. When constant returns to scale are present, the $LRAC$ curve is horizontal.

Economies of Scale at Campus Sweaters The economies of scale and diseconomies of scale at Campus Sweaters arise from the firm's production function in Table 10.4. With 1 machine and 1 worker, the firm produces 4 sweaters a day. With 2 machines and 2 workers, total cost doubles but

FIGURE 10.9 Long-Run Average Cost Curve

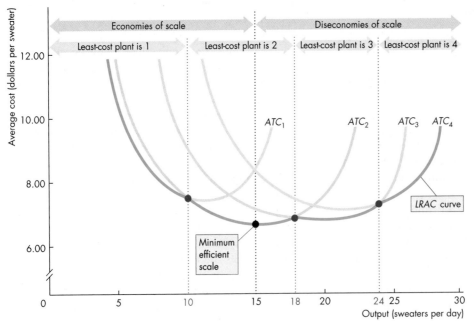

The long-run average cost curve traces the lowest attainable ATC when both labour and capital change. The green arrows highlight the output range over which each plant achieves the lowest ATC. Within each range, to change the quantity produced, the firm changes the quantity of labour it employs.

Along the $LRAC$ curve, economies of scale occur if average cost falls as output increases; diseconomies of scale occur if average cost rises as output increases. Minimum efficient scale is the output at which average cost is lowest, 15 sweaters a day.

ECONOMICS IN ACTION

Produce More to Cut Cost

Why do GM, Ford, and the other automakers have expensive equipment lying around that isn't fully used? You can answer this question with what you've learned in this chapter.

The basic answer is that auto production enjoys economies of scale. A larger output rate brings a lower long-run average cost—the firm's $LRAC$ curve slopes downward.

An auto producer's average total cost curves look like those in the figure. To produce 20 vehicles an hour, the firm installs the plant with the short-run average total cost curve ATC_1. The average cost of producing a vehicle is $20,000.

Producing 20 vehicles an hour doesn't use the plant at its lowest possible average total cost. If the firm could sell enough cars for it to produce 40 vehicles an hour, the firm could use its current plant and produce at an average cost of $15,000 a vehicle.

But if the firm planned to produce 40 vehicles an hour, it would not stick with its current plant. The firm would install a bigger plant with the short-run average total cost curve ATC_2 and produce 40 vehicles an hour for $10,000 a car.

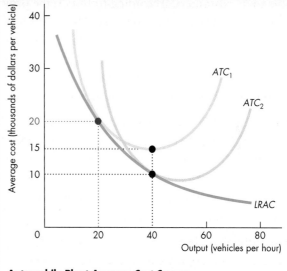

Automobile Plant Average Cost Curves

output more than doubles to 15 sweaters a day, so average cost decreases and Campus Sweaters experiences economies of scale. With 4 machines and 4 workers, total cost doubles again but output less than doubles to 26 sweaters a day, so average cost increases and the firm experiences diseconomies of scale.

Minimum Efficient Scale   A firm's **minimum efficient scale** is the *smallest* output at which long-run average cost reaches its lowest level. At Campus Sweaters, the minimum efficient scale is 15 sweaters a day.

The minimum efficient scale plays a role in determining market structure. In a market in which the minimum efficient scale is small relative to market demand, the market has room for many firms, and the market is competitive. In a market in which the minimum efficient scale is large relative to market demand, only a small number of firms, and possibly only one firm, can make a profit and the market is either an oligopoly or monopoly. We will return to this idea in the next four chapters.

REVIEW QUIZ

1 What does a firm's production function show and how is it related to a total product curve?

2 Does the law of diminishing returns apply to capital as well as labour? Explain why or why not.

3 What does a firm's $LRAC$ curve show? How is it related to the firm's short-run ATC curves?

4 What are economies of scale and diseconomies of scale? How do they arise? What do they imply for the shape of the $LRAC$ curve?

5 What is a firm's minimum efficient scale?

Work these questions in Study Plan 10.4 and get instant feedback.   MyLab Economics

◆ *Economics in the News* on pp. 246–247 applies what you've learned about a firm's cost curves. It looks at IKEA's cost curves and explains how increasing plant size (store size) can lower average total cost.

A Long-Run Decision for IKEA

IKEA Has Announced a $13.5-Million Investment to Increase Space at Its Edmonton Store by 10 Percent

IKEA Edmonton broke ground in July 2016 on a warehouse expansion project set to open by summer 2017 that will improve its existing services and make more stock available to its customers. According to IKEA, the project will add some 29,000 square feet of space to the existing warehouse. The expansion will increase the amount of space at the Edmonton location by roughly 10 percent, according to an article in the *Edmonton Journal*. Sales at the Edmonton location have increased almost 10 percent year-over-year, according to the *Journal*, thanks to low pricing and a weaker Canadian dollar, which have encouraged Canadians to stay home and work on home improvements.

Calgary IKEA is undergoing a similar warehouse expansion at the same time. According to IKEA, both Alberta expansions are part of IKEA Canada's ambition to become accessible to as many people as possible. IKEA's goal is to double its presence in Canada by 2025. Stefan Sjostrand, IKEA Canada's president, said, "With sales increasing at both locations, there is a need to expand our warehouses to better serve our valued customers in Alberta."

The Edmonton IKEA is one of 12 stores across Canada, and currently employs 342 co-workers. Sjostrand was quoted as saying that the company will consider hiring more employees if growth continues to be strong.

Sources: Based on Ameya Charnalia, "IKEA Invests $13.5M to Expand Edmonton Store," *Edmonton Journal*, June 25, 2016, and www.ikea.com/ca/en/about_ikea/newsitem/2016_alberta_expansion_plan

ESSENCE OF THE STORY

- IKEA will expand its Edmonton store by 10 percent.

- The expanded store will employ 342 workers.

- Sales at the Edmonton store have increased almost 10 percent a year.

- If sales growth continues beyond 2017, the company will hire more workers.

MyLab Economics Economics in the News

ECONOMIC ANALYSIS

- IKEA's decision to expand its Edmonton store is a long-run decision about the cost-minimizing plant size.

- IKEA plans an expansion from 300,000 square feet to 330,000 square feet, which is and remains one of the company's smaller stores (see the table).

- A firm chose this plant size to minimize its long-run average total cost.

- We don't know IKEA's costs, but we can gain insight into the firm's decisions with an example.

- Figure 1 graphs the (assumed) marginal cost (MC) and average total cost (ATC) curves for the Edmonton store.

- IKEA can serve 500 customers per hour in this store at a minimum average total cost of $10 per customer.

- When 10 percent more customers per hour turn up, IKEA must hire more workers and install more checkouts. The store becomes congested and marginal cost increases sharply, which increases average total cost.

- To avoid the higher average total cost, IKEA is expanding its store.

- Figure 2 shows IKEA's average total cost with a larger store. To make the effects of scale clear, we'll compare the Edmonton store with the store in Seoul, South Korea, IKEA's largest.

- The Edmonton store's ATC curve is ATC_0, and ATC_1 is the average total cost curve for a store like the one in Seoul, South Korea, with a capacity of 640,000 square feet.

Plant Sizes of Some IKEA Stores

Location	Square feet
Seoul, South Korea	640,000
Stockholm, Sweden	594,167
Montreal, Quebec	469,694
Beijing, China	452,000
Tokyo, Japan	430,000
London, England	398,000
Paris, France	390,729
Edmonton, Alberta, in 2018	330,000
Halifax, Nova Scotia	328,000
Edmonton, Alberta, in 2016	300,000

- In our example, IKEA can serve 1,000 customers per hour in the larger store at minimum average total cost.

- Figure 2 also shows IKEA's long-run average cost curve ($LRAC$).

- At low output levels, the average total cost of serving a customer is lower at the smaller store, and at high output levels, the average total cost is lower at the larger store.

- Economies of scale enable IKEA to serve a larger number of customers at the Seoul store at a lower average total cost than in the Edmonton store.

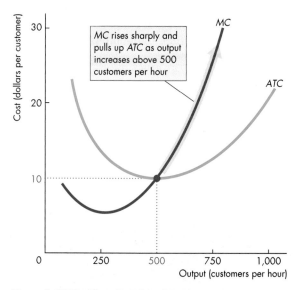

Figure 1 IKEA's Short-Run Cost Curves

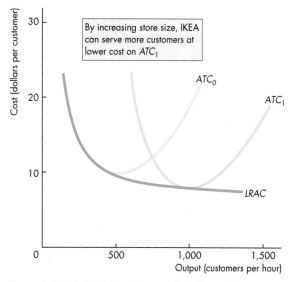

Figure 2 IKEA's Long-Run Average Cost Curve

WORKED PROBLEM

MyLab Economics Work this problem in Chapter 10 Study Plan.

The table provides data about a firm's short-run costs. It shows the firm's total cost, *TC*, when output is zero, and marginal cost, *MC*, at four levels of output.

Output	MC	TC	TFC	TVC	ATC	AFC	AVC
0		$12	?	?			
	$10						
1		?	?	?	?	?	?
	$2						
2		?	?	?	?	?	?
	$6						
3		?	?	?	?	?	?
	$22						
4		?	?	?	?	?	?

Questions

1. Fill in the cells marked "?" to record the firm's costs: *TC*, *TFC*, *TVC*, *ATC*, *AFC*, and *AVC* at each output.
2. Draw a graph of the total cost curves, and a graph of the average and marginal cost curves.

Solutions

1. a. Begin by using the fact that marginal cost, *MC*, is the change in total cost, *TC*, when output increases by 1 unit. This fact means that *TC* at 1 unit equals *TC* at zero units plus *MC* of the first unit. *TC* is $12 at zero and *MC* of the first unit is $10, so *TC* at 1 unit equals $22. The rest of the *TC* column is calculated in the same way. For example, *TC* at 4 units is $52, which equals $30 + $22.

b. *TFC* equals *TC* at zero output, so you can fill in the *TFC* column as $12 at each quantity of output.

c. Because *TC* = *TFC* + *TVC*, you can fill in the *TVC* column as *TVC* = *TC* − *TFC*. For example, at 1 unit of output, *TVC* = $22 − $12 = $10.

d. Average cost equals *TC* ÷ output, so to fill in the *ATC*, *AFC*, and *AVC* columns, divide the numbers for *TC*, *TFC*, and *TVC* by the output level. For example, *ATC* at 3 units of output is $30 ÷ 3 = $10.

Output	MC	TC	TFC	TVC	ATC	AFC	AVC
0		$12	$12	$0			
	$10						
1		$22	$12	$10	$22	$12	$10
	$2						
2		$24	$12	$12	$12	$6	$6
	$6						
3		$30	$12	$18	$10	$4	$6
	$22						
4		$52	$12	$40	$13	$3	$10

Key Point: Given a firm's total cost at zero output and its marginal cost at each output, by using the relationships among the cost concepts, we can calculate the total costs and the average costs at each output.

2. The key figure (a) graphs the total cost curves and the key figure (b) graphs the marginal and average cost curves.

Key Point: The marginal cost curve intersects the average cost curves at their minimum points.

Key Figure

MyLab Economics Interactive Animation

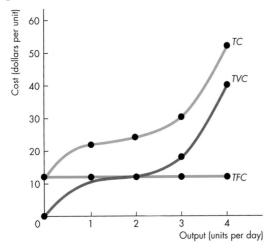

(a) Total Cost Curves

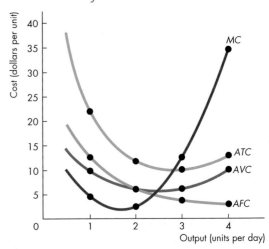

(b) Average and Marginal Cost Curves

SUMMARY

Key Points

Economic Cost and Profit (pp. 228–230)

- Firms hire and organize factors of production to produce and sell goods and services.
- A firm's goal is to maximize economic profit, which is total revenue minus total cost measured as the opportunity cost of production.
- A firm's opportunity cost of production is the sum of the cost of resources bought in the market, using the firm's own resources, and resources supplied by the firm's owner.
- Normal profit is the opportunity cost of entrepreneurship and is part of the firm's opportunity cost.
- In the short run, the quantity of at least one factor of production is fixed and the quantities of the other factors of production can be varied.
- In the long run, the quantities of all factors of production can be varied.

Working Problems 1 and 2 will give you a better understanding of a firm's decision time frames.

Short-Run Technology Constraint (pp. 231–234)

- A total product curve shows the quantity a firm can produce with a given quantity of capital and different quantities of labour.
- Initially, the marginal product of labour increases as the quantity of labour increases, because of increased specialization and the division of labour.
- Eventually, marginal product diminishes because an increasing quantity of labour must share a fixed quantity of capital—the law of diminishing returns.

- Initially, average product increases as the quantity of labour increases, but eventually average product diminishes.

Working Problems 3 to 6 will give you a better understanding of a firm's short-run technology constraint.

Short-Run Cost (pp. 235–241)

- As output increases, total fixed cost is constant, and total variable cost and total cost increase.
- As output increases, average fixed cost decreases and average variable cost, average total cost, and marginal cost decrease at low outputs and increase at high outputs. These cost curves are U-shaped.

Working Problems 7 to 11 will give you a better understanding of a firm's short-run cost.

Long-Run Cost (pp. 242–245)

- A firm has a set of short-run cost curves for each different plant. For each output, the firm has one least-cost plant. The larger the output, the larger is the plant that will minimize average total cost.
- The long-run average cost curve traces out the lowest attainable average total cost at each output when both capital and labour inputs can be varied.
- With economies of scale, the long-run average cost curve slopes downward. With diseconomies of scale, the long-run average cost curve slopes upward.

Working Problems 12 to 14 will give you a better understanding of a firm's long-run cost.

Key Terms

MyLab Economics Key Terms Quiz

Average fixed cost, 236
Average product, 231
Average total cost, 236
Average variable cost, 236
Constant returns to scale, 244
Diminishing marginal returns, 233
Diseconomies of scale, 244
Economic depreciation, 229
Economic profit, 228

Economies of scale, 244
Firm, 228
Implicit rental rate, 228
Law of diminishing returns, 233
Long run, 230
Long-run average cost curve, 243
Marginal cost, 236
Marginal product, 231
Minimum efficient scale, 245

Normal profit, 229
Short run, 230
Sunk cost, 230
Total cost, 235
Total fixed cost, 235
Total product, 231
Total variable cost, 235

STUDY PLAN PROBLEMS AND APPLICATIONS

MyLab Economics Work Problems 1 to 14 in Chapter 10 Study Plan and get instant feedback.

Economic Cost and Profit (Study Plan 10.1)

1. Joe, who has no skills, no job experience, and no alternative job, runs a shoeshine stand. Other shoeshine operators earn $10,000 a year. Joe pays rent of $2,000 a year, and his total revenue is $15,000 a year. Joe spent $1,000 on equipment and used his credit card to buy it. The interest on a credit card balance is 20 percent a year. At the end of the year, Joe was offered $500 for his business and its equipment. Calculate Joe's opportunity cost of production and economic profit.

2. **Macy's Is Closing Another 100 Stores**

   Macy's will close 15 percent of its department stores and employees at closed stores may be offered jobs in nearby stores. Premiere Macy's locations could be scaled back.

   Walmart plans to shut down 269 stores.

   Nearly 44,000 retail workers have been laid off in 2016.

   Amazon and other online retailers are expanding.

   Source: CNNMoney, August 11, 2016

   Which of the items in the news clip involves a short-run decision and which involves a long-run decision? Explain.

Short-Run Technology Constraint (Study Plan 10.2)

Use the following table to work Problems 3 to 6. Sue's Surfboards' total product schedule is:

Labour (workers per week)	Output (surfboards per week)
1	30
2	70
3	120
4	160
5	190
6	210
7	220

3. Calculate the average product of labour and draw the average product curve.
4. Calculate the marginal product of labour and draw the marginal product curve.
5. Over what output range does Sue's Surfboards:
   a. Enjoy the benefits of increased specialization and the division of labour?

   b. Experience diminishing marginal product of labour?

6. Explain how it is possible for a firm to experience simultaneously an increasing *average* product but a diminishing *marginal* product.

Short-Run Cost (Study Plan 10.3)

Use the table in Problem 3 to work Problems 7 to 11. Sue's Surfboards hires workers at $500 a week and its total fixed cost is $1,000 a week.

7. Calculate total cost, total variable cost, and total fixed cost of each output in the table. Plot these points and sketch the short-run total cost curves.
8. Calculate average total cost, average fixed cost, average variable cost, and marginal cost of each output in the table and plot these cost curves.
9. Use graphs to show the connections between Sue's *AP, MP, AVC,* and *MC* curves.
10. If the rent Sue's Surfboards pays rises by $200 a week, how do Sue's Surfboards' short-run average cost curves and marginal cost curve change?
11. If the wage rate rises by $100 a week, explain how Sue's Surfboards' short-run average cost curves and marginal cost curve change.

Long-Run Cost (Study Plan 10.4)

Use the following data to work Problems 12 to 14. Jackie's Canoe Rides rents canoes at $100 per day and pays $50 per day for each canoe operator it hires. The table shows the firm's production function.

Labour (workers per day)	Output (rides per day)			
	Plant 1	Plant 2	Plant 3	Plant 4
10	20	40	55	65
20	40	60	75	85
30	65	75	90	100
40	75	85	100	110
Canoes	**10**	**20**	**30**	**40**

12. Graph the *ATC* curves for Plant 1 and Plant 2. Explain why these *ATC* curves differ.
13. Graph the *ATC* curves for Plant 3 and Plant 4. Explain why these *ATC* curves differ.
14. a. On Jackie's *LRAC* curve, what is the average cost of producing 40, 75, and 85 rides a week?

    b. What is Jackie's minimum efficient scale?

    c. Does Jackie's production function feature economies of scale or diseconomies of scale?

ADDITIONAL PROBLEMS AND APPLICATIONS

MyLab Economics You can work these problems in Homework or Test if assigned by your instructor.

Economic Cost and Profit

15. In 2016, Toni taught music and earned $20,000. She also earned $4,000 by renting out her basement. On January 1, 2017, she quit teaching, stopped renting out her basement, and began to use it as the office for her new Web site design business. She took $2,000 from her savings account to buy a computer.

During 2017, she paid $1,500 for the lease of a Web server and $1,750 for high-speed Internet service. Her total revenue from Web site designing was $45,000 and she earned interest at 5 percent a year on her savings account balance. Normal profit was $55,000 a year. At the end of 2017, Toni could have sold her computer for $500. Calculate Toni's opportunity cost of production and her economic profit in 2017.

16. **Staples Closing Another 70 Stores as North American Sales Sink**
Staples closed 48 of its North American stores in 2016 and will close another 70 in 2017. The firm has expanded its e-commerce, and has focused on buying small business-to-business service providers beyond office supplies companies that employ 10 to 200 employees. It has added 1,000 people to its sales force.
Source: *Fortune*, March 9, 2017

a. Which of Staples' decisions is a short-run decision and which is a long-run decision?

b. Why is Staples' long-run decision riskier than its short-run decision?

17. **The Sunk-Cost Fallacy**
You have good tickets to a basketball game an hour's drive away. There's a blizzard raging outside, and the game is being televised. What do you do: go to the game or watch it on TV?
Source: *Slate*, September 9, 2005

a. What type of cost is your expenditure on tickets?

b. Why is the ticket price irrelevant to your decision to stay at home or to go to the game?

Short-Run Technology Constraint

18. Terri runs a rose farm. One worker produces 1,000 roses a week; hiring a second worker doubles her total product; hiring a third worker doubles her output again; hiring a fourth worker increased her total product but by only 1,000 roses. Construct Terri's marginal product and average product schedules. Over what range of workers do marginal returns increase?

Short-Run Cost

19. The news clip in Problem 16 sets out Staples' business decisions. Explain how Staples' short-run decision will change its average variable cost and its short-run ATC curve.

20. Bill's Bakery has a fire and Bill loses some of his cost data. The bits of paper that he recovers after the fire provide the information in the following table (all the cost numbers are dollars).

TP	AFC	AVC	ATC	MC
10	120	100	220	
				80
20	*A*	*B*	150	
				90
30	40	90	130	
				130
40	30	*C*	*D*	
				E
50	24	108	132	

Bill asks you to come to his rescue and provide the missing data in the five spaces identified as *A*, *B*, *C*, *D*, and *E*.

Use the following table to work Problems 21 and 22. ProPainters hires students at $250 a week to paint houses. It leases equipment at $500 a week. The table sets out its total product schedule.

Labour (students)	Output (houses painted per week)
1	2
2	5
3	9
4	12
5	14
6	15

21. If ProPainters paints 12 houses a week, calculate its total cost, average total cost, and marginal cost. At what output is average total cost a minimum?

22. Explain why the gap between ProPainters' total cost and total variable cost is the same no matter how many houses are painted.

23. **Sushi Under Intense Price Pressure**

    The price of flavoured hake, used by sushi bars in place of crabmeat, has increased by 33 percent over the past three years. Crabmeat is up about 50 percent. Californian sushi rice has increased in price by about 25 percent in the past two years. The wholesale price of sushi-grade sockeye salmon has fluctuated between $11 and $15 a kilogram. The price of avocados has fluctuated between $40 and $60 a case.

    Source: *Vancouver Sun*, May 28, 2015

    a. Do the fluctuations in the prices of items in the news clip change a sushi bar's fixed cost, variable cost, or marginal cost?

    b. Explain how the price fluctuations influence a sushi bar's short-run cost curves.

Long-Run Cost

Use the table in Problem 21 and the following information to work Problems 24 and 25.

If ProPainters doubles the number of students it hires and doubles the amount of equipment it leases, it experiences diseconomies of scale.

24. Explain how the *ATC* curve with one unit of equipment differs from that when ProPainters uses double the amount of equipment.

25. Explain what might be the source of the diseconomies of scale that ProPainters experiences.

Use the following information to work Problems 26 to 28.

The table shows the production function of Bonnie's Balloon Rides. Bonnie's pays $500 a day for each balloon it rents and $25 a day for each balloon operator it hires.

Labour (workers per day)	Output (rides per day)			
	Plant 1	**Plant 2**	**Plant 3**	**Plant 4**
10	6	10	13	15
20	10	15	18	20
30	13	18	22	24
40	15	20	24	26
50	16	21	25	27
Balloons (number)	1	2	3	4

26. Graph the *ATC* curves for Plant 1 and Plant 2. Explain why these *ATC* curves differ.

27. Graph the *ATC* curves for Plant 3 and Plant 4. Explain why these *ATC* curves differ.

28. a. On Bonnie's *LRAC* curve, what is the average cost of producing 15 rides and 18 rides a day?

    b. Explain how Bonnie's uses its long-run average cost curve to decide how many balloons to rent.

Economics in the News

29. After you have studied *Economics in the News* on pp. 246–247, answer the following questions.

    a. Explain the distinction between the short run and the long run and identify when IKEA would want to make each type of decision.

    b. Explain economies of scale. Does IKEA reap economies of scale in the example on p. 247?

    c. Amend the graph in Fig. 2 on p. 247 to illustrate IKEA's *ATC* curve for its expanded Edmonton store.

30. **Self-Serve Beer Stations Cut Labour Costs**

    A new technology lets beer drinkers draw their own taps, like the soda fountain at McDonald's. The technology can measure and charge by the sip. It costs $25,000 for a wall-mounted, 20-tap system, plus a monthly maintenance fee.

    Source: *The Toronto Star*, October 9, 2015

    a. What is the total fixed cost of operating one self-serve system? What are its variable costs of providing self-serve beer?

    b. Explain how the fixed costs, variable costs, and total costs of beer served by a person differ from those of self-served beer.

    c. Sketch the marginal cost and average cost curves implied by your answer to part (b).

11

PERFECT COMPETITION

After studying this chapter, you will be able to:

◆ Define perfect competition

◆ Explain how a firm makes its output decision

◆ Explain how price and output are determined in perfect competition

◆ Explain why firms enter and leave a market

◆ Predict the effects of technological change in a competitive market

◆ Explain why perfect competition is efficient

Six million "apps" have been created for tablets and smartphones. Most of these apps are the work of individuals in intense competition with each other. No single app creator can influence the price of an app, but each can and must decide how many hours to work and how many apps to produce.

In this chapter, we study producers who, like small app developers, are in intense competition—in *perfect competition*. At the end of the chapter, in *Economics in the News*, we apply the perfect competition model to the highly competitive market in apps.

◆ What Is Perfect Competition?

The firms that you study in this chapter face the force of raw competition. We call this extreme form of competition perfect competition. **Perfect competition** is a market in which

- Many firms sell identical products to many buyers.
- There are no restrictions on entry into the market.
- Established firms have no advantage over new ones.
- Sellers and buyers are well informed about prices.

Farming, fishing, wood pulping and paper milling, the manufacture of paper cups and shopping bags, grocery and fresh flower retailing, photo finishing, lawn services, plumbing, painting, dry cleaning, and laundry services are all examples of highly competitive industries.

How Perfect Competition Arises

Perfect competition arises if the minimum efficient scale of a single producer is small relative to the market demand for the good or service. In this situation, there is room in the market for many firms. A firm's *minimum efficient scale* is the smallest output at which long-run average cost reaches its lowest level. (See Chapter 10, p. 245.)

In perfect competition, each firm produces a good that has no unique characteristics, so consumers don't care which firm's good they buy.

Price Takers

Firms in perfect competition are price takers. A **price taker** is a firm that cannot influence the market price because its production is an insignificant part of the total market.

Imagine that you are a wheat farmer in Manitoba. You have 500 hectares planted—which sounds like a lot. But compared to the millions of hectares across the Canadian prairies and the U.S. Midwest as well as the millions more in Argentina, Australia, and Ukraine, your 500 hectares are just a drop in the ocean. Nothing makes your wheat any better than any other farmer's, and all the buyers of wheat know the price at which they can do business.

If the market price of wheat is $300 a tonne, then that is the highest price you can get for your wheat. Ask for $310 and no one will buy from you. Offer it for $290 and you'll be sold out in a flash and have given away $10 a tonne. You take the market price.

Economic Profit and Revenue

A firm's goal is to maximize *economic profit*, which is equal to total revenue minus total cost. Total cost is the *opportunity cost* of production, which includes *normal profit*. (See Chapter 10, p. 229.)

A firm's **total revenue** equals the price of its output multiplied by the number of units of output sold (price × quantity). **Marginal revenue** is the change in total revenue that results from a one-unit increase in the quantity sold. Marginal revenue is calculated by dividing the change in total revenue by the change in the quantity sold.

Figure 11.1 illustrates these revenue concepts. In part (a), the market demand curve, D, and market supply curve, S, determine the market price. The market price is $25 a sweater. Campus Sweaters is just one of many producers of sweaters, so the best it can do is to sell its sweaters for $25 each.

Total Revenue Total revenue is equal to the price multiplied by the quantity sold. In the table in Fig. 11.1, if Campus Sweaters sells 9 sweaters, its total revenue is $225 (9 × $25).

Figure 11.1(b) shows the firm's total revenue curve (*TR*), which graphs the relationship between total revenue and the quantity sold. At point *A* on the *TR* curve, the firm sells 9 sweaters and has a total revenue of $225. Because each additional sweater sold brings in a constant amount—$25—the total revenue curve is an upward-sloping straight line.

Marginal Revenue Marginal revenue is the change in total revenue that results from a one-unit increase in quantity sold. In the table in Fig. 11.1, when the quantity sold increases from 8 to 9 sweaters, total revenue increases from $200 to $225, so marginal revenue is $25 a sweater.

Because the firm in perfect competition is a price taker, the change in total revenue that results from a one-unit increase in the quantity sold equals the market price. *In perfect competition, the firm's marginal revenue equals the market price.* Figure 11.1(c) shows the firm's marginal revenue curve (*MR*) as the horizontal line at the market price.

Demand for the Firm's Product The firm can sell any quantity it chooses at the market price. So the demand curve for the firm's product is a horizontal line at the market price, the same as the firm's marginal revenue curve.

FIGURE 11.1   Demand, Price, and Revenue in Perfect Competition

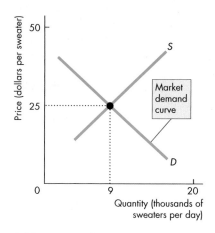

(a) Sweater market

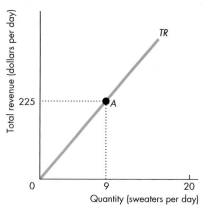

(b) Campus Sweaters' total revenue

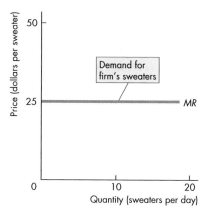

(c) Campus Sweaters' marginal revenue

Quantity sold (Q) (sweaters per day)	Price (P) (dollars per sweater)	Total revenue (TR = P × Q) (dollars)	Marginal revenue (MR = ΔTR/ΔQ) (dollars per additional sweater)
8	25	200	
			25
9	25	225	
			25
10	25	250	

In part (a), market demand and market supply determine the market price (and quantity). Part (b) shows the firm's total revenue curve (*TR*). Point *A* corresponds to the second row of the table—Campus Sweaters sells 9 sweaters at $25 a sweater, so total revenue is $225. Part (c) shows the firm's marginal revenue curve (*MR*). This curve is also the demand curve for the firm's sweaters. The demand for sweaters from Campus Sweaters is perfectly elastic at the market price of $25 a sweater.

MyLab Economics Animation

A horizontal demand curve illustrates a perfectly elastic demand, so the demand for the firm's product is perfectly elastic. A sweater from Campus Sweaters is a *perfect substitute* for a sweater from any other factory. But the *market* demand for sweaters is *not* perfectly elastic: Its elasticity depends on the substitutability of sweaters for other goods and services.

The Firm's Decisions

The goal of the competitive firm is to maximize economic profit, given the constraints it faces. To achieve its goal, a firm must decide:

1. How to produce at minimum cost
2. What quantity to produce
3. Whether to enter or exit a market

You've already seen how a firm makes the first decision. It does so by operating with the plant that minimizes long-run average cost—by being on its

long-run average cost curve. We'll now see how the firm makes the other two decisions. We start by looking at the firm's output decision.

REVIEW QUIZ

1 Why is a firm in perfect competition a price taker?
2 In perfect competition, what is the relationship between the demand for the firm's output and the market demand?
3 In perfect competition, why is a firm's marginal revenue curve also the demand curve for the firm's output?
4 What decisions must a firm make to maximize profit?

Work these questions in Study Plan 11.1 and get instant feedback.   MyLab Economics

The Firm's Output Decision

A firm's cost curves (total cost, average cost, and marginal cost) describe the relationship between its output and costs (see Chapter 10, pp. 235–236). And a firm's revenue curves (total revenue and marginal revenue) describe the relationship between its output and revenue (pp. 254–255). From the firm's cost curves and revenue curves, we can find the output that maximizes the firm's economic profit.

Figure 11.2 shows how to do this for Campus Sweaters. The table lists the firm's total revenue and total cost at different outputs, and part (a) of the figure shows the firm's total revenue curve, *TR*, and total cost curve, *TC*. These curves are graphs of numbers in the first three columns of the table.

Economic profit equals total revenue minus total cost. The fourth column of the table in Fig. 11.2 shows the economic profit made by Campus Sweaters, and part (b) of the figure graphs these numbers as its economic profit curve, *EP*.

Campus Sweaters maximizes its economic profit by producing 9 sweaters a day: Total revenue is $225, total cost is $183, and economic profit is $42. No other output rate achieves a larger profit.

At outputs of less than 4 sweaters and more than 12 sweaters a day, Campus Sweaters would incur an economic loss. At either 4 or 12 sweaters a day, Campus Sweaters would make zero economic profit, called a *break-even point*.

FIGURE 11.2 Total Revenue, Total Cost, and Economic Profit

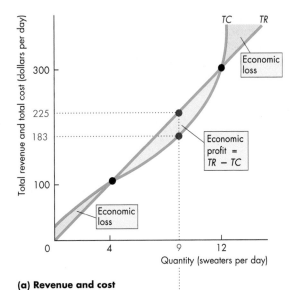

(a) Revenue and cost

(b) Economic profit and loss

Quantity (Q) (sweaters per day)	Total revenue (TR) (dollars)	Total cost (TC) (dollars)	Economic profit (TR − TC) (dollars)
0	0	22	−22
1	25	45	−20
2	50	66	−16
3	75	85	−10
4	100	100	0
5	125	114	11
6	150	126	24
7	175	141	34
8	200	160	40
9	225	183	42
10	250	210	40
11	275	245	30
12	300	300	0
13	325	360	−35

The table lists Campus Sweaters' total revenue, total cost, and economic profit. Part (a) of the figure graphs the total revenue and total cost curves, and part (b) graphs economic profit.

Campus Sweaters makes maximum economic profit, $42 a day ($225 − $183), when it produces 9 sweaters a day. At outputs of 4 sweaters and 12 sweaters a day, Campus Sweaters makes zero economic profit—these are break-even points. At an output less than 4 sweaters and greater than 12 sweaters a day, Campus Sweaters incurs an economic loss.

MyLab Economics Animation

Marginal Analysis and the Supply Decision

Another way to find the profit-maximizing output is to use marginal analysis, which compares marginal revenue, *MR*, with marginal cost, *MC*. As output increases, the firm's marginal revenue is constant but its marginal cost eventually increases.

If marginal revenue exceeds marginal cost ($MR > MC$), then the revenue from selling one more unit exceeds the cost of producing it and an increase in output increases economic profit. If marginal revenue is less than marginal cost ($MR < MC$), then the revenue from selling one more unit is less than the cost of producing that unit and a *decrease* in output *increases* economic profit. If marginal revenue equals marginal cost ($MR = MC$), then the revenue from selling one more unit equals the cost incurred to produce that unit. Economic profit is maximized and either an increase or a decrease in output decreases economic profit.

Figure 11.3 illustrates these propositions. If Campus Sweaters increases its output from 8 sweaters to 9 sweaters a day, marginal revenue ($25) exceeds marginal cost ($23), so by producing the 9th sweater economic profit increases by $2 from $40 to $42 a day. The blue area in the figure shows the increase in economic profit when the firm increases production from 8 to 9 sweaters per day.

If Campus Sweaters increases its output from 9 sweaters to 10 sweaters a day, marginal revenue ($25) is less than marginal cost ($27), so by producing the 10th sweater, economic profit decreases. The last column of the table shows that economic profit decreases from $42 to $40 a day. The red area in the figure shows the economic loss that arises from increasing production from 9 to 10 sweaters a day.

Campus Sweaters maximizes economic profit by producing 9 sweaters a day, the quantity at which marginal revenue equals marginal cost.

A firm's profit-maximizing output is its quantity supplied at the market price. The quantity supplied at a price of $25 a sweater is 9 sweaters a day. If the price were higher than $25 a sweater, the firm would increase production. If the price were lower than $25 a sweater, the firm would decrease production. These profit-maximizing responses to different market prices are the foundation of the law of supply:

Other things remaining the same, the higher the market price of a good, the greater is the quantity supplied of that good.

FIGURE 11.3   Profit-Maximizing Output

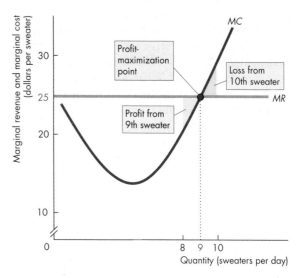

Quantity (Q) (sweaters per day)	Total revenue (TR) (dollars)	Marginal revenue (MR) (dollars per additional sweater)	Total cost (TC) (dollars)	Marginal cost (MC) (dollars per additional sweater)	Economic profit (TR − TC) (dollars)
7	175		141		34
		25		19	
8	200		160		40
		25		23	
9	**225**		**183**		**42**
		25		27	
10	250		210		40
		25		35	
11	275		245		30

The firm maximizes profit by producing the output at which marginal revenue equals marginal cost and marginal cost is increasing. The table and figure show that marginal cost equals marginal revenue and economic profit is maximized when Campus Sweaters produces 9 sweaters a day. The table shows that if Campus Sweaters increases output from 8 to 9 sweaters, marginal cost is $23, which is less than the marginal revenue of $25. If output increases from 9 to 10 sweaters, marginal cost is $27, which exceeds the marginal revenue of $25. If marginal revenue exceeds marginal cost, an increase in output increases economic profit. If marginal revenue is less than marginal cost, an increase in output decreases economic profit. If marginal revenue equals marginal cost, economic profit is maximized.

_____ MyLab Economics Animation and Draw Graph _____

Temporary Shutdown Decision

You've seen that a firm maximizes profit by producing the quantity at which marginal revenue (price) equals marginal cost. But suppose that at this quantity, price is less than average total cost. In this case, the firm incurs an economic loss. Maximum profit is a loss (a minimum loss). What does the firm do?

If the firm expects the loss to be permanent, it goes out of business. But if it expects the loss to be temporary, the firm must decide whether to shut down temporarily and produce no output, or to keep producing. To make this decision, the firm compares the loss from shutting down with the loss from producing and takes the action that minimizes its loss.

Loss Comparisons A firm's economic loss equals total fixed cost, *TFC*, plus total variable cost minus total revenue. Total variable cost equals average variable cost, *AVC*, multiplied by the quantity produced, *Q*, and total revenue equals price, *P*, multiplied by the quantity, *Q*. So:

$$\text{Economic loss} = TFC + (AVC - P) \times Q.$$

If the firm shuts down, it produces no output ($Q = 0$). The firm has no variable costs and no revenue but it must pay its fixed costs, so its economic loss equals total fixed cost.

If the firm produces, then in addition to its fixed costs, it incurs variable costs. But it also receives revenue. Its economic loss equals total fixed cost—the loss when shut down—plus total variable cost minus total revenue. If total variable cost exceeds total revenue, this loss exceeds total fixed cost and the firm shuts down. Equivalently, if average variable cost *exceeds* price, this loss exceeds total fixed cost and the firm *shuts down*.

The Shutdown Point A firm's **shutdown point** is the price and quantity at which it is indifferent between producing and shutting down. The shutdown point occurs at the price and the quantity at which average variable cost is a minimum. At the shutdown point, the firm is minimizing its loss and its loss equals total fixed cost. If the price falls below minimum average variable cost, the firm shuts down temporarily and continues to incur a loss equal to total fixed cost. At prices above minimum average variable cost but below average total cost, the firm produces the loss-minimizing output and incurs a loss, but a loss that is less than total fixed cost.

Figure 11.4 illustrates the firm's shutdown decision and the shutdown point that we've just described for Campus Sweaters.

The firm's average variable cost curve is *AVC* and the marginal cost curve is *MC*. Average variable cost has a minimum of $17 a sweater when output is 7 sweaters a day. The *MC* curve intersects the *AVC* curve at its minimum. (We explained this relationship in Chapter 10; see pp. 236–237.)

The figure shows the marginal revenue curve *MR* when the price is $17 a sweater, a price equal to minimum average variable cost. Marginal revenue equals marginal cost at 7 sweaters a day, so this quantity maximizes economic profit (minimizes economic loss). The *ATC* curve shows that the firm's average total cost of producing 7 sweaters a day is $20.14 a sweater. The firm incurs a loss equal to $3.14 a sweater on 7 sweaters a day, so its loss is $22 a day. The table in Fig. 11.2 shows that Campus Sweaters' loss equals its total fixed cost.

FIGURE 11.4 The Shutdown Decision

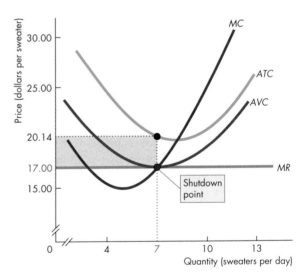

The shutdown point is at minimum average variable cost. At a price below minimum average variable cost, the firm shuts down and produces no output. At a price equal to minimum average variable cost, the firm is indifferent between shutting down and producing no output or producing the output at minimum average variable cost. Either way, the firm minimizes its economic loss and incurs a loss equal to total fixed cost.

MyLab Economics Animation and Draw Graph

FIGURE 11.5   A Firm's Supply Curve

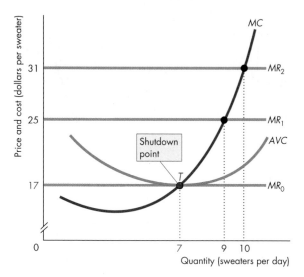

(a) Marginal cost and average variable cost

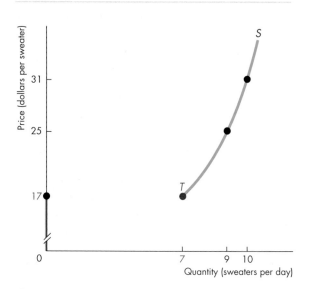

(b) Campus Sweaters' short-run supply curve

Part (a) shows the firm's profit-maximizing output at various market prices. At $25 a sweater, it produces 9 sweaters, and at $17 a sweater, it produces 7 sweaters. At all prices below $17 a sweater, Campus Sweaters produces nothing. Its shutdown point is T. Part (b) shows the firm's supply curve—the quantity of sweaters it produces at each price. Its supply curve is made up of the marginal cost curve at all prices above minimum average variable cost and the vertical axis at all prices below minimum average variable cost.

MyLab Economics Animation and Draw Graph

The Firm's Supply Curve

A perfectly competitive firm's supply curve shows how its profit-maximizing output varies as the market price varies, other things remaining the same. The supply curve is derived from the firm's marginal cost curve and average variable cost curves. Figure 11.5 illustrates the derivation of the supply curve.

When the price *exceeds* minimum average variable cost (more than $17), the firm maximizes profit by producing the output at which marginal cost equals price. If the price rises, the firm increases its output—it moves up along its marginal cost curve.

When the price is *less* than minimum average variable cost (less than $17 a sweater), the firm maximizes profit by temporarily shutting down and producing no output. The firm produces zero output at all prices below minimum average variable cost.

When the price *equals* minimum average variable cost, the firm maximizes profit *either* by temporarily shutting down and producing no output *or* by producing the output at which average variable cost is a minimum—the shutdown point, T. The firm never produces a quantity between zero and the quantity at the shutdown point T (a quantity greater than zero and less than 7 sweaters a day).

The firm's supply curve in Fig. 11.5(b) runs along the y-axis from a price of zero to a price equal to minimum average variable cost, jumps to point T, and then, as the price rises above minimum average variable cost, follows the marginal cost curve.

◆ REVIEW QUIZ

1 Why does a firm in perfect competition produce the quantity at which marginal cost equals price?

2 What is the lowest price at which a firm produces an output? Explain why.

3 What is the relationship between a firm's supply curve, its marginal cost curve, and its average variable cost curve?

Work these questions in Study Plan 11.2 and get instant feedback.   MyLab Economics

So far, we've studied a single firm in isolation. We've seen that the firm's profit-maximizing decision depends on the market price, which it takes as given. How is the market price determined? Let's find out.

Output, Price, and Profit in the Short Run

To determine the price and quantity in a perfectly competitive market, we need to know how market demand and market supply interact. We start by studying a perfectly competitive market in the short run. The short run is a situation in which the number of firms is fixed.

Market Supply in the Short Run

The **short-run market supply curve** shows the quantity supplied by all the firms in the market at each price when each firm's plant and the number of firms remain the same.

You've seen how an individual firm's supply curve is determined. The market supply curve is derived from the individual supply curves. The quantity supplied by the market at a given price is the sum of the quantities supplied by all the firms in the market at that price.

Figure 11.6 shows the supply curve for the competitive sweater market. In this example, the market consists of 1,000 firms exactly like Campus Sweaters. At each price, the quantity supplied by the market is 1,000 times the quantity supplied by a single firm.

The table in Fig. 11.6 shows the firm's and the market's supply schedules and how the market supply curve is constructed. At prices below $17 a sweater, every firm in the market shuts down; the quantity supplied by the market is zero. At $17 a sweater, each firm is indifferent between shutting down and producing nothing or operating and producing 7 sweaters a day. Some firms will shut down, and others will supply 7 sweaters a day. The quantity supplied by each firm is *either* 0 or 7 sweaters, and the quantity supplied by the market is *between* 0 (all firms shut down) and 7,000 (all firms produce 7 sweaters a day each).

The market supply curve is a graph of the market supply schedules, and the points on the supply curve *A* through *D* represent the rows of the table.

To construct the market supply curve, we sum the quantities supplied by all the firms at each price. Each of the 1,000 firms in the market has a supply schedule like Campus Sweaters. At prices below $17 a sweater, the market supply curve runs along the *y*-axis. At $17 a sweater, the market supply curve is horizontal—supply is perfectly elastic. As the price

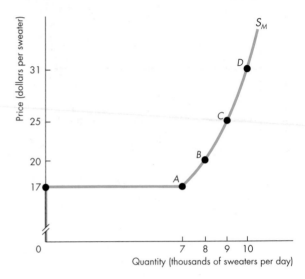

FIGURE 11.6 Short-Run Market Supply Curve

	Price (dollars per sweater)	Quantity supplied by Campus Sweaters (sweaters per day)	Quantity supplied by market (sweaters per day)
A	17	0 or 7	0 to 7,000
B	20	8	8,000
C	25	9	9,000
D	31	10	10,000

The market supply schedule is the sum of the supply schedules of all the individual firms. A market that consists of 1,000 identical firms has a supply schedule similar to that of one firm, but the quantity supplied by the market is 1,000 times as large as that of the one firm (see the table). The market supply curve is S_M. Points *A*, *B*, *C*, and *D* correspond to the rows of the table. At the shutdown price of $17 a sweater, each firm produces either 0 or 7 sweaters a day and the quantity supplied by the market is between 0 and 7,000 sweaters a day. The market supply is perfectly elastic at the shutdown price.

————— MyLab Economics Animation —————

rises above $17 a sweater, each firm increases its quantity supplied and the quantity supplied by the market increases by 1,000 times that of one firm.

Short-Run Equilibrium

Market demand and short-run market supply determine the market price and market output. Figure 11.7(a) shows a short-run equilibrium. The short-run supply curve, S, is the same as S_M in Fig. 11.6. If the market demand curve is D_1, the market price is $20 a sweater. Each firm takes this price as given and produces its profit-maximizing output, which is 8 sweaters a day. Because the market has 1,000 identical firms, the market output is 8,000 sweaters a day.

A Change in Demand

Changes in demand bring changes to short-run market equilibrium. Figure 11.7(b) shows these changes.

If demand increases and the demand curve shifts rightward to D_2, the market price rises to $25 a sweater. At this price, each firm maximizes profit by increasing its output to 9 sweaters a day. The market output increases to 9,000 sweaters a day.

If demand decreases and the demand curve shifts leftward to D_3, the market price falls to $17. At this

price, each firm maximizes profit by decreasing its output. If each firm produces 7 sweaters a day, the market output decreases to 7,000 sweaters a day.

If the demand curve shifts farther leftward than D_3, the market price remains at $17 a sweater because the market supply curve is horizontal at that price. Some firms continue to produce 7 sweaters a day, and others temporarily shut down. Firms are indifferent between these two activities, and whichever they choose, they incur an economic loss equal to total fixed cost. The number of firms continuing to produce is just enough to satisfy the market demand at a price of $17 a sweater.

Profits and Losses in the Short Run

In short-run equilibrium, although the firm produces the profit-maximizing output, it does not necessarily end up making an economic profit. It might do so, but it might alternatively break even or incur an economic loss. Economic profit (or loss) per sweater is price, P, minus average total cost, ATC. So economic profit (or loss) is $(P - ATC) \times Q$. If price equals

FIGURE 11.7   Short-Run Equilibrium

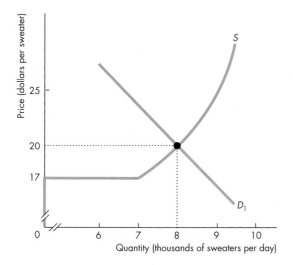

(a) Equilibrium

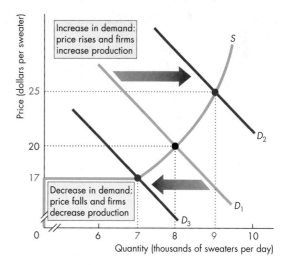

(b) Change in equilibrium

In part (a), the market supply curve is S and the market demand curve is D_1. The market price is $20 a sweater. At this price, each firm produces 8 sweaters a day and the market produces 8,000 sweaters a day.

In part (b), if the market demand increases to D_2, the price rises to $25 a sweater. Each firm produces 9 sweaters

a day and the market output is 9,000 sweaters. If the market demand decreases to D_3, the price falls to $17 a sweater and each firm decreases its output. If each firm produces 7 sweaters a day, the market output is 7,000 sweaters a day.

average total cost, a firm breaks even—the entrepreneur makes normal profit. If price exceeds average total cost, a firm makes an economic profit. If price is less than average total cost, a firm incurs an economic loss. Figure 11.8 shows these three possible short-run profit outcomes for Campus Sweaters. These outcomes correspond to the three different levels of market demand that we've just examined.

Three Possible Short-Run Outcomes

Figure 11.8(a) corresponds to the situation in Fig. 11.7(a) where the market demand is D_1. The equilibrium price of a sweater is $20 and the firm produces 8 sweaters a day. Average total cost is $20 a sweater. Price equals average total cost (ATC), so the firm breaks even (makes zero economic profit).

Figure 11.8(b) corresponds to the situation in Fig. 11.7(b) where the market demand is D_2. The equilibrium price of a sweater is $25 and the firm produces 9 sweaters a day. Here, price exceeds average total cost, so the firm makes an economic profit. Its economic profit is $42 a day, which equals $4.67 per sweater ($25.00 − $20.33) multiplied by 9, the

profit-maximizing number of sweaters produced. The blue rectangle shows this economic profit. The height of that rectangle is profit per sweater, $4.67, and the length is the quantity of sweaters produced, 9 a day. So the area of the rectangle is economic profit of $42 a day.

Figure 11.8(c) corresponds to the situation in Fig. 11.7(b) where the market demand is D_3. The equilibrium price of a sweater is $17. Here, the price is less than average total cost, so the firm incurs an economic loss. Price and marginal revenue are $17 a sweater, and the profit-maximizing (in this case, loss-minimizing) output is 7 sweaters a day. Total revenue is $119 a day (7 × $17). Average total cost is $20.14 a sweater, so the economic loss is $3.14 per sweater ($20.14 − $17.00). This loss per sweater multiplied by the number of sweaters is $22. The red rectangle shows this economic loss. The height of that rectangle is economic loss per sweater, $3.14, and the length is the quantity of sweaters produced, 7 a day. So the area of the rectangle is the firm's economic loss of $22 a day. If the price dips below $17 a sweater, the firm temporarily shuts down and incurs an economic loss equal to total fixed cost.

FIGURE 11.8   Three Short-Run Outcomes for the Firm

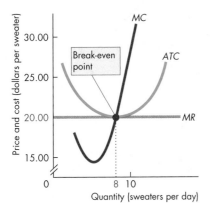

(a) Break even

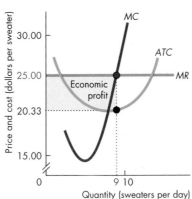

(b) Economic profit

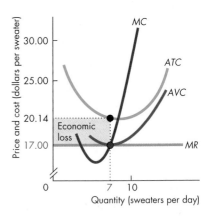

(c) Economic loss

In the short run, the firm might break even (make zero economic profit), make an economic profit, or incur an economic loss. In part (a), the price equals minimum average total cost. At the profit-maximizing output, the firm breaks even and makes zero economic profit. In part (b), the market price is $25 a sweater. At the profit-maximizing output,

the price exceeds average total cost and the firm makes an economic profit, which is equal to the area of the blue rectangle. In part (c), the market price is $17 a sweater. At the profit-maximizing output, the price is below minimum average total cost and the firm incurs an economic loss, which is equal to the area of the red rectangle.

MyLab Economics Animation

ECONOMICS IN ACTION

A Temporary Shutdown

An increase in the supply of coal from low-cost Australian producers, combined with a decrease in the demand for coal by China, lowered the price of coal from US$257 per tonne in 2011, to US$131 per tonne in 2014, and to US$106 per tonne in 2015.

Faced with this low market price, mining company Teck Resources decided to shut down its six coal mines in British Columbia and Alberta for three weeks during the summer of 2015.

The temporary shutdown decreased the firm's coal production by 1.5 million tonnes—22 percent of its total output.

Teck Resources made this decision because its average variable cost was greater than US$106 per tonne.

By shutting down for three weeks, Teck Resources avoided paying its variable cost and incurred an economic loss equal to total fixed cost, the minimum possible economic loss.

REVIEW QUIZ

1 How do we derive the short-run market supply curve in perfect competition?
2 In perfect competition, when market demand increases, explain how the price of the good and the output and profit of each firm changes in the short run.
3 In perfect competition, when market demand decreases, explain how the price of the good and the output and profit of each firm changes in the short run.

Work these questions in Study Plan 11.3 and get instant feedback. 　MyLab Economics

◆ Output, Price, and Profit in the Long Run

In short-run equilibrium, a firm might make an economic profit, incur an economic loss, or break even. Although each of these three situations is a short-run equilibrium, only one of them is a long-run equilibrium. The reason is that in the long run, firms can enter or exit the market.

Entry and Exit

Entry occurs in a market when new firms come into the market and the number of firms increases. Exit occurs when existing firms leave a market and the number of firms decreases.

Firms respond to economic profit and economic loss by either entering or exiting a market. New firms enter a market in which existing firms are making an economic profit. Firms exit a market in which they are incurring an economic loss. Temporary economic profit and temporary economic loss don't trigger entry and exit. It's the prospect of persistent economic profit or loss that triggers entry and exit.

Entry and exit change the market supply, which influences the market price, the quantity produced by each firm, and its economic profit (or loss).

If firms enter a market, supply increases and the market supply curve shifts rightward. The increase in supply lowers the market price and eventually eliminates economic profit. When economic profit reaches zero, entry stops.

If firms exit a market, supply decreases and the market supply curve shifts leftward. The market price rises and economic loss decreases. Eventually, economic loss is eliminated and exit stops.

To summarize:

■ New firms enter a market in which existing firms are making an economic profit.

■ As new firms enter a market, the market price falls and the economic profit of each firm decreases.

■ Firms exit a market in which they are incurring an economic loss.

■ As firms leave a market, the market price rises and the economic loss incurred by the remaining firms decreases.

■ Entry and exit stop when firms make zero economic profit.

A Closer Look at Entry

The sweater market has 800 firms with cost curves like those in Fig. 11.9(a). The market demand curve is D, the market supply curve is S_1, and the price is $25 a sweater in Fig. 11.9(b). Each firm produces 9 sweaters a day and makes an economic profit.

This economic profit is a signal for new firms to enter the market. As entry takes place, supply increases and the market supply curve shifts rightward toward S^*. As supply increases with no change in demand, the market price gradually falls from $25 to $20 a sweater. At this lower price, each firm makes zero economic profit and entry stops.

Entry results in an increase in market output, but each firm's output *decreases*. Because the price falls, each firm moves down its supply curve and produces less. Because the number of firms increases, the market produces more.

A Closer Look at Exit

The sweater market has 1,200 firms with cost curves like those in Fig. 11.9(a). The market demand curve is D, the market supply curve is S_2, and the price is $17 a sweater in Fig. 11.9(b). Each firm produces 7 sweaters a day and incurs an economic loss.

This economic loss is a signal for firms to exit the market. As exit takes place, supply decreases and the market supply curve shifts leftward toward S^*. As supply decreases with no change in demand, the market price gradually rises from $17 to $20 a sweater. At this higher price, losses are eliminated, each firm makes zero economic profit, and exit stops.

Exit results in a decrease in market output, but each firm's output *increases*. Because the price rises, each firm moves up its supply curve and produces more. Because the number of firms decreases, the market produces less.

FIGURE 11.9 Entry, Exit, and Long-Run Equilibrium

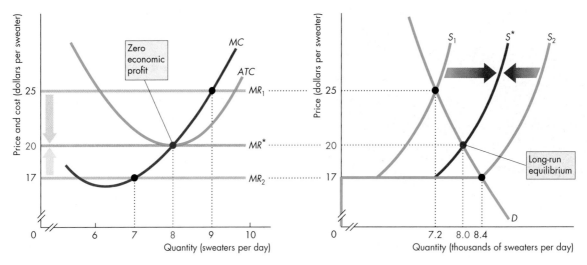

(a) Campus Sweaters

(b) The sweater market

Each firm has cost curves like those of Campus Sweaters in part (a). The market demand curve is D in part (b).

When the market supply curve in part (b) is S_1, the price is $25 a sweater. In part (a), each firm produces 9 sweaters a day and makes an economic profit. Profit triggers the entry of new firms, and as new firms enter, the market supply curve shifts rightward, from S_1 toward S^*. The price falls from $25 to $20 a sweater, and the quantity produced increases from 7,200 to 8,000 sweaters. Each firm decreases its output to 8 sweaters a day and its economic profit falls to zero.

When the market supply curve is S_2, the price is $17 a sweater. In part (a), each firm produces 7 sweaters a day and incurs an economic loss. Loss triggers exit, and as firms exit, the market supply curve shifts leftward, from S_2 toward S^*. The price rises from $17 to $20 a sweater, and the quantity produced decreases from 8,400 to 8,000 sweaters. Each firm increases its output from 7 to 8 sweaters a day and its economic profit rises to zero.

MyLab Economics Animation

ECONOMICS IN ACTION

Entry and Exit

An example of entry and falling prices occurred during the 1980s and 1990s in the personal computer market. When IBM introduced its first PC in 1981, IBM had little competition. The price was $7,000 (about $18,750 in today's money) and IBM made a large economic profit selling the new machine.

Observing IBM's huge success, new firms such as Gateway, NEC, Dell, and a host of others entered the market with machines that were technologically identical to IBM's. In fact, they were so similar that they came to be called "clones." The massive wave of entry into the personal computer market increased the market supply and lowered the price. The economic profit for all firms decreased.

Today, a $500 computer is vastly more powerful than its 1981 ancestor that cost 38 times as much.

The same PC market that saw entry during the 1980s and 1990s has seen some exit more recently. In 2001, IBM, the firm that first launched the PC, announced that it was exiting the market. The intense competition from Gateway, NEC, Dell, and others that entered the market following IBM's lead lowered the price and eliminated the economic profit. So IBM now concentrates on servers and other parts of the computer market.

IBM exited the PC market because it was incurring economic losses. Its exit decreased market supply and made it possible for the remaining firms in the market to make zero economic profit.

International Harvester, a manufacturer of farm equipment, provides another example of exit. For decades, people associated the name "International Harvester" with tractors, combines, and other farm machines. But International Harvester wasn't the only maker of farm equipment. The market became intensely competitive, and the firm began to incur economic losses. Now the firm has a new name, Navistar International, and it doesn't make tractors any more. After years of economic losses and shrinking revenues, it got out of the farm-machine business in 1985 and started to make trucks.

International Harvester exited because it was incurring an economic loss. Its exit decreased supply and made it possible for the remaining firms in the market to break even.

Long-Run Equilibrium

You've now seen how economic profit induces entry, which in turn eliminates the profit. You've also seen how economic loss induces exit, which in turn eliminates the loss.

When economic profit and economic loss have been eliminated and entry and exit have stopped, a competitive market is in *long-run equilibrium*.

You've seen how a competitive market adjusts toward its long-run equilibrium. But a competitive market is rarely *in* a state of long-run equilibrium. Instead, it is constantly and restlessly evolving toward long-run equilibrium. The reason is that the market is constantly bombarded with events that change the constraints that firms face.

Markets are constantly adjusting to keep up with changes in tastes, which change demand, and changes in technology, which change costs.

In the next sections, we're going to see how a competitive market reacts to changing tastes and technology and how the market guides resources to their highest-valued use.

◆ REVIEW QUIZ

1 What triggers entry in a competitive market? Describe the process that ends further entry.

2 What triggers exit in a competitive market? Describe the process that ends further exit.

Work these questions in Study Plan 11.4 and get instant feedback.   MyLab Economics

◆ Changes in Demand and Supply as Technology Advances

The arrival of high-speed Internet service increased the demand for personal computers and the demand for music and movie downloads. At the same time, the arrival of these technologies decreased the demand for the services of bricks-and-mortar stores.

What happens in a competitive market when the demand for its product changes? The perfect competition model can answer this question.

A Decrease in Demand

Bricks-and-mortar retailers are in long-run equilibrium making zero economic profit when the arrival of the high-speed Internet brings an increase in online shopping and a decrease in the demand for traditional retail services. The equilibrium price of retail services falls and stores incur economic losses. As the losses seem permanent, stores start to close.

Supply decreases and the price stops falling and then begins to rise. Eventually, enough firms have exited for the supply and the decreased demand to be in balance at a price that enables the firms in the market to return to zero economic profit—long-run equilibrium.

Figure 11.10 illustrates the process. In the market in part (a), demand is D_0, supply is S_0, price is P_0, and market output is Q_0. The firm in part (b) maximizes profit with marginal revenue, MR_0, equal to marginal cost, MC, at output q_0. Economic profit is zero.

Market demand decreases and the demand curve shifts leftward to D_1 in Fig. 11.10(a). The price falls to P_1, and the quantity supplied decreases from Q_0 to Q_1 as the market moves down its short-run supply curve S_0. In Fig. 11.10(b), the firm maximizes profit by producing q_1, where marginal revenue MR_1 equals MC. The market is now in short-run equilibrium in which each firm incurs an economic loss.

The economic loss brings exit and short-run supply decreases—the market supply curve starts to shift

FIGURE 11.10 A Decrease in Demand

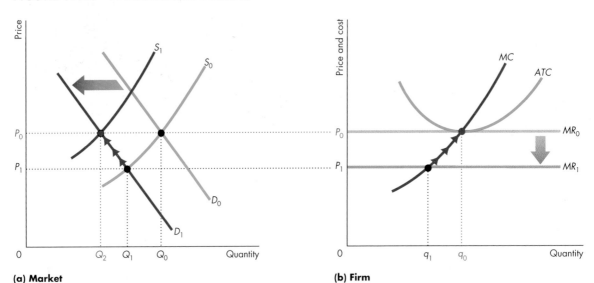

(a) Market

(b) Firm

A market starts out in long-run competitive equilibrium. Part (a) shows the market demand curve D_0, the market supply curve S_0, the market price P_0, and the equilibrium quantity Q_0. Each firm sells its output at the price P_0, so its marginal revenue curve is MR_0 in part (b). Each firm produces q_0 and makes zero economic profit.

Market demand decreases from D_0 to D_1 in part (a) and the market price falls to P_1. Each firm maximizes profit by increasing its output to q_1 in part (b), and the market

output decreases to Q_1 in part (a). Firms now incur economic losses. Firms exit the market, and as they do so, the market supply curve gradually shifts leftward, from S_0 toward S_1. This shift gradually raises the market price from P_1 back to P_0. While the price is below P_0, firms make economic losses, so firms keep exiting the market. Once the price has returned to P_0, each firm makes zero economic profit and there is no incentive for firms to exit. Each firm produces q_0, and the market output is Q_2.

leftward. The decrease in supply raises the market price and firms increase output—move up along their marginal cost or supply curve in Fig. 11.10(b).

Eventually, exit shifts the supply curve to S_1 in Fig. 11.10(a). The market price has returned to its original level, P_0. At this price, each firm produces q_0, the same as the quantity produced before the decrease in demand. Market output is Q_2 in a long-run equilibrium.

The difference between the initial long-run equilibrium and the new long-run equilibrium is the number of firms in the market. A decrease in demand has

decreased the number of firms. In the process of moving from the initial equilibrium to the new one, each firm incurs an economic loss.

An Increase in Demand

An *increase* in demand triggers a similar but opposite response: It brings a higher price, economic profits, and entry. Entry increases supply, which lowers the price to its original level and economic profit returns to zero in a new long-run equilibrium. *Economics in the News* below looks at an example.

◆ ECONOMICS IN THE NEWS

Vinyl's Comeback

Best Vinyl Record Stores in Toronto
Vinyl records have returned over the past few years and their popularity shows no signs of slowing down. Toronto has some excellent vinyl record shops that cover every musical genre.

Source: toronto.com, May 26, 2017

THE PROBLEM

Provide a graphical analysis to explain why vinyl record shops entered the market and the effects of entry in the market for record store services.

THE SOLUTION

- With demand D_0 and supply S_0, Q_0 customers are served at a price P_0 in part (a) of Fig. 1.
- With marginal revenue MR_0 and marginal cost MC, a record store serves q_0 customers in long-run equilibrium in part (b) of Fig. 1.

- Demand increases to D_1, the price rises to P_1, and marginal revenue rises to MR_1. Customers increase to q_1 (and Q_1) and stores make an economic profit.
- Anticipating profit opportunities, stores enter and the market supply increases to S_1.
- Eventually, entry lowers the market price to P_0 and returns economic profit to zero.

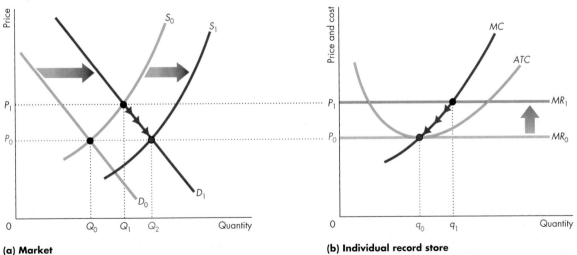

(a) Market

(b) Individual record store

Figure 1 The Market for Record Store Services

Technological Advances Change Supply

We've studied the effects of technological change on demand, and to isolate those effects we've kept the individual firm's cost curves unchanged. But new technologies also lower production costs. We now study those effects of advancing technology.

Starting from a long-run equilibrium, when a new technology becomes available that lowers production costs, the first firms to use it make economic profit. But as more firms begin to use the new technology, market supply increases and the price falls. At first, new-technology firms continue to make positive economic profits, so more enter. But firms that continue to use the old technology incur economic losses. Why? Initially they were making zero economic profit and now with the lower price they incur economic losses. So old-technology firms exit.

Eventually, all the old-technology firms have exited and enough new-technology firms have entered to increase the market supply to a level that lowers the price to equal the minimum average total cost using the new technology. In this situation, all the firms, all of which are now new-technology firms, are making zero economic profit.

Figure 11.11 illustrates the process that we've just described. Part (a) shows the market demand and supply curves and market equilibrium. Part (b) shows the cost and revenue curves for a firm using the original old technology. Initially these are the only firms. Part (c) shows the cost and revenue curves for a firm using a new technology after it becomes available.

In part (a), the demand curve is D and initially the supply curve is S_0, so the price is P_0 and the equilibrium quantity is Q_0.

In part (b), marginal revenue is MR_0 and each firm produces q_0 where MR_0 equals MC_{Old}. Economic profit is zero and firms are producing at minimum average total cost on the curve ATC_{Old}.

When a new technology becomes available, average total cost and marginal cost of production fall, and firms that use the new technology produce with the average total cost curve ATC_{New} and marginal cost curve MC_{New} in part (c).

When one firm adopts the new technology, it is too small to influence supply, so the price remains at P_0 and the firm makes an economic profit. But economic profit brings entry of new-technology firms. Market supply increases and the price falls.

FIGURE 11.11 A Technological Advance Lowers Production Costs

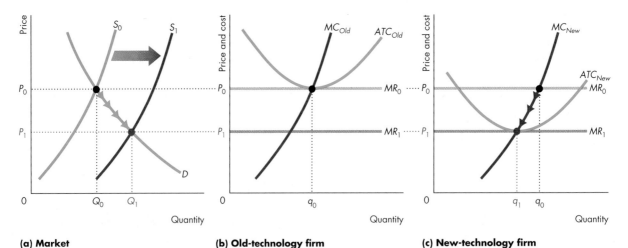

(a) Market   **(b) Old-technology firm**   **(c) New-technology firm**

In part (a), the demand curve is D and initially the supply curve is S_0. The price is P_0 and the equilibrium quantity is Q_0. In part (b), marginal revenue is MR_0 and each firm produces q_0 where MR_0 equals MC_{Old}. Economic profit is zero.

A new technology becomes available with lower costs of ATC_{New} and MC_{New} in part (c). A firm that uses this technology produces q_0 where MR_0 equals MC_{New}.

As more firms use this technology, market supply increases and the market price falls. With price below P_0 and above P_1, old-technology firms incur economic losses and exit the market while new-technology firms make economic profits and new firms enter the market.

In the new long-run equilibrium, the old-technology firms have gone. New-technology firms increase the market supply to S_1. The price falls to P_1, marginal revenue is MR_1, and each firm produces q_1 where MR_1 equals MC_{New}.

MyLab Economics Animation

ECONOMICS IN THE NEWS

The Falling Cost of Sequencing DNA

Illumina Promises to Sequence Human Genome for $100—But Not Quite Yet

Illumina, a maker of DNA sequencers, is developing a technology that lowers the cost of decoding a human genome from $1,000 to $100—although that decrease will not come for years.

Source: *Forbes*, January 9, 2017

SOME DATA

The graph shows how the cost of sequencing a person's entire genome has fallen. Illumina (in the news clip) is one of around 40 firms competing to develop a machine that can lower that cost from the current $1,000 to around $100. Many dozens of firms operate DNA sequencing machines and sell their services in a competitive market.

THE QUESTIONS

- What are the competitive markets in the news clip?
- Are any of these markets in long-run equilibrium?
- Are any firms in these markets likely to be making an economic profit?
- Are any of the firms in these markets likely to be incurring an economic loss?
- Are these markets likely to be experiencing entry, exit, or both? If both, which is likely to be greater?
- Who gains from the advances in DNA sequencing technology in the short run and in the long run: producers, or consumers, or both?

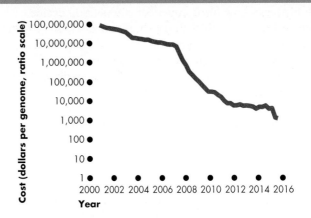

Figure 1 Cost per Genome
Source of data: National Human Genome Research Institute.

THE ANSWERS

- The markets are for DNA sequencing machines and for DNA sequencing services.
- With massive ongoing technological change, neither market is likely to be in long-run equilibrium.
- Firms using the latest technology are likely to be making economic profit.
- Firms using the older technology are likely to be incurring economic loss.
- New-technology firms are entering and old-technology firms are exiting, but with a falling price, there is more entry than exit.
- In the short run, firms gain from higher profit and consumers gain from the lower price. In the long run, economic profit will be zero but consumers will continue to gain from the low price.

— MyLab Economics Economics in the News —

With price below P_0, old-technology firms incur an economic loss and exit. With price above P_1, new-technology firms make an economic profit and enter. When a new long-run equilibrium is achieved, the old-technology firms have gone. The new-technology firms that have entered have shifted the supply curve to S_1. The price is P_1, marginal revenue is MR_1, and each firm in Fig. 11.11(c) produces q_1, where MR_1 equals MC_{New}.

Technological change brings only temporary gains to producers. But the lower prices and better products that technological advances bring are permanent gains for consumers.

REVIEW QUIZ

Describe what happens to output, price, and economic profit in the short run and in the long run in a competitive market following:

1 An increase in demand
2 A decrease in demand
3 The adoption of a new technology that lowers production costs

Work these questions in Study Plan 11.5 and get instant feedback.   MyLab Economics

◆ Competition and Efficiency

You've seen how firms in perfect competition decide the quantity to produce in the short run and in the long run. You've also seen how these individual decisions determine the market supply that interacts with market demand to determine the equilibrium price and quantity.

We're now going to use what you've learned to gain a deeper understanding of why competition achieves an efficient allocation of resources.

Efficient Use of Resources

Resource use is efficient when we produce the goods and services that people value most highly (see Chapter 2, pp. 37–39, and Chapter 5, p. 116). If it is possible to make someone better off without anyone else becoming worse off, resources are *not* being used efficiently. For example, suppose we produce a computer that no one wants and no one will ever use and, at the same time, some people are clamouring for more video games. If we produce fewer computers and reallocate the unused resources to produce more video games, some people will be better off and no one will be worse off. So the initial resource allocation was inefficient.

We can test whether resources are allocated efficiently by comparing marginal social benefit and marginal social cost. In the computer and video games example, the marginal social benefit of a video game exceeds its marginal social cost; the marginal social cost of a computer exceeds its marginal social benefit. So by producing fewer computers and more video games, we move resources toward a higher-valued use.

Choices, Equilibrium, and Efficiency

We can use what you have learned about the decisions of consumers and firms and equilibrium in a competitive market to describe an efficient use of resources.

Choices Consumers allocate their budgets to get the most value possible out of them. We derive a consumer's demand curve by finding how the best budget allocation changes as the price of a good changes. So consumers get the most value out of their resources at all points along their demand curves. If the people who consume a good or service are the

only ones who benefit from it, then the market demand curve measures the benefit to the entire society and is the marginal social benefit curve.

Competitive firms produce the quantity that maximizes profit. We derive the firm's supply curve by finding the profit-maximizing quantity at each price. So firms get the most value out of their resources at all points along their supply curves. If the firms that produce a good or service bear all the costs of producing it, then the market supply curve measures the marginal cost to the entire society and the market supply curve is the marginal social cost curve.

Equilibrium and Efficiency Resources are used efficiently when marginal social benefit equals marginal social cost. Competitive equilibrium achieves this efficient outcome because, with no externalities, price equals marginal social benefit for consumers, and price equals marginal social cost for producers.

The gains from trade are the sum of consumer surplus and producer surplus. The gains from trade for consumers are measured by *consumer surplus*, which is the area below the demand curve and above the price paid. (See Chapter 5, p. 113.) The gains from trade for producers are measured by *producer surplus*, which is the area above the supply curve and below the price received. (See Chapter 5, p. 115.) The total gains from trade equals *total surplus*—the sum of consumer surplus and producer surplus. When the market for a good or service is in equilibrium, the gains from trade are maximized.

Efficiency in the Sweater Market Figure 11.12 illustrates the efficiency of perfect competition in the sweater market. Part (a) shows the market, and part (b) shows Campus Sweaters.

In part (a), consumers get the most value from their budgets at all points on the market demand curve, $D = MSB$. Producers get the most value from their resources at all points on the market supply curve, $S = MSC$. At the equilibrium quantity and price, marginal social benefit equals marginal social cost, and resources are allocated efficiently. Consumer surplus is the green area, producer surplus is the blue area, and *total surplus* (the sum of producer surplus and consumer surplus) is maximized.

In part (b) Campus Sweaters (and every other firm) makes zero economic profit, and each firm has the plant that enables it to produce at the lowest possible average total cost. Consumers are as well off as

FIGURE 11.12 Efficiency of Perfect Competition

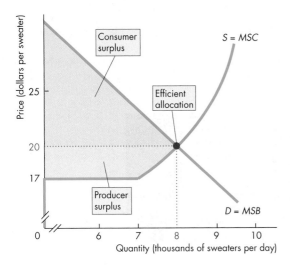

(a) The sweater market

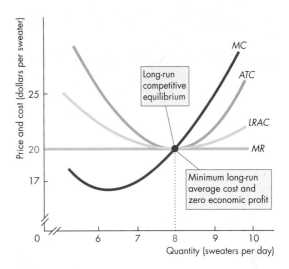

(b) Campus Sweaters

In part (a), market demand, *D*, and market supply, *S*, determine the equilibrium price and quantity. Consumers have made the best available choices on the demand curve, and firms are producing at least cost on the supply curve. Marginal social

benefit, *MSB*, equals marginal social cost, *MSC*, so resources are used efficiently. In part (b), Campus Sweaters produces at the lowest possible long-run average total cost and makes zero economic profit.

MyLab Economics Animation and Draw Graph

possible because the good cannot be produced at a lower cost and the equilibrium price equals that least possible cost.

When firms in perfect competition are away from long-run equilibrium, either entry or exit moves the market toward the situation depicted in Fig. 11.12. During this process, the market is efficient because marginal social benefit equals marginal social cost. But it is only in long-run equilibrium that economic profit is driven to zero and consumers pay the lowest feasible price.

◆ You've now completed your study of perfect competition. *Economics in the News* on pp. 272–273 gives you an opportunity to use what you have learned to understand the market for smartphone and tablet computer "apps."

Although many markets approximate the model of perfect competition, many do not. In Chapter 12, we study markets at the opposite extreme of market power: monopoly. Then in the following chapters we'll study markets that lie between perfect competition

and monopoly. In Chapter 13, we study monopolistic competition and in Chapter 14, we study oligopoly. When you have completed this study, you'll have a toolkit that will enable you to understand the variety of real-world markets.

REVIEW QUIZ

1 State the conditions that must be met for resources to be allocated efficiently.
2 Describe the choices that consumers make and explain why consumers are efficient on the market demand curve.
3 Describe the choices that producers make and explain why producers are efficient on the market supply curve.
4 Explain why resources are used efficiently in a competitive market.

Work these questions in Study Plan 11.6 and get instant feedback. MyLab Economics

Perfect Competition in Smartphone Apps

Apple's Gift to Schools: Free App Development Curriculum

In May 2017, Apple launched a new app development curriculum designed for students who want to pursue careers in the fast-growing app economy. The curriculum is available as a free download from Apple's iBooks Store.

A few months later, Apple announced the same app development curriculum will now be offered in more than 30 community colleges across the country in the 2017–2018 school year, providing opportunities to millions of students to build apps that will prepare them for careers in software development and information technology.

Created by engineers and educators at Apple, the full-year App Development with Swift course teaches students how to build apps using Swift, which is an open source programming language that emphasizes safety, performance, and modern software design patterns. The course takes students with no programming experience and enables them to build fully functional apps of their own design.

Apple's app economy supports 1.5 million jobs in the United States. In 2016, U.S. software developers earned $5 billion through the App Store, a 40 percent increase over 2015. Since the App Store launched, Apple has paid out $16 billion to U.S. developers, over one-quarter of total App Store earnings.

The first iPhone hit the market in 2006, and 10 years later, Apple celebrated the sale of its one billionth iPhone.

Sources: Based on Greg Toppo, "Apple's Gift to Schools: Free App Development Curriculum," *USA TODAY*, May 24, 2017, and Apple press releases.

ESSENCE OF THE STORY

- Apple sold its billionth iPhone in July 2016, 10 years after its launch.

- Providing the materials at no charge, Apple is creating a high school and college course to teach mobile app development.

- More than 30 community colleges will teach the course to millions of students during the 2017–2018 school year.

MyLab Economics Economics in the News

ECONOMIC ANALYSIS

- The iPhone, iPad, and Android smartphones and tablet computers have created a large demand for apps.

- Although apps are not like wheat or sweaters and come in thousands of varieties, the market for apps is highly competitive and we can use the perfect competition model to explain what is happening in that market.

- The market began to operate in 2008, when the first app developers got to work using a software development kit made available by Apple.

- During 2009 through 2016, the number of iPhone and Android smartphone apps increased dramatically. By 2016, there were 2.2 million iPhone apps, 2.8 million Android apps, and 1.5 million others.

- The increase in the number of devices in use increased the demand for apps.

- Thousands of developers, most of them individuals, saw a profit opportunity and got to work creating apps. Their entry into the market increased the supply of apps.

- But the demand for apps kept growing and despite the entry of more developers, profit opportunities remained.

- Figure 1 illustrates the market for apps. In 2016, the demand for apps was D_0 and the supply was S_0. The equilibrium price was P_0 and the quantity was Q_0.

- Figure 2 illustrates the cost and revenue curves of an individual app developer. With marginal revenue MR_0 and marginal cost MC, the developer maximizes profit by producing an app that sells q_0 units.

- Average total cost of an app (on the ATC curve) is less than the price, so the developer makes an economic profit.

- Economic profit brings entry, so in Fig. 1, supply increases in 2017 to S_1. But the demand for apps also keeps increasing and in 2017 the demand curve is D_1.

- The equilibrium quantity increases to Q_1, and this quantity is produced by an increased number of developers—each producing q_0 units and each continuing to make an economic profit.

- The developer's cost curves in Fig. 2 are unchanged, but as development tools improve, development costs will fall and the cost curves will shift downward, which will further increase supply.

- At some future date, market supply will increase by enough to eliminate economic profit and the market for apps will be in long-run equilibrium. That date is unknown but likely will be a long way off.

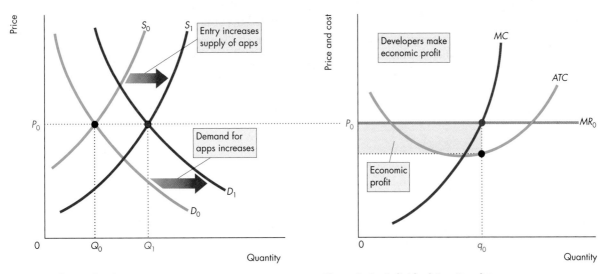

Figure 1 The Market for Apps

Figure 2 An Individual App Developer

WORKED PROBLEM

MyLab Economics You can work this problem in Chapter 11 Study Plan.

The table provides data on a market demand schedule (top two rows) and a firm's average and marginal cost schedules (bottom four rows).

Price P ($)	24	20	16	12	8
Quantity	3,000	4,000	5,000	6,000	7,000
Firm's output	1	2	3	4	5
MC ($)	11.00	11.13	12.00	13.63	16.00
ATC ($)	13.50	12.25	12.00	12.19	12.70
AVC ($)	11.25	11.13	11.25	11.63	12.25

Questions

1. What is the firm's shutdown point?
2. If there are 1,000 identical firms in the market, what is the market price and quantity?
3. With 1,000 firms, will firms enter or exit?
4. Calculate the long-run equilibrium price, quantity, and number of firms.

Solutions

1. The firm will stop producing if the market price falls below minimum AVC. In the table, AVC is at a minimum of $11.13 when 2 units are produced, so that is the shutdown point.

Key Point: A firm shuts down if the market price is *less* than minimum AVC.

2. The first step is to find the market supply schedule. The firm supplies the quantity at which

marginal cost equals market price and its supply curve is its MC curve above the shutdown point. The market supply curve is the sum of the 1,000 firms' supply curves. For example, at a price (MC) of $12, the quantity supplied is 3,000 units—one point on the supply curve.

The second step is to find the price at which the quantity supplied by 1,000 firms equals quantity demanded. When the price (MC) is $16, each firm produces 5 units, so the quantity supplied by the market is 5,000 units. At $16, the quantity demanded is 5,000 units, so the market price is $16 and the quantity is 5,000 units.

Key Point: Each firm supplies the quantity at which marginal cost equals market price.

3. Firms will enter if the price exceeds ATC and exit if the price is below ATC. In the equilibrium above, P is $16 and ATC is $12.70, so firms enter.

Key Point: Firms enter when $P > ATC$.

4. In long-run equilibrium, economic profit is zero, so $P = ATC$. Firms maximize profit, so $P = MC$. This outcome occurs at minimum ATC. From the table, minimum ATC is $12 and the firm's output is 3 units. At $12, 6,000 units are demanded, so firms enter until this quantity is supplied. The number of firms increases to 2,000 (6,000 units divided by 3 units per firm).

Key Point: In long-run equilibrium, economic profit is zero and the market price equals minimum ATC.

Key Figure

MyLab Economics Interactive Animation

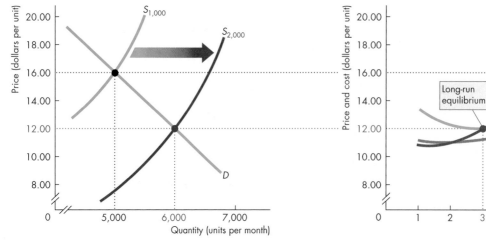

(a) Market

(b) Individual firm

SUMMARY

Key Points

What Is Perfect Competition? (pp. 254–255)

- In perfect competition, many firms sell identical products to many buyers; there are no restrictions on entry; sellers and buyers are well informed about prices.
- A perfectly competitive firm is a price taker.
- A perfectly competitive firm's marginal revenue always equals the market price.

Working Problem 1 will give you a better understanding of perfect competition.

The Firm's Output Decision (pp. 256–259)

- The firm produces the output at which marginal revenue (price) equals marginal cost.
- In short-run equilibrium, a firm can make an economic profit, incur an economic loss, or break even.
- If price is less than minimum average variable cost, the firm temporarily shuts down.
- At prices below minimum average variable cost, a firm's supply curve runs along the y-axis; at prices above minimum average variable cost, a firm's supply curve is its marginal cost curve.

Working Problems 2 to 5 will give you a better understanding of a firm's output decision.

Output, Price, and Profit in the Short Run (pp. 260–263)

- The market supply curve shows the sum of the quantities supplied by each firm at each price.
- Market demand and market supply determine price.
- A firm might make a positive economic profit, a zero economic profit, or incur an economic loss.

Working Problem 6 will give you a better understanding of output, price, and profit in the short run.

Output, Price, and Profit in the Long Run (pp. 263–265)

- Economic profit induces entry and economic loss induces exit.
- Entry increases supply and lowers price and profit. Exit decreases supply and raises price and profit.
- In long-run equilibrium, economic profit is zero. There is no entry or exit.

Working Problem 7 will give you a better understanding of output, price, and profit in the long run.

Changes in Demand and Supply as Technology Advances (pp. 266–269)

- A permanent increase in demand leads to a larger market output and a larger number of firms. A permanent decrease in demand leads to a smaller market output and a smaller number of firms.
- New technologies lower the cost of production, increase supply, and in the long run lower the price and increase the quantity.

Working Problem 8 will give you a better understanding of changes in demand and supply as technology advances.

Competition and Efficiency (pp. 270–271)

- Resources are used efficiently when we produce goods and services in the quantities that people value most highly.
- Perfect competition achieves an efficient allocation. In long-run equilibrium, consumers pay the lowest possible price and marginal social benefit equals marginal social cost.

Working Problem 9 will give you a better understanding of competition and efficiency.

Key Terms

MyLab Economics Key Terms Quiz

Marginal revenue, 254

Perfect competition, 254

Price taker, 254

Short-run market supply curve, 260

Shutdown point, 258

Total revenue, 254

STUDY PLAN PROBLEMS AND APPLICATIONS

MyLab Economics Work Problems 1 to 9 in Chapter 11 Study Plan and get instant feedback.

What Is Perfect Competition? (Study Plan 11.1)

1. Lin's makes fortune cookies. Anyone can make and sell fortune cookies, so there are dozens of producers. All fortune cookies are the same and buyers and sellers know this fact. In what type of market does Lin's operate? What determines the price of fortune cookies? What determines Lin's marginal revenue?

The Firm's Output Decision (Study Plan 11.2)

Use the following table to work Problems 2 to 4. Pat's Pizza Kitchen is a price taker and the table shows its costs of production.

Output (pizzas per hour)	Total cost (dollars per hour)
0	10
1	21
2	30
3	41
4	54
5	69

2. Calculate Pat's profit-maximizing output and economic profit if the market price is (i) $14 a pizza, (ii) $12 a pizza, and (iii) $10 a pizza.

3. What is Pat's shutdown point and what is Pat's economic profit if it shuts down temporarily?

4. Derive Pat's supply curve.

5. The market for paper is perfectly competitive and 1,000 firms produce paper. The table sets out the market demand schedule for paper.

Price (dollars per box)	Quantity demanded (thousands of boxes per week)
3.65	500
5.20	450
6.80	400
8.40	350
10.00	300
11.60	250
13.20	200

The table in the next column sets out the costs of each producer of paper.

Calculate the market price, the market output, the quantity produced by each firm, and the firm's economic profit or loss.

Output (boxes per week)	Marginal cost (dollars per additional box)	Average variable cost	Average total cost
		(dollars per box)	
200	6.40	7.80	12.80
250	7.00	7.00	11.00
300	7.65	7.10	10.43
350	8.40	7.20	10.06
400	10.00	7.50	10.00
450	12.40	8.00	10.22
500	20.70	9.00	11.00

Output, Price, and Profit in the Short Run

(Study Plan 11.3)

6. In Problem 5, the market demand decreases and the demand schedule becomes:

Price (dollars per box)	Quantity demanded (thousands of boxes per week)
2.95	500
4.13	450
5.30	400
6.48	350
7.65	300
8.83	250
10.00	200
11.18	150

If firms have the same costs set out in Problem 5, what is the market price and the firm's economic profit or loss in the short run?

Output, Price, and Profit in the Long Run

(Study Plan 11.4)

7. In Problem 5, in the long run what is the market price and the quantity of paper produced? What is the number of firms in the market?

Changes in Demand and Supply as Technology Advances (Study Plan 11.5)

8. If the market demand for paper remains the same as in Problem 6, calculate the market price, market output, and the economic profit or loss of each firm.

Competition and Efficiency (Study Plan 11.6)

9. In perfect competition in long-run equilibrium, can consumer surplus or producer surplus be increased? Explain your answer.

ADDITIONAL PROBLEMS AND APPLICATIONS

MyLab Economics You can work these problems in Homework or Test if assigned by your instructor.

What Is Perfect Competition?

Use the following news clip to work Problems 10 to 12.

Money in the Tank

Two gas stations stand on opposite sides of the road: Rutter's Farm Store and Sheetz gas station. Rutter's doesn't even have to look across the highway to know when Sheetz changes its price for a gallon of gas. When Sheetz raises the price, Rutter's pumps are busy. When Sheetz lowers prices, there's not a car in sight. Both gas stations survive, but each has no control over the price.

Source: *The Mining Journal*, May 24, 2008

10. In what type of market do these gas stations operate? What determines the price of gasoline and the marginal revenue from gasoline?

11. Describe the elasticity of demand that each of these gas stations faces.

12. Why does each of these gas stations have so little control over the price of the gasoline it sells?

The Firm's Output Decision

13. The figure shows the costs of Quick Copy, one of many copy shops near campus.

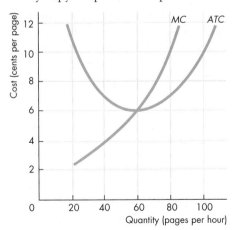

If the market price of copying is 10¢ a page, calculate Quick Copy's
a. Profit-maximizing output
b. Economic profit

14. The market for smoothies is perfectly competitive. The table in the next column sets out the market demand schedule.

Price (dollars per smoothie)	Quantity demanded (smoothies per hour)
1.90	1,000
2.00	950
2.20	800
2.91	700
4.25	550
5.25	400
5.50	300

Each of the 100 producers of smoothies has the following costs when it uses its least-cost plant:

Output (smoothies per hour)	Marginal cost (dollars per additional smoothie)	Average variable cost	Average total cost
		(dollars per smoothie)	
3	2.50	4.00	7.33
4	2.20	3.53	6.03
5	1.90	3.24	5.24
6	2.00	3.00	4.67
7	2.91	2.91	4.34
8	4.25	3.00	4.25
9	8.00	3.33	4.44

a. What is the market price of a smoothie?

b. What is the market quantity of smoothies?

c. How many smoothies does each firm sell?

d. What is the economic profit made or economic loss incurred by each firm?

15. **GM to Cut Production and Jobs**

General Motors will temporarily idle five U.S. assembly plants that build sedans and coupes, such as the Chevrolet Cruze, Cadillac CTS, and Chevy Camaro, as American motorists by the millions shift from passenger cars to utility vehicles and other light trucks.

Source: *The Toronto Star*, December 21, 2016

a. Explain how the shutdown decision will affect GM's *TFC, TVC*, and *TC*.

b. Under what conditions would this shutdown decision maximize GM's economic profit (or minimize its loss)? Explain your answer.

c. Under what conditions will GM start producing the sedans and coupes again? Explain your answer.

Output, Price, and Profit in the Short Run

16. **Dark Clouds Loom for Farmers as Corn Price Languishes**

    Global corn acreage expanded by 18 percent over the past 10 years and Minnesota farms are producing a near-record amount of corn at a time when its price is low.

    Source: *Star Tribune*, August 1, 2016

    Why did the price of corn fall in 2016? Draw a graph to show the short-run effect on an individual farmer's economic profit.

Output, Price, and Profit in the Long Run

17. In Problem 14, do firms enter or exit the market for smoothies in the long run? What is the market price and the equilibrium quantity in the long run?

18. In Problem 15, under what conditions would GM stop producing the Cadillac CTS and exit the market for sedans? Explain your answer.

19. **Kraft Heinz Cutting Jobs and Closing Plant**

    Kraft Heinz is closing its plant in St. Marys, Ontario, believed to employ some 200 people. In 2013, Heinz closed its century-old plant in Leamington, Ontario, laying off around 740 people. After these closures and others in the United States, Kraft Heinz will have 41 plants in North America that employ about 18,000 people.

    Source: *Canadian Manufacturing*, November 5, 2015

    a. Was Kraft Heinz making a shutdown or exit decision?

    b. Under what conditions would this decision maximize Kraft Heinz's economic profit?

    c. How might Kraft Heinz's decision affected the economic profit of other firms?

Changes in Demand and Supply as Technology Advances

20. **4K Ultra HD TV: Consumers Enjoy Picture Quality, Boosting Disc Sales**

    As the average price of a 4K Ultra HD television fell below $1,000, the quantity bought increased. About 9 million were bought between 2012 and 2015, 10 million in 2016, and an anticipated 15 million in 2017. Improved streaming services have also boosted 4K TV sales. Sales of movie discs and 4K Ultra HD Blu-ray Disc players have increased.

    Source: *USA TODAY*, January 4, 2017

    a. Explain how the advance in TV technology will influence the markets for streaming services and Blu-ray discs and players in the short run and in the long run. Illustrate your explanation with a graph.

    b. Explain how the markets for streaming services and Blu-ray discs and players will influence the market for 4K HD TVs.

Competition and Efficiency

21. In a perfectly competitive market, each firm maximizes its profit by choosing only the quantity to produce and, regardless of whether the firm makes an economic profit or incurs an economic loss, the short-run equilibrium is efficient. Is the statement true? Explain why or why not.

Economics in the News

22. After you have studied *Economics in the News* on pp. 272–273, answer the following questions.

    a. What are the features of the market for apps that make it competitive?

    b. Does the information provided in the news article suggest that the app market is in long-run equilibrium? Explain why or why not.

    c. How would an advance in development technology that lowered a developer's costs change the market supply and the developer's marginal revenue, marginal cost, average total cost, and economic profit?

    d. Illustrate your answer to part (c) with an appropriate graphical analysis.

23. **China's Phone Makers Look to India for Growth**

    China produces smartphones, and hundreds of millions of Chinese have bought one. With intense competition among more than 150 brands, China's smartphone producers are looking to capture the Indian market.

    Source: *The New York Times*, May 12, 2015

    a. Explain the effects of the increase in Indian demand for smartphones on the market for smartphones and on an individual smartphone producer in the short run.

    b. Draw a graph to illustrate your explanation in part (a).

12

MONOPOLY

After studying this chapter, you will be able to:

◆ Explain how monopoly arises

◆ Explain how a single-price monopoly determines its output and price

◆ Compare the performance and efficiency of single-price monopoly and competition

◆ Explain how price discrimination increases profit

◆ Explain how monopoly regulation influences output, price, economic profit, and efficiency

Google and Microsoft are big players in the markets for Web search and advertising and for computer operating systems, markets that are obviously not perfectly competitive.

In this chapter, we study markets dominated by one big firm. We call such a market *monopoly*. We study the performance and the efficiency of monopoly and compare it with perfect competition.

In *Economics in the News* at the end of the chapter, we look at the remarkable success of Google and ask whether Google is serving the social interest or violating Canadian, U.S., and European antitrust laws.

Monopoly and How It Arises

A **monopoly** is a market with a single firm that produces a good or service with no close substitutes and that is protected by a barrier that prevents other firms from entering that market.

How Monopoly Arises

Monopoly arises for two key reasons:

- No close substitutes
- Barrier to entry

No Close Substitutes If a good has a close substitute, even though only one firm produces it, that firm effectively faces competition from the producers of the substitute. A monopoly sells a good or service that has no good substitutes. Tap water and bottled water are close substitutes for drinking, but for showering or washing a car, tap water has no effective substitutes, and a local public utility that supplies tap water is a monopoly.

Barrier to Entry A constraint that protects a firm from potential competitors is called a **barrier to entry**. There are three types of barrier to entry:

- Natural
- Ownership
- Legal

Natural Barrier to Entry A natural barrier to entry creates a **natural monopoly**: a market in which economies of scale enable one firm to supply the entire market at the lowest possible cost. The firms that deliver gas, water, and electricity to our homes are examples of natural monopoly.

Figure 12.1 illustrates an electric power natural monopoly. When the market demand curve is *D*, and the long-run average cost curve is *LRAC*, the firm has economies of scale and can supply the entire market of 4 million kilowatt-hours at 5 cents per kilowatt-hour. If two firms shared the market equally, it would cost each firm 10 cents per kilowatt-hour to produce a total of 4 million kilowatt-hours.

Ownership Barrier to Entry An ownership barrier to entry occurs if one firm owns a significant portion of a key resource. An example of this type of monopoly occurred during the last century when De Beers controlled up to 90 percent of the world's supply of diamonds. (Today, its share is only 65 percent.)

FIGURE 12.1 Natural Monopoly

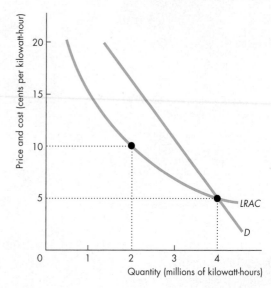

The market demand curve for electric power is *D*, and the long-run average cost curve is *LRAC*. Economies of scale exist over the entire *LRAC* curve. One firm can distribute 4 million kilowatt-hours at a cost of 5 cents a kilowatt-hour. This same total output costs 10 cents a kilowatt-hour with two firms. One firm can meet the market demand at a lower cost than two or more firms can. The market is a natural monopoly.

——————— MyLab Economics Animation ———————

Legal Barrier to Entry A legal barrier to entry creates a **legal monopoly**: a market in which competition and entry are restricted by the granting of a public franchise, government licence, patent, or copyright.

A *public franchise* is an exclusive right granted to a firm to supply a good or service. An example is Canada Post, which has the exclusive right to deliver residential mail. A *government licence* controls entry into particular occupations, professions, and industries. Examples of this type of barrier to entry occur in medicine and other professional services.

A *patent* is an exclusive right granted to the inventor of a product or service. A *copyright* is an exclusive right granted to the author or composer of a literary, musical, dramatic, or artistic work. Patents encourage the *invention* of new products and production methods. They also stimulate *innovation*—the use of new inventions—by encouraging inventors to publicize their discoveries and offer them for use under licence. Patents have stimulated innovations in areas as diverse as soybean seeds, pharmaceuticals, memory chips, and video games.

ECONOMICS IN ACTION
Two Information-Age Monopolies

Information-age technologies have created some big natural monopolies—firms with large plant costs but almost zero marginal cost, so they experience economies of scale.

Two of these firms are Microsoft and Google. The figures show their market shares. Microsoft provides 92 percent of the market for personal computer operating systems, and Google provides 80 percent of Internet search.

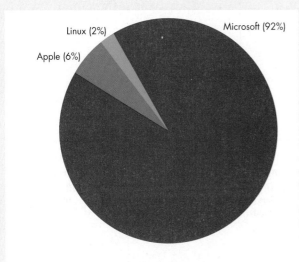

Figure 1 Operating Systems Market Shares

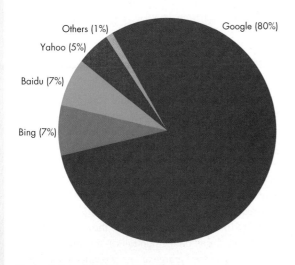

Figure 2 Search Engines Market Shares

Monopoly Price-Setting Strategies

A major difference between monopoly and competition is that a monopoly sets its own price. In doing so, the monopoly faces a market constraint: To sell a larger quantity, the monopoly must set a lower price. There are two monopoly situations that create two pricing strategies:

- Single price
- Price discrimination

Single Price A **single-price monopoly** is a firm that must sell each unit of its output for the same price to all its customers. De Beers sells diamonds (of a given size and quality) for the same price to all its customers. If it tried to sell at a low price to some customers and at a higher price to others, only the low-price customers would buy from De Beers. Others would buy from De Beers' low-price customers. De Beers is a *single-price* monopoly.

Price Discrimination When a firm practises **price discrimination**, it sells different units of a good or service for different prices. Many firms price discriminate. Microsoft sells its Windows and Office software at different prices to different buyers. Computer manufacturers who install the software on new machines, students and teachers, governments, and businesses all pay different prices. Pizza producers offer a second pizza for a lower price than the first one. These are examples of *price discrimination*.

When a firm price discriminates, it looks as though it is doing its customers a favour. In fact, it is charging the highest possible price for each unit sold and making the largest possible profit.

REVIEW QUIZ

1 How does monopoly arise?
2 How does a natural monopoly differ from a legal monopoly?
3 Distinguish between a price-discriminating monopoly and a single-price monopoly.

Work these questions in Study Plan 12.1 and get instant feedback.   MyLab Economics

We start with a single-price monopoly and see how it makes its decisions about the quantity to produce and the price to charge to maximize its profit.

◆ A Single-Price Monopoly's Output and Price Decision

To understand how a single-price monopoly makes its output and price decision, we must first study the link between price and marginal revenue.

Price and Marginal Revenue

Because in a monopoly there is only one firm, the demand curve facing the firm is the market demand curve. Let's look at Bobbie's Barbershop, the sole supplier of haircuts in Trout River, Newfoundland. The table in Fig. 12.2 shows the market demand schedule. At a price of $20, Bobbie sells no haircuts. The lower the price, the more haircuts per hour she can sell. For example, at $12, consumers demand 4 haircuts per hour (row E).

Total revenue (TR) is the price (P) multiplied by the quantity sold (Q). For example, in row D, Bobbie sells 3 haircuts at $14 each, so total revenue is $42. *Marginal revenue* ($MR$) is the change in total revenue (ΔTR) resulting from a one-unit increase in the quantity sold. For example, if the price falls from $16 (row C) to $14 (row D), the quantity sold increases from 2 to 3 haircuts. Total revenue increases from $32 to $42, so the change in total revenue is $10. Because the quantity sold increases by 1 haircut, marginal revenue equals the change in total revenue and is $10. Marginal revenue is placed between the two rows to emphasize that marginal revenue relates to the *change* in the quantity sold.

Figure 12.2 shows the market demand curve and marginal revenue curve (MR) and also illustrates the calculation we've just made. Notice that at each level of output, marginal revenue is less than price—the marginal revenue curve lies *below* the demand curve.

Why is marginal revenue *less* than price? It is because when the price is lowered to sell one more unit, two opposing forces affect total revenue. The lower price results in a revenue loss on the original units sold and a revenue gain on the additional quantity sold. For example, at a price of $16 a haircut, Bobbie sells 2 haircuts (point C). If she cuts the price to $14, she sells 3 haircuts and has a revenue gain of $14 on the third haircut. But she now receives only $14 on each of the first 2 haircuts—$2 less than before. As a result, she loses $4 of revenue on the first 2 haircuts. To calculate marginal revenue, she must deduct this amount from the revenue gain of $14. So marginal revenue is $10, which is less than the price.

FIGURE 12.2 Demand and Marginal Revenue

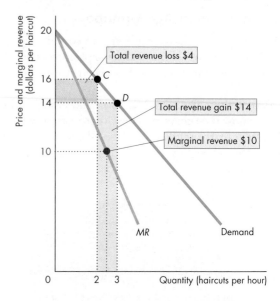

Price (P) (dollars per haircut)	Quantity demanded (Q) (haircuts per hour)	Total revenue (TR = P × Q) (dollars)	Marginal revenue (MR = ΔTR/ΔQ) (dollars per haircut)
A 20	0	0	
			18
B 18	1	18	
			14
C 16	**2**	**32**	
			10
D 14	**3**	**42**	
			6
E 12	4	48	
			2
F 10	5	50	

The table shows the demand schedule. Total revenue (TR) is price multiplied by quantity sold. For example, in row C, the price is $16 a haircut, Bobbie sells 2 haircuts, and total revenue is $32. Marginal revenue (MR) is the change in total revenue that results from a one-unit increase in the quantity sold. For example, when the price falls from $16 to $14 a haircut, the quantity sold increases from 2 to 3, an increase of 1 haircut, and total revenue increases by $10. Marginal revenue is $10. The demand curve and the marginal revenue curve, MR, are based on the numbers in the table and illustrate the calculation of marginal revenue when the price falls from $16 to $14 a haircut.

MyLab Economics Animation and Draw Graph

Marginal Revenue and Elasticity

A single-price monopoly's marginal revenue is related to the *elasticity of demand* for its good. The demand for a good can be *elastic* (the elasticity is greater than 1), *inelastic* (the elasticity is less than 1), or *unit elastic* (the elasticity is equal to 1). Demand is *elastic* if a 1 percent fall in the price brings a greater than 1 percent increase in the quantity demanded. Demand is *inelastic* if a 1 percent fall in the price brings a less than 1 percent increase in the quantity demanded. Demand is *unit elastic* if a 1 percent fall in the price brings a 1 percent increase in the quantity demanded. (See Chapter 4, pp. 88–90.)

If demand is elastic, a fall in the price brings an increase in total revenue—the revenue gain from the increase in quantity sold outweighs the revenue loss from the lower price—and marginal revenue is *positive*. If demand is inelastic, a fall in the price brings a decrease in total revenue—the revenue gain from the increase in quantity sold is outweighed by the revenue loss from the lower price—and marginal revenue is *negative*. If demand is unit elastic, total revenue does not change—the revenue gain from the increase in the quantity sold offsets the revenue loss from the lower price—and marginal revenue is *zero*. (See Chapter 4, p. 92.)

Figure 12.3 illustrates the relationship between marginal revenue, total revenue, and elasticity. As the price gradually falls from $20 to $10 a haircut, the quantity demanded increases from 0 to 5 haircuts an hour. Over this output range, marginal revenue is positive in part (a), total revenue increases in part (b), and the demand for haircuts is elastic. As the price falls from $10 to $0 a haircut, the quantity of haircuts demanded increases from 5 to 10 an hour. Over this output range, marginal revenue is negative in part (a), total revenue decreases in part (b), and the demand for haircuts is inelastic. When the price is $10 a haircut, marginal revenue is zero in part (a), total revenue is at a maximum in part (b), and the demand for haircuts is unit elastic.

In Monopoly, Demand Is Always Elastic
The relationship between marginal revenue and elasticity of demand that you've just discovered implies that a profit-maximizing monopoly never produces an output in the inelastic range of the market demand curve. If it did so, it could charge a higher price, produce a smaller quantity, and increase its profit. Let's now look at a monopoly's price and output decision.

FIGURE 12.3 Marginal Revenue and Elasticity

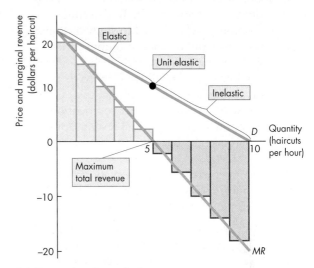

(a) Demand and marginal revenue curves

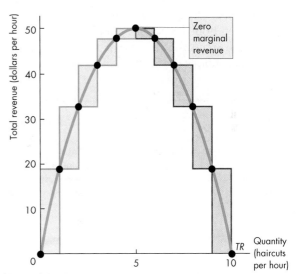

(b) Total revenue curve

In part (a), the demand curve is *D* and the marginal revenue curve is *MR*. In part (b), the total revenue curve is *TR*. Over the range 0 to 5 haircuts an hour, a price cut increases total revenue, so marginal revenue is positive—as shown by the blue bars. Demand is elastic. Over the range 5 to 10 haircuts an hour, a price cut decreases total revenue, so marginal revenue is negative—as shown by the red bars. Demand is inelastic. At 5 haircuts an hour, total revenue is maximized and marginal revenue is zero. Demand is unit elastic.

MyLab Economics Animation

Price and Output Decision

A monopoly sets its price and output at the levels that maximize economic profit. To determine this price and output level, we need to study the behaviour of both cost and revenue as output varies. A monopoly faces the same types of technology and cost constraints as a competitive firm, so its costs (total cost, average cost, and marginal cost) behave just like those of a firm in perfect competition. And a monopoly's revenues (total revenue, price, and marginal revenue) behave in the way we've just described.

Table 12.1 provides information about Bobbie's costs, revenues, and economic profit, and Fig. 12.4 shows the same information graphically.

Maximizing Economic Profit You can see in Table 12.1 and Fig. 12.4(a) that total cost (*TC*) and total revenue (*TR*) both rise as output increases, but *TC* rises at an increasing rate and *TR* rises at a decreasing rate. Economic profit, which equals *TR* minus *TC*, increases at small output levels, reaches a maximum, and then decreases. The maximum profit ($12) occurs when Bobbie sells 3 haircuts for $14 each. If she sells 2 haircuts for $16 each or 4 haircuts for $12 each, her economic profit will be only $8.

Marginal Revenue Equals Marginal Cost You can see Bobbie's marginal revenue (*MR*) and marginal cost (*MC*) in Table 12.1 and Fig. 12.4(b).

When Bobbie increases output from 2 to 3 haircuts, *MR* is $10 and *MC* is $6. *MR* exceeds *MC* by $4 and Bobbie's profit increases by that amount. If Bobbie increases output from 3 to 4 haircuts, *MR* is $6 and *MC* is $10. In this case, *MC* exceeds *MR* by $4, so profit decreases by that amount. When *MR* exceeds *MC*, profit increases if output increases. When *MC* exceeds *MR*, profit increases if output *decreases*. When *MC* equals *MR*, profit is maximized.

Figure 12.4(b) shows the maximum profit as price (on the demand curve *D*) minus average total cost (on the *ATC* curve) multiplied by the quantity produced—the blue rectangle.

Maximum Price the Market Will Bear Unlike a firm in perfect competition, a monopoly influences the price of what it sells. But a monopoly doesn't set the price at the maximum *possible* price. At the maximum possible price, the firm would be able to sell only one unit of output, which in general is less than the profit-maximizing quantity. Rather, a monopoly produces the profit-maximizing quantity and sells that quantity for the highest price it can get.

TABLE 12.1 A Monopoly's Output and Price Decision

Price (P) (dollars per haircut)	Quantity demanded (Q) (haircuts per hour)	Total revenue (TR = P × Q) (dollars)	Marginal revenue (MR = ΔTR/ΔQ) (dollars per haircut)	Total cost (TC) (dollars)	Marginal cost (MC = ΔTC/ΔQ) (dollars per haircut)	Profit (TR − TC) (dollars)
20	0	0		20		−20
			 18		 1	
18	1	18		21		−3
			 14		 3	
16	2	32		24		+8
			 10		 6	
14	**3**	**42**		**30**		**+12**
			 6		 10	
12	4	48		40		+8
			 2		 15	
10	5	50		55		−5

This table gives the data needed to find the profit-maximizing output and price. Total revenue (*TR*) equals price multiplied by the quantity sold. Profit equals total revenue minus total cost (*TC*).

Profit is maximized when 3 haircuts are sold at a price of $14 each. Total revenue is $42, total cost is $30, and economic profit is $12 ($42 − $30).

FIGURE 12.4   A Monopoly's Output and Price

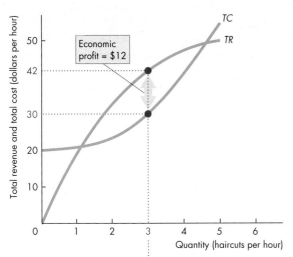

(a)   Total revenue and total cost curves

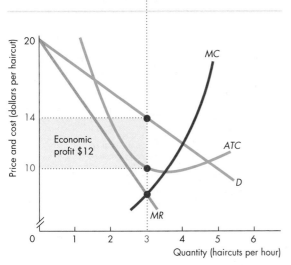

(b) Demand and marginal revenue and cost curves

In part (a), economic profit is the vertical distance equal to total revenue (*TR*) minus total cost (*TC*) and it is maximized at 3 haircuts an hour.

In part (b), economic profit is maximized when marginal cost (*MC*) equals marginal revenue (*MR*). The profit-maximizing output is 3 haircuts an hour. The price is determined by the demand curve (*D*) and is $14 a haircut. The average total cost of a haircut is $10, so economic profit, the blue rectangle, is $12—the profit per haircut ($4) multiplied by 3 haircuts.

———— MyLab Economics Animation and Draw Graph ————

All firms maximize profit by producing the output at which marginal revenue equals marginal cost. For a competitive firm, price equals marginal revenue, so price also equals marginal cost. For a monopoly, price exceeds marginal revenue, so price also exceeds marginal cost.

A monopoly charges a price that exceeds marginal cost, but does it always make an economic profit? In Fig. 12.4(b), Bobbie produces 3 haircuts an hour. Her average total cost is $10 (on the *ATC* curve) and her price is $14 (on the *D* curve), so her profit per haircut is $4 ($14 minus $10). Bobbie's economic profit is shown by the area of the blue rectangle, which equals the profit per haircut ($4) multiplied by the number of haircuts (3), for a total of $12.

If firms in a perfectly competitive market make a positive economic profit, new firms enter. That does *not* happen in monopoly. Barriers to entry prevent new firms from entering the market, so a monopoly can make a positive economic profit and might continue to do so indefinitely. Sometimes that economic profit is large, as in the international diamond business.

Bobbie makes a positive economic profit. But suppose that Bobbie's landlord increases the rent on her shop. If Bobbie pays an additional $12 an hour for rent, her fixed cost increases by $12 an hour. Her marginal cost and marginal revenue don't change, so her profit-maximizing output remains at 3 haircuts an hour. Her profit decreases by $12 an hour to zero. If Bobbie's rent increases by more than $12 an hour, she incurs an economic loss. If this situation were permanent, Bobbie would go out of business.

◆   REVIEW QUIZ

1   What is the relationship between marginal cost and marginal revenue when a single-price monopoly maximizes profit?
2   How does a single-price monopoly determine the price it will charge its customers?
3   What is the relationship between price, marginal revenue, and marginal cost when a single-price monopoly is maximizing profit?
4   Why can a monopoly make a positive economic profit even in the long run?

Work these questions in Study Plan 12.2 and get instant feedback.   MyLab Economics

Single-Price Monopoly and Competition Compared

Imagine a market that is made up of many small firms operating in perfect competition. Then imagine that a single firm buys out all these small firms and creates a monopoly.

What will happen in this market? Will the price rise or fall? Will the quantity produced increase or decrease? Will economic profit increase or decrease? Will either the original competitive situation or the new monopoly situation be efficient?

These are the questions we're now going to answer. First, we look at the effects of monopoly on the price and quantity produced. Then we turn to the questions about efficiency.

Comparing Price and Output

Figure 12.5 shows the market we'll study. The market demand curve is D. The demand curve is the same regardless of how the industry is organized. But the supply side and the equilibrium are different in monopoly and competition. First, let's look at the case of perfect competition.

Perfect Competition Initially, with many small perfectly competitive firms in the market, the market supply curve is S. This supply curve is obtained by summing the supply curves of all the individual firms in the market.

In perfect competition, equilibrium occurs where the supply curve and the demand curve intersect. The price is P_C, and the quantity produced by the industry is Q_C. Each firm takes the price P_C and maximizes its profit by producing the output at which its own marginal cost equals the price. Because each firm is a small part of the total industry, there is no incentive for any firm to try to manipulate the price by varying its output.

Monopoly Now suppose that this industry is taken over by a single firm. Consumers do not change, so the market demand curve remains the same as in the case of perfect competition. But now the monopoly recognizes this demand curve as a constraint on the price at which it can sell its output. The monopoly's marginal revenue curve is MR.

The monopoly maximizes profit by producing the quantity at which marginal revenue equals marginal cost. To find the monopoly's marginal cost curve, first recall that in perfect competition, the market supply curve is the sum of the supply curves of the firms in the industry. Also recall that each firm's supply curve is its marginal cost curve (see Chapter 11, p. 259). So when the market is taken over by a single firm, the competitive market's supply curve becomes the monopoly's marginal cost curve. To remind you of this fact, the supply curve is also labelled MC.

The output at which marginal revenue equals marginal cost is Q_M. This output is smaller than the competitive output Q_C. And the monopoly charges the price P_M, which is higher than P_C. We have established that

> Compared to a perfectly competitive market, a single-price monopoly produces a smaller output and charges a higher price.

We've seen how the output and price of a monopoly compare with those in a competitive market. Let's now compare the efficiency of the two types of market.

FIGURE 12.5 Monopoly's Smaller Output and Higher Price

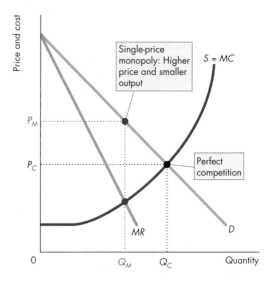

A competitive market produces the quantity Q_C at price P_C. A single-price monopoly produces the quantity Q_M at which marginal revenue equals marginal cost and sells that quantity for the price P_M. Compared to perfect competition, a single-price monopoly produces a smaller output and charges a higher price.

MyLab Economics Animation

Efficiency Comparison

Perfect competition (with no externalities) is efficient. Figure 12.6(a) illustrates the efficiency of perfect competition and serves as a benchmark against which to measure the inefficiency of monopoly. Along the demand and marginal social benefit curve ($D = MSB$), consumers are efficient. Along the supply curve and marginal social cost curve ($S = MSC$), producers are efficient. In competitive equilibrium, the price is P_C, the quantity is Q_C, and marginal social benefit equals marginal social cost.

Consumer surplus is the green triangle under the demand curve and above the equilibrium price (see Chapter 5, p. 113). *Producer surplus* is the blue area above the supply curve and below the equilibrium price (see Chapter 5, p. 115). Total surplus (consumer surplus and producer surplus) is maximized.

Also, in long-run competitive equilibrium, entry and exit ensure that each firm produces its output at the minimum possible long-run average cost.

To summarize: At the competitive equilibrium, marginal social benefit equals marginal social cost; total surplus is maximized; firms produce at the lowest possible long-run average cost; and resource use is efficient.

Figure 12.6(b) illustrates the inefficiency of monopoly and the sources of that inefficiency. A monopoly produces Q_M and sells its output for P_M. The smaller output and higher price drive a wedge between marginal social benefit and marginal social cost and create a *deadweight loss*. The grey triangle shows the deadweight loss, and its magnitude is a measure of the inefficiency of monopoly.

Consumer surplus shrinks for two reasons. First, consumers lose by having to pay more for the good. This loss to consumers is a gain for monopoly and increases the producer surplus. Second, consumers lose by getting less of the good, and this loss is part of the deadweight loss.

Although the monopoly gains from a higher price, it loses some producer surplus because it produces a smaller output. That loss is another part of the deadweight loss.

A monopoly produces a smaller output than perfect competition and faces no competition, so it does not produce at the lowest possible long-run average cost. As a result, monopoly damages the consumer interest in three ways: A monopoly produces less, increases the cost of production, and raises the price by more than the increased cost of production.

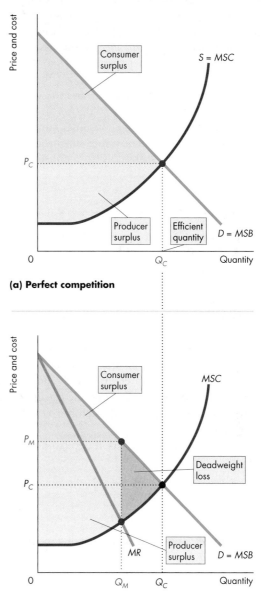

FIGURE 12.6   Inefficiency of Monopoly

(a) Perfect competition

(b) Monopoly

In perfect competition in part (a), output is Q_C and the price is P_C. Marginal social benefit (*MSB*) equals marginal social cost (*MSC*); total surplus, the sum of consumer surplus (the green triangle) and producer surplus (the blue area), is maximized; and in the long run, firms produce at the lowest possible average cost. Monopoly in part (b) produces Q_M and raises the price to P_M. Consumer surplus shrinks, the monopoly gains, and a deadweight loss (the grey triangle) arises.

—— MyLab Economics Animation and Draw Graph ——

Redistribution of Surpluses

You've seen that monopoly is inefficient because marginal social benefit exceeds marginal social cost and there is deadweight loss—a social loss. But monopoly also brings a *redistribution* of surpluses.

Some of the lost consumer surplus goes to the monopoly. In Fig. 12.6, the monopoly takes the difference between the higher price, P_M, and the competitive price, P_C, on the quantity sold, Q_M. So the monopoly takes that part of the consumer surplus. This portion of the loss of consumer surplus is not a loss to society. It is a redistribution from consumers to the monopoly producer.

Rent Seeking

You've seen that monopoly creates a deadweight loss and is inefficient. But the social cost of monopoly can exceed the deadweight loss because of an activity called rent seeking. Any surplus—consumer surplus, producer surplus, or economic profit—is called **economic rent**. The pursuit of wealth by capturing economic rent is called **rent seeking**.

You've seen that a monopoly makes its economic profit by diverting part of consumer surplus to itself—by converting consumer surplus into economic profit. So the pursuit of economic profit by a monopoly is rent seeking. It is the attempt to capture consumer surplus.

Rent seekers pursue their goals in two main ways. They might:

- Buy a monopoly
- Create a monopoly

Buy a Monopoly To rent seek by buying a monopoly, a person searches for a monopoly that is for sale at a lower price than the monopoly's economic profit. Trading of taxicab licences is an example of this type of rent seeking. In some cities, taxicabs are regulated. The city restricts both the fares and the number of taxis that can operate so that operating a taxi results in economic profit. A person who wants to operate a taxi must buy a licence from someone who already has one.

People rationally devote time and effort to seeking out profitable monopoly businesses to buy. In the process, they use scarce resources that could otherwise have been used to produce goods and services. The value of this lost production is part of the social cost of monopoly. The amount paid for a monopoly is *not*

a social cost because the payment transfers an existing producer surplus from the buyer to the seller.

Create a Monopoly Rent seeking by creating a monopoly is mainly a political activity. It takes the form of lobbying and trying to influence the political process. Such influence might be sought by making campaign contributions in exchange for legislative support or by indirectly seeking to influence political outcomes through publicity in the media or more direct contacts with politicians and bureaucrats. An example of a monopoly created in this way is the cable television monopoly created and regulated by the Canadian Radio-Television and Telecommunications Commission (CRTC). Another is a regulation that restricts "split-run" magazines. These are regulations that restrict output and increase price.

This type of rent seeking is a costly activity that uses up scarce resources. Taken together, firms spend billions of dollars lobbying MPs, MPPs, and bureaucrats in the pursuit of licences and laws that create barriers to entry and establish a monopoly.

Rent-Seeking Equilibrium

Barriers to entry create monopoly. But there is no barrier to entry into rent seeking. Rent seeking is like perfect competition. If an economic profit is available, a new rent seeker will try to get some of it. And competition among rent seekers pushes up the price that must be paid for a monopoly, to the point at which the rent seeker makes zero economic profit by operating the monopoly. For example, competition for the right to operate a taxi leads to a price of $300,000 in Toronto and $200,000 in Montreal for a taxi licence, which is sufficiently high to eliminate the economic profit made by a taxi operator.

Figure 12.7 shows a rent-seeking equilibrium. The cost of rent seeking is a fixed cost that must be added to a monopoly's other costs. Rent seeking and rent-seeking costs increase to the point at which no economic profit is made. The average total cost curve, which includes the fixed cost of rent seeking, shifts upward until it just touches the demand curve. Economic profit is zero. It has been lost in rent seeking.

Consumer surplus is unaffected, but the deadweight loss from monopoly is larger. The deadweight loss now includes the original deadweight loss triangle plus the lost producer surplus, shown by the enlarged grey area in Fig. 12.7.

FIGURE 12.7 Rent-Seeking Equilibrium

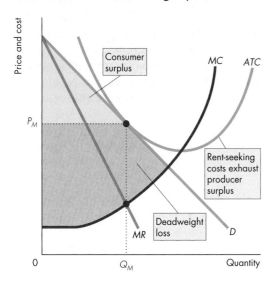

With competitive rent seeking, a single-price monopoly uses all its economic profit to maintain its monopoly. The firm's rent-seeking costs are fixed costs. They add to total fixed cost and to average total cost. The *ATC* curve shifts upward until, at the profit-maximizing price, the firm breaks even.

————— MyLab Economics Animation —————

REVIEW QUIZ

1 Why does a single-price monopoly produce a smaller output and charge more than the price that would prevail if the market were perfectly competitive?

2 How does a monopoly transfer consumer surplus to itself?

3 Why is a single-price monopoly inefficient?

4 What is rent seeking and how does it influence the inefficiency of monopoly?

Work these questions in Study Plan 12.3 and get instant feedback. MyLab Economics

So far, we've considered only a single-price monopoly. But many monopolies do not operate with a single price. Instead, they price discriminate. Let's now see how a price-discriminating monopoly works.

 Price Discrimination

You encounter *price discrimination*—selling a good or service at a number of different prices—when you travel, go to the movies, get your hair cut, visit an art museum or theme park, or buy pizza. These are all examples of firms with market power, setting the prices of an identical good or service at different levels for different customers.

Not all price *differences* are price *discrimination*: Many reflect differences in production costs. For example, real-time meters for electricity enable power utilities to charge a different price at peak-load times than during the night. Because it costs more per kilowatt-hour to generate electricity at peak-load times, this price difference reflects production cost differences and is not price discrimination.

At first sight, price discrimination appears to be inconsistent with profit maximization. Why would a movie theatre allow children to see movies at a discount? Why would a hairdresser charge students and senior citizens less? Aren't these firms losing profit by being nice to their customers? The answer, as you are about to discover, is that price discrimination is profitable: It increases economic profit.

But to be able to price discriminate, the firm must sell a product that cannot be resold; and it must be possible to identify and separate different buyer types.

Two Ways of Price Discriminating

Firms price discriminate in two broad ways. They discriminate:

- Among groups of buyers
- Among units of a good

Discriminating Among Groups of Buyers People differ in the value they place on a good—their marginal benefit and willingness to pay. Some of these differences are correlated with features such as age, employment status, and other easily distinguished characteristics. When such a correlation is present, firms can profit by price discriminating among the different groups of buyers.

For example, salespeople and other business travellers know that a face-to-face sales meeting with a customer might bring a large and profitable order. So for these travellers, the marginal benefit from a trip is large and the price that such a traveller is willing to pay for a trip is high. In contrast, for a leisure traveller, any of several different trips and even no trip at all are options. So for leisure travellers, the marginal benefit of a trip is small and the price that such a traveller is willing to pay for a trip is low. Because the price that business travellers are willing to pay exceeds what leisure travellers are willing to pay, it is possible for an airline to price discriminate between these two groups and increase its profit. We'll return to this example of price discrimination below.

Discriminating Among Units of a Good Everyone experiences diminishing marginal benefit, so if all the units of the good are sold for a single price, buyers end up with a consumer surplus equal to the value they get from each unit minus the price paid for it.

A firm that price discriminates by charging a buyer one price for a single item and a lower price for a second or third item can capture some of the consumer surplus. Buy one pizza and get a second one for a lower price is an example of this type of price discrimination.

Increasing Profit and Producer Surplus

By getting buyers to pay a price as close as possible to their maximum willingness to pay, a monopoly captures the consumer surplus and converts it into producer surplus. And more producer surplus means more economic profit.

To see why more producer surplus means more economic profit, recall some definitions. With total revenue *TR* and total cost *TC*,

$$\text{Economic profit} = TR - TC.$$

Producer surplus is total revenue minus the area under the marginal cost curve. But the area under the marginal cost curve is total *variable* cost, *TVC*. So producer surplus equals total revenue minus *TVC*, or

$$\text{Producer surplus} = TR - TVC.$$

You can see that the difference between economic profit and producer surplus is the same as the difference between *TC* and *TVC*. But *TC* minus *TVC* equals total *fixed* cost, *TFC*. So

$$\text{Economic profit} = \text{Producer surplus} - TFC.$$

For a given level of total fixed cost, anything that increases producer surplus also increases economic profit.

Let's now see how price discrimination works by looking at a price-discriminating airline.

A Price-Discriminating Airline

Inter-City Airlines has a monopoly on passenger flights between two cities. Figure 12.8 shows the market demand curve, *D*, for travel on this route. It also shows Inter-City Airlines' marginal revenue curve, *MR*, and marginal cost curve, *MC*. Inter-City's marginal cost is a constant $40 per trip. (It is easier to see how price discrimination works for a firm with constant marginal cost.)

Single-Price Profit Maximization As a single-price monopoly, Inter-City maximizes profit by producing the quantity of trips at which *MR* equals *MC*, which is 8,000 trips a week, and charging $120 a trip. With a marginal cost of $40 a trip, producer surplus is $80 a trip, and Inter-City's producer surplus is $640,000 a week, shown by the area of the blue rectangle. Inter-City's customers enjoy a consumer surplus shown by the area of the green triangle.

FIGURE 12.8 A Single Price of Air Travel

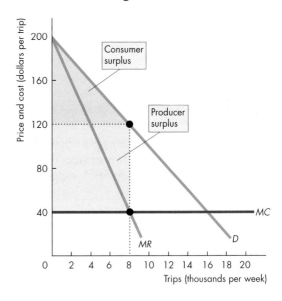

Inter-City Airlines has a monopoly on an air route with a market demand curve D. Inter-City's marginal cost, MC, is $40 per trip. As a single-price monopoly, Inter-City's marginal revenue curve is MR. Profit is maximized by selling 8,000 trips a week at $120 a trip. Producer surplus is $640,000 a week—the blue rectangle—and Inter-City's customers enjoy a consumer surplus—the green triangle.

———— MyLab Economics Animation ————

Discrimination Between Two Types of Travellers

Inter-City surveys its customers and discovers that they are all business travellers. It also surveys people who are *not* its customers and discovers that they are mainly people who travel for leisure. These people travel by bus or car, but would travel by air at a low fare. Inter-City would like to attract some of these travellers and knows that to do so, it must offer a fare below the current $120 a trip. How can it do that?

Inter-City digs more deeply into its survey results and discovers that its current customers always plan their travel less than two weeks before departure. In contrast, the people who travel by bus or car know their travel plans at least two weeks ahead of time.

Inter-City sees that it can use what it has discovered about its current and potential new customers to separate the two types of travellers into two markets: one market for business travel and another for leisure travel.

Figure 12.9 shows Inter-City's two markets. Part (a), the market for business travel, is the same as Fig. 12.8. Part (b) shows the market for leisure travel. No leisure traveller is willing to pay the business fare of $120 a trip, so at that price, the quantity demanded in part (b) is zero. The demand curve D_L is the demand for travel on this route after satisfying the demand of business travellers. Inter-City's marginal cost remains at $40 a trip, so its marginal revenue curve is MR_L. Inter-City maximizes profit by setting the leisure fare at $80 a trip and attracting 4,000 leisure travellers a week. Inter-City's producer surplus increases by $160,000 a week—the area of the blue rectangle in Fig. 12.9(b)—and leisure travellers enjoy a consumer surplus—the area of the green triangle.

Inter-City announces its new fare schedule: no restrictions, $120, and 14-day advance purchase, $80. Inter-City increases its passenger count by 50 percent and increases its producer surplus by $160,000.

FIGURE 12.9   Price Discrimination

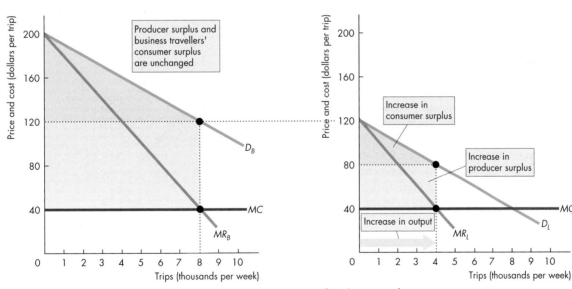

(a) Business travel

(b) Leisure travel

Inter-City separates its market into two types of travel: business travel with no restrictions in part (a) and leisure travel that requires a 14-day advance purchase in part (b). For business travel, the profit-maximizing price is $120 a trip with 8,000 trips a week. For leisure travel, the profit-maximizing price is $80 a trip with 4,000 trips a week.

Inter-City continues to make the same producer surplus on business travel as it did with a single price, and business travellers continue to enjoy the same consumer surplus. But in part (b), Inter-City sells 4,000 trips to leisure travellers, which increases its producer surplus—the blue rectangle—and increases consumer surplus—the green triangle.

Discrimination Among Several Types of Travellers

Pleased with the success of its price discrimination between business and leisure travellers, Inter-City sees that it might be able to profit even more by dividing its customers into a larger number of types. So it does another customer survey, which reveals that some business travellers are willing to pay $160 for a fully refundable, unrestricted ticket while others are willing to pay only $120 for a nonrefundable ticket. So applying the same principles as it used to discriminate between business and leisure travellers, Inter-City now discriminates between business travellers who want a refundable ticket and those who want a nonrefundable ticket.

Another survey of leisure travellers reveals that they fall into two goups: those who are able to plan 14 days ahead and others who can plan 21 days ahead. So Inter-City discriminates between these two groups with two fares: an $80 and a $60 fare.

By offering travellers four different fares, the airline increases its producer surplus and increases its economic profit. But why only four fares? Why not keep looking for even more traveller types and offer even more fares?

Perfect Price Discrimination

Firms try to capture an ever larger part of consumer surplus by devising a host of special conditions, each one of which appeals to a tiny segment of the market but at the same time excludes others from taking advantage of a lower price. The more consumer surplus a firm is able to capture, the closer it gets to the extreme case called **perfect price discrimination**, which occurs if a firm can sell each unit of output for the highest price someone is willing to pay for it. In this extreme (hypothetical) case consumer surplus is eliminated and captured as producer surplus.

With perfect price discrimination, something special happens to marginal revenue—the market demand curve becomes the marginal revenue curve. The reason is that when the monopoly cuts the price to sell a larger quantity, it sells only the marginal unit at the lower price. All the other units continue to be sold for the highest price that each buyer is willing to pay. So for the perfect price discriminator, marginal revenue *equals* price and the market demand curve becomes the monopoly's marginal revenue curve.

With marginal revenue equal to price, Inter-City can obtain even greater producer surplus by increasing output up to the point at which price (and marginal revenue) equals marginal cost.

So Inter-City seeks new travellers who will not pay as much as $60 a trip but who will pay more than $40, its marginal cost. Inter-City offers a variety of vacation specials at different low fares that appeal only to new travellers. Existing customers continue to pay the higher fares and some, with further perks and frills that have no effect on cost, are induced to pay fares going all the way up to $200 a trip.

With all these special conditions and fares, Inter-City increases its output to the quantity demanded at marginal cost, extracts the entire consumer surplus on that quantity, and maximizes economic profit.

Figure 12.10 shows the outcome with perfect price discrimination and compares it with the single-price monopoly outcome. The range of business-class fares extract the entire consumer surplus from this group. The new leisure-class fares going down to $40 a trip attract an additional 8,000 travellers and take the entire consumer surplus of leisure travellers. Inter-City makes the maximum possible economic profit.

FIGURE 12.10 Perfect Price Discrimination

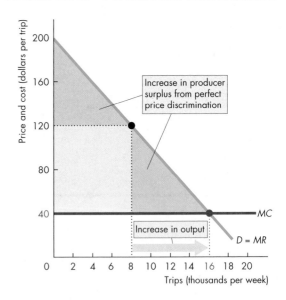

Dozens of fares discriminate among many different types of business travellers, and many new low fares with restrictions appeal to leisure travellers. With perfect price discrimination, the market demand curve becomes Inter-City's marginal revenue curve. Producer surplus is maximized when the lowest fare equals marginal cost. Inter-City sells 16,000 trips and makes the maximum possible economic profit.

Would it bother you to hear how
little I paid for this flight?

From William Hamilton, "Voodoo Economics," © 1992 by
The Chronicle Publishing Company, p. 3.
Reprinted with permission of Chronicle Books.

Efficiency and Rent Seeking with Price Discrimination

With perfect price discrimination, output increases to
the point at which price equals marginal cost. This output is identical to that of perfect competition. Perfect
price discrimination pushes consumer surplus to zero
but increases the monopoly's producer surplus to equal
the total surplus in perfect competition. With perfect
price discrimination, no deadweight loss is created, so
perfect price discrimination achieves efficiency.

> The more perfectly the monopoly can price
> discriminate, the closer its output is to the compet-
> itive output and the more efficient is the outcome.

But the outcomes of perfect competition and
perfect price discrimination differ. First, how total
surplus is distributed is not the same. In perfect
competition, total surplus is shared by consumers
and producers, while with perfect price discrimination, the monopoly takes it all. Second, because the
monopoly takes all the total surplus, rent seeking is
profitable.

People use resources in pursuit of economic rent,
and the bigger the rents, the more resources are used
in pursuing them. With free entry into rent seeking,
the long-run equilibrium outcome is that rent seekers
use up the entire producer surplus.

Real-world airlines are as creative as Inter-City
Airlines, as you can see in the cartoon! Disney Corporation is creative too in extracting consumer surplus,
as *Economics in Action* shows.

We next study some key monopoly policy issues.

ECONOMICS IN ACTION

Attempting Perfect Price Discrimination

If you want to spend a day at Disney World, it will cost
you $107. You can spend a second consecutive day for
an extra $92, a third day for $90, and a fourth day for
$61. Three more days to complete a week cost $20 each
and yet more days, up to 10, cost only $10 a day.

The Disney Corporation hopes that it has read your
willingness to pay correctly and not left you with too
much consumer surplus.

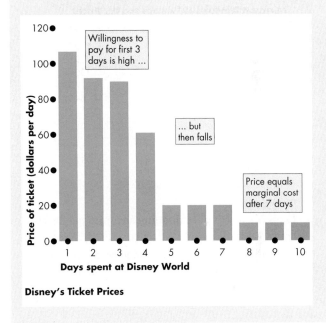

Disney's Ticket Prices

◆ REVIEW QUIZ

1 What is price discrimination and how is it used
to increase a monopoly's profit?

2 Explain how consumer surplus changes when a
monopoly price discriminates.

3 Explain how consumer surplus, economic
profit, and output change when a monopoly
perfectly price discriminates.

4 What are some of the ways that real-world
airlines price discriminate?

Work these questions in Study Plan 12.4 and
get instant feedback.   MyLab Economics

ECONOMICS IN THE NEWS

Microsoft Monopoly

Microsoft Announces Windows 10 Release Date

Microsoft announced that its Windows 10 operating system will be released on July 29, 2015. The operating system is designed to run on a wide range of devices and will be updated.

Source: *Time*, June 1, 2015

SOME DATA

Microsoft Windows 10 Versions and U.S. Prices

Version	Price
Pro from Microsoft	199.99
Home from Microsoft	119.99
OEM from Amazon	136.48
OEM	77.50
Student from Microsoft	64.95

THE QUESTIONS

- Is Microsoft a monopoly?
- Is Microsoft a natural monopoly or a legal monopoly?
- Does Microsoft price discriminate or do the different prices of Windows reflect cost differences?
- Sketch a demand curve for Windows, Microsoft's marginal cost curve, and the distribution of the total surplus between consumers and Microsoft.

THE ANSWERS

- Microsoft controls 92 percent of the market for computer operating systems, and almost 100 percent of the non-Apple market, which makes it an effective monopoly.
- Microsoft is a natural monopoly. It has large fixed costs and almost zero marginal cost, so its long-run average cost curve (*LRAC*) slopes downward and economies of scale are achieved when the *LRAC* curve intersects the demand curve.
- Microsoft sells Windows for a number of different prices to different market segments and the marginal cost of a Windows licence is the same for all market segments, so Microsoft is a price-discriminating monopoly.

- The figure illustrates the demand curve, *D*, and marginal cost curve, *MC*, for Windows licences.
- Using the U.S. prices in the data table, the figure shows how Microsoft converts consumer surplus into producer surplus by price discriminating.
- Because Microsoft also price discriminates among its different national markets, it gains even more producer surplus than the figure illustrates.

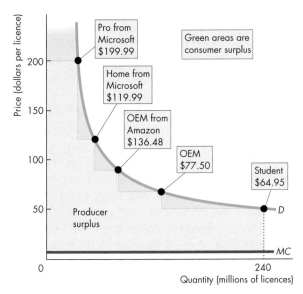

Microsoft Grabs Consumer Surplus

Microsoft has sold 200 million Windows 10 licences at different prices in different national markets.

◆ Monopoly Regulation

Natural monopoly presents a dilemma. With economies of scale, it produces at the lowest possible cost. But with market power, it has an incentive to raise the price above the competitive price and produce too little—to operate in the self-interest of the monopolist and not in the social interest.

Regulation—rules administered by a government agency to influence prices, quantities, entry, and other aspects of economic activity in a firm or industry—is a possible solution to this dilemma.

To implement regulation, the government establishes agencies to oversee and enforce the rules. For example, the Canadian Transportation Agency regulates transport under federal jurisdiction, including rail, air, marine transportation, and some interprovincial commercial motor transport. The National Energy Board regulates international and interprovincial aspects of the oil, gas, and electric utility industries.

Deregulation is the process of removing regulation of prices, quantities, entry, and other aspects of economic activity in a firm or industry. During the past 30 years, deregulation has occurred in many Canadian markets, including domestic rail and air transportation, telephone service, natural gas, and grain transportation. In 2012, wheat handling and marketing were deregulated.

Regulation is a possible solution to the dilemma presented by natural monopoly but not a guaranteed solution. There are two theories about how regulation actually works: the *social interest theory* and the *capture theory*.

The **social interest theory** is that the political and regulatory process relentlessly seeks out inefficiency and introduces regulation that eliminates deadweight loss and allocates resources efficiently.

The **capture theory** is that regulation serves the self-interest of the producer, who captures the regulator and maximizes economic profit. Regulation that benefits the producer but creates a deadweight loss gets adopted because the producer's gain is large and visible while each individual consumer's loss is small and invisible. No individual consumer has an incentive to oppose the regulation, but the producer has a big incentive to lobby for it.

We're going to examine efficient regulation that serves the social interest and see why it is not a simple matter to design and implement such regulation.

Efficient Regulation of a Natural Monopoly

A cable TV company is a *natural monopoly*—it can supply the entire market at a lower price than two or more competing firms can. Shaw Communications provides cable TV to households in Western Canada. The firm has invested heavily in satellite receiving dishes, cables, and control equipment and so has large fixed costs. These fixed costs are part of the firm's average total cost. Its average total cost decreases as the number of households served increases because the fixed cost is spread over a larger number of households.

Unregulated, Shaw produces the quantity that maximizes profit. Like all single-price monopolies, the profit-maximizing quantity is less than the efficient quantity, and underproduction results in a deadweight loss.

How can Shaw be regulated to produce the efficient quantity of cable TV service? The answer is by being regulated to set its price equal to marginal cost, known as the **marginal cost pricing rule**. The quantity demanded at a price equal to marginal cost is the efficient quantity—the quantity at which marginal benefit equals marginal cost.

Figure 12.11 illustrates the marginal cost pricing rule. The demand curve for cable TV is D. Shaw's marginal cost curve is MC. That marginal cost curve is (assumed to be) horizontal at $10 per household per month—that is, the cost of providing each additional household with a month of cable programming is $10. The efficient outcome occurs if the price is regulated at $10 per household per month with 10 million households served.

But there is a problem: At the efficient output, average total cost exceeds marginal cost, so a firm that uses marginal cost pricing incurs an economic loss. A cable TV company that is required to use a marginal cost pricing rule will not stay in business for long. How can the firm cover its costs and, at the same time, obey a marginal cost pricing rule?

There are two possible ways of enabling the firm to cover its costs: price discrimination and a two-part price (called a *two-part tariff*).

For example, local telephone companies offer plans at a fixed monthly price that give access to the cellphone network and unlimited free calls. The price of a call (zero) equals the marginal cost of a call. Similarly, a cable TV operator can charge a one-time connection fee that covers its fixed cost and then charge a monthly fee equal to marginal cost.

FIGURE 12.11   Regulating a Natural Monopoly

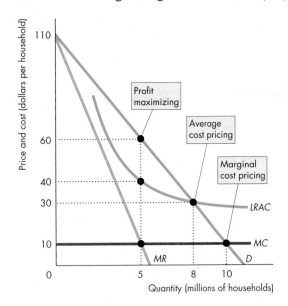

A natural monopoly cable TV supplier faces the demand curve *D*. The firm's marginal cost is constant at $10 per household per month, as shown by the curve labelled *MC*. The long-run average cost curve is *LRAC*.

Unregulated, as a profit-maximizer, the firm serves 5 million households at a price of $60 a month. An efficient marginal cost pricing rule sets the price at $10 a month. The monopoly serves 10 million households and incurs an economic loss. A second-best average cost pricing rule sets the price at $30 a month. The monopoly serves 8 million households and earns zero economic profit.

—————— MyLab Economics Animation ——————

Second-Best Regulation of a Natural Monopoly

A natural monopoly cannot always be regulated to achieve an efficient outcome. There are two possible ways of enabling a regulated monopoly to avoid an economic loss:

- Average cost pricing
- Government subsidy

Average Cost Pricing The **average cost pricing rule** sets price equal to average total cost. With this rule the firm produces the quantity at which the average

total cost curve cuts the demand curve. This rule results in the firm making zero economic profit—breaking even. But because for a natural monopoly average total cost exceeds marginal cost, the quantity produced is less than the efficient quantity and a deadweight loss arises.

Figure 12.11 illustrates the average cost pricing rule. The price is $30 a month and 8 million households get cable TV.

Government Subsidy A government subsidy is a direct payment to the firm equal to its economic loss. To pay a subsidy, the government must raise the revenue by taxing some other activity. You saw in Chapter 6 that taxes themselves generate deadweight loss.

And the Second-Best Is ... Which is the better option, average cost pricing or marginal cost pricing with a government subsidy? The answer depends on the relative magnitudes of the two deadweight losses. Average cost pricing generates a deadweight loss in the market served by the natural monopoly. A subsidy generates deadweight losses in the markets for the items that are taxed to pay for the subsidy. The smaller deadweight loss is the second-best solution to regulating a natural monopoly. Making this calculation in practice is too difficult, so average cost pricing is generally preferred to a subsidy.

Implementing average cost pricing presents the regulator with a challenge because it is not possible to be sure what a firm's costs are. So regulators use one of two practical rules:

- Rate of return regulation
- Price cap regulation

Rate of Return Regulation Under **rate of return regulation**, a firm must justify its price by showing that its return on capital doesn't exceed a specified target rate. This type of regulation can end up serving the self-interest of the firm rather than the social interest. The firm's managers have an incentive to inflate costs by spending on items such as private jets, free hockey tickets (disguised as public relations expenses), and lavish entertainment. Managers also have an incentive to use more capital than the efficient amount. The rate of return on capital is regulated but not the total return on capital, and the greater the amount of capital, the greater is the total return.

Price Cap Regulation For the reason that we've just examined, rate of return regulation is increasingly being replaced by price cap regulation. A **price cap regulation** is a price ceiling—a rule that specifies the highest price the firm is permitted to set. This type of regulation gives a firm an incentive to operate efficiently and keep costs under control. Price cap regulation has become common for the electricity and telecommunications industries and is replacing rate of return regulation.

To see how a price cap works, let's suppose that the cable TV operator is subject to this type of regulation. Figure 12.12 shows that without regulation, the firm maximizes profit by serving 5 million households and charging a price of $60 a month. If a price cap is set at $30 a month, the firm is permitted to sell

any quantity it chooses at that price or at a lower price. At 5 million households, the firm now incurs an economic loss. It can decrease the loss by increasing its output to 8 million households. But to increase output further, the firm would have to lower the price and again it would incur a loss. So the profit-maximizing quantity is 8 million households—the same as with average cost pricing.

Notice that a price cap lowers the price and increases output. This outcome is in sharp contrast to the effect of a price ceiling in a competitive market that you studied in Chapter 6 (pp. 132–134). The reason is that in a monopoly, the unregulated equilibrium output is *less* than the competitive equilibrium output, and the price cap regulation replicates the conditions of a competitive market.

In Fig. 12.12, the price cap delivers average cost pricing. In practice, the regulator might set the cap too high. For this reason, price cap regulation is often combined with *earnings sharing regulation*—a regulation that requires firms to make refunds to customers when profits rise above a target level.

FIGURE 12.12 Price Cap Regulation

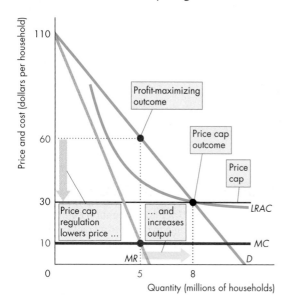

A natural monopoly cable TV supplier faces the demand curve *D*. The firm's marginal cost is constant at $10 per household per month, as shown by the curve labelled *MC*. The long-run average cost curve is *LRAC*.

Unregulated, the firm serves 5 million households at a price of $60 a month. A price cap sets the maximum price at $30 a month. The firm has an incentive to minimize cost and serve the quantity of households that demand service at the price cap. The price cap regulation lowers the price and increases the quantity.

———— MyLab Economics Animation ————

REVIEW QUIZ

1 What is the pricing rule that achieves an efficient outcome for a regulated monopoly? What is the problem with this rule?

2 What is the average cost pricing rule? Why is it not an efficient way of regulating monopoly?

3 What is a price cap? Why might it be a more effective way of regulating monopoly than rate of return regulation?

4 Compare the consumer surplus, producer surplus, and deadweight loss that arise from average cost pricing with those that arise from profit-maximization pricing and marginal cost pricing.

Work these questions in Study Plan 12.5 and get instant feedback.   MyLab Economics

◆ You've now completed your study of monopoly. *Economics in the News* on pp. 298–299 looks at Google's dominant position in the market for Internet search advertising.

In the next chapter, we study markets that lie between the extremes of perfect competition and monopoly and that blend elements of the two.

Is Google Misusing Monopoly Power?

E.U. Slaps Google with New Competition Complaints

The Financial Times

July 14, 2016

Google's regulatory woes in Europe deepened on Thursday as Brussels served the U.S. tech group with a fresh antitrust complaint and separate new evidence attempting to hone its first competition case.

Margrethe Vestager, the E.U.'s competition commissioner, issued two separate "statements of objections" against the company for misusing its market clout in online advertising and shopping, writes Alex Barker in Brussels.

"Google has come up with many innovative products that have made a difference to our lives. But that doesn't give Google the right to deny other companies the chance to compete and innovate," said Ms Vestager.

The advertising charges—covering Google businesses such as AdWords—stem from a longstanding Commission investigation into concerns about Google's contracts with websites to which it delivers search ads.

Brussels also acted on worries that Google restricts advertisers from moving their search advertising campaigns from AdWords to the platforms of competitors. ...

A spokesperson for Google said: "We believe that our innovations and product improvements have increased choice for European consumers and promote competition. We'll examine the Commission's renewed cases and provide a detailed response in the coming weeks."

Ms Vestager repeated the commission's long-standing accusation that Google abuses its market position by placing its own products higher in search results, in areas such as online shopping. "We see it happen very, very, very often," said Ms Vestager. "This is where we have the strongest evidence."

Alex Barker and Robert Cookson, Published July 14, 2016, *Financial Times*

ESSENCE OF THE STORY

- The European Union's competition commissioner says Google misuses its market power in online advertising and shopping.

- One claim is that Google restricts advertisers from moving their search advertising campaigns from Google AdWords to the platforms of competitors.

- Another claim is that Google abuses its market position by placing its own online shopping products higher in search results.

- Google says its innovations and product improvements increase choice and promote competition.

ECONOMIC ANALYSIS

- Google gets its revenue by selling advertisements associated with search keywords.

- Google sells keywords based on a combination of willingness to pay and the number of clicks an advertisement receives, with bids starting at 5 cents per click.

- Google has steadily improved its search engine and refined and simplified its interface with both searchers and advertisers to make searches more powerful and advertising more effective.

- Figure 1 shows Google's extraordinary success in terms of its revenue, cost, and profit.

- Google could have provided a basic search engine with none of the features of today's Google.

- If Google had followed this strategy, people seeking information would have used other search engines and advertisers would have been willing to pay lower prices for Google ads.

- Google would have faced the market described in Fig. 2 and earned a small economic profit.

- Instead, Google improved its search engine and the effectiveness of advertising. The demand for Google ads increased.

- By selling keywords to the highest bidder, Google is able to achieve perfect price discrimination.

- Figure 3 shows the consequences of Google's successful strategy. With perfect price discrimination, Google's producer surplus is maximized. Google produces the efficient quantity of search and advertising by accepting ads at prices that exceed or equal marginal cost.

- Google does not appear to be acting against the social interest.

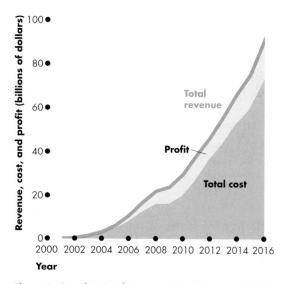

Figure 1 Google's Total Revenue, Total Cost, and Profit

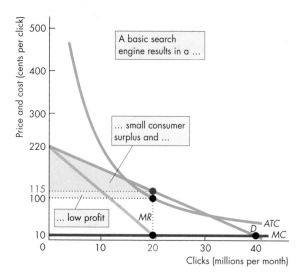

Figure 2 Basic Search Engine

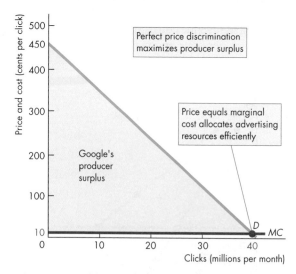

Figure 3 Google with AdWords and Other Features

WORKED PROBLEM

MyLab Economics Work this problem in Chapter 12 Study Plan.

Tanya's Tattoos is a local monopoly. Columns 1 and 2 of the table set out the market demand schedule and columns 2 and 3 set out the total cost schedule.

Price (dollars per tattoo)	Quantity (tattoos per hour)	Total cost (dollars per hour)
60	0	30
50	1	50
40	2	70
30	3	90
20	4	110

Questions

1. If Tanya's Tattoos is a single-price monopoly, what is Tanya's profit-maximizing quantity? What price does Tanya's charge? What are its economic profit and producer surplus?
2. If Tanya's Tattoos can perfectly price discriminate, what is its profit-maximizing quantity? What are its economic profit and producer surplus?

Solutions

1. The profit-maximizing quantity is that at which marginal cost equals marginal revenue. Marginal cost—the increase in total cost when output increases by one unit—is $20 at all output levels. Marginal revenue—the change in total revenue when output increases by one unit—is calculated in the table at the top of the next column.

   Marginal revenue equals marginal cost of $20 at 2 tattoos per hour (midway between $30 and

Demand schedule		Total revenue (dollars per hour)	Marginal revenue (dollars per tattoo)
Price (dollars per tattoo)	Quantity (tattoos per hour)		
60	0	0	
			 50
50	1	50	
			 30
40	2	80	
			 10
30	3	90	
			.... −10
20	4	80	

   $10). So this quantity maximizes profit. The highest price of a tattoo at which 2 tattoos per hour can be sold is $40, so total revenue is $80. Total cost is $70, so economic profit is $10. TFC (TC at zero output) = $30, so TVC = $40 and producer surplus = $TR - TVC$ = $40.

   Key Point: Profit is maximized when marginal cost equals marginal revenue.

2. If Tanya can perfectly price discriminate, she produces 4 tattoos per hour and sells one for $50, one for $40, one for $30, and one for $20. Total revenue is $140 per hour. Total cost is $110 per hour, so economic profit is $30 per hour. Producer surplus = $TR - TVC$, which is $140 − $80 = $60 per hour.

   Key Point: With perfect price discrimination, a firm charges the highest price that each buyer is willing to pay and increases production to the quantity at which the lowest price equals marginal cost.

Key Figure

MyLab Economics Interactive Animation

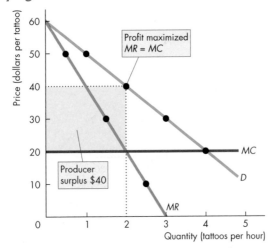

(a) Single-price monopoly

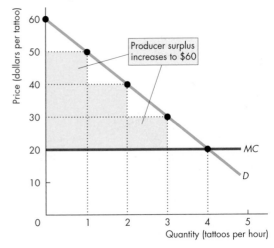

(b) Price-discriminating monopoly

SUMMARY

Key Points

Monopoly and How It Arises (pp. 280–281)

- A monopoly is a market with a single supplier of a good or service that has no close substitutes and in which barriers to entry prevent competition.
- Barriers to entry may be legal (public franchise, licence, patent, or copyright), ownership (one firm controls a resource), or natural (created by economies of scale).
- A monopoly might be able to price discriminate when there is no resale possibility.
- Where resale is possible, a firm charges one price.

Working Problem 1 will give you a better understanding of monopoly and how it arises.

A Single-Price Monopoly's Output and Price Decision (pp. 282–285)

- A monopoly's demand curve is the market demand curve and a single-price monopoly's marginal revenue is less than price.
- A monopoly maximizes profit by producing the output at which marginal revenue equals marginal cost and by charging the maximum price that consumers are willing to pay for that output.

Working Problems 2 to 4 will give you a better understanding of a single-price monopoly's output and price decision.

Single-Price Monopoly and Competition Compared (pp. 286–289)

- A single-price monopoly charges a higher price and produces a smaller quantity than a perfectly competitive market.
- A single-price monopoly restricts output and creates a deadweight loss.

- The total loss that arises from monopoly equals the deadweight loss plus the cost of the resources devoted to rent seeking.

Working Problem 5 will give you a better understanding of the comparison of single-price monopoly and perfect competition.

Price Discrimination (pp. 289–294)

- Price discrimination converts consumer surplus into economic profit.
- Perfect price discrimination extracts the entire consumer surplus; each unit is sold for the maximum price that each consumer is willing to pay; the quantity produced is the efficient quantity.
- Rent seeking with perfect price discrimination might eliminate the entire consumer surplus and producer surplus.

Working Problem 6 will give you a better understanding of price discrimination.

Monopoly Regulation (pp. 295–297)

- Monopoly regulation might serve the social interest or the interest of the monopoly (the monopoly captures the regulator).
- Price equal to marginal cost achieves efficiency but results in economic loss.
- Price equal to average cost enables the firm to cover its cost but is inefficient.
- Rate of return regulation creates incentives for inefficient production and inflated cost.
- Price cap regulation with earnings sharing regulation can achieve a more efficient outcome than rate of return regulation.

Working Problems 7 to 9 will give you a better understanding of monopoly regulation.

Key Terms

MyLab Economics Key Terms Quiz

Average cost pricing rule, 296
Barrier to entry, 280
Capture theory, 295
Deregulation, 295
Economic rent, 288
Legal monopoly, 280

Marginal cost pricing rule, 295
Monopoly, 280
Natural monopoly, 280
Perfect price discrimination, 292
Price cap regulation, 297
Price discrimination, 281

Rate of return regulation, 296
Regulation, 295
Rent seeking, 288
Single-price monopoly, 281
Social interest theory, 295

STUDY PLAN PROBLEMS AND APPLICATIONS

MyLab Economics Work problems 1 to 9 in Chapter 12 Study Plan and get instant feedback.

Monopoly and How It Arises (Study Plan 12.1)

1. Canada Post has a monopoly on residential mail delivery. Pfizer Inc. makes Lipitor, a prescription drug that lowers cholesterol. Rogers Communications is the sole provider of cable television service in some parts of Ontario.

   Are any of these firms protected by a barrier to entry? Do any of these firms produce a good or service that has a substitute? Might any of them be able to profit from price discrimination? Explain your answers.

A Single-Price Monopoly's Output and Price Decision (Study Plan 12.2)

Use the following table to work Problems 2 to 4.
Minnie's Mineral Springs is a single-price monopoly. Columns 1 and 2 of the table set out the market demand schedule for Minnie's water, and columns 2 and 3 set out Minnie's total cost schedule.

Price (dollars per bottle)	Quantity (bottles per hour)	Total cost (dollars per hour)
10	0	1
8	1	3
6	2	7
4	3	13
2	4	21
0	5	31

2. Calculate Minnie's marginal revenue schedule and draw a graph of the market demand curve and Minnie's marginal revenue curve.
   Explain why Minnie's marginal revenue is less than the price.

3. At what price is Minnie's total revenue maximized and over what price range is the demand for water elastic? Why will Minnie not produce a quantity at which the market demand is inelastic?

4. Calculate Minnie's profit-maximizing output and price and economic profit.

Single-Price Monopoly and Competition Compared (Study Plan 12.3)

5. Use the data in Problem 2 to work this problem.
   a. Use a graph to illustrate the producer surplus generated from Minnie's Mineral Springs' water production and consumption.

   b. Is Minnie's an efficient producer of water? Explain your answer.

   c. Suppose that new wells were discovered nearby to Minnie's and Minnie's faced competition from new producers. Explain what would happen to Minnie's output, price, and profit.

Price Discrimination (Study Plan 12.4)

6. La Bella Pizza can produce a pizza for a marginal cost of $2. Its price of a pizza is $15.
   a. Could La Bella Pizza make a larger economic profit by offering a second pizza for $5? Use a graph to illustrate your answer.
   b. How might La Bella Pizza make even more economic profit? Would it then be more efficient than when it charged $15 for each pizza?

Monopoly Regulation (Study Plan 12.5)

Use the following figure to work Problems 7 to 9.
Calypso, a natural gas distributor, is a natural monopoly that cannot price discriminate. The figure shows Calypso's costs and the market demand for natural gas.

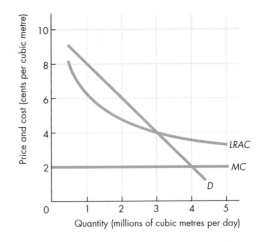

What quantity will Calypso produce, what price will it charge, and what will be the total surplus and deadweight loss if Calypso is:

7. An unregulated profit-maximizing firm?

8. Regulated to make zero economic profit?

9. Regulated to be efficient?

ADDITIONAL PROBLEMS AND APPLICATIONS

MyLab Economics You can work these problems in Homework or Test if assigned by your instructor.

Monopoly and How It Arises

Use the following list, which gives some information about seven firms, to answer Problems 10 and 11.

- Coca-Cola cuts its price below that of Pepsi in an attempt to increase its market share.
- A single firm, protected by a barrier to entry, produces a personal service that has no close substitutes.
- A barrier to entry exists, but the good has some close substitutes.
- A firm offers discounts to students and seniors.
- A firm can sell any quantity it chooses at the going price.
- The government issues Nike an exclusive licence to produce golf balls.
- A firm experiences economies of scale even when it produces the quantity that meets the entire market demand.

10. In which of the seven cases might monopoly arise?

11. Which of the seven cases are natural monopolies and which are legal monopolies? Which can price discriminate, which cannot, and why?

A Single-Price Monopoly's Output and Price Decision

Use the following information to work Problems 12 to 16.

Hot Air Balloon Rides is a single-price monopoly. Columns 1 and 2 of the table set out the market demand schedule, and columns 2 and 3 set out the total cost schedule:

Price (dollars per ride)	Quantity (rides per month)	Total cost (dollars per month)
220	0	80
200	1	160
180	2	260
160	3	380
140	4	520
120	5	680

12. Construct Hot Air's total revenue and marginal revenue schedules.

13. Draw a graph of the market demand curve and Hot Air's marginal revenue curve.

14. Find Hot Air's profit-maximizing output and price and calculate the firm's economic profit.

15. If the government imposes a tax on Hot Air's profit, how do its output and price change?

16. If instead of taxing Hot Air's profit, the government imposes a sales tax on balloon rides of $30 a ride, what are the new profit-maximizing quantity, price, and economic profit?

17. The figure illustrates the situation facing the publisher of the only newspaper containing local news in an isolated community.

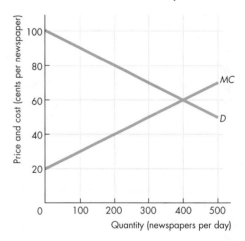

a. On the graph, mark the profit-maximizing quantity and price and the publisher's total revenue per day.

b. At the price charged, is the demand for this newspaper elastic or inelastic? Why?

Single-Price Monopoly and Competition Compared

18. Show on the graph in Problem 17 the consumer surplus from newspapers and the deadweight loss created by the monopoly. Explain why this market might encourage rent seeking.

19. If the newspaper market in Problem 17 were perfectly competitive, what would be the quantity, price, consumer surplus, and producer surplus? Mark each on the graph.

20. **U.S. Supreme Court Rules for Samsung in Smartphone Patent Dispute**

    In a decision over Samsung's use of iPhone design elements, the Supreme Court gave Samsung a chance to recover some of the nearly $400 million it had previously been ordered to pay Apple.

    Source: *The Financial Times*, December 6, 2016

a. If Samsung and other smartphone producers had been prevented from entering the market by Apple patents, leaving Apple with a monopoly in the smartphone market, who would benefit and who would lose?

b. Compared to a smartphone monopoly, who would benefit and who would lose if hundreds of firms entered the smartphone market, each producing an identical smartphone, making the market perfectly competitive?

c. Explain which market would be efficient: a perfectly competitive one or a monopoly.

Price Discrimination

21. **Amazon Kills Unlimited Online Storage Plans**

    Amazon launched unlimited data storage for $59.99 per year in 2015. In 2017, it replaced its unlimited deal with a tiered pricing system. Now Amazon offers 100 gigabytes of storage for $11.99 yearly and larger storage at $59.99 yearly per terabyte.

    Source: theverge.com, June 8, 2017

    a. Explain why Amazon's new data plans might be price discrimination.

    b. Draw a graph to illustrate the original plan and the new plans.

Monopoly Regulation

22. **Is It Time to Break Up Google?**

    Google has an 80 percent market share in search advertising. It is a monopoly. In the early 20th century, Supreme Court Justice Louis Brandeis said, "in a democratic society the existence of large centers of private power is dangerous to the continuing vitality of a free people." He believed that unless it is a natural monopoly it should be broken up.

    Source: *The New York Times*, April 22, 2017

    a. How would we test whether Google is a monopoly in the Internet advertising market?

    b. Explain why the Internet advertising market might be a natural monopoly.

    c. How does Google's dominant position as a provider of Internet advertising influence the price and quantity in this market?

    d. How would breaking Google into two providers of Internet advertising influence the price and quantity in this market?

Economics in the News

23. After you have studied *Economics in the News* on pp. 298–299, answer the following questions.

    a. Why do the European regulators say that Google is misusing its monopoly power? Do you agree? Explain why or why not.

    b. Explain why it would be inefficient to regulate Google to make it charge the same price per keyword click to all advertisers.

    c. Explain why selling keywords to the highest bidder can lead to an efficient allocation of advertising resources.

24. **FCC Helps AT&T and Verizon Charge More by Ending Broadband Price Caps**

    The U.S. Federal Communications Commission has eliminated price caps on broadband service in a county if 50 percent of potential customers live within a half mile of a location served by a competitive provider or if 75 percent of a county's census blocks have a cable provider. Effectively, the FCC says a local market is competitive even when there is only one broadband provider.

    Source: *Wired*, April 20, 2017

    a. What barriers to entry exist in the broadband Internet service market?

    b. How can a price cap on broadband service achieve a more efficient outcome?

    c. Draw a graph to illustrate the effects of eliminating a price cap in the broadband Internet service market on the price, quantity, total surplus, and deadweight loss.

25. **Intel and Samsung Gang Up on Qualcomm, Backing FTC Monopoly Suit**

    The U.S. Federal Trade Commission says Qualcomm is trying to corner the market for chips used in smartphones.

    Qualcomm has a set of patents that Intel says prevent it from competing in the smartphone chips market.

    Samsung claims its in-house chip unit is artificially held back by Qualcomm's unwillingness to licence its technology.

    Source: *Bloomberg*, May 12, 2017

    a. What are the barriers to entry in the smartphone chip market?

    b. Show in a graph how the price and the quantity of smartphone chips are determined.

13 MONOPOLISTIC COMPETITION

After studying this chapter, you will be able to:

◆ Define and identify monopolistic competition and other market structures

◆ Explain how a firm in monopolistic competition determines its price and output in the short run and the long run

◆ Explain why advertising costs are high and why firms in monopolistic competition use brand names

You know that you have a lot of choice when you shop for a new smartphone. But did you know that more than 100 firms produce close to 9,000 different phones to choose among? Smartphone producers compete, but each has a monopoly on its own special kind of phone—the market is an example of monopolistic competition.

The model of monopolistic competition helps us to understand the competition that we see every day. And in *Economics in the News*, at the end of the chapter, we apply the model to the market for smartphones.

◆ Monopolistic Competition and Other Market Structures

You have studied perfect competition and monopoly and now know how these markets work. While the perfect competition and monopoly models enable us to understand many real-world markets, they don't work for all. The markets you are now going to learn about are competitive but not perfectly competitive, and the firms in these markets have some power to set their prices, as monopolies do. We call this type of market *monopolistic competition*

What Is Monopolistic Competition?

Monopolistic competition is a market structure in which:

- A large number of firms compete.
- Each firm produces a differentiated product.
- Firms compete on product quality, price, and marketing.
- Firms are free to enter and exit the industry.

Large Number of Firms In monopolistic competition, as in perfect competition, the industry consists of a large number of firms. The presence of a large number of firms has three implications for the firms in the industry.

Small Market Share In monopolistic competition, each firm supplies a small part of the total industry output. Consequently, each firm has only limited power to influence the price of its product. Each firm's price can deviate from the average price of other firms by only a relatively small amount.

Ignore Other Firms A firm in monopolistic competition must be sensitive to the average market price of the product, but the firm does not pay attention to any one individual competitor. All the firms are relatively small, so no one firm can dictate market conditions and the actions of no one firm directly affect the actions of the other firms.

Collusion Impossible Firms in monopolistic competition would like to be able to conspire to fix a higher price—called *collusion*. But because the number of firms in monopolistic competition is large, coordination is difficult and collusion is not possible.

Product Differentiation A firm practises **product differentiation** if it makes a product that is slightly different from the products of competing firms. A differentiated product is one that is a close substitute but not a perfect substitute for the products of the other firms. Some people are willing to pay more for one variety of the product, so when its price rises, the quantity demanded of that variety decreases, but it does not (necessarily) decrease to zero.

For example, Adidas, Asics, Brooks, Fila, New Balance, Nike, Puma, Reebok, and others all make differentiated running shoes. If the price of Adidas running shoes rises and the prices of the other shoes remain constant, Adidas sells fewer shoes and the other producers sell more. But Adidas shoes don't disappear unless the price rises by a large enough amount.

Competing on Quality, Price, and Marketing Product differentiation enables a firm to compete with other firms in three areas: product quality, price, and marketing.

Quality The quality of a product is the physical attributes that make it different from the products of other firms. Quality includes design, reliability, the service provided to the buyer, and the buyer's ease of access to the product. Quality lies on a spectrum that runs from high to low. Some firms offer high-quality products. They are well designed and reliable, and the customer receives quick and efficient service. Other firms offer a lower-quality product that is poorly designed, that might not work perfectly, and that is not supported by effective customer service.

Price Because of product differentiation, a firm in monopolistic competition faces a downward-sloping demand curve. So, like a monopoly, the firm can set both its price and its output. But there is a tradeoff between the product's quality and price. A firm that makes a high-quality product can charge a higher price than a firm that makes a low-quality product.

Marketing Because of product differentiation, a firm in monopolistic competition must market its product. Marketing takes two main forms: advertising and packaging. A firm that produces a high-quality product wants to sell it for a suitably high price. To be able to do so, it must advertise and package its product in a way that convinces buyers that they are getting the higher quality for which they are paying a higher price. For example, pharmaceutical companies advertise and package their brand-name drugs to persuade buyers that these items are superior to the lower-priced generic alternatives. Similarly, a low-quality producer uses advertising and packaging to persuade buyers that although the quality is low, the low price more than compensates for this fact.

Entry and Exit Monopolistic competition has no barriers to prevent new firms from entering the industry in the long run. Consequently, a firm in monopolistic competition cannot make an economic profit in the long run. When existing firms make an economic profit, new firms enter the industry. This entry lowers prices and eventually eliminates economic profit. When firms incur economic losses, some firms leave the industry in the long run. This exit increases prices and eventually eliminates the economic loss.

In long-run equilibrium, firms neither enter nor leave the industry and the firms in the industry make zero economic profit.

Identifying Monopolistic Competition

We've defined monopolistic competition and described its features. But how do we recognize it in real-world markets? What is a large enough number of firms and how free must entry be for a market to be competitive?

Many factors must be taken into account to determine which market structure describes a particular real-world market. But the key factors are the number of firms in a market and the share of the market served by the largest firms. To determine whether a market is sufficiently competitive to be classified as monopolistic competition, economists use indexes called measures of concentration. Let's look at two of these measures.

Measures of Concentration

The two main measures of market concentration are:

- The four-firm concentration ratio
- The Herfindahl-Hirschman Index

The Four-Firm Concentration Ratio The **four-firm concentration ratio** is the percentage of the total revenue accounted for by the four largest firms in an industry. This concentration ratio ranges from almost zero for perfect competition to 100 percent for monopoly. This ratio is the main measure used to assess market structure.

A low concentration ratio indicates a high degree of competition, and a high concentration ratio indicates an absence of competition. A monopoly has a concentration ratio of 100 percent—the largest (and only) firm has 100 percent of the total revenue. A four-firm concentration ratio that exceeds 60 percent is regarded as an indication of a market that is highly concentrated and dominated by a few firms. A ratio

of less than 60 percent is regarded as an indication of a competitive market.

Table 13.1 shows the calculation of a four-firm concentration ratio. In this example, the market has 14 firms. The largest four have 80 percent of the total revenue, so the four-firm concentration ratio is 80 percent, which indicates an absence of competition.

The Herfindahl-Hirschman Index The **Herfindahl-Hirschman Index (HHI)** is the square of the percentage market share of each firm summed over the largest 50 firms (or summed over all the firms if there are fewer than 50) in a market.

For example, if there are 4 firms in a market and the market shares of the firms are 50 percent, 25 percent, 15 percent, and 10 percent, the Herfindahl-Hirschman Index is:

$$HHI = 50^2 + 25^2 + 15^2 + 10^2 = 3,450$$

In perfect competition, the HHI is small. For example, if each of the largest 50 firms in an industry has a market share of 0.1 percent, then the HHI is $0.1^2 \times 50$, which equals 0.5. For a monopoly, the HHI is 10,000. There is only one firm and it has 100 percent of the market: $100^2 = 10,000$.

The HHI can be used to identify monopolistic competition. A market in which the HHI is between 1,500 and 2,500 is regarded as being competitive. These markets are considered to be examples of monopolistic competition. But a market in which the HHI exceeds 2,500 is regarded as being concentrated and uncompetitive.

TABLE 13.1 Calculating a Four-Firm Concentration Ratio

Firm	Total Revenue (millions of dollars)
Top, Inc.	200
ABC, Inc.	250
Big, Inc.	150
XYZ, Inc.	100
Largest 4 firms	700
Other 10 firms	175
Industry	875

Four-firm concentration ratio = 700 ÷ 875 × 100 = 80%

A market with a high concentration ratio and high HHI is called an *oligopoly*. You will learn how an oligopoly works in the next chapter.

Table 13.2 summarizes the characteristics of the four market structures, along with the measures of concentration and some examples of each.

Limitations of a Concentration Measure

The three main limitations of using only concentration measures as determinants of market structure are their failure to take proper account of:

The four market structures: perfect competition, monopolistic competition, oligopoly, and monopoly.

- The geographical scope of the market
- Barriers to entry and firm turnover
- Market and industry correspondence

Geographical Scope of the Market Concentration measures take a national view of the market. Many goods are sold in a *national* market, but some are sold in a *regional* or in a *global* market. The concentration measures for newspapers are low, indicating competition, but in most cities the newspaper industry is highly concentrated. The concentration measures for automobiles are high, indicating little competition, but the three biggest North American car makers compete with foreign car makers in a highly competitive global market.

Barriers to Entry and Firm Turnover Some markets are highly concentrated, but entry is easy and the turnover of firms is large. For example, small towns have few cafes, but no restrictions hinder a new cafe from opening and many attempt to do so.

Also, a market with a few firms might be competitive because of *potential entry*. The firms face competition from the many potential firms that will enter the market if economic profit opportunities arise.

Market and Industry Correspondence To calculate concentration ratios, Statistics Canada classifies each firm as being in a particular industry. But markets do not always correspond closely to industries for two main reasons.

TABLE 13.2 Market Structure

Characteristics	Perfect competition	Monopolistic competition	Oligopoly	Monopoly
Number of firms in industry	Many	Many	Few	One
Product	Identical	Differentiated	Either identical or differentiated	No close substitutes
Barriers to entry	None	None	Moderate	High
Firm's control over price	None	Some	Considerable	Considerable or regulated
Concentration ratio	0	Low	High	100
HHI (approx. ranges)	Close to 0	Less than 2,500	More than 2,500	10,000
Examples	Wheat, honey	Pizza, clothing	Airplanes	Cable TV

ECONOMICS IN ACTION

Monopolistic Competition Today

These 10 industries operate in monopolistic competition. The number of firms in the industry is shown in parentheses after the name of the industry. The red bars show the percentage of industry revenue of the 4 largest firms. The blue bars show the percentage of industry revenue by the next 4 largest firms, and the orange bars show the percentage of industry revenue by the next 12 largest firms. So the entire length of the combined red, blue, and orange bars shows the percentage of industry revenue of the 20 largest firms. The Herfindahl-Hirschman Index is shown on the right.

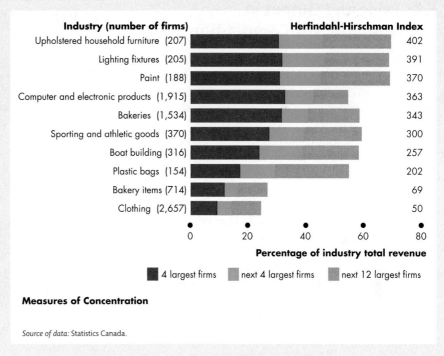

Measures of Concentration

Source of data: Statistics Canada.

First, markets are often narrower than industries. For example, the pharmaceutical industry, which has a low concentration ratio, operates in many separate markets for individual products—for example, measles vaccine and cancer drugs. These drugs do not compete with each other, so this industry, which looks competitive, includes firms that are monopolies (or near monopolies) in individual drug markets.

Second, most firms make several products. For example, Westinghouse makes electrical equipment and, among other things, gas-fired incinerators and plywood. So this one firm operates in at least three separate markets, but Statistics Canada classifies Westinghouse as being in the electrical goods and equipment industry. The fact that Westinghouse competes with other producers of plywood does not show up in the concentration numbers for the plywood market.

Despite their limitations, concentration measures do provide a basis for determining the degree of competition in a market when they are combined with information about the geographical scope of the market, barriers to entry, and the extent to which large, multiproduct firms straddle a variety of markets.

REVIEW QUIZ

1 What are the features of monopolistic competition?
2 How do firms in monopolistic competition compete?
3 How do we identify monopolistic competition?
4 What are the two measures of concentration? Explain how each measure is calculated.
5 Under what conditions do the measures of concentration give a good indication of the degree of competition in a market?
6 Provide some examples of industries near your school that operate in monopolistic competition (excluding those in the figure above).

Work these questions in Study Plan 13.1 and get instant feedback.   MyLab Economics

You now know what monopolistic competition is and how to identify it in real-world markets. Your next task is to see how prices and quantities are determined in monopolistic competition.

◆ Price and Output in Monopolistic Competition

Suppose you've been hired by Michael Budman and Don Green, the co-founders of Roots Canada Ltd., to manage the production and marketing of Roots jackets. Think about the decisions that you must make at Roots. First, you must decide on the design and quality of jackets and on your marketing program. Second, you must decide on the quantity of jackets to produce and the price at which to sell them.

We'll suppose that Roots has already made its decisions about design, quality, and marketing, and now we'll concentrate on its output and pricing decisions. We'll study quality and marketing decisions in the next section.

For a given quality of jackets and marketing activity, Roots faces given costs and market conditions. Given its costs and the demand for its jackets, how does Roots decide the quantity of jackets to produce and the price at which to sell them?

The Firm's Short-Run Output and Price Decision

In the short run, a firm in monopolistic competition makes its output and price decision just like a monopoly firm does. Figure 13.1 illustrates this decision for Roots jackets.

The demand curve for Roots jackets is *D*. This demand curve tells us the quantity of Roots jackets demanded at each price, given the prices of other jackets. It is not the demand curve for jackets in general.

The *MR* curve shows the marginal revenue curve associated with the demand curve for Roots jackets. It is derived in the same way as the marginal revenue curve of a single-price monopoly that you studied in Chapter 12.

The *ATC* curve and the *MC* curve show the average total cost and the marginal cost of producing Roots jackets.

Roots' goal is to maximize its economic profit. To do so, it produces the output at which marginal revenue equals marginal cost. In Fig. 13.1, this output is 125 jackets a day. Roots charges the price that buyers are willing to pay for this quantity, which is determined by the demand curve. This price is $75 per jacket. When Roots produces 125 jackets a day, its average total cost is $25 per jacket and it makes an economic profit of $6,250 a day ($50 per jacket

FIGURE 13.1 Economic Profit in the Short Run

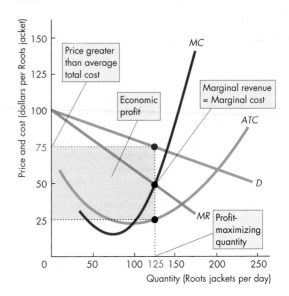

Roots maximizes profit by producing the quantity at which marginal revenue equals marginal cost, 125 jackets a day, and charging the price of $75 a jacket. This price exceeds the average total cost of $25 a jacket, so the firm makes an economic profit of $50 a jacket. The blue rectangle illustrates economic profit, which equals $6,250 a day ($50 a jacket multiplied by 125 jackets a day).

—— MyLab Economics Animation and Draw Graph ——

multiplied by 125 jackets a day). The blue rectangle shows Roots' economic profit.

Profit Maximizing Might Be Loss Minimizing

Figure 13.1 shows that Roots is making a large economic profit. But such an outcome is not inevitable. A firm might face a level of demand for its product that is too low for it to make an economic profit.

Excite@Home was such a firm. Offering high-speed Internet service over the same cable that provides television, Excite@Home hoped to capture a large share of the Internet portal market in competition with AOL, MSN, and a host of other providers.

Figure 13.2 illustrates the situation facing Excite@Home in 2001. The demand curve for its portal service is *D*, the marginal revenue curve is *MR*, the average total cost curve is *ATC*, and the marginal cost curve is *MC*. Excite@Home maximized profit—

FIGURE 13.2 Economic Loss in the Short Run

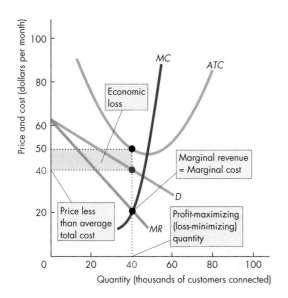

Profit is maximized where marginal revenue equals marginal cost. The loss-minimizing quantity is 40,000 customers. The price of $40 a month is less than the average total cost of $50 a month, so the firm incurs an economic loss of $10 a customer. The red rectangle illustrates economic loss, which equals $400,000 a month ($10 a customer multiplied by 40,000 customers).

MyLab Economics Animation

equivalently, it minimized its loss—by producing the output at which marginal revenue equals marginal cost. In Fig. 13.2, this output is 40,000 customers. Excite@Home charged the price that buyers were willing to pay for this quantity, which was determined by the demand curve and which was $40 a month. With 40,000 customers, Excite@Home's average total cost was $50 per customer, so it incurred an economic loss of $400,000 a month ($10 a customer multiplied by 40,000 customers). The red rectangle shows Excite@Home's economic loss.

So far, the firm in monopolistic competition looks like a single-price monopoly. It produces the quantity at which marginal revenue equals marginal cost and then charges the price that buyers are willing to pay for that quantity, as determined by the demand curve. The key difference between monopoly and monopolistic competition lies in what happens next when firms either make an economic profit or incur an economic loss.

Long Run: Zero Economic Profit

A firm like Excite@Home is not going to incur an economic loss for long. Eventually, it goes out of business. Also, there is no restriction on entry into monopolistic competition, so if firms in an industry are making economic profit, other firms have an incentive to enter that industry.

As the Gap and other firms start to make jackets similar to those made by Roots, the demand for Roots jackets decreases. The demand curve for Roots jackets and the marginal revenue curve shift leftward. As these curves shift leftward, the profit-maximizing quantity and price fall.

Figure 13.3 shows the long-run equilibrium. The demand curve for Roots jackets and the marginal revenue curve have shifted leftward. The firm produces 75 jackets a day and sells them for $25 each. At this output level, average total cost is also $25 per jacket.

FIGURE 13.3 Output and Price in the Long Run

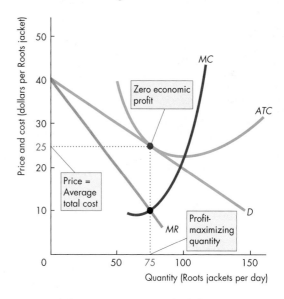

Economic profit encourages entry, which decreases the demand for each firm's product. When the demand curve touches the ATC curve at the quantity at which MR equals MC, the market is in long-run equilibrium. The output that maximizes profit is 75 jackets a day, and the price is $25 per jacket. Average total cost is also $25 per jacket, so economic profit is zero.

MyLab Economics Animation

So Roots is making zero economic profit on its jackets. When all the firms in the industry are making zero economic profit, there is no incentive for new firms to enter.

If demand is so low relative to costs that firms incur economic losses, exit will occur. As firms leave an industry, the demand for the products of the remaining firms increases and their demand curves shift rightward. The exit process ends when all the firms in the industry are making zero economic profit.

Monopolistic Competition and Perfect Competition

Figure 13.4 compares monopolistic competition and perfect competition and highlights two key differences between them:

- Excess capacity
- Markup

Excess Capacity A firm has **excess capacity** if it produces less than its **efficient scale**, which is the quantity at which average total cost is a minimum—the quantity at the bottom of the U-shaped *ATC* curve. In Fig. 13.4, the efficient scale is 100 jackets a day. Roots in part (a) produces 75 Roots jackets a day and has *excess capacity* of 25 jackets a day. But if all jackets are alike and are produced by firms in perfect competition, each firm in part (b) produces 100 jackets a day, which is the efficient scale. Average total cost is the lowest possible only in *perfect* competition.

You can see the excess capacity in monopolistic competition all around you. Family restaurants (except for the truly outstanding ones) almost always have some empty tables. You can always get a pizza delivered in less than 30 minutes. It is rare that every pump at a gas station is in use with customers waiting in line. Many realtors are ready to help you find or sell a home. These industries are examples of monopolistic competition. The firms have excess capacity.

FIGURE 13.4 Excess Capacity and Markup

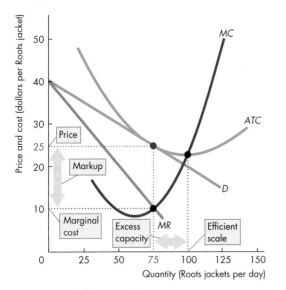

(a) Monopolistic competition

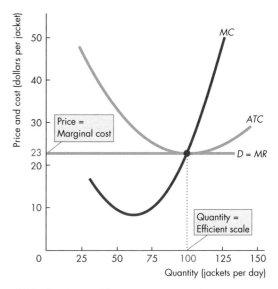

(b) Perfect competition

The efficient scale is 100 jackets a day. In monopolistic competition in the long run, because the firm faces a downward-sloping demand curve for its product, the quantity produced is less than the efficient scale and the firm has excess capacity. Price exceeds marginal cost by the amount of the markup.

In contrast, because in perfect competition the demand for each firm's product is perfectly elastic, the quantity produced in the long run equals the efficient scale and price equals marginal cost. The firm produces at the least possible cost and there is no markup.

MyLab Economics Animation and Draw Graph

They could sell more by cutting their prices, but they would then incur economic losses.

Markup A firm's **markup** is the amount by which price exceeds marginal cost. Figure 13.4(a) shows Roots' markup. In perfect competition, marginal cost always equals price, so there is no markup. Figure 13.4(b) shows this case. In monopolistic competition, buyers pay a higher price than in perfect competition and also pay more than marginal cost.

Is Monopolistic Competition Efficient?

Resources are used efficiently when marginal social benefit equals marginal social cost. Price equals marginal social benefit and the firm's marginal cost equals marginal social cost (assuming there are no external benefits or costs). So if the price of a Roots jacket exceeds the marginal cost of producing it, the quantity of Roots jackets produced is less than the efficient quantity. And you've just seen that in long-run equilibrium in monopolistic competition, price *does* exceed marginal cost. So is the quantity produced in monopolistic competition less than the efficient quantity?

Making the Relevant Comparison Two economists meet in the street, and one asks the other, "How is your husband?" The quick reply is "Compared to what?" This bit of economic wit illustrates a key point: Before we can conclude that something needs fixing, we must check out the available alternatives.

The markup that drives a gap between price and marginal cost in monopolistic competition arises from product differentiation. Roots jackets are not quite the same as jackets from other producers—Banana Republic, CK, Diesel, DKNY, Earl Jackets, Gap, Levi's, Ralph Lauren, or any of the other dozens of producers—so the demand for Roots jackets is not perfectly elastic. The only way in which the demand for Roots jackets might be perfectly elastic is if there were only one kind of jacket and all firms made it. In this situation, Roots jackets would be indistinguishable from all other jackets and they wouldn't even have identifying labels.

If there were only one kind of jacket, the total benefit of jackets would almost certainly be less than it is with variety. People value variety—not only because it enables each person to select what he or she likes best but also because it provides an external benefit. Most of us enjoy seeing variety in the choices of others. Contrast a scene from the China of the 1960s, when everyone wore a Mao tunic, with the China of today, when everyone wears the clothes of their own choosing. Or contrast a scene from the Germany of the 1930s, when almost everyone who could afford a car owned a first-generation Volkswagen Beetle, with the world of today with its enormous variety of styles and types of automobiles.

If people value variety, why don't we see infinite variety? The answer is that variety is costly. Each different variety of any product must be designed, and then customers must be informed about it. These initial costs of design and marketing—called setup costs—mean that some varieties that are too close to others already available are just not worth creating.

The Bottom Line Product variety is both valued and costly. The efficient degree of product variety is the one for which the marginal social benefit of product variety equals its marginal social cost. The loss that arises because the quantity produced is less than the efficient quantity is offset by the gain that arises from having a greater degree of product variety. So compared to the alternative—product uniformity—monopolistic competition might be efficient.

◆ REVIEW QUIZ

1 How does a firm in monopolistic competition decide how much to produce and at what price to offer its product for sale?

2 Why can a firm in monopolistic competition make an economic profit only in the short run?

3 Why do firms in monopolistic competition operate with excess capacity?

4 Why is there a price markup over marginal cost in monopolistic competition?

5 Is monopolistic competition efficient?

Work these questions in Study Plan 13.2 and get instant feedback.   MyLab Economics

---

You've seen how the firm in monopolistic competition determines its output and price in both the short run and the long run when it produces a given product and undertakes a *given* marketing effort. But how does the firm choose its product quality and marketing effort? We'll now study these decisions.

◆ Product Development and Marketing

When Roots made its output and pricing decisions that we've just studied, it had already made its product quality and marketing decisions. We'll now look at these decisions and see how they influence the firm's output, price, and economic profit.

Product Development

The prospect of new firms entering the industry keeps firms in monopolistic competition on their toes! To enjoy economic profits, they must continually seek ways of keeping one step ahead of imitators—other firms who imitate the success of profitable firms.

To maintain economic profit, a firm must either develop an entirely new product, or develop a significantly improved product that provides it with a competitive edge, even if only temporarily. A firm that introduces a new or improved and more differentiated product faces a demand that is less elastic and is able to increase its price and make an economic profit. Eventually, imitators will make close substitutes for the firm's new product and compete away the economic profit arising from an initial advantage. So to restore economic profit, the firm must develop another new or seriously improved product.

Profit-Maximizing Product Development The decision to develop a new or improved product is based on the same type of profit-maximizing calculation that you've already studied.

Product development is a costly activity, but it also brings in additional revenue. The firm must balance the cost and revenue at the margin.

The marginal dollar spent on developing a new or improved product is the marginal cost of product development. The marginal dollar that the new or improved product earns for the firm is the marginal revenue of product development. At a low level of product development, the marginal revenue from a better product exceeds the marginal cost. At a high level of product development, the marginal cost of a better product exceeds the marginal revenue.

When the marginal cost and marginal revenue of product development are equal, the firm is undertaking the profit-maximizing amount of product development.

Efficiency and Product Development Is the profit-maximizing amount of product development also the efficient amount? Efficiency is achieved if the marginal social benefit of a new and improved product equals its marginal social cost.

The marginal social benefit of an improved product is the increase in price that consumers are willing to pay for it. The marginal social cost is the amount that the firm must pay to make the improvement. Profit is maximized when marginal *revenue* equals marginal cost. But in monopolistic competition, marginal revenue is less than price, so product development is probably not pushed to its efficient level.

Monopolistic competition brings many product changes that cost little to implement and are purely cosmetic, such as improved packaging or a new scent in laundry detergent. Even when there is a truly improved product, it is never as good as the consumer would like and for which the consumer is willing to pay a higher price. For example, "The Legend of Zelda: Skyward Sword" is regarded as an almost perfect and very cool game, but users complain that it isn't quite perfect. It is a game whose features generate a marginal revenue equal to the marginal cost of creating them.

Advertising

A firm with a differentiated product needs to ensure that its customers know how its product is different from the competition. A firm also might attempt to create a consumer perception that its product is different, even when that difference is small. Firms use advertising and packaging to achieve this goal.

Advertising Expenditures Firms in monopolistic competition incur huge costs to ensure that buyers appreciate and value the differences between their own products and those of their competitors. So a large proportion of the price that we pay for a good covers the cost of selling it, and this proportion is increasing. Advertising in newspapers and magazines and on radio, television, and the Internet is the main selling cost. But it is not the only one. Selling costs include the cost of shopping malls that look like movie sets, glossy catalogues and brochures, and the salaries, airfares, and hotel bills of salespeople.

Advertising expenditures affect the profits of firms in two ways: They increase costs, and they change demand. Let's look at these effects.

ECONOMICS IN ACTION

The Cost of Selling a Pair of Shoes

When you buy a pair of running shoes that cost you $110, you're paying $14.25 for the materials from which the shoes are made, $4.25 for the services of the Malaysian worker who made the shoes, and $8.25 for the production and transportation services of a manufacturing firm in Asia and a shipping company. These numbers total $26.75. You pay $5.25 to the Canadian government in import duty. So we've now accounted for a total of $32. Where did the other $78 go? It is the cost of advertising, retailing, and other sales and distribution services.

The selling costs associated with running shoes are not unusual. Almost everything that you buy includes a selling cost component that exceeds one-half of the total cost. Your clothing, food, electronic items, DVDs, magazines, and even your textbooks cost more to sell than they cost to manufacture.

Advertising costs are only a part, and often a small part, of total selling costs. For example, Nike spends about $6.25 on advertising per pair of shoes sold.

For the North American economy as a whole, there are some 20,000 advertising agencies, which employ more than 200,000 people and have revenue of $45 billion. These numbers are only part of the total cost of advertising because firms have their own internal advertising departments, the costs of which we can only guess.

But the biggest part of selling costs is not the cost of advertising. It is the cost of retailing services. The retailer's selling costs (and economic profit) are often as much as 50 percent of the price you pay.

| Raw materials $14.25 | Production costs $12.50 | Import duty $5.25 | Selling costs $78 |

Selling Costs and Total Cost Selling costs are fixed costs and they increase the firm's total cost. So like the fixed cost of producing a good, advertising costs per unit decrease as the quantity produced increases.

Figure 13.5 shows how selling costs change a firm's average total cost. The blue curve shows the average total cost of production. The red curve shows the firm's average total cost of production plus advertising. The height of the red area between the two curves shows the average fixed cost of advertising. The *total* cost of advertising is fixed. But the *average* cost of advertising decreases as output increases.

Figure 13.5 shows that if advertising increases the quantity sold by a large enough amount, it can lower average total cost. For example, if the quantity sold increases from 25 jackets a day with no advertising to 100 jackets a day with advertising, average total cost falls from $60 to $40 a jacket. The reason is that although the *total* fixed cost has increased, the greater fixed cost is spread over a greater output, so average total cost decreases.

FIGURE 13.5 Selling Costs and Total Cost

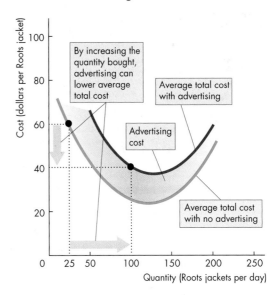

Selling costs such as the cost of advertising are fixed costs. When added to the average total cost of production, selling costs increase average total cost by a greater amount at small outputs than at large outputs. If advertising enables the quantity to increase from 25 jackets a day to 100 jackets a day, average total cost *falls* from $60 to $40 a jacket.

MyLab Economics Animation

Selling Costs and Demand Advertising and other selling efforts change the demand for a firm's product. But how? Does demand increase or does it decrease? The most natural answer is that advertising increases demand. By informing people about the quality of its products or by persuading people to switch from the products of other firms, a firm might expect to increase the demand for its own products.

But all firms in monopolistic competition advertise, and all seek to persuade customers that they have the best deal. If advertising enables a firm to survive, the number of firms in the market might increase. And to the extent that the number of firms does increase, advertising *decreases* the demand faced by any one firm. It also makes the demand for any one firm's product more elastic. So advertising can end up not only lowering average total cost but also lowering the markup and the price.

Figure 13.6 illustrates this possible effect of advertising. In part (a), with no advertising, the demand for Roots jackets is not very elastic. Profit is

maximized at 75 jackets per day, and the markup is large. In part (b), advertising, which is a fixed cost, increases average total cost from ATC_0 to ATC_1 but leaves marginal cost unchanged at MC. Demand becomes much more elastic, the profit-maximizing quantity increases, and the markup shrinks.

Using Advertising to Signal Quality

Some advertising, like the Roger Federer Rolex watch ad in glossy magazines or the ones that Coke and Pepsi spend a huge number of dollars on, seems hard to understand. There doesn't seem to be any concrete information about a watch in a tennis player's smile. And surely everyone knows about Coke and Pepsi. What is the gain from pouring millions of dollars into advertising these well-known colas?

One answer is that advertising is a signal to the consumer of a high-quality product. A **signal** is an action taken by an informed person (or firm) to send a message to uninformed people. Think about two colas:

FIGURE 13.6 Advertising and Markup

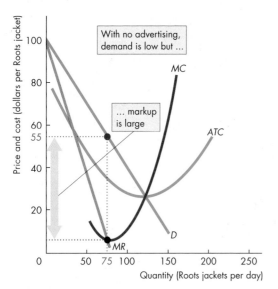

(a) No firms advertise

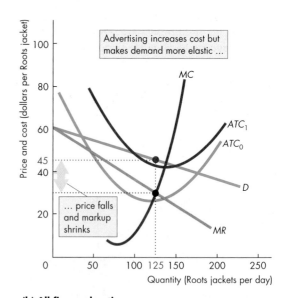

(b) All firms advertise

If no firms advertise, demand for each firm's product is low and not very elastic. The profit-maximizing output is small, the markup is large, and the price is high.

Advertising increases average total cost and shifts the ATC curve upward from ATC_0 to ATC_1. If all firms advertise, the demand for each firm's product becomes more elastic. Output increases, the price falls, and the markup shrinks.

Coke and Oke. Oke knows that its cola is not very good and that its taste varies a lot depending on which cheap batch of unsold cola it happens to buy each week. So Oke knows that while it could get a lot of people to try Oke by advertising, they would all quickly discover what a poor product it is and switch back to the cola they bought before. Coke, in contrast, knows that its product has a high-quality, consistent taste and that once consumers have tried it, there is a good chance they'll never drink anything else. On the basis of this reasoning, Oke doesn't advertise but Coke does. And Coke spends a lot of money to make a big splash.

Cola drinkers who see Coke's splashy ads know that the firm would not spend so much money advertising if its product were not truly good. So consumers reason that Coke is indeed a really good product. The flashy expensive ad has signalled that Coke is really good without saying anything about Coke.

Notice that if advertising is a signal, it doesn't need any specific product information. It just needs to be expensive and hard to miss. That's what a lot of advertising looks like. So the signalling theory of advertising predicts much of the advertising that we see.

Brand Names

Many firms create and spend a lot of money promoting a brand name. Why? What benefit does a brand name bring to justify the sometimes high cost of establishing it?

The basic answer is that a brand name provides information to consumers about the quality of a product and is an incentive to the producer to achieve a high and consistent quality standard.

To see how a brand name helps the consumer, think about how you use brand names to get information about quality. You're on a road trip, and it is time to find a place to spend the night. You see roadside advertisements for Holiday Inn, Joe's Motel, and Annie's Driver's Stop. You know about Holiday Inn because you've stayed in it before. You've also seen their advertisements and know what to expect. You have no information at all about Joe's and Annie's. They might be better than the lodgings you do know about, but without that knowledge, you're not going to try them. You use the brand name as information and stay at Holiday Inn.

This same story explains why a brand name provides an incentive to achieve high and consistent quality. Because no one would know whether Joe's and Annie's were offering a high standard of service, they have no incentive to do so. But equally, because everyone expects a given standard of service from Holiday Inn, a failure to meet a customer's expectation would almost surely lose that customer to a competitor. So Holiday Inn has a strong incentive to deliver what it promises in the advertising that creates its brand name.

Efficiency of Advertising and Brand Names

To the extent that advertising and brand names provide consumers with information about the precise nature of product differences and product quality, they benefit the consumer and enable a better product choice to be made. But the opportunity cost of the additional information must be weighed against the gain to the consumer.

The final verdict on the efficiency of monopolistic competition is ambiguous. In some cases, the gains from extra product variety offset the selling costs and the extra cost arising from excess capacity. The tremendous varieties of books, magazines, clothing, food, and drinks are examples of such gains. It is less easy to see the gains from being able to buy a brand-name drug with the identical chemical composition to that of a generic alternative, but many people willingly pay more for the brand-name alternative.

◆ REVIEW QUIZ

1 How, other than by adjusting price, do firms in monopolistic competition compete?

2 Why might product innovation be efficient and why might it be inefficient?

3 Explain how selling costs influence a firm's cost curves and its average total cost.

4 Explain how advertising influences the demand for a firm's product.

5 Are advertising and brand names efficient?

Work these questions in Study Plan 13.3 and get instant feedback.   MyLab Economics

---

◆ Monopolistic competition is one of the most common market structures that you encounter in your daily life. *Economics in the News* on pp. 318–319 applies the model of monopolistic competition to the market for smartphones and shows why you can expect continual innovation and the introduction of new phones from Apple, Samsung, and the many other smartphone producers.

Product Differentiation in Smartphones

How the iPhone Triumphed in Business

The Financial Times
May 17, 2017

Billions, the television series about a hedge fund manager, played by Damian Lewis, is typical of US entertainment shows, in that Apple iPhones and MacBook computers feature so heavily they almost deserve their own credit. …

In recent years, iPhone sales made up 40 per cent of the US smartphone market. Because they work for years and their looks do not age, most of the billion-plus iPhones sold over the past decade are likely to be still in use—one for every seven people on the planet. Not bad. …

The iPhone, while remaining expensive, has become the phone to own across class and national boundaries. How has this happened? …

The reasons why the iPhone triumphed über alles in business is not complicated.

First, the Apple ecosystem for music, movies and the rest sucks you in. It works well and changing to Android is a faff. So it is not quite a question of consumers taking delight in their iPhones, but of simplicity.

The second element of the device's appeal is its image. …

Could the iPhone's seemingly unassailable position continue for another 10 years? Or will it inevitably do a BlackBerry?

The iPhone 8 is expected in the autumn and it is difficult to imagine how the new model will keep momentum going.

The Galaxy S8, regarded by many as the best phone ever, makes the current iPhones look rather conservative. But the last thing Apple would want is for their 8 to resemble a me-too Samsung. ….

Jonathan Margolis, Published May 17, 2017, *Financial Times*

ESSENCE OF THE STORY

- The iPhone has a 40 percent share of the U.S. smartphone market.
- Although its price is high, the iPhone is the preferred choice of all classes and nations.
- The iPhone's success arises from its simplicity and its image.
- To maintain its market share, Apple must create a better product.
- Samsung's Galaxy S8 is regarded by many as the best phone.
- Apple must avoid making iPhone 8 resemble the Galaxy S8.

ECONOMIC ANALYSIS

■ The market for smartphones is an example of monopolistic competition.

■ More than 100 firms compete in a market with up to 9,000 differentiated phones.

■ Although the phones are differentiated, most of them are close substitutes for each other.

■ Close substitutes have highly elastic demand, so markups are low and economic profit is competed away.

■ To make an economic profit, a firm must keep innovating.

■ The market for smartphones has seen a sequence of innovation since the first iPhone was launched in 2007.

■ The iPhone 7 innovations were new camera systems, a longer battery life, and water and dust resistance.

■ By creating a differentiated product, Apple was able to bring to the market a product sufficiently differentiated from its competitors to earn an economic profit.

■ The monopolistic competition model explains what is now happening at Apple and what the future holds.

■ Figure 1 shows the market for Apple's iPhone 7. (The numbers are assumptions but are ballpark realistic.)

■ Because Apple's smartphone differs from other phones and has features that users value, the demand curve, *D*, and marginal revenue curve, *MR*, provide a large short-run profit opportunity.

■ The marginal cost curve is *MC* and the average total cost curve is *ATC*. Apple maximizes its economic profit by producing the quantity at which marginal revenue equals marginal cost.

■ This quantity of phones can be sold for $600 each.

■ The blue rectangle shows Apple's economic profit.

■ Because Apple makes an economic profit, other phone producers will innovate to create a yet better smartphone to take some of the market.

■ Figure 2 shows the impact on Apple of competition from other producers.

■ The demand for the Apple phone decreases as the market is shared with the other phones.

■ Apple's profit-maximizing price for the iPhone falls, and in the long run economic profit is eliminated.

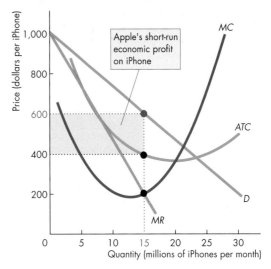

Figure 1 Apple's Economic Profit in the Short Run

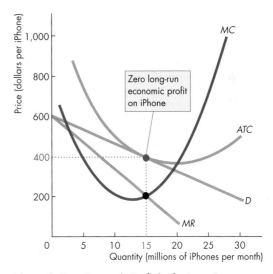

Figure 2 Zero Economic Profit in the Long Run

■ With zero economic profit, Apple (along with the other producers) has an incentive to develop an even better differentiated phone and start the cycle described here all over again, making an economic profit with a new phone in the short run.

WORKED PROBLEM

MyLab Economics Work this problem in Chapter 13 Study Plan.

The table provides information about Prue's Personal Trainer Service, a firm that is in monopolistic competition with similar firms that offer slightly differentiated services.

Demand schedule		Production costs	
Price (dollars per session)	Quantity (sessions per hour)	MC (dollars per session)	ATC (dollars per session)
45	0		..
		12	
40	1		33
		5	
35	2		19
		7	
30	3		15
		27	
25	4		18

Questions

1. Calculate Prue's profit-maximizing quantity and price.
2. What is Prue's markup and does she have excess capacity?
3. Is Prue in a long-run equilibrium?

Solutions

1. The profit-maximizing quantity is that at which marginal cost equals marginal revenue. The table above provides the marginal cost data. For example, the marginal cost of the 4th session per hour is $27. The table below shows the calculation of marginal revenue. Multiply quantity by price to find total revenue (third column) and then calculate the change in total revenue when the quantity increases by 1 session (fourth column).

Demand schedule		Total revenue (dollars per hour)	Marginal revenue (dollars per session)
Price (dollars per session)	Quantity (sessions per hour)		
45	0	0	
			40
40	1	40	
			30
35	2	70	
			20
30	3	90	
			10
25	4	100	

When the number of sessions increases from 2 to 3 an hour, marginal revenue ($20) exceeds marginal cost ($7), so profit increases. But when the number of sessions increases from 3 to 4 an hour, marginal cost ($27) exceeds marginal revenue ($10), so profit decreases. So 3 sessions an hour maximizes Prue's profit. The highest price at which 3 sessions an hour can be sold is $30 a session, which is the profit-maximizing price.

Key Point: To maximize profit, increase production if $MR > MC$ and decrease production if $MR < MC$.

2. To find Prue's markup, we compare price and marginal cost. Use the fact that $MC = ATC$ at minimum ATC and notice that minimum ATC is $15 a session at 3 sessions an hour. The price is $30 a session, so the markup is 100 percent. Prue is producing at minimum ATC, which is the efficient scale, so she has no excess capacity.

Key Point: Markup is the amount by which price exceeds marginal cost; and excess capacity is the gap between output and the efficient scale.

3. In the long run, entry decreases demand and drives economic profit to zero. Prue is making a profit of $45 an hour (price of $30 a session minus ATC of $15 a session, multiplied by 3 sessions an hour). So Prue is not in a long-run equilibrium.

Key Point: Entry decreases the demand for the firm's good or service and economic profit falls to zero.

The figure shows Prue's short-run equilibrium.

Key Figure

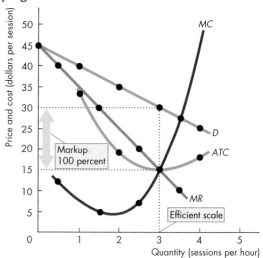

MyLab Economics Interactive Animation

SUMMARY

Key Points

Monopolistic Competition and Other Market Structures (pp. 306–309)

- Monopolistic competition occurs when a large number of firms compete with each other on product quality, price, and marketing.
- The four-firm concentration ratio and the Herfindahl-Hirschman Index (HHI) along with other information indicate the degree of competition in a market.

Working Problems 1 and 2 will give you a better understanding of what monopolistic competition is.

Price and Output in Monopolistic Competition (pp. 310–313)

- Each firm in monopolistic competition faces a downward-sloping demand curve and produces the profit-maximizing quantity.

- Entry and exit result in zero economic profit and excess capacity in long-run equilibrium.

Working Problems 3 to 8 will give you a better understanding of price and output in monopolistic competition.

Product Development and Marketing (pp. 314–317)

- Firms in monopolistic competition innovate and develop new products.
- Advertising expenditures increase total cost, but average total cost might fall if the quantity sold increases by enough.
- Advertising expenditures might increase demand, but demand might decrease if competition increases.
- Whether monopolistic competition is inefficient depends on the value we place on product variety.

Working Problem 9 will give you a better understanding of product development and marketing.

Key Terms

MyLab Economics Key Terms Quiz

Efficient scale, 312
Excess capacity, 312
Four-firm concentration ratio, 307

Herfindahl-Hirschman Index, 307
Markup, 313
Monopolistic competition, 306

Product differentiation, 306
Signal, 316

STUDY PLAN PROBLEMS AND APPLICATIONS

MyLab Economics Work Problems 1 to 9 in Chapter 13 Study Plan and get instant feedback.

Monopolistic Competition and Other Market Structures (Study Plan 13.1)

1. Which of the following items are sold by firms in monopolistic competition? Explain your selections.
   - Cable television service
   - Wheat
   - Athletic shoes
   - Soft drinks
   - Toothbrushes
   - Ready-mix concrete

2. The four-firm concentration ratio for audio equipment makers is 30, and for electric lamp makers it is 89. The HHI for audio equipment makers is 415, and for electric lamp makers it is 2,850. Which of these markets is an example of monopolistic competition?

Price and Output in Monopolistic Competition (Study Plan 13.2)

Use the following information to work Problems 3 and 4.

Sara is a dot.com entrepreneur who has established a Web site at which people can design and buy sweatshirts. Sara pays $1,000 a week for her Web server and Internet connection. The sweatshirts that her customers design are made to order by another firm, and Sara pays this firm $20 a sweatshirt. Sara has no other costs. The table sets out the demand schedule for Sara's sweatshirts.

Price (dollars per sweatshirt)	Quantity demanded (sweatshirts per week)
0	100
20	80
40	60
60	40
80	20
100	0

3. Calculate Sara's profit-maximizing output, price, and economic profit.

4. a. Do you expect other firms to enter the Web sweatshirt business and compete with Sara?

   b. What happens to the demand for Sara's sweatshirts in the long run? What happens to Sara's economic profit in the long run?

Use the following figure, which shows the situation facing Flight Inc., a producer of running shoes, to work Problems 5 to 8.

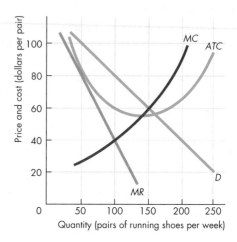

5. What quantity does Flight produce, what price does it charge, and what is its economic profit?

6. In the long run, how does Flight change its price and the quantity it produces? What happens to the market output of running shoes?

7. Does Flight have excess capacity in the long run? If it has excess capacity in the long run, why doesn't it decrease its plant size?

8. Is the market for running shoes efficient or inefficient in the long run? Explain your answer.

Product Development and Marketing (Study Plan 13.3)

9. Suppose that Roots' marginal cost of a jacket is a constant $100 and the total fixed cost at one of its stores is $2,000 a day. This store sells 20 jackets a day, which is its profit-maximizing number of jackets. Then the stores nearby start to advertise their jackets. The Roots store now spends $2,000 a day advertising its jackets, and its profit-maximizing number of jackets sold jumps to 50 a day.

   a. What is this store's average total cost of a jacket sold (i) before the advertising begins and (ii) after the advertising begins?

   b. Can you say what happens to the price of a Roots jacket, Roots' markup, and Roots' economic profit? Why or why not?

ADDITIONAL PROBLEMS AND APPLICATIONS

MyLab Economics You can work these problems in Homework or Test if assigned by your instructor.

Monopolistic Competition and Other Market Structures

10. Which of the following items are sold by firms in monopolistic competition? Explain your selection.
    - Orange juice
    - Canned soup
    - Tablet computers
    - Chewing gum
    - Breakfast cereals
    - Corn

11. The HHI for automobiles is 2,350, for sporting goods it is 161, for batteries it is 2,883, and for jewellery it is 81. Which of these markets is an example of monopolistic competition?

Price and Output in Monopolistic Competition

Use the following data to work Problems 12 and 13.

Lorie teaches singing. Her fixed costs are $1,000 a month, and it costs her $50 of labour to give one class. The table shows the demand schedule for Lorie's singing lessons.

Price (dollars per lesson)	Quantity demanded (lessons per month)
0	250
50	200
100	150
150	100
200	50
250	0

12. Calculate Lorie's profit-maximizing output, price, and economic profit.

13. a. Do you expect other firms to enter the market for singing lessons and compete with Lorie?

    b. What happens to the demand for Lorie's lessons in the long run? What happens to Lorie's economic profit in the long run?

Use the figure in the next column, which shows the situation facing Mike's Bikes, a producer of mountain bikes, to work Problems 14 to 18. The demand and costs of other mountain bike producers are similar to those of Mike's Bikes.

14. What quantity does the firm produce and what is its price? Calculate the firm's economic profit or economic loss.

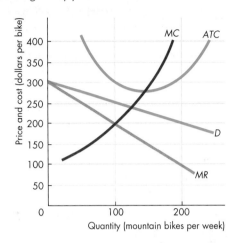

15. What will happen to the number of firms producing mountain bikes in the long run?

16. a. How will the price of a mountain bike and the number of bikes produced by Mike's Bikes change in the long run?

    b. How will the quantity of mountain bikes produced by all firms change in the long run?

17. Is there any way for Mike's Bikes to avoid having excess capacity in the long run?

18. Is the market for mountain bikes efficient or inefficient in the long run? Explain your answer.

Use this news clip to work Problems 19 and 20.

'The Lunatic Fringe of Extreme Beer' Now Available in Dayton

Samuel Adams Utopias is an ultra-rich, port-like beer, which is meant to be sipped and not guzzled. It has a high 28 percent alcohol content. Its price tag is $199 for a ceramic decanter containing 24 ounces. This volume is the equivalent of two cans of beer, or a bit less than a standard-sized (750-ml) bottle of wine.

Source: dayton.com, November 18, 2016

19. a. Explain how Samuel Adams has differentiated its Utopias to compete with other beer brands in terms of quality, price, and marketing.

    b. Predict whether Samuel Adams produces Utopias at, above, or below the efficient scale in the short run.

    c. Predict whether Samuel Adams produces Utopias at, above, or below the efficient scale in the long run.

20. a. Predict whether the $199 price tag on the Utopias is at, above, or below marginal cost: (i) in the short run and (ii) in the long run.

    b. Do you think that Samuel Adams' Utopias makes the market for beer inefficient?

Use the following news clip to work Problems 21 and 22.

Women's Golf Clubs

A quarter of golfers today are women and the number keeps growing. And golf club manufacturers are paying attention and developing a market for women's clubs. Callaway and fourteen other firms are players in this market.

Source: Thoughtco.com, February 20, 2017

21. a. How are golf club manufacturers attempting to maintain economic profit?

    b. Draw a graph to illustrate the cost curves and revenue curves of Callaway in the market for golf clubs for women.

    c. Show on your graph in part (b) the short-run economic profit.

22. a. Explain why the economic profit that Callaway makes on golf clubs for women is likely to be temporary.

    b. Draw a graph to illustrate the cost curves and revenue curves of Callaway in the market for golf clubs for women in the long run. Mark the firm's excess capacity.

Product Development and Marketing

Use the following data to work Problems 23 to 25.
Bianca bakes delicious cookies. Her total fixed cost is $40 a day, and her average variable cost is $1 a bag. Few people know about Bianca's Cookies, and she is maximizing her profit by selling 10 bags a day for $5 a bag. Bianca thinks that if she spends $50 a day on advertising, she can increase her market share and sell 25 bags a day for $5 a bag.

23. If Bianca's advertising works as she expects, can she increase her economic profit by advertising?

24. If Bianca advertises, will her average total cost increase or decrease at the quantity produced?

25. If Bianca advertises, will she continue to sell her cookies for $5 a bag or will she change her price?

Use the following news clip to work Problems 26 and 27.

How Uniqlo Will Conquer U.S. Consumerism

Uniqlo's marketing seeks to associate the brand with sustainable quality for all activities and differentiate it from fast-fashion competitors. Uniqlo launched its first global marketing campaign last year costing $6.1 million. The firm's fall collection is built around a series of technological improvements to enhance comfort and make cold weather enjoyable.

Source: *Advertising Age*, March 29, 2017

26. a. What is the main objective of Uniqlo's marketing plan?

    b. Is Uniqlo's marketing expenditure of $6.1 million a fixed cost or a variable cost?

27. How does Uniqlo's marketing change the firm's cost curves and revenue curves and its economic profit? Does average total cost at the profit-maximizing output increase or decrease?

28. **Amazon May Be Sprinting into Athletic Apparel**

    People increasingly wear their workout clothes outside the gym and athletic clothing sales in the U.S. increased by 15 percent in 2015 and 12 percent in 2016. Amazon wants to get into this $44 billion market, which is currently dominated by Nike and Under Armour.

    Source: CBS News, January 4, 2017

    How will Amazon's entry into the athletic clothing market influence Nike and Under Armour? Illustrate your answer with a graph.

Economics in the News

29. After you have studied *Economics in the News* on pp. 318–319, answer the following questions.

    a. Why did Apple improve the cameras and battery in iPhone 7?

    b. How would Apple's cost curves (*MC* and *ATC*) have been different if they had not made improvements in iPhone 7?

    c. How do you think the launch of a new iPhone influences the demand for other firms' smartphones?

    d. Explain the effects of the introduction of a new iPhone on Samsung and other firms in the market for smartphones.

    e. Draw a graph to illustrate your answer to part (c). Explain your answer.

    f. What do you predict will happen to the markup in the market for smartphones?

    g. What do you predict will happen to excess capacity in the market for smartphones? Explain your answer.

14

OLIGOPOLY

After studying this chapter, you will be able to:

- ◆ Define and identify oligopoly
- ◆ Use game theory to explain how price and output are determined in oligopoly
- ◆ Use game theory to explain other strategic decisions
- ◆ Describe the anti-combine laws that regulate oligopoly

Chances are that your cellphone service provider is Rogers, Bell, or Telus. Nine out of ten Canadians have plans with these firms. Similarly, the chip in your computer was made by either Intel or AMD; the battery in your TV remote by Duracell or Energizer; and the airplane that takes you on a long-distance trip by Boeing or the European firm Airbus.

How does a market work when only two or a handful of firms compete? To answer this question, we use the model of oligopoly.

At the end of the chapter, in *Economics in the News*, we'll look at the market for cellphone service and see why Rogers, Bell, and Telus charge such high prices.

◆ What Is Oligopoly?

Oligopoly, like monopolistic competition, lies between perfect competition and monopoly. The firms in oligopoly might produce an identical product and compete only on price, or they might produce a differentiated product and compete on price, product quality, and marketing. **Oligopoly** is a market structure in which:

- Natural or legal barriers prevent the entry of new firms.
- A small number of firms compete.

Barriers to Entry

Natural or legal barriers to entry can create oligopoly. You saw in Chapter 12 how economies of scale and demand form a natural barrier to entry that can create a *natural monopoly*. These same factors can create a *natural oligopoly*.

Figure 14.1 illustrates two natural oligopolies. The demand curve, D (in both parts of the figure), shows the demand for taxi rides in a town. If the average

total cost curve of a taxi company is ATC_1 in part (a), the market is a natural **duopoly**—an oligopoly market with two firms. You can probably see some examples of duopoly where you live. Some cities have only two taxi companies, two car rental firms, two copy centres, or two college bookstores.

The lowest price at which the firm in Fig. 14.1(a) would remain in business is $10 a ride. At that price, the quantity of rides demanded is 60 a day, the quantity that can be provided by just two firms. There is no room in this market for three firms. But if there were only one firm, it would make an economic profit and a second firm would enter to take some of the business and economic profit.

If the average total cost curve of a taxi company is ATC_2 in part (b), the efficient scale of one firm is 20 rides a day. This market is large enough for three firms.

A legal oligopoly arises when a legal barrier to entry protects the small number of firms in a market. A city might license two taxi firms or two bus companies, for example, even though the combination of demand and economies of scale leaves room for more than two firms.

FIGURE 14.1   Natural Oligopoly

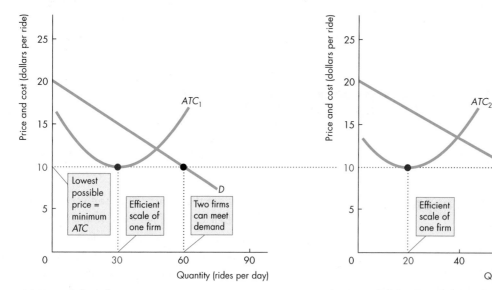

(a) Natural duopoly

(b) Natural oligopoly with three firms

The minimum average total cost of producing a ride is $10, so $10 a ride is the lowest possible price that a firm can charge. When a firm produces the efficient scale of 30 rides a day, two firms can satisfy the market demand. This market is a natural oligopoly with two firms—a natural duopoly.

When the efficient scale of one firm is 20 rides per day, three firms can satisfy the market demand at the lowest possible price. This natural oligopoly has three firms.

ECONOMICS IN ACTION

Oligopoly Today

The markets listed in the figure are oligopolies. Although in some of them the number of firms (in parentheses) is large, the share of the market held by the four largest firms (the red bars) is close to 100 percent.

The most concentrated markets—cigarettes, motor vehicles, breakfast cereals, chocolates, pet food, and batteries—are dominated by one or two firms.

If you want to buy a battery for your TV remote or toothbrush, you'll find it hard to avoid buying a Duracell or an Energizer.

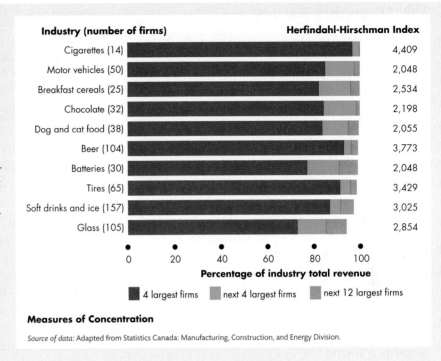

Industry (number of firms)	Herfindahl-Hirschman Index
Cigarettes (14)	4,409
Motor vehicles (50)	2,048
Breakfast cereals (25)	2,534
Chocolate (32)	2,198
Dog and cat food (38)	2,055
Beer (104)	3,773
Batteries (30)	2,048
Tires (65)	3,429
Soft drinks and ice (157)	3,025
Glass (105)	2,854

Percentage of industry total revenue

■ 4 largest firms   ■ next 4 largest firms   ■ next 12 largest firms

Measures of Concentration

Source of data: Adapted from Statistics Canada: Manufacturing, Construction, and Energy Division.

Small Number of Firms

Because barriers to entry exist, oligopoly consists of a small number of firms, each of which has a large share of the market. Such firms are interdependent, and they face a temptation to cooperate to increase their joint economic profit.

Interdependence With a small number of firms in a market, each firm's actions influence the profits of all the other firms. When Penny Stafford opened her coffee shop in Lethbridge, Alberta, a nearby Starbucks coffee shop took a hit. Within days, Starbucks began to attract Penny's customers with enticing offers and lower prices. Starbucks survived, but Penny eventually went out of business. Penny Stafford and Starbucks were interdependent.

Temptation to Cooperate When a small number of firms share a market, they can increase their profits by forming a cartel and acting like a monopoly. A **cartel** is a group of firms acting together—colluding—to limit output, raise the price, and increase economic profit. Cartels are illegal, but they do operate in some markets. But for reasons that you'll discover in this chapter, cartels tend to break down.

Examples of Oligopoly

Economics in Action above shows some examples of oligopoly. The dividing line between oligopoly and monopolistic competition is hard to pin down. As a practical matter, we identify oligopoly by looking at concentration ratios, the Herfindahl-Hirschman Index (HHI), and information about the geographical scope of the market and barriers to entry. The HHI that divides oligopoly from monopolistic competition is generally taken to be 2,500. An HHI below 2,500 is usually an example of monopolistic competition, and a market in which the HHI exceeds 2,500 is usually an example of oligopoly.

◆ REVIEW QUIZ

1 What are the two distinguishing characteristics of oligopoly?
2 Why are firms in oligopoly interdependent?
3 Why do firms in oligopoly face a temptation to collude?
4 Can you think of some examples of oligopolies that you buy from?

Work these questions in Study Plan 14.1 and get instant feedback.   MyLab Economics

◆ Oligopoly Games

Economists think about oligopoly as a game between two or a few players, and to study oligopoly markets they use game theory. **Game theory** is a set of tools for studying *strategic behaviour*—behaviour that takes into account the expected behaviour of others and the recognition of mutual interdependence. Game theory was invented by John von Neumann in 1937 and extended by von Neumann and Oskar Morgenstern in 1944 (see p. 351). Today, it is one of the major research fields in economics.

Game theory seeks to understand oligopoly as well as other forms of economic, political, social, and even biological rivalries by using a method of analysis specifically designed to understand games of all types, including the familiar games of everyday life (see Talking with Thomas Hubbard on p. 352). To lay the foundation for studying oligopoly games, we first think about the features that all games share.

What Is a Game?

What is a game? At first thought, the question seems silly. After all, there are many different games. There are ball games and parlour games, games of chance and games of skill. But what is it about all these different activities that makes them games? What do all these games have in common? All games share four common features:

- Rules
- Strategies
- Payoffs
- Outcome

We're going to look at these features of games by playing a game called "the prisoners' dilemma." The prisoners' dilemma game displays the essential features of many games, including oligopoly games, and it gives a good illustration of how game theory works and generates predictions.

The Prisoners' Dilemma

Art and Bob have been caught red-handed stealing a car. Facing airtight cases, they will receive a sentence of two years each for their crime. During his interviews with the two prisoners, the Crown attorney begins to suspect that he has stumbled on the two people who were responsible for a multimillion-dollar bank robbery some months earlier. But this is just a suspicion. He has no evidence on which he can convict them of the greater crime unless he can get them to confess. But how can he extract a confession? The answer is by making the prisoners play a game. The Crown attorney makes the prisoners play the following game.

Rules Each prisoner (player) is placed in a separate room and cannot communicate with the other prisoner. Each is told that he is suspected of having carried out the bank robbery and that:

> If both of them confess to the larger crime, each will receive a sentence of 3 years for both crimes.

> If he alone confesses and his accomplice does not, he will receive only a 1-year sentence while his accomplice will receive a 10-year sentence.

Strategies In game theory, **strategies** are all the possible actions of each player. Art and Bob each have two possible actions:

1. Confess to the bank robbery.
2. Deny having committed the bank robbery.

Because there are two players, each with two strategies, there are four possible outcomes:

1. Both confess.
2. Both deny.
3. Art confesses and Bob denies.
4. Bob confesses and Art denies.

Payoffs Each prisoner can work out his *payoff* in each of these situations, and we can tabulate the four possible payoffs for each of the prisoners in what is called a payoff matrix for the game. A **payoff matrix** is a table that shows the payoffs for every possible action by each player for every possible action by each other player.

Table 14.1 shows a payoff matrix for Art and Bob. The squares show the payoffs for each prisoner—the red triangle in each square shows Art's and the blue triangle shows Bob's. If both prisoners confess (top left), each gets a prison term of 3 years. If Bob confesses but Art denies (top right), Art gets a 10-year sentence and Bob gets a 1-year sentence. If Art confesses and Bob denies (bottom left), Art gets a 1-year sentence and Bob gets a 10-year sentence. Finally, if both of them deny (bottom right), neither can be convicted of the bank robbery charge but both are sentenced for the car theft—a 2-year sentence.

Outcome The choices of both players determine the outcome of the game. To predict that outcome, we use an equilibrium idea proposed by John Nash of Princeton University (who received the Nobel Prize for Economic Science in 1994 and was the subject of the 2001 movie *A Beautiful Mind*). In **Nash equilibrium**, player *A* takes the best possible action given the action of player *B* and player *B* takes the best possible action given the action of player *A*.

In the case of the prisoners' dilemma, the Nash equilibrium occurs when Art makes his best choice given Bob's choice and when Bob makes his best choice given Art's choice.

To find the Nash equilibrium, we compare all the possible outcomes associated with each choice and eliminate those that are dominated—that are not as good as some other choice. Let's find the Nash equilibrium for the prisoners' dilemma game.

Finding the Nash Equilibrium Look at the situation from Art's point of view. If Bob confesses (top row), Art's best action is to confess because in that case, he is sentenced to 3 years rather than 10 years. If Bob denies (bottom row), Art's best action is still to confess because in that case, he receives 1 year rather than 2 years. So Art's best action is to confess.

Now look at the situation from Bob's point of view. If Art confesses (left column), Bob's best action is to confess because in that case, he is sentenced to 3 years rather than 10 years. If Art denies (right column), Bob's best action is still to confess because in that case, he receives 1 year rather than 2 years. So Bob's best action is to confess.

Because each player's best action is to confess, each does confess, each goes to jail for 3 years, and the Crown attorney has solved the bank robbery. This is the Nash equilibrium of the game.

The Nash equilibrium for the prisoners' dilemma is called a **dominant-strategy equilibrium**, which is an equilibrium in which the best strategy of each player is to cheat (confess) *regardless of the strategy of the other player*.

The Dilemma The dilemma arises as each prisoner contemplates the consequences of his decision and puts himself in the place of his accomplice. Each knows that it would be best if both denied. But each also knows that if he denies it is in the best interest of the other to confess. So each considers whether to deny and rely on his accomplice to deny or to confess

TABLE 14.1   Prisoners' Dilemma Payoff Matrix

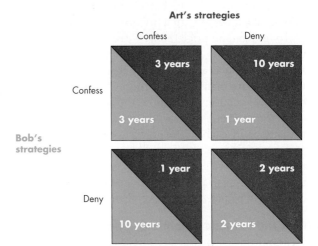

Each square shows the payoffs for the two players, Art and Bob, for each possible pair of actions. In each square, the red triangle shows Art's payoff and the blue triangle shows Bob's. For example, if both confess, the payoffs are in the top left square. The equilibrium of the game is for both players to confess and each gets a 3-year sentence.

———————— MyLab Economics Animation ——

hoping that his accomplice denies but expecting him to confess. The dilemma leads to the equilibrium of the game.

A Bad Outcome For the prisoners, the equilibrium of the game, with each confessing, is not the best outcome. If neither of them confesses, each gets only 2 years for the lesser crime. Isn't there some way in which this better outcome can be achieved? It seems that there is not, because the players cannot communicate with each other. Each player can put himself in the other player's place, and so each player can figure out that there is a best strategy for each of them. The prisoners are indeed in a dilemma. Each knows that he can serve 2 years *only* if he can trust the other to deny. But each prisoner also knows that it is *not* in the best interest of the other to deny. So each prisoner knows that he must confess, thereby delivering a bad outcome for both.

The firms in an oligopoly are in a similar situation to Art and Bob in the prisoners' dilemma game. Let's see how we can use this game to understand oligopoly.

An Oligopoly Price-Fixing Game

We can use game theory and a game like the prisoners' dilemma to understand price fixing, price wars, and other aspects of the behaviour of firms in oligopoly. We'll begin with a price-fixing game.

To understand price fixing, we're going to study the special case of duopoly—an oligopoly with two firms. Duopoly is easier to study than oligopoly with three or more firms, and it captures the essence of all oligopoly situations. Somehow, the two firms must share the market. And how they share it depends on the actions of each. We're going to describe the costs of the two firms and the market demand for the item they produce. We're then going to see how game theory helps us to predict the prices charged and the quantities produced by the two firms in a duopoly.

Cost and Demand Conditions Two firms, Trick and Gear, produce switchgears. They have identical costs. Figure 14.2(a) shows their average total cost curve (*ATC*) and marginal cost curve (*MC*). Figure 14.2(b) shows the market demand curve for switchgears (*D*). The two firms produce identical switchgears, so one firm's switchgear is a perfect substitute for the other's, and the market price of each firm's product is identical. The quantity demanded depends on that price—the higher the price, the smaller is the quantity demanded.

This industry is a natural duopoly. Two firms can produce this good at a lower cost than either one firm or three firms can. For each firm, average total cost is at its minimum when production is 3,000 units a week. When price equals minimum average total cost, the total quantity demanded is 6,000 units a week, and two firms can just produce that quantity.

Collusion We'll suppose that Trick and Gear enter into a collusive agreement. A **collusive agreement** is an agreement between two (or more) producers to form a cartel to restrict output, raise the price, and increase profits. Such an agreement is illegal in Canada and is undertaken in secret. The firms in a cartel can pursue two startegies:

- Comply
- Cheat

A firm that complies carries out the agreement. A firm that cheats breaks the agreement to its own benefit and to the cost of the other firm.

Because each firm has two strategies, there are four possible combinations of actions for the firms:

1. Both firms comply.
2. Both firms cheat.
3. Trick complies and Gear cheats.
4. Gear complies and Trick cheats.

FIGURE 14.2 Costs and Demand

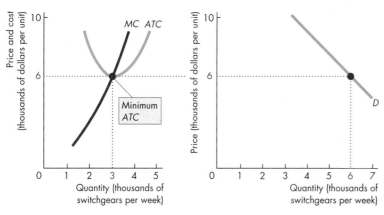

(a) Individual firm

(b) Industry

The average total cost curve for each firm is *ATC*, and the marginal cost curve is *MC* (part a). Minimum average total cost is $6,000 a unit, and it occurs at a production of 3,000 units a week.

Part (b) shows the market demand curve. At a price of $6,000, the quantity demanded is 6,000 units per week. The two firms can produce this output at the lowest possible average cost. If the market had one firm, it would be profitable for another to enter. If the market had three firms, one would exit. There is room for only two firms in this industry. It is a natural duopoly.

MyLab Economics Animation

Colluding to Maximize Profits Let's work out the payoffs to the two firms if they collude to make the maximum profit for the cartel by acting like a monopoly. The calculations that the two firms perform are the same calculations that a monopoly performs. (You can refresh your memory of these calculations by looking at Chapter 12, pp. 284–285.) The only thing that the firms in duopoly must do beyond what a monopoly does is to agree on how much of the total output each of them will produce.

Figure 14.3 shows the price and quantity that maximize industry profit for the duopoly. Part (a) shows the situation for each firm, and part (b) shows the situation for the industry as a whole. The curve labelled *MR* is the industry marginal revenue curve. This marginal revenue curve is like that of a single-price monopoly (Chapter 12, p. 282). The curve labelled MC_I is the industry marginal cost curve if each firm produces the same quantity of output. This curve is constructed by adding together the outputs of the two firms at each level of marginal cost. Because the two firms are the same size, at each level of marginal cost, the industry output is twice the output of one firm. The curve MC_I in part (b) is twice as far to the right as the curve *MC* in part (a).

To maximize industry profit, the firms in the duopoly agree to restrict output to the rate that makes the industry marginal cost and marginal revenue equal. That output rate, as shown in part (b), is 4,000 units a week. The demand curve shows that the highest price for which the 4,000 switchgears can be sold is $9,000 each. Trick and Gear agree to charge this price.

To hold the price at $9,000 a unit, production must be 4,000 units a week. So Trick and Gear must agree on output rates for each of them that total 4,000 units a week. Let's suppose that they agree to split the market equally so that each firm produces 2,000 switchgears a week. Because the firms are identical, this division is the most likely.

The average total cost (*ATC*) of producing 2,000 switchgears a week is $8,000, so the profit per unit is $1,000 and economic profit is $2 million (2,000 units × $1,000 per unit). The economic profit of each firm is represented by the blue rectangle in Fig. 14.3(a).

We have just described one possible outcome for a duopoly game: The two firms collude to produce the monopoly profit-maximizing output and divide that output equally between themselves. From the industry point of view, this solution is identical to a monopoly. A duopoly that operates in this way is indistinguishable from a monopoly. The economic profit that is made by a monopoly is the maximum total profit that can be made by the duopoly when the firms collude.

But with price greater than marginal cost, either firm might think of trying to increase profit by cheating on the agreement and producing more than the agreed amount. Let's see what happens if one of the firms does cheat in this way.

FIGURE 14.3   Colluding to Make Monopoly Profits

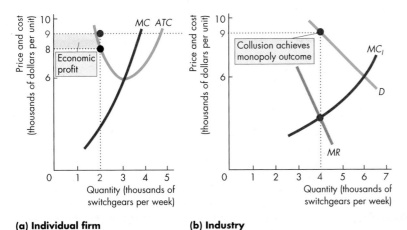

(a) Individual firm   **(b) Industry**

The industry marginal cost curve, MC_I in part (b), is the horizontal sum of the two firms' marginal cost curves, *MC* in part (a). The industry marginal revenue curve is *MR*. To maximize profit, the firms produce 4,000 units a week (the quantity at which marginal revenue equals marginal cost). They sell that output for $9,000 a unit. Each firm produces 2,000 units a week. Average total cost is $8,000 a unit, so each firm makes an economic profit of $2 million (blue rectangle)—2,000 units multiplied by $1,000 profit a unit.

One Firm Cheats on a Collusive Agreement To set the stage for cheating on their agreement, Trick convinces Gear that demand has decreased and that it cannot sell 2,000 units a week. Trick tells Gear that it plans to cut its price so that it can sell the agreed 2,000 units each week. Because the two firms produce an identical product, Gear matches Trick's price cut but still produces only 2,000 units a week.

In fact, there has been no decrease in demand. Trick plans to increase output, which it knows will lower the price, and Trick wants to ensure that Gear's output remains at the agreed level.

Figure 14.4 illustrates the consequences of Trick's cheating. Part (a) shows Gear (the complier); part (b) shows Trick (the cheat); and part (c) shows the industry as a whole. Suppose that Trick increases output to 3,000 units a week. If Gear sticks to the agreement to produce only 2,000 units a week, total output is now 5,000 a week, and given demand in part (c), the price falls to $7,500 a unit.

Gear continues to produce 2,000 units a week at a cost of $8,000 a unit and incurs a loss of $500 a unit, or $1 million a week. This economic loss is shown by the red rectangle in part (a). Trick produces 3,000 units a week at a cost of $6,000 a unit. With a price

of $7,500, Trick makes a profit of $1,500 a unit and therefore an economic profit of $4.5 million. This economic profit is the blue rectangle in part (b).

We've now described a second possible outcome for the duopoly game: One of the firms cheats on the collusive agreement. In this case, the industry output is larger than the monopoly output and the industry price is lower than the monopoly price. The total economic profit made by the industry is also smaller than the monopoly's economic profit. Trick (the cheat) makes an economic profit of $4.5 million, and Gear (the complier) incurs an economic loss of $1 million. The industry makes an economic profit of $3.5 million. This industry profit is $0.5 million less than the economic profit that a monopoly would make, but it is distributed unevenly. Trick makes a bigger economic profit than it would under the collusive agreement, while Gear incurs an economic loss.

A similar outcome would arise if Gear cheated and Trick complied with the agreement. The industry profit and price would be the same, but in this case, Gear (the cheat) would make an economic profit of $4.5 million and Trick (the complier) would incur an economic loss of $1 million.

Let's next see what happens if both firms cheat.

FIGURE 14.4 One Firm Cheats

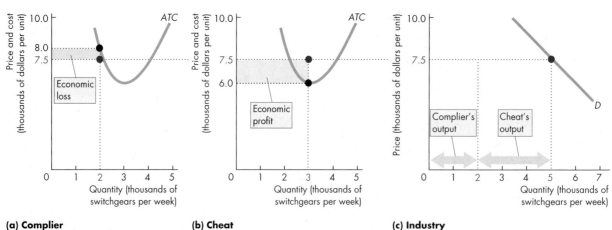

(a) Complier   **(b) Cheat**   **(c) Industry**

One firm, shown in part (a), complies with the agreement and produces 2,000 units. The other firm, shown in part (b), cheats on the agreement and increases its output to 3,000 units a week. Given the market demand curve, shown in part (c), and with a total production of 5,000 units a week, the price falls

to $7,500 a unit. At this price, the complier in part (a) incurs an economic loss of $1 million ($500 per unit × 2,000 units), shown by the red rectangle. In part (b), the cheat makes an economic profit of $4.5 million ($1,500 per unit × 3,000 units), shown by the blue rectangle.

Both Firms Cheat Suppose that both firms cheat and that each firm behaves like the cheating firm that we have just analyzed. Each tells the other that it is unable to sell its output at the going price and that it plans to cut its price. But because both firms cheat, each will propose a successively lower price. As long as price exceeds marginal cost, each firm has an incentive to increase its production—to cheat. Only when price equals marginal cost is there no further incentive to cheat. This situation arises when the price has reached $6,000. At this price, marginal cost equals price. Also, price equals minimum average total cost. At a price less than $6,000, each firm incurs an economic loss. At a price of $6,000, each firm covers all its costs and makes zero economic profit. Also, at a price of $6,000, each firm wants to produce 3,000 units a week, so the industry output is 6,000 units a week. Given the demand conditions, 6,000 units can be sold at a price of $6,000 each.

Figure 14.5 illustrates the situation just described. Each firm, in part (a), produces 3,000 units a week, and its average total cost is a minimum ($6,000 per unit). The market as a whole, in part (b), operates at the point at which the market demand curve (D) intersects the industry marginal cost curve (MC_I). Each firm has lowered its price and increased its output to try to gain an advantage over the other firm. Each has pushed this process as far as it can without incurring an economic loss.

We have now described a third possible outcome of this duopoly game: Both firms cheat. If both firms cheat on the collusive agreement, the output of each firm is 3,000 units a week and the price is $6,000 a unit. Each firm makes zero economic profit.

The Payoff Matrix Now that we have described the strategies and payoffs in the duopoly game, we can summarize the strategies and the payoffs in the form of the game's payoff matrix. Then we can find the Nash equilibrium.

Table 14.2 sets out the payoff matrix for this game. It is constructed in the same way as the payoff matrix for the prisoners' dilemma in Table 14.1. The squares show the payoffs for the two firms—Gear and Trick. In this case, the payoffs are profits. (For the prisoners' dilemma, the payoffs were losses.)

The table shows that if both firms cheat (top left), they achieve the perfectly competitive outcome—each firm makes zero economic profit. If both firms comply (bottom right), the industry makes the monopoly profit and each firm makes an economic profit of $2 million. The top right and bottom left squares show the payoff if one firm cheats while the other complies. The firm that cheats makes an economic profit of $4.5 million, and the one that complies incurs a loss of $1 million.

Nash Equilibrium in the Duopolists' Dilemma The duopolists have a dilemma like the prisoners' dilemma. Do they comply or cheat? To answer this question, we must find the Nash equilibrium.

FIGURE 14.5 Both Firms Cheat

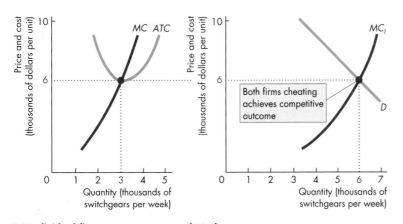

(a) Individual firm   **(b) Industry**

If both firms cheat by increasing production, the collusive agreement collapses. The limit to the collapse is the competitive equilibrium. Neither firm will cut its price below $6,000 (minimum average total cost) because to do so will result in losses. In part (a), each firm produces 3,000 units a week at an average total cost of $6,000. In part (b), with a total production of 6,000 units, the price falls to $6,000. Each firm now makes zero economic profit. This output and price are the ones that would prevail in a competitive industry.

TABLE 14.2 Duopoly Payoff Matrix

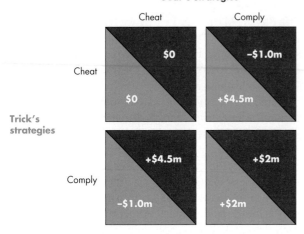

Gear's strategies

Cheat | Comply

Trick's strategies

Cheat: $0 / $0, –$1.0m / +$4.5m

Comply: +$4.5m / –$1.0m, +$2m / +$2m

Each square shows the payoffs from a pair of actions. For example, if both firms comply with the collusive agreement, the payoffs are recorded in the bottom right square. The red triangle shows Gear's payoff, and the blue triangle shows Trick's. In Nash equilibrium, both firms cheat.

—— MyLab Economics Animation ——

Look at things from Gear's point of view. Gear reasons as follows: Suppose that Trick cheats. If I comply, I will incur an economic loss of $1 million. If I also cheat, I will make zero economic profit. Zero is better than *minus* $1 million, so I'm better off if I cheat. Now suppose Trick complies. If I cheat, I will make an economic profit of $4.5 million, and if I comply, I will make an economic profit of $2 million. Profit of $4.5 million is better than $2 million, so I'm better off if I cheat. So regardless of whether Trick cheats or complies, Gear's best strategy is to cheat.

Trick comes to the same conclusion as Gear because the two firms face an identical situation. So both firms cheat. The Nash equilibrium of the duopoly game is that both firms cheat. Although the industry has only two firms, they charge the same price and produce the same quantity as those in a competitive industry. Also, as in perfect competition, each firm makes zero economic profit.

Economics in Action (opposite) and *Economics in the News* (p. 337) look at some other prisoners' dilemma games. But not all games are prisoners' dilemmas, as you'll now see.

ECONOMICS IN ACTION

A Game in the Market for Tissues

Anti-Viral Kleenex and Puffs Plus Lotion didn't get developed because Kimberly-Clark (Kleenex) and P&G (Puffs) were thinking about helping you cope with a miserable cold. These new-style tissues and other innovations in the quality of facial tissues are the product of a costly research and development (R&D) game.

The table below illustrates the game (with hypothetical numbers). Each firm can spend either $25 million or nothing on R&D. If neither firm spends, Kimberly-Clark makes an economic profit of $70 million and P&G of $30 million (bottom right). If each firm spends on R&D, Kimberly-Clark's economic profit is $45 million and P&G's is $5 million (top left). The other parts of the matrix show the economic profits for each when one spends on R&D and the other doesn't.

Confronted with these payoffs, Kimberly-Clark sees that it gets a bigger profit if it spends on R&D regardless of what P&G does. P&G reaches the same conclusion: It, too, gets a bigger profit by spending on R&D regardless of what Kimberly-Clark does.

Because R&D is the best strategy for both players, it is the Nash equilibrium—a *dominant-strategy Nash equilibrium*.

The outcome of this game is that both firms conduct R&D. They make less profit than they would if they could collude to achieve the cooperative outcome of no R&D. But you get a better Kleenex or Puffs tissue.

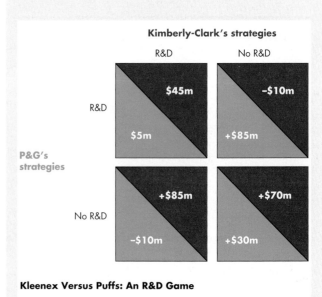

Kimberly-Clark's strategies

R&D | No R&D

P&G's strategies

R&D: $45m / $5m, –$10m / +$85m

No R&D: +$85m / –$10m, +$70m / +$30m

Kleenex Versus Puffs: An R&D Game

A Game of Chicken

The Nash equilibrium for the prisoners' dilemma is unique: Both players cheat (confess). Not all games have a unique equilibrium, and one that doesn't is a game called "chicken."

An Example of the Game of Chicken A graphic, if disturbing, version of "chicken" has two cars racing toward each other. The first driver to swerve and avoid a crash is the "chicken." The payoffs are a big loss for both if no one "chickens out;" zero for both if both "chicken out;" and zero for the chicken and a gain for the one who stays the course. If player 1 swerves, player 2's best strategy is to stay the course; and if player 1 stays the course, player 2's best strategy is to swerve.

An Economic Example of Chicken An economic game of chicken can arise when research and development (R&D) creates a new technology that cannot be kept secret or patented, so both firms benefit from the R&D of either firm. The chicken in this case is the firm that does the R&D.

Suppose, for example, that either Apple or Nokia spends $9 million developing a new touch-screen technology that both would end up being able to use regardless of which of them developed it.

Table 14.3 illustrates a payoff matrix for the game that Apple and Nokia play. Each firm has two strategies: Do the R&D ("chicken out") or do not do the R&D. Each entry shows the additional profit (the profit from the new technology minus the cost of the research), given the strategies adopted.

If neither firm does the R&D, each makes zero additional profit. If both firms conduct the R&D, each firm makes an additional $5 million. If one of the firms does the R&D ("chickens out"), the chicken makes $1 million and the other firm makes $10 million. Confronted with these payoffs, the two firms calculate their best strategies. Nokia is better off doing R&D if Apple does no R&D. Apple is better off doing R&D if Nokia does no R&D. There are two Nash equilibrium outcomes: Only one firm does the R&D, but we can't predict which one.

You can see that an outcome with no firm doing R&D isn't a Nash equilibrium because one firm would be better off doing it. Also, both firms doing R&D isn't a Nash equilibrium because one firm would be better off *not* doing it. To decide *which* firm does the R&D, the firms might toss a coin, called a mixed strategy.

TABLE 14.3 An R&D Game of Chicken

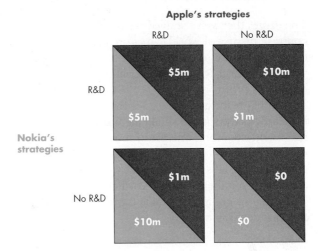

If neither firm does the R&D, their payoffs are in the bottom right square. When one firm "chickens out" and does the R&D while the other does no R&D, their payoffs are in the top right and bottom left squares. When both "chicken out" and do the R&D, the payoffs are in the top left square. The red triangle shows Apple's payoff, and the blue triangle shows Nokia's. The equilibrium for this R&D game of chicken is for only one firm to undertake the R&D. We cannot tell which firm will do the R&D and which will not.

REVIEW QUIZ

1 What are the common features of all games?
2 Describe the prisoners' dilemma game and explain why the Nash equilibrium delivers a bad outcome for both players.
3 Why does a collusive agreement to restrict output and raise the price create a game like the prisoners' dilemma?
4 What creates an incentive for firms in a collusive agreement to cheat and increase output?
5 What is the equilibrium strategy for each firm in a duopolists' dilemma and why do the firms not succeed in colluding to raise the price and profits?
6 Describe the payoffs for an R&D game of chicken and contrast them with the payoffs in a prisoners' dilemma game.

Work these questions in Study Plan 14.2 and get instant feedback. MyLab Economics

Repeated Games and Sequential Games

The games that we've studied are played just once. In contrast, many real-world games are played repeatedly. This feature of games turns out to enable real-world duopolists to cooperate, collude, and make a monopoly profit.

Another feature of the games that we've studied is that the players move simultaneously. But in many real-world situations, one player moves first and then the other moves—the play is sequential rather than simultaneous. This feature of real-world games creates a large number of possible outcomes.

We're now going to examine these two aspects of strategic decision making.

A Repeated Duopoly Game

If two firms play a game repeatedly, one firm has the opportunity to penalize the other for previous "bad" behaviour. If Gear cheats this week, perhaps Trick will cheat next week. Before Gear cheats this week, won't it consider the possibility that Trick will cheat next week? What is the equilibrium of this game?

Actually, there is more than one possibility. One is the Nash equilibrium that we have just analyzed. Both players cheat, and each makes zero economic profit forever. In such a situation, it will never pay for one of the players to start complying unilaterally because to do so would result in a loss for that player and a profit for the other. But a **cooperative equilibrium** in which the players make and share the monopoly profit is possible.

A cooperative equilibrium might occur if cheating is punished. There are two extremes of punishment. The smallest penalty is called "tit for tat." A *tit-for-tat strategy* is one in which a player cooperates in the current period if the other player cooperated in the previous period, but cheats in the current period if the other player cheated in the previous period. The most severe form of punishment is called a trigger strategy. A *trigger strategy* is one in which a player cooperates if the other player cooperates but plays the Nash equilibrium strategy forever thereafter if the other player cheats.

In the duopoly game between Gear and Trick, a tit-for-tat strategy keeps both players cooperating and making monopoly profits. Let's see why with an example.

Table 14.4 shows the economic profit that Trick and Gear will make over a number of periods under two alternative sequences of events: colluding and cheating with a tit-for-tat response by the other firm.

If both firms stick to the collusive agreement in period 1, each makes an economic profit of $2 million. Suppose that Trick contemplates cheating in period 1. The cheating produces a quick $4.5 million economic profit and inflicts a $1 million economic loss on Gear. But a cheat in period 1 produces a response from Gear in period 2. If Trick wants to get back into a profit-making situation, it must return to the agreement in period 2 even though it knows that Gear will punish it for cheating in period 1. So in period 2, Gear punishes Trick and Trick cooperates. Gear now makes an economic profit of $4.5 million, and Trick incurs an economic loss of $1 million. Adding up the profits over two periods of play, Trick would have made more profit by cooperating—$4 million compared with $3.5 million.

What is true for Trick is also true for Gear. Because each firm makes a larger profit by sticking with the collusive agreement, both firms do so and the monopoly price, quantity, and profit prevail.

In reality, whether a cartel works like a one-play game or a repeated game depends primarily on the

---

TABLE 14.4   Cheating with Punishment

Period of play	Collude		Cheat with tit-for-tat	
	Trick's profit (millions of dollars)	Gear's profit (millions of dollars)	Trick's profit (millions of dollars)	Gear's profit (millions of dollars)
1	2	2	4.5	−1.0
2	2	2	−1.0	4.5
3	2	2	2.0	2.0
4	•	•	•	•

If duopolists repeatedly collude, each makes a profit of $2 million per period of play. If one player cheats in period 1, the other player plays a tit-for-tat strategy and cheats in period 2. The profit from cheating can be made for only one period and must be paid for in the next period by incurring a loss. Over two periods of play, the best that a duopolist can achieve by cheating is a profit of $3.5 million, compared to an economic profit of $4 million by colluding.

◆ ECONOMICS IN THE NEWS

Airbus Versus Boeing

Airbus Is Shopping a New Jet to Compete with Boeing's Future Airliner

Airbus and Boeing are competing to produce an inexpensive midsize airliner that can seat around 250 people and fly up to 5,000 nautical miles, or 10 hours. To meet this demand, Boeing is considering developing a new small twin-aisle jet to be called the 797 at an estimated cost of $15 billion. Airbus is looking at a lower-cost option of upgrading its A321neo airliner with new carbon fiber wings and a longer cabin that seats more than 240 and can fly longer distances.

Source: CNNMoney, May 9, 2017

SOME ASSUMPTIONS

- If Airbus upgrades the A321neo and Boeing develops the 797, each firm's economic profit will increase by $10 billion.
- If Airbus upgrades the A321neo and Boeing drops the 797 plan and sticks with its current planes, Airbus will take market share from Boeing. Airbus will see economic profit increase by $20 billion and Boeing will incur a loss of $10 billion.
- If Boeing develops the 797 and Airbus drops its upgrade idea and sticks with its current planes, Boeing will take market share from Airbus. Boeing will see economic profit increase by $20 billion and Airbus will incur a loss of $10 billion.
- If both firms abandon development and upgrade plans, their economic profit is $15 billion higher because they avoid a large development expense.

THE QUESTIONS

- In what type of market are Airbus and Boeing competing?
- Given the assumptions above, will Airbus upgrade the A321neo? Will Boeing develop the 797? To answer this question, set out the payoff matrix for the game that Airbus and Boeing are playing and find the Nash equilibrium.

THE ANSWERS

- Airbus and Boeing are a duopoly.
- The table illustrates the payoff matrix for the game between Airbus and Boeing.
- Regardless of what Boeing does, Airbus is better off upgrading the A321neo.

- And regardless of what Airbus does, Boeing is better off developing the 797.
- The outcome is a dominant-strategy Nash equilibrium.
- Airbus upgrades the A321neo and Boeing develops the 797.
- The airplane development game played by Airbus and Boeing brings ever better planes.

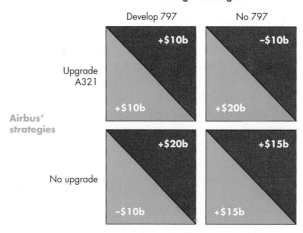

Duopoly Game: Market for Airplanes

The A321neo and 797 in a development game

number of players and the ease of detecting and punishing cheating. The larger the number of players, the harder it is to maintain a cartel.

Games and Price Wars A repeated duopoly game can help us understand real-world behaviour and, in particular, price wars. Some price wars can be interpreted as the implementation of a tit-for-tat strategy. But the game is a bit more complicated than the one we've looked at because the players are uncertain about the demand for the product.

Playing a tit-for-tat strategy, firms have an incentive to stick to the monopoly price. But fluctuations in demand lead to fluctuations in the monopoly price, and sometimes, when the price changes, it might seem to one of the firms that the price has fallen because the other has cheated. In this case, a price war will break out. The price war will end only when each firm is satisfied that the other is ready to cooperate again. There will be cycles of price wars and the restoration of collusive agreements. Fluctuations in the world price of oil might be interpreted in this way.

Some price wars arise from the entry of a small number of firms into an industry that had previously been a monopoly. Although the industry has a small number of firms, the firms are in a prisoners' dilemma and they cannot impose effective penalties for price cutting. The behaviour of prices and outputs in the computer chip industry during 1995 and 1996 can be explained in this way. Until 1995, the market for Pentium chips for IBM-compatible computers was dominated by one firm, Intel Corporation, which was able to make maximum economic profit by producing the quantity of chips at which marginal cost equalled marginal revenue. The price of Intel's chips was set to ensure that the quantity demanded equalled the quantity produced. Then in 1995 and 1996, with the entry of a small number of new firms, the industry became an oligopoly. If the firms had maintained Intel's price and shared the market, together they could have made economic profits equal to Intel's profit. But the firms were in a prisoners' dilemma, so prices fell toward the competitive level.

Let's now study a sequential game. There are many such games, and the one we'll examine is among the simplest. It has an interesting implication and it will give you the flavour of this type of game. The sequential game that we'll study is an entry game in a contestable market.

A Sequential Entry Game in a Contestable Market

If two firms play a sequential game, one firm makes a decision at the first stage of the game and the other makes a decision at the second stage.

We're going to study a sequential game in a **contestable market**—a market in which firms can enter and leave so easily that firms in the market face competition from *potential* entrants. Examples of contestable markets are routes served by airlines and by barge companies that operate on the major waterways. These markets are contestable because firms could enter if an opportunity for economic profit arose and could exit with no penalty if the opportunity for economic profit disappeared.

If the Herfindahl-Hirschman Index (Chapter 13, pp. 307–308) is used to determine the degree of competition, a contestable market appears to be uncompetitive. But a contestable market can behave as if it were perfectly competitive. To see why, let's look at an entry game for a contestable air route.

A Contestable Air Route Agile Air is the only firm operating on a particular route. Demand and cost conditions are such that there is room for only one airline to operate. Wanabe Inc. is another airline that could offer services on the route.

We describe the structure of a sequential game by using a *game tree* like that in Fig. 14.6. At the first stage, Agile Air must set a price. Once the price is set and advertised, Agile can't change it. That is, once set, Agile's price is fixed and Agile can't react to Wanabe's entry decision. Agile can set its price at either the monopoly level or the competitive level.

At the second stage, Wanabe must decide whether to enter or to stay out. Customers have no loyalty (there are no frequent-flyer programs) and they buy from the lowest-price firm. So if Wanabe enters, it sets a price just below Agile's and takes all the business.

Figure 14.6 shows the payoffs from the various decisions (Agile's in the red triangles and Wanabe's in the blue triangles).

To decide on its price, Agile's CEO reasons as follows: Suppose that Agile sets the monopoly price. If Wanabe enters, it earns 90 (think of all payoff numbers as thousands of dollars). If Wanabe stays out, it earns nothing. So Wanabe will enter. In this case Agile will lose 50.

Now suppose that Agile sets the competitive price. If Wanabe stays out, it earns nothing, and if it enters,

FIGURE 14.6 Agile Versus Wanabe: A Sequential Entry Game in a Contestable Market

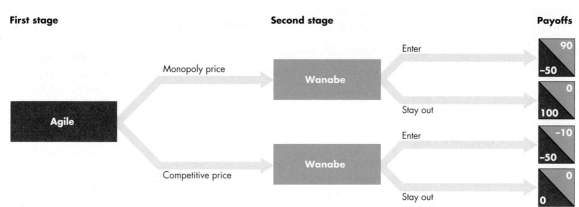

If Agile sets the monopoly price, Wanabe makes 90 (thousand dollars) by entering and earns nothing by staying out. So if Agile sets the monopoly price, Wanabe enters.

If Agile sets the competitive price, Wanabe earns nothing if it stays out and incurs a loss if it enters. So if Agile sets the competitive price, Wanabe stays out.

MyLab Economics Animation

it loses 10, so Wanabe will stay out. In this case, Agile will make zero economic profit.

Agile's best strategy is to set its price at the competitive level and make zero economic profit. The option of earning 100 by setting the monopoly price with Wanabe staying out is not available to Agile. If Agile sets the monopoly price, Wanabe enters, undercuts Agile, and takes all the business.

In this example, Agile sets its price at the competitive level and makes zero economic profit. A less costly strategy, called **limit pricing**, sets the price at the highest level that inflicts a loss on the entrant. Any loss is big enough to deter entry, so it is not always necessary to set the price as low as the competitive price. In the example of Agile and Wanabe, at the competitive price Wanabe incurs a loss of 10 if it enters. A smaller loss would still keep Wanabe out.

This game is interesting because it points to the possibility of a monopoly behaving like a competitive industry and serving the social interest without regulation. But the result is not general and depends on one crucial feature of the setup of the game: At the second stage, Agile is locked in to the price set at the first stage.

If Agile could change its price in the second stage, it would want to set the monopoly price if Wanabe stayed out—100 with the monopoly price beats zero with the competitive price. But Wanabe can figure out what Agile would do, so the price set at the first stage

has no effect on Wanabe. Agile sets the monopoly price and Wanabe might either stay out or enter.

We've looked at two of the many possible repeated and sequential games, and you've seen how these types of games can provide insights into the complex forces that determine prices and profits.

REVIEW QUIZ

1 If a prisoners' dilemma game is played repeatedly, what punishment strategies might the players employ and how does playing the game repeatedly change the equilibrium?

2 If a market is contestable, how does the equilibrium differ from that of a monopoly?

Work these questions in Study Plan 14.3 and get instant feedback. MyLab Economics

So far, we've studied oligopoly with unregulated market power. Firms like Trick and Gear are free to collude to maximize their profit with no concern for the consumer or the law.

But when firms collude to achieve the monopoly outcome, they also have the same effects on efficiency and the social interest as monopoly. Profit is made at the expense of consumer surplus and a deadweight loss arises. Your next task is to see how Canada's anti-combine law limits market power.

◆ Anti-Combine Law

Anti-combine law is the law that regulates oligopolies and prevents them from becoming monopolies or behaving like monopolies. Anti-combine law can work in the social interest to maximize total surplus or in the self-interest of producers to maximize producer surpluses. We'll describe Canada's anti-combine law and examine some recent cases.

Canada's Anti-Combine Law

Canada's anti-combine law dates from 1889. At that time, monopoly was a major political issue and people were concerned about the absence of competition in industries as diverse as sugar and groceries, biscuits and confectionery, coal, binder twine, agricultural implements, stoves, coffins, eggs, and fire insurance.

Canada's anti-combine law today is defined in the Competition Act of 1986, which is described in Table 14.5. The Act established a Competition Bureau and a Competition Tribunal. The Competition Act distinguishes between criminal and noncriminal practices.

Criminal offences include conspiring to fix prices, bid-rigging, and false advertising. It is also a criminal offence for a manufacturer to set the price at which a retailer must sell its products—called resale price maintenance. The courts handle alleged criminal offences, and the standard level of proof beyond a reasonable doubt must be established.

Noncriminal offences are mergers, abuse of a dominant market position, refusal to deal, and other actions designed to limit competition such as exclusive dealing. The Director of the Competition Bureau sends alleged violations of a noncriminal nature to the Competition Tribunal for examination.

Some Major Anti-Combine Cases

To see how the Competition Act has been working, we'll look at a few cases. The first case we'll examine is important because it confirms the Competition Tribunal's power to enforce its orders.

TABLE 14.5   Canada's Anti-Combine Law: The Competition Act, 1986

Abuse of Dominant Position

79 (1) Where on application by the Director, the Tribunal finds that:

    (a) one or more persons substantially or completely control, throughout Canada or any area thereof, a class or species of business,

    (b) that person or those persons have engaged in or are engaging in a practice of anti-competitive acts, and

    (c) the practice has had, is having or is likely to have the effect of preventing or lessening competition substantially in a market,

the Tribunal may make an order prohibiting all or any of those persons from engaging in that practice.

Mergers

92 (1) Where on application by the Director, the Tribunal finds that a merger or proposed merger prevents or lessens, or is likely to prevent or lessen, competition substantially … the Tribunal may … [,] in the case of a completed merger, order any party to the merger or any other person

    (i) to dissolve the merger …

    (ii) to dispose of assets and shares …

    [or]

in the case of a proposed merger, make an order directed against any party to the proposed merger or any other person

    (i) ordering the person … not to proceed with the merger

Source: Competition Act, R.S.C., 1985, c. C-34. Published by the Government of Canada, © 2014.

Chrysler In 1986, Chrysler stopped supplying autoparts to Richard Brunet, a Montreal auto dealer. Chrysler also discouraged other dealers from supplying Brunet. The Competition Tribunal claimed that Chrysler wanted Brunet's business for itself and ordered Chrysler to resume doing business with Brunet. Chrysler did not resume sending supplies and the Tribunal cited Chrysler for contempt. Appeals against this ruling eventually reached the Supreme Court of Canada, which confirmed the Tribunal's power over contempt for its ruling. The Tribunal subsequently dropped its contempt charge.

The second case we'll look at concerns aspartame, the sweetener in many soft drinks.

NutraSweet NutraSweet, the maker of aspartame, tried to gain a monopoly in aspartame. It did so by licensing the use of its "swirl" only on products for which it had an exclusive deal. On October 4, 1990, the Competition Tribunal ruled that this action was an abuse of dominant position and unduly limited competition. The Competition Tribunal told NutraSweet that it may not enforce existing contracts, enter into new contracts in which it is the exclusive supplier, or give inducements to encourage the display of its "swirl." As a result of this case, competition increased and the price of aspartame fell in Canada.

The third case we'll examine concerns a publication that is now struggling to stay alive: the Yellow Pages.

Bell Canada Entrepises Two subsidiaries of Bell Canada Enterprises have a 90 percent share of the market for the publication of telephone directories in their territories. These companies tie the sale of advertising services to the sale of advertising space in the Yellow Pages. If you want to advertise in the Yellow Pages, you must buy the advertising services of one of these two companies. As a result, other advertising agencies cannot effectively compete for business in Yellow Pages advertising.

The Director of the Competition Bureau applied for an order prohibiting the tied-sale practice of these two companies.

Other Recent Cases The Competition Bureau has investigated several high-profile cases in the past few years. These include two proposed mergers between big Canadian banks, a movie theatre merger when Cineplex Galaxy acquired Famous Players, a retail gasoline price-fixing cartel in Quebec, and the ownership transfer and relocation policies of the NHL when Jim Balsillie tried to buy the Nashville Predators.

We look at each of these cases in the following *Economics in Action* boxes.

ECONOMICS IN ACTION

Mergers Blocked

In January 1998, the Royal Bank of Canada and the Bank of Montreal announced that they wanted to merge and create a new bank. Soon after, in April 1998, CIBC and TD Bank announced their desire to combine.

After some months of deliberation, in December 1998, the Finance Minister, Paul Martin, told the banks that they could not proceed with their proposed mergers.

Why the Merger Was Blocked The Finance Minister said that the bank mergers were not in the public interest because they would result in:

- Too much concentration of economic power in the hands of too few financial institutions

- Reduced competition in the financial services markets
- Reduced Government of Canada flexibility to address future concerns

A Competition Bureau report agreed.

Competition Bureau's View The Competition Bureau investigated the impact of the proposed bank mergers on competition in the banking industry. The Bureau concluded that the mergers would substantially lessen competition and would result in bank branches being closed. Canadians would end up paying higher prices for reduced banking services.

Bank mergers in Canada are now so politically sensitive that any future attempts to merge will require the sanction of the federal government.

ECONOMICS IN ACTION

Cineplex Galaxy Acquires Famous Players

In 2004, Cineplex Galaxy bought Famous Players. But before the deal could be confirmed, the Competition Bureau needed to vet and approve it.

The Firms There were two firms in the deal:

1. Cineplex Galaxy operated 86 theatres with 775 screens under the Cineplex Odeon and Galaxy brands in British Columbia, Alberta, Saskatchewan, Manitoba, Ontario, and Quebec.

2. Famous Players operated 77 theatres and 768 screens in the same six provinces as Cineplex Galaxy. The firm operated a number of brands other than its own name, including Coliseum, Colossus, Paramount, and SilverCity.

By number of theatres and screens, Cineplex Galaxy was larger but Famous Players had larger box-office receipts.

The Markets There isn't just one Canadian market for movie theatres. Each urban area is a separate market.

Barriers to Entry The Competition Bureau identified three barriers to entry into the movie-theatre industry:

1. Access to high box-office movies
2. Access to suitable locations
3. Sunk costs and risks

Access to Movies The distribution policies of the major movie studios and distributors make entry risky. A new entrant cannot be sure before entering that the studios and distributors will provide it with movies capable of generating box-office revenue. So entry is highly risky.

Access to Locations During the late 1990s, a major building program created a large number of new stadium theatres, all of which occupied the best sites. As a consequence, it is difficult today to acquire a suitable site or location for a new movie theatre in many urban markets.

Sunk Costs and Risks Most new movie theatres are stadium-seating complexes that are single-purpose buildings. They are costly to build but have no resale

value so the cost of building them is a sunk cost, which makes entry very risky.

Concentration and Competition After the Merger With Cineplex Galaxy and Famous Players operating as a single firm, many urban markets would become highly concentrated.

The Competition Bureau identified 17 local markets. In seven of them, the new merged firm would have had 100 percent market share and in five others, they would be near monopolies.

A few areas would have competition: in Montreal from Cinémas Guzzo; and in Montreal, Ottawa, and Toronto from AMC, a large U.S. operator. Outside of these major cities, the merged firm would have faced either no competition or very limited competition from small local firms.

The Competition Bureau's Decision The Competition Bureau examined the competitive impact of the merger in each of the cities where Famous Players and Cineplex Galaxy competed and determined that the merger would likely reduce competition substantially in 17 of these areas. The Bureau was concerned about both price and nonprice competition on such factors as theatre quality and film choice.

To resolve these concerns, in 17 cities the Bureau required the new firm to sell 35 of its theatres.

The general rule the Bureau employed was to reduce the new firm's market share in each city to a level similar to the pre-merger market share of the larger of Cineplex or Famous Players.

Source: The Competition Bureau, *Acquisitions of Famous Players by Cineplex Galaxy*.

ECONOMICS IN ACTION

Price Fixing

In June 2008, during a period of rapidly rising oil and gasoline prices, the Competition Bureau laid criminal charges against a number of individuals and companies in Victoriaville, Thetford Mines, Magog, and Sherbrooke (all in Quebec) for fixing the price of gasoline at the pump.

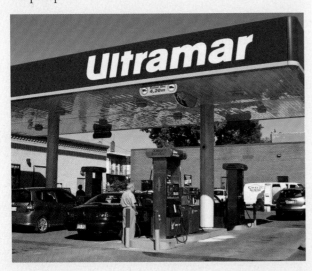

Price-fixing cartels are hard to detect. Evidence of identical prices does not prove the operation of a price-fixing agreement. Firms in perfect competition charge identical prices. Canadian law requires the Competition Bureau to provide evidence that proves, beyond a reasonable doubt, that the competitors have an agreement to fix prices.

In the Quebec gas prices case, the Competition Bureau used wiretaps and searches and took advantage of an immunity program that encourages people who are themselves breaking the law to provide evidence to investigators.

After extensive investigations, evidence emerged that gas retailers had made agreements by telephone on the prices they would charge. The evidence suggested that the overwhelming majority of gasoline retailers in these markets participated in the cartel.

The Court imposed fines totalling more than $2 million against the companies that pleaded guilty.

The Competition Bureau's investigation into potential price-fixing in the retail gasoline market continues in other markets in Canada.

Source: Adapted from the Competition Bureau, *Competition Bureau Uncovers Gasoline Cartel in Quebec.*

ECONOMICS IN ACTION

Abuse of Dominant Position

In May 2007, Jim Balsillie did a tentative deal to buy the NHL team called Nashville Predators with the intention, it was believed, of relocating the team to Hamilton, Ontario.

Locating the Predators in Hamilton would take some of the market from the Toronto Maple Leafs, who would demand compensation. The Buffalo Sabres might also be damaged and demand compensation, although NHL rules do permit relocation outside a radius of 80 kilometres of an existing team.

NHL policy requires that before a relocation can be accepted, a new owner must make a good faith effort to keep the team in its city. Balsillie, it was claimed, had made no such attempt, and the NHL prevented him from completing the deal.

Following intense discussion in the media, the Competition Bureau investigated whether the NHL's transfer of ownership and relocation policies were anticompetitive or merely designed to protect the interests of the league.

After a major and highly detailed investigation, the Competition Bureau concluded that the NHL's policies were not anticompetitive and did not constitute an abuse of a dominant position. Rather, their aim was to maintain healthy rivalries among teams, to attract the largest possible audiences, and to encourage the investment in sports facilities by local governments.

Source: The Competition Bureau, *NHL Ownership Transfer and Relocation Policies.*

◆ REVIEW QUIZ

1 What is the Act of Parliament that provides our anti-combine law?
2 What actions violate the anti-combine law?
3 Under what circumstances is a merger unlikely to be approved?

Work these questions in Study Plan 14.4 and get instant feedback. MyLab Economics

◆ Oligopoly is a market structure that you often encounter in your daily life. *Economics in the News* on pp. 344–345 looks at a game played in the market for cellphone service.

Oligopoly Games in Cellphone Service

Trudeau Minister Says Canada's Cellular Plans Are Too Expensive

Bloomberg News
June 5, 2017

Canada's Liberal government is picking a fight with the country's telecommunications giants.

Internet and cell services still aren't available for many rural and low-income Canadians, and prices are higher than in other developed countries, Innovation Minister Navdeep Bains said in a speech at the Canadian Telecom Summit on Monday.

"Access isn't the only challenge, the bigger barrier is price," Bains said. "The digital divide is unacceptable." …

Rogers Communications Inc., Telus Corp. and BCE Inc. still own more than 90 percent of the wireless market and dominate television and Internet service across the country. Prices, especially for cellphone service, are generally higher than in Europe and the U.S. Carriers argue this is because Canada, with a small population spread over a massive area, demands larger and more expensive infrastructure investment to maintain network quality.

Bains ordered the country's telecommunications regulator to review its recent decision that allows wireless network owners to refuse access for smaller companies that don't have their own cell towers in a certain geographic area.

That decision effectively shuts down prospects for companies like Sugar Wireless, which mostly uses wi-fi service to connect its users and pays to roam on other networks when wi-fi isn't available. It's a model that's been employed with success in the U.S. by firms such as Republic Wireless.

ESSENCE OF THE STORY

- Rogers, Telus, and Bell (BCE) own more than 90 percent of the wireless market.

- Cellphone services aren't available for many rural and low-income Canadians.

- The prices of cellphone services are higher in Canada than in Europe, the United States, and other developed countries.

- Cellphone service providers say Canada's small population spread over a massive area makes their costs high.

- A recent decision by the regulator allows Rogers, Telus, and Bell to block access for smaller companies to their cellular networks.

- The Innovation Minister ordered a review of this decision.

ECONOMIC ANALYSIS

- The Canadian market in cellphone service is dominated by three firms: Rogers, Telus, and Bell.

- Figure 1 shows the shares in this market. You can see that Rogers has 34 percent of the market, Bell 29 percent, and Telus 28 percent. Another four smaller firms share the remaining 9 percent.

- Canada's cellphone services prices are high and the three big firms raise their prices together.

- They are able to set high prices because the operate behind a barrier to entry and they play a repeated game.

- If they played a one-shot game, they would be stuck in the prisoners' dilemma, shown in Table 1.

- Being a prisoners' dilemma like that on p. 329, the game has a dominant-strategy Nash equilibrium.

- If Rogers raised its price and Bell didn't, Rogers would lose market share and its profit would fall; and if Bell raised its prices and Rogers didn't, Rogers would take market share and Bell would have lower profit.

- The Nash equilibrium is to set low prices.

- But if the game is repeated with a tit-for-tat punishment strategy like that on p. 336, the firms can break free from the prisoners' dilemma.

- Table 2 summarizes what each player can anticipate if it doesn't cooperate with the others in raising the price.

- In the repeated game, Rogers knows that it will be punished for not going along with a price rise, so its gain from holding the current price is temporary and it will incur a loss in the second period as punishment.

- That is, to restore cooperation with the price hike, Rogers will have to be the only firm with a higher price in the second period.

- The situation is symmetric for Rogers' competitors.

- So after two plays of the game, neither Rogers nor its competitors will have benefited from a price hike.

- The best strategy for all players is to set high prices.

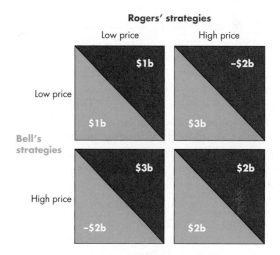

Table 1 Cellphone Service Prisoners' Dilemma

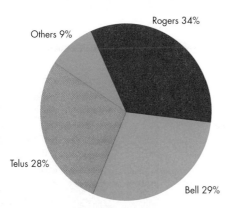

Figure 1 Market Shares in Cellphone Service

TABLE 2   Cheating with Punishment

Period of play	Collude		Cheat with tit-for-tat	
	Rogers' profit (billions of dollars)	Bell's profit (billions of dollars)	Rogers' profit (billions of dollars)	Bell's profit (billions of dollars)
1	1	1	2	−2
2	1	1	−2	2
3	1	1	1	1
4	·	·	·	·

WORKED PROBLEM

MyLab Economics Work this problem in Chapter 14 Study Plan.

Black and White are the two and only producers of piano keys. The firms are identical. They have the same technologies and costs, and they produce the same quantities of piano keys. Their keys are identical too, so they sell for the same price regardless of whether Black or White produces them.

The firms are busy and operating at capacity output. But profit margins are thin and they are making zero economic profit.

Despite it being illegal, the two firms decide to collude: to restrict output and raise the price. The deal is that each of them cuts output to 50 percent of the current level and raises the price.

With the deal in place, the firms can earn the maximum monopoly profit and share it equally.

But each firm wants a bigger share of the market and to get back to the original output level. They each know, though, that if only one of them increases output, profit will increase for the one with larger output and the other will incur an economic loss. They also know that if both of them increase production, they will be back in the situation before the deal.

Questions

1. Describe the game played by Black and White.
2. Make up some profit numbers for Black and White that are consistent with the above account of their situation. Construct a payoff matrix for the game they are playing, and find the equilibrium of the game.

Solutions

1. The game played by Black and White is a duopoly prisoners' dilemma cartel game.

   Each player has two strategies: To keep the cartel agreement or to break the cartel agreement. The payoffs are symmetric.

   If both keep the agreement, they each earn 50 percent of the maximum attainable monopoly profit.

   If both break the agreement, they each earn zero economic profit.

   If one of them breaks the agreement, the breaker earns a profit that is larger than 50 percent of the monopoly profit and the other incurs a loss.

   The game is a prisoners' dilemma because each knows that the joint best outcome requires

keeping the agreement and that the other has an incentive to break it.

Key Point: A duopoly price-fixing game is a prisoners' dilemma in which the firms might keep or break an agreement to collude—might comply or cheat.

2. The table below shows a payoff matrix with profit (and loss) numbers that are consistent with the story about Black and White.

   If both break the agreement (top left), they earn zero economic profit ($0 in the table).

   If both keep the agreement (bottom right), they earn a monopoly profit and share it equally ($10m each in the table).

   If one keeps the agreement and the other breaks it (top right and bottom left), the keeper incurs a loss (–$5m in the table) and the breaker gets a profit larger than half the monopoly profit ($14m in the table).

   The Nash equilibrium is for both firms to break the agreement and make zero economic profit.

   For each firm, breaking the agreement is the best strategy regardless of the strategy of the other player.

   If the other firm keeps the agreement, then the firm that breaks it increases its profit by $4m.

   But if the other firm also breaks the agreement, then breaking the agreement avoids economic loss.

Key Point: The Nash equilibrium of a prisoners' dilemma is not the best joint outcome.

Key Table

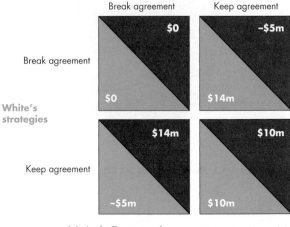

MyLab Economics Interactive Animation

◆ SUMMARY

Key Points

What Is Oligopoly? (pp. 326–327)

- Oligopoly is a market in which a small number of firms compete.

Working Problems 1 to 3 will give you a better understanding of what oligopoly is.

Oligopoly Games (pp. 328–335)

- Oligopoly is studied by using game theory, which is a method of analyzing strategic behaviour.
- In a prisoners' dilemma game, two prisoners acting in their own self-interest harm their joint interest.
- An oligopoly (duopoly) price-fixing game is a prisoners' dilemma in which the firms might collude or cheat.
- In Nash equilibrium, both firms cheat and output and price are the same as in perfect competition.
- Firms' decisions about advertising and R&D can be studied by using game theory.

Working Problems 4 to 6 will give you a better understanding of oligopoly games.

Repeated Games and Sequential Games (pp. 336–339)

- In a repeated game, a punishment strategy can produce a cooperative equilibrium in which price and output are the same as in a monopoly.
- In a sequential contestable market game, a small number of firms can behave like firms in perfect competition.

Working Problem 7 will give you a better understanding of repeated and sequential games.

Anti-Combine Law (pp. 340–343)

- Anti-combine law provides an alternative way for the government to control monopoly and monopolistic practices.
- The Competition Act of 1986 sets out Canada's anti-combine law and established a Competition Bureau and a Competition Tribunal.
- Criminal activity is handled by the courts; violations of a noncriminal nature are examined by the Competition Tribunal.

Working Problem 8 will give you a better understanding of anti-combine law.

Key Terms

MyLab Economics Key Terms Quiz

Anti-combine law, 340
Cartel, 327
Collusive agreement, 330
Contestable market, 338
Cooperative equilibrium, 336

Dominant-strategy equilibrium, 329
Duopoly, 326
Game theory, 328
Limit pricing, 339
Nash equilibrium, 329

Oligopoly, 326
Payoff matrix, 328
Strategies, 328

STUDY PLAN PROBLEMS AND APPLICATIONS

MyLab Economics Work Problems 1 to 8 in Chapter 14 Study Plan and get instant feedback.

What Is Oligopoly? (Study Plan 14.1)

1. **WestJet Targets Air Canada**

   WestJet has signed a deal to buy at least 10 Boeing 787 airplanes to use on international routes and challenge Air Canada. The decision raised the issue of whether Canada can sustain two international airlines.

   > Source: *The Globe and Mail*, May 3, 2017

   Sketch the market demand and cost curves that describe the situation if Canada can sustain two international airlines.

2. **Energizer Versus Duracell**

   In the year to March 2017, Duracell's share of the battery market fell from 47.7 percent to 44.5 percent and Energizer's share grew from 29.6 percent to 32.9 percent.

   > Source: *Seeking Alpha*, April 27, 2017

   In what type of market are batteries sold? Explain your answer.

3. **CRTC Rejects Appeal by Small Internet Players Over Wireless Access**

   Canada's telecom regulator, the CRTC, has confirmed its ruling that wireless carriers are not required to share access to their networks with companies that don't own cellular airwaves of their own.

   > Source: *The Globe and Mail*, February 18, 2016

   Explain why the CRTC ruling described in the news clip creates a barrier to entry in the wireless Internet market and explain why the ruling might create an oligopoly even if there is no natural oligopoly in wireless Internet service.

Oligopoly Games (Study Plan 14.2)

4. Consider a game with two players who cannot communicate, and in which each player is asked a question. The players can answer honestly or lie. If both answer honestly, each receives $100. If one player answers honestly and the other lies, the liar receives $500 and the honest player gets nothing. If both lie, then each receives $50.
   a. Describe the strategies and the payoffs.
   b. Construct the payoff matrix.
   c. What is the equilibrium of this game?
   d. Compare this game to the prisoners' dilemma. Are the games similar or different? Explain.

5. Soapy Inc. and Suddies Inc., the only laundry detergent producers, collude and agree to share the market equally. If neither firm cheats, each makes $1 million. If one firm cheats, it makes $1.5 million, while the complier incurs a loss of $0.5 million. If both cheat, they break even. Neither firm can monitor the other's actions.
   a. What are the strategies in this game? Construct the payoff matrix for this game.
   b. If the game is played only once what is the equilibrium? Is it a dominant-strategy equilibrium? Explain.

6. **If You Hate Flying Now, Just Wait**

   After the airline industry was deregulated, a series of mergers created a four-carrier oligopoly with an 85 percent market share. Reduced competition brought worse service and higher fares. With Washington's refusal to rein in the unfettered airline industry, flying is going to get more uncomfortable.

   > Source: *The Washington Post*, May 3, 2017

   a. Explain how airline mergers might (i) increase fares or (ii) lower airline production costs.
   b. Explain how lower costs might be passed on to travellers or boost airlines' profits. What does the news clip say happened and how would you explain that outcome?

Repeated Games and Sequential Games (Study Plan 14.3)

7. If Soapy Inc. and Suddies Inc. play the game in Problem 5 repeatedly, on each round of play:
   a. What strategies might each firm adopt?
   b. Can the firms adopt a strategy that gives the game a cooperative equilibrium?
   c. Would one firm still be tempted to cheat in a cooperative equilibrium? Explain your answer.

Anti-Combine Law (Study Plan 14.4)

8. Apple conspired with five publishers to undercut Amazon's 90 percent share of the e-book market, which caused e-book prices to rise to $12.99 or $14.99 from the $9.99 that Amazon charged.

   > Source: *Financial Post*, July 10, 2013

   Explain why this conspiracy to raise prices violates the anti-combine law.

ADDITIONAL PROBLEMS AND APPLICATIONS

MyLab Economics You can work these problems in Homework or Test if assigned by your instructor.

What Is Oligopoly?

9. **Monster Hopes for Jump From NASCAR Deal**

   Red Bull and Monster, the two main players in the $8.3 billion U.S. energy-drink market, invest heavily in sponsoring motor racing. And Monster has now signed a multiyear deal to name the Monster Energy NASCAR Cup Series. Red Bull has a 38 percent market share and Monster a 27 percent share. Overall market growth is expected to be 3.1 percent a year over the next five years

   Source: *Los Angeles Times*, January 4, 2017

   a. Describe the structure of the energy-drink market.

   b. What might be the reason that two firms dominate the energy-drink market?

Oligopoly Games

Use the following data to work Problems 10 and 11. Bud and Wise are the only two producers of aniseed beer, a New Age product designed to displace root beer. Bud and Wise are trying to figure out how much of this new beer to produce. They know:

(i) If they both produce 10,000 litres a day, they will make the maximum attainable joint economic profit of $200,000 a day, or $100,000 a day each.

(ii) If either firm produces 20,000 litres a day while the other produces 10,000 litres a day, the one that produces 20,000 litres will make an economic profit of $150,000 and the other will incur an economic loss of $50,000.

(iii) If both produce 20,000 litres a day, each firm will make zero economic profit.

10. Construct a payoff matrix for the game that Bud and Wise must play.

11. Find the Nash equilibrium of the game that Bud and Wise play.

12. **Cartel Flexes Maple Syrup Muscle**

   Quebec is the world's largest maple syrup producer, and in the spring of 2017, its production increased by 4 million pounds over the previous year to 152.2 million pounds. The Federation of Quebec Maple Syrup Producers regulates how much farmers can sell and it increased production quotas in a bid to restore market share lost to U.S. producers in the past decade. Quebec farmers oppose the federation's quota on output, and some producers exceed their quotas and sell on a black market. U.S. producers increased their share of the world market with a 23 percent increase in output in 2016.

   Source: *Bloomberg News*, June 1, 2017

   a. If the Quebec and U.S. maple syrup producers become a profit-maximizing colluding oligopoly, explain how they would influence the price of maple syrup.

   b. Draw a graph to illustrate your answer to (a).

   c. Why is it difficult for a Quebec cartel to act like a monopoly? Use the ideas of game theory to explain.

13. Suppose that Mozilla and Microsoft each develop their own versions of an amazing new Web browser that allows advertisers to target consumers with great precision. Also, the new browser is easier and more fun to use than existing browsers. Each firm is trying to decide whether to sell the browser or to give it away. What are the likely benefits from each action? Which action is likely to occur?

14. Why do Coca-Cola and PepsiCo spend huge amounts on advertising? Do they benefit? Does the consumer benefit? Explain your answer by constructing a game to illustrate the choices Coca-Cola and PepsiCo make.

Use the following news clip to work Problems 15 and 16.

Who's Winning Console Wars?

Sony, Microsoft, and Nintendo dominate the video game console market. Nintendo has a new hybrid handheld and home console called the Switch. Sony has a new PlayStation VR headset. Microsoft plans to launch a more powerful Xbox One.

   Source: *USA TODAY*, April 28, 2017

15. a. Thinking about competition in game consoles as a game, describe the firms' strategies.

   b. What, based on the information provided, turned out to be the equilibrium of the game?

16. Can you think of reasons why the three consoles are different?

Repeated Games and Sequential Games

17. If Bud and Wise in Problem 10 play the game repeatedly, what is the equilibrium of the game?

18. Agile Airlines' profit on a route on which it has a monopoly is $10 million a year. Wanabe Airlines is considering entering the market and operating on this route. Agile warns Wanabe to stay out and threatens to cut the price so that if Wanabe enters it will make no profit. Wanabe determines that the payoff matrix for the game in which it is engaged with Agile is shown in the table.

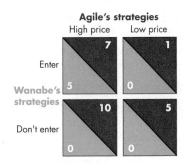

Agile's strategies

Does Wanabe believe Agile's assertion? Does Wanabe enter or not? Explain.

19. **Swatch Is Taking on Silicon Valley**

Swatch, Switzerland's largest watchmaker, is developing an alternative to Apple's iOS and Google's Android operating systems for smartwatches. Swatch says its technology will need less battery power and will protect data better.

Source: *The Toronto Star*, March 17, 2017

What type of market does the news clip imply best describes the markets for smartwatches and their operating systems?

Anti-Combine Law

Use the following news clip to work Problems 20 and 21.

Gadgets for Sale ... or Not

How come the prices of some gadgets, like the iPod, are the same no matter where you shop? No, the answer isn't that Apple illegally manages prices. In reality, Apple uses an accepted retail strategy called minimum advertised price to discourage resellers from discounting. The minimum advertised price (MAP) is the absolute lowest price of a product that resellers can advertise. Marketing subsidies offered by a manufacturer to its resellers usually keep the price at or above the MAP. Stable prices are important to the company

that is both a manufacturer and a retailer. If Apple resellers advertised the iPod below cost, they could squeeze the Apple Stores out of their own markets. The downside to the price stability is that by limiting how low sellers can go, MAP keeps prices artificially high (or at least higher than they might otherwise be with unfettered price competition).

Source: *Slate*, December 22, 2006

20. a. Describe the practice of resale price maintenance that violates the anti-combine law.

b. Describe the MAP strategy used by Apple and explain how it differs from a resale price maintenance agreement that would violate the anti-combine law.

21. Why might the MAP strategy be against the social interest and benefit only the producer?

Economics in the News

22. After you have studied *Economics in the News* on pp. 344–345, answer the following questions.

a. What are the strategies of Rogers, Bell, and Telus in the market for cellphone service?

b. If Rogers, Bell, and Telus played a one-shot game, how would the outcome be different?

c. Why is a tit-for-tat punishment strategy needed to get the firms out of a prisoners' dilemma?

d. How would you expect the entry of a fourth big player, such as U.S. Verizon, to change the game and its outcome?

23. **After a Surge in Orders, Airlines Balk at Big Jets**

Boeing and Airbus are the main producers of commercial airplanes and dominate the markets for wide-bodied super jumbos and for smaller planes. Passenger traffic is predicted to create a demand for 9,000 smaller, more fuel-efficient wide-bodied planes over the next 20 years.

Source: *The New York Times*, June 19, 2017

a. Thinking of competition between Boeing and Airbus as a game, what are the strategies and the payoffs?

b. Set out a hypothetical payoff matrix for the game you've described in part (a). What is the equilibrium of the game?

c. Do you think the market for commercial airplanes is efficient? Explain and illustrate your answer.

Managing Change and Limiting Market Power

Our economy is constantly changing. Every year, new goods appear and old ones disappear. New firms are born, and old ones die. This process of change is initiated and managed by firms operating in markets.

When a new product appears, just one or two firms sell it: Apple and IBM were the only producers of personal computers; Microsoft was (and almost still is) the only producer of the PC operating system; Intel was the only producer of the PC chip. These firms had enormous power to determine the quantity to produce and the price of their products.

In many markets, entry eventually brings competition. Even with just two rivals, the industry changes its face in a dramatic way. *Strategic interdependence* is capable of leading to an outcome like perfect competition.

With the continued arrival of new firms in an industry, the market becomes competitive. But in most markets, the competition isn't perfect: it becomes *monopolistic competition* with each firm selling its own differentiated product.

Often, an industry that is competitive becomes less so as the bigger and more successful firms in the industry begin to swallow up the smaller firms, either by driving them out of business or by acquiring their assets. Through this process, an industry might return to oligopoly or even monopoly. You can see such a movement in the auto and banking industries today.

By studying firms and markets, we gain a deeper understanding of the forces that allocate resources and begin to see the invisible hand at work.

PART FOUR

UNDERSTANDING FIRMS AND MARKETS

John von Neumann *was one of the great minds of the twentieth century. Born in Budapest, Hungary, in 1903, Johnny, as he was known, showed early mathematical brilliance. He was 25 when he published the article that changed the social sciences and began a flood of research on* **game theory**—*a flood that has not subsided. In that article, von Neumann proved that in a zero-sum game (such as sharing a pie), there exists a best strategy for each player.*

Von Neumann did more than invent game theory: He also invented and built the first practical computer, and he worked on the Manhattan Project, which developed the atomic bomb during World War II.

Von Neumann believed that the social sciences would progress only if they used their own mathematical tools, not those of the physical sciences.

"Real life consists of bluffing, of little tactics of deception, of asking yourself what is the other man going to think I mean to do."

JOHN VON NEUMANN, told to Jacob Bronowski (in a London taxi) and reported in *The Ascent of Man.*

351

THOMAS HUBBARD is the John L. and Helen Kellogg Distinguished Professor of Management and Strategy at the Kellogg School of Management, Northwestern University and a research fellow at the National Bureau of Economic Research.

Professor Hubbard is an empirical economist. His work is driven by data. The central problems that unify much of his work are the limits to information and the fact that information is costly to obtain. Professor Hubbard studies the ways in which information problems influence the organization of firms; the extent to which firms make or buy what they sell; and the structure and performance of markets.

His work appears in the leading journals such as the *American Economic Review*, the *Quarterly Journal of Economics*, and the *Rand Journal of Economics*. He is a co-editor of the *Journal of Industrial Economics*.

Michael Parkin and Robin Bade talked with Thomas Hubbard about his research and what we learn from it about the choices that firms make and their implications for market structure and performance.

Professor Hubbard, you have made important contributions to our understanding of outsourcing: whether a firm will make it or buy it. Can you summarize what economists know about this issue?

If there is one thing that Coase (Ronald Coase, see p. 395) taught us about the boundaries of the firm, it is that when thinking about whether to do something internally or to outsource it, a very useful starting point is to make the decision on a transaction-by-transaction basis.

The way I like to think about it is to boil it down to the theory of markets and incentives. Markets provide strong incentives but not necessarily good incentives. So when you outsource something, you rely on a market mechanism rather than on something within a firm that is less than a market mechanism. By outsourcing, you expose people to a strong market incentive. Now that can be good, and it is good most of the time. Strong market incentives get people to do things that the market rewards. Market rewards are generally quite valuable, but in some circumstances what the market rewards

> **Markets provide strong incentives but not necessarily good incentives.**

isn't what the buyer would want to reward. So there's a tradeoff. Strong incentives are sometimes good and sometimes bad. Therefore, keeping things inside the firm provides a weaker incentive. Sometimes that is good.

Can you provide an example?

Think about McDonald's. McDonald's is not one firm, but many firms because a lot of the outlets are owned and managed by franchisees while McDonald's owns and manages others internally.

McDonald's thinks about whether to run one of its restaurants itself or to franchise it out. One thing that it has in mind is that if it franchises it out, then the franchisor is going to be exposed to very strong market incentives. Now under some circumstances this is great. The franchisee treats the business as if he owns it. So the good part about it is the franchisee works hard to try to develop his business.

But a flip side to the franchisee's treating the business as his own is that it can be harmful for the McDonald's brand.

---

*Read the full interview with Thomas Hubbard in MyLab Economics.

PART FIVE **MARKET FAILURE AND GOVERNMENT**

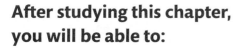

EXTERNALITIES

After studying this chapter, you will be able to:

◆ Explain how externalities arise

◆ Explain why external costs bring market failure and overproduction and how property rights and public choices might achieve an efficient outcome

◆ Explain why external benefits bring market failure and underproduction and how public choices might achieve an efficient outcome

How can we use less fossil fuels to generate electricity and reduce carbon emissions that bring climate change? How can we ensure that we spend enough on our schools, colleges, and universities to provide everyone with a quality education?

These are the questions we study in this chapter. They arise because some of our choices impose costs on or bring benefits to others that we don't think about when we make those choices.

In *Economics in the News* at the end of the chapter, we look at the way Canadian provinces are trying to cut carbon emissions and fight climate change.

Externalities in Our Lives

An **externality** is a cost of or a benefit from an action that falls on someone other than the person or firm choosing the action. We call an externality that imposes a cost a **negative externality**; and we call an externality that provides a benefit a **positive externality**.

We identify externalities as four types:

- Negative production externalities
- Positive production externalities
- Negative consumption externalities
- Positive consumption externalities

Negative Production Externalities

Burning coal to generate electricity emits carbon dioxide that is warming the planet. Logging and the clearing of forests is destroying the habitat of wildlife and also adding carbon dioxide to the atmosphere. These activities are negative production externalities, the costs of which are borne by everyone, and even by future generations.

Noise is another negative production externality. When the Rogers Cup tennis tournament is being played in Toronto, players, spectators, and television viewers around the world share a cost that local residents experience every day: the noise of airplanes taking off from Pearson International Airport. Aircraft noise imposes a cost on millions of people who live under the flight paths to airports in every major city.

Positive Production Externalities

To produce orange blossom honey, a honey producer locates beehives next to an orange orchard. The honeybees collect pollen and nectar from the orange blossoms to make the honey. At the same time, they transfer pollen between the blossoms, which helps to fertilize the blossoms. Two positive production externalities are present in this example. The honey producer gets a positive production externality from the owner of the orange orchard; and the orange grower gets a positive production externality from the honey producer.

Negative Consumption Externalities

Negative consumption externalities are a source of irritation for most of us. Smoking tobacco in a confined space creates fumes that many people find unpleasant and that pose a health risk. So smoking in restaurants and on airplanes generates a negative externality. To avoid this negative externality, many restaurants and all airlines ban smoking. But while a smoking ban avoids a negative consumption externality for most people, it imposes a negative external cost on smokers who would prefer to enjoy the consumption of tobacco while dining or taking a plane trip.

Noisy parties and outdoor rock concerts are other examples of negative consumption externalities. They are also examples of the fact that a simple ban on an activity is not a solution. Banning noisy parties avoids the external cost on sleep-seeking neighbours, but it results in the sleepers imposing an external cost on the fun-seeking partygoers.

Permitting dandelions to grow in lawns, not picking up leaves in the fall, allowing a dog to bark loudly or to foul a neighbour's lawn, and letting a cellphone ring in class are other examples of negative consumption externalities.

Positive Consumption Externalities

When you get a flu vaccination, you lower your risk of being infected. If you avoid the flu, your neighbour, who didn't get vaccinated, has a better chance of remaining healthy. Flu vaccinations generate positive consumption externalities.

When the owner of a historic building restores it, everyone who sees the building gets pleasure from it. Similarly, when someone erects a spectacular home—such as those built by Frank Lloyd Wright during the 1920s and 1930s—or other exciting building—such as the CN Tower in Toronto or the Sydney Opera House in Australia—an external consumption benefit flows to everyone who has an opportunity to view it.

Education, which we examine in more detail in this chapter, is a major example of this type of externality.

REVIEW QUIZ

1 What are the four types of externality?
2 Provide an example of each type of externality that is different from the ones described above.

Work these questions in Study Plan 15.1 and get instant feedback.　　MyLab Economics

We're now going to examine the market failure that arises from an externality and the ways in which it can be avoided. We begin by looking at a negative production externality: pollution.

ECONOMICS IN ACTION

Opposing Trends: Success and Failure

The trends in the air quality of Canadian cities and in global greenhouse gas concentrations are starkly opposed. The concentrations of air pollutants in Canadian cities is decreasing, as it has done so for many years. In contrast, the concentration of greenhouse gases (mainly carbon dioxide) in the global atmosphere is increasing and posing an ever more urgent problem.

Air Pollution Trends

Figure 1 shows the trends in the concentrations of four main pollutants of the air of Canada's cities between 2000 and 2014. With the exception of ozone, the concentrations of these pollutants decreased.

Environment Canada regulations have cut emissions of nitrogen dioxide to 60 percent of its 2000 level, and of volatile organic compounds and sulphur dioxide to around 34 percent of their 2000 levels.

These reductions in air pollution are even more impressive seen against the trends in economic activity. Between 2000 and 2014, total production in Canada increased by 32 percent, vehicle kilometres travelled increased by 41 percent, and the population increased by 16 percent.

Canada's air also compares favourably with that of other countries. No Canadian city, even on a bad day, experiences a smoggy dawn like that of Los Angeles.

Global CO$_2$ and Temperature Trends

Figure 2 shows the global trends in carbon dioxide (CO$_2$) concentration and temperature.

Both trends are starkly upward. CO$_2$ concentration has increased by 50 percent since 1850, and global temperature has been rising for more than 100 years.

Scientists agree that the scale on which we burn fossil fuels is the major source of the rising CO$_2$ trend. There is more uncertainty about the effect of the increase in CO$_2$ on global temperature, but the consensus is that the effect is significant.

Stopping the rising CO$_2$ trend requires joint action by the governments of every nation. First steps in this direction were taken at a 2015 United Nations climate change conference in Paris where 197 countries agreed to limit greenhouse gases emitted by human activity to the level that can be absorbed naturally, and to keep global temperatures "well below" 2°C above pre-industrial levels.

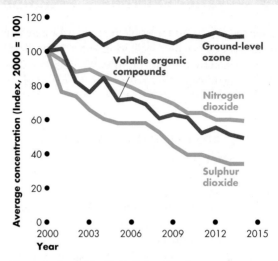

Figure 1 Canadian Air Pollution Trends

Source of data: Environment Canada.

Los Angeles still has a smoggy dawn on some days

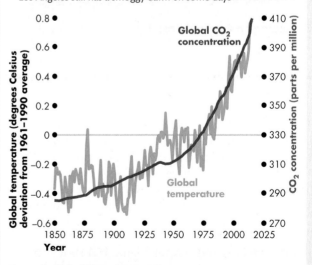

Figure 2 Global Warming Trends

Sources of data: Temperature: Met Office Hadley Centre (combined land and oceans); CO$_2$: Scripps Institution of Oceanography, Mauna Loa Observatory, Hawaii, data since 1960 and ice-core estimates before 1960.

◆ Negative Externality: Pollution

To see the effects and possible remedies for a negative production externality, we'll look at the example of production activities that pollute. We begin by distinguishing among three costs: private, external, and social.

Private, External, and Social Cost

A *private cost* of production is a cost that is borne by the producer of a good or service. *Marginal cost* is the cost of producing an *additional unit* of a good or service. So **marginal private cost** (*MC*) is the cost of producing an additional unit of a good or service that is borne by its producer.

An *external cost* is a cost of producing a good or service that is *not* borne by the producer but borne by other people. A **marginal external cost** is the cost of producing an additional unit of a good or service that falls on people other than the producer.

Marginal social cost (*MSC*) is the marginal cost incurred by the producer and by everyone else on whom the cost falls—by society. It is the sum of marginal private cost and marginal external cost. That is,

$$MSC = MC + \text{Marginal external cost.}$$

We express costs in dollars, but we must always remember that a cost is an opportunity cost—something real, such as clean air or a clean river, is given up to get something.

Valuing an External Cost Economists use market prices to put a dollar value on the external cost of pollution. For example, suppose that there are two similar rivers, one polluted and the other clean. Ten identical homes are built along the side of each river. The homes on the clean river rent for $2,000 per month, and those on the polluted river rent for $1,500 per month. If the pollution is the only detectable difference between the two rivers and the two locations, the rent difference of $500 per month is the pollution cost per home. With 10 homes on the side of a polluted river, the external cost of pollution is $5,000 per month.

External Cost and Output Figure 15.1 shows an example of the relationship between output and cost in a paint industry that pollutes rivers. The marginal cost curve, *MC*, describes the marginal private cost borne by the paint producers, which increases as the quantity of paint produced increases.

FIGURE 15.1 An External Cost

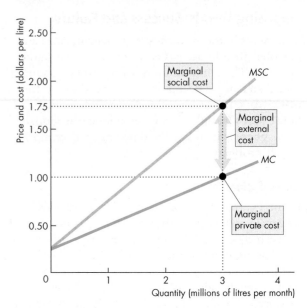

The *MC* curve shows the marginal private cost borne by the factories that produce paint. The *MSC* curve shows the sum of marginal private cost and marginal external cost. When output is 3 million litres of paint per month, marginal private cost is $1.00 per litre, marginal external cost is 75¢ per litre, and marginal social cost is $1.75 per litre.

—— MyLab Economics Animation ——

If a firm pollutes a river, it imposes an external cost borne by other users of the river. Pollution and its marginal external cost increase with the amount of paint produced.

The marginal social cost curve, *MSC*, is found by adding marginal external cost to marginal private cost. So a point on the *MSC* curve shows the sum of the marginal private cost and marginal external cost at a given level of output.

For example, if 3 million litres of paint per month are produced, marginal private cost is $1.00 per litre, marginal external cost is 75¢ per litre, and marginal social cost is $1.75 per litre.

Let's now see how much paint gets produced and how much pollution gets created.

Equilibrium and Amount of Pollution Equilibrium in the market for paint determines the amount of pollution. Figure 15.2 has the same *MC* and *MSC* curves as Fig. 15.1 and also has a market demand and marginal social benefit curve, *D = MSB*. Equilibrium occurs at a price of $1.00 per litre and 3 million litres

FIGURE 15.2   Inefficiency with an External Cost

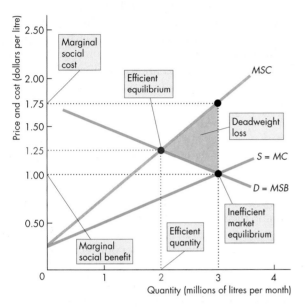

The factories' marginal private cost curve is the market supply curve, *S = MC*. The market demand curve is the marginal social benefit curve, *D = MSB*. The market equilibrium occurs at a price of $1.00 per litre and 3 million litres per month. This outcome is inefficient because marginal social cost exceeds marginal social benefit. The efficient quantity of paint is 2 million litres per month. The grey triangle shows the deadweight loss created by the pollution.

———MyLab Economics Animation and Draw Graph———

per month. This equilibrium is one with *inefficient overproduction* (Chapter 5, p. 118) because marginal social cost at $1.75 per litre exceeds marginal social benefit at $1.00 per litre.

The efficient equilibrium occurs where marginal social benefit *equals* marginal social cost at 2 million litres of paint per month. Too much paint is produced, too much pollution is created, and the area of the deadweight loss triangle measures the society's loss.

The deadweight loss arises because the paint factories only take their private cost into account when making their production decision. If some method can be found to get paint factories to create less pollution and eliminate the deadweight loss, everyone—the owners of paint factories and the residents of the riverside homes—can gain. So, what can be done to fix the inefficiency that arises from an external

cost? Three approaches are available and we will examine each of them. They are:

- Establish property rights
- Mandate clean technology
- Tax or price pollution

Establish Property Rights

Property rights are legally established titles to the ownership, use, and disposal of factors of production and goods and services that are enforceable in the courts. Property rights are a foundation stone of the market economy. But they don't apply to all property. Establishing property rights can confront producers with the costs of their actions and provide the incentives that allocate resources efficiently.

To see how property rights work, suppose that the paint producers have property rights on a river and the homes alongside it—they *own* the river and the homes. The rental income that the paint producers are able to make on the homes depends on the amount of pollution they create. Using the earlier example, people are willing to pay a rent of $2,000 a month to live alongside a pollution-free river but only $1,500 a month to live with the pollution created by producing 3 million litres of paint per month.

The forgone rental income from homes alongside a polluted river is an opportunity cost of producing paint. The paint producers must now decide how to respond to this cost. There are two possible responses:

- Use an abatement technology
- Produce less and pollute less

Use an Abatement Technology An **abatement technology** is a production technology that reduces or prevents pollution. The catalytic converter in every car is an example of an abatement technology. Its widespread adoption (with lead-free gasoline) has dramatically reduced pollution from highway vehicles and helped to achieve an improvement in air quality.

Abatement technologies exist to eliminate or reduce pollution from electricity generation and many industrial processes, including the manufacture of paint.

Produce Less and Pollute Less An alternative to incurring the cost of using an abatement technology is to use the polluting technology but cut production, reduce pollution, and get a higher income from renting homes by the river. The decision turns on cost: Firms will choose the least-cost alternative.

Efficient Market Equilibrium Figure 15.3 illustrates the efficient market outcome. With property rights in place, the paint producers face the pollution costs or the abatement costs, whichever is lower. The *MSC* curve includes the cost of producing paint plus *either* the cost of abatement *or* the cost of pollution (forgone rent), whichever is lower. This curve, labelled $S = MC = MSC$, is now the market supply curve.

Market equilibrium occurs at a price of $1.25 per litre and 2 million litres of paint per month. This outcome is efficient.

If the forgone rent is less than the abatement cost, the factories will still create some pollution, but it will be the efficient quantity. If the abatement cost is lower than the forgone rent, the factories will stop polluting. But they will produce the efficient quantity because marginal cost includes the abatement cost.

FIGURE 15.3 Property Rights Achieve an Efficient Outcome

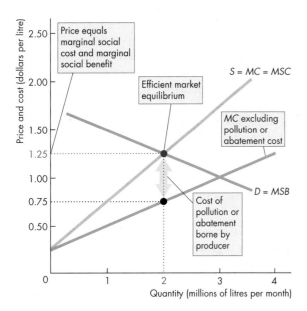

With property rights, the marginal cost curve that excludes pollution and abatement costs shows only part of the producers' marginal cost. The marginal cost of producing paint now includes the cost of pollution—the external cost—or the cost of abatement. So the market supply curve is $S = MC = MSC$. Market equilibrium occurs at a price of $1.25 per litre and 2 million litres of paint per month. Marginal social cost equals marginal social benefit, so the outcome is efficient.

MyLab Economics Animation

The Coase Theorem Does it matter whether the polluter or the victim of the pollution owns the resource that might be polluted? Until 1960, everyone thought that it did matter. But in 1960, Ronald Coase (see p. 395) had a remarkable insight that we now call the Coase theorem.

The **Coase theorem** is the proposition that if property rights exist and the transactions costs of enforcing them are low, then private transactions are efficient and it doesn't matter who has the property rights.

Application of the Coase Theorem Suppose that instead of the paint factories owning the homes, the residents own their homes and the river. Now the factories must pay a fee to the homeowners for the right to dump their waste. The greater the quantity of waste dumped into the river, the more the factories must pay. So again, the factories face the opportunity cost of the pollution they create. The quantity of paint produced and the amount of waste dumped are the same whoever owns the homes and the river. If the factories own them, they bear the cost of pollution because they receive a lower income from home rents. If the residents own the homes and the river, the factories bear the cost of pollution because they must pay a fee to the homeowners. In both cases, the factories bear the cost of their pollution and dump the efficient amount of waste into the river.

The Coase solution works only when transactions costs are low. **Transactions costs** are the opportunity costs of conducting a transaction. For example, when you buy a house, you pay an agent to help you find the best place and a lawyer to run checks that assure you that the seller owns the property and that after you've paid for it, the ownership has been properly transferred to you. These costs are transactions costs.

In the example of the homes alongside a river, the transactions costs that are incurred by a small number of paint factories and a few homeowners might be low enough to enable them to negotiate the deals that produce an efficient outcome. But in many situations, transactions costs are so high that it would be inefficient to incur them. In these situations, the Coase solution is not available.

Mandate Clean Technology

When property rights are too difficult to define and enforce, public choices are made. Regulation is a government's most likely response.

Most countries regulate what may be dumped in rivers and lakes and emitted into the atmosphere. The environmental resources of Canada are heavily regulated.

Canadian Environmental Regulation Environment Canada, the government department charged with monitoring and protecting the environment, was created by the Department of the Environment Act of 1985.

Environment Canada monitors air pollution with its National Air Pollution Surveillance Program and has issued thousands of regulations that require chemical plants and power utilities to adopt best-practice pollution abatement technologies and limit their emissions of specified air pollutants. Other regulations have been issued that govern road vehicle emission limits, which must be met by vehicle manufacturers.

Although direct regulation can and has reduced emissions and improved air quality, economists are generally skeptical about this approach. Abatement is not always the least-cost solution. Also, government agencies are not well placed to find the cost-minimizing solution to a pollution problem. Individual firms seeking to minimize cost and maximize profit and responding to price signals are more likely to achieve an efficient outcome. We'll now examine these other approaches to pollution.

Tax or Cap and Price Pollution

Governments use two main methods of confronting polluters with the costs of their decisions:

- Taxes
- Cap-and-trade

Taxes Governments can use taxes as an incentive for producers to cut back the pollution they create. Taxes used in this way are called **Pigovian taxes**, in honour of Arthur Cecil Pigou, the British economist who first worked out this method of dealing with external costs during the 1920s.

By setting the tax equal to the marginal external cost (or marginal abatement cost if it is lower), firms can be made to behave in the same way as they would if they bore the cost of the externality directly.

To see how government actions can change the outcome in a market with external costs, let's return to the example of paint factories and the river. Assume that the government has assessed the marginal external cost of pollution accurately and

imposes a tax on the factories that exactly equals this cost. The producers are now confronted with the social cost of their actions. The market equilibrium is one in which price equals marginal social cost—an efficient outcome.

Figure 15.4 illustrates the effects of a Pigovian tax on paint factory pollution. The curve $D = MSB$ is the market demand and the marginal social benefit curve. The curve MC is the marginal cost curve. The tax equals the marginal external cost of the pollution. We add this tax to the marginal private cost to find the market supply curve, the curve labelled $S = MC + tax = MSC$. This curve is the market supply curve because it tells us the quantity supplied at each price, given the factories' marginal cost and the tax they must pay. This curve is also the marginal social cost curve because the pollution tax has been set equal to the marginal external cost.

FIGURE 15.4 A Pollution Tax to Achieve an Efficient Outcome

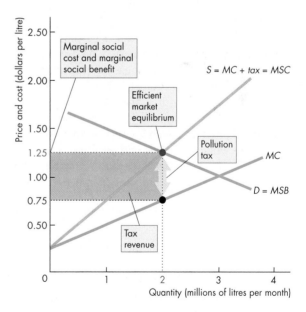

When the government imposes a pollution tax equal to the marginal external cost of pollution, the market supply curve becomes the marginal private cost curve, MC, plus the tax—the curve $S = MC + tax$. Market equilibrium occurs at a price of $1.25 per litre and a quantity of 2 million litres of paint per month. This equilibrium is efficient because marginal social cost equals marginal social benefit. The purple rectangle shows the government's tax revenue.

———— MyLab Economics Animation and Draw Graph ————

ECONOMICS IN ACTION

Taxing Carbon Emissions

British Columbia, Ireland, and the United Kingdom are making their carbon footprints smaller.

British Columbia's Carbon Tax

Introduced in 2008 at $10 per tonne of carbon emitted, British Columbia's tax increased each year to its final rate of $30 per tonne in 2012. The tax applies to all forms of carbon emission from coal, oil, and natural gas. The tax is revenue-neutral, which means that other taxes, personal and corporate income taxes, are cut by the amount raised by the carbon tax. Between 2008 and 2012, carbon emissions fell by 17 percent.

Ireland's Carbon Tax

Since 2010, Ireland has taxed kerosene, gas oil, liquid petroleum gas, fuel oil, natural gas, and solid fuels. The tax rate in 2017 was 30 euros ($34) per tonne of CO_2 emitted. Emissions have fallen since the tax was introduced, but a recession contributed to this fall.

U.K. Tax on Gasoline

The United Kingdom doesn't call its gasoline tax a carbon tax, but it has the same effect on drivers. The figure shows the U.K. price of gasoline compared with that in three other countries. The enormous differences arise almost entirely from tax differences.

An effect of these price differences is that cars in the United Kingdom get an average of 13.5 kilometres per litre while in Canada and the United States, the average is 8.13 kilometres per litre. A high gas tax cuts carbon emissions by inducing people to drive smaller cars and to drive less.

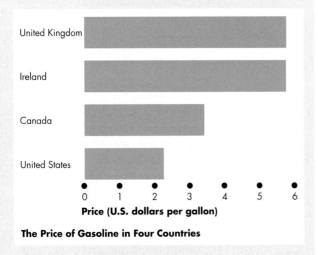

The Price of Gasoline in Four Countries

Demand and supply now determine the market equilibrium price at $1.25 per litre and a quantity of 2 million litres of paint a month. At this quantity of paint production, the marginal social cost is $1.25 and the marginal social benefit is $1.25, so the market outcome is efficient. The factories incur a marginal private cost of 75¢ per litre and pay a pollution tax of 50¢ per litre. The government collects tax revenue of $1 million per month.

Cap-and-Trade A cap is an upper limit. You've met the idea of a government imposing an upper limit before when you learned about production quotas (Chapter 6, p. 143) and import quotas (Chapter 7, p. 164). A cap is a quota—a pollution quota.

A government that uses this method must first estimate the efficient quantity of pollution and set the overall cap at that level.

A pollution quota or cap must somehow be allocated to individual firms (and possibly even households). In an efficient allocation of pollution quotas, each firm has the same marginal social cost. So to make an efficient allocation of the cap across firms, the government would need to know each firm's marginal production cost and marginal abatement cost.

A Pigovian tax doesn't have this problem because each firm chooses how much to produce and pollute taking the tax into account. Because all firms face the same market price, they also incur the same marginal social cost.

Cap-and-trade avoids the need to know each firm's cost by allowing them to trade in a market for pollution permits. Firms that have a low marginal abatement cost sell permits and make big cuts in pollution. Firms that have a high marginal abatement cost buy permits and make smaller cuts or perhaps even no cuts in pollution.

The market in permits determines the equilibrium price of pollution and each firm, confronted with that price, maximizes profit by setting its marginal pollution cost or marginal abatement cost, whichever is lower, equal to the market price of a permit.

By confronting polluters with a price of pollution, trade in pollution permits can achieve the same efficient outcome as a Pigovian tax.

We'll return to cap-and-trade in *Economics in the News* at the end of this chapter when we see how Quebec and Ontario are using this method of tackling the carbon emissions that bring global warming and climate change.

◆ AT **ISSUE**

Should We Be Doing More to Reduce Carbon Emissions?

Economists agree that tackling the global-warming problem requires changes in the incentives that people face. The cost of carbon-emitting activities must rise and the cost of clean-energy technologies must fall.

Disagreement centres on *how* to change incentives. Should more countries set targets for cutting carbon emissions at a faster rate? And should they introduce a carbon tax, emissions charges, or cap-and-trade to cut emissions? Should clean-energy research and development be subsidized?

Yes: *The Stern Review*	No: **The Copenhagen Consensus**

Yes: *The Stern Review*

- Confronting emitters with a tax or price on carbon imposes low present costs for high future benefits.

- The cost of reducing greenhouse gas emissions to safe levels can be kept to 1 percent of global income each year.

- The future benefits are incomes at least 5 percent and possibly 20 percent higher than they will be with inaction every year forever.

- Climate change is a global problem that requires an international coordinated response.

- Unlike most taxes, which bring deadweight loss, a carbon tax eliminates (or reduces) deadweight loss.

- Strong, deliberate policy action is required to change the incentives that emitters face.

- Policy actions should include:
  1. Emissions limits and emissions trading
  2. Increased subsidies for energy research and development, including the development of low-cost clean technology for generating electricity
  3. Reduced deforestation and research into new drought and flood-resilient crop varieties

No: The Copenhagen Consensus

- Confronting emitters with a tax or price on carbon imposes high present costs and low future benefits.

- Unless the entire world signs onto an emissions reduction program, free riders will increase their emissions and carbon leakage will occur.

- A global emissions reduction program and carbon tax would lower living standards in the rich countries and slow the growth rate of living standards in developing countries.

- Technology is already advancing and the cost of cleaner energy is falling.

- Fracking technology has vastly expanded the natural gas deposits that can be profitably exploited and replacing coal with gas halves the carbon emissions from electricity generation.

- Free-market price signals will allocate resources to the development of new technologies that stop and eventually reverse the upward trend in greenhouse gases.

Economist Nicholas Stern, principal author of *The Stern Review on the Economics of Climate Change*.

Greenhouse gas emission is "the greatest market failure the world has ever seen."

He believes that to avoid the risk of catastrophic climate change, the upward CO_2 trend must be stopped.

Bjørn Lomborg, President of the Copenhagen Consensus and author of *The Skeptical Environmentalist*.

"For little environmental benefit, we could end up sacrificing growth, jobs, and opportunities for the big majority, especially in the developing world."

ECONOMICS IN ACTION

A Global Prisoners' Dilemma

China, the United States, and the European Union create 52 percent of global carbon emissions. Another six large countries create a further 21 percent (see Fig. 1).

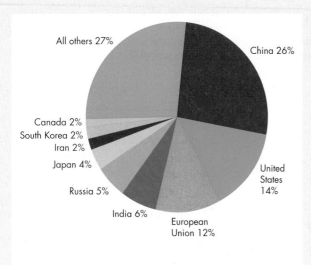

Figure 1 The Global Distribution of CO₂ Emissions

Cutting global carbon emissions is a *prisoners' dilemma* (see pp. 328–329). The payoff matrix opposite illustrates the dilemma. The strategies for the United States and other countries are to keep increasing carbon emissions or to cut them.

Cutting emissions requires using production technologies with higher private costs, but higher private costs make the nation's exporters less competitive in world markets. By letting others cut their emissions and continuing to use low-cost carbon-emitting technologies, a nation can gain a competitive advantage.

In the payoff matrix below, India is better off increasing emissions regardless of what others do; and the others are better off increasing their emissions regardless of what India does. The *Nash equilibrium* (see p. 329) is for all countries to keep increasing their emissions. But the world is better off if all cut.

The challenge is to find a cooperative outcome that avoids this prisoners' dilemma.

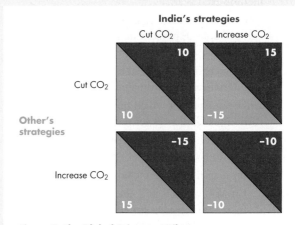

Figure 2 The Global Prisoners' Dilemma

Coping with Global Externalities

Canada has cut the emissions of local air pollutants and made its own air cleaner by adopting the measures you've just seen. But no country, even a big country such as the United States that accounts for 20 percent of the value of global output and 14 percent of carbon emissions, can solve the problem of global warming and climate change alone. Coping with this problem requires public choices at a *global* level, choices by all governments, which are much harder to make and coordinate.

A lower CO₂ concentration in the world's atmosphere is a global *public good*. And like all public goods, it brings a *free-rider problem* (see Chapter 16, p. 377). Without a mechanism to ensure participation in a global carbon-reduction program, countries are in a *prisoners' dilemma* (see *Economics in Action* above).

◆ REVIEW QUIZ

1 What is the distinction between private cost and social cost?
2 How do external costs prevent a competitive market from allocating resources efficiently?
3 How can external costs be eliminated by assigning property rights?
4 How do taxes, pollution charges, and cap-and-trade work to reduce emissions?

Work these questions in Study Plan 15.2 and get instant feedback.　　　MyLab Economics

Your next task is to study a positive externality: the external benefit that arises from knowledge gained through education and research.

◆ Positive Externality: Knowledge

Knowledge comes from education and research. To study the economics of knowledge, we distinguish between private benefits and social benefits.

Private Benefits and Social Benefits

A *private benefit* is a benefit that the consumer of a good or service receives. *Marginal benefit* is the benefit from an additional unit of a good or service. So **marginal private benefit** (*MB*) is the benefit that the consumer of a good or service receives from an additional unit of it.

The *external benefit* from a good or service is the benefit that someone other than the consumer of the good or service receives. University graduates generate many external benefits. On average, they are better citizens, have lower crime rates, and are more tolerant of the views of others. They enable the success of high-quality newspapers and television channels, music, theatre, and other organized social activities that bring benefits to many other people.

A **marginal external benefit** is the benefit from an additional unit of a good or service that people *other than its consumer* enjoy. The benefit that your friends and neighbours get from your university education is its marginal external benefit.

Marginal social benefit (*MSB*) is the marginal benefit enjoyed by society—by the consumer of a good or service (marginal private benefit) and by others (the marginal external benefit). That is,

$$MSB = MB + \text{Marginal external benefit.}$$

Figure 15.5 shows an example of the relationship between marginal private benefit, marginal external benefit, and marginal social benefit. The marginal benefit curve, *MB*, describes the marginal private benefit enjoyed by the people who receive a university education. Marginal private benefit decreases as the number of students enrolled increases.

In the example in Fig. 15.5, when 15 million students enroll in university, the marginal external benefit is $15,000 per student per year. The marginal social benefit curve, *MSB*, is the sum of marginal private benefit and marginal external benefit at each number of students enrolled. For example, when 15 million students a year enroll, the marginal private benefit is $10,000 per student and the marginal external benefit is $15,000 per student, so the marginal social benefit is $25,000 per student.

FIGURE 15.5 An External Benefit

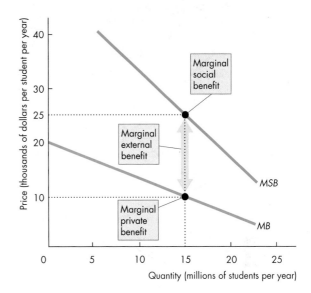

The *MB* curve shows the marginal private benefit enjoyed by the people who receive a university education. The *MSB* curve shows the sum of marginal private benefit and marginal external benefit. When 15 million students attend university, the marginal private benefit is $10,000 per student, the marginal external benefit is $15,000 per student, and the marginal social benefit is $25,000 per student.

———— MyLab Economics Animation ————

When people make schooling decisions, they ignore its external benefits and consider only their private benefits. So if education were provided by private schools that charged full-cost tuition, the market would produce too few graduates.

Figure 15.6 illustrates this private underprovision. The supply curve is the marginal social cost curve, *S = MSC*. The demand curve is the marginal private benefit curve, *D = MB*. Market equilibrium occurs at a tuition of $15,000 per student per year with 7.5 million students per year. At this equilibrium, the marginal social benefit of $38,000 per student exceeds the marginal social cost by $23,000 per student. Too few students enroll in university. The efficient number is 15 million per year, where marginal social benefit equals marginal social cost. The grey triangle shows the deadweight loss created.

FIGURE 15.6 Inefficiency with an External Benefit

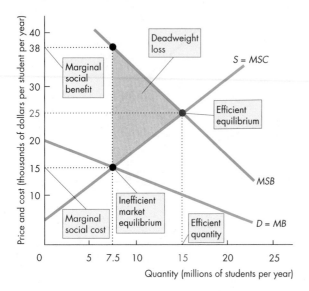

The market demand curve is the marginal private benefit curve, $D = MB$. The supply curve is the marginal social cost curve, $S = MSC$. Market equilibrium at a tuition of $15,000 a year and 7.5 million students is inefficient because marginal social benefit exceeds marginal social cost. The efficient quantity is 15 million students. A deadweight loss arises (grey triangle) because too few students enroll in university.

———MyLab Economics Animation and Draw Graph———

Underproduction similar to that in Fig. 15.6 would occur in elementary school and high school if public education were left to an unregulated market. When children learn basic reading, writing, and number skills, they receive the private benefit of increased earning power. But even these basic skills bring the external benefit of developing better citizens.

External benefits also arise from the discovery of new knowledge. When Isaac Newton worked out the formulas for calculating the rate of response of one variable to another—calculus—everyone was free to use his method. When a spreadsheet program called VisiCalc was invented, Lotus Corporation and Microsoft were free to copy the basic idea and create 1-2-3 and Excel. When the first shopping mall was built and found to be a successful way of arranging retailing, everyone was free to copy the idea, and malls sprouted like mushrooms.

Once someone has discovered a basic idea, others can copy it. Because they do have to work to copy an idea, they face an opportunity cost, but they do not usually have to pay a fee for the idea. When people make decisions, they ignore the external benefits and consider only the private benefits.

When people make decisions about the amount of education or research to undertake, they balance the marginal private cost against the marginal private benefit. They ignore the external benefit. As a result, if we left education and research to unregulated market forces, we would get too little of these activities.

To get closer to producing the efficient quantity of a good with an external benefit, we make public choices, through governments, to modify the market outcome.

Government Actions in the Face of External Benefits

Four devices that governments can use to achieve a more efficient allocation of resources in the presence of external benefits are:

- Public production
- Private subsidies
- Vouchers
- Patents and copyrights

Public Production With **public production**, a good or service is produced by a public authority that receives its revenue from the government. The education services produced by public universities and colleges and public schools are examples of public production.

Figure 15.7 shows how public production might overcome underprovision. Public provision cannot lower the cost of production, so marginal social cost is the same as before. Marginal private benefit and marginal external benefit are also the same as before.

The efficient quantity occurs where marginal social benefit equals marginal social cost. In Fig. 15.7, this quantity is 15 million students. Tuition is set to ensure that the efficient number of students enrolls. That is, tuition is set equal to the marginal private benefit at the efficient quantity. In Fig. 15.7, tuition is $10,000 a year. The rest of the cost of the public university is borne by the taxpayers and, in this example, is $15,000 per student per year.

FIGURE 15.7 Public Production to Achieve an Efficient Outcome

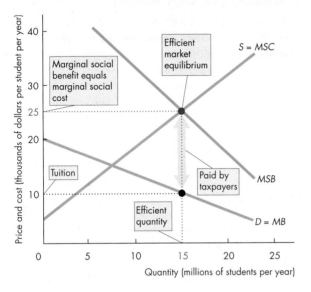

FIGURE 15.8 Private Subsidy to Achieve an Efficient Outcome

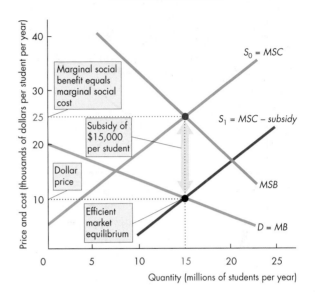

With public production, marginal social benefit equals marginal social cost with 15 million students enrolled per year, the efficient quantity. Tuition is set at $10,000 per student per year, equal to marginal private benefit. Taxpayers cover the other $15,000 of cost per student per year.

With a subsidy of $15,000 per student, the supply curve is $S_1 = MSC - subsidy$. The equilibrium price is $10,000 per year, and the market equilibrium is efficient with 15 million students enrolled per year. Marginal social benefit equals marginal social cost.

MyLab Economics Animation and Draw Graph

MyLab Economics Animation

Private Subsidies A *subsidy* is a payment by the government to private producers. By making the subsidy depend on the level of output, the government can induce private decision makers to consider external benefits when they make their choices.

Figure 15.8 shows how a subsidy to private universities would work. In the absence of a subsidy, the market supply curve is $S_0 = MSC$. The demand curve is the marginal private benefit curve, $D = MB$. If the government provides a subsidy of $15,000 per student per year, we must subtract the subsidy from the universities' marginal cost to find the new market supply curve. That curve is $S_1 = MSC - subsidy$. The market equilibrium is tuition of $10,000 a year and 15 million students a year. The marginal social cost of educating 15 million students is $25,000 and the marginal social benefit is $25,000, so the subsidy has achieved an efficient outcome. The tuition plus the subsidy equals the universities' marginal cost.

Vouchers A **voucher** is a token that the government provides to households, which they can use to buy specified goods or services. Milton Friedman, recipient of the 1976 Nobel Prize for economic science, long advocated vouchers as a means of providing parents with greater choice and control over the education of their children. Some people advocate them for college and university so that students can both receive financial help and exercise choice.

A school voucher would allow parents to choose the school their children will attend and to use the voucher to pay part of the cost. The school cashes the vouchers to pay its bills. A voucher provided to a university student would work in a similar way. Because vouchers can be spent only on a specified item, they increase the willingness to pay for that item and so increase the demand for it.

Figure 15.9 shows how a voucher system would work. The government provides a voucher per

FIGURE 15.9 Voucher to Achieve an Efficient Outcome

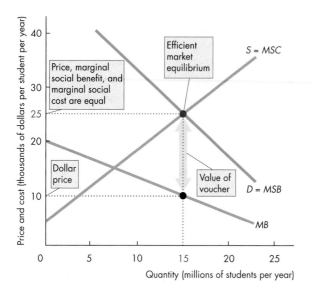

The efficient number of students is 15 million per year—the number at which marginal social benefit equals marginal social cost. With the demand and marginal private benefit curve, $D = MSB$, the tuition at which the efficient number will enroll is $10,000 per year. If students pay this tuition price, the taxpayer must somehow pay the rest, which equals the marginal external benefit at the efficient quantity—$15,000 per student per year.

MyLab Economics Animation

student equal to the marginal external benefit. Parents (or students) use these vouchers to supplement the dollars they pay for education. The marginal social benefit curve becomes the demand for university education, $D = MSB$. The market equilibrium occurs at a price of $25,000 per student per year, and 15 million students attend university. Each student pays $10,000 tuition, and schools collect an additional $15,000 per student from the voucher.

If the government estimates the value of the external benefit correctly and makes the value of the voucher equal the marginal external benefit, the outcome from the voucher scheme is efficient. Marginal social cost equals marginal social benefit, and the deadweight loss is eliminated.

Vouchers are similar to subsidies, but their advocates say that they are more efficient than subsidies because the consumer can monitor school performance more effectively than the government can.

ECONOMICS IN ACTION
Education Efficiency and School Choices

Competition among suppliers is a source of efficiency. It keeps costs in check and it encourages innovation that benefits the consumer. Is there enough competition among Canada's schools?

Almost 93 percent of Canadians in grades K-12 attend a public school. The other 7 percent attend independent schools or (0.4 percent) get home schooling—see Fig. 1.

But the near monopoly of the public school sector doesn't lack competition within it. Anglophone, Francophone, and religious schools compete for public funding and students.

Alberta has the most competitive school system and is the only province to have established another alternative to public schools—charter schools. A *charter school* is funded like a regular public school but is free to make its own education policy.

This model of schooling, while rare in Canada, has become popular in the United States and has received high marks for the quality of education it achieves and the low cost at which it operates.

Today, around 4,000 charter schools in 40 U.S. states are teaching more than 1 million students. Are charter schools succeeding? Success has two dimensions: educational standards attained and cost per

Patents and Copyrights Knowledge might be an exception to the principle of diminishing marginal benefit. Additional knowledge (about the right things) makes people more productive. And there seems to be no tendency for the additional productivity from additional knowledge to diminish.

For example, in just 15 years, advances in knowledge about microprocessors have given us a sequence of processor chips that has made our personal computers increasingly powerful. Each advance in knowledge about how to design and manufacture a processor chip has brought ever larger increments in performance and productivity. Similarly, each advance in knowledge about how to design and build an airplane has brought apparently ever larger increments in performance: Orville and Wilbur Wright's 1903 Flyer was a one-seat plane that could hop a farmer's field. The Lockheed Constellation, designed in 1949, was an airplane that could fly 120 passengers from New York to London, but with two refuelling stops in Newfoundland and Ireland. Today, a Boeing 747 can carry 400 people nonstop from student. Charter schools perform well on both dimensions. They achieve high standards and cost less. In the United States, charter school students achieve better test scores in math and reading than equivalent students who apply to but randomly don't get into a charter school.

Charter schools also achieve this higher standard at lower cost. For example, in New York, the cost per student in charter schools is 18 percent less than in regular public schools.

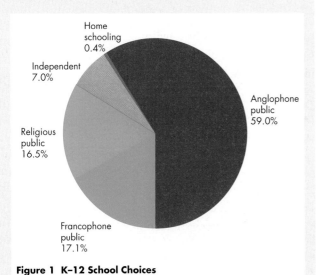

Figure 1 K–12 School Choices

Singapore to New York (flights of 15,325 kilometres that take 20 hours). Similar examples can be found in agriculture, biogenetics, communications, engineering, entertainment, and medicine.

One reason why the stock of knowledge increases without diminishing returns is the sheer number of different techniques that can in principle be tried. Paul Romer, an economist at Stanford University, explains this fact: "Suppose that to make a finished good, 20 different parts have to be attached to a frame, one at a time. A worker could proceed in numerical order, attaching part one first, then part two. ... Or the worker could proceed in some other order, starting with part 10, then adding part seven ... With 20 parts, ... there are [more] different sequences ... than the total number of seconds that have elapsed since the big bang created the universe, so we can be confident that in all activities, only a very small fraction of the possible sequences have ever been tried."*

_____

*Paul Romer, "Ideas and Things," in The Future Surveyed, supplement to *The Economist*, September 11, 1993.

Think about all the processes, all the products, and all the different bits and pieces that go into each, and you can see that we have only begun to scratch the surface of what is possible.

Because knowledge is productive and generates external benefits, it is necessary to use public policies to ensure that those who develop new ideas have incentives to encourage an efficient level of effort. The main way of providing the right incentives uses the central idea of the Coase theorem and assigns property rights—called **intellectual property rights**—to creators. The legal device for establishing intellectual property rights is the patent or copyright. A **patent** or **copyright** is a government-sanctioned exclusive right granted to the inventor of a good, service, or productive process to produce, use, and sell the invention for a given number of years. A patent enables the developer of a new idea to prevent others from benefiting freely from an invention for a limited number of years.

Although patents encourage invention and innovation, they do so at an economic cost. While a patent is in place, its holder has a monopoly. And monopoly is another source of inefficiency (see Chapter 12). But without a patent, the effort to develop new goods, services, or processes is diminished and the flow of new inventions is slowed. So the efficient outcome is a compromise that balances the benefits of more inventions against the cost of temporary monopoly in new inventions.

◆ **REVIEW QUIZ**

1 What is special about knowledge that creates external benefits?

2 How might governments use public provision, private subsidies, and vouchers to achieve an efficient amount of education?

3 How might governments use public provision, private subsidies, vouchers, and patents and copyrights to achieve an efficient amount of research and development?

Work these questions in Study Plan 15.3 and get instant feedback.   MyLab Economics

◆ *Economics in the News* on pp. 368–369 looks at the effects of a cap-and-trade scheme on the efficient use of fuels that emit carbon dioxide.

A Carbon Reduction Plan

Ontario Set for First Cap-and-Trade Auction as Provinces Watch Closely

The Toronto Star
March 21, 2017

Ontario's cap-and-trade system aimed at lowering greenhouse gas emissions begins in earnest Wednesday with its first auction, which other provinces said they will be watching closely as they consider their own carbon pricing plans.

The provincial Liberal government hopes the auction—held every three months—will bring in $1.9 billion a year, or $8 billion by the end of 2020, to be invested in programs that reduce emissions and help businesses and consumers adapt to a low-carbon economy.

Under the plan, businesses will have limits—or caps—on the amount of pollution they can emit. Companies that exceed those limits, which will be reduced each year, can buy permits or allowances through auctions or from other companies that come in under their limits. …

Ontario plans to link its cap-and-trade system with a joint Quebec-California market next year. …

Ontario is capping emission allowances at roughly 142 megatonnes this year, declining about 4 percent each year to 2020, when the Liberals hope to have achieved a 15-percent reduction in greenhouse gas emissions over 1990 levels.

As the emissions cap declines, the government hopes companies have more incentive to invest in technologies that cut their emissions.

Carbon market expert Nicolas Girod said he expects the first auction to be close to fully subscribed. However, some businesses may sit this one out and some may be waiting until the market is linked with the California-Quebec one, he said. …

Prime Minister Justin Trudeau has said all provinces must set up a cap-and-trade system or impose a price on carbon of at least $10 per tonne starting next year. …

© The Canadian Press

ESSENCE OF THE STORY

- Ontario is capping carbon emissions and creating a cap-and-trade system jointly with Quebec and California.

- The goal is to cut carbon emissions to 15 percent below 1990 levels by 2020.

- Ontario's carbon emissions cap-and-trade system held its first quarterly auction in April 2017.

- Prime Minister Trudeau wants all provinces to establish a cap-and-trade system or impose a price on carbon of at least $10 per tonne starting in 2018.

ECONOMIC ANALYSIS

- Carbon emissions from using fossil fuels to generate electricity are a negative externality that make the marginal social cost of electricity exceed its marginal private cost.

- Left to unregulated market forces, there is an inefficient overproduction of electricity generated using carbon-emitting fuels, and a deadweight loss is created. The California, Quebec, and Ontario cap-and-trade program seeks to address this problem.

- Figure 1 illustrates the problem. The demand for and marginal social benefit of electricity is $D = MSB$. The supply of electricity from carbon-emitting generators and the marginal private cost curve is $S = MC$. The marginal social cost curve is MSC. The efficient quantity of carbon-emitting electricity is 1.5 terawatt-hours per year. But the equilibrium quantity is 2.0 terawatt-hours per year, so overproduction brings a deadweight loss as shown by the area of the grey triangle.

- A cap-and-trade program decreases the use of carbon-emitting fuels and will eventually bring an end to their use. The program achieves this outcome by making power utilities pay for carbon allowances that makes emitting carbon as costly as using a clean alternative.

- The inefficiency arising from carbon emissions and its deadweight loss is eliminated by making marginal benefit and market price equal to marginal *social* cost.

- Figure 2 illustrates how this outcome is achieved. The market demand and marginal social benefit curve $D = MSB$ is unchanged. Marginal social cost is the marginal cost of using clean fuel, shown by MSC_{Clean}. The marginal cost curve for carbon-emitting generation is MC_{Carbon}, but this marginal cost curve is no longer the supply curve.

- A program caps the output of carbon-emitting generators at the efficient quantity of 1.5 terawatt-hours per year—the quantity at which marginal social benefit equals marginal social cost.

- At this quantity, the market price of electricity is $50 per megawatt-hour and the marginal cost of a carbon-emitting generator is $25 per megawatt-hour, so utilities would profit from increasing production.

- To increase production, a utility must buy carbon permits. With all carbon-emitting utilities trying to buy permits, the price of a permit rises and only stops rising when it reaches $25 per megawatt-hour and the profit from increasing production is zero.

- The cost of producing electricity from fossil fuels is now the same as the cost of using a clean technology, so as

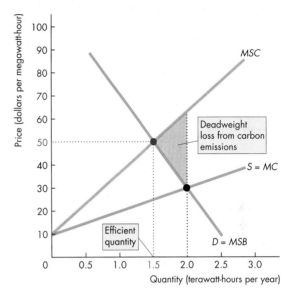

Figure 1 Inefficient Carbon-Emitting Generation

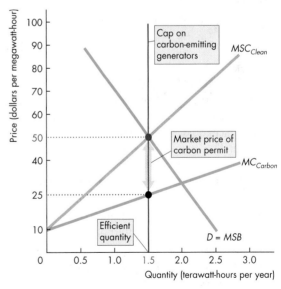

Figure 2 Efficient Generation with Cap-and-Trade

carbon-emitting generators reach the end of their productive lives, utililties will have an incentive to switch to a clean alternative technology.

- The model in Fig. 2 prices carbon allowances to achieve the efficient outcome, but the current cap-and trade system prices carbon too low because the cap is too high and too large a carbon allowance has been allocated.

369

WORKED PROBLEM

MyLab Economics Work this problem in Chapter 15 Study Plan.

The first two columns of the table show the demand schedule for fitness sessions with independent coaches; the second and third columns show the coaches' marginal cost. Fitness creates an external benefit and the marginal external benefit is $10 per session. The market for fitness sessions is competitive.

Price (dollars per session)	Quantity (sessions per month)	Marginal cost (dollars per session)
10	800	30
15	600	25
20	400	20
25	200	15
30	0	10

Questions

1. What is the market-determined quantity of fitness sessions per month and what is the price of a session?
2. Calculate the marginal social benefit from fitness at each quantity of sessions.
3. What is the efficient number of fitness sessions per month?

Solutions

1. In the market for fitness sessions, the supply schedule is the same as the marginal cost schedule. The demand schedule is also the marginal private benefit schedule, so price equals marginal private benefit. The quantity of sessions is that at which marginal private benefit equals marginal cost: 400 sessions per month. The price is $20 a session.

Key Point: The market outcome is determined by marginal private benefit and marginal cost.

2. Marginal social benefit (*MSB*) equals the sum of marginal private benefit (*MB*), which equals the market price, and the marginal external benefit of $10 per session.

   The table below shows the calculations.

Quantity (sessions per month)	MB (sessions per month)	MSB (dollars per session)
800	10	20
600	15	25
400	20	30
200	25	35
0	–	–

For example, the marginal social benefit from 600 sessions per month equals the marginal private benefit of $15 per session plus the marginal external benefit of $10 per session, which equals $25 per session.

Key Point: The marginal social benefit from a service that creates a positive externality is the sum of the marginal private benefit and the marginal external benefit.

3. To find the efficient number of fitness sessions, we need to determine the number of sessions per month at which the marginal social benefit (*MSB*) equals marginal cost (*MC*).

   The table below combines the data from the other two tables.

Quantity (sessions per month)	MSB (sessions per month)	MC (dollars per session)
800	20	30
600	**25**	**25**
400	30	20
200	35	15
0	–	10

By inspecting the table above, you can see that *MSB* equals *MC* at 600 sessions per month, so that is the efficient quantity.

Key Point: The efficient quantity of a service that creates a positive externality is the quantity at which marginal social benefit from the service equals the marginal cost of producing the service.

Key Figure

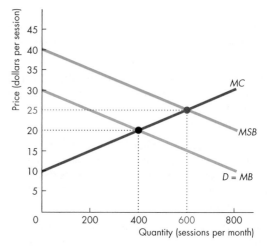

MyLab Economics Interactive Animation

SUMMARY

Key Points

Externalities in Our Lives (pp. 354–355)

■ An externality can arise from either a production activity or a consumption activity.

■ A negative externality imposes an external cost. A positive externality provides an external benefit.

Working Problems 1 and 2 will give you a better understanding of the externalities in our lives.

Negative Externality: Pollution (pp. 356–362)

■ A competitive market would produce too much of a good that has external production costs.

■ External costs are costs of production that fall on people other than the producer of a good or service. Marginal social cost equals marginal private cost plus marginal external cost.

■ Producers take account only of marginal private cost and produce more than the efficient quantity when there is a marginal external cost.

■ Sometimes it is possible to overcome a negative externality by assigning a property right.

■ When property rights cannot be assigned, governments might overcome externalities by using taxes or cap-and-trade.

Working Problems 3 to 7 will give you a better understanding of the external costs of pollution.

Positive Externality: Knowledge (pp. 363–367)

■ External benefits are benefits that are received by people other than the consumer of a good or service. Marginal social benefit equals marginal private benefit plus marginal external benefit.

■ External benefits from education arise because better-educated people tend to be better citizens, commit fewer crimes, and support social activities.

■ External benefits from research arise because once someone has worked out a basic idea, others can copy it.

■ Vouchers or subsidies to schools or the provision of public education below cost can achieve a more efficient provision of education.

Working Problems 8 to 10 will give you a better understanding of the external benefit from knowledge.

Key Terms

MyLab Economics Key Terms Quiz

Abatement technology, 357
Coase theorem, 358
Copyright, 367
Externality, 354
Intellectual property rights, 367
Marginal external benefit, 363
Marginal external cost, 356

Marginal private benefit, 363
Marginal private cost, 356
Marginal social benefit, 363
Marginal social cost, 356
Negative externality, 354
Patent, 367
Pigovian taxes, 359

Positive externality, 354
Property rights, 357
Public production, 364
Transactions costs, 358
Voucher, 365

STUDY PLAN PROBLEMS AND APPLICATIONS

MyLab Economics Work Problems 1 to 10 in Chapter 15 Study Plan and get instant feedback.

Externalities in Our Lives (Study Plan 15.1)

1. Describe three consumption activities that create external costs.

2. Describe three production activites that create external benefits.

Negative Externality: Pollution (Study Plan 15.2)

Use the following figure, which illustrates the market for tomatoes, to work Problems 3 to 6.

Suppose that the tomato grower uses a chemical to control insects and waste flows into the town's river. The marginal social cost of producing the tomatoes is double the marginal private cost.

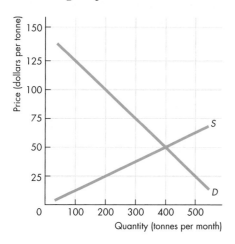

3. If no one owns the river and the town takes no action to control the waste, what is the quantity of tomatoes and the deadweight loss created?

4. a. If the town owns the river and makes the tomato grower pay the cost of pollution, how many tomatoes are produced? What does the grower pay the town per tonne of tomatoes produced?

   b. If the tomato grower owns the river and rents it to the town, how many tomatoes are produced? How is the rent paid by the town to the grower (per tonne of tomatoes produced) influenced by tomato growing?

   c. Compare the quantities of tomatoes produced in parts (a) and (b) and explain the relationship between these quantities.

5. If no one owns the river and the city introduces a pollution tax, what is the tax per tonne of

tomatoes produced that achieves an efficient outcome?

6. Compare the outcomes when property rights exist and when the pollution tax achieves the efficient amount of waste.

7. **Bloor St. Bike Lanes Find Strong Support**

   A survey finds 75 percent of people who live in the area say bike lanes are worth the tradeoffs of increased traffic congestion and loss of parking. A study shows that bike lanes on Bloor increased car travel time by more than 8 minutes.

   Source: *Toronto Star*, June 5, 2017

   How do bike lanes change externalites and could bike lanes on Bloor St. make the Toronto road system more efficient?

Positive Externality: Knowledge (Study Plan 15.3)

Use the following figure, which shows the demand for university education, to work Problems 8 to 10.

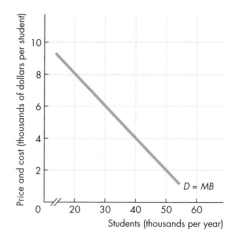

The marginal cost is a constant $6,000 per student per year. The marginal external benefit from a university education is a constant $4,000 per student per year.

8. What is the efficient number of students? If all universities are private, how many people enroll in university and what is the tuition?

9. If the government provides public universities, what tuition will achieve the efficient number of students? How much will taxpayers have to pay?

10. If the government offers students vouchers, what is the value of the voucher that will achieve the efficient number of students?

ADDITIONAL PROBLEMS AND APPLICATIONS

MyLab Economics You can work these problems in Homework or Test if assigned by your instructor.

Externalities in Our Lives

11. Which of the following activities creates an externality? If it does, is it a positive or negative production or consumption externality?
    - A sunset over the Pacific Ocean
    - An increase in the number of graduates
    - A person talks on a cellphone while driving
    - A bakery bakes bread

12. What externalities arise from smoking tobacco products and how do we deal with them?

13. What externalities arise from beautiful and ugly buildings and how do we deal with them?

Negative Externality: Pollution

14. Betty and Anna work at the same office in Toronto and they have to attend a meeting in Montreal. They decide to drive to the out-of-town meeting together. Betty is a cigarette smoker and her marginal benefit from smoking a package of cigarettes a day is $40. Cigarettes are $6 a pack. Anna dislikes cigarette smoke, and her marginal benefit from a smoke-free environment is $50 a day. What is the outcome if:
    a. Betty drives her car with Anna as a passenger?
    b. Anna drives her car with Betty as a passenger?

Use the following figure, which illustrates the market for a pesticide with no government intervention, to work Problems 15 to 18.

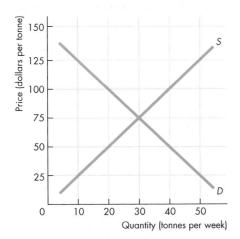

When factories produce pesticide, they also create waste, which they dump into a lake near the town. The marginal external cost of the waste is equal to the marginal private cost of producing the pesticide

(that is, the marginal social cost of producing the pesticide is double the marginal private cost).

15. What quantity of pesticide is produced if no one owns the lake? What is the efficient quantity?

16. If the town owns the lake, what is the quantity of pesticide produced and how much does the town charge the factories to dump waste?

17. If the pesticide factories own the lake, how much pesticide is produced?

18. If no one owns the lake and the government levies a pollution tax, what is the tax that achieves the efficient outcome?

Use the following table to work Problems 19 to 21.
The first two columns of the table show the demand schedule for electricity from a coal-burning utility; the second and third columns show the utility's cost of producing electricity. The marginal external cost of the pollution created equals the marginal cost.

Price (cents per kilowatt)	Quantity (kilowatts per day)	Marginal cost (cents per kilowatt)
4	500	10
8	400	8
12	300	6
16	200	4
20	100	2

19. With no government action to control pollution, what is the quantity of electricity produced, the price of electricity, and the marginal external cost of the pollution generated?

20. With no government action to control pollution, what is the marginal social cost of the electricity generated and the deadweight loss created?

21. If the government levies a pollution tax such that the utility produces the efficient quantity, what is the price of electricity, the tax levied, and the government's tax revenue per day?

Use the following news clip to work Problems 22 and 23.

How to Dispose of Mercury-Filled Light Bulbs

Compact fluorescent light bulbs (CFLs) contain mercury and 1,150 kilograms of this toxic substance end up in Canadian landfills each year. A new federal law provides guidance on how to dispose of CFLs in an environmentally responsible way.

Source: CBC News, June 26, 2017

22. a. What is the external cost that arises from CFLs?

    b. Draw a graph to illustrate and explain why the market for CFLs is inefficient.

    c. How could the market for CFLs be made to operate efficiently? List all the methods you can think of.

23. Explain how the market for CFLs could be made to operate efficiently. Draw a graph to illustrate your answer.

Positive Externality: Knowledge

Use the following data to work Problems 24 to 27.
The table shows the demand for university education.

Price (dollars per student)	Quantity (students per year)
6,000	10,000
5,000	20,000
4,000	30,000
3,000	40,000
2,000	50,000

The marginal cost of educating a student is a constant $4,000 a year and education creates an external benefit of a constant $2,000 per student per year.

24. If all universities are private and the market for education is competitive, calculate the number of students, the tuition, and the deadweight loss.

25. If all universities are public, calculate the tuition that will achieve the efficient number of students. How much will taxpayers have to pay?

26. If the government decides to subsidize private universities, what subsidy will achieve the efficient number of students?

27. If all universities are private and the government offers vouchers to those who enroll, calculate the value of the voucher that will achieve the efficient number of students.

Use the following news clip to work Problems 28 to 30.

Budget Boosts Funding for the Arts

Canada's biggest arts and cultural institutions, including the CBC and Radio-Canada, are getting a $182 million budget increase over the next five years.

Source: CBC News, March 22, 2016

28. What external benefits are associated with the arts and public broadcast services?

29. Draw a graph to illustrate and explain why the market for arts creates a deadweight loss.

30. Draw a graph to illustrate and explain how the budget increase described in the newsclip might improve efficiency.

Economics in the News

31. After you have studied *Economics in the News* on pp. 368–369, answer the following questions.

    a. What are the marginal private costs of and marginal private benefits from using carbon-free resources to generate electricity?

    b. What are the marginal social costs of and marginal social benefits from using carbon-free resources to generate electricity?

    c. How will a cap-and-trade scheme change the price that households pay for electricity?

    d. How will a cap-and-trade scheme change the efficiency of electricity production?

16

PUBLIC GOODS AND COMMON RESOURCES

After studying this chapter, you will be able to:

◆ Distinguish among private goods, public goods, and common resources

◆ Explain how the free-rider problem arises and how the quantity of public goods is determined

◆ Explain the tragedy of the commons and its possible solutions

The Gardiner Expressway, an 18-kilometre link between highways to the east and west of downtown Toronto, is undergoing major repairs. The Gardiner is a small part of the 17,000 kilometres of expressways in Canada built and maintained by governments. But why governments? Why not private firms? And are governments efficient in their provision of expressways and other goods and services?

These are the questions we study in this chapter. In *Economics in the News* at the end of the chapter, we return to the Gardiner Expressway and look at the problem of keeping it in a good state of repair.

Classifying Goods and Resources

Goods, services, and resources differ in the extent to which people can be *excluded* from consuming them and the extent to which one person's consumption *rivals* the consumption of others.

Excludable

A good is **excludable** if it is possible to prevent someone from enjoying its benefits. Brinks security services, Cooke Aquaculture's fish, and a U2 concert are examples. People must pay to consume them.

A good is **nonexcludable** if it is impossible (or extremely costly) to prevent anyone from benefiting from it. The services of the Calgary police, fish in the Atlantic Ocean, and a concert on network television are examples. When a police cruiser enforces the speed limit, everyone on the highway benefits; anyone with a boat can fish in the ocean; and anyone with a TV can watch a network broadcast.

Rival

A good is **rival** if one person's use of it decreases the quantity available for someone else. A Brinks truck can't deliver cash to two banks at the same time. A fish can be consumed only once.

A good is **nonrival** if one person's use of it does not decrease the quantity available for someone else. The services of the police and a concert on network television are nonrival. One person's benefit doesn't lower the benefit of others.

A Fourfold Classification

Figure 16.1 classifies goods, services, and resources into four types.

FIGURE 16.1 Fourfold Classification of Goods

	Excludable	Nonexcludable
Rival	**Private goods** Food and drink Car House	**Common resources** Fish in ocean Atmosphere National parks
Nonrival	**Natural monopoly goods** Internet Cable television Bridge or tunnel	**Public goods** National defence The law Air traffic control

A private good is rival and excludable: You must pay to get it and you alone enjoy it. A public good is nonrival and nonexcludable: You and everyone else enjoy it without paying for it. A common resource is rival but nonexcludable. And a natural monopoly good is nonrival but excludable.

MyLab Economics Animation

Private Goods A **private good** is both rival and excludable. A can of Coke and a fish on Cooke Aquaculture's farm are examples of private goods.

Public Goods A **public good** is both nonrival and nonexcludable. A public good can be consumed simultaneously by everyone, and no one can be excluded from enjoying its benefits. National defence is the best example of a public good. Another is weather forecasting.

Common Resources A **common resource** is rival and nonexcludable. A unit of a common resource can be used only once, but no one can be prevented from using what is available. Ocean fish are a common resource. They are rival because a fish taken by one person isn't available for anyone else, and they are nonexcludable because it is difficult to prevent people from catching them.

Natural Monopoly Goods A **natural monopoly good** is nonrival but excludable. Consumers can be excluded if they don't pay, but adding one more user doesn't rival other users, so marginal cost is zero. The fixed cost of producing such a good is usually high, so economies of scale exist over the entire range of output for which there is a demand (see p. 280). Examples of natural monopoly goods are the Internet, cable television, and an uncongested bridge or tunnel.

REVIEW QUIZ

1. Distinguish among public goods, private goods, common resources, and natural monopoly goods.
2. Provide examples of goods (or services or resources) in each of the four categories that differ from the examples in this section.

Work these questions in Study Plan 16.1 and get instant feedback. MyLab Economics

Public Goods

Why does the government provide our weather forecasting? Why don't we buy our weather forecasts from North Pole Weather, Inc., a private firm that competes for our dollars in the marketplace in the same way that McDonald's does? The answer is that weather forecasting is a public good—nonexcludable and nonrival—and it has a free-rider problem.

The Free-Rider Problem

A *free rider* enjoys the benefits of a good or service without paying for it. Because a public good is provided for everyone to use and no one can be excluded from its benefits, no one has an incentive to pay his or her share of the cost. Everyone has an incentive to free ride. The **free-rider problem** is that the market would provide an inefficiently small quantity of a public good. Marginal social benefit from the public good would exceed its marginal social cost and a deadweight loss would arise.

Let's look at the marginal social benefit and marginal social cost of a public good.

Marginal Social Benefit from a Public Good

Lisa and Max (the only people in an imagined society) value weather forecasts. Figures 16.2(a) and 16.2(b) graph their marginal benefits from a weather satellite system as MB_L for Lisa and MB_M for Max. A person's marginal benefit from a public good, like that from a private good, diminishes as the quantity of the good increases—the marginal benefit curves slope downward.

Figure 16.2(c) shows the marginal *social* benefit curve, *MSB*. Because everyone gets the same quantity of a public good, its marginal social benefit curve is the sum of the marginal benefits of all individuals at each *quantity*—it is the *vertical* sum of the individual *MB* curves. So the *MSB* curve in part (c) is the marginal social benefit curve for the economy made up of Lisa and Max. For each satellite, Lisa's marginal benefit is added to Max's marginal benefit to calculate the marginal social benefit from that satellite.

Contrast the *MSB* curve for a public good with that of a private good. To obtain the economy's *MSB* curve for a private good, we *sum the quantities demanded* by all individuals at each price—we sum the individual marginal benefit curves *horizontally* (see Chapter 5, p. 112).

FIGURE 16.2 Benefits of a Public Good

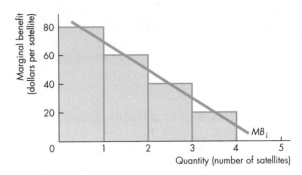

(a) Lisa's marginal benefit

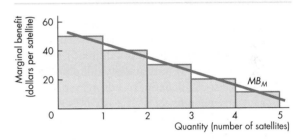

(b) Max's marginal benefit

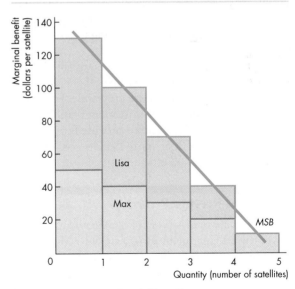

(c) Economy's marginal social benefit

The marginal social benefit at each quantity of the public good is the sum of the marginal benefits of all individuals. The marginal benefit curves are MB_L for Lisa and MB_M for Max. The economy's marginal social benefit curve is *MSB*.

MyLab Economics Animation

Marginal Social Cost of a Public Good

The marginal social cost of a public good is determined in exactly the same way as that of a private good—see p. 356. The principle of increasing marginal cost applies to the cost of a public good, so the marginal social cost curve of a public good slopes upward.

Efficient Quantity of a Public Good

To determine the efficient quantity of a public good, we use the same principles that you learned in Chapter 5 and have used repeatedly: Find the quantity at which marginal social benefit equals marginal social cost.

Figure 16.3 shows the marginal social benefit curve, *MSB*, and the marginal social cost curve, *MSC*, for weather satellites. (Now think of society as consisting of Lisa and Max and 30 million others.)

If marginal social benefit exceeds marginal social cost, as it does when fewer than 2 satellites are provided, resources can be used more efficiently by increasing the quantity. The extra benefit exceeds the extra cost. If marginal social cost exceeds marginal social benefit, as it does when more than 2 satellites are provided, resources can be used more efficiently by decreasing the quantity. The saving in cost exceeds the loss of benefit.

If marginal social benefit equals marginal social cost, as it does when exactly 2 satellites are provided, resources cannot be used more efficiently. To provide more than 2 satellites would cost more than the additional coverage is worth, and to provide fewer satellites lowers the benefit by more than its cost saving. Resources are allocated efficiently.

Inefficient Private Provision

Could a private firm—North Pole Weather, Inc.—deliver the efficient quantity of satellites? Most likely it couldn't because no one would have an incentive to buy his or her share of the satellite system. Everyone would reason as follows: "The number of satellites provided by North Pole Weather, Inc., is not affected by my decision to pay my share or not. But my own private consumption will be greater if I free ride and do not pay my share of the cost of the satellite system. If I don't pay, I enjoy the same level of security and I can buy more private goods. I will spend my money on private goods and free ride on the public good." Such reasoning is the free-rider problem. If everyone reasons the same way, North Pole Weather,

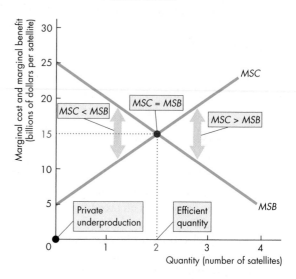

FIGURE 16.3 The Efficient Quantity of a Public Good

With fewer than 2 satellites, marginal social benefit, *MSB*, exceeds marginal social cost, *MSC*. With more than 2 satellites, *MSC* exceeds *MSB*. Only with 2 satellites is *MSC* equal to *MSB* and the number of satellites is efficient.

—— MyLab Economics Animation

Inc. has no revenue and so provides no satellites. Because the efficient level is 2 satellites, private provision is inefficient.

Efficient Public Provision

The political process might be efficient or inefficient. We look first at an efficient outcome. There are two political parties: Greens and Blues. They agree on all issues except for the number of satellites. The Greens want 3 satellites, and the Blues want 1 satellite. But both parties want to get elected, so they run a voter survey and discover the marginal social benefit curve of Fig. 16.4. They also consult with satellite producers to establish the marginal cost schedule. The parties then do a "what-if" analysis. If the Greens propose 3 satellites and the Blues propose 1 satellite, the voters will be equally unhappy with both parties. Compared to the efficient quantity, the Blues want an underprovision of 1 satellite and the Greens want an overprovision of 1 satellite. The deadweight losses are equal. So the election would be too close to call.

Contemplating this outcome, the Greens realize that they are too hawkish to get elected. They figure

FIGURE 16.4   An Efficient Political Outcome

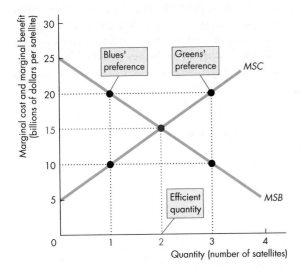

The Blues would like to provide 1 satellite and the Greens would like to provide 3 satellites. The political outcome is 2 satellites because unless each party proposes 2 satellites, the other party will beat it in an election.

MyLab Economics Animation

the road. If Chrysler designs a new van with a sliding door on the driver's side, most likely Ford will too.

For the political process to deliver the efficient outcome that you've just seen, voters must be well informed, evaluate the alternatives, and vote in the election. Political parties must be well informed about voter preferences. As the next section shows, we can't expect to achieve this outcome.

Inefficient Public Overprovision

If competition between two political parties is to deliver the efficient quantity of a public good, bureaucrats must cooperate and help to achieve this outcome. In the case of satellites, bureaucrats in the Department of Weather Forecasting (DWF) must cooperate and accept this outcome.

Objective of Bureaucrats   Bureaucrats want to maximize their department's budget because a bigger budget brings greater status and more power. So the DWF's objective is to maximize the satellite budget.

Figure 16.5 shows the outcome if the DWF is successful in the pursuit of its goal. The DWF might try to persuade the politicians that 2 satellites cost more

that if they scale back to 2 satellites, they will win the election if the Blues propose 1 satellite. The Blues reason in a similar way and figure that if they increase the number of satellites to 2, they can win the election if the Greens propose 3 satellites.

So they both propose 2 satellites. The voters are indifferent between the parties, and each party receives 50 percent of the vote.

Regardless of which party wins the election, 2 satellites are provided and this quantity is efficient. Competition in the political marketplace results in the efficient provision of a public good.

The Principle of Minimum Differentiation   The tendency for competitors to make themselves similar to appeal to the maximum number of clients or voters is called the **principle of minimum differentiation**. This principle describes the behaviour of political parties. It also explains why fast-food restaurants cluster in the same block and even why new auto models have similar features. If McDonald's opens a new restaurant, it is likely that Wendy's will open near to McDonald's rather than a kilometre down

FIGURE 16.5   Bureaucratic Overprovision

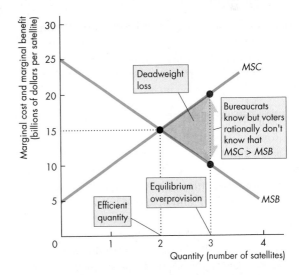

Well-informed bureaucrats want to maximize their budget and rationally ignorant voters enable the bureaucrats to go some way toward achieving their goal. A public good might be inefficiently overprovided with a deadweight loss.

MyLab Economics Animation

than the originally budgeted amount; or the DWF might press its position more strongly and argue for more than 2 satellites. In Fig. 16.5, the DWF persuades the politicians to provide 3 satellites.

Why don't the politicians block the DWF? Won't overproducing satellites cost future votes? It will if voters are well informed and know what is best for them. But voters might not be well informed, and well-informed interest groups might enable the DWF to achieve its objective and overcome the objections of the politicians.

Rational Ignorance A principle of the economic analysis of public choices is that it is rational for a voter to be ignorant about an issue unless that issue has a perceptible effect on the voter's economic welfare. **Rational ignorance** is the decision not to acquire information because the cost of doing so exceeds the expected benefit.

For example, each voter knows that he or she can make virtually no difference to the Government of Canada's weather forecasting. Each voter also knows that it would take an enormous amount of time and effort to become even moderately well informed about alternative weather technologies. So voters remain relatively uninformed about the technicalities of weather issues. Although we are using weather forecasting as an example, the same reasoning applies to all aspects of government economic activity.

All voters are consumers of weather forecasts, but not all voters work in industries involved in weather forecasting. Only a small number of voters are in this latter category. Voters who own or work for firms that produce components of satellites have a direct personal interest in weather satellites because it affects their incomes and careers. These voters have an incentive to become well informed about weather forecasting issues and to operate a political lobby aimed at furthering their own self-interests.

In collaboration with the bureaucrats who are responsible for the provision of a public good, informed voters who produce that public good exert a larger influence than do the relatively uninformed voters who only use the public good.

When the rationality of the uninformed voter and special interest groups are taken into account, the political equilibrium provides public goods in excess of the efficient quantity. So in the satellite example, 3 or more satellites might be installed rather than the efficient quantity of 2 satellites.

ECONOMICS IN ACTION

Is a Lighthouse a Public Good?

Canada's first lighthouse was built at Louisbourg, Nova Scotia, in 1730.

For two centuries, economists used the lighthouse as an example of a public good. No one can be prevented from seeing its warning light—*nonexcludable*—and one person seeing its light doesn't prevent someone else from doing so too—*nonrival*.

Ronald Coase, who won the 1991 Nobel Prize for ideas he first developed when he was an undergraduate at the London School of Economics, discovered that before the nineteenth century, lighthouses in England were built and operated by private corporations that earned profits by charging tolls on ships docking at nearby ports. A ship that refused to pay the lighthouse toll was *excluded* from the port.

So the benefit arising from the services of a lighthouse is *excludable*. Because the services provided by a lighthouse are nonrival but excludable, a lighthouse is an example of a natural monopoly good and not a public good.

Two Types of Political Equilibrium

We've seen that two types of political equilibrium are possible: efficient and inefficient. These two types of political equilibrium correspond to two theories of government:

- Social interest theory
- Public choice theory

Social Interest Theory Social interest theory predicts that governments make choices that achieve an efficient provision of public goods. This outcome occurs in a perfect political system in which voters are fully informed about the effects of policies and refuse to vote for outcomes that can be improved upon.

Public Choice Theory Public choice theory predicts that governments make choices that result in inefficient overprovision of public goods. This outcome occurs in political markets in which voters are rationally ignorant and base their votes only on issues that they know affect their own net benefit. Voters pay more attention to their self-interests as producers than their self-interests as consumers, and public officials also act in their own self-interest. The result is government failure that parallels market failure.

Why Government Is Large and Growing

Now that we know how the quantity of public goods is determined, we can explain part of the reason for the growth of government. Government grows in part because the demand for some public goods increases at a faster rate than the demand for private goods. There are two possible reasons for this growth:

- Voter preferences
- Inefficient overprovision

Voter Preferences The growth of government can be explained by voter preferences in the following way. As voters' incomes increase (as they do in most years), the demand for many public goods increases more quickly than income. (Technically, the income elasticity of demand for many public goods is greater than 1—see Chapter 4, pp. 95–96.) These goods include public health, education, weather forecasting, highways, airports, and air traffic control systems. If politicians did not support increases in expenditures on these items, they would not get elected.

Inefficient Overprovision Inefficient overprovision might explain the size of government but not its growth rate. It (possibly) explains why government is larger than its efficient scale, but it does not explain why governments use an increasing proportion of total resources.

Voters Strike Back

If government grows too large relative to the value that voters place on public goods, there might be a voter backlash against government programs and a large bureaucracy. Electoral success during the 1990s at the provincial and federal levels required politicians of all parties to embrace smaller, leaner, and more efficient government. But promising to trim the bureaucracy and eliminate waste turns out to be much easier than delivering more efficient government, so overspending persists.

Another way in which voters—and politicians—can try to counter the tendency of bureaucrats to expand their budgets is to privatize the production of public goods. Government provision of a public good does not automatically imply that a government-operated bureau must produce the good. Garbage collection (a public good) is often done by a private firm, and in the United Kingdom and United States, even prisons are provided by private firms.

REVIEW QUIZ

1 What is the free-rider problem? Why do free riders make the private provision of a public good inefficient?
2 Under what conditions will competition among politicians for votes result in an efficient provision of a public good?
3 How do rationally ignorant voters and budget-maximizing bureaucrats prevent the political marketplace from delivering the efficient quantity of a public good?

Work these questions in Study Plan 16.2 and get instant feedback.   MyLab Economics

You've seen how public goods create a free-rider problem that would result in the underprovision of such goods. We're now going to learn about common resources and see why they result in the opposite problem—the overuse of such resources.

◆ Common Resources

Overgrazing the pastures around a village in Middle Ages England and overfishing the cod stocks of the North Atlantic Ocean during the recent past are tragedies of the commons. The **tragedy of the commons** is the overuse of a common resource that arises when its users have no incentive to conserve it and use it sustainably.

To study the tragedy of the commons and its possible remedies, we'll focus on a recent and current tragedy—overfishing and depleting the stock of Atlantic cod. We begin by thinking about the sustainable use of a renewable resource.

Sustainable Use of a Renewable Resource

A *renewable natural resource* is one that replenishes itself by the birth and growth of new members of the population. Fish, trees, and the fertile soil are all examples of this type of resource.

Focusing on fish, the sustainable catch is the quantity that can be caught year after year without depleting the stock. This quantity depends on the stock and in the interesting way illustrated in Fig. 16.6.

If the stock of fish is small, the quantity of new fish born is also small, so the sustainable catch is small.

FIGURE 16.6 Sustainable Catch

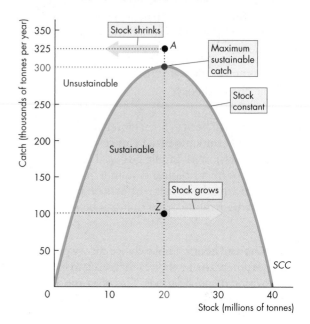

As the fish stock increases (on the *x*-axis), the sustainable catch (on the *y*-axis) increases to a maximum. As the stock increases further, the fish must compete for food and the sustainable catch falls. If the catch exceeds the sustainable catch, such as at point *A*, the fish stock diminishes. If the catch is less than the sustainable catch, such as at point *Z*, the fish stock increases.

— MyLab Economics Animation —

ECONOMICS IN ACTION
The Original Tragedy of the Commons

The term "tragedy of the commons" comes from fourteenth-century England, where areas of rough grassland surrounded villages. The commons were open to all and used for grazing cows and sheep owned by the villagers.

Because the commons were open to all, no one had an incentive to ensure that the land was not overgrazed. The result was a severe overgrazing situation and the number of cows and sheep that could feed on the commons kept falling as the overgrazing continued.

During the sixteenth century, the price of wool increased and England became a wool exporter to the world. Sheep farming became profitable, and sheep owners wanted to gain more effective control of the land they used. So the commons were gradually privatized and enclosed. Overgrazing ended, and land use became more efficient.

ECONOMICS IN ACTION
One of Today's Tragedies of the Commons

Before 1970, Atlantic cod was abundant. It was fished for many centuries and was a major food source for the first European settlers in North America. During the sixteenth century, hundreds of European ships caught large quantities of cod in the northwest Atlantic off the coast of what is now New England and Newfoundland. By 1620, there were more than 1,000 fishing boats in the waters off Newfoundland, and in 1812 about 1,600 boats. During these years, cod were huge fish, typically weighing in at more than 110 kilograms and measuring 1 to 2 metres in length.

Most of the fishing done during these years used lines and productivity was low. But low productivity limited the catch and enabled cod to be caught sustainably for hundreds of years.

The situation changed dramatically during the 1960s with the introduction of high-efficiency nets (called trawls, seines, and gill nets), sonar technology to find fish concentrations, and large ships with efficient processing and storage facilities. These technological advances brought soaring cod harvests. In less than a decade, cod landings increased from less than 300,000 tonnes a year to 800,000 tonnes.

This volume of cod could not be taken without a serious collapse in the remaining stock, and by the 1980s it became vital to regulate cod fishing. But regulation was of limited success and stocks continued to fall.

In 1992, a total ban on cod fishing in the North Atlantic stabilized the population but at a very low level. Two decades of ban have enabled the species to repopulate, and it is now hoped that one day cod fishing will return, but at a low and sustainable rate.

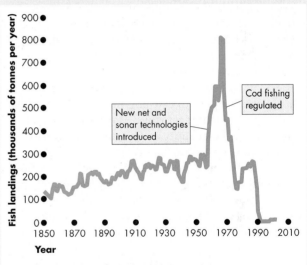

The Atlantic Cod Catch: 1850–2005

Source of data for graph: Millenium Ecosystem Assessment.
Source of information in text: Codfishes—Atlantic cod and its fishery, science.jrank.org.

If the fish stock is large, many fish are born, but they must compete with each other for food so only a small number survive to reproduce and to grow large enough to catch.

Between a small and a large stock is a quantity of fish stock that maximizes the sustainable catch. In Fig. 16.6, this fish stock is 20 million tonnes and the sustainable catch is 300,000 tonnes a year. The maximum sustainable catch arises from a balancing of the birth of new fish from the stock and the availability of food to sustain the fish popuation.

If the quantity of fish caught is less than the sustainable catch, the fish stock grows; if the quantity caught exceeds the sustainable catch, the fish stock shrinks; and if the quantity caught equals the sustainable catch, the fish stock remains constant and is available for future generations of fishers in the same quantity that is available today.

If the fish stock exceeds the level that maximizes the sustainable catch, overfishing isn't a problem. But if the fish stock is less than the level that maximizes the sustainable catch, overfishing depletes the stock.

The Overuse of a Common Resource

Why might a fish stock be overused? Why might overfishing occur? The answer is that fishers face only their own private cost and don't face the cost they impose on others—external cost. The *social* cost of fishing combines the *private* cost and *external* cost. Let's examine the costs of catching fish to see how the presence of external cost brings overfishing.

Marginal Private Cost You can think of the *marginal private cost* of catching fish as the additional cost incurred by keeping a boat and crew at sea for long enough to increase the catch by one tonne. Keeping a fishing boat at sea for an additional amount of time eventually runs into *diminishing marginal returns* (see p. 233). As the crew gets tired and the storage facilities get overfull, the catch per hour decreases. The cost of keeping the boat at sea for an additional hour is constant, so the marginal cost of catching fish increases as the quantity caught increases.

You've just seen that the *principle of increasing marginal cost* applies to catching fish just as it applies to other production activities: Marginal private cost increases as the quantity of fish caught increases.

The marginal private cost of catching fish determines an individual fisher's supply of fish. A profit-maximizing fisher is willing to supply the quantity at which the market price of fish covers the marginal private cost. And the market supply is the sum of the quantities supplied by each individual fisher.

Marginal External Cost The *marginal external cost* of catching fish is the cost per additional tonne that one fisher's production imposes on all other fishers. This additional cost arises because one fisher's catch decreases the remaining stock, which in turn decreases the renewal rate of the stock and makes it harder for others to find and catch fish.

Marginal external cost also increases as the quantity of fish caught increases. If the quantity of fish caught is so large that it drives the species to near extinction, the marginal external cost becomes infinitely large.

Marginal Social Cost The *marginal social cost* of catching fish is the marginal private cost plus the marginal external cost. Because both of its components increase as the quantity caught increases, marginal social cost also increases with the quantity of fish caught.

Marginal Social Benefit and Demand The marginal social benefit from fish is the price that consumers are willing to pay for an additional kilogram of fish. Marginal social benefit decreases as the quantity of fish consumed increases, so the demand curve, which is also the marginal social benefit curve, slopes downward.

Overfishing Equilibrium Figure 16.7 illustrates overfishing and how it arises. The market demand curve for fish is the marginal social benefit curve, *MSB*. The market supply curve is the marginal *private* cost curve, *MC*. Market equilibrium occurs at the intersection point of these two curves. The equilibrium quantity is 800,000 tonnes per year and the equilibrium price is $10 per kilogram.

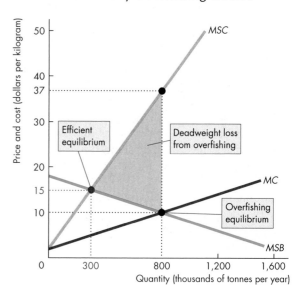

FIGURE 16.7 Why Overfishing Occurs

The supply curve is the marginal private cost curve, *MC*. The demand curve is the marginal social benefit curve, *MSB*. Market equilibrium occurs at a quantity of 800,000 tonnes and a price of $10 per kilogram.

The marginal social cost curve is *MSC* and at the market equilibrium there is overfishing—marginal social cost exceeds marginal social benefit.

The quantity at which *MSC* equals *MSB* is the efficient quantity, 300,000 tonnes per year. The grey triangle shows the deadweight loss from overfishing.

MyLab Economics Animation and Draw Graph

At this market equilibrium, overfishing is running down the fish stock. Figure 16.7 illustrates why overfishing occurs. At the market equilibrium quantity, marginal social benefit (and willingness to pay) is $10 per kilogram, but the marginal social cost exceeds this amount. The marginal external cost is the cost of running down the fish stock.

Efficient Equilibrium What is the efficient use of a common resource? It is the use of the resource that makes the marginal social benefit from the resource equal to the marginal social cost of using it.

In Fig. 16.7, the efficient quantity of fish is 300,000 tonnes per year—the quantity that makes marginal social cost (on the *MSC* curve) equal to marginal social benefit (on the *MSB* curve). At this quantity, the marginal catch of each individual fisher costs society what people are willing to pay for it.

Deadweight Loss from Overfishing Deadweight loss measures the cost of overfishing. The grey triangle in Fig. 16.7 illustrates this loss. It is the marginal social cost minus the marginal social benefit from all the fish caught in excess of the efficient quantity.

Achieving an Efficient Outcome

Defining the conditions under which a common resource is used efficiently is easier than delivering those conditions. To use a common resource efficiently, it is necessary to design an incentive mechanism that confronts the users of the resource with the marginal *social* consequences of their actions. The same principles apply to common resources as those that you met earlier in Chapter 15 when you studied the external cost of pollution.

The three main methods that might be used to achieve the efficient use of a common resource are:

- Property rights
- Production quotas
- Individual transferable quotas (ITQs)

Property Rights A common resource that no one owns and that anyone is free to use contrasts with *private property*, which is a resource that *someone* owns and has an incentive to use in the way that maximizes its value. One way of overcoming the tragedy of the commons is to convert a common resource to private property. By assigning private property rights to what was previously a common resource, its owner faces

the same conditions as society faces. It doesn't matter who owns the resource.

The users of the resource will be confronted with the full cost of using it because they either own it or pay a fee to the owner for permission to use it.

When private property rights over a resource are established and enforced, the *MSC* curve becomes the marginal *private* cost curve, and the use of the resource is efficient.

Figure 16.8 illustrates an efficient outcome with property rights. The supply curve $S = MC = MSC$ and the demand curve, the marginal social benefit curve, determine the equilibrium price and quantity. The price equals both marginal social benefit and marginal social cost and the quantity is efficient.

FIGURE 16.8 Property Rights Achieve an Efficient Outcome

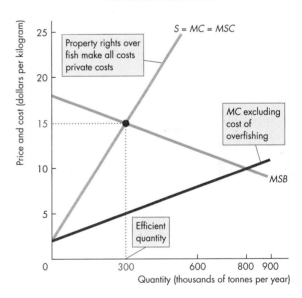

With private property rights, fishers pay the owner of the fish stock for permission to fish and face the full social cost of their actions. The marginal cost curve includes the external cost, so the supply curve is the marginal private cost curve and the marginal social cost curve, $S = MC = MSC$.

Market equilibrium occurs at $15 per kilogram and, at that price, the quantity is 300,000 tonnes per year. At this quantity, marginal social cost equals marginal social benefit, and the quantity of fish caught is efficient.

The property rights convert the fish stock from a common resource to a private resource and it is used efficiently.

——————— MyLab Economics Animation ———

The private property solution to the tragedy of the commons *is* available in some cases. It was the solution to the original tragedy of the commons in England's Middle Ages. It is also a solution that has been used to prevent overuse of the airwaves that carry cellphone services. The right to use this space (called the frequency spectrum) has been auctioned by governments to the highest bidders. The owner of each part of the spectrum is the only one permitted to use it (or to license someone else to use it).

But assigning private property rights is not always feasible. It would be difficult, for example, to assign private property rights to the oceans. It would not be impossible, but the cost of enforcing private property rights over thousands of hectares of ocean would be high. It would be even more difficult to assign and protect private property rights to the atmosphere.

In some cases, there is an emotional objection to assigning private property rights. Critics of it have a moral objection to someone owning a resource that they regard as public. In the absence of property rights, some form of government intervention is used, one of which is a production quota.

Production Quotas A *production quota* is an upper limit to the quantity of a good that may be produced in a specified period. The quota is allocated to individual producers, so each producer has its own quota.

You studied the effects of a production quota in Chapter 6 (pp. 143–144) and learned that a quota can drive a wedge between marginal social benefit and marginal social cost and create deadweight loss. In that earlier example, the market was efficient without a quota. But in the case of common resources, the market overuses the resource and produces an inefficient quantity. A production quota in this market brings a move towards a more efficient outcome.

Figure 16.9 shows a quota that achieves an efficient outcome. The quota limits the catch (production) to 300,000 tonnes, the efficient quantity at which marginal social benefit, *MSB*, equals marginal social cost, *MSC*. If everyone sticks to their own quota, the outcome is efficient. But implementing a production quota has two problems.

First, it is in every fisher's self-interest to catch more fish than the quantity permitted under the quota. The reason is that price exceeds marginal private cost, so by catching more fish, a fisher gets a higher income. If enough fishers break the quota, overfishing and the tragedy of the commons remain.

Second, marginal cost is not, in general, the same for all producers—as we're assuming here. Efficiency

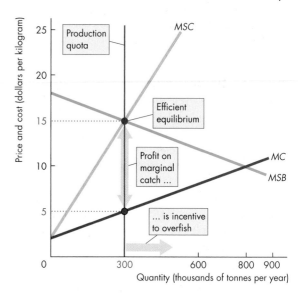

FIGURE 16.9 A Production Quota to Use a Common Resource Efficiently

A quota of 300,000 tonnes that limits production to this quantity raises the price to $15 per kilogram and lowers marginal cost to $5 per kilogram. A fisher who cheats and produces more than the alloted quota increases his profit by $10 per kilogram. If all (or most) fishers cheat, production exceeds the quota and there is a return to overfishing.

MyLab Economics Animation

requires that the quota be allocated to the producers with the lowest marginal cost. But bureaucrats who allocate quotas do not have information about the marginal cost of individual producers. Even if they tried to get this information, producers would have an incentive to lie about their costs so as to get a bigger quota.

So where producers are difficult, or very costly, to monitor or where marginal cost varies across producers, a production quota cannot achieve an efficient outcome.

Individual Transferable Quotas Where producers are difficult to monitor or where marginal cost varies across producers, a more sophisticated quota system can be effective. It is an **individual transferable quota (ITQ)**, which is a production limit that is assigned to an individual who is then free to transfer (sell) the quota to someone else. A market in ITQs emerges and ITQs are traded at their market price.

The market price of an ITQ is the highest price that someone is willing to pay for one. That price is marginal social benefit minus marginal cost. The price of an ITQ will rise to this level because fishers who don't have a quota would be willing to pay this amount to get one.

A fisher with an ITQ could sell it for the market price, so by not selling the ITQ the fisher incurs an opportunity cost. The marginal cost of fishing, which now includes the opportunity cost of the ITQ, equals the marginal social benefit from the efficient quantity.

Figure 16.10 illustrates how ITQs work. Each fisher receives an allocation of ITQs and the total catch permitted by the ITQs is 300,000 tonnes per year. Fishers trade ITQs: Those with low marginal cost buy ITQs from those with high marginal cost and the market price of an ITQ settles at $10 per kilogram of fish. The marginal private cost of fishing now becomes the original marginal private cost, *MC*, plus the price of the ITQ. The marginal private cost curve shifts upward from *MC* to *MC* + *price of ITQ* and each fisher is confronted with the marginal *social* cost of fishing. No one has an incentive to exceed the quota because to do so would send marginal cost above price and result in a loss on the marginal catch. The outcome is efficient.

FIGURE 16.10 ITQs to Use a Common Resource Efficiently

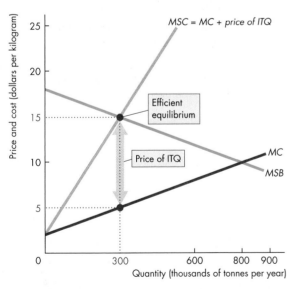

ITQs are issued on a scale that keeps output at the efficient level. The market price of an ITQ equals the marginal social benefit minus marginal cost. Because each user of the common resource faces the opportunity cost of using the resource, self-interest achieves the social interest.

———— MyLab Economics Animation ————

ECONOMICS IN ACTION
ITQs Work

Iceland introduced the first ITQs in 1984 to conserve its stocks of lobster. In 1986, New Zealand and a bit later Australia introduced ITQs to conserve fish stocks in the South Pacific and Southern Oceans. The evidence from these countries suggests that ITQs work well.

ITQs help maintain fish stocks, but they also reduce the size of the fishing industry. This consequence of ITQs puts them against the self-interest of fishers. In all countries, the fishing industry opposes restrictions on its activities, but in Australia and New Zealand, the opposition is not strong enough to block ITQs.

In the United States the opposition has been harder to overcome, and in 1996 Congress passed the Sustainable Fishing Act that put a moratorium on ITQs. This moratorium was lifted in 2004, and since then ITQs have been applied to 28 fisheries from the Gulf of Alaska to the Gulf of Mexico. Economists have studied the effects of ITQs extensively and agree that they work. ITQs offer an effective tool for achieving an efficient use of the stock of ocean fish.

Opposition to ITQs has prevented them from being adopted in Canada. One Parliamentary committee in Ottawa even went so far as to argue that evidence from Australia and New Zealand should not be used to justify ITQs in Canada.

REVIEW QUIZ

1 What is the tragedy of the commons? Give two examples, including one from your province.
2 Describe the conditions under which a common resource is used efficiently.
3 Review three methods that might achieve the efficient use of a common resource and explain the obstacles to efficiency.

Work these questions in Study Plan 16.3 and get instant feedback.   MyLab Economics

◆ *Economics in the News* on pp. 388–389 looks at the problem of keeping highway infrastructure in a good state of repair.

Maintainting the Transportation Infrastucture

Mayor Won't Reopen Gardiner Repair Debate Despite $1B Cost Spike

In September 2015, Toronto city staff estimated the cost to repair the entire Gardiner Expressway at $2.57 billion. Less than a year later, the estimated cost was projected to be $3.64 billion.

With uncertainty over federal funding, the city planners have been studying alternative revenue sources and estimated that a $2 toll on the Gardiner Expressway and Don Valley Parkway would raise almost $5 billion over 30 years.

Mayor John Tory opposed further debate about the project even though the cost had ballooned by more than $1 billion, and agreed with the city manager's recommendation to council that revenue should be raised by putting tolls on the Gardiner and Don Valley Parkway.

The *Toronto Star* reported Tory as saying, "the Gardiner is going to be part of our transportation infrastructure going forward for a long time to come," and "at least we're getting realistic numbers now."

"We have had discussions on a number of these projects over and over and over again. No matter what decision is made, no matter by how big a margin at city council, there are always those who want to reopen them, usually the people on the losing end of the vote."

Sources: Based on Powell, Betsy, "Tory Won't Reopen Gardiner Repair Debate Despite $1B Cost Spike," *Toronto Star*, November 28, 2016; and City of Toronto Staff Report "Tolling Options for the Gardiner Expressway and Don Valley Parkway," September 10, 2015.

ESSENCE OF THE STORY

- The estimated cost of repairing the Gardiner Expressway has jumped from $2.6 billion to $3.6 billion.

- Toronto Mayor John Tory says the council's decision stands and it is now time to get on with raising money to do the job.

- A report recommends putting tolls on the Gardiner and the Don Valley Parkway.

- City staff estimate that a $2 toll would raise close to $5 billion over 30 years.

MyLab Economics Economics in the News

ECONOMIC ANALYSIS

- Canada's road transportation infrastructure is constructed and maintained by all levels of government.

- Toronto's Gardiner Expressway was constructed and is maintained by the City of Toronto.

- To maintain any highway requires continuous repairs and eventually major refurbishment or replacement.

- The Gardiner Expressway was constructed 60 years ago and is undergoing a major overhaul.

- The City of Toronto considered a variety of proposals that include tearing down the Gardiner and replacing it with either a surface or tunnel expressway.

- The City government decision was to undertake major repairs that cost $3.6 billion.

- You can explain the problem of expressway maintenance and Mayor Tory's support for the complete repair of the Gardiner by using the tools you've learned in this chapter.

- In Fig. 1, the x-axis measures the number of kilometres of expressway repaired and the y-axis measures the marginal benefit and cost of repairs. All the numbers are assumptions but calibrated to the Toronto numbers.

- The MSC curve shows the marginal social cost of repairing a kilometre of expressway and the MSB curve shows the marginal social benefit.

- If the city allocated only $2 billion to the Gardiner project, only 12 kilometres of the expressway could be repaired. Given the (assumed) MSB and MSC curves, the efficient quantity is 18 kilometres.

- Because the number of kilometres repaired is less than the efficient quantity, a deadweight loss arises.

- The efficient use of resources occurs, shown in Fig. 2, when all 18 kilometres of the Gardiner are repaired at a cost of $0.2 billion per kilometre, with a total expenditure of $3.6 billion.

- Comparing the outcomes in Fig. 1 and Fig. 2, a political party can propose an expressway repair and tax program that achieves an efficient outcome.

- The efficient size of the repair project is paid for by the people who benefit from the restored expressway—its users—by a road toll.

- A road toll set at the efficient level would both pay for the repairs and provide an incentive for people to use public transit and ease congestion on the expressway.

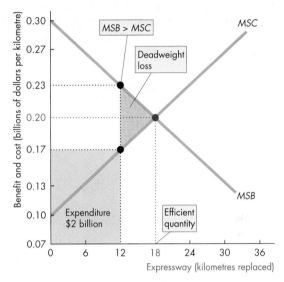

Figure 1 Underprovision of Expressway

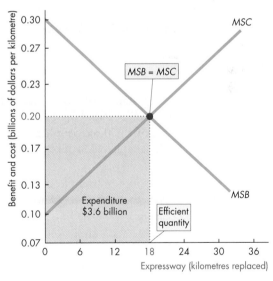

Figure 2 Efficient Provision of Expressway

WORKED PROBLEM

MyLab Economics Work this problem in Chapter 16 Study Plan.

The table sets out the marginal benefits that Ann, Sue, and Zack receive from spraying their shared swamp to control mosquitoes. The marginal social cost (*MSC*) is a constant $12 per spray.

Number of sprays (per season)	Marginal benefit		
	Ann	Sue	Zack
	(dollars per spray)		
0	5	10	15
1	4	8	12
2	3	6	9
3	2	4	6
4	1	2	3
5	0	0	0

Questions

1. What is the marginal social benefit of mosquito control at each quantity of sprays?
2. What is the efficient number of sprays per season?

Solutions

1. Mosquito control is a public good, so its marginal social benefit (*MSB*) is found by summing the marginal benefits of the three people at each quantity of sprays. The table below records the calculations.

   At 2 sprays per season, for example, *MSB* is $18 per spray, which is the sum of $3 (Ann), $6 (Sue), and $9 (Zack).

   The other rows of the table show the *MSB* for other quantities of sprays.

   Figure 1 illustrates the *MSB* calculation.

Number of sprays (per season)	Marginal benefit			*MSB*
	Ann	Sue	Zack	
	(dollars per spray)			
0	5	10	15	30
1	4	8	12	24
2	3	6	9	18
3	2	4	6	12
4	1	2	3	4
5	0	0	0	0

Key Point: The marginal social benefit curve of a public good is the *vertical* sum of the individual marginal benefit curves.

2. To find the efficient number of sprays, we need to determine the number of sprays per season at which the *MSB* equals the *MSC* of $12.

   The table shows that *MSB* equals $12 at 3 sprays per season, so that is the efficient quantity.

Key Point: The efficient quantity of a public good is that at which its marginal social benefit equals its marginal social cost.

Key Figures

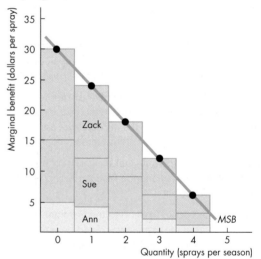

Figure 1 Marginal Social Benefit

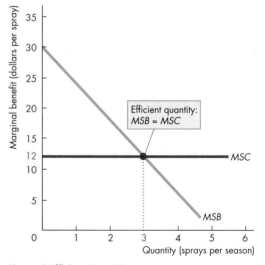

Figure 2 Efficient Quantity

MyLab Economics Interactive Animation

◆   **SUMMARY**

Key Points

Classifying Goods and Resources (p. 376)

- A private good is a good or service that is rival and excludable.
- A public good is a good or service that is nonrival and nonexcludable.
- A common resource is a resource that is rival but nonexcludable.
- A natural monopoly good is a good or service that is nonrival and excludable.

Working Problems 1 and 2 will give you a better understanding of classifying goods and resources.

Public Goods (pp. 377–381)

- Because a public good is a good or service that is *nonrival* and *nonexcludable*, it creates a *free-rider problem*. No one has an incentive to pay their share of the cost of providing a public good.
- The efficient level of provision of a public good is that at which marginal social benefit equals marginal social cost.

- Competition between political parties can lead to the efficient scale of provision of a public good.
- Bureaucrats who maximize their budgets and voters who are rationally ignorant can lead to the inefficient overprovision of a public good—government failure.

Working Problems 3 to 6 will give you a better understanding of public goods.

Common Resources (pp. 382–387)

- Common resources create a problem that is called the *tragedy of the commons*—no one has a private incentive to conserve the resources and use them at an efficient rate.
- A common resource is used to the point at which the marginal social (private) benefit equals the marginal private cost.
- A common resource might be used efficiently by creating a private property right, setting a quota, or issuing individual transferable quotas.

Working Problems 7 to 9 will give you a better understanding of common resources.

Key Terms

MyLab Economics Key Terms Quiz

Common resource, 376
Excludable, 376
Free-rider problem, 377
Individual transferable quota
   (ITQ), 386

Natural monopoly good, 376
Nonexcludable, 376
Nonrival, 376
Principle of minimum
   differentiation, 379

Private good, 376
Public good, 376
Rational ignorance, 380
Rival, 376
Tragedy of the commons, 382

STUDY PLAN PROBLEMS AND APPLICATIONS

MyLab Economics Work Problems 1 to 9 in Chapter 16 Study Plan and get instant feedback.

Classifying Goods and Resources (Study Plan 16.1)

1. Classify each of the following items as excludable, nonexcludable, rival, or nonrival. Explain your answer.
   - A Big Mac
   - A bridge
   - A view of the sunset
   - A hurricane warning system

2. Classify each of the following items as a public good, a private good, a natural monopoly good, or a common resource. Explain your answer.
   - Highway police services
   - Internet service
   - A Tim Hortons coffee
   - Fish in the Atlantic ocean
   - Purolator courier service

Public Goods (Study Plan 16.2)

3. For each of the following goods, explain why a free-rider problem arises or how it is avoided.
   - Canada Day fireworks display
   - TransCanada Highway in Manitoba
   - Wireless Internet access in a hotel
   - The public library in your city

4. The table sets out the benefits that Terri and Sue receive from on-campus police at night:

Police officers on duty	Marginal benefit	
	Terri	Sue
(number per night)	(dollars per police officer)	
1	18	22
2	14	18
3	10	14
4	6	10
5	2	6

Suppose that Terri and Sue are the only students on campus at night. Draw a graph to show the marginal social benefit from the on-campus police at night.

Use the data on mosquito control in the table in the next column to work Problems 5 and 6.

5. What quantity of spraying would a private firm provide? What is the efficient quantity of spraying? In a single-issue election on mosquito control, what quantity would the winner provide?

Quantity (hectares sprayed per day)	Marginal social cost	Marginal social benefit
	(thousands of dollars per day)	
1	2	10
2	4	8
3	6	6
4	8	4
5	10	2

6. If the government appoints a bureaucrat to run the program, would mosquito spraying most likely be underprovided, overprovided, or provided at the efficient quantity?

Common Resources (Study Plan 16.3)

Use the following figure to work Problems 7 to 9. The figure shows the market for North Atlantic tuna.

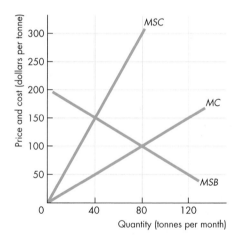

7. a. What is the quantity of tuna that fishers catch and the price of tuna? Is the tuna stock being used efficiently? Explain why or why not.

   b. What would be the price of tuna if the stock of tuna is used efficiently?

8. a. With a quota of 40 tonnes a month for the tuna fishing industry, what is the equilibrium price of tuna and the quantity of tuna that fishers catch?

   b. Is the equilibrium an overfishing equilibrium?

9. If the government issues ITQs to individual fishers that limit the total catch to the efficient quantity, what is the market price of an ITQ?

ADDITIONAL PROBLEMS AND APPLICATIONS

MyLab Economics You can work these problems in Homework or Test if assigned by your instructor.

Classifying Goods and Resources

10. Classify each of the following items as excludable, nonexcludable, rival, or nonrival and explain your classification.
    - Firefighting service
    - A Starbucks coffee
    - A view of Niagara Falls
    - Jasper National Park
    - A Google search

11. Classify each of the following items as a public good, a private good, a natural monopoly good, or a common resource and explain your classification.
    - A car licence
    - Tuna in the Pacific Ocean
    - Airline service within Canada
    - A cinema
    - A local storm-water system

Public Goods

Use the following table to work Problems 12 and 13. The table sets out the marginal benefits that Sam and Nick receive from the town's street lighting:

| Number of street lights | Marginal benefit | |
| | Sam | Nick |
	(dollars per street light)	
1	10	12
2	8	9
3	6	6
4	4	3
5	2	0

12. a. Is the town's street lighting a private good, a public good, or a common resource?

    b. Suppose that Sam and Nick are the only residents of the town. Draw a graph to show the marginal social benefit from the town's street lighting.

13. What is the principle of diminishing marginal benefit? Does Sam's, Nick's, or the society's marginal benefit diminish faster?

Use the following news clip to work Problems 14 and 15.

Threatened by Free Riders

Some parents refuse to get their children vaccinated against infectious diseases like measles and preventable infectious disease is returning to the developed world. A measles outbreak that began at California's Disneyland has health officials warning of worse to come. Parents who don't vaccinate are free riders.

Source: Washingtonpost.com, February 3, 2015

14. Explain why someone in a rich country who has not opted out on medical or religious grounds and refuses to be vaccinated is called a "free rider."

15. Explain why a measles vaccination is not a public good but why, nonetheless, an efficient outcome can be achieved by making it compulsory and paid for by government.

Use the following news clip to work Problems 16 and 17.

Higher Gas Tax and Road Tolls Can Fund Infrastructure

A Trent University road-pricing expert says Ontario should immediately and substantially raise the gas tax and begin creating more road tolls to pay for transportation infrastructure.

Source: *The Toronto Star*, July 15, 2015

16. Why are the gas tax and road tolls likely to be good tools to finance transportation infrastructure?

17. Explain how a rise in the gas tax and a road toll would enable the transportation infrastructure to be efficiently maintained and illustrate your analysis with an appropriate graph.

Common Resources

18. **In Quebec, an Economic Plan**
    As the polar ice caps recede, Canada plans Asian shipping routes and sustainable developments for its northern lands. "We're building a parallel canal to the Panama Canal for Chinese and Indian ships, so they can accelerate the transport of goods," says Jean Charest, the premier of Quebec. Charest announced Quebec's Plan Nord: a plan to develop the north by opening mines, building infrastructure to mines, boosting tourism, and establishing sustainable logging.

    Source: *Fortune*, June 3, 2011

    Which items in the news clip are common resources? Which items are public goods? Which activities are likely to increase climate change? Explain your answers.

19. If hikers were required to pay a fee to use the Overlander Trail in Jasper National Park,
    a. Would the use of this common resource be more efficient?
    b. Would it be even more efficient if the most popular spots along the trail had the highest prices?
    c. Why do you think we don't see more market solutions to the tragedy of the commons?

Use the following information to work Problems 20 to 22.

A spring runs under a village. Everyone can sink a well on her or his land and take water from the spring. The following figure shows the marginal social benefit from water and the marginal cost of taking it.

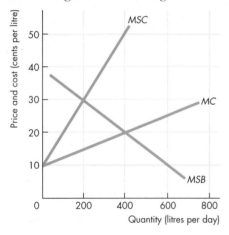

20. What is the quantity of water taken and what is the private cost of the water taken?

21. What is the efficient quantity of water taken and the marginal social cost at the efficient quantity?

22. If the village council sets a quota on the total amount of water such that the spring is used efficiently, what would be the quota and the market value of the water taken per day?

23. **Athabasca Fishery Declining**
    A new biology study finds that Arctic grayling has virtually disappeared from the northeast rivers. The causes include forestry and oilsands development, overfishing, and water quality.
    Source: *The Calgary Herald*, February 2, 2015
    a. Explain the tragedy of the commons described in this news clip.

b. How might this tragedy of the commons have been avoided?
c. Illustrate your answer to (b) with a graphical analysis.

Economics in the News

24. After you have studied *Economics in the News* on pp. 388–389, answer the following questions.
    a. What are some of the benefits of a well-maintained transportation infrastructure such as the Gardiner Expressway?
    b. What are some of the costs of keeping transportation infrastructure such as the Gardiner Expressway well maintained?
    c. What determines the efficient amount of expressway maintenance and what might lead to underprovision or overprovision of maintenance?
    d. How would you expect Toronto's population growth to influence the marginal social benefit from the Gardiner Expressway?
    e. Illustrate your answer to part (d) by drawing a version of Fig. 2 on p. 389 that shows the effect of an increase in the population.

25. **Trump Confronts NATO's Free Riders**
    NATO is a 28-nation defence alliance that regards an attack on one member as an attack on every member. To provide the agreed level of mutual support, NATO members commit to spending at least 2 percent of their gross domestic product on defence. But only the United States, Britain, Poland, Estonia, and Greece beat 2 percent. France, Germany, and Canada fall short.
    Source: *The Chicago Tribune*, February 16, 2017
    a. Explain the free-rider problem described in this news clip.
    b. Does the free-rider problem in international defence mean that the world has too little defence against aggression?
    c. How do nations try to overcome the free-rider problem among nations?

Making the Rules

UNDERSTANDING MARKET FAILURE AND GOVERNMENT

Creating a system of responsible democratic government is a huge entreprise, and one that could easily go wrong. Creating a constitution that made despotic and tyrannical rule impossible was relatively easy. And we achieved such a constitution for Canada by using some sound economic ideas. We designed a sophisticated system of incentives—of carrots and sticks—to make the government responsive to public opinion and to limit the ability of individual self-interests to gain at the expense of the majority. But they were not able to create a constitution that effectively blocks the ability of special interest groups to capture the consumer and producer surpluses that result from specialization and exchange.

We have created a system of government to deal with four market failures: (1) monopoly, (2) externalities, (3) public goods, and (4) common resources.

Government might help cope with these market failures, but government does not eliminate the pursuit of self-interest. Voters, politicians, and bureaucrats pursue their self-interest, sometimes at the expense of the social interest, and instead of market failure, we get government failure.

Many economists have thought long and hard about the problems discussed in Part Five, but none has had as profound an effect on our ideas in this area as Ronald Coase.

Ronald Coase *(1910–2013), was born in England and educated at the London School of Economics, where he was deeply influenced by his teacher, Arnold Plant, and by the issues of his youth: communist central planning versus free markets.*

Professor Coase lived in the United States from 1951 until his death in 2013. He first visited America as a 20-year-old on a travelling scholarship during the depths of the Great Depression. It was on this visit, and before he had completed his Bachelor's degree, that he conceived the ideas that 60 years later were to earn him the 1991 Nobel Prize for Economic Science.

Ronald Coase discovered and clarified the significance of transactions costs and property rights for the functioning of the economy. He revolutionized the way we think about property rights and externalities and opened up the growing field of law and economics.

"The question to be decided is: Is the value of fish lost greater or less than the value of the product which contamination of the stream makes possible?"

RONALD H. COASE
The Problem of Social Cost

CAROLINE M. HOXBY is the Allie S. Freed Professor of Economics at Harvard University. Born in Cleveland, Ohio, she was an undergraduate at Harvard and a graduate student at Oxford and MIT.

Professor Hoxby is a leading student of the economics of education. She has written many articles on this topic and has published books entitled *The Economics of School Choice* and *College Choices* (both University of Chicago Press, 2003 and 2004, respectively). She is Program Director of the Economics of Education Program at the National Bureau of Economic Research, serves on several other national boards that study education issues, and has advised or provided testimony to several state legislatures and the United States Congress.

Michael Parkin and Robin Bade talked with Caroline Hoxby about her work and the progress that economists have made in understanding how the financing and the provision of education influence the quality of education and the equality of access to it.

Why did you decide to become an economist?

I've wanted to be an economist from about the age of 13. That was when I took my first class in economics (an interesting story in itself) and discovered that all of the thoughts swimming around in my head belonged to a "science" and there was an entire body of people who understood this science—a lot better than I did, anyway. I can still recall reading *The Wealth of Nations* for the first time; it was a revelation.

What drew you to study the economics of education?

We all care about education, perhaps because it is the key means by which opportunity is (or should be) extended to all in the United States. Also, nearly everyone now acknowledges that highly developed countries like the United States rely increasingly on education as the engine of economic growth. Thus, one reason I was drawn to education is its importance. However, what primarily drew me was that education issues were so clearly begging for economic analysis and that there was so little of it. I try hard to understand educational institutions and problems, but I insist on bringing economic logic to bear on educational issues.

What can economists say about the alternative methods of financing education? Is there a voucher solution that could work?

There is definitely a voucher solution that could work because vouchers are inherently an extremely flexible policy. …

> **Economists should say to policymakers: "Tell me your goals; I'll design you a voucher."**

Any well-designed voucher system will give schools an incentive to compete. However, when designing vouchers, we can also build in remedies for a variety of educational problems. Vouchers can be used to ensure that disabled children get the funding they need and the program choices they need.

Compared to current school finance programs, vouchers can do a better job of ensuring that low-income families have sufficient funds to invest in the child's education. Well-designed vouchers can encourage schools to make their student bodies socio-economically diverse.

Economists should say to policymakers: "Tell me your goals; I'll design you a voucher."

*Read the full interview with Caroline Hoxby in MyLab Economics.

17 MARKETS FOR FACTORS OF PRODUCTION

After studying this chapter, you will be able to:

◆ Describe the anatomy of factor markets

◆ Explain how the value of marginal product determines the demand for a factor of production

◆ Explain how wage rates and employment are determined and how labour unions influence labour markets

◆ Explain how capital and land rental rates and natural resource prices are determined

Uber and Airbnb, the two big players in the "sharing economy," are transforming the way we get a taxi ride or book a room. And they are bringing protests from traditional taxi and hotel operators. How are these new technologies changing the jobs people do and the wages they earn? How are they changing the way we use our capital?

In this chapter, we study factor markets—the markets for labour, capital, and natural resources. In *Economics in the News* at the end of the chapter we look at the effects that Uber has had on the market for taxi drivers in major cities.

◆ The Anatomy of Factor Markets

The four factors of production are:

- Labour
- Capital
- Land (natural resources)
- Entrepreneurship

Let's take a brief look at the anatomy of the markets in which these factors of production are traded.

Markets for Labour Services

Labour services are the physical and mental work effort that people supply to produce goods and services. A labour market is a collection of people and firms who trade labour services. The price of labour services is the wage rate.

Some labour services are traded day by day. These services are called *casual labour*. People who pick fruit and vegetables often just show up at a farm and take whatever work is available that day. But most labour services are traded on a job contract.

Most labour markets have many buyers and many sellers and are competitive. In these markets, supply and demand determine the wage rate and quantity of labour employed. Jobs expand when demand increases and jobs disappear when demand decreases.

In some labour markets, a labour union operates like a monopoly on the supply side of the labour market. In this type of labour market, a bargaining process between the union and the employer determines the wage rate.

We'll study both competitive labour markets and labour unions in this chapter.

Markets for Capital Services

Capital consists of the tools, instruments, machines, buildings, and other constructions that have been produced in the past and that businesses now use to produce goods and services. These physical objects are themselves goods—capital goods. Capital goods are traded in goods markets, just as bottled water and toothpaste are. The price of a dump truck, a capital good, is determined by supply and demand in the market for dump trucks. This market is not a market for capital services.

A market for *capital services* is a *rental market*—a market in which the services of capital are hired.

An example of a market for capital services is the vehicle rental market in which Avis, Budget, Hertz,

U-Haul, and many other firms offer automobiles and trucks for hire. The price in a capital services market is a *rental rate*.

Most capital services are not traded in a market. Instead, a firm buys capital and uses it itself. The services of the capital that a firm owns and operates have an implicit price that arises from depreciation and interest costs (see Chapter 10, p. 229). You can think of this price as the implicit rental rate of capital. Firms that buy capital and use it themselves are *implicitly* renting the capital to themselves.

Markets for Land Services and Natural Resources

Land consists of all the gifts of nature—natural resources. The market for land as a factor of production is the market for the *services of land*—the use of land. The price of the services of land is a rental rate.

Most natural resources, such as farmland, can be used repeatedly. But a few natural resources are nonrenewable. **Nonrenewable natural resources** are resources that can be used only once. Examples are oil, natural gas, and coal. The prices of nonrenewable natural resources are determined in global *commodity markets* and are called *commodity prices*.

Entrepreneurship

Entrepreneurial services are not traded in markets. Entrepreneurs receive the profit or bear the loss that results from their business decisions.

◆ REVIEW QUIZ

1 What are the factors of production and their prices?
2 What is the distinction between capital and the services of capital?
3 What is the distinction between the price of capital equipment and the rental rate of capital?

Work these questions in Study Plan 17.1 and get instant feedback.   MyLab Economics

The rest of this chapter explores the influences on the demand and supply of factors of production. We begin by studying the demand for a factor of production.

The Demand for a Factor of Production

The demand for a factor of production is a **derived demand**—it is derived from the demand for the goods and services that the labour produces. You've seen, in Chapters 10 through 14, how a firm determines its profit-maximizing output. The quantities of factors of production demanded are a consequence of the firm's output decision. A firm hires the quantities of factors of production that produce the firm's profit-maximizing output.

To decide the quantity of a factor of production to hire, a firm compares the cost of hiring an additional unit of the factor with its value to the firm. The cost of hiring an additional unit of a factor of production is the factor price. The value to the firm of hiring one more unit of a factor of production is called the factor's **value of marginal product**. We calculate the value of marginal product as the price of a unit of output multiplied by the marginal product of the factor of production.

To study the demand for a factor of production, we'll use labour as the example. But what you learn here about the demand for labour applies to the demand for all factors of production.

Value of Marginal Product

Table 17.1 shows you how to calculate the value of marginal product of labour at Angelo's Bakery. The first two columns show Angelo's total product

schedule—the number of loaves per hour that each quantity of labour can produce. The third column shows the marginal product of labour—the change in total product that results from a one-unit increase in the quantity of labour employed. (See Chapter 10, pp. 231–234 for a refresher on product schedules.)

Angelo can sell bread at the going market price of $2 a loaf. Given this information, we can calculate the value of marginal product (fourth column). It equals price multiplied by marginal product. For example, the marginal product of hiring the second worker is 6 loaves. Each loaf sold brings in $2, so the value of marginal product of the second worker is $12 (6 loaves at $2 each).

A Firm's Demand for Labour

The value of marginal product of labour tells us what an additional worker is worth to a firm. It tells us the revenue that the firm earns by hiring one more worker. The wage rate tells us what an additional worker costs a firm.

The value of marginal product of labour and the wage rate together determine the quantity of labour demanded by a firm. Because the value of marginal product decreases as the quantity of labour employed increases, there is a simple rule for maximizing profit: Hire the quantity of labour at which the value of marginal product equals the wage rate.

If the value of marginal product of labour exceeds the wage rate, a firm can increase its profit by hiring

---

TABLE 17.1 Value of Marginal Product at Angelo's Bakery

Quantity of labour (L) (workers)	Total product (TP) (loaves per hour)	Marginal product ($MP = \Delta TP/\Delta L$) (loaves per worker)	Value of marginal product ($VMP = MP \times P$) (dollars per worker)
A 0	0		14
		 7	
B 1	7		12
		.... **6**	
C 2	13		10
		 5	
D 3	18		8
		 4	
E 4	22		6
		 3	
F 5	25		

The value of marginal product of labour equals the price of the product multiplied by the marginal product of labour. If Angelo's hires 2 workers, the marginal product of the second worker is 6 loaves (in the third column). The price of a loaf is $2, so the value of marginal product of the second worker is $2 a loaf multiplied by 6 loaves, which is $12 (in the fourth column).

one more worker. If the wage rate exceeds the value of marginal product of labour, a firm can increase its profit by firing one worker. But if the wage rate equals the value of marginal product of labour, the firm cannot increase its profit by changing the number of workers it employs. The firm is making the maximum possible profit, so:

> The quantity of labour demanded by a firm is the quantity at which the value of marginal product of labour equals the wage rate.

A Firm's Demand for Labour Curve

A firm's demand for labour curve is derived from its value of marginal product curve. Figure 17.1 shows these two curves. Figure 17.1(a) shows the value of marginal product curve at Angelo's Bakery. The blue bars graph the numbers in Table 17.1. The curve labelled *VMP* is Angelo's value of marginal product curve.

If the wage rate falls and other things remain the same, a firm hires more workers. Figure 17.1(b) shows Angelo's demand for labour curve.

Suppose the wage rate is $10 an hour. You can see in Fig. 17.1(a) that if Angelo hires 2 workers, the value of marginal product of labour is $12 an hour. At a wage rate of $10 an hour, Angelo makes a profit of $2 an hour on the second worker. If Angelo hires a third worker, the value of marginal product of that worker is $10 an hour. So on this third worker, Angelo breaks even.

If Angelo hired 4 workers, his profit would fall. The fourth worker generates a value of marginal product of only $8 an hour but costs $10 an hour, so Angelo does not hire the fourth worker. When the wage rate is $10 an hour, the quantity of labour demanded by Angelo is 3 workers.

Figure 17.1(b) shows Angelo's demand for labour curve, *D*. At $10 an hour, the quantity of labour demanded by Angelo is 3 workers. If the wage rate increased to $12 an hour, Angelo would decrease the quantity of labour demanded to 2 workers. If the wage rate decreased to $8 an hour, Angelo would increase the quantity of labour demanded to 4 workers.

A change in the wage rate brings a change in the quantity of labour demanded and a movement along the demand for labour curve.

A change in any other influence on a firm's labour-hiring plans changes the demand for labour and shifts the demand for labour curve.

FIGURE 17.1   The Demand for Labour at Angelo's Bakery

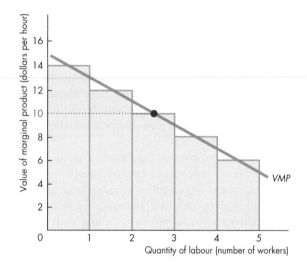

(a) Value of marginal product

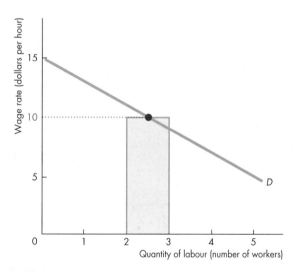

(b) Demand for labour

Angelo's Bakery can sell any quantity of bread at $2 a loaf. The blue bars in part (a) represent the firm's value of marginal product of labour (based on Table 17.1). The line labelled *VMP* is the firm's value of marginal product curve. Part (b) shows Angelo's demand for labour curve. Angelo hires the quantity of labour that makes the value of marginal product equal to the wage rate. The demand for labour curve slopes downward because the value of marginal product diminishes as the quantity of labour employed increases.

——— MyLab Economics Animation and Draw Graph ———

Changes in a Firm's Demand for Labour

A firm's demand for labour depends on:

- The price of the firm's output
- The prices of other factors of production
- Technology

The Price of the Firm's Output The higher the price of a firm's output, the greater is the firm's demand for labour. The price of a firm's output affects the firm's demand for labour through its influence on the value of marginal product of labour. A higher price for the firm's output increases the value of marginal product of labour. A change in the price of a firm's output leads to a shift in the firm's demand for labour curve. If the price of the firm's output increases, the demand for labour increases and the demand for labour curve shifts rightward.

For example, if the price of bread increased to $3 a loaf, the value of marginal product of Angelo's fourth worker would increase from $8 an hour to $12 an hour. At a wage rate of $10 an hour, Angelo would now hire 4 workers instead of 3.

The Prices of Other Factors of Production If the price of using capital decreases relative to the wage rate, a firm substitutes capital for labour and increases the quantity of capital it uses. Usually, the demand for labour will decrease when the price of using capital falls. For example, if the price of a bread-making machine falls, Angelo might decide to install one machine and lay off a worker. But the demand for labour could increase if the lower price of capital led to a sufficiently large increase in the scale of production. For example, with cheaper machines available, Angelo might install a machine and hire more labour to operate it. This type of factor substitution occurs in the long run when the firm can change the size of its plant.

Technology New technologies decrease the demand for some types of labour and increase the demand for other types. For example, if a new automated bread-making machine becomes available, Angelo might install one of these machines and fire most of his workforce—a decrease in the demand for bakery workers. But the firms that manufacture and service automated bread-making machines hire more labour, so there is an increase in the demand for this type of labour. An event similar to this one occurred during the 1990s when the introduction of electronic telephone exchanges decreased the demand for telephone operators and increased the demand for computer programmers and electronic engineers.

Table 17.2 summarizes the influences on a firm's demand for labour.

TABLE 17.2   A Firm's Demand for Labour

The Law of Demand

(Movements along the demand curve for labour)

The quantity of labour demanded by a firm

Decreases if:	*Increases if:*
■ The wage rate increases	■ The wage rate decreases

Changes in Demand

(Shifts in the demand curve for labour)

A firm's demand for labour

Decreases if:	*Increases if:*
■ The price of the firm's output decreases	■ The price of the firm's output increases
■ The price of a substitute for labour falls	■ The price of a substitute for labour rises
■ The price of a complement of labour rises	■ The price of a complement of labour falls
■ A new technology or new capital decreases the marginal product of labour	■ A new technology or new capital increases the marginal product of labour

---

◆ REVIEW QUIZ

1 What is the value of marginal product of labour?
2 What is the relationship between the value of marginal product of labour and the marginal product of labour?
3 How is the demand for labour derived from the value of marginal product of labour?
4 What are the influences on the demand for labour?

Work these questions in Study Plan 17.2 and get instant feedback.   MyLab Economics

Labour Markets

Labour services are traded in many different labour markets. Examples are markets for bakery workers, van drivers, crane operators, computer support specialists, air traffic controllers, surgeons, and economists. Some of these markets, such as the market for bakery workers, are local. They operate in a given neighbourhood or town. Some labour markets, such as the market for air traffic controllers, are national. Firms and workers search across the nation for the right match of worker and job. And some labour markets are global, such as the market for superstar hockey, basketball, and soccer players.

We'll look at a local market for bakery workers as an example. First, we'll look at a *competitive* labour market. Then, we'll see how monopoly elements can influence a labour market.

A Competitive Labour Market

A competitive labour market is one in which many firms demand labour and many households supply labour.

Market Demand for Labour Earlier in the chapter, you saw how an individual firm decides how much labour to hire. The market demand for labour is derived from the demand for labour by individual firms. We determine the market demand for labour by adding together the quantities of labour demanded by all the firms in the market at each wage rate. (The market demand for a good or service is derived in a similar way—see Chapter 5, pp. 112–113.)

Because each firm's demand for labour curve slopes downward, the market demand for labour curve also slopes downward.

The Market Supply of Labour The market supply of labour is derived from the supply of labour decisions made by individual households.

Individual's Labour Supply Decision People can allocate their time to two broad activities: labour supply and leisure. (Leisure is a catch-all term. It includes all activities other than supplying labour.) For most people, leisure is more fun than work, so to induce them to work they must be offered a wage.

Think about the labour supply decision of Jill, one of the workers at Angelo's Bakery. Let's see how the wage rate influences the quantity of labour she is willing to supply.

Reservation Wage Rate Jill enjoys her leisure time, and she would be pleased if she didn't have to spend her time working at Angelo's Bakery. But Jill wants to earn an income, and as long as she can earn a wage rate of at least $5 an hour, she's willing to work. This wage is called her *reservation wage*. At any wage rate above her reservation wage, Jill supplies some labour.

The wage rate at Angelo's is $10 an hour, and at that wage rate, Jill chooses to work 30 hours a week. At a wage rate of $10 an hour, Jill regards this use of her time as the best available. Figure 17.2 illustrates.

Backward-Bending Labour Supply Curve If Jill were offered a wage rate between $5 and $10 an hour, she would want to work a few hours a week. If she were offered a wage rate above $10 an hour, she would want to work more hours a week, but only up to a

---

FIGURE 17.2 Jill's Labour Supply Curve

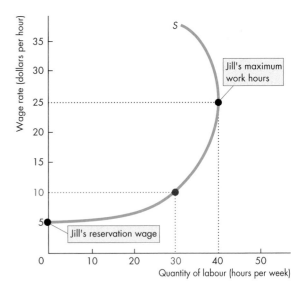

Jill's labour supply curve is *S*. Jill supplies no labour at wage rates below her reservation wage of $5 an hour. As the wage rate rises above $5 an hour, the quantity of labour that Jill supplies increases to a maximum of 40 hours a week at a wage rate of $25 an hour. As the wage rate rises above $25 an hour, Jill supplies a decreasing quantity of labour: her labour supply curve bends backward. The income effect on the demand for leisure dominates the substitution effect.

point. If Jill could earn $25 an hour, she would be willing to work 40 hours a week (and earn $1,000 a week). But at a wage rate above $25 an hour, with the goods and services that Jill can buy for $1,000, her priority would be a bit more leisure time. So if the wage rate increased above $25 an hour, Jill would cut back on her work hours and take more leisure. Jill's labour supply curve eventually bends backward.

Jill's labour supply decisions are influenced by a substitution effect and an income effect.

Substitution Effect At wage rates below $25 an hour, the higher the wage rate Jill is offered, the greater is the quantity of labour that she supplies. Jill's wage rate is her *opportunity cost of leisure*. If she leaves work an hour early to catch a movie, the cost of that extra hour of leisure is the wage rate that Jill forgoes. The higher the wage rate, the less willing Jill is to forgo the income and take the extra leisure time. This tendency for a higher wage rate to induce Jill to work longer hours is a *substitution effect*.

Income Effect The higher Jill's wage rate, the higher is her income. A higher income, other things remaining the same, induces Jill to increase her demand for most goods and services. Leisure is one of those goods. Because an increase in income creates an increase in the demand for leisure, it also creates a decrease in the quantity of labour supplied.

Market Supply Curve The market supply curve shows the quantity of labour supplied by all households in a particular job market. It is found by adding together the quantities supplied by all households to the job market at each wage rate, so the greater the number of households (the greater is the working-age population), the greater is the market supply of labour.

Despite the fact that an individual's labour supply curve eventually bends backward, the market supply curve of labour slopes upward. The higher the wage rate for bakery workers, the greater is the quantity of bakery workers supplied in that labour market.

One reason why the market supply curve doesn't bend backward is that different households have different reservation wage rates and different wage rates at which their labour supply curves bend backward.

Also, along a supply curve in a particular job market, the wage rates available in other job markets remain the same. For example, along the supply curve of bakers, the wage rates of salespeople and all other types of labour are constant.

Let's now look at labour market equilibrium.

Competitive Labour Market Equilibrium Labour market equilibrium determines the wage rate and employment. In Fig. 17.3, the market demand curve for bakery workers is *D* and the market supply curve of bakery workers is *S*. The equilibrium wage rate is $10 an hour, and the equilibrium quantity is 300 bakery workers. If the wage rate exceeded $10 an hour, there would be a surplus of bakery workers. More people would be looking for jobs in bakeries than firms were willing to hire. In such a situation, the wage rate would fall as firms found it easy to hire people at a lower wage rate. If the wage rate were less than $10 an hour, there would be a shortage of bakery workers. Firms would not be able to fill all the positions they had available. In this situation, the wage rate would rise as firms found it necessary to offer higher wages to attract labour. Only at a wage rate of $10 an hour are there no forces operating to change the wage rate.

FIGURE 17.3 The Market for Bakery Workers

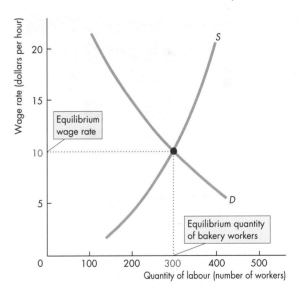

A competitive labour market coordinates firms' and households' plans. The market is in equilibrium—the quantity of labour demanded equals the quantity supplied—at a wage rate of $10 an hour when 300 workers are employed. If the wage rate exceeds $10 an hour, the quantity supplied exceeds the quantity demanded and the wage rate will fall. If the wage rate is below $10 an hour, the quantity demanded exceeds the quantity supplied and the wage rate will rise.

MyLab Economics Animation

ECONOMICS IN ACTION

Wage Rates in Canada

In 2015, the average hourly wage in Canada was $25.19. The figure shows the average hourly wage rates for 12 jobs selected from the hundreds of jobs for which Statistics Canada reports wage rate data.

You can see that a senior manager, on average, earns more than three times as much per hour as a chef or cook and twice as much as a construction worker. Remember that these numbers are averages. Some senior managers earn much more and some earn less than the average.

Many more occupations earn a wage rate below the national average than above it. Most of the occupations that earn more than the national average require a university degree and postgraduate training.

Earning differences are explained by differences in the value of marginal product of the skills in the various occupations and in market power.

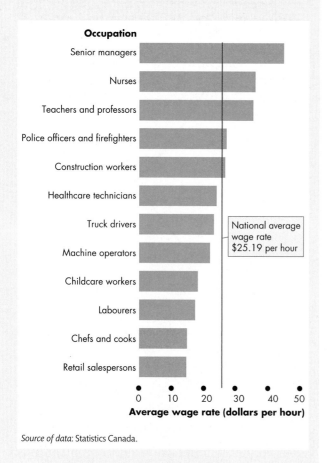

Source of data: Statistics Canada.

Differences and Trends in Wage Rates

You can use what you've learned about labour markets to explain some of the differences in wage rates across occupations and the trends in wage rates.

Wage rates are unequal, and *Economics in Action* on this page shows a sample of the inequality in wages in 2015. The differences in wage rates across occupations are driven by differences in demand and supply in labour markets. The highest wage rates are earned in occupations where the value of marginal product is highest and where few people have the ability and training to perform the job.

Rising Wage Rates Wage rates increase over time and trend upward. The reason is that the value of marginal product of labour also increases over time. Technological change and the new types of capital that it brings make workers more productive. With greater labour productivity, the demand for labour increases, which increases the wage rate. Even jobs in which physical productivity doesn't increase, experience increases in the *value* of marginal product. Childcare is an example. A worker can't care for an increasing number of children, but an increasing number of parents who earn high wages are willing to hire childcare workers. The *value* of marginal product of these workers increases, so the demand for their services increases, and so does their wage rate.

Increased Wage Inequality In recent years wage inequality has increased. High wage rates have increased more rapidly than the low ones, and some low wage rates have stagnated or even fallen. The reasons are complex and not fully understood, but the best explanation is that there is an interaction between technology and education.

The new information technologies of the 1990s and 2000s made well-educated, skilled workers more productive, so it raised their wage rates. For example, the computer created the jobs and increased the wage rates of computer programmers and electronic engineers.

These same technologies destroyed some low-skilled jobs. For example, the ATM took the jobs and lowered the wage rate of bank tellers, and automatic telephones took the jobs of telephone operators.

Another reason for increased inequality is that globalization has brought increased competition for low-skilled workers and at the same time opened global markets for high-skilled workers.

A Labour Market with a Union

A **labour union** is an organized group of workers that aims to increase the wage rate and influence other job conditions. Let's see what happens when a union enters a competitive labour market.

Influences on Labour Supply One way of raising the wage rate is to decrease the supply of labour. In some labour markets, a union can restrict supply by controlling entry into apprenticeship programs or by influencing job qualification standards. Markets for skilled workers, doctors, dentists, and lawyers are the easiest ones to control in this way.

If there is an abundant supply of nonunion labour, a union can't decrease supply. For example, in the market for farm labour in southern California, the flow of nonunion labour from Mexico makes it difficult for a union to control the supply.

On the demand side of the labour market, the union faces a tradeoff: The demand for labour curve slopes downward, so restricting supply to raise the wage rate costs jobs. For this reason, unions also try to influence the demand for union labour.

Influences on Labour Demand A union tries to increase the demand for the labour of its members in four main ways:

1. Increasing the value of marginal product of its members by organizing and sponsoring training schemes and apprenticeship programs, and by professional certification.
2. Lobbying for import restrictions and encouraging people to buy goods made by unionized workers.
3. Supporting minimum wage laws, which increase the cost of employing low-skilled labour and lead firms to substitute high-skilled union labour for low-skilled nonunion labour.
4. Lobbying for restrictive immigration laws to decrease the supply of foreign workers.

Labour Market Equilibrium with a Union Figure 17.4 illustrates what happens to the wage rate and employment when a union successfully enters a competitive labour market. With no union, the demand curve is D_C, the supply curve is S_C, the wage rate is $10 an hour, and 300 workers have jobs.

Now a union enters this labour market. First, look at what happens if the union has sufficient control over the supply of labour to be able to restrict supply

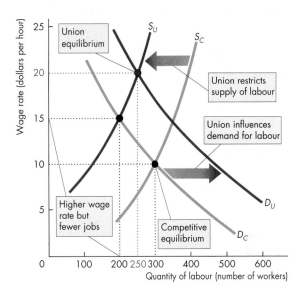

FIGURE 17.4   A Union Enters a Competitive Labour Market

In a competitive labour market, the demand curve is D_C and the supply curve is S_C. The wage rate is $10 an hour and 300 workers are employed. If a union decreases the supply of labour and the supply of labour curve shifts to S_U, the wage rate rises to $15 an hour and employment decreases to 200 workers. If the union can also increase the demand for labour and shift the demand for labour curve to D_U, the wage rate rises to $20 an hour and 250 workers are employed.

———— MyLab Economics Animation and Draw Graph ————

below its competitive level—to S_U. If that is all the union is able to do, employment falls to 200 workers and the wage rate rises to $15 an hour.

Suppose now that the union is also able to increase the demand for labour to D_U. The union can get an even bigger increase in the wage rate and with a smaller fall in employment. By maintaining the restricted labour supply at S_U, the union increases the wage rate to $20 an hour and achieves an employment level of 250 workers.

Because a union restricts the supply of labour in the market in which it operates, the union's actions spill over into nonunion markets. Workers who can't get union jobs must look elsewhere for work. This action increases the supply of labour in nonunion markets and lowers the wage rate in those markets. This spillover effect further widens the gap between union and nonunion wages.

Monopsony in the Labour Market Not all labour markets in which unions operate are competitive. Rather, some are labour markets in which the employer possesses market power and the union enters to try to counteract that power.

A market in which there is a single buyer is called a **monopsony**. A monopsony labour market has one employer. Provincial governments are the major employer of healthcare professionals. In some communities, a mining company is the major employer. These firms have monopsony power.

A monopsony acts on the buying side of a market in a similar way to a monopoly on the selling side. The firm maximizes profit by hiring the quantity of labour that makes the marginal cost of labour equal to the value of marginal product of labour and by paying the lowest wage rate at which it can attract this quantity of labour.

Figure 17.5 illustrates a monopsony labour market. Like all firms, a monopsony faces a downward-sloping value of marginal product curve, *VMP*, which is its demand for labour curve, *D*—the curve labelled *VMP* = *D* in the figure.

What is special about monopsony is the marginal cost of labour. For a firm in a competitive labour market, the marginal cost of labour is the wage rate. For a monopsony, the marginal cost of labour exceeds the wage rate. The reason is that being the only buyer in the market, the firm faces an upward-sloping supply of labour curve—the curve *S* in the figure.

To attract one more worker, the monopsony must offer a higher wage rate. But it must pay this higher wage rate to all its workers, so the marginal cost of a worker is the wage rate plus the increased wage bill that arises from paying all the workers the higher wage rate.

The supply curve is now the average cost of labour curve and the relationship between the supply curve and the marginal cost of labour curve, *MCL*, is similar to that between a monopoly's demand curve and marginal revenue curve (see p. 282). The relationship between the supply curve and the *MCL* curve is also similar to that between a firm's average cost curve and marginal cost curve (see pp. 240–241).

To find the profit-maximizing quantity of labour to hire, the monopsony sets the marginal cost of labour equal to the value of marginal product of labour. In Fig. 17.5, this outcome occurs when the firm employs 100 workers.

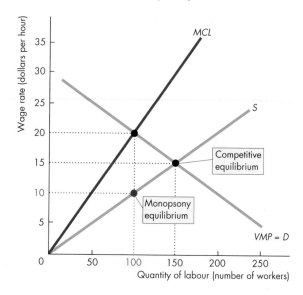

FIGURE 17.5 A Monopsony Labour Market

A monopsony is a market structure in which there is a single buyer. A monopsony in the labour market has a value of marginal product curve *VMP* = *D* and faces a labour supply curve *S*. The marginal cost of labour curve is *MCL*. Making the marginal cost of labour equal to the value of marginal product of labour maximizes profit. The monopsony hires 100 hours of labour and pays the lowest wage rate for which that quantity of labour will work—$10 an hour.

MyLab Economics Animation

To hire 100 workers, the firm must pay $10 an hour (on the supply of labour curve). Each worker is paid $10 an hour, but the value of marginal product of labour is $20 an hour, so the firm makes an economic profit of $10 an hour on the marginal worker.

If the labour market in Fig. 17.5 were competitive, the equilibrium wage rate and employment would be determined by the demand and supply curves. The wage rate would be $15 an hour and 150 workers would be employed. So compared with a competitive labour market, a monopsony pays a lower wage rate and employs fewer workers.

A Union and a Monopsony A union is like a monopoly. If the union (monopoly seller) faces a monopsony buyer, the situation is called **bilateral monopoly**. An example of bilateral monopoly is the National Hockey League (the owners) and the National Hockey League

◆ AT **ISSUE**

Monopoly Power for Evil or Good?

The standard view of economists is that monopoly is bad. It prevents resources from being used efficiently, and on any criterion of fairness or equity, monopoly is unfair. It fails to serve the social interest.

We normally think of a monopoly as a big firm that gouges its customers. But a surprising monopoly (and monopsony) has attracted attention—the National Collegiate Athletic Association (NCAA).

Does the NCAA do a good job at efficiently allocating the talents of college athletes and providing those athletes with a fair return for their efforts?

The standard economist's view is that the NCAA doesn't serve the social interest. But there is an opposing view.

Let's look at both sides of this argument.

The Standard View

Robert Barro expresses the standard economist view. While acknowledging that the NCAA has boosted the productivity of college sports programs, he says that the NCAA monopoly:

- Suppresses financial competition in college sports.

- Restricts scholarships and other payments to college athletes.

- Prevents college basketball players who come from poor families from accumulating wealth during a college career.

- Keeps poor students poor.

Despite doing these bad things, the NCAA manages to convince most people that the bad guys are the colleges that violate NCAA rules by attempting to pay their athletes competitive wages.

An Opposing View

Richard B. McKenzie of the University of California, Irvine, and Dwight R. Lee of the University of Georgia, in their book, *In Defense of Monopoly: How Market Power Fosters Creative Production* (University of Michigan Press, 2008), say the NCAA:

- Helps its members to cooperate to everyone's benefit.

- Has enabled healthy growth of college athletics over the past 50 years.

- Has generated economic profits for member schools.

- Does not lower student athletes' wages.

- Has stimulated the demand for student athletes and increased their wages and employment opportunities.

- Permitting NCAA colleges to pay athletes competitive wages is misguided.

The contenders for best monopoly in America include the Post Office, Microsoft, and the NCAA. And the winner is … the NCAA.

Robert Barro, "The Best Little Monopoly in America," *BusinessWeek*, December 9, 2002

The Connecticut Huskies celebrate their victory at the 2014 NCAA National Championship.

Players' Association (the union of players). The NHL and the NHPLA negotiate a multi-year salary deal.

In bilateral monopoly, the outcome is determined by bargaining, which depends on the costs that each party can inflict on the other. The firm can shut down temporarily and lock out its workers, and the workers can shut down the firm by striking. Each party estimates the other's strength and what it will lose if it does not agree to the other's demands.

Usually, an agreement is reached without a strike or a lockout. The threat is usually enough to bring the bargaining parties to an agreement. When a strike or lockout does occur, it is because one party has mis-judged the costs each party can inflict on the other. Such an event occurred in December 2012 when negotiations over a new collective bargaining agree-ment failed and owners locked out the players. Fifty-eight percent of the regular season was cancelled. Teams lost billions in revenue from tickets, media, sponsorships, and concessions, while players lost salaries.

In the example in Fig. 17.5, if the union and employer are equally strong, and each party knows the strength of the other, they will agree to split the gap between $10 (the wage rate on the supply curve) and $20 (the wage rate on the demand curve) and agree to a wage rate of $15 an hour.

You've now seen that in a monopsony, a union can bargain for a higher wage rate without sacrific-ing jobs. A similar outcome can arise in a monop-sony labour market when a minimum wage law is enforced. Let's look at the effect of a minimum wage.

Monopsony and the Minimum Wage In a competi-tive labour market, a minimum wage that exceeds the equilibrium wage decreases employment (see Chapter 6, pp. 135–136). In a monopsony labour market, a minimum wage can increase both the wage rate and employment. Let's see how.

Figure 17.6 shows a monopsony labour market without a union. The wage rate is $10 an hour and 100 workers are employed.

A minimum wage law is passed that requires employers to pay at least $15 an hour. The monop-sony now faces a perfectly elastic supply of labour at $15 an hour up to 150 workers (along the minimum wage line). To hire more than 150 workers, a wage rate above $15 an hour must be paid (along the sup-ply curve). Because the wage rate is $15 an hour up to 150 workers, the marginal cost of labour is also $15 an hour up to 150 workers. To maximize profit, the monopsony sets the marginal cost of labour

FIGURE 17.6   Minimum Wage Law in Monopsony

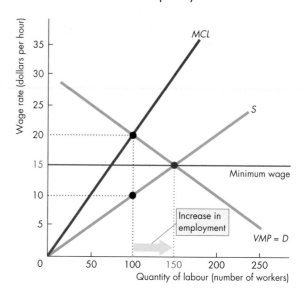

In a monopsony labour market, the wage rate is $10 an hour and 100 workers are hired. If a minimum wage law increases the wage rate to $15 an hour, the wage rate rises to this level and employment increases to 150 workers.

——— MyLab Economics Animation and Draw Graph ———

equal to the value of marginal product of labour (on the demand curve). That is, the monopsony hires 150 workers and pays $15 an hour. The minimum wage law has succeeded in raising the wage rate and increasing the number of workers employed.

◆◆◆   **REVIEW QUIZ**

1 What determines the amount of labour that households plan to supply?

2 How are the wage rate and employment deter-mined in a competitive labour market?

3 How do labour unions influence wage rates?

4 What is a monopsony and why is a monopsony able to pay a lower wage rate than a firm in a competitive labour market?

5 How is the wage rate determined when a union faces a monopsony?

6 What is the effect of a minimum wage law in a monopsony labour market?

Work these questions in Study Plan 17.3 and get instant feedback.   MyLab Economics

Capital and Natural Resource Markets

The markets for capital and land can be understood by using the same basic ideas that you've seen when studying a competitive labour market. But markets for nonrenewable natural resources are different. We'll now examine three groups of factor markets:

- Capital rental markets
- Land rental markets
- Nonrenewable natural resource markets

Capital Rental Markets

The demand for capital is derived from the *value of marginal product of capital*. Profit-maximizing firms hire the quantity of capital services that makes the value of marginal product of capital equal to the *rental rate of capital*. The *lower* the rental rate of capital, other things remaining the same, the *greater* is the quantity of capital demanded. The supply of capital responds in the opposite way to the rental rate. The *higher* the rental rate, other things remaining the same, the *greater* is the quantity of capital supplied. The equilibrium rental rate makes the quantity of capital demanded equal to the quantity supplied.

Figure 17.7 illustrates the rental market for tower cranes—capital used to construct high-rise buildings. The value of marginal product and the demand curve is $VMP = D$. The supply curve is S. The equilibrium rental rate is $1,000 per day and 100 tower cranes are rented.

Rent-Versus-Buy Decision Some capital services are obtained in a rental market like the market for tower cranes. And as with tower cranes, many of the world's large airlines rent their airplanes. But not all capital services are obtained in a rental market. Instead, firms buy the capital equipment that they use. You saw in Chapter 10 (pp. 228–229) that the cost of the services of the capital that a firm owns and operates itself is an implicit rental rate that arises from depreciation and interest costs. Firms that buy capital *implicitly* rent the capital to themselves.

The decision to obtain capital services in a rental market rather than buy capital and rent it implicitly is made to minimize cost. The firm compares the cost of explicitly renting the capital and the cost of buying and implicitly renting it. This decision is the same as

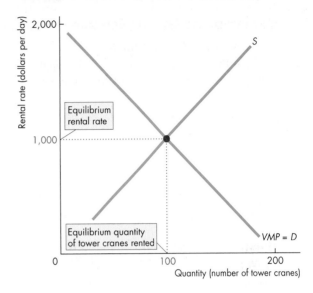

FIGURE 17.7 A Rental Market for Capital

The value of marginal product of tower cranes, *VMP*, determines the demand, *D*, for tower crane rentals. With the supply curve *S*, the equilibrium rental rate is $1,000 a day and 100 cranes are rented.

———— MyLab Economics Animation ————

the one that a household makes in deciding whether to rent or buy a home.

To make a rent-versus-buy decision, a firm must compare a cost incurred in the *present* with a stream of rental costs incurred over some *future* period. The Mathematical Note (pp. 416–417) explains how to make this comparison by calculating the *present value* of a future amount of money. If the *present value* of the future rental payments of an item of capital equipment exceeds the cost of buying the capital, the firm will buy the equipment. If the *present value* of the future rental payments of an item of capital equipment is less than the cost of buying the capital, the firm will rent (or lease) the equipment.

Land Rental Markets

The demand for land is based on the *value of marginal product of land* in the same way as the demand for labour and the demand for capital are based on the value of marginal product of labour and capital. Profit-maximizing firms rent the quantity of land at

ECONOMICS IN THE NEWS

The Growth of the Sharing Economy

Airbnb Not Hurting Boston Hotels

Researchers at Boston University find that the rapid expansion of Airbnb has not stopped Boston hotels from getting more business.

Source: *BU Today*, June 21, 2017

THE DATA

Airbnb	Quantity (thousands of rooms)	Price (dollars per room)
Sep 2015	129	183
Sep 2016	390	159

Hotels	Quantity (thousands of rooms)	Price (dollars per room)
Sep 2015	1,564	209
Sep 2016	1,622	219

THE QUESTIONS

■ What are the factors of production mentioned in the news clip?

■ What do the data tables tell us?

■ Provide a graphical illustration of the markets for Airbnb rooms and hotel rooms in September 2015 and September 2016.

THE ANSWERS

■ The factors of production are capital: the Airbnb platform, private homes and rooms offered for rent on Airbnb, and hotel rooms.

■ The data tables tell us that the quantity of Airbnb rooms more than tripled and the average price (rental rate) fell. Also, the quantity of hotel rooms increased slightly and the average price increased.

■ Figure 1 illustrates the market for Airbnb rooms in September 2015 and September 2016.

■ As more people discovered Airbnb, both supply and demand for Airbnb rooms increased. Supply increased from S_0 to S_1 and demand increased from D_0 to D_1.

■ The increase in supply was greater than the increase in demand.

■ The equilibrium quantity of Airbnb rooms increased from 129,000 in 2015 to 390,000 in 2016.

■ Because supply increased by more than demand, the equilibrium price fell from $183 to $159 per room.

■ Figure 2 illustrates the market for hotel rooms in September 2015 and September 2016.

■ Despite the expansion of Airbnb, the demand for hotel rooms increased from D_0 to D_1.

■ The equilibrium quantity of rooms increased from 1,564,000 in 2015 to 1,622,000 in 2016.

■ The equilibrium price increased from $209 to $219 per room.

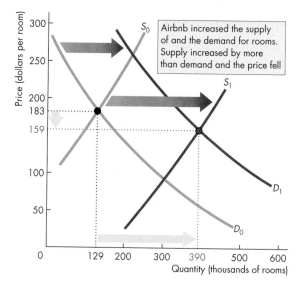

Figure 1 The Boston Market for Airbnb

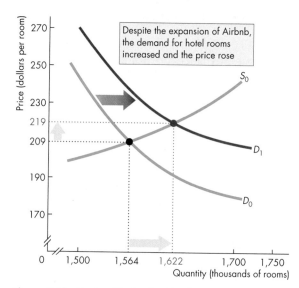

Figure 2 The Boston Market for Hotel Rooms

which the value of marginal product of land is equal to the *rental rate of land*. The *lower* the rental rate, other things remaining the same, the *greater* is the quantity of land demanded.

But the supply of land is special: Its quantity is fixed, so the quantity supplied cannot be changed by people's decisions. The supply of each particular block of land is perfectly inelastic.

The equilibrium rental rate makes the quantity of land demanded equal to the quantity available. Figure 17.8 illustrates the market for a 10-hectare block of land on Yonge Street in Toronto. The quantity supplied is fixed and the supply curve is *S*. The value of marginal product and the demand curve is *VMP = D*. The equilibrium rental rate is $1,000 a hectare per day.

The rental rate of land is high in Toronto because the willingness to pay for the services produced by that land is high, which in turn makes the *VMP* of land high. A Big Mac costs more at McDonald's on Yonge Street than at McDonald's on Mountain Road, Moncton, but not because the rental rate of land is higher in Toronto. The rental rate of land is higher in Toronto because of the greater willingness to pay for a Big Mac (and other goods and services) in Toronto.

FIGURE 17.8   A Rental Market for Land

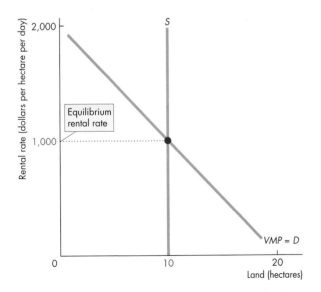

The value of marginal product of a 10-hectare block, *VMP*, determines the rental demand, *D*, for this land. With the supply curve *S*, the block rents for $10,000 a day.

Nonrenewable Natural Resource Markets

The nonrenewable natural resources are oil, gas, and coal. Burning one of these fuels converts it to energy and other by-products, and the used resource cannot be re-used. The natural resources that we use to make metals are also nonrenewable, but they can be used again, at some cost, by recycling them.

Oil, gas, and coal are traded in global commodity markets. The price of a given grade of crude oil is the same in New York, London, and Singapore. Traders, linked by telephone and the Internet, operate these markets around the clock every day of the year.

Demand and supply determine the prices and the quantities traded in these commodity markets. We'll look at the influences on demand and supply by considering the global market for crude oil.

The Demand for Oil   The two key influences on the demand for oil are:

1. The *value of marginal product* of oil
2. The expected future price of oil

The value of marginal product of oil is the *fundamental* influence on demand. It works in exactly the same way for a nonrenewable resource as it does for any other factor of production. The greater the quantity of oil used, the smaller is the value of marginal product of oil. Diminishing value of marginal product makes the demand curve slope downward. The lower the price, the greater is the quantity demanded.

The higher the expected future price of oil, the greater is the present demand for oil. The expected future price is a *speculative* influence on demand. Oil in the ground and oil in storage tanks are inventories that can be held or sold. A trader might plan to buy oil to hold now and to sell it later for a profit. Instead of buying oil to hold and sell later, the trader could buy a bond and earn interest. The interest forgone is the opportunity cost of holding the oil. If the price of oil is expected to rise by a bigger percentage than the interest rate, a trader will hold oil and incur the opportunity cost. In this case, the return from holding oil exceeds the return from holding bonds.

The Supply of Oil   The three key influences on the supply of oil are:

1. The known oil reserves
2. The scale of current oil production facilities
3. The expected future price of oil

Known oil reserves refers to the oil that has been discovered and can be extracted with today's technology. This quantity increases over time because advances in technology enable ever-less accessible sources to be discovered. The greater the size of known reserves, the greater is the supply of oil. But this influence on supply is small and indirect. It operates by changing the expected distant future price of oil. Even a major new discovery of oil would have a negligible effect on the current supply of oil.

The scale of current oil production facilities is the *fundamental* influence on the supply of oil. Producing oil is like any production activity: It is subject to increasing marginal cost. The increasing marginal cost of extracting oil means that the supply curve of oil slopes upward. The higher the price of oil, the greater is the quantity supplied. When new oil wells are sunk or when new faster pumps are installed, the supply of oil increases. When existing wells run dry, the supply of oil decreases. Over time, the factors that increase supply are more powerful than those that decrease supply, so changes in the scale of current oil production facilities increase the supply of oil.

Speculative forces based on expectations about the future price also influence the supply of oil. The *higher* the expected future price of oil, the *smaller* is the present supply of oil. A trader with an oil inventory might plan to sell now or to hold and sell later. You've seen that interest forgone is the opportunity cost of holding the oil. If the price of oil is expected to rise by a bigger percentage than the interest rate, it is profitable to incur the opportunity cost of holding oil rather than selling it immediately.

The Equilibrium Price of Oil The demand for oil and the supply of oil determine the equilibrium price and quantity traded. Figure 17.9 illustrates the market equilibrium.

The value of marginal product of oil, *VMP*, is the *fundamental determinant of demand*, and the marginal cost of extraction, *MC*, is the *fundamental determinant of supply*. Together, they determine the *market fundamentals price*.

If expectations about the future price are also based on fundamentals, the equilibrium price is the market fundamentals price. But if expectations about the future price of oil depart from what the market fundamentals imply, *speculation* can drive a wedge between the equilibrium price and the market fundamentals price.

FIGURE 17.9   A Nonrenewable Natural Resource Market

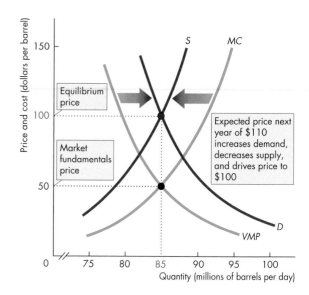

The value of marginal product of a natural resource, *VMP*, and the marginal cost of extraction, *MC*, determine the *market fundamentals* price. Demand, *D*, and supply, *S*, which determine the equilibrium price, are influenced by the expected future price. Speculation can bring a gap between the market fundamentals price and the equilibrium price.

MyLab Economics Animation

The Hotelling Principle Harold Hotelling, an economist at Columbia University, had an incredible idea: Traders expect the price of a nonrenewable natural resource to rise at a rate equal to the interest rate. We call this idea the **Hotelling Principle**. Let's see why it is correct.

You've seen that the interest rate is the opportunity cost of holding an oil inventory. If the price of oil is expected to rise at a rate that exceeds the interest rate, it is profitable to hold a bigger inventory. Demand increases, supply decreases, and the price rises. If the interest rate exceeds the rate at which the price of oil is expected to rise, it is not profitable to hold an oil inventory. Demand decreases, supply increases, and the price falls. But if the price of oil is expected to rise at a rate equal to the interest rate, holding an inventory of oil is just as good as holding bonds. Demand and supply don't change and the price does not change. Only when the price of oil is expected to rise at a rate equal to the interest rate is the price at its equilibrium.

ECONOMICS IN ACTION

The World and Canadian Markets for Oil

The world produced 92 million barrels of oil per day in 2016 and the price was a low $40 a barrel.

Canada produced 1.8 billion barrels in 2016, which is close to 4 percent of global production. This quantity is more than enough for Canada's use of crude oil. But we sell two-thirds of our production to the United States and we buy a small quantity of the oil that we use from Africa, Europe, the Middle East, Mexico, and Venezuela (see Fig. 1).

Transportation costs explain these movements of oil. It is easy and cheap to pipe oil from Alberta into the United States and Western Canada, and to transport oil in tankers from the rest of the world to Eastern Canada.

As a net exporter, Canada benefits from a high oil price and the Hotelling Principle tells us that we can expect that price to rise at a rate equal to the interest rate. That doesn't mean that the price will rise at this rate. As you can see in Fig. 2, the price of oil over the past 60 years has not followed the path predicted by the Hotelling Principle.

The forces that influence expectations are not well understood. The expected future price of oil depends on its expected future rate of use and the rate of discovery of new sources of supply. One person's expectation about a future price also depends on guesses about other people's expectations. These guesses can

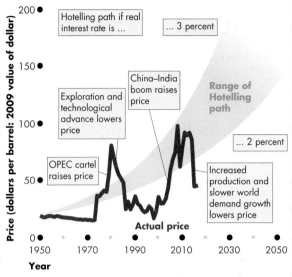

Figure 2 The Price of Oil and Its Hotelling Path

Source of data: U.S. Energy Information Administration.

change abruptly and become self-reinforcing. When the expected future price of oil changes for whatever reason, demand and supply change, and so does the price. Prices in speculative markets are always volatile.

REVIEW QUIZ

1 What determines demand and supply in rental markets for capital and land?
2 What determines the demand for a nonrenewable natural resource?
3 What determines the supply of a nonrenewable natural resource?
4 What is the market fundamentals price and how might it differ from the equilibrium price?
5 Explain the Hotelling Principle.

Work these questions in Study Plan 17.4 and get instant feedback.   MyLab Economics

◆ *Economics in the News* on pp. 414–415 looks at the impact on the taxi industry of Uber, a big player in the gig and sharing economy.

The next chapter looks more closely at the distribution of income and its trends. The chapter also looks at the efforts by governments to redistribute income and modify the market outcome.

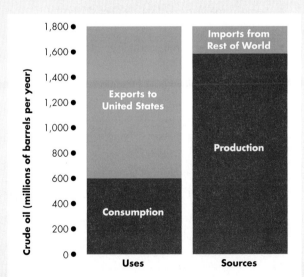

Figure 1 Canada's Uses and Sources of Oil

Source of data: Statistics Canada, Table 126-0001.

The Gig and Sharing Economy

Study Explores the Impact of Uber on the Taxi Industry

Forbes
January 26, 2017

Oxford Martin School's Carl Benedikt Frey …[has examined]… the impact Uber has had on the income of taxi drivers in a range of U.S. cities.

Despite widespread protests against the sharing economy platform, the analysis revealed that the impact was muted. For instance, whilst it typically resulted in a fall in income of around 10% among salaried drivers, it resulted in a 50% rise in the number of self-employed drivers in a city. …

"Uber is the flagship of the sharing economy," Frey says. "But what our study shows is that even in one of the sharing economy's most exposed industries, traditional jobs have not been displaced.

"The effects are complex; while some have seen a loss in income, Uber has created more jobs than it has destroyed, demonstrated by the staggering expansion of self-employment following its introduction."

What's more, employment rose not just in self-employed drivers, but also in traditional taxi services.

It's also noticeable that Uber drivers were found to earn more than those in traditional taxi services. This is largely due to the fact that the Uber software allows drivers to better optimize their time and services.

"The higher hourly earnings among self-employed drivers suggest that capacity utilization, in terms of the time spent in the car with a passenger, has increased with Uber, as its platform allows for better matching between drivers and passengers. But for traditional taxi drivers the effect has been the opposite, with a decline in the amount of time they have a passenger in their vehicle," Frey says. …

ESSENCE OF THE STORY

- The arrival of Uber in a U.S. city has the following effects.
- It lowers the income of salaried taxi drivers by 10 percent.
- It increases the number of self-employed drivers by 50 percent.
- It increases employment of traditional taxi drivers.
- Its software allows drivers to better optimize their time, which enables them to earn more than traditional taxi drivers.
- It decreases the amount of time a traditional taxi driver has a passenger.

ECONOMIC ANALYSIS

- Uber is a matching platform for connecting self-employed drivers and passengers.

- The Uber technology has created an incentive for people to become self-employed Uber drivers and for passengers to use the services of these drivers.

- Wage-employed taxi drivers—full-time, wage-earning taxi drivers—have demonstrated against Uber and tried to block its entry into their markets, fearing that it would take their jobs or lower their incomes.

- How has Uber changed the labour markets for self-employed and wage-employed taxi drivers?

- This question has been answered by three economists at the University of Oxford Martin School, whose work is reported in the news article.*

- Their answer: The number of self-employed drivers increased by at least 50 percent and their wage rate increased by 10 percent; and the wage rate of wage-employed drivers fell by 10 percent but their employment level increased.

- We can explain these changes, and the surprising increase in employment of wage-employed drivers, by applying the competitive labour market model to the two markets for taxi drivers.

- Figure 1 shows what has happened in the market for self-employed drivers. (The numbers are assumed and chosen to illustrate the effects as clearly as possible.)

- The supply curve is S and before Uber, the demand curve was D_0. The wage rate was $12 an hour and the drivers worked a total of 50,000 hours per day.

- The Uber technology increased the demand for self-employed drivers to D_1. This increase in demand increased both the wage rate and total hours worked.

- Figure 2 shows what has happened in the market for wage-employed drivers. (Again, the numbers are assumed to illustrate the effects as clearly as possible.)

- The Uber technology decreased the demand for wage-employed drivers from D_0 to D_1.

- The Oxford researchers say that employment of wage-employed drivers *increased*. To get this outcome, either the supply curve of these drivers is backward-bending, or the supply of wage-employed drivers increased.

---

*Thor Berger, Chinchih Chen, and Carl Frey, "Drivers of Disruption? The Uber Effect," Oxford Martin School, January 2017.

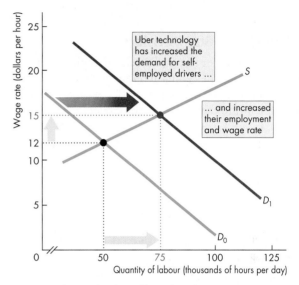

Figure 1 The Market for Self-Employed Taxi Drivers

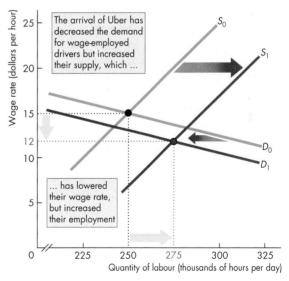

Figure 2 The Market for Wage-Employed Taxi Drivers

- We will assume that the publicity surrounding the arrival of Uber increased awareness and attracted more people to taxi driving, which increased the supply of wage-employed drivers.

- The supply curve of wage-employed drivers shifted rightward from S_0 to S_1.

- The combined effect of the decrease in demand and increase in supply lowered the wage rate and increased employment.

MATHEMATICAL NOTE

Present Value and Discounting

Rent-Versus-Buy Decision

To decide whether to rent an item of capital equipment or to buy the capital and implicitly rent it, a firm must compare the present expenditure on the capital with the future rental cost of the capital.

Comparing Current and Future Dollars

To compare a present expenditure with a future expenditure, we convert the future expenditure to its "present value."

The *present value* of a future amount of money is the amount that, if invested today, will grow to be as large as that future amount when the interest that it will earn is taken into account.

So the present value of a future amount of money is smaller than the future amount. The calculation that we use to convert a future amount of money to its present value is called *discounting*.

The easiest way to understand discounting and present value is to first consider its opposite: How a present value grows to a future amount of money because of *compound interest*.

Compound Interest

Compound interest is the interest on an initial investment plus the interest on the interest that the investment has previously earned. Because of compound interest, a present amount of money (a present value) grows into a larger future amount. The future amount is equal to the present amount (present value) plus the interest it will earn in the future. That is,

Future amount = Present value + Interest income.

The interest in the first year is equal to the present value multiplied by the interest rate, r, so

Amount after 1 year = Present value + ($r \times$ Present value)

or

Amount after 1 year = Present value $\times$ $(1 + r)$.

If you invest $100 today and the interest rate is 10 percent a year ($r = 0.1$), 1 year from today you will have $110—the original $100 plus $10 interest.

Check that the above formula delivers that answer:

$$\$100 \times 1.1 = \$110.$$

If you leave this $110 invested to earn 10 percent during a second year, at the end of that year you will have

Amount after 2 years = Present value $\times$ $(1 + r)^2$.

With the numbers of the previous example, you invest $100 today at an interest rate of 10 percent a year ($r = 0.1$). After 1 year, you will have $110—the original $100 plus $10 interest. And after 2 years, you will have $121. In the second year, you earned $10 on your initial $100 plus $1 on the $10 interest that you earned in the first year.

Check that the above formula delivers that answer:

$$\$100 \times (1.1)^2 = \$100 \times 1.21 = \$121.$$

If you leave your $100 invested for n years, it will grow to

Amount after n years = Present value $\times$ $(1 + r)^n$.

With an interest rate of 10 percent a year, your $100 will grow to $195 after 7 years ($n = 7$)—almost double the present value of $100.

Discounting a Future Amount

We have just calculated future amounts 1 year, 2 years, and n years in the future, knowing the present value and the interest rate. To calculate the present value of these future amounts, we just work backward.

To find the present value of an amount 1 year in the future, we divide the future amount by $(1 + r)$. That is,

$$\text{Present value} = \frac{\text{Amount of money 1 year in future}}{(1 + r)}$$

Let's check that we can use the present value formula by calculating the present value of $110 1 year from now when the interest rate is 10 percent a year.

You'll be able to guess that the answer is $100 because we just calculated that $100 invested today at 10 percent a year becomes $110 in 1 year. So the present value of $110 to be received 1 year from today is $100. But let's use the formula. Putting the numbers into the above formula, we have

$$\text{Present value} = \frac{\$110}{(1 + 0.1)}$$

$$= \frac{\$110}{1.1} = \$100.$$

To calculate the present value of an amount of money 2 years in the future, we use the formula:

$$\text{Present value} = \frac{\substack{\text{Amount of money} \\ \text{2 years in future}}}{(1 + r)^2}$$

Use this formula to calculate the present value of $121 to be received 2 years from now at an interest rate of 10 percent a year. With these numbers, the formula gives

$$\text{Present value} = \frac{\$121}{(1 + 0.1)^2}$$

$$= \frac{\$121}{(1.1)^2}$$

$$= \frac{\$121}{1.21}$$

$$= \$100.$$

We can calculate the present value of an amount of money n years in the future by using the general formula

$$\text{Present value} = \frac{\substack{\text{Amount of money} \\ n \text{ years in future}}}{(1 + r)^n}$$

For example, if the interest rate is 10 percent a year, $100 to be received 10 years from now has a present value of $38.55. That is, if $38.55 is invested today at 10 percent a year it will accumulate to $100 in 10 years.

Present Value of a Sequence of Future Amounts

You've seen how to calculate the present value of an amount of money to be received 1 year, 2 years, and n years in the future. Most practical applications of present value calculate the present value of a sequence of future amounts of money that are spread over several years. An airline's payment of rent for the lease of airplanes is an example.

To calculate the present value of a sequence of amounts over several years, we use the formula you have learned and apply it to each year. We then sum the present values for all the years to find the present value of the sequence of amounts.

For example, suppose that a firm expects to pay $100 a year for each of the next 5 years and the interest rate is 10 percent a year ($r = 0.1$). The present value (PV) of these five payments of $100 each is calculated by using the following formula:

$$PV = \frac{\$100}{1.1} + \frac{\$100}{1.1^2} + \frac{\$100}{1.1^3} + \frac{\$100}{1.1^4} + \frac{\$100}{1.1^5},$$

which equals

$$PV = \$90.91 + \$82.64 + \$75.13 + \$68.30$$
$$+ \$62.09 = \$379.07.$$

You can see that the firm pays $500 over 5 years. But because the money is paid in the future, it is not worth $500 today. Its present value is only $379.07. And the farther in the future the money is paid, the smaller is its present value. The $100 paid 1 year in the future is worth $90.91 today, but the $100 paid 5 years in the future is worth only $62.09 today.

The Decision

If this firm could lease a machine for 5 years at $100 a year or buy the machine for $500, it would jump at leasing. Only if the firm could buy the machine for less than $379.07 would it want to buy.

Many personal and business decisions turn on calculations like the one you've just made. A decision to buy or rent an apartment, to buy or lease a car, and to pay off a student loan or let the loan run another year can all be made using the above calculation.

MyLab Economics Work this Problem in Chapter 17 Study Plan.

Tom hires workers to pack the tomatoes he grows. The market for tomatoes is perfectly competitive, and the price of tomatoes is $2 a box. The labour market is competitive, and the market wage rate is $16 an hour. The table shows the workers' total product schedule.

Number of workers	Quantity produced (boxes packed per hour)
1	14
2	26
3	36
4	44
5	50

Questions

1. Calculate the marginal product of the third worker hired and that worker's value of marginal product.

2. How many workers will Tom hire to maximize profit and what will the workers produce?

3. If the market wage rate rises to $20 an hour, how many workers will Tom hire?

Solutions

1. Marginal product (*MP*) of the third worker equals the total product (*TP*) of 3 workers (36 boxes) minus the *TP* of 2 workers (26 boxes), so the *MP* of the third worker is 10 boxes of tomatoes.

   The third worker's value of marginal product (*VMP*) equals the third worker's *MP* (10 boxes of tomatoes an hour) multiplied by the price of a box of tomatoes ($2), so the *VMP* of the third worker equals $20 an hour.

   The figure shows the *VMP* of each worker.

   Key Point: The value of marginal product of labour is the marginal product of labour multiplied by the market price of the good produced by the labour.

2. Tom maximizes profit by hiring the number of workers at which *VMP* equals the market wage rate. The table in the next column shows the calculations.

   The market wage rate is $16 an hour, so Tom hires the number of workers at which the *VMP* equals $16 an hour. You can see in the table that *VMP* equals $16 an hour when Tom hires the fourth worker. So Tom maximizes profit when he hires

Number of workers	TP (boxes per hour)	MP (boxes per worker)	VMP (dollars per hour)
1	14		
		 12	24
2	26		
		 10	20
3	36		
		 8	**16**
4	44		
		 6	12
5	50		

4 workers who produce 44 boxes of tomatoes. Tom sells the tomatoes for $88 and pays the wages of $64, so his profit is $24 an hour. The figure shows this equality.

Key Point: The firm maximizes profit by hiring the quantity of labour at which the value of marginal product of labour equals the market wage rate.

3. If the market wage rate rises to $20 an hour, the *VMP* of labour does not change and remains the same as in the table above. But now with a wage rate of $20 an hour, Tom hires fewer workers. The *VMP* equals $20 an hour when Tom hires the third worker. So Tom cuts the number of workers to 3.

Key Point: When the market wage rate rises, the firm maximizes profit by hiring fewer workers.

Key Figure

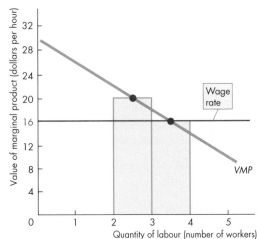

MyLab Economics Interactive Animation

◆ SUMMARY

Key Points

The Anatomy of Factor Markets (p. 398)

- The factor markets are the job markets for labour; the rental markets (often implicit rental markets) for capital and land; and the global commodity markets for nonrenewable natural resources.
- The services of entrepreneurs are not traded on a factor market.

Working Problem 1 will give you a better understanding of the anatomy of factor markets.

The Demand for a Factor of Production (pp. 399–401)

- The value of marginal product determines the demand for a factor of production.
- The value of marginal product decreases as the quantity of the factor employed increases.
- The firm employs the quantity of each factor of production that makes the value of marginal product equal to the factor price.

Working Problems 2 to 6 will give you a better understanding of the demand for a factor of production.

Labour Markets (pp. 402–408)

- The value of marginal product of labour determines the demand for labour. A rise in the wage rate brings a decrease in the quantity demanded.
- The quantity of labour supplied depends on the wage rate. At low wage rates, a rise in the wage rate increases the quantity supplied. Beyond a high enough wage rate, a rise in the wage rate decreases the quantity supplied—the supply curve eventually bends backward.

- Demand and supply determine the wage rate in a competitive labour market.
- A labour union can raise the wage rate by restricting the supply or increasing the demand for labour.
- A monopsony can lower the wage rate below the competitive level.
- A union or a minimum wage in a monopsony labour market can raise the wage rate without a fall in employment.

Working Problems 7 to 9 will give you a better understanding of labour markets.

Capital and Natural Resource Markets (pp. 409–413)

- The value of marginal product of capital (or land) determines the demand for capital (or land).
- Firms make a rent-versus-buy decision by choosing the option that minimizes cost.
- The supply of land is inelastic and the demand for land determines the rental rate.
- The demand for a nonrenewable natural resource depends on the value of marginal product and on the expected future price.
- The supply of a nonrenewable natural resource depends on the known reserves, the cost of extraction, and the expected future price.
- The price of nonrenewable natural resources can differ from the market fundamentals price because of speculation based on expectations about the future price.
- The price of a nonrenewable natural resource is expected to rise at a rate equal to the interest rate.

Working Problem 10 will give you a better understanding of capital and natural resource markets.

Key Terms

MyLab Economics Key Terms Quiz

Bilateral monopoly, 406
Derived demand, 399
Hotelling Principle, 412
Labour union, 405

Monopsony, 406
Nonrenewable natural resources, 398
Value of marginal product, 399

STUDY PLAN PROBLEMS AND APPLICATIONS

MyLab Economics Work Problems 1 to 10 in Chapter 17 Study Plan and get instant feedback.

The Anatomy of Factor Markets (Study Plan 17.1)

1. Tim is opening a new online store. He plans to hire two workers at $10 an hour. Tim is also considering buying or leasing some new computers. The purchase price of a computer is $900 and after three years it is worthless. The annual cost of leasing a computer is $450.

   a. In which factor markets does Tim operate?

   b. What is the price of the capital equipment and the rental rate of capital?

The Demand for a Factor of Production
(Study Plan 17.2)

Use the following data to work Problems 2 to 6. Wanda's is a fish store that hires students to pack the fish. Students can pack the following amounts of fish:

Number of students	Quantity of fish packed (kilograms per hour)
1	20
2	50
3	90
4	120
5	145
6	165
7	180
8	190

The fish market is competitive and the price of fish is 50¢ a kilogram. The market for packers is competitive and their market wage rate is $7.50 an hour.

2. Calculate the value of marginal product of labour and draw the value of marginal product curve.

3. a. Find Wanda's demand for labour curve.

   b. How many students does Wanda's employ?

Use the following additional data to work Problems 4 and 5.

The market price of fish falls to 33.33¢ a kilogram, but the packers' wage rate remains at $7.50 an hour.

4. How does the students' marginal product change? How does the value of marginal product of labour change?

5. How does Wanda's demand for labour change? What happens to the number of students that Wanda's employs?

6. At Wanda's fish store, packers' wages increase to $10 an hour, but the price of fish remains at 50¢ a kilogram.

   a. What happens to the value of marginal product of labour?

   b. What happens to Wanda's demand for labour curve?

   c. How many students does Wanda's employ?

Labour Markets (Study Plan 17.3)

Use the following news clip to work Problems 7 to 9.

Theatre Jobs Skew White and Male, Study Finds

Equity (The Actors' Equity Association) is a labour union that represent live-theatre actors and stage managers. A study by the union shows that women and minorities get fewer jobs and lower pay than white men. Equity recently hired its first diversity director and will try to diversify its own organization as well as meet with producers, writers, and others to discuss challenges facing the industry.

Source: *The New York Times*, June 26, 2017

7. What is the goal of Equity?

8. Why is Equity seeking greater diversity?

9. How can Equity try to change the demand for female and minority labour?

Capital and Natural Resource Markets
(Study Plan 17.4)

10. **Land Prices Reflect Farm Incomes**
    Bank CEOs predict that farmland prices will fall by 3.1 percent over the next 12 months. Lower farm income resulted in tighter restrictions on bank loans to farmers.

    Source: *Today's Producer*, June 21, 2017

    a. Why does the price of farmland reflect farm incomes? In your answer include a discussion of the demand for and supply of land.

    b. Use a graph to show why the price of farmland is expected to fall.

    c. Is the supply of farmland perfectly inelastic?

ADDITIONAL PROBLEMS AND APPLICATIONS

MyLab Economics You can work these problems in Homework or Test if assigned by your instructor.

The Anatomy of Factor Markets

11. Venus is opening a tennis school. She plans to hire a marketing graduate to promote and manage the school at $20 an hour. Venus is also considering buying or leasing a new tennis ball machine. The purchase price of the machine is $1,000 and after three years it is worthless. The annual cost of leasing the machine is $500.

   a. In which factor markets does Venus operate?

   b. What is the price of the capital equipment and the rental rate of capital?

The Demand for a Factor of Production

Use the following data to work Problems 12 to 15.

Kaiser's Ice Cream Parlour hires workers to produce milkshakes. The market for milkshakes is perfectly competitive, and the price of a milkshake is $4. The labour market is competitive, and the wage rate is $40 a day. The table shows the workers' total product schedule.

Number of workers	Quantity produced (milkshakes per day)
1	7
2	21
3	33
4	43
5	51
6	55

12. Calculate the marginal product of hiring the fourth worker and the fourth worker's value of marginal product.

13. How many workers will Kaiser's hire to maximize its profit and how many milkshakes a day will Kaiser's produce?

14. If the price of a milkshake rises to $5, how many workers will Kaiser's hire?

15. Kaiser's installs a new machine for making milkshakes that increases the productivity of workers by 50 percent. If the price of a milkshake remains at $4 and the wage rises to $48 a day, how many workers does Kaiser's hire?

16. **Tesla $350 million Gigafactory Hiring 500 Workers**

   Tesla has partnered with Panasonic to increase production of lithium-ion batteries and drivetrains for its mass-market Model 3 car in a massive factory in Nevada. The electric carmaker will spend $350 million and hire 500 workers. The Model 3 will be priced at $35,000.

   Source: *Business Insider*, January 18, 2017

   a. Explain how the price of an electric car influences the market for factory labour in Nevada.

   b. Draw a graph to illustrate the effects of an increase in the demand for electric cars on the market for factory labour in Nevada.

Labour Markets

Use the following news clip to work Problems 17 and 18.

New Labour Laws in Chile Embolden Striking Miners

Workers at BHP Billiton's Escondida mine in Chile, the world's largest copper mine, have been strengthened by new labour laws and are striking for higher pay. This strike and another at the world's second-largest mine in Indonesia have sent the price of copper to a 20-month high.

   Source: Reuters, February 15, 2017

17. How would the wage rate and employment for the Escondida miners be determined in a competitive market?

18. a. Explain how it is possible that the mine workers are being paid less than the wage that would be paid in a competitive labour market.

   b. Explain how the Escondida miners' union might be able to raise their wage rate.

Use the following news clip to work Problems 19 to 22.

Walmart Ups Pay Well Above Minimum Wage

Walmart announced it will pay 500,000 workers at least $9 an hour from April 2015 and at least $10 an hour from February 2016. The union-backed group OUR Walmart took credit for the company's announcement but a leader of the group said the improved wages fell short of what was needed. Black Friday protesters were demanding $15 an hour.

   Source: CNNMoney, February 19, 2015

19. a. Assuming that Walmart has market power in a labour market, explain how the firm could use that market power in setting wages.

    b. Draw a graph to illustrate how Walmart might use labour market power to set wages.

20. a. Explain how OUR Walmart would attempt to counteract Walmart's wage offers in a bilateral monopoly.

    b. Explain how the wage rate would be determined if the market were a bilateral monopoly.

21. Based upon evidence presented in this article, does Walmart function as a monopsony in labour markets, or is the market for retail labour competitive? Explain.

22. If the market for retail labour is competitive, explain the effect of OUR Walmart on the wage rate and employment. Draw a graph to illustrate your answer.

Capital and Natural Resource Markets

23. New technology has allowed oil to be pumped from much deeper offshore oil fields than before. For example, 28 deep-ocean rigs operate in the deep waters of the Gulf of Mexico.

    a. What effect do you think deep-ocean sources have had on the world oil price?

    b. Who will benefit from drilling for oil in the Gulf of Mexico? Explain your answer.

24. Water is a natural resource that is plentiful in Canada but not plentiful in Arizona.

    a. If Canadians start to export bulk water to Arizona, what do you predict will be the effect on the price of bulk water?

    b. Will Canada eventually run out of water?

    c. Do you think the Hotelling Principle applies to Canada's water? Explain why or why not.

25. **Land Rush in Permian Basin, Where Oil Is Stacked Like a Layer Cake**

    The Permian Basin, which straddles Texas and New Mexico, is hot. Oil companies spent more than $25 billion buying into it during the second half of 2016. The reason: Its geology is ideal for hydraulic fracturing, and well served with pipelines. Its oil shale fields are profitable even when oil sells for only $40 a barrel.

    Source: *The New York Times*, January 17, 2017

    a. Explain why the demand for land in the Permian basin increased.

    b. When an oil company buys land and the right to its oil reserves, what is its assumption about the future price of oil?

    c. What could cause the price of oil to fall in the future?

Economics in the News

26. After you have studied *Economics in the News* on pp. 414–415, answer the following questions.

    a. How is the demand for self-employed Uber drivers determined?

    b. How is the demand for regular wage-employed taxi drivers determined?

    c. Which of the influences on the demand for self-employed drivers changed to increase the demand when Uber arrived?

    d. Which of the influences on the demand for wage-employed drivers changed to decrease the demand when Uber arrived?

    e. Explain the two possible reasons why a decrease in the demand for wage-employed drivers can result in an increase in their level of employment.

    f. Illustrate with a graph the backward-bending supply curve explanation for the fall in the wage rate and increase in employment of wage-employed drivers.

Mathematical Note

27. Keshia is opening a new bookkeeping service. She is considering buying or leasing some new laptop computers. The purchase price of a laptop is $1,500 and after three years it is worthless. The annual lease rate is $550 per laptop. The value of marginal product of one laptop is $700 a year. The value of marginal product of a second laptop is $625 a year. The value of marginal product of a third laptop is $575 a year. And the value of marginal product of a fourth laptop is $500 a year.

    a. How many laptops will Keshia lease or buy?

    b. If the interest rate is 4 percent a year, will Keshia lease or buy her laptops?

    c. If the interest rate is 6 percent a year, will Keshia lease or buy her laptops?

18 ECONOMIC INEQUALITY

After studying this chapter, you will be able to:

◆ Describe the distributions of income and wealth and the trends in economic inequality in Canada

◆ Describe the distribution of income and the trends in inequality in selected countries and the world

◆ Explain the sources of economic inequality and its trends

◆ Describe the scale of government income redistribution in Canada

Every night in Vancouver, a city with mansions that are home to some of the wealthiest Canadians, around 2,500 people sleep outside without shelter. In Toronto, where a luxury penthouse sells for $30 million, more than 5,000 people seek a bed every night in a shelter for the homeless. Extreme poverty and extreme wealth exist side by side in every major Canadian city and in all parts of the world.

In this chapter, we study economic inequality—its extent, its sources, and the things governments do to make it less extreme. And in *Economics in the News* at the end of the chapter, we look at the income gap between the rich and the poor and the forces that are widening it.

◆ Measuring Economic Inequality

Statistics Canada provides measures of economic inequality based on three definitions of income: market income, total income, and after-tax income. **Market income** equals the wages, interest, rent, and profit earned in factor markets before paying income taxes. **Total income** equals market income plus cash payments to households by governments. **After-tax income** equals total income minus tax payments by households to governments.

The Distribution of Income

Figure 18.1 shows the distribution of annual after-tax income across the 15 million households in Canada in 2015. Note that the *x*-axis measures household after-tax income and the *y*-axis is percentage of households.

The most common household income, called the *mode* income, was received by the 10.8 percent of the households whose incomes fell between $30,000 and $39,999.

The middle level of household income in 2015, called the *median* income, was $56,000. Fifty percent of households have an income that exceeds the median and fifty percent have an income below the median.

The *average* household money income in 2015, also called the *mean* income, was $69,100. This number equals total household after-tax income divided by the 15 million households.

You can see in Fig. 18.1 that the mode income is less than the median income and that the median income is less than the mean income. This feature of the distribution of income tells us that there are more households with low incomes than with high incomes. It also tells us that some of the high incomes are very high.

The income distribution in Fig. 18.1 is called a *positively skewed* distribution, which means that it has a long tail of high values. This distribution shape contrasts with the bell distribution of people's heights. In a bell-shaped distribution, the mean, median, and mode are all equal.

Another way of looking at the distribution of income is to measure the percentage of total income received by each given percentage of households. Data are reported for five groups—called *quintiles*

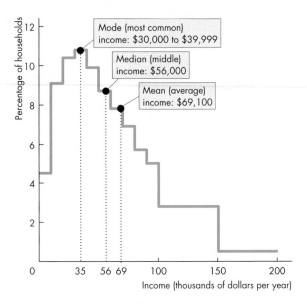

FIGURE 18.1   The Distribution of Income in Canada in 2015

The distribution of after-tax income is positively skewed. The mode (most common) income is less than the median (middle) income, which in turn is less than the mean (average) income. The distribution shown here ends at $200,000 because data above that level are not available, but the distribution goes up to several million dollars a year.

Source of data: Statistics Canada, CANSIM Table 206–0012.

——————— MyLab Economics Animation ———————

or fifth shares—each consisting of 20 percent of households.

Figure 18.2 shows the distribution based on these shares in 2015. The poorest 20 percent of households received 7.2 percent of total after-tax income; the second poorest 20 percent received 13.0 percent; the third 20 percent received 17.8 percent; the fourth 20 percent received 23.3 percent; and the highest 20 percent received 38.7 percent of total after-tax income.

The distribution of income in Fig. 18.1 and the quintile shares in Fig. 18.2 tell us that income is distributed unequally. But we need a way of comparing the distribution of income in different periods and using different measures. A clever graphical tool called the *Lorenz curve* enables us to make such comparisons.

FIGURE 18.2 Quintile Shares in Canada in 2015

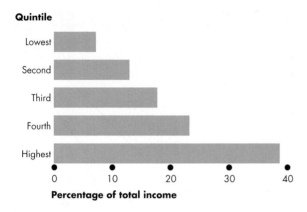

Quintile

Households (quintile)	Income (percentage of total income)
Lowest	7.2
Second	13.0
Third	17.8
Fourth	23.3
Highest	38.7

In 2015, the poorest 20 percent of households received 7.2 percent of total income; the second poorest 20 percent received 13.0 percent; the middle 20 percent received 17.8 percent; the next highest 20 percent received 23.3 percent; and the highest 20 percent received 38.7 percent.

Source of data: Statistics Canada, CANSIM Table 206-0032.

———— MyLab Economics Animation ————

The Income Lorenz Curve

The income **Lorenz curve** graphs the cumulative percentage of income against the cumulative percentage of households. Figure 18.3 shows the income Lorenz curve using the quintile shares from Fig. 18.2. The table shows the percentage of income of each quintile group. For example, row *A* tells us that the lowest quintile of households receives 7.2 percent of total income. The table also shows the *cumulative* percentages of households and income. For example, row *B* tells us that the lowest two quintiles (40 percent of households) receive 20.2 percent of total income (7.2 percent for the lowest quintile plus 13.0 percent for the next lowest).

FIGURE 18.3 The Income Lorenz Curve in 2015

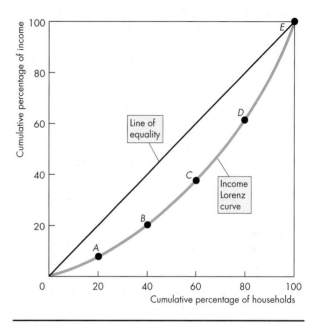

	Households		Income	
	Quintile	Cumulative percentage	Percentage	Cumulative percentage
A	Lowest	20	7.2	7.2
B	Second	40	13.0	20.2
C	Third	60	17.8	38.0
D	Fourth	80	23.3	61.3
E	Highest	100	38.7	100.0

The cumulative percentage of income is graphed against the cumulative percentage of households. Points *A* through *E* on the Lorenz curve correspond to the rows of the table. If incomes were distributed equally, each 20 percent of households would receive 20 percent of total income and the Lorenz curve would fall along the line of equality. The Lorenz curve shows that income is unequally distributed.

Source of data: Statistics Canada, CANSIM Table 206-0032.

———— MyLab Economics Animation and Draw Graph ————

The Lorenz curve provides a direct visual clue about the degree of income inequality by comparing it with the line of equality. This line, identified in Fig. 18.3, shows what the Lorenz curve would be if everyone had the same level of income.

If income were distributed equally across all the households, each quintile would receive 20 percent of total income and the cumulative percentages of income received would equal the cumulative percentages of households, so the Lorenz curve would be the straight line labelled "Line of equality."

The actual distribution of income shown by the curve labelled "Income Lorenz curve" can be compared with the line of equality. The closer the Lorenz curve is to the line of equality, the more equal is the distribution of income.

The Distribution of Wealth

The distribution of wealth provides another way of measuring economic inequality. A household's **wealth** is the value of the things that it owns.

Figure 18.4 shows the Lorenz curve for wealth in Canada in 2005. The median household wealth in 2005 was $148,350. By looking closely at Fig. 18.4, you can see that wealth is extremely unequally distributed. The poorest 40 percent of households owns only 2.1 percent of total wealth (row *A'* in the table), and the wealthiest 10 percent of households owns 51.0 percent of total wealth (row *G'*).

The Lorenz curve for wealth is much farther away from the line of equality than is the Lorenz curve for income: The distribution of wealth is much more unequal than the distribution of income.

Wealth or Income?

We've seen that wealth is much more unequally distributed than is income. Which distribution provides the better description of the degree of inequality? To answer this question, we need to think about the connection between wealth and income.

Wealth is a *stock* and income is the *flow* of earnings that results from the stock of wealth. Suppose that a person owns assets worth $1 million—has a wealth of $1 million. If the rate of return on assets is 5 percent a year, then this person receives an income of $50,000 a year from those assets. We can describe this person's economic condition by using either the wealth of $1 million or the income of $50,000. When the rate of return is 5 percent a year, $1 million of wealth equals $50,000 of income in perpetuity. Wealth and income are just different ways of looking at the same thing.

But in Fig. 18.4, the distribution of wealth is more unequal than the distribution of income. Why?

FIGURE 18.4 Lorenz Curves for Income and Wealth

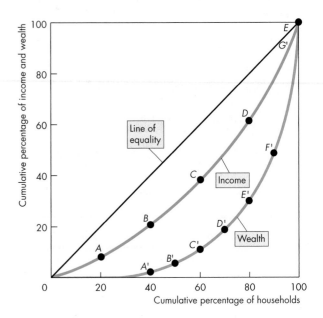

	Households		Wealth	
	Percentage	Cumulative percentage	Percentage	Cumulative percentage
A' Lowest 40	40		2.1	2.1
B' Next 10	50		3.4	5.5
C' Next 10	60		5.6	11.1
D' Next 10	70		7.6	18.7
E' Next 10	80		11.5	30.2
F' Next 10	90		18.8	49.0
G' Highest 10	100		51.0	100.0

The cumulative percentage of wealth is graphed against the cumulative percentage of households. Points *A'* through *G'* on the Lorenz curve for wealth correspond to the rows of the table. By comparing the Lorenz curves for income and wealth, we can see that wealth is distributed much more unequally than is income.

Sources of data: Statistics Canada, Survey of Financial Security (SFS) and authors' calculations.

MyLab Economics Animation

It is because the wealth data do not include the value of *human capital*, while the income data measure income from all wealth, including human capital.

Think about Lee and Peter who have the same income and wealth. Lee's wealth is human capital and his entire income is from employment. Peter's wealth is investments in stocks and bonds and his entire income is from these investments.

The national survey of wealth excludes human capital, so Peter looks more wealthy than Lee, although they have equal wealth. The bias in wealth measurement means that the income distribution is a more accurate measure of economic inequality than the wealth distribution.

Annual or Lifetime Income and Wealth?

A typical household's income changes over its life cycle. Income starts out low, grows to a peak, and then falls after retirement. Like income, wealth starts out low, grows to a peak at the point of retirement, and falls after retirement.

Because of these life-cycle patterns, the distributions of annual income and wealth in a given year are much more unequal than the distributions of lifetime income and wealth.

Inequality in annual income and wealth data overstates lifetime inequality because households are at different stages in their life cycles.

ECONOMICS IN ACTION
The Rich Get Richer

Figure 1 shows how the distribution of after-tax income changed between 1976 and 2015. The share of total income received by the highest 20 percent of households increased and the share received by the next highest 20 percent decreased. The shares of the other three quintiles didn't change much.

The quintile data in Fig. 1 mask the most interesting change in inequality, which is the changing share of the super rich. Figure 2 shows what has been happening to the income share of the top *one* percent.

Michael Veall of McMaster University compiled these Canadian data from tax returns as part of a global, multi-country study.

You can see that after decades of a falling income share—called the "Great Compression"—the income share received by the top one percent began a steady climb starting in 1979. By 2010 the top one percent were receiving 12 percent of total income.

No one knows for sure *why* the trend to greater inequality occurred, so it is not known whether the trend will persist or cycle back to a new "Great Compression."

We'll explore a leading explanation for the rise in inequality later in this chapter (on p. 432).

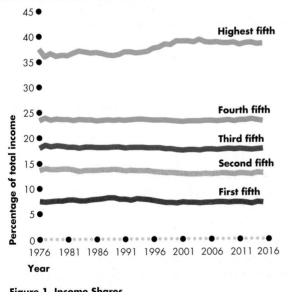

Figure 1 Income Shares

Source of data: Statistics Canada, CANSIM Table 206–0032.

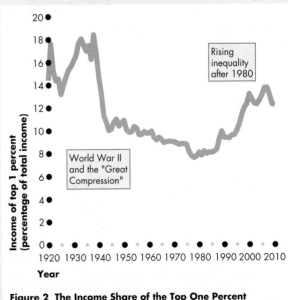

Figure 2 The Income Share of the Top One Percent

Source of data: The World Top Incomes Database, http://topincomes.g-mond.parisschoolofeconomics.eu

Trends in Inequality

Economics in Action on the previous page looks at the trend in inequality as measured by changes in quintile shares. A more direct measure of inequality is called the **Gini ratio**, which equals the ratio of the area between the line of equality and the Lorenz curve to the entire area beneath the line of equality. The larger the Gini ratio, the greater is the degree of income inequality. If income is equally distributed, the Lorenz curve is the same as the line of equality, so the Gini ratio is zero. If one person has all the income and everyone else has none, the Gini ratio is 1.

Figure 18.5 shows the Canadian Gini ratio from 1976 to 2015. The first thing that stands out in this graph is the rising trend. But looking in more detail at the timing of the rise in the Gini ratio, you can see that the main increase occurred during the 1990s. From 1976 to 1990, the ratio fluctuated but had no rising trend. And after 2000, it stopped increasing. The timing of the increase is a clue to its cause, which we explore on p. 433.

FIGURE 18.5 The Canadian Gini Ratio: 1976–2015

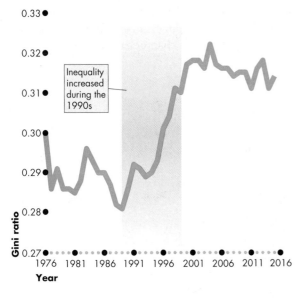

Inequality increased during the 1990s

Measured by the Gini ratio, the distribution of income in Canada became more unequal from 1976 to 2015. The percentage of income earned by the richest households increased through these years. Some increase in inequality occurred during the 1980s, but most of the increase occurred during the 1990s. Since 2000, the Gini ratio has fluctuated but has not continued an upward trend.

Source of data: Statistics Canada, CANSIM Table 206-0033.

—— MyLab Economics Animation ——

ECONOMICS IN ACTION
School Pays

The lowest incomes are earned by people who scratch out a living doing seasonal work on farms. But the poorest Canadians are people who earn nothing and rely on handouts to survive. The incidence of poverty varies systematically depending on household characteristics, and six characteristics stand out:

- Education
- Labour force status
- Source of income
- Household type
- Age of householder
- Number of children

Education Education makes a huge difference to a household's income and to the risk of being poor. A person who has not completed high school has the highest risk of being poor. University graduates and those with a post-graduate or professional degree have the lowest risk of being poor.

Labour Force Status Households that are in the labour force, even if unemployed, tend to have higher incomes than those not in the labour force—either they've retired or they have become discouraged by a persistent failure to find a suitable job.

Source of Income A household that earns its income either by working or from its wealth is unlikely to be poor and a household that receives its income in the form of a transfer payment from the government is more likely to be poor.

Household Type Households with two parents present are unlikely to be poor. The poorest household is most likely to be one with a single female parent—almost 50 percent of whom are poor.

Age of Householder The youngest and the oldest households have lower incomes and a greater incidence of poverty than middle-aged households.

Number of Children On average, the more children in a household, the smaller is the income per person and the more likely the household is to be poor.

Poverty

Poverty is a state in which a family's income is too low to be able to buy the quantities of food, shelter, and clothing that are deemed necessary.

Poverty is both an absolute and a relative concept. Millions of people in Africa and Asia live, barely, in absolute poverty with incomes of less than $400 a year.

In Canada, poverty is identified in relative terms using the concept of the **low-income cut-off**, defined as the income level below which a family normally spends 63.6 percent or more of its income on food, shelter, and clothing. (The low-income cut-off is determined separately for each family type.)

How much poverty (defined as the percentage of families with incomes below the low-income cut-off) is there in Canada, and is the problem getting worse or better? Figure 18.6 answers this question.

The incidence of poverty has fluctuated between a low of 10.5 percent in 1989 and a high of 14.2 percent in 2015. Starting in 1990, the poverty trend has been upward. On average, 12.7 percent of Canadian families (a bit more than one in eight) have incomes below the low-income cut-off.

FIGURE 18.6 The Incidence of Low Income

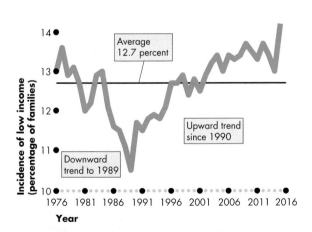

The incidence of low income in Canada has fluctuated between 10.5 percent and 14.2 percent of families. On average, 12.7 percent of families have incomes below the low-income cut-off.

Source of data: Statistics Canada, CANSIM Table 206–0042.

— MyLab Economics Animation —

ECONOMICS IN ACTION

How Long Does a Spell of Poverty Last?

Most poverty is temporary and short-lived. The figure shows the numbers: 75 percent of those in poverty remain in that state for less than 1 year and another 8 percent of those in poverty remain so for 1 year. Poverty rates for people who are in that state for 2 years or more are very low.

Given that the average poverty rate is 12.7 percent of families, around 2 percent of families experience poverty that persists for more than 2 years.

The duration of poverty, like its level, depends on household characteristics, and education is the key. The least well educated tend to be those who experience the most persistent poverty.

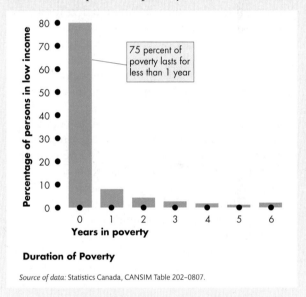

Duration of Poverty

Source of data: Statistics Canada, CANSIM Table 202–0807.

◆ **REVIEW QUIZ**

1 Which is distributed more unequally, income or wealth? Why? Which is the better measure?

2 How has the distribution of income changed in the past few decades?

3 What are the main characteristics of people who earn high incomes and who earn low incomes?

4 What is poverty and how does its incidence vary across families?

5 How long does a spell of poverty usually last?

Work these questions in Study Plan 18.1 and get instant feedback. MyLab Economics

◆ Inequality in the World Economy

Which countries have the greatest economic inequality and which have the least and the greatest equality? Where does Canada rank? Is it one of the most equal or most unequal or somewhere in the middle? And how much inequality is there in the world as a whole when we consider the entire world as a single global economy?

We'll answer these questions by first looking at the income distribution in a selection of countries and then by examining features of the global distribution of income.

Income Distributions in Selected Countries

By inspecting the income distribution data for every country, we can compare the degree of income inequality and identify the countries with the most and the least inequality.

Figure 18.7 summarizes some extremes and shows where Canada lies in the range of degrees of income inequality.

Look first at the numbers in the table. They tell us that in Brazil and South Africa, the poorest 20 percent of households receive only 2 percent of total income while the highest 20 percent receive 65 percent of total income. An average person in the highest quintile receives 32.5 times the income of an average person in the lowest quintile.

Contrast these numbers with those for Finland and Sweden. In these countries, the poorest 20 percent receive 8 percent of total income and the highest 20 percent receive 35 percent. So an average person in the highest quintile receives 4.4 times the income of an average person in the lowest quintile.

The numbers for Canada lie between these extremes, with an average person in the highest quintile receiving just under 5.6 times the income received by an average person in the lowest quintile.

Brazil and South Africa are extremes not matched in any other major country or region. Inequality is large in these countries because they have a relatively small but rich European population and a large and relatively poor indigenous population.

Finland and Sweden are extremes, but they are not unusual. Income distributions similar to these are found in many European countries in which governments pursue aggressive income redistribution policies.

We look next at the global income distribution.

FIGURE 18.7 Lorenz Curves Compared

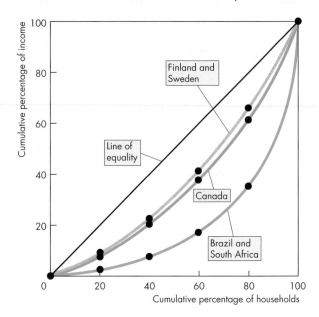

Households (quintile)	Percentage of total income[1]		
	Brazil and South Africa	Canada	Finland and Sweden
Lowest	2	7	8
Second	5	13	14
Third	10	18	20
Fourth	18	23	23
Highest	65	39	35

The table shows the percentages of total income received by each quintile. The figure shows the cumulative percentage of income graphed against the cumulative percentage of households. The data and the Lorenz curves show that income is distributed most unequally in Brazil and South Africa and least unequally in Finland and Sweden. The degree of income inequality in Canada lies between these extremes.

Sources of data: Brazil, South Africa, Finland, and Sweden, Klaus W. Deininger and Lyn Squire, Measuring Income Inequality Database, World Bank, go.worldbank.org/. Canada, see Fig. 18.2.

[1]The data are based on income *after* redistribution. See pp. 437–439 for an account of income redistribution in Canada.

MyLab Economics Animation

Global Inequality and Its Trends

The global distribution of income is much more unequal than the distribution within any one country. The reason is that many countries, especially in Africa and Asia, are in a pre-industrial stage of economic development and are poor, while industrial countries such as Canada, the United States, and those in Western Europe are rich. When we look at the distribution of income across the entire world population that goes from the low income of the poorest African to the high income of the richest North American, we observe a very large degree of inequality.

To put some raw numbers on this inequality, start with the poorest. Measured in the value of the Canadian dollar in 2005, a total of 3 billion people or 50 percent of the world population live on $2.50 a day or less. Another 2 billion people or 30 percent of the world population live on more than $2.50 but less than $10 a day. So 5 billion people or 80 percent of the world population live on $10 a day or less.

In contrast, in rich Canada, the average person has an income of $164 per day and the lowest income in the highest income quintile is $240 a day.

So the average Canadian earns 66 times the income of one of the world's 3 billion poorest people and more than 16.4 times the income of 80 percent of the people who live in developing economies. A Canadian with the lowest income in the highest income quintile earns 96 times that of the world's poorest people but only 9 times that of an average Canadian in the lowest quintile.

World Gini Ratio We can compare world inequality with Canadian inequality by comparing Gini ratios. You saw that the Canadian Gini ratio in 2011 was 0.31. The world Gini ratio was 0.64. Interpreting the Gini ratio in terms of the Lorenz curve, the world Lorenz curve lies much farther from the line of equality than the Canadian Lorenz curve.

World Trend You saw (in Fig. 18.5 on p. 428) that incomes have become more unequal in Canada—the Gini ratio has increased. The same trends are found in most economies. Increased income inequality is a big issue in two of the world's largest and poorer nations, China and India. In these two economies, urban middle classes are getting richer at a faster pace than the rural farmers.

Despite greater inequality within countries, the world is becoming *less* unequal. Figure 18.8 shows this trend towards less inequality as measured by the

FIGURE 18.8 The World Gini Ratio: 1970–2005

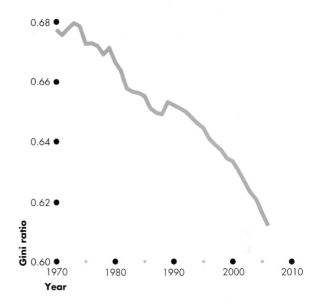

Measured by the Gini ratio, the distribution of income in the entire world became more equal between 1970 and 2005.

Source of data: Xavier Sala-i-Martin and Maxim Pinkovskiy, "Parametric estimations of the world distribution of income," 22 January 2010, http://www.voxeu.org/article/parametric-estimations-world-distribution-income.

——————— MyLab Economics Animation ———————

world Gini ratio. How can the world income distribution become less unequal while individual countries become more unequal? The answer is that average incomes in poorer countries are rising much faster than average incomes in rich countries. While the gap between rich and poor is widening *within* countries, it is narrowing *across* countries.

◆ REVIEW QUIZ

1 In which countries are incomes distributed most unequally and least unequally?

2 Which income distribution is more unequal and why: the income distribution in Canada or in the entire world?

3 How can incomes become *more* unequally distributed within countries and *less* unequally distributed across countries?

Work these questions in Study Plan 18.2 and get instant feedback.   MyLab Economics

The Sources of Economic Inequality

We've described some key facts about economic inequality and its trends and our task now is to explain those facts. We began this task in Chapter 17 by learning about the forces that influence demand and supply in the markets for labour, capital, and land. We're now going to deepen our understanding of these forces.

Inequality arises from unequal labour market outcomes and from unequal ownership of capital. We'll begin by looking at labour markets and three features of them that contribute to differences in income:

- Human capital
- Discrimination
- Contests among superstars

Human Capital

A clerk in a law firm earns less than one-tenth of the amount earned by the lawyer he assists. An operating room assistant earns less than one-tenth of the amount earned by the surgeon with whom she works. A bank teller earns less than one-tenth of the amount earned by the bank's CEO. Some of the differences in these earnings arise from differences in human capital.

To see the influence of human capital on labour incomes, consider the example of a law clerk and the lawyer he assists. (The same reasoning can be applied to an operating room assistant and surgeon, or a bank teller and bank CEO.)

Demand, Supply, and Wage Rates A lawyer performs many tasks that a law clerk cannot perform. Imagine an untrained law clerk cross-examining a witness in a complicated trial. The tasks that the lawyer performs are valued highly by her clients who willingly pay for her services. Using a term that you learned in Chapter 17, a lawyer has a high *value of marginal product*, and a higher value of marginal product than her law clerk. But you also learned in Chapter 17 that the value of marginal product of labour determines the demand for labour. So, because a lawyer has a high value of marginal product, there is also a high demand for her services.

To become a lawyer, a person must acquire human capital. But human capital is costly to acquire. This cost—an opportunity cost—includes expenditures on tuition and textbooks. It also includes forgone earnings during the years spent in university and law school. It might also include low earnings doing on-the-job training in a law office during the summer.

Because the human capital needed to supply lawyer services is costly to acquire, a person's willingness to supply these services reflects this cost. The supply of lawyer services is smaller than the supply of law-clerk services.

The demand for and supply of each type of labour determine the wage rates that each type earns. Lawyers earn a higher wage rate than law clerks because the demand for lawyers is greater and the supply of lawyers is smaller. The gap between the wage rates reflects the higher value of marginal product of a lawyer (demand) and the cost of acquiring human capital (supply).

Do Education and Training Pay? You know that a lawyer earns much more than a law clerk, but does human capital add more to earning power generally and on average? The answer is that it does. Rates of return on high school and post-secondary education have been estimated to be in the range of 5 percent to 10 percent a year after allowing for inflation, which suggests that a university degree is a better investment than almost any other that a person can undertake.

Human capital differences help to explain much of the inequality that we observe. High-income households tend to be better educated, middle-aged, married couples. Human capital differences are correlated with these household characteristics. Education contributes directly to human capital. Age contributes indirectly to human capital because older workers have more experience than younger workers. Human capital differences can also explain a small part of the inequality associated with sex. A larger proportion of men than women have completed four years of university.

These differences in education levels between the sexes are becoming smaller, and today more women than men are enrolled in university, so this source of differences in average earnings is gradually being eliminated. But it remains a source of the difference in the average earnings of men and women.

Career interruptions can decrease human capital. A person (most often a woman) who interrupts a career to raise young children usually returns to the labour force with a lower earning capacity than a similar person who has kept working. Likewise, a person who has suffered a spell of unemployment often finds a new job at a lower wage rate than that of a similar person who has not been unemployed.

Trends in Inequality Explained by a Race Between Technology and Education You've seen that high-income households have earned an increasing share of total income while lower-income households have earned a decreasing share: Why?

Harvard University economists Claudia Goldin and Lawrence Katz have amassed a heap of data that point towards an answer. They say there is a race between technological change and the education needed to work with the new technologies, and for now, technology is winning.

A related idea is that information technologies such as computers and laser scanners are *substitutes* for low-skilled labour: They perform tasks that previously low-skilled labour did. The introduction of these technologies has lowered the value of marginal product and the demand for low-skilled labour.

These same technologies require high-skilled labour to design, program, and run them. High-skilled labour and the information technologies are *complements*. So the introduction of these technologies has increased the value of marginal product and the demand for high-skilled labour.

As changes in information technology have increased the growth rate of the demand for high-skilled labour, trends in schooling have lowered the growth rate of the supply of high-skilled labour. Since 1995, the trend growth rate of human capital through education has slowed. Before 1995, the percentage of the labour force with a university degree was growing at a rate of 4 percent a year. After 1995, that growth rate slowed to about 2 percent a year.

The combination of the above two forces has lowered the earnings of low-skilled labour and increased the earnings of high-skilled labour.

Figure 18.9 illustrates this outcome. In Fig. 18.9(a), the demand for low-skilled labour decreases from D_0 to D_1 and the supply of low-skilled labour increases from S_0 to S_1. The wage rate falls from \$10 per hour to \$8 per hour. In Fig. 18.9(b), the demand for high-skilled labour increases from D_0 to D_1 and the supply of high-skilled labour decreases from S_0 to S_1. The wage rate rises from \$20 per hour to \$25 per hour.

The wider wage gap increases the income share of the highest quintile and lowers the shares of the lower quintiles.

FIGURE 18.9 Explaining the Trend in Income Distribution

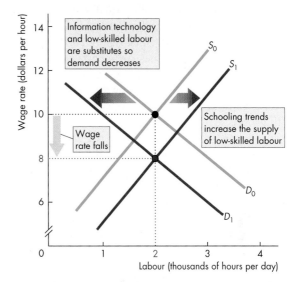

(a) The market for low-skilled labour

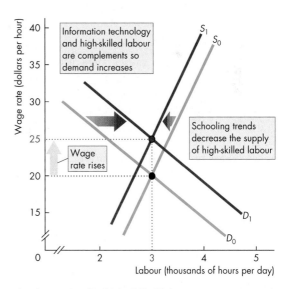

(b) The market for high-skilled labour

In part (a), the demand for low-skilled labour decreases, the supply of low-skilled labour increases, and the wage rate of low-skilled labour falls.

In part (b), the demand for high-skilled labour increases, the supply of high-skilled labour decreases, and the wage rate of high-skilled labour rises. Inequality increases.

⎯⎯ MyLab Economics Animation ⎯⎯

Discrimination

Human capital differences can explain some of the economic inequality that we observe. Discrimination is another possible source of inequality.

Suppose that females and males have identical abilities as investment advisors. Figure 18.10 shows the supply curves of females, S_F in part (a), and of males, S_M in part (b). The value of marginal product of investment advisors, shown by the two curves labelled VMP in parts (a) and (b), is the same for both groups.

If everyone is free of sex-based prejudice, the market determines a wage rate of $40,000 a year for investment advisors. But if the customers are prejudiced against women, this prejudice is reflected in the wage rate and employment.

Suppose that the perceived value of marginal product of the females, when discriminated against, is VMP_{DA}. Suppose that the perceived value of marginal product for males, the group discriminated in favour of, is VMP_{DF}. With these VMP curves, females earn $20,000 a year and only 1,000 females work as investment advisors; males earn $60,000 a year and 3,000 of them work as investment advisors.

Counteracting Forces Economists disagree about whether prejudice actually causes wage differentials, and one line of reasoning implies that it does not. In the above example, customers who buy from men pay a higher service charge for investment advice than do the customers who buy from women. This price difference acts as an incentive to encourage people who are prejudiced to buy from the people against whom they are prejudiced. This force could be strong enough to eliminate the effects of discrimination altogether.

Suppose, as is true in manufacturing, that a firm's customers never meet its workers. If such a firm discriminates against women (or against visible minorities), it can't compete with firms that hire these groups because the firm that discriminates has higher costs than those of the nonprejudiced firms. Only firms that do not discriminate survive in a competitive industry.

Whether because of discrimination or some other cause, women on average do earn lower incomes than men. Another possible source of the lower wage rates of women arises from differences in the relative degree of specialization of women and men.

FIGURE 18.10 Discrimination

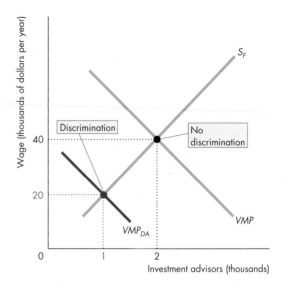

(a) Females

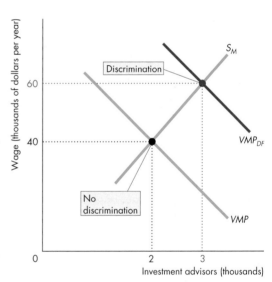

(b) Males

With no discrimination, the wage rate is $40,000 a year and 2,000 of each group are hired. With discrimination against women, the value of marginal product curve in part (a) is VMP_{DA} and that in part (b) is VMP_{DF}. The wage rate for women falls to $20,000 a year, and only 1,000 are employed. The wage rate for men rises to $60,000 a year, and 3,000 are employed.

———— MyLab Economics Animation ————

Differences in the Degree of Specialization Couples must choose how to allocate their time between working for a wage and doing jobs in the home, such as cooking, cleaning, shopping, organizing vacations, and, most important, bearing and raising children. Let's look at the choices of Bob and Sue.

Bob might specialize in earning an income and Sue in taking care of the home. Or Sue might specialize in earning an income and Bob in taking care of the home. Or both of them might earn an income and share home production jobs.

The allocation they choose depends on their preferences and on their earning potential. The choice of an increasing number of households is for each person to diversify between earning an income and doing some household chores. But in most households, Bob will specialize in earning an income and Sue will both earn an income and bear a larger share of the task of running the home. With this allocation, Bob will probably earn more than Sue. If Sue devotes time and effort to ensuring Bob's mental and physical well-being, the quality of Bob's market labour will be higher than it would be if he were diversified. If the roles were reversed, Sue would be able to supply market labour that earns more than Bob's.

To test whether the degree of specialization accounts for earnings differences between the sexes, economists have compared the incomes of never-married men and women. They have found that, on the average, with equal amounts of human capital, the wages of these two groups are the same.

Contests Among Superstars

The differences in income that arise from differences in human capital are important and affect a large proportion of the population. But human capital differences can't account for some of the really large income differences.

The super rich—those in the top 1 percent of the income distribution—earn vastly more than can be explained by human capital differences. What makes a person super rich?

A clue to the answer is provided by thinking about the super rich in tennis and golf. What makes tennis players and golfers special is that their earnings depend on where they finish in a tournament. When Petra Kvitová won the Wimbledon Championship in 2014, she received £1,760,000, or $3,257,000. The runner-up in this event, Eugenie Bouchard, received £880,000. So Petra earned twice the amount earned by Eugenie. And Petra earned 65 times the amount received by the players who lost in the first round of the tournament.

It is true that Petra Kvitová has a lot of human capital. She practises hard and long and is a remarkable athlete. But anyone who is good enough to get into a tennis Grand Slam tournament is similarly well equipped with human capital and has spent a similar number of long hours in training and practice. It isn't human capital that explains the differences in earnings. It is the tournament and the prize differences that accounts for the large differences in earnings.

Three questions jump out: First, why do we reward superstar tennis players (and golfers) with prizes for winning a contest? Second, why are the prizes so different? And third, do the principles that apply on the tennis court (and golf course) apply more generally?

Why Prizes for a Contest? The answer to this question (which was noted in Chapter 5, p. 110) is that contests with prizes do a good job of allocating scarce resources efficiently when the efforts of the participants are hard to monitor and reward directly. There is only one winner, but many people work hard in an attempt to be that person. So a lot of diligent effort is induced by a contest.

Why Are Prizes So Different? The prizes need to be hugely different to induce enough effort. If the winner received 10 percent more than the runner-up, the gain from being the winner would be insufficient to encourage anyone to work hard enough. Someone would win, but no one would put in much effort. Tennis matches would be boring, golf scores would be high, and no one would be willing to pay to see these sports. Big differences are necessary to induce a big enough effort to generate the quality of performance that people are willing to pay to see.

Does the Principle Apply More Generally? Winner-takes-all isn't confined to tennis and golf. Movie stars; superstars in baseball, basketball, football, and hockey; and top corporate executives can all be viewed as participants in contests that decide the winners. The prize for the winner is an income around double that of the runner-up and many multiples of the incomes of those who drop out earlier in the tournament.

Do Contests Among Superstars Explain the Trend?

Contests among superstars can explain large differences in incomes. But can contests explain the trend towards greater inequality with an increasing share of total income going to the super rich thereby boosting the income share of the highest quintile?

An idea first suggested by University of Chicago economist Sherwin Rosen suggests that a winner-takes-all contest can explain the trend. The key is that globalization has increased the market reach of the winner and increased the spread between the winner and the runners-up.

Global television audiences now watch all the world's major sporting events, and the total revenue generated by advertising spots during these events has increased. Competition among networks and cable and satellite television distributors has increased the fees that event organizers receive. And to attract the top star performers, prize money has increased and the winner gets the biggest share of the prize pot.

So the prizes in sports have become bigger and the share of income going to the "winner" has increased.

A similar story can be told about superstars and the super rich in business. As the cost of doing business on a global scale has fallen, more and more businesses have become global in their reach. Not only are large multinational corporations sourcing their inputs from far afield and selling in every country, they are also recruiting their top executives from a global talent pool. With a larger source of talent, and a larger total revenue, firms must make the "prize"—the reward for the top job—more attractive to compete for the best managers.

We've examined some sources of inequality in the labour market. Let's now look at the way inequality arises from unequal ownership of capital.

Unequal Wealth

You've seen that wealth inequality—excluding human capital—is much greater than income inequality. This greater wealth inequality arises from two sources: life-cycle saving patterns and transfers of wealth from one generation to the next.

Life-Cycle Saving Patterns Over a family's life cycle, wealth starts out at zero or perhaps less than zero. A student who has financed education all the way through graduate school might have lots of human capital and an outstanding student loan of $60,000. This person has negative wealth. Gradually loans get paid off and a retirement fund is accumulated. At the point of retiring from full-time work, the family has maximum wealth. Then, during its retirement years, the family spends its wealth. This life-cycle pattern means that much of the wealth is owned by people in their sixties.

Intergenerational Transfers Some households inherit wealth from the previous generation. Some save more than enough on which to live during retirement and transfer wealth to the next generation. But these intergenerational transfers of wealth do not always increase wealth inequality. If a generation that has a high income saves a large part of that income and leaves wealth to a succeeding generation that has a lower income, this transfer decreases the degree of inequality. But one feature of intergenerational transfers of wealth leads to increased inequality: wealth concentration through marriage.

Marriage and Wealth Concentration People tend to marry within their own socioeconomic class—a phenomenon called *assortative mating*. In everyday language, "like attracts like." Although there is a good deal of folklore that "opposites attract," perhaps such Cinderella tales appeal to us because they are so rare in reality. Wealthy people seek wealthy partners.

Because of assortative mating, wealth becomes more concentrated in a small number of families and the distribution of wealth becomes more unequal.

◆ REVIEW QUIZ

1 What role does human capital play in accounting for income inequality?

2 What role might discrimination play in accounting for income inequality?

3 What role might contests among superstars play in accounting for income inequality?

4 How might technological change and globalization explain trends in the distribution of income?

5 Does inherited wealth make the distribution of income less equal or more equal?

Work these questions in Study Plan 18.3 and get instant feedback.   MyLab Economics

Next, we're going to see how taxes and Canadian government programs redistribute income and decrease the degree of economic inequality.

◆ Income Redistribution

The three main ways in which governments in Canada redistribute income are:

- Income taxes
- Income maintenance programs
- Subsidized services

Income Taxes

Income taxes may be progressive, regressive, or proportional. A **progressive income tax** is one that taxes income at an average rate that increases as income increases. A **regressive income tax** is one that taxes income at an average rate that decreases as income increases. A **proportional income tax** (also called a *flat-rate income tax*) is one that taxes income at a constant rate, regardless of the level of income.

The income tax rates that apply in Canada are composed of two parts: federal and provincial taxes. The highest income tax rates are in Quebec and the lowest are in Alberta. There is variety in the detailed tax arrangements in the individual provinces, but the tax system, at both the federal and provincial levels, is progressive.

The poorest Canadians pay no income tax. Even those who earn $30,000 a year pay a very low rate of income tax. Those whose incomes are $50,000 a year pay about 21 percent of their income in income taxes; those whose incomes are $100,000 a year pay about 28 percent in income tax; and as incomes increase, the average tax rate increases to 45 percent or higher.

Income Maintenance Programs

Three main types of programs redistribute income by making direct payments (in cash, services, or vouchers) to people in the lower part of the income distribution. They are:

- Social security
- Employment insurance
- Welfare

Social Security Four government programs—Old Age Security (OAS), Guaranteed Income Supplement (GIS), the Allowance, and the Allowance for the Survivor (AS)—ensure a minimum level of income for senior citizens. Cash payments to retired or disabled workers or their surviving spouses are paid for by compulsory payroll taxes on both employers and employees. In 2017, the maximum OAS was $583.74 a month, the maximum GIS for a single person was $871.86, the maximum Allowance was $1,108.59, and the maximum AS was $1,321.46.

Employment Insurance To provide an income to unemployed workers, the federal government has established an unemployment compensation program. The Employment Insurance program is funded by employee and employer contributions, and after a qualifying period the worker is entitled to receive a benefit if he or she becomes unemployed. In 2017, the maximum EI benefit was 55 percent of average weekly earnings up to a maximum of $534 per week, adjusted for the unemployment rate in his or her region of Canada.

Welfare Other welfare programs provide income maintenance for families and persons. They are:

1. Canada Social Transfer (CST), in support of post-secondary education, social assistance, and social services, including early childhood development, is administered by the provinces and provides basic assistance to cover the cost of food, clothing, personal and household items, and, in some provinces and territories, regularly recurring special needs.
2. Canada/Quebec Pension Plans, funded equally by employee and employer contributions, provide retirement benefits, survivor benefits, disability benefits, and death benefits.
3. Workers' Compensation, a provincial program funded by employers, is designed to provide financial assistance to, as well as medical care and rehabilitation of, workers injured at work.

Subsidized Services

A great deal of redistribution takes place through the provision of subsidized services—services provided by the government at prices below the cost of production. The taxpayers who consume these goods and services receive a transfer in kind from the taxpayers who do not consume them. The two most important areas in which this form of redistribution takes place are education—both kindergarten through Grade 12 and college and university—and healthcare.

ECONOMICS IN ACTION

Income Redistribution: Only the Richest Pay

To determine the scale of income redistribution, we need to compare the distribution of *market income* with the distribution of *after-tax income*. The data available on benefits exclude the value of subsidized services (such as the value of university education and healthcare services), so the resulting distribution might understate the total amount of redistribution from the rich to the poor.

The figures show the scale of redistribution based on the calculations just described. In Fig. 1, the blue Lorenz curve describes the market distribution of income and the green Lorenz curve shows the distribution of income after all taxes and benefits. (The Lorenz curve based on total income—market income plus transfer payments from governments—lies between these two curves.)

The distribution after taxes and benefits is much less unequal than the market distribution. In 2015, the lowest 10 percent of households received only 0.3 percent of market income but 2.6 percent of after-tax income. The second-lowest 10 percent of households received 7.5 percent of market income but 8.3 percent of after-tax income. The highest 10 percent of households received 29.1 percent of market income but only 23.5 percent of after-tax income.

Figure 2 highlights the percentage of total income redistributed among the ten 10-percent groups (called deciles). The share of total income received by the lowest six deciles (60 percent) of households increased. The share received by the lowest decile increased by 2.3 percent, and the share received by the second-lowest decile increased by 2.4 percent. The share of total income received by the seventh decile fell slightly. And the share of total income received by the highest decile fell by 5.6 percent of total income.

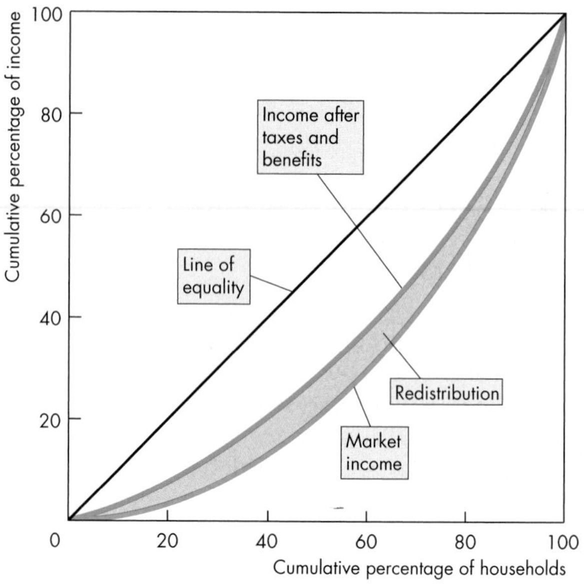

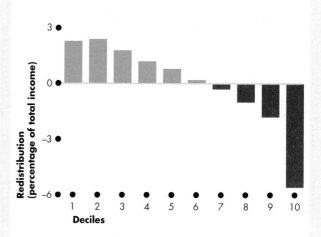

Figure 1 Income Distribution Before and After Redistribution

Figure 2 The Scale of Redistribution

Source of data: Statistics Canada, CANSIM Table 202–0701.

Canadian students enrolled in the universities in Ontario pay annual tuition fees of around $5,000. This tuition fee is much less than the cost of a year's education. The cost of a year of university education is about $20,000. Thus families with members enrolled in these institutions receive a benefit from the government of about $15,000 per student per year. Those with several college or university students receive proportionately higher benefits.

Government provision of healthcare to all residents has brought high-quality and high-cost healthcare to millions of people who earn too little to buy such services themselves. As a result, this program has contributed to reducing inequality.

The Big Tradeoff

The redistribution of income creates what has been called the **big tradeoff**, a tradeoff between equity and efficiency.

You learned in Chapter 5 that there are two views about equity (or fairness): the *fair-rules* view and the *fair-results* view. The fair-rules view doesn't present a tradeoff between equity and efficiency because voluntary transactions are efficient, and even if they result in inequality they are considered fair.

The big tradeoff arises from the fair-results view of equity. On this view, more equal is fairer: less equal is less fair. But there is a tradeoff—a big tradeoff—because redistributing income and wealth to achieve greater equality ends up creating inefficiencies.

There are two sources of inefficiency from redistributing income and wealth:

- Administrative cost
- Deadweight loss

Administrative Cost A dollar collected from a rich person does not translate into a dollar received by a poor person. Some of the dollar collected gets used up in the process of redistribution. Tax-collecting agencies such as the Canada Revenue Agency and welfare-administering agencies (as well as tax accountants and lawyers) use skilled labour, computers, and other scarce resources to do their work. The bigger the scale of redistribution, the greater is the opportunity cost of administering it.

But the cost of collecting taxes and making welfare payments is a small part of the total cost of redistribution.

Deadweight Loss The bigger cost of redistributing income and wealth arises from allocative inefficiency—from deadweight loss—of taxes and benefits.

Greater equality can be achieved only by taxing productive activities—from taxing work and saving. Taxing people's income from their work and saving lowers the after-tax income they receive. This lower after-tax income makes them work and save less, which in turn results in smaller output and less consumption not only for the rich who pay the taxes but also for the poor who receive the benefits.

It is not only taxpayers who face weaker incentives to work. Benefit recipients also face weaker incentives. In fact, under the welfare arrangements that prevail in Canada today, households that benefit most from welfare face the weakest incentive to work. When a welfare recipient gets a job, benefits are withdrawn and eligibility for support is withdrawn. In effect, these households face a marginal tax rate of more than 100 percent on their earnings. This arrangement locks poor households in a welfare trap.

So the scale and methods of income redistribution must pay close attention to the incentive effects of taxes and benefits.

A Major Welfare Challenge

The poorest people in Canada are women who have not completed high school, have a child (or children), and live without a partner. Single mothers present a major welfare challenge. Their numbers are large—approximately 1 million—and their economic plight and the economic prospects for their children are serious.

For physically fit single mothers, the long-term solution to their problem is education and on-the-job training—acquiring human capital. The short-term solution is welfare. But welfare must be designed to minimize the disincentive to pursue the long-term goal. This is the central challenge in designing an effective welfare program.

◆▶ REVIEW QUIZ

1 How do governments in Canada redistribute income?
2 Describe the scale of redistribution in Canada.
3 What is the big tradeoff? Why does it arise?
4 What is one of the major welfare challenges today and how is it being tackled in Canada?

Work these questions in Study Plan 18.4 and get instant feedback.   MyLab Economics

◆ We've examined economic inequality in Canada. We've seen how inequality arises and that on some measures, inequality has been increasing. *Economics in the News* on pp. 440–441 looks at the effects of information-age technology on the increasing inequality that began during the early 1980s and continues today.

The Rich–Poor Gap Widens in Canada's Most Unequal Places

Two Canadian Cities Are by Far the Country's Most Unequal

Research by Chartered Professional Accountants of Canada reported in *Global News* found that Calgary and Toronto are the most unequal places in Canada.

The finding agrees with and reinforces an earlier study by Statistics Canada, which also shows that both cities saw a large increase in inequality over the 30 years to 2014.

Between 1982 and 2014, Toronto's income gap doubled. In 2014, the average income of people in the top one percent was 12 times that of the median earner. That's up from six times the median income earned in 1982. The numbers are similar for Calgary.

And for Canada, the top one percent earn 11.6 times as much as the median earner, up from 7.6 in 1982.

Reporting the Statistics Canada study, *Huffington Post Canada* notes that financial centres such as Toronto and New York attract many high earners. And although the oil industry pays high salaries, it's not very labour intensive, meaning that it hires fewer people, per dollar of revenue, than other industries.

The Statistics Canada study shows that in 2014, one in five of the top one-percenters were women, up from one in ten in 1982.

The study also shows that more of Canada's one-percenters are working for an income and living less off accumulated wealth. The share of one-percenters whose income came from wages was 65 percent in 2014, up from 49 percent in the early 1980s.

Sources: Based on Statistics Canada, "Canadian Megatrends: The Fall and Rise of Canada's Top Income Earners," *The Daily*, December 16, 2016; Tencer, Daniel, "2 Canadian Cities Are by Far the Country's Most Unequal," *Huffington Post Canada*, December 16, 2016; and *Global News*, July 14, 2017.

ESSENCE OF THE STORY

- A Statistics Canada report shows that Toronto and Calgary have the largest rich–poor gaps in the country.

- Today, Toronto's top one percent earn 12 times as much as the city's median earners, up from 6 times the median income earned in 1982. Calgary's data are similar.

- For Canada as a whole, the top one percent earn 11.6 times as much as the median earner, up from 7.6 in 1982.

- Women accounted for 20 percent of the top one percent in 2014, up from 10 percent in 1982.

- More top earners get their income from work, up from 49 percent in 1982 to 65 percent in 2014.

MyLab Economics Economics in the News

ECONOMIC ANALYSIS

- The news article reports that the gap between top incomes and bottom incomes is greatest and has widened in Calgary and Toronto.

- The article also reports that more high incomes come from work and that women account for an increasing percentage of high earners.

- You can understand the forces that have brought increased inequality in major cities by applying the model that you saw on pp. 432–433.

- Figure 1 illustrates the job market for retail sales clerks, an example of lower-skilled workers, who are being replaced by computers and robots in a transition to online retailing.

- In 2017, the demand curve for retail sales clerks, derived from their value of marginal product, was LD_0, and their supply curve was LS.

- The equilibrium wage rate in 2017 was $10 per hour and 50,000 retail sales clerks were employed.

- Computers and robots are lowering the value of marginal product of retail sales clerks, which is decreasing the demand for these workers. By the 2030s, demand will have decreased to (an assumed) LD_1.

- If there is no change in supply, the wage rate of retail sales clerks will fall to $9 per hour and the number of jobs will have decreased by 40 percent to 30,000.

- Figure 2 illustrates the job market for engineers—chemical engineers in Calagary and financial engineers in Toronto—examples of higher-skilled workers, who are becoming more productive by using computers and artifical intelligence robots to work with.

- In 2017, the demand curve for high-skilled workers, derived from their value of marginal product, was LD_0, and the supply curve of these workers was LS.

- The equilibrium wage rate in 2017 was $40 per hour and 20,000 engineers were employed.

- Computers and robots are raising the value of marginal product of engineers, which is increasing the demand for these workers. By the 2030s, demand will have increased to (an assumed) LD_1.

- If there is no change in supply, the wage rate of engineers will rise to $44 per hour and the number of jobs will have increased by 50 percent to 30,000.

- In this example, the income gap will have increased from $30 an hour in 2017 to $35 an hour in the 2030s.

- The prediction that the income gap will continue to widen might turn out to be wrong.

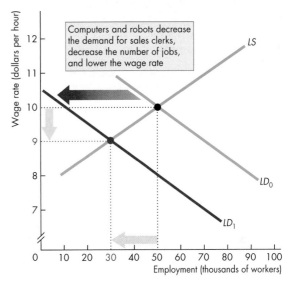

Figure 1 The Job Market for Retail Sales Clerks

Computers and robots decrease the demand for sales clerks, decrease the number of jobs, and lower the wage rate

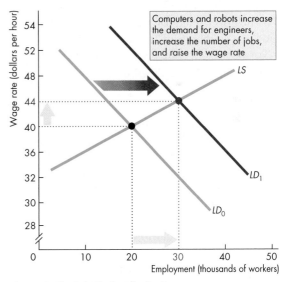

Figure 2 The Job Market for Engineers

Computers and robots increase the demand for engineers, increase the number of jobs, and raise the wage rate

- Advances in technology have been lowering the value of marginal product of low-skilled workers since the Industrial Revolution of the 1770s, but low-skilled workers have found new jobs and enjoyed rising wage rates and, over long periods, the income gap has narrowed.

- If the labour market is efficient, the income gap will narrow again.

- Computers and robots have expanded production possibilities but they have not abolished scarcity, and when wants are unsatisfied, new jobs are created.

WORKED PROBLEM

MyLab Economics Work this problem in Chapter 18 Study Plan.

The table shows the quintile shares of income in South Africa and Norway.

Households (quintile)	Norway (percentage of total income)	South Africa
Lowest	10	3
Second	16	5
Third	19	8
Fourth	22	16
Highest	33	68

Questions

1. Make a table to show the cumulative percentage of income against the cumulative percentage of households in Norway and find five points on the Lorenz curve for Norway.
2. Is income in Norway distributed more equally or less equally than in South Africa? Explain.
3. If the government of South Africa redistributed income so that its distribution matched that of Norway, which quintiles would see their incomes increase and which would decrease?

Solutions

1. To make a cumulative distribution table start with the lowest quintile (20 percent of households) who receive 10 percent of total income. Now add the income share of the second 20 percent of households to show that the lowest 40 percent of households receive $10 + 16 = 26$ percent of income. Repeating: The lowest 60 percent receive $26 + 19 = 45$ percent of income, the lowest 80 percent receive $45 + 22 = 67$ percent, and 100 percent receive $67 + 33 = 100$ percent.

Households		Income	
Percentage	Cumulative percentage	Percentage	Cumulative percentage
Lowest 20	20	10	10
Second 20	40	16	26
Third 20	60	19	45
Fourth 20	80	22	67
Highest 20	100	33	100

The Lorenz curve shows the percentages of total income received by the cumulative percentages of households. The rows of the table in the next column show the five points. See the blue curve in the figure.

Households (percentage)	Cumulative percentage
Lowest 20	10
Lowest 40	26
Lowest 60	45
Lowest 80	67
All 100	100

Key Point: To calculate the cumulative distribution, start with the lowest quintile's share and then add the next higher quintile's share one at a time.

2. Each quintile in Norway except the highest quintile receives a larger percentage of income than does the corresponding quintile in South Africa. So income is more equally distributed in Norway than in South Africa. See the figure.

Key Point: The closer is the Lorenz curve to the line of equality, the more equal is the distribution.

3. To make South Africa's distribution match Norway's, the lowest quintile would have to receive an additional 7 percent of income. The second quintile would have to receive an additional 11 percent, the third quintile an additional 11 percent, and the fourth quintile an additional 6 percent. The second and third quintiles would receive the biggest increase, and only the highest quintile would have a smaller income.

Key Point: To make the distribution more equal, redistribute income from the highest to the others.

Key Figure

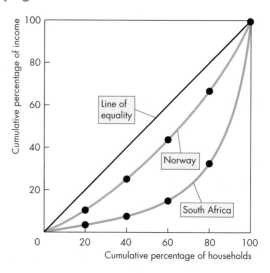

MyLab Economics Interactive Animation

SUMMARY

Key Points

Measuring Economic Inequality (pp. 424–429)

- In 2015, the mode after-tax household income was between $30,000 and $39,999 a year, the median after-tax income was $56,000, and the mean after-tax income was $69,100.
- The income distribution is positively skewed.
- In 2015, the poorest 20 percent of households received 7.2 percent of total after-tax income and the wealthiest 20 percent received 38.7 percent of total after-tax income.
- Wealth is distributed more unequally than income because the wealth data exclude the value of human capital.
- Between 1976 and 2015, the distribution of income has become more unequal.
- Education, type of household, and age and sex of householder all influence household income.

Working Problems 1 and 2 will give you a better understanding of economic inequality in Canada.

Inequality in the World Economy (pp. 430–431)

- Incomes are distributed most unequally in Brazil and South Africa and least unequally in Finland, Sweden, and some other European economies.
- The Canadian income distribution lies between the extremes.
- The distribution of income across individuals in the global economy is much more unequal than in Canada.
- The global income distribution has been getting less unequal as rapid income growth in China and India has lifted millions from poverty.

Working Problems 3 to 5 will give you a better understanding of economic inequality in the world economy.

The Sources of Economic Inequality (pp. 432–436)

- Inequality arises from differences in human capital and from contests among superstars.
- Trends in the distribution of human capital and in the rewards to superstars that arise from technological change and globalization can explain some of the trend in increased inequality.
- Inequality might arise from discrimination.
- Inequality between men and women might arise from differences in the degree of specialization.
- Intergenerational transfers of wealth lead to increased inequality, and assortative mating tends to concentrate wealth.

Working Problem 6 will give you a better understanding of the sources of economic inequality.

Income Redistribution (pp. 437–439)

- Governments redistribute income through progressive income taxes, income maintenance programs, and subsidized services.
- Redistribution increases the share of total income received by the lowest 60 percent of households and decreases the share of total income received by the two highest quintiles.
- Because the redistribution of income weakens incentives, it creates a tradeoff between equity and efficiency.
- Effective redistribution seeks to support the long-term solution to low income, which is education and job training—acquiring human capital.

Working Problems 7 and 8 will give you a better understanding of income redistribution.

Key Terms

MyLab Economics Key Terms Quiz

After-tax income, 424
Big tradeoff, 439
Gini ratio, 428
Lorenz curve, 425

Low-income cut-off, 429
Market income, 424
Poverty, 429
Progressive income tax, 437

Proportional income tax, 437
Regressive income tax, 437
Total income, 424
Wealth, 426

STUDY PLAN PROBLEMS AND APPLICATIONS

MyLab Economics Work Problems 1 to 8 in Chapter 18 Study Plan and get instant feedback.

Measuring Economic Inequality (Study Plan 18.1)

1. What is after-tax income? Describe the distribution of after-tax income in Canada in 2015.

2. The table shows after-tax income shares in Canada in 1986.

Households (quintile)	After-tax income (percent of total)
Lowest	5.5
Second	11.4
Third	17.6
Fourth	24.7
Highest	40.8

   a. Draw a Lorenz curve for Canada in 1986 and compare it with the Lorenz curve in 2015 shown in Fig. 18.3 on p. 425.

   b. Was Canadian after-tax income distributed more equally or less equally in 2015 than it was in 1986?

Inequality in the World Economy (Study Plan 18.2)

3. Incomes in China and India are a small fraction of incomes in Canada. But incomes in China and India are growing at more than twice the rate of those in Canada.

   a. Explain how economic inequality in China and India is changing relative to that in Canada.

   b. Explain how the world Lorenz curve and world Gini ratio are changing.

Use the following table to work Problems 4 and 5. The table shows the income shares in the United States and the United Kingdom.

Households (quintile)	U.S. income	U.K. income
	(percentage of total)	
Lowest	3	3
Second	9	5
Third	15	14
Fourth	23	25
Highest	50	53

4. Draw the U.K. Lorenz curve and compare it with Canada's Lorenz curve in Fig. 18.3 on p. 425. In which country is income less equally distributed?

5. Draw the U.S. Lorenz curve and compare it with Canada's Lorenz curve in Fig. 18.3 on p. 425. In which country is income less equally distributed?

The Sources of Economic Inequality (Study Plan 18.3)

6. The following figure shows the market for low-skilled labour.

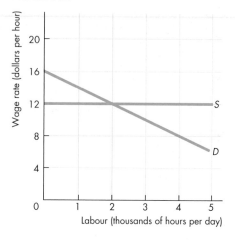

The value of marginal product of high-skilled workers is $16 an hour greater than that of low-skilled workers at each quantity of labour. The cost of acquiring human capital adds $12 an hour to the wage that must be offered to attract high-skilled labour.

   Compare the equilibrium wage rates of low-skilled labour and high-skilled labour. Explain why the difference between these wage rates equals the cost of acquiring human capital.

Income Redistribution (Study Plan 18.4)

Use the following table to work Problems 7 and 8. The table shows three redistribution schemes.

Before-tax income (dollars)	Plan A tax (dollars)	Plan B tax (dollars)	Plan C tax (dollars)
10,000	1,000	1,000	2,000
20,000	2,000	4,000	2,000
30,000	3,000	9,000	2,000

7. Which scheme has a proportional tax? Which scheme has a regressive tax? Which scheme has a progressive tax?

8. a. Which scheme will increase economic inequality? Explain why.

   b. Which scheme will reduce economic inequality? Explain why.

   c. Which scheme will have no effect on economic inequality? Explain why.

ADDITIONAL PROBLEMS AND APPLICATIONS

MyLab Economics You can work these problems in Homework or Test if assigned by your instructor.

Measuring Economic Inequality

Use the following table to work Problems 9 and 10. The table shows the distribution of market income in Canada in 2011.

Households (quintiles)	Market income (percentage of total)
Lowest	1.0
Second	7.2
Third	14.6
Fourth	24.9
Highest	52.3

9. a. What is the definition of market income?

   b. Draw the Lorenz curve for the distribution of market income.

10. Compare the distribution of market income with the distribution of after-tax income shown in Fig. 18.3 on p. 425. Which distribution is more unequal and why?

Inequality in the World Economy

Use the following table to work Problems 11 to 13. The table shows shares of income in Australia.

Households (quintile)	Income share (percentage of total)
Lowest	7
Second	13
Third	18
Fourth	24
Highest	38

11. Draw the Lorenz curve for the income distribution in Australia and in Brazil and South Africa (use the data in Fig. 18.7 on p. 430). Is income distributed more equally or less equally in Brazil and South Africa than in Australia?

12. Is the Gini ratio for Australia larger or smaller than that for Brazil and South Africa? Explain your answer.

13. What are some reasons for the differences in the distribution of income in Australia and in Brazil and South Africa?

The Sources of Economic Inequality

14. The figure shows the market for a group of workers who are discriminated against. Suppose that other workers in the same industry are not discriminated against and their value of marginal product is perceived to be twice that of the workers who are discriminated against. Suppose also that the supply of these other workers is 2,000 hours per day less at each wage rate.

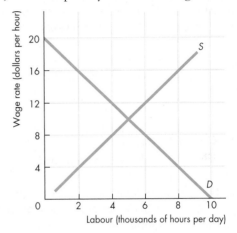

a. What is the wage rate of the workers who are discriminated against?

b. What is the quantity of workers employed who are discriminated against?

c. What is the wage rate of the workers who do not face discrimination?

d. What is the quantity of workers employed who do not face discrimination?

15. **StatsCan on Gender Pay Gap: Women Earn 87¢ to Men's $1**

The average hourly earnings of Canadian women aged 25 to 54 is 87 percent that of men. The rising educational attainment of women has shrunk the gender wage gap from 77 percent in 1981, but education hasn't ended the gap. Women with a higher degree earn 90 percent of what similarly qualified men earn. The main source of the gap is that women work in lower-paid jobs like teaching, nursing, and social work.

Source: CBC News Business, March 9, 2017

a. Explain why women earn less than men and why the gap has shrunk.

b. Draw a graph to illustrate why discrimination could result in female workers getting paid less than male workers for some jobs.

c. Explain how market competition could potentially eliminate a wage differential arising from discrimination.

Income Redistribution

16. Use the information provided in Problem 9 and in Fig. 18.3 on p. 425.

    a. What is the percentage of total income that is redistributed from the highest income group?

    b. What percentages of total income are redistributed to the lower income groups?

17. Describe the effects of increasing the amount of income redistribution in Canada to the point at which the lowest income group receives 15 percent of total income and the highest income group receives 30 percent of total income.

Use the following news clip to work Problems 18 and 19.

Income Gap Growing

In 2009, people in the highest quintile had 24.6 times as much market income as those in the lowest quintile, but after taxes and transfers the people in the highest quintile had 9.1 times as much income as those in the lowest quintile.

In 1989, the people in the highest quintile had 7.2 times more income after taxes and transfers than those in the lowest quintile.

In 1990, 82.9 percent of the unemployed received unemployment benefits. In 2009, 47.8 percent of the unemployed received unemployment benefits.

Source: Conference Board of Canada, July 13, 2011

18. Explain what the information provided in the news clip implies about the effects of income redistribution policies on the income gap between the richest and poorest Canadians.

19. How have changes in Employment Insurance changed the income gap between the richest and the poorest Canadians?

Economics in the News

20. After you have studied *Economics in the News* on pp. 440–441, answer the following questions.

    a. What information in the news article is consistent with the view that information-age technology is a source of increased inequality?

    b. If the labour market is efficient and more people become high-skilled workers and more jobs are created for low-skilled workers, how would the wage gap change?

    c. Draw a graph to illustrate your answer to (b).

21. **Best and Worst Graduate Degrees for Jobs in 2016**

    Average tuition for a master's degree ranges from $30,000 at public universities to $40,000 at private schools. But a graduate degree can be a good investment. PayScale's numbers for the median salary earned with its pick for the best five graduate degrees are master's in biostatistics, $105,900; master's in statistics, $113,700; Ph.D. in computer science, $147,400; Ph.D. in economics, $125,800; and a master's in applied math, $124,900. The median salaries for PayScale's five worst graduate degrees are $46,600 with a master of fine arts, $48,700 in early childhood education, $59,900 in divinity and elementary education, and $58,200 in reading and literacy.

    Source: *Fortune*, March 21, 2016

    a. Why do people with different graduate degrees have different salaries?

    b. Draw a graph of the labour markets for Ph.D. economists and early childhood educators to illustrate your explanation of the differences in the salaries of these two groups.

For Whom?

UNDERSTANDING FACTOR MARKETS AND INEQUALITY

During the past 35 years, the gap between the richest and the poorest in Canada has widened. But millions in Asia have been lifted from poverty and are now enjoying a high and rapidly rising standard of living. What are the forces that generate these trends? The answer to this question is the forces of demand and supply in factor markets. These forces determine wages, interest rates, rents, and the prices of natural resources. These forces also determine people's incomes.

In Canada, human capital and entrepreneurship are the most prized resources, and their incomes have grown most rapidly. In Asia, labour has seen its wage rates transformed. And in all regions rich in oil, incomes have risen on the back of high and fast-rising energy prices.

Many outstanding economists have advanced our understanding of factor markets and the role they play in helping to resolve the conflict between the demands of humans and the resources available. One of them was Thomas Robert Malthus.

Another was Harold Hotelling, whose prediction of an ever-rising price of nonrenewable natural resources implies an ever-falling rate of their use and an intensifying search for substitutes.

Yet another was Julian Simon, who challenged both the Malthusian gloom and the Hotelling Principle. He believed that people are the "ultimate resource" and predicted that a rising population lessens the pressure on natural resources. A bigger population provides a larger number of resourceful people who can discover more efficient ways of using scarce resources.

Thomas Robert Malthus *(1766–1834), an English clergyman and economist, was an extremely influential social scientist. In his best-selling* An Essay on the Principle of Population, *published in 1798, he predicted that population growth would outstrip food production and said that wars, famine, and disease were inevitable unless population growth was held in check by marrying at a late age and living a celibate life. (He married at 38 a wife of 27—marriage ages that he recommended for others.)*

Malthus had a profound influence on Charles Darwin, who got the key idea that led him to the theory of natural selection from An Essay on the Principle of Population. *But it was also Malthus' gloomy predictions that made economics the "dismal science."*

The passion between the sexes has appeared in every age to be so nearly the same, that it may always be considered, in algebraic language, as a given quantity.

THOMAS ROBERT MALTHUS
An Essay on the Principle of Population

RAJ CHETTY is Professor of Economics at Stanford University. He was an undergraduate at Harvard University, earning his BA *summa cum laude* in 2000, and a graduate student, completing his Ph.D. in 2003.

His list of honours is extraordinarily long and includes the 2013 John Bates Clark Medal of the American Economic Association, awarded to the best economist under 40 years of age; the National Tax Association Best Dissertation Prize in 2003; and the Harris, Hoopes, and Williams Prizes for the best thesis and undergraduate in economics at Harvard in 2000.

Professor Chetty's research combines empirical evidence and economic theory to help design more effective government policies regarding taxation, unemployment insurance, and education. His current research focuses on equality of opportunity: How can we give children from disadvantaged backgrounds better chances of succeeding? Chetty has published more than 20 papers in leading journals on a wide range of policy issues and come up with interesting answers, some of which he describes here.

Every economics student learns that tax incidence and deadweight loss depend on elasticities of supply and demand, and that one of the most crucial elasticities is that of the supply of labour. What does your work tell us about this elasticity? Is labour supply elastic or inelastic?

It is true that labour supply elasticity is a key determinant of the deadweight loss from income taxation. If people are very responsive in how much they work, that is, if labour supply is very elastic with respect to tax rates, then having high tax rates will generate a lot of inefficiency.

My work has shown that the picture is actually quite a bit more complicated than that because there are many other factors that affect how people respond to tax changes beyond what we have in standard economic models.

To take one example, we usually assume that people perfectly understand and pay attention to the complicated income tax system that we face today. But we have a number of studies showing that, in fact, many people aren't aware of tax rates they face, don't really pay attention to tax changes, and may not, at least in the short run, respond by changing the amount they work when the tax code is changed in complicated ways.

The bottom line is that labour supply might be somewhat elastic in the long run if you've got very high tax rates, say, as in European economies for 50 years consistently. People might start to think "Oh, I don't get to keep so much of my paycheque, maybe it doesn't pay to work." With a short-run tax increase of 5 or 10 percent, our growing sense is that people may not respond as much, and labour supply may not be very elastic.

> ... labour supply might be somewhat elastic in the long run ... [but in the short run] may not be very elastic.

*Read the full interview with Raj Chetty in MyLab Economics.

Abatement technology A production technology that reduces or prevents pollution. (p. 357)

Absolute advantage A person has an absolute advantage if that person is more productive than another person. (p. 40)

After-tax income Total income minus tax payments by households to governments. (p. 424)

Allocative efficiency A situation in which goods and services are produced at the lowest possible cost and in the quantities that provide the greatest possible benefit. We cannot produce more of any good without giving up some of another good that we *value more highly*. (p. 37)

Anti-combine law A law that regulates oligopolies and prevents them from becoming monopolies or behaving like monopolies. (p. 340)

Average cost pricing rule A rule that sets price to cover cost including normal profit, which means setting the price equal to average total cost. (p. 296)

Average fixed cost Total fixed cost per unit of output. (p. 236)

Average product The average product of a factor of production. It equals total product divided by the quantity of the factor employed. (p. 231)

Average total cost Total cost per unit of output. (p. 236)

Average variable cost Total variable cost per unit of output. (p. 236)

Barrier to entry A natural or legal constraint that protects a firm from potential competitors. (p. 280)

Behavioural economics A study of the ways in which limits on the human brain's ability to compute and implement rational decisions influences economic behaviour—both the decisions that people make and the consequences of those decisions for the way markets work. (p. 196)

Benefit The benefit of something is the gain or pleasure that it brings and is determined by preferences. (p. 9)

Big tradeoff The tradeoff between efficiency and fairness. (pp. 121, 439)

Bilateral monopoly A situation in which a monopoly seller faces a monopsony buyer. (p. 406)

Black market An illegal market in which the equilibrium price exceeds the legally imposed price ceiling. (p. 132)

Budget line The limit to a household's consumption choices. It marks the boundary between those combinations of goods and services that a household can afford to buy and those that it cannot afford. (pp. 182, 206)

Capital The tools, equipment, buildings, and other constructions that businesses use to produce goods and services. (p. 4)

Capital accumulation The growth of capital resources, including *human capital*. (p. 45)

Capture theory A theory that regulation serves the self-interest of the producer, who captures the regulator and maximizes economic profit. (p. 295)

Cartel A group of firms acting together—colluding—to limit output, raise the price, and increase economic profit. (p. 327)

Ceteris paribus Other things being equal—all other relevant things remaining the same. (p. 26)

Change in demand A change in buyers' plans that occurs when some influence on those plans other than the price of the good changes. It is illustrated by a shift of the demand curve. (p. 62)

Change in supply A change in sellers' plans that occurs when some influence on those plans other than the price of the good changes. It is illustrated by a shift of the supply curve. (p. 67)

Change in the quantity demanded A change in buyers' plans that occurs when the price of a good changes but all other influences on buyers' plans remain unchanged. It is illustrated by a movement along the demand curve. (p. 65)

Change in the quantity supplied A change in sellers' plans that occurs when the price of a good changes but all other influences on sellers' plans remain unchanged. It is illustrated by a movement along the supply curve. (p. 68)

Coase theorem The proposition that if property rights exist, if only a small number of parties are involved, and transactions costs are low, then private transactions are efficient and it doesn't matter who has the property rights. (p. 358)

Collusive agreement An agreement between two (or more) producers to form a cartel to restrict output, raise the price, and increase profits. (p. 330)

Command system A method of allocating resources by the order (command) of someone in authority. In a firm a managerial hierarchy organizes production. (p. 110)

Common resource A resource that is rival and nonexcludable. (p. 376)

Comparative advantage A person or country has a comparative advantage in an activity if that person or country can perform the activity at a lower opportunity cost than anyone else or any other country. (p. 40)

Competitive market A market that has many buyers and many sellers, so no single buyer or seller can influence the price. (p. 60)

Complement A good that is used in conjunction with another good. (p. 63)

Constant returns to scale Features of a firm's technology that lead to constant long-run average cost as output increases. When constant returns to scale are present, the *LRAC* curve is horizontal. (p. 244)

Consumer equilibrium A situation in which a consumer has allocated all his or her available income in the way that, given the prices of goods and services, maximizes his or her total utility. (p. 185)

Consumer surplus The excess of the benefit received from a good over the amount paid for it. It is calculated as the marginal benefit (or value) of a good minus its price, summed over the quantity bought. (p. 113)

Contestable market A market in which firms can enter and leave so easily that firms in the market face competition from *potential* entrants. (p. 338)

Cooperative equilibrium The outcome of a game in which the players make and share the monopoly profit. (p. 336)

Copyright A government-sanctioned exclusive right granted to an inventor of a good, service, or productive process to produce, use, and sell the invention for a given number of years. (p. 367)

Cross elasticity of demand The responsiveness of the demand for a good to a change in the price of a substitute or complement, other things remaining the same. It is calculated as the percentage change in the quantity demanded of the good divided by the percentage change in the price of the substitute or complement. (p. 96)

Deadweight loss A measure of inefficiency. It is equal to the decrease in total surplus that results from an inefficient level of production. (p. 118)

Demand The entire relationship between the price of the good and the quantity demanded of it when all other influences on buyers' plans remain the same. It is illustrated by a demand curve and described by a demand schedule. (p. 61)

Demand curve A curve that shows the relationship between the quantity demanded of a good and its price when all other influences on consumers' planned purchases remain the same. (p. 62)

Deregulation The process of removing regulation of prices, quantities, entry, and other aspects of economic activity in a firm or industry. (p. 295)

Derived demand Demand for a factor of production—it is derived from the demand for the goods and services produced by that factor. (p. 399)

Diminishing marginal rate of substitution The general tendency for a person to be willing to give up less of good *y* to get one more unit of good *x*, while at the same time remaining indifferent as the quantity of good *x* increases. (p. 210)

Diminishing marginal returns The tendency for the marginal product of an additional unit of a factor of production to be less than the marginal product of the previous unit of the factor. (p. 233)

Diminishing marginal utility The tendency for marginal utility to decrease as the quantity consumed of a good increases. (p. 184)

Direct relationship A relationship between two variables that move in the same direction. (p. 20)

Diseconomies of scale Features of a firm's technology that make average total cost rise as output increases—the *LRAC* curve slopes upward. (p. 244)

Dominant-strategy equilibrium An equilibrium in which the best strategy for each player is to cheat *regardless of the strategy of the other player*. (p. 329)

Dumping The sale by a foreign firm of exports at a lower price than the cost of production. (p. 168)

Duopoly An oligopoly market in which two producers of a good or service compete. (p. 326)

Economic depreciation The *fall* in the market value of a firm's capital over a given period. (p. 229)

Economic growth The expansion of production possibilities. (p. 45)

Economic model A description of some aspect of the economic world that includes only those features of the world that are needed for the purpose at hand. (p. 11)

Economic profit A firm's total revenue minus its total cost, with total cost measured as the opportunity cost of production. (p. 228)

Economic rent Any surplus—consumer surplus, producer surplus, or economic profit. (p. 288)

Economics The social science that studies the *choices* that individuals, businesses, governments, and entire societies make as they cope with *scarcity* and the *incentives* that influence and reconcile those choices. (p. 2)

Economies of scale Features of a firm's technology that make average total cost fall as output increases—the *LRAC* curve slopes downward. (p. 244)

Efficient Resource use is efficient if it is *not* possible to make someone

better off without making someone else worse off. (p. 5)

Efficient scale The quantity at which average total cost is a minimum— the quantity at the bottom of the U-shaped *ATC* curve. (p. 312)

Elastic demand Demand with a price elasticity greater than 1; other things remaining the same, the percentage change in the quantity demanded exceeds the percentage change in price. (p. 90)

Elasticity of supply The responsiveness of the quantity supplied of a good to a change in its price, other things remaining the same. (p. 98)

Entrepreneurship The human resource that organizes the other three factors of production: labour, land, and capital. (p. 4)

Equilibrium price The price at which the quantity demanded equals the quantity supplied. (p. 70)

Equilibrium quantity The quantity bought and sold at the equilibrium price. (p. 70)

Excess capacity A firm has excess capacity if it produces below its efficient scale. (p. 312)

Excludable A good or service or a resource is excludable if it is possible to prevent someone from enjoying the benefit of it. (p. 376)

Exports The goods and services that we sell to people in other countries. (p. 156)

Externality A cost or a benefit that arises from an action that falls on someone other than the person or firm choosing the action. (p. 354)

Factors of production The productive resources used to produce goods and services. (p. 3)

Firm An economic unit that hires factors of production and organizes those factors to produce and sell goods and services. (pp. 48, 228)

Four-firm concentration ratio A measure of market power that is calculated as the percentage of the value of sales accounted for by the four largest firms in an industry. (p. 307)

Free-rider problem The problem that the market would provide an inefficiently small quantity of a public good. (p. 377)

Game theory A set of tools for studying strategic behaviour—behaviour that takes into account the expected behaviour of others and the recognition of mutual interdependence. (p. 328)

Gini ratio The ratio of the area between the line of equality and the Lorenz curve to the entire area beneath the line of equality. (p. 428)

Goods and services The objects that people value and produce to satisfy human wants. (p. 3)

Herfindahl–Hirschman Index A measure of market power that is calculated as the square of the market share of each firm (as a percentage) summed over the largest 50 firms (or over all firms if there are fewer than 50) in a market. (p. 307)

Hotelling Principle The idea that traders expect the price of a nonrenewable natural resource to rise at a rate equal to the interest rate. (p. 412)

Human capital The knowledge and skill that people obtain from education, on-the-job training, and work experience. (p. 3)

Implicit rental rate The firm's opportunity cost of using its own capital. (p. 228)

Import quota A restriction that limits the quantity of a good that may be imported in a given period. (p. 164)

Imports The goods and services that we buy from people in other countries. (p. 156)

Incentive A reward that encourages an action or a penalty that discourages one. (p. 2)

Income effect The effect of a change in income on buying plans, other things remaining the same. (p. 215)

Income elasticity of demand The responsiveness of demand to a change in income, other things remaining the same. It is calculated as the percentage change in the quantity demanded divided by the percentage change in income. (p. 95)

Indifference curve A line that shows combinations of goods among which a consumer is *indifferent*. (p. 209)

Individual transferable quota (ITQ) A production limit that is assigned to an individual who is free to transfer (sell) the quota to someone else. (p. 386)

Inelastic demand A demand with a price elasticity between 0 and 1; the percentage change in the quantity demanded is less than the percentage change in price. (p. 89)

Inferior good A good for which demand decreases as income increases. (p. 64)

Intellectual property rights Property rights for discoveries owned by creators of knowledge. (p. 367)

Interest The income that capital earns. (p. 4)

Inverse relationship A relationship between variables that move in opposite directions. (p. 21)

Labour The work time and work effort that people devote to producing goods and services. (p. 3)

Labour union An organized group of workers that aims to increase the wage rate and influence other job conditions. (p. 405)

Land The "gifts of nature" that we use to produce goods and services. (p. 3)

Law of demand Other things remaining the same, the higher the price of a good, the smaller is the quantity demanded of it; the lower the price of a good, the larger is the quantity demanded of it. (p. 61)

Law of diminishing returns As a firm uses more of a variable factor of production with a given quantity of the fixed factor of production, the marginal product of the variable factor of production eventually diminishes. (p. 233)

Law of supply Other things remaining the same, the higher the price of a good, the greater is the quantity supplied of it; the lower the price of a good, the smaller is the quantity supplied. (p. 66)

Legal monopoly A market in which competition and entry are restricted by the granting of a public franchise, government licence, patent, or copyright. (p. 280)

Limit pricing The practice of setting the price at the highest level that inflicts a loss on an entrant. (p. 339)

Linear relationship A relationship between two variables that is illustrated by a straight line. (p. 20)

Long run The time frame in which the quantities of *all* factors of production can be varied. (p. 230)

Long-run average cost curve The relationship between the lowest attainable average total cost and output when the firm can change both the plant it uses and the quantity of labour it employs. (p. 243)

Lorenz curve A curve that graphs the cumulative percentage of income or wealth against the cumulative percentage of households. (p. 425)

Low-income cut-off The income level below which a family normally spends 63.6 percent or more of its income on food, shelter, and clothing. (p. 429)

Macroeconomics The study of the performance of the national economy and the global economy. (p. 2)

Margin When a choice is made by comparing a little more of something with its cost, the choice is made at the margin. (p. 10)

Marginal benefit The benefit that a person receives from consuming one more unit of a good or service. It is measured as the maximum amount that a person is willing to pay for one more unit of the good or service. (pp. 10, 38)

Marginal benefit curve A curve that shows the relationship between the marginal benefit of a good and the quantity of that good consumed. (p. 38)

Marginal cost The *opportunity cost* of producing *one* more unit of a good or service. It is the best alternative forgone. It is calculated as the increase in total cost divided by the increase in output. (pp. 10, 37, 236)

Marginal cost pricing rule A rule that sets the price of a good or service equal to the marginal cost of producing it. (p. 295)

Marginal external benefit The benefit from an additional unit of a good or service that people other than the consumer enjoy. (p. 363)

Marginal external cost The cost of producing an additional unit of a good or service that falls on people other than the producer. (p. 356)

Marginal private benefit The benefit from an additional unit of a good or service that the consumer of that good or service receives. (p. 363)

Marginal private cost The cost of producing an additional unit of a good or service that is borne by the producer of that good or service. (p. 356)

Marginal product The increase in total product that results from a one-unit increase in the variable input, with all other inputs remaining the same. It is calculated as the increase in total product divided by the increase in the variable input employed, when the quantities of all other inputs remain the same. (p. 231)

Marginal rate of substitution The rate at which a person will give up good y (the good measured on the y-axis) to get an additional unit of good x (the good measured on the x-axis) while at the same time remaining indifferent (remaining on the same indifference curve) as the quantity of x increases. (p. 210)

Marginal revenue The change in total revenue that results from a one-unit increase in the quantity sold. It is calculated as the change in total revenue divided by the change in quantity sold. (p. 254)

Marginal social benefit The marginal benefit enjoyed by society—by the consumer of a good or service (marginal private benefit) plus the marginal benefit enjoyed by others (marginal external benefit). (p. 363)

Marginal social cost The marginal cost incurred by the producer and by everyone else on whom the cost falls—by society. It is the sum of marginal private cost and marginal external cost. (p. 356)

Marginal utility The *change* in total utility resulting from a one-unit increase in the quantity of a good consumed. (p. 183)

Marginal utility per dollar The marginal utility from a good that results from spending one more dollar on it. It is calculated as the marginal utility from the good divided by its price. (p. 186)

Market Any arrangement that enables buyers and sellers to get information and to do business with each other. (p. 48)

Market failure A situation in which a market delivers an inefficient outcome. (p. 118)

Market income The wages, interest, rent, and profit earned in factor markets and before paying income taxes. (p. 424)

Markup The amount by which the firm's price exceeds its marginal cost. (p. 313)

Microeconomics The study of the choices that individuals and businesses make, the way these choices interact in markets, and the influence of governments. (p. 2)

Minimum efficient scale The *smallest* quantity of output at which the long-run average cost reaches its lowest level. (p. 245)

Minimum wage A regulation that makes the hiring of labour below a specified wage rate illegal. The lowest wage at which a firm may legally hire labour. (p. 135)

Money Any commodity or token that is generally acceptable as a means of payment. (p. 48)

Money price The number of dollars that must be given up in exchange for a good or service. (p. 60)

Monopolistic competition A market structure in which a large number of firms make similar but slightly different products and compete on product quality, price, and marketing, and firms are free to enter or exit the market. (p. 306)

Monopoly A market structure in which there is one firm, which produces a good or service that has no close substitutes and in which the firm is protected from competition by a barrier preventing the entry of new firms. (p. 280)

Monopsony A market in which there is a single buyer. (p. 406)

Nash equilibrium The outcome of a game that occurs when player A takes the best possible action given the action of player B and player B takes the best possible action given the action of player A. (p. 329)

Natural monopoly A market in which economies of scale enable one firm to supply the entire market at the lowest possible cost. (p. 280)

Natural monopoly good A good that is nonrival and excludable. When buyers can be excluded if they don't pay but the good is nonrival, marginal cost is zero. (p. 376)

Negative externality An externality that arises from either production or consumption and that imposes an external cost. (p. 354)

Negative relationship A relationship between variables that move in opposite directions. (p. 21)

Neuroeconomics The study of the activity of the human brain when a person makes an economic decision. (p. 197)

Nonexcludable A good or service or a resource is nonexcludable if it is impossible (or extremely costly) to prevent someone from enjoying its benefits. (p. 376)

Nonrenewable natural resources Natural resources that can be used only once. (p. 398)

Nonrival A good or service or a resource is nonrival if its use by one person does not decrease the quantity available for someone else. (p. 376)

Normal good A good for which demand increases as income increases. (p. 64)

Normal profit The return to entrepreneurship is normal profit and it is the profit that an entrepreneur earns *on average*. (p. 229)

Offshore outsourcing A Canadian firm buys finished goods, components, or services from firms in other countries. (p. 169)

Oligopoly A market structure in which a small number of firms compete. (p. 326)

Opportunity cost The highest-valued alternative that we must give up to get something. (pp. 9, 35)

Patent A government-sanctioned exclusive right granted to an inventor of a good, service, or productive process to produce, use, and sell the invention for a given number of years. (p. 367)

Payoff matrix A table that shows the payoffs for every possible action by each player for every possible action by each other player. (p. 328)

Perfect competition A market in which there are many firms each selling an identical product; there are many buyers; there are no restrictions on entry into the industry; firms in the industry have no advantage over potential new entrants; and firms and buyers are well informed about the price of each firm's product. (p. 254)

Perfectly elastic demand Demand with an infinite price elasticity; the quantity demanded changes by an infinitely large percentage in response to a tiny price change. (p. 89)

Perfectly inelastic demand Demand with a price elasticity of zero; the quantity demanded remains constant when the price changes. (p. 89)

Perfect price discrimination Price discrimination that occurs when a firm sells each unit of output for the highest price that anyone is willing to pay for it. The firm extracts the entire consumer surplus. (p. 292)

Pigovian taxes Taxes that are used as an incentive for producers to cut back on an activity that creates an external cost. (p. 359)

Positive externality An externality that arises from either production or consumption and that creates an external benefit. (p. 354)

Positive relationship A relationship between two variables that move in the same direction. (p. 20)

Poverty A state in which a household's income is too low to be able to buy the quantities of food, shelter, and clothing that are deemed necessary. (p. 429)

Preferences A description of a person's likes and dislikes and the intensity of those feelings. (pp. 9, 38, 183)

Price cap A regulation that makes it illegal to charge a price higher than a specified level. (p. 132)

Price cap regulation A rule that specifies the highest price that the firm is permitted to set—a price ceiling. (p. 297)

Price ceiling A regulation that makes it illegal to charge a price higher than a specified level. (p. 132)

Price discrimination The practice of selling different units of a good or service for different prices. (p. 281)

Price effect The effect of a change in the price of a good on the quantity of the good consumed, other things remaining the same. (p. 213)

Price elasticity of demand A units-free measure of the responsiveness of the quantity demanded of a good to a change in its price, when all other influences on buyers' plans remain the same. (p. 88)

Price floor A regulation that makes it illegal to trade at a price lower than a specified level. (p. 135)

Price taker A firm that cannot influence the price of the good or service it produces. (p. 254)

Principle of minimum differentiation The tendency for competitors to make themselves similar to appeal to the maximum number of clients or voters. (p. 379)

Private good A good or service that is both rival and excludable. (p. 376)

Producer surplus The excess of the amount received from the sale of a good or service over the cost of producing it. It is calculated as the price of a good minus the marginal cost (or minimum supply-price), summed over the quantity sold. (p. 115)

Product differentiation Making a product slightly different from the product of a competing firm. (p. 306)

Production efficiency A situation in which goods and services are produced at the lowest possible cost. (p. 35)

Production possibilities frontier The boundary between those combinations of goods and services that can be produced and those combinations that cannot. (p. 34)

Production quota An upper limit to the quantity of a good that may be produced in a specified period. (p. 143)

Profit The income earned by entrepreneurship. (p. 4)

Progressive income tax A tax on income at an average rate that increases as income increases. (p. 437)

Property rights The social arrangements that govern the ownership, use, and disposal of anything that people value. Property rights are enforceable in the courts. (pp. 48, 357)

Proportional income tax A tax on income at a constant rate, regardless of the level of income. (p. 437)

Public good A good or service that is both nonrival and nonexcludable. It can be consumed simultaneously by everyone and no one can be excluded from enjoying its benefits. (p. 376)

Public production The production of a good or service by a public authority that receives its revenue from the government. (p. 364)

Quantity demanded The amount of a good or service that consumers plan to buy during a given time period at a particular price. (p. 61)

Quantity supplied The amount of a good or service that producers plan to sell during a given time period at a particular price. (p. 66)

Rate of return regulation A regulation that requires the firm to justify its price by showing that its return on capital doesn't exceed a specified target rate. (p. 296)

Rational choice A choice that compares costs and benefits and achieves the greatest benefit over cost for the person making the choice. (p. 9)

Rational ignorance The decision not to acquire information because the cost of doing so exceeds the expected benefit. (p. 380)

Real income A household's income expressed as a quantity of goods that the household can afford to buy. (p. 207)

Regressive income tax A tax on income at an average rate that decreases as income increases. (p. 437)

Regulation Rules administered by a government agency to influence prices, quantities, entry, and other aspects of economic activity in a firm or industry. (p. 295)

Relative price The ratio of the price of one good or service to the price of another good or service. A relative price is an opportunity cost. (pp. 60, 207)

Rent The income that land earns. (p. 4)

Rent ceiling A regulation that makes it illegal to charge a rent higher than a specified level. (p. 132)

Rent seeking The lobbying for special treatment by the government to create economic profit or to divert consumer surplus or producer surplus away from others. The pursuit of wealth by capturing economic rent. (pp. 171, 288)

Rival A good, service, or a resource is rival if its use by one person decreases the quantity available for someone else. (p. 376)

Scarcity Our inability to satisfy all our wants. (p. 2)

Scatter diagram A graph that plots the value of one variable against the value of another variable for a number of different values of each variable. (p. 18)

Search activity The time spent looking for someone with whom to do business. (p. 132)

Self-interest The choices that you think are the best ones available for you are choices made in your self-interest. (p. 5)

Short run The time frame in which the quantity of at least one factor of production is fixed and the quantities

of the other factors can be varied. The fixed factor is usually capital—that is, the firm uses a given plant. (p. 230)

Short-run market supply curve A curve that shows the quantity supplied in a market at each price when each firm's plant and the number of firms remain the same. (p. 260)

Shutdown point The price and quantity at which the firm is indifferent between producing the profit-maximizing output and shutting down temporarily. The shutdown point occurs at the price and the quantity at which average variable cost is a minimum. (p. 258)

Signal An action taken by an informed person (or firm) to send a message to uninformed people. (p. 316)

Single-price monopoly A monopoly that must sell each unit of its output for the same price to all its customers. (p. 281)

Slope The change in the value of the variable measured on the y-axis divided by the change in the value of the variable measured on the x-axis. (p. 24)

Social interest Choices that are the best ones for society as a whole. (p. 5)

Social interest theory A theory that the political and regulatory process relentlessly seeks out inefficiency and introduces regulation that eliminates deadweight loss and allocates resources efficiently. (p. 295)

Strategies All the possible actions of each player in a game. (p. 328)

Subsidy A payment made by the government to a producer. (p. 144)

Substitute A good that can be used in place of another good. (p. 63)

Substitution effect The effect of a change in price of a good or service on the quantity bought when the consumer (hypothetically) remains indifferent between the original and the new consumption situations—that is, the consumer remains on the same indifference curve. (p. 216)

Sunk cost The past expenditure on a plant that has no resale value. (p. 230)

Supply The entire relationship between the price of a good and the

quantity supplied of it when all other influences on producers' planned sales remain the same. It is described by a supply schedule and illustrated by a supply curve. (p. 66)

Supply curve A curve that shows the relationship between the quantity supplied of a good and its price when all other influences on producers' planned sales remain the same. (p. 66)

Symmetry principle A requirement that people in similar situations be treated similarly. (p. 122)

Tariff A tax that is imposed by the importing country when an imported good crosses its international boundary. (p. 161)

Tax incidence The division of the burden of the tax between the buyer and the seller. (p. 137)

Technological change The development of new goods and of better ways of producing goods and services. (p. 45)

Total cost The cost of all the productive resources that a firm uses. (p. 235)

Total fixed cost The cost of the firm's fixed inputs. (p. 235)

Total income Market income plus cash payments to households by governments. (p. 424)

Total product The maximum output that a given quantity of labour can produce. (p. 231)

Total revenue The value of a firm's sales. It is calculated as the price of the good multiplied by the quantity sold. (pp. 92, 254)

Total revenue test A method of estimating the price elasticity of demand by observing the change in total revenue that results from a change in the price, when all other influences on the quantity sold remain the same. (p. 92)

Total surplus The sum of consumer surplus and producer surplus. (p. 116)

Total utility The total benefit that a person gets from the consumption of all the different goods and services. (p. 183)

Total variable cost The cost of all the firm's variable inputs. (p. 235)

Tradeoff A constraint that involves giving up one thing to get something else. (p. 9)

Tragedy of the commons The absence of incentives to prevent the overuse and depletion of a commonly owned resource. (p. 382)

Transactions costs The opportunity costs of making trades in a market. The costs that arise from finding someone with whom to do business, of reaching an agreement about the price and other aspects of the exchange, and of ensuring that the terms of the agreement are fulfilled. (pp. 119, 358)

Unit elastic demand Demand with a price elasticity of 1; the percentage change in the quantity demanded equals the percentage change in price. (p. 89)

Utilitarianism A principle that states that we should strive to achieve "the greatest happiness for the greatest number of people." (p. 120)

Utility The benefit or satisfaction that a person gets from the consumption of goods and services. (p. 183)

Value of marginal product The value to the firm of hiring one more unit of a factor of production. It is calculated as the price of a unit of output multiplied by the marginal product of the factor of production. (p. 399)

Voucher A token that the government provides to households, which they can use to buy specified goods and services. (p. 365)

Wages The income that labour earns. (p. 4)

Wealth The value of all the things that people own—the market value of their assets—at a point in time. (p. 426)

Note: Key terms and the pages on which they are defined are **bolded.** References to "*f*" denote a figure and "*t*" denote a table.

A

abatement technology, 357
ability to pay, 62
ability-to-pay principle, 142
absolute advantage, 40
absolute value, 89
abuse of dominant position, 340*t,* 343
accounting profit, 228
administrative costs, 439
advertising, 314–317, 316*f*
affordable quantities, 206
Africa, 145, 167, 431
after-tax income, 424, 427, 427*f,* 438
age, 428
Agricultural Revolution, 57
air pollution, 355, 356–362
Airbnb, 397, 410
Airbus, 337
Alberta, and inequality, 438
Alberta labour market, 414–415
allocative efficiency, 37–39, 39*f*
the Allowance, 437
the Allowance for the Survivor (AS), 437
alternatives to the market, 119
analytical skills, 13
Anarchy, State, and Utopia (Nozick), 122
anti-combine cases, 340–341
anti-combine law, 340–343
app development curriculum, 272–273
Apple, 272–273, 318–319, 351
Asia, 145, 431, 447
assortative mating, 436
Athey, Susan, 179, 180
Atlantic cod, 383
auctions, 179
Australia, 145, 387
auto production, 245
average cost, 236, 240, 240*f*
average cost curves, 236–237, 237*f*
average cost pricing rule, 296
average fixed cost, 236, 241*t*
average fixed cost curve, 237
average grades, 234
average income, 424
average price, 88–89
average product, 231, 231*t,* 240
average quantity, 88–89
average total cost, 236, 241*t*
average total cost curve, 236–237
average variable cost, 236, 241*t*
average variable cost curve, 236, 237
axes, 17, 20

B

Bains, Navdeep, 344
Balsillie, Jim, 341, 343

bank mergers, 341
Bank of Canada, 11
Bank of Montreal, 341
banking crisis. *See* financial crisis
barriers to entry, 280, 288, 308, 326
Barro, Robert, 407
BCE Inc., 344
behavioural economics, 196–197
Bell Canada, 170, 198
Bell Canada Enterprises, 341
benefit, 9
    external benefit, 119, 363–367,
        363*f,* 364*f*
    marginal benefit. *See* marginal benefit
    marginal external benefit, 363
    marginal private benefit, 363
    marginal social benefit, 112*f,* 113,
        287, 363
    measurement of, 9
    private benefit, 363
benefits principle, 142
Bentham, Jeremy, 120, 225
Berkeley, California, 102–103
best affordable choice, 212–213,
    212*f,* 214
big tradeoff, 121, 142, **439**
bilateral monopoly, 406–408
Biocom, 6
black market, 132–133
Boeing, 337
Boorstin, Daniel J., 179
bounded rationality, 196
bounded self-interest, 196–197
bounded willpower, 196
brand names, 317
Brazil, 3, 3*f,* 167, 430, 430*f*
break even, 262*f*
break-even point, 256
British Columbia's carbon tax, 360
Brunet, Richard, 341
BSE (mad cow disease), 167
budget equation, 207–208
budget line, 182, 182*f,* **206,**
    206*f,* 207
    best affordable point, 213
    budget equation, 207–208
    and change in prices, 207–208,
        208*f*
bureaucrats, 379–380
buyers
    penalties, and illegal goods markets,
        146–147
    price discrimination among groups
        of buyers, 289–290
    tax on, 138, 139*f*

C

Calgary, Alberta, 440
Campolieti, Michele, 136
Canada
    anti-combine law, 340
    charter school, 366
    distribution of income, 424, 424*f,* 431
    exports, 156, 158
    farm subsidies, 145
    imports, 156, 157
    Lorenz curve, 430*f*
    most equal places in, 438–439
    most unequal places in, 438–439
    NAFTA. *See* North American Free
        Trade Agreement (NAFTA)
    production in, 3*f*
    production possibilities, 46
    rich-poor gap, 440–441
    subsidies, 167
    university tuition, 218–219
    unlimited data, 198–199
    U.S.-Canada lumber dispute, 166
    wage rates, 404
Canada Post, 281
Canada/Quebec Pension Plans, 437
Canada Revenue Agency (CRA), 121,
    228, 439
Canada Social Transfer (CST), 437
Canadian Automobile Association
    (CAA), 124
Canadian Centre for Policy Alternatives
    (CCPA), 438
Canadian Food Inspection Agency, 167
Canadian Radio-Television and
    Telecommunications
    Commission (CRTC), 288
Canadian Telecom Summit, 344
Canadian Transportation Agency, 295
Cancún, 167
cap-and-trade, 360, 368–369
capital, 4, 398
    demand for capital, 410
    diminishing marginal product
        of capital, 242
    human capital, 427, 432–433, 447
    implicit rental rate, 228
    rental rate of capital, 410
    value of marginal product of
        capital, 410
capital accumulation, 45
capital rental markets, 410, 410*f*
capital services, 398
capital services markets, 398
capture theory, 295
carbon emissions, 7, 360, 361, 362, 369
carbon reduction plan, 368–369

carbon tax, 360
Card, David, 136
career interruptions, 432–433
cartel, 327
cartels, 343
casual labour, 398
causation, 20
cause and effect, 11
CBC News, 198
cellphone plans, 198–199, 344
cellphone service, 344–345
cellular providers, 198–199
Central America, 145, 167
central economic planning, 48
central planning, 8
centrally planned socialism, 8
ceteris paribus, 26–27
change in demand, 62–64, 72, 72*f*
   change in demand and supply in
      opposite directions, 76–77, 77*f*
   change in demand and supply in same
      direction, 76, 76*f*
   changes in both demand and supply,
      76–77, 76*f*, 77*f*
   decrease in demand, 72, 266–267
   increase in demand, 63*f*, 72, 267
   labour demand, changes in, 401, 401*f*
   and marginal utility, 190
   and short-run market
      equilibrium, 261
   and technology advances,
      266–267, 266*f*
change in supply, 67–69, 69*f*, 74, 74*f*
   change in demand and supply in
      opposite directions, 76–77, 77*f*
   change in demand and supply
      in same direction, 76, 76*f*
   changes in both demand and supply,
      76–77, 76*f*, 77*f*
   decrease in supply, 74
   increase in supply, 68*f*, 74
   and state of nature, 68
   and technological advances,
      268–269
change in the quantity demanded,
   64–65, 65*f*, 190
change in the quantity supplied,
   68–69, 69*f*
charter school, 366–367
cheap foreign labour, 168–169
cheating, 144, 332–333, 332*f*, 333*f*,
   336, 336*f*
Chetty, Raj, 448
child labour, 169
children, number of, 428
China
   access to markets, 167

carbon emissions, 7, 362
   and centrally planned socialism, 8
   chocolate consumption, 73
   income inequality, 431
   and international trade, 156
   pollution, 169
   what is produced, 3, 3*f*
chocolate, 36, 73
choice. *See* consumer choice
Chrysler, 341
CIBC, 341
Cineplex Galaxy, 341, 342
circular flows through markets, 48, 49*f*
citrus greening, 78–79
clean technology, 358–359
climate change, 7
close substitutes, 211
Coase, Ronald, 380, 395
Coase theorem, 358
cocoa, 36, 73
cod industry, 383
collusion, 327, 330–333, 331*f*
collusive agreement, 330, 332
Colombia, 75
command system, 110
commodity markets, 398
commodity prices, 398
common resources, 119, 376,
   382–387
   deadweight loss from overuse, 385
   efficient equilibrium, 385
   efficient outcome, 385–387
   individual transferable quota (ITQ),
      386–387, 387*f*
   marginal external cost, 384
   marginal private cost, 384
   marginal social benefit, 384
   marginal social cost, 384
   overfishing, 384–385, 384*f*
   overuse of, 384–385
   production quota, 386, 386*f*
   property rights, 385–386, 385*f*
   sustainable use of renewable resource,
      382–383, 382*f*
   tragedy of the commons, 382
comparative advantage, 40, 42,
   156, 169
Competition Act, 340, 340*t*
Competition Bureau, 340, 341,
   342, 343
Competition Tribunal, 340, 341
competitive equilibrium, 116
competitive labour market, 402–403
competitive market, 60
   efficiency of, 116–119, 116*f*
   fairness of, 120–122
   resource allocation, 112–115

complement, 63, 211–212, 433
   and cross elasticity of demand,
      97–98
   in production, 67
concentration measures, 307–309
   barriers to entry, 308
   firm turnover, 308
   four-firm concentration
      ratio, 307
   geographic scope of the
      market, 308
   Herfindahl-Hirschman Index
      (HHI), 307–308
   limitations of, 308
   market and industry correspondence,
      308–309
constant returns to scale, 244
constraints, 66
   resources, 66
   technology constraint, 66, 231–234
consumer choice
   behavioural economics, 196–197
   best affordable choice, 212–213,
      212*f*, 214
   change in income, 215*f*
   change in price, 213–215
   choosing at the margin, 186–187
   consumption choices, 182–184,
      206–208
   and efficient use of resources, 270
   and incentives, 2, 10
   income effect, 215, 215*f*,
      216–217, 217*f*
   inferior goods, 217
   margin, choosing at, 10
   neuroconomics, 197
   new ways of explaining consumer
      choice, 196–197
   predicting consumer choices,
      212–217
   price effect, 213–215, 213*f*, 216*f*
   rational choice, 9
   self-interest *vs.* social interest, 5–7
   student budget and choice, 218–219
   substitution effect, 216, 216*f*
   as tradeoff, 9
   understanding households'
      choices, 225
   unlimited data, 198–199
   utility-maximizing choices, 185–188
consumer equilibrium, 185
consumer surplus, 113, 113*f*
   gains from trade, 270
   with no international trade,
      159*f*, 160*f*
   and price discrimination, 293
   and value, 193

consumption
    negative consumption
        externalities, 354
    positive consumption
        externalities, 354
consumption choices, 182–184
    consumption possibilities, 182,
        206–208
    preferences, 183–184
consumption possibilities, 182,
    206–208
contest, 110
contestable market, 338, 339*f*
contests among superstars, 435–436
Cook, Tim, 272
cooperative equilibrium, 336
coordinates, 17
Copenhagen Consensus, 361
copyright, 280, 366**–367**
correlation, 20
cost
    administrative costs, 439
    average cost, 236, 240, 240*f*
    average fixed cost, 236, 241*t*
    average total cost, 236, 241*t*
    average variable cost, 236, 241*t*
    of economic growth, 45
    external cost, 119, 356, 356*f*
    fixed cost, 241, 241*t*
    glossary of costs, 241*t*
    long-run cost, 242–245
    marginal cost. *See* marginal cost
    marginal external cost, 356
    marginal social cost, 287, 356
    and minimum supply-price, 114
    oligopoly price-fixing game,
        330, 330*f*
    opportunity cost. *See* opportunity cost
    output cost, 241*t*
    private cost, 356
    production costs, 268, 268*f*
    selling costs, 315–316, 315*f*
    short-run cost, 235–241
    sunk cost, 230
    total cost, 235, 241*t*, 256, 256*f*,
        315, 315*f*
    total fixed cost, 235, 241*t*
    total product cost, 241*t*
    total variable cost, 235, 238,
        238*f*, 241*t*
    transactions costs, 119, 358
    variable cost, 241, 241*t*
    vs. price, 114
cost curves
    average fixed cost curve, 237
    average total cost curve, 236–237
    average variable cost curve, 236, 237

checkout cost curves, 238–239
    long-run average cost curve,
        243–244, 244*f*
    marginal cost curve. *See* marginal
        cost curve
    and prices of factors of
        production, 241
    and product curves, 238–240
    shifts in, 240–241
    and technology, 240–241
    total cost curves, 235*f*, 285*f*
Council on Foreign Relations, 172
countervailing duties, 168
critical-thinking skills, 13
cross elasticity of demand, 96–98,
    97*f*, 101
Cuba, 8
currency markets, 60
curve, 20
curved line, slope of, 25–26, 25*f*, 26*f*

D
De Beers, 280, 281
deadweight loss, 118
    income redistribution, 439
    minimum wage, 136
    monopoly, 287
    from overuse of a common
        resource, 385
    and perfect price discrimination, 293
    pollution, 357
    and regulation, 295, 296
    tariffs, 163
decision time frames, 230
degree of substitutability,
    211–212, 211*f*
Dell, 265
demand, 61–65
    change in demand. *See* change in
        demand
    change in the quantity demanded,
        64–65, 65*f*
    and consumer surplus, 113, 113*f*
    demand curve. *See* demand curve
    demand schedule, 62
    derived demand, 399
    elastic demand, 90, 90*f*, 93, 283
    elasticities of demand. *See* elasticity
        of demand
    and expected future income and
        credit, 64
    and expected future prices, 63–64
    for a factor of production,
        399–401
    fundamental determinant of
        demand, 412
    fundamental influence, 411

and human capital, 432
    and income, 64
    income elastic demand, 95, 96
    income inelastic demand, 95–96
    individual demand, 112–113, 112*f*
    inelastic demand, 89, 90*f*, 93, 283
    labour demand, 399–400,
        400*f*, 402
    law of demand, 61
    and marginal revenue, 282, 282*f*
    and marginal social benefit, 384
    market demand, 112–113, 112*f*
    market demand for labour, 402
    for oil, 411
    oligopoly price-fixing game,
        330, 330*f*
    in perfect competition, 254–255,
        255*f*
    perfectly elastic demand, 89–90, 90*f*,
        140, 140*f*
    perfectly inelastic demand, 89, 90*f*,
        140, 140*f*
    and population, 64
    and preferences, 64
    price elasticity of demand. *See* price
        elasticity of demand
    and prices of related goods, 63
    quantity demanded, 61
    and selling costs, 316
    speculative influence, 411
    unit elastic demand, 89, 283
    willingness to pay and value,
        112, 112*f*
demand curve, 61–62, 62*f*,
    80, 80*f*
    elasticity along linear demand
        curve, 91, 91*f*
    equation, 80
    and income effect, 215, 215*f*
    as marginal benefit curve, 112
    movement along, 65
    and price effect, 213*f*, 215
    shift of, 65
demand schedule, 62
Department of Finance, 11
Department of the Environment
    Act, 359
depreciation, 228, 229
deregulation, 295
derived demand, 399
developing nations
    exploitation of, 169
    and farm subsidies, 145
    and market access, 167
diamond-water paradox, 193
diminishing marginal product of
    capital, 242

diminishing marginal rate of substitution, 210
diminishing marginal returns, 233, 384
diminishing marginal utility, 183–**184**
diminishing returns, 242
  see also law of diminishing returns
direct relationship, 20, 21*f*
The Discoverers (Boorstin), 179
discrimination, 134, 434–435, 434*f*
diseconomies of scale, 244
Disney Corporation, 293
divisible goods, 206
DNA sequencing, 269
Doha Development Agenda, 167
Doha Round, 167
domestic jobs, 168
dominant-strategy equilibrium, 329
dominant-strategy Nash equilibrium, 334
Duflo, Esther, 58
dumping, 168
duopolist's dilemma, 333–334
duopoly, 326, 326*f,* 330

E
e-commerce markets, 60
earnings sharing regulation, 297
Eastern Europe, 169
eBay, 179
economic accounting, 228–229, 229*t*
economic coordination, 48–49
economic data, graphing, 18
economic depreciation, 229
economic growth, 45, 45*f*
  changes in what we produce, 46–47, 47*f*
  cost of, 45
  nation's economic growth, 46
economic inequality
  annual *vs.* lifetime income and wealth, 427
  and contests among superstars, 435–436
  and discrimination, 434–435, 434*f*
  Gini ratio, 428, 428*f*
  and human capital, 432–433
  income distribution, 424, 424*f*
  income redistribution, 437–439
  Lorenz curve, 424, 425–426, 425*f*
  measurement of, 424–429
  poverty, 429, 429*f*
  sources of, 432–436
  trends in inequality, 428
  understanding, 447
  and unequal wealth, 436
  wealth distribution, 426
  in the world economy, 430–431

economic instability, 7
economic loss, in short run, 261–262, 262*f,* 311*f*
economic model, 11, 20–23
economic profit, 228, 256, 256*f,* 262*f,* 284, 290
  monopolistic competition, in short run, 310, 310*f*
  perfect competition, 254–255
  zero economic profit, 311–312
economic rent, 288
economic way of thinking, 9–10
economics, 2
  behavioural economics, 196–197
  birth of, 57
  definition of, 2
  economic way of thinking, 9–10
  macroeconomics, 2
  microeconomics, 2
  neuroconomics, 197
  as policy tool, 11
  scope of economics, 9
  as social science, 11
  two big economic questions, 3–7
economies of scale, 244–245
economists, 12–13
  earnings of economics majors, 13, 13*f*
  jobs for an economics major, 12
  skills needed for economics jobs, 13
education, 428, 432–433
education efficiency, 366
efficiency, 120
  see also efficient
  of advertising, 317
  allocative efficiency, 37–39, 39*f*
  and the big tradeoff, 121
  of brand names, 317
  of competitive equilibrium, 116
  of competitive market, 116–119, 116*f*
  and consumer choice, 270
  of education, 366
  and equilibrium, 270
  fair results view, 121
  fair rules view, 122
  and monopolistic competition, 313
  in monopoly, 287, 287*f*
  perfect competition, 270–271, 270*f,* 287, 287*f*
  with price discrimination, 293
  private provision of a public good, 378–379, 379*f*
  and product development, 314
  production efficiency, 35
  resources, use of, 37–39, 270
  and social interest, 5

  with specialization and trade, 44
  and taxes, 139, 139*f*
efficient, 5
  see also efficiency
efficient market equilibrium, 358
efficient scale, 312
elastic demand, 90, 90*f,* 93, 283
elastic supply, 98–99, 99*f*
elasticity of demand
  cross elasticity of demand, 96–98, 97*f,* 101
  income elasticity of demand, 95–96, 101
  magnitude of, 89
  and marginal revenue, 283, 283*f*
  and minus sign, 89
  and peanut butter markets, 97
  price elasticity of demand. *See* price elasticity of demand
  and tax incidence, 140, 140*f*
elasticity of supply, 98–100, 101
  calculation of, 98–99
  influencing factors, 99–100
  and resource substitution possibilities, 99–100
  and tax incidence, 141, 141*f*
  time frame for supply decision, 100
Employment and Social Development Canada, 121
Employment Insurance program, 437
endowment effect, 197
energy drinks, 59, 78
entrepreneurship, 4, 229, 398, 447
entry
  monopolistic competition, 307
  perfect competition, 263, 264, 264*f,* 265
the environment
  air quality, 355
  cap-and-trade, 360, 368–369
  carbon emissions, 360, 361, 362, 369
  carbon reduction plan, 368–369
  clean technology, 358–359
  climate change, 7
  global externalities, coping with, 362
  global greenhouse gas concentrations, 355
  lax environmental standards, 169
  pollution, 169, 356–362
Environment Canada, 355, 359
equality of opportunity, 122
equilibrium, 70
  see also market equilibrium
  competitive equilibrium, 116
  consumer equilibrium, 185
  cooperative equilibrium, 336

dominant-strategy equilibrium, 329
dominant-strategy Nash
    equilibrium, 334
and efficiency, 270
efficient market equilibrium, 358, 385
labour market equilibrium, 403, 405
long-run equilibrium, 264*f*, 265
in market with exports, 158*f*
in market with imports, 157*f*
Nash equilibrium, 329, 333–334, 362
with no international trade,
    157*f*, 158*f*
oil price, 412
overfishing equilibrium, 384–385
political equilibrium, 381
and pollution, amount of, 356–357
rent-seeking equilibrium, 288, 289*f*
short-run equilibrium, 261–262
and tax on sellers, 138
equilibrium price, 70, 132, 135
equilibrium quantity, 70, 143
equity, 120
European Union, 298
    access to markets of developing
        nations, 167
    carbon emissions, 7, 362
    distribution of income, 431
    farm subsidies, 145
    regulatory barriers, 167
    subsidies, 167
excess capacity, 312–313, 312*f*
excludable, 376, 380
exit
    monopolistic competition, 307
    perfect competition, 263–264, 264*f*,
        265
expected future credit, 64
expected future income, 64
expected future prices, 63–64, 68
expenditure, and price elasticity of
    demand, 94
export subsidies, 167
exports, 156
    Canada, 158, 158*f*
    gains and losses, 160, 160*f*
external benefit, 119, 363–367,
    363*f*, 364*f*
external cost, 119, 356, 356*f*
externality, 119, **354**
    knowledge, 363–367
    negative consumption externalities, 354
    negative externality, 354, 356–362
    negative production externalities, 354
    in our lives, 354
    pollution, 356–362
    positive consumption externalities, 354
    positive externality, 354, 363–367
    positive production externalities, 354

F
Facebook, 14, 281
factor markets, 48
    anatomy of, 398
    capital rental markets, 410, 410*f*
    capital services markets, 398
    labour markets, 398, 402–409
    land rental markets, 410–411, 411*f*
    land services markets, 398
    natural resources market, 398
    nonrenewable natural resource
        markets, 411–412, 412*f*
    understanding, 447
factors of production, 3, 60, 398
    see also specific factors of production
    demand for, 399–401
    factor markets. *See* factor markets
    fixed factors of production, 230
    prices of, 67, 241, 401
    value of marginal product, 399,
        399*f*, 400*f*
fair-results view, 120–121
    big tradeoff, 439
    rent ceilings, 134
fair-rules view, 122
    big tradeoff, 439
    rent ceilings, 134
fair shares, 5–6
fairness, 5
    of competitive market, 120–122
    fair results view, 120–121
    fair rules view, 122
    of minimum wage, 135–136
    principles of fairness, 120
    rent ceiling, 134
    and taxes, 142
Famous Players, 341, 342
Fang, Tony, 136
farm subsidies, 144–145
federal taxes, 437
FedEx, 281
Fight for $15 & Fairness, 148
financial capital, 4
financial crisis, 7
financial property, 48
Finland, 430, 430*f*
firm
    turnover, and concentration
        measures, 308
firm, 48, 228
    accounting profit, 228
    decision time frames, 230
    decisions, 229, 255
    economic accounting, 228–229,
        229*t*
    economic problem of the firm,
        228–230
    goal of, 228

labour demand, 399–400, 400*f*,
    401, 401*f*
labour demand curve, 400, 400*f*
opportunity cost of production,
    228–229
output decision, 256–259
owner's labour services, 229
price of output, 401
price taker, 254
resources bought in the market, 228
resources owned by the firm,
    228–229
resources supplied by firm's
    owner, 229
supply curve, 259, 259*f*
first-come, first-served, 110–111,
    119, 134
fixed cost, 241, 241*t*
flat-rate income tax, 437
Florida, 78
flow, 426
force, 111
forgone interest, 229
four-firm concentration ratio, 307
free-rider problem, 362, **377**
free trade, 161*f*, 163*f*, 165*f*, 171
    see also international trade
free trade obstacles, 172–173
Friedman, Milton, 365
fundamental determinant of
    demand, 412
fundamental determinant of
    supply, 412

G
gains from trade, 40–44, 43*f*
    achieving gains from trade, 42–43
    and consumer surplus, 270
    and offshore outsourcing, 169
    producer surplus, 270
Galaxy S8, 318
game of chicken, 335, 335*f*
game theory, 328, 351
    duopolist's dilemma, 333–334
    game of chicken, 335, 335*f*
    games, 328
    Nash equilibrium, 329, 333–334
    oligopoly price-fixing game,
        330–334
    payoff matrix, 328, 329*f*, 333, 334*f*
    prisoners' dilemma, 328–329
    repeated games, 336–338
    sequential games, 338–339, 339*f*
    strategies, 328
game tree, 338, 339*f*
Gardiner Expressway, 375, 388–389
Gates, Bill, 7
Gateway, 265

General Agreement on Tariffs and Trade (GATT), 162
generator shortage case study, 122
Geneva, 167
Germany, 156
gig economy, 414
Gini ratio, 428, 428*f*, 431, 431*f*
global carbon emissions, 362
global financial crisis. *See* financial crisis
global greenhouse gas concentrations, 355
global inequality, 430–431
global markets. *See* international trade
globalization, 6
Goldin, Claudia, 433
goods, 60
    classification of, 376, 376*f*
    divisible goods, 206
    excludable, 376, 380
    indivisible goods, 206
    inferior good, 64, 95, 96, 217
    natural monopoly good, 376
    nonexcludable, 376, 380
    nonrival, 376
    normal good, 64, 95
    private good, 376
    public goods, 119, 362, 376
        see also public goods
    related goods, 63
    rival, 376
goods and services, 3
    see also goods; services
goods markets, 48
Google, 279, 281, 298–299
government
    action in the market. *See* government action in markets
    intervention. *See* government action in markets
    licence, 280
    size and growth, 381
government action in markets
    copyright, 366–367
    in face of external benefits, 364–367
    market failure and government, 395
    and markets for illegal goods, 146–147, 146*f*
    minimum wage, 135–136, 137*f*
    patents, 366–367
    private subsidies, 365, 365*f*
    production quotas, 143–144, 143*f*
    public production, 364, 365*f*
    rent ceiling, 132–134
    subsidies, 144–145, 145*f*
    taxes, 137–142
    voucher, 365–366, 366*f*
graphs
    axes, 17, 20
    breaks in the axes, 20

ceteris paribus, 26–27
coordinates, 17
correlation and causation, 20
curve, 20
economic data, 18
in economic models, 20–23
graphing data, 17–20, 17*f*, 18*f*
misleading graphs, 20
more than two variables, 26–27, 27*f*
origin, 17
scatter diagram, 18–20, 19*f*
slope, 23, 24–26
variables that are unrelated, 23, 23*f*
variables that have maximum or minimum, 22, 23*f*
variables that move in opposite directions, 21–22
variables that move in same direction, 20–21
when other things change, 27
x-coordinate, 17
y-coordinate, 17
Great Compression, 427
Great Depression, 170
grocery self-checkouts, 238
growth. *See* economic growth
Guaranteed Income Supplement (GIS), 437
Gunderson, Morley, 136

H
health, safety, and regulation barriers, 167
Herfindahl-Hirschman Index (HHI), 307–308, 327, 338
HHI, 307–308
highway, economic model of, 125
Hong Kong, 46, 167
Hotelling, Harold, 412
Hotelling Principle, 412, 413, 447
household type, 428
housing market with rent ceiling, 132–134
housing shortage, 132
how, 3
Hoxby, Caroline, 396
Hubbard, Thomas, 328, 352
human capital, 3, 427, 432–433, 447
    and capital accumulation, 45
    measure of, 4*f*
Hurricane Katrina, 122
Huu-ay-aht First Nation, 50

I
IBM, 265, 351
Iceland, 387
IKEA Canada, 246–247

illegal drugs
    legalization of, 147
    market for, 146–147, 146*f*
    taxation of, 147
illegal goods markets, 146–147, 146*f*
implicit rental rate, 228, 238
import quota, 164–165, 164*f*
imports, 156
    Canada, 157, 157*f*
    gains and losses, 159, 159*f*
In Defense of Monopoly: How Market Power Fosters Creative Production (McKenzie and Lee), 407
incentive, 2, 10
    to cheat, 144
    to overproduce, 144
income
    after-tax income, 424, 427, 427*f*, 438
    annual *vs.* lifetime, 427
    average income, 424
    change in income, 208, 208*f*, 215, 215*f*
    and demand, 64
    distribution of. *See* income distribution
    expected future income, 64
    and labour, 4
    Lorenz curve, 426*f*
    market income, 424, 438
    mean income, 424
    median income, 424
    mode income, 424
    proportion spent on good, 90–91
    real income, 207, 208
    redistribution of. *See* income redistribution
    rise in income, and marginal utility, 192, 192*f*
    source of income, 428
    total income, 424
    vs. wealth, 426–427
income distribution, 424, 424*f*
    Canada, 424, 424*f*, 431
    explanation of trend in, 433, 433*f*
    selected countries, 430, 430*f*
income effect, 61, 215, 215*f*, 216–217, 217*f*, 403
income elastic demand, 95, 96
income elasticity of demand, 95–96, 101
income inelastic demand, 95–96
income maintenance programs, 437
income redistribution, 437–439
    administrative costs, 439
    big tradeoff, 439
    deadweight loss, 439
    income maintenance programs, 437
    income taxes, 437
    major welfare challenge, 439

market income *vs.* after-tax income, 438
scale of, 438, 438*f*
subsidized services, 437–438
income taxes, 437
increasing marginal returns, 232–233
India, 7, 95, 167, 431
indifference curve, 209
close substitutes, 211
complements, 211–212
degree of substitutability, 211–212, 211*f*
diminishing marginal rate of substitution, 210
flat indifference curve, 210
highest attainable indifference curve, 213
marginal rate of substitution, 210, 210*f*
preference map, 209, 209*f*
and preferences, 209–212
steep indifference curve, 210
individual demand, 112–113, 112*f*
individual supply, 114, 114*f*
individual transferable quota (ITQ), 386–387, 387*f*
indivisible goods, 206
Industrial Revolution, 57
inefficiency
with external benefit, 364*f*
with external cost, 357
of minimum wage, 136, 137*f*
in monopoly, 287, 287*f*
overproduction, 145, 357
private provision of a public good, 378
and production quota, 144
public overprovision, 379–380, 379*f*, 381
rent ceiling, 133, 133*f*
without specialization and trade, 44
inelastic demand, 89, 90*f*, 93, 283
inelastic supply, 98–99, 99*f*
inequality. *See* economic inequality
infant industry, 168
inferior good, 64, 95, 96, 217
information-age monopolies, 7, 281
Information Revolution, 7, 57
innovation, 281
inputs, 60
Intel Corporation, 338, 351
intellectual property, 48
intellectual property rights, 367
interdependence, 327, 351
interest, 4, 229
intergenerational transfers, 436
International Harvester, 265

international trade
case against protection, 168–171
current state of, 156
drivers of, 156
free trade obstacles, 172–173
how global markets work, 156–158
net gain from trade, 158–159
restrictions, 161–167
winners and losers, 159–160
international trade restrictions
case against protection, 168–171
cheap foreign labour, competition with, 168–169
compensation of losers, 171
domestic jobs, 168
dumping, 168
exploitation of developing nations, 169
export subsidies, 167
health, safety, and regulation barriers, 167
import quota, 164–165, 164*f*
infant industry, 168
lax environmental standards, 169
offshore outsourcing, 169
other import barriers, 167
reasons for, 170–171
rent seeking, 171
tariff revenue, 170
tariffs, 161–163, 161*f*, 163*f*
trade wars, avoidance of, 170
voluntary export restraint, 167
Internet, 14
inverse relationship, 21, 21*f*
invisible hand, 6, 8, 117
iPhone, 318–319
Ireland, 360

J
Japan, 167
Jevons, William Stanley, 196
jobs for economics majors, 12–13
just-affordable combinations, 185

K
Karns, Scott, 94
Karns Foods, 94
Katz, Lawrence, 433
Kennesaw State University, 97
key money, 132
Kimberly-Clark, 334
known oil reserves, 412
Krueger, Alan, 136

L
labour, 3
and income, 4
owner's labour services, 229
quality of labour, 3

labour demand, 399–400, 400*f*, 401, 401*f*, 402, 405
labour demand curve, 400, 400*f*
labour force status, 428
labour market
Alberta labour market, 414–415
minimum wage, 135–136
monopsony, 406–408, 406*f*, 408*f*
labour market equilibrium, 403, 405
labour markets, 398, 402–409
competitive labour market, 402–403
with unions, 405–408
wage rate differences and trends, 404
labour services, 398
labour supply, 402–403, 405
labour supply curve, 402–403, 402*f*
labour union, 398, 405–408, 405*f*
labour demand, influences on, 405
labour market equilibrium, 405
labour supply, influences on, 405
monopsony, 406–408, 406*f*, 408*f*
Laidler, David, 11
land, 3
land rental markets, 410–411, 411*f*
land services markets, 398
law of demand, 61
law of diminishing returns, 233, 236
law of supply, 66
learning-by-doing, 168
Lee, Dwight R., 407
legal barrier to entry, 280
legal monopoly, 280
legal system, 111
leisure, opportunity cost of, 403
Levitt, Steven D., 226
life-cycle saving patterns, 436
Life Technologies Corp., 269
lighthouses, 380
limit pricing, 339
line of equality, 426
linear equation, 28
linear relationship, 20–21, 28, 28*f*
liquefied natural gas export facility, 50–51
living standards. *See* standard of living
living wage, 120
Lockheed Constellation, 366
Lomborg, Bjorn, 361
long run, 230
long-run average cost curve, 243–244, 244*f*
long-run cost, 242–245
long-run average cost curve, 243–244, 244*f*
production function, 242, 242*t*
and short-run cost, 242–243
long-run equilibrium, 264*f*, 265
long-run supply, 100

Lorenz curve, 424, 425–426, 425*f,* 426*f,* 430
loss comparisons, 258
lottery, 111, 134
Lotus Corporation, 364
Louis Dreyfus Co., 78
low-income cut-off, 429
lumber dispute, 166
luxuries, 90, 95

M
Macdonald, David, 438
macroeconomics, 2
Madagascar, 75
majority rule, 110, 119
Malthus, Thomas Robert, 447
Mankiw, N. Gregory, 170
margin, 10
marginal analysis, 257
marginal benefit, 10, 38, 363
   measures of, 62
   and preferences, 38, 38*f*
   principle of decreasing marginal benefit, 38
   vs. marginal cost, 38
marginal benefit curve, 38, 38*f,* 112
marginal cost, 10, 37, 236, 240, 240*f,* 241*t,* 356
   and marginal revenue, 284
   minimum supply price, 67
   price and quantity supplied, 66
   and production possibilities frontier, 37, 37*f*
   and production quota, 144
   and subsidies, 144
   and supply, 113–114
   vs. marginal benefit, 38
marginal cost curve, 114, 236, 237*f,* 285*f*
marginal cost pricing rule, 295
marginal external benefit, 363
marginal external cost, 356, 384
marginal private benefit, 363
marginal private cost, 356, 384
marginal product, 231, 231*t,* 233*f,* 240, 240*f*
marginal product curve, 232–233
marginal product of capital, 242
marginal rate of substitution, 210, 210*f,* 213
marginal returns
   diminishing marginal returns, 233, 384
   increasing marginal returns, 232–233
marginal revenue, 254, 255*f,* 282
   and demand, 282, 282*f*
   and elasticity, 283, 283*f*
   and marginal cost, 284
   and price, 282

marginal revenue curve, 285*f*
marginal social benefit, 112*f,* 113, 287
marginal social benefit, 363
   and demand, 384
   overuse of a common resource, 384
   from a public good, 377, 377*f*
marginal social benefit curve, 377, 377*f*
marginal social benefit (MSB) curve, 113
marginal social cost, 287, 356, 378, 384
marginal utility, 183–184, 184*f,* 186
   see also utility
   change in demand, 190
   change in quantity demanded, 190
   choosing at the margin, 186–187
   diminishing marginal utility, 183–184
   equalizing marginal utility per dollar, 186, 187*f,* 189–190
   fall in price, 189–190, 190*f*
   marginal calculations, 186–187
   marginal utility per dollar, 186, 189
   paradox of value, 193, 193*f*
   positive marginal utility, 183
   power of marginal analysis, 188
   predictions of marginal utility theory, 189–194
   rise in income, 192, 192*f*
   rise in price, 191, 191*f*
   utility-maximizing choices, 185–188
marginal utility per dollar, 186
market, 48
   alternatives to the market, 119
   buyers and sellers, 60
   for chocolate and cocoa, 73
   circular flows through markets, 48, 49*f*
   for coffee, 75
   commodity markets, 398
   competitive market, 60
   contestable market, 338, 339*f*
   coordination of decisions, 49
   currency markets, 60
   e-commerce markets, 60
   with exports, 158, 158*f*
   factor markets. See factor markets
   goods markets, 48
   how markets work, 179
   for illegal goods, 146–147, 146*f*
   with imports, 157, 157*f*
   market structure. See market structure
   oil, world and Canadian markets for, 413
market capitalism, 8
market demand, 112–113, 112*f*
market demand curve, 112, 112*f,* 113
market demand for labour, 402
market equilibrium, 70–71, 70*f,* 81, 81*f*
   equation, 81
   price above equilibrium, 71
   price adjustments, 71

   price as regulator, 70–71
   price below equilibrium, 71
market failure, 118
   externalities, 119
   and monopoly, 119
   price and quantity regulations, 118
   public goods and common resources, 119
   sources of, 118–119
   taxes and subsidies, 118
   transaction costs, 119
   understanding, 395
market fundamentals price, 412
market income, 424, 438
market power, limiting, 351
market price, 110
market structure, 308*t*
   see also specific market structures
market supply, 114, 114*f*
market supply curve, 114, 114*f,* 403
market supply of labour, 402–403
market value, 229
marketing, 306–307, 314–317
markup, 312*f,* **313,** 316*f*
marriage, and wealth concentration, 436
Marshall, Alfred, 179
Marshall, Mary Paley, 179
Martin, Paul, 341
Marx, Karl, 8
math skills, 13
Mathews, Timothy, 97
maximum points, 22, 23*f*
maximum profit, 8
Mazumdar-Shaw, Kiran, 6
McKenzie, Richard B., 407
mean income, 424
measures of concentration. See concentration measures
median income, 424
mergers, 340*t,* 341
Mexico, 169, 172–173
   see also North American Free Trade Agreement (NAFTA)
microeconomics, 2
Microsoft, 7, 279, 281, 294, 351, 364
Mill, John Stuart, 120
minimum efficient scale, 245, 254
minimum points, 22, 23*f*
minimum supply-price, 114
minimum wage, 131, 135–136, 135*f,* 137*f,* 148–149, 408, 408*f*
misleading graphs, 20
mixed economy, 8
mode income, 424
model. *See* economic model
model economy, 34
momentary supply, 100
money, 48

money price, **60**
monopolistic competition, **306**, 351
   advertising, 314–317
   collusion not possible, 306
   economic profit in short run,
      310, 310*f*
   efficiency, 313
   entry and exit, 307
   excess capacity, 312–313, 312*f*
   identifying, **307**
   ignore other firms, 306
   large number of firms, 306
   long run output and price,
      311–312, 311*f*
   marketing, 306, 314–317
   markup, 312*f*, 313
   measures of concentration, 307–309
   price, competing on, 306
   price and output, 310–313
   product development, 314
   product differentiation, 306
   profit maximization, 310–311
   quality, competing on, 306
   short-run output and price
      decision, 310
   small market share, 306
   today, 307
   vs. perfect competition, 312–313, 312*f*
   zero economic profit, 311–312
monopoly, **280**
   barrier to entry, 280
   bilateral monopoly, 406–408
   efficiency, 287, 287*f*
   elastic demand, 283
   good *vs.* bad, 407
   how monopoly arises, 280
   information-age monopolies, 7, 281
   and market failure, 119
   maximization of profit, 284
   natural monopoly, 280, 280*f*,
      295–297, 326
   no close substitutes, 280
   output in, 286, 286*f*
   price and output decision, 282–285,
      284*t*, 285*f*
   price cap regulation, 297, 297*f*
   price discrimination, 281, 289–293
   price in, 286, 286*f*
   price-setting strategies, 281
   rate of return regulation, 296
   redistribution of surpluses, 288
   regulation of, 295–297, 296*f*
   rent seeking, 288
   rent-seeking equilibrium, 288, 289*f*
   single-price monopoly, 281, 282–285
   vs. perfect competition, 286–288
monopsony, **406**–408, 406*f*, 408*f*
Montreal, Quebec, 124

Morgenstern, Oskar, 328
Multifibre Arrangement, 168

N
Nash, John, 329
Nash equilibrium, 329, 333–334, 362
Nashville Predators, 341, 343
National Air Pollution Surveillance
      Program, 359
National Collegiate Athletic Association
      (NCAA), 407
national comparative advantage, 156
national defence, 119
National Energy Board, 295
National Hockey League, 341, 343,
      406–408
National Hockey League Players'
      Association, 406–408
natural barrier to entry, 280
natural disaster, 122
natural monopoly, 280, 280*f*,
      295–297, 326
natural monopoly good, 376
natural oligopoly, 326, 326*f*
natural resources, 3, 33
natural resources market, 398
nature, 68
near-slave labour, 169
NEC, 265
necessities, 90, 95
negative consumption externalities, 354
negative externality, 354, 356–362
negative production externalities, 354
negative relationship, 21, 21*f*, 29, 29*f*
negative slope, 24*f*
neuroconomics, 197
New Zealand, 145, 387
Newton, Isaac, 364
Nielsen, 78
no close substitutes, 280
nonexcludable, 376, 380
nonrenewable natural resource markets,
      411–412, 412*f*
nonrenewable natural resources, 398
nonrival, 376
normal good, 64, 95
normal profit, 229, 254
normative statements, 11
North American Free Trade Agreement
      (NAFTA), 167, 168–169, 171
North Korea, 8, 110
Nozick, Robert, 122
NutraSweet, 341

O
obesity crisis, 87
Occupy Wall Street, 8
offshore outsourcing, 169, 170

oil, 411–413
Old Age Security (OAS), 437
oligopoly, 308, **326**–327
   anti-combine law, 340–343
   barriers to entry, 326
   cellphone service, 344–345
   examples of, 327
   games. *See* game theory
   interdependence, 327
   natural oligopoly, 326, 326*f*
   price-fixing game, 330–334
   small number of firms, 327
   temptation to cooperate, 327
   today, 327
Ontario, 148, 368–369
opportunity cost, 9–10, **35**
   of cocoa, 36
   and human capital, 432
   of increase in an activity, 10
   increasing opportunity cost, 35–36
   and international trade, 156
   of leisure, 403
   and price, 60
   of production, 228–229, 254
   and production possibilities frontier,
      35–36, 37*f*
   ratio, 35
   and value of search time, 132
oral communication skills, 13
orange juice, 59, 78–79
origin, 17
output
   and external cost, 356
   in long run, 263–265
   in monopolistic competition, 310–313
   in monopoly, 286, 286*f*
   output decision, 256–259
   in perfect competition, 286
   production function, 242
   profit-maximizing output, 257, 257*f*
   in short run, 260–262, 310
   and short-run cost, 235–241, 243*f*
   and short-run technology constraint,
      231–234
   single-price monopoly, output decision,
      282–285, 284*t*, 285*f*
output cost, 241*t*
outsourcing, 169
overfishing, 384–385, 384*f*
overproduction, 118, 118*f*, 144, 145, 357
overprovision, 379–380, 379*f*, 381
ownership barrier to entry, 280

P
paradox of value, 193, 193*f*
patents, 280, 366–**367**
payoff matrix, 328, 329*f*, 333, 334*f*
peanut butter, 94, 97

percentage change, 89
perfect competition, 254–255
    economic profit and revenue, 254–255
    efficiency, 270–271, 270*f*, 287, 287*f*
    firm decisions, 255
    firm's output decision, 256–259
    firm's supply curve, 259, 259*f*
    how perfect competition arises, 254
    long-run output, price, and profit,
        263–265
    marginal analysis and the supply
        decision, 257
    marginal revenue, and market
        price, 254
    output in, 286
    price in, 255*f*, 286
    price taker, 254
    revenue in, 254–255, 255*f*
    short-run output, price, and profit,
        260–262
    in smartphone apps, 272–273
    technological advances, 266–269
    temporary shutdown decision, 258
    vs. monopolistic competition,
        312–313, 312*f*
    vs. single-price monopoly, 286–288
perfect price discrimination, 292,
    292*f*, 293
perfectly elastic demand, 89–90, 90*f*,
    140, 140*f*
perfectly elastic supply, 99*f*, 141
perfectly inelastic demand, 89, 90*f*,
    140, 140*f*
perfectly inelastic supply, 99*f*, 141
personal characteristics, 111
P&G, 334
Pigou, Arthur Cecil, 359
Pigovian taxes, 359
plant, 230
policy tool, economics as, 11
political equilibrium, 381
pollution, 356–362
population, and demand, 64
positive consumption externalities, 354
positive externality, 354, 363–367
positive marginal utility, 183
positive production externalities, 354
positive relationship, 20, 21*f*, 29
positive slope, 24*f*
positive statements, 11
positively skewed distribution, 424
poverty, 121, **429,** 429*f*, 447
PPF. See production possibilities
    frontier *(PPF)*
preference map, 209, 209*f*
preferences, 9, 38, 183
    and consumption choices, 183–184
    and demand, 64

    and indifference curves, 209–212
    and marginal benefit, 38
    and marginal benefit curve, 38*f*
    marginal utility, 183–184, 184*f*
    revealing preferences, 188
    total utility, 183, 184*f*
    voter preferences, 381
    vs. production possibilities, 38
present value, 410
price
    above equilibrium, 71
    adjustments, 71
    average price, 88–89
    below equilibrium, 71
    change in, and budget line,
        207–208, 208*f*
    change in, and consumer choice,
        213–215
    change in, predictions of, 72–77
    commodity prices, 398
    equilibrium oil price, 412
    equilibrium price, 70, 132, 135
    expected future prices, 63–64, 68
    of factors of production, 67, 241, 401
    fall in price, and marginal utility,
        189–190, 190*f*
    of firm's output, 401
    limit pricing, 339
    in long run, 263–265
    and marginal revenue, 282
    market fundamentals price, 412
    market price, 110
    maximum price market will bear,
        284–285
    minimum supply price, 67
    minimum supply-price, 114
    money price, 60
    in monopolistic competition, 306,
        310–313
    in monopoly, 286, 286*f*
    monopoly price-setting strategies, 281
    and opportunity cost, 60
    in perfect competition, 255*f*, 286
    and production quota, 144
    as regulator, 70–71
    of related goods, 63
    of related goods produced, 67
    relative price, 60, 61, 207, 208, 213
    rise in price, and marginal utility,
        191, 191*f*
    in short run, 260–262, 310
    and shortage, 71
    single-price monopoly, price decision,
        282–285, 284*t*, 285*f*
    and subsidies, 144
    and surplus, 71
    time elapsed since price change, and
        elasticity, 91

    vs. cost, 114
    vs. value, 112
price cap, 132
price cap regulation, 297, 297*f*
price differences, 289
price discrimination, 281, 289–293
    airline example, 290–292, 290*f*, 291*f*
    among groups of buyers, 289–290
    among units of a good, 290
    efficiency with, 293
    increasing profit and producer
        surplus, 290
    perfect price discrimination, 292,
        292*f*, 293
    rent seeking with, 293
price effect, 213–215, 213*f*, 216*f*
price elasticity of demand, 88–94, 101
    see also elasticity of demand
    along linear demand curve, 91, 91*f*
    calculation of, 88–89, 89*f*
    and expenditure, 94
    factors influencing, 90–91
    for food, 93, 93*f*
    minus sign and elasticity, 89
    peanut butter, 94
    percentages and proportions, 89
    in real world, 93
    and total revenue, 92, 92*f*
    units-free measure, 89
price fixing, 343
price floor, 135, 143
price gouging, 123
price index, 60
price regulation, 118
price taker, 254
price wars, 338
Prince Edward Island, 438
principle of decreasing marginal benefit, 38
principle of increasing marginal cost, 384
**principle of minimum
    differentiation, 379**
prisoners' dilemma, 328–329
    bad outcome, 329
    the dilemma, 329
    dominant-strategy equilibrium, 329
    global carbon emissions, 362
    Nash equilibrium, 329, 333–334
    outcome, 329
    payoff matrix, 328, 329*f*, 333, 334*f*
    rules, 328
    strategies, 328
private benefit, 363
private cost, 356
private good, 376
private property, 385
private subsidies, 365, 365*f*
prizes, 435

producer surplus, 115, 115*f*, 290
    gains from trade, 270
    with no international trade, 159*f*, 160*f*
    and price discrimination, 290
product
    average product, 231, 231*t*, 240, 240*f*
    demand for firm's product, 254–255
    development, 314
    marginal product, 231, 231*t*, 233*f*,
      240, 240*f*
    total product, 231, 231*t*, 233*f*, 238, 238*f*
    variety, 313
product curves, 231–234
    average product curve, 234, 234*f*
    and cost curves, 238–240
    marginal product curve, 232–233
    total product curve, 232, 232*f*
product differentiation, 306, 318–319
product schedules, 231
production
    auto production, 245
    negative production externalities, 354
    opportunity cost of production,
      228–229, 254
    positive production externalities, 354
    produce more to cut cost, 245
    public production, 364, 365*f*
production costs, 268, 268*f*
production efficiency, 35
production function, 242, 242*t*
production possibilities frontier
      (PPF), 34, 34*f*, 41*f*, 232
    cocoa production, 36
    efficiency and inefficiency, 44
    Liz-Joe economy and its *PPF*, 44, 44*f*
    and marginal cost, 37, 37*f*
    and opportunity cost, 35–36, 37*f*
    outward-bowed *PPF*, 44
    tradeoff along, 35
production quota, 386, 386*f*
production quotas, 143–144, 143*f*
profit, 4
    accounting profit, 228
    economic profit. *See* economic profit
    increasing, and price discrimination, 290
    in long run, 263–265
    maximum profit, 8
    normal profit, 229, 254
    in short run, 260–262
profit maximization
    collusion, 331, 331*f*
    monopolistic competition, 310–311
    product development, 314
    profit-maximizing output, 257, 257*f*
progressive income tax, 437
prohibition, 147
property rights, 48, 357–358, 358*f*,
    385–386, 385*f*

proportional income tax, 437
proportionate change, 89
provincial taxes, 437
public choice theory, 381
public franchise, 280
public goods, 119, 362, **376,** 377–381
    efficient private provision, 378–379,
      379*f*
    efficient quantity, 378, 378*f*
    free-rider problem, 377
    government size and growth, 381
    inefficient private provision, 378
    inefficient public overprovision,
      379–380, 379*f*
    lighthouses, 380
    marginal social benefit, 377, 377*f*
    marginal social cost, 378
    political equilibrium, 381
    principle of minimum
      differentiation, 379
public production, 364, 365*f*
Purolator, 281

Q
Qatar, 167
quality
    advertising, as signal of quality, 316–317
    and monopolistic competition, 306
quantity
    affordable quantities, 206
    average quantity, 88–89
    change in, predictions of, 72–77
    equilibrium quantity, 143
    produced, and subsidies, 144
    public good, efficient quantity of,
      378, 378*f*
    unaffordable quantities, 206
quantity demanded, 61
quantity regulation, 118
quantity supplied, 66
Quebec City, Quebec, 124
Quebec gas prices case, 343

R
Ragan, Christopher, 11
rate of return regulation, 296, **296**
rational choice, 9
rational ignorance, 380
Rawls, John, 121
real income, 207, 208
real property, 48
recorded music, 194–195
Reddish, Angela, 11
redistribution of surpluses, 288
regressive income tax, 437
regulation, 295
    clean technology, 358–359
    earnings sharing regulation, 297

    efficient regulation of a natural
      monopoly, 295
    of monopoly, 295–297, 296*f*
    price cap regulation, 297, 297*f*
    rate of return regulation, 296
    second-best regulation of a natural
      monopoly, 296–297
regulatory barriers, 167
related goods, 63
relative price, 60, 61, **207,** 208, 213
renewable natural resource, 382–383
rent, 4
rent ceiling, 132–134, 133*f*
    black market, 132–133
    fairness of, 134
    housing shortage, 132
    inefficiency, 133, 133*f*
    rent control winners, 134
    search activity, 132
rent seeking, 171, 288, 293
rent-seeking equilibrium, 288, 289*f*
rent *vs.* buy decision, 410
rental market, 398
rental rate, 398
rental rate of capital, 410
repeated games, 336–338
Republic Wireless, 344
research and development game of
      chicken, 335, 335*f*
reservation wage rate, 402
resource allocation
    in competitive markets, 112–115
    resource allocation methods,
      110–111
resource allocation methods, 110–111
    command system, 110
    contest, 110
    first-come, first-served, 110–111
    force, 111
    lottery, 111
    majority rule, 110
    market price, 110
    personal characteristics, 111
resources
    bought in the market, 228
    classification of, 376
    common resources, 119, 376,
      382–387
    as constraint, 66
    efficient use of, 37–39, 270
    misallocated resources, 35
    natural resources, 3, 33
    nonrenewable natural resources, 398
    owned by the firm, 228
    renewable natural resource, 382–383
    substitution possibilities, 99–100
    supplied by firm's owner, 229
    unused resources, 35

revenue
    and economic profit, 254–255
    marginal revenue. *See* marginal revenue
    in perfect competition, 254–255, 255*f*
    total revenue, 254, 255*f*, 256, 256*f*, 282
rich-poor gap, 440–441
rival, 376
Rogers Communications Inc., 198, 344
Romer, Paul, 367
Rosen, Sherwin, 436
Royal Bank of Canada, 170, 341
Rudd Center for Food Policy and
        Obesity, 102
rule of law, 111
running shoes, 315
Russia, 7

S
saving patterns, 436
scarcity, 2, 34, 134
scatter diagram, 18–20, 19*f*
school choices, 366
search activity, 132
Sears Canada, 170
self-checkouts, 238
self-interest, 5
    bounded self-interest, 196–197
    and majority rule, 119
    and social interest, 5–7, 10, 167
    vs. selfish actions, 10
selfish actions, 10
sellers
    penalties, and illegal goods market,
        146, 147
    tax on, 138, 138*f*
selling costs, 315–316, 315*f*
sequential games, 338–339, 339*f*
services, 60
sharing economy, 397, 410, 414–415
Shaw Communications, 295
short run, 230
short-run cost, 235–241, 243*f*
    average cost, 236
    and long-run cost, 242–243
    marginal cost, 236
    total cost, 235
short-run equilibrium, 261–262, 261*f*
**short-run market supply curve,
        260,** 260*f*
short-run supply, 100
short-run technology constraint,
        231–234
    product curves, 231–234
    product schedules, 231
shortage, 71
shutdown decision, 258, 258*f*
shutdown point, 258
signal, 316–317

Simon, Julian, 447
single-price monopoly, 281, 282–285
    see also monopoly
Sjostrand, Stefan, 246
slope, 23, **24**
    across an arc, 25–26, 26*f*
    of a curved line, 25–26, 25*f*, 26*f*
    negative slope, 24*f*
    at a point, 25, 25*f*
    positive slope, 24*f*
    of a relationship, 24–26
    of a straight line, 24–25, 24*f*, 28–29, 28*f*
    of total product curve, 232
smartphone apps, 272–273
smartphones, and product differentiation,
        318–319
Smith, Adam, 8, 57, 117, 225
Smoot-Hawley tariff, 170
smoothies, 59, 78
social interest, 5
    and climate change, 7
    and economic instability, 7
    and efficiency, 5
    and fair shares, 5–6
    and globalization, 6
    and information-age monopolies, 7
    and resource allocation, 112
    and self-interest, 5–7, 10, 167
social interest theory, 295, 381
social loss
    import quota, 164–165
    tariffs, 162–164, 163*f*
social science, and economics, 11
social security, 437
socialism, 8
society, and scarcity, 2
softwood lumber imports, 166
South Africa, 167, 430, 430*f*
South America, 145, 167
Soviet Union, 8
specialization, 40, 435
spillover effect, 405
standard of living, 45
Starbucks, 230
Statistics Canada, 148, 424, 438, 440
Steelhead LNG, 50–51
Stern, Nicholas, 361
stock, 426
straight line
    equations of straight lines, 28–29
    linear relationship, 20–21, 28, 28*f*
    negative relationships, 29, 29*f*
    position of the line, 29
    positive relationships, 29
    slope of, 24–25, 24*f*, 28–29, 28*f*
    y-axis intercept, 28, 28*f*
strategic behaviour, 328
strategic interdependence, 351

strategies, 328
student budget and choice, 218–219
subsidized services, 437–438
subsidy, 118, **144**–145, 145*f*
    export subsidies, 167
    natural monopoly, 296
    private subsidies, 365, 365*f*
substitutes, 61, **63**
    close substitutes, 211
    closeness of, and elasticity of
        demand, 90
    and cross elasticity of demand, 96–97
    degree of substitutability, 211–212, 211*f*
    for low-skilled labour, 433
    no close substitutes, 280
    in production, 67
    resource substitution possibilities,
        99–100
substitution effect, 61, **216,** 216*f*, 403
sugar-sweetened drinks, 87, 102–103
Sugar Wireless, 344
sunk cost, 230
super rich, 435–436
superstars, contests among, 435–436
suppliers, number of, 68
supply, 66–69
    change in supply. *See* change in supply
    change in the quantity supplied,
        68–69, 69*f*
    cost and minimum supply-price, 114
    decision, and marginal analysis, 257
    elastic supply, 98–99, 99*f*
    elasticity of supply, 98–100
    and expected future prices, 68
    fundamental determinant of
        supply, 412
    fundamental influences, 412
    and human capital, 432
    individual supply, 114, 114*f*
    inelastic supply, 98–99, 99*f*
    law of supply, 66
    long-run supply, 100
    and marginal cost, 113–114
    market supply, 114, 114*f*
    market supply of labour, 402–403
    minimum supply price, 67
    momentary supply, 100
    and number of suppliers, 68
    of oil, 411–412
    perfectly elastic supply, 99*f*, 141
    perfectly inelastic supply, 99*f*, 141
    and prices of factors of production, 67
    and prices of related goods
        produced, 67
    and producer surplus, 115, 115*f*
    and production quota, 143
    quantity supplied, 66
    short-run supply, 100

speculative influences, 412
and state of nature, 68
and subsidies, 144
supply curve. *See* supply curve
supply schedule, 66
and technological change, 68
time frame for supply decision, 100
unit elastic supply, 99*f*
supply curve, 66, 67*f*, 80, 80*f*
   equation, 80
   of firm, 259, 259*f*
   as marginal cost curve, 114
   short-run market supply curve,
     260, 260*f*
supply schedule, 66
surplus, 71
   consumer surplus. *See* consumer
     surplus
   producer surplus. *See* producer surplus
   redistribution of surpluses, 288
   total surplus, 116, 270, 293
sustainable use of renewable resource,
   382–383, 382*f*
Sweden, 430, 430*f*
symmetry principle, 122

T
Tanzania, 95
tariffs, 161–163
   countervailing duties, 168
   deadweight loss, 163
   effects of, 161–162, 161*f*
   reduction in, 162
   tariff revenue, 170
   two-part tariff, 295
   winners, losers and social loss,
     162–164, 163*f*
tax incidence, 137
   and elasticity of demand, 140, 140*f*
   and elasticity of supply, 141, 141*f*
taxes, 118, 137–142
   ability-to-pay principle, 142
   benefits principle, 142
   big tradeoff, 142
   buyers, tax on, 138, 138*f*
   carbon tax, 360
   and efficiency, 139, 139*f*
   equivalence of tax on buyers and
     sellers, 138–139
   evasion, and illegal trading, 147
   and fairness, 142
   on illegal drugs, 147
   income taxes, 437
   perfectly elastic demand, 140, 140*f*
   perfectly elastic supply, 141
   perfectly inelastic demand, 140, 140*f*
   perfectly inelastic supply, 141
   Pigovian taxes, 359

and pollution, 359–360, 359*f*
sellers, tax on, 138, 138*f*
tax incidence. *See* tax incidence
vs. prohibition, 147
as wedge, 139, 139*f*
who pays the most tax, 142
taxi industry, 414–415
TD Bank, 341
technological advance. *See* technological
   change
technological change, 45
   and changes in demand and supply,
     266–269
   and production costs, 268, 268*f*
   and supply, 68
technology
   abatement technology, 357
   clean technology, 358–359
   as constraint, 66, 231–234
   and cost curves, 240–241
   and labour demand, 401
   short-run technology constraint,
     231–234
   and trends in inequality, 433
Teck Resources, 263
Telus Corp., 198, 344
temperature, and utility, 194
temporary shutdown decision, 258
theft, 111
A Theory of Justice (Rawls), 121
tissue market, 334
tit-for-tat strategy, 336
Toronto, Ontario, 124–125, 440
total cost, 235, 241*t*, 256, 256*f*,
   315, 315*f*
total cost curves, 235*f*, 285*f*
total fixed cost, 235, 241*t*
total income, 424
total product, 231, 231*t*, 233*f*, 238, 238*f*
total product cost, 241*t*
total product curve, 232, 232*f*
total revenue, 92, 92*f*, **254,** 255*f*, 256,
   256*f*, 282
total revenue curve, 283*f*, 285*f*
total revenue test, 92
total surplus, 116, 270, 293
total utility, 183, 184*f*, 185
total variable cost, 235, 238,
   238*f*, 241*t*
trade wars, 170
tradeoff, 9
   along production possibilities
     frontier, 35
   big tradeoff, 121, 439
   choice as tradeoff, 9
traffic bottlenecks, 124–125
traffic flow, 109, 124–125
tragedy of the commons, 382, 383

training. *See* education
transactions costs, 119, 358
transportation infrastructure, 388–389
trigger strategy, 336
tuition fees, 218–219
two big economic questions, 3–7
two-part tariff, 295

U
Uber, 397, 414–415
unaffordable quantities, 206
underproduction, 118, 118*f*, 364
unemployment
   benefits, 169
   and minimum wage, 135, 135*f*, 136
unfair results, 120–121
unit elastic demand, 89, 283
unit elastic supply, 99*f*
United Kingdom, 360
United States
   access to markets of developing
     nations, 167
   carbon emissions, 7, 362
   charter school, 366–367
   college costs, 218–219
   distribution of income, 431
   farm subsidies, 145
   financial crisis, 7
   and individual transferable
     quotas, 387
   and international trade, 156
   Mexico, and the wall, 172–173
   NAFTA. *See* North American Free
     Trade Agreement (NAFTA)
   rent ceilings, 134
   Smoot-Hawley tariff, 170
   subsidies, 167
   Sustainable Fishing Act, 387
   Trump administration, 166, 172–173
   unlimited data, 198–199
   U.S.-Canada lumber dispute, 166
units-free measure, 89
University of Georgia, 218
University of Windsor, 218–219
university tuition, 218–219
unlimited data, 198–199
U.S. Federal Reserve, 7
U.S. International Trade Commission,
   166, 168
utilitarianism, 120–121, 121*f*
utility, 183
   recorded music, 194–195
   schedules, 184
   temperature, analogy to, 194
   total utility, 183, 184*f*, 185
   units of utility, 188
   utility-maximizing choices,
     185–188

utility-maximizing choices
  see also marginal utility
  choosing at the margin, 186–187
  equalizing marginal utility per dollar,
    186, 187*f*
  just-affordable combinations, 185
  marginal calculations, 186–187
  marginal utility per dollar, 186
  power of marginal analysis, 188
  spreadsheet solution, 185
  utility-maximizing rule, 186

V
value, 112
  and marginal benefit, 112
  market value, 229
  paradox of value, 193, 193*f*
  vs. price, 112
value of marginal product, 399, 399*f*,
    400*f*, 411, 412, 432
value of marginal product of capital, 410
value of marginal product of land,
    410–411
Vancouver, B.C., 124
vanilla bean, 75
variable cost, 241, 241*t*
variables
  more than two variables, 26–27, 27*f*
  that are unrelated, 23, 23*f*

that have maximum or minimum,
    22, 23*f*
that move in opposite directions,
    21–22
that move in the same direction,
    20–21
Veall, Michael, 427
vinyl record stores, 267
voluntary export restraint, 167
von Neumann, John, 328, 351
voters, 381
voucher, 365–366, 366*f*

W
wage inequality, 404
wage rates, 404, 432
wages, 4
wants, 61
war, 111
water-diamond paradox, 193
wealth, 426
  annual *vs.* lifetime, 427
  distribution of wealth, 426
  intergenerational transfers, 436
  life-cycle saving patterns, 436
  Lorenz curve, 426*f*
  marriage, and wealth
    concentration, 436
  rich-poor gap, 440–441

super rich, 435–436
unequal wealth, 436
vs. income, 426–427
Wealth of Nations (Smith), 57
welfare challenge, 439
welfare programs, 437
what, 3
who, 4
willingness to pay, 38, 62, 112
wireless companies, 344
Workers' Compensation, 437
world Gini ratio, 431, 431*f*
world inequality, 430–431
World Trade Organization (WTO),
    167, 168
Wright, Orville and Wilbur, 366
writing skills, 13
Wynne, Kathleen, 148

X
x-coordinate, 17

Y
y-axis intercept, 28, 28*f*
Yellow Pages, 341

Z
zero economic profit, 311–312
Zuckerberg, Mark, 14

Chapter 1: p. 1: D. Hurst/Alamy Stock Photo; p. 6 (top): Adek Berry/AFP/Getty Images; p. 6 (bottom): STR New/Reuters; p. 7 (left): Christian Prandl/Imagebroker/Alamy; p. 7 (right): Snap Happy/Fotolia; p. 8 (left): Brendan McDermid/Reuters; p. 8 (right): Pictorial Press Ltd/Alamy Stock Photo; p. 12: Courtesy of Courtney Roofing; p. 14: Karelnoppe/Fotolia

Chapter 2: p. 33: Agus D. Laksono/Alamy Stock Photo; p. 57: Bettmann/Getty Images; p. 58: Eric Fougere/VIP Images/Corbis/Getty Images

Chapter 3: p. 59: Ian Dagnall/Alamy Stock Photo; p. 73: Poplis, Paul/the food passionates/Corbis; p. 75: Uber Images/Shutterstock

Chapter 4: p. 87: Monticello/Shutterstock

Chapter 5: p. 109: Benoit Daoust/Shutterstock; p. 117: Stephen Coburn/Shutterstock; p. 123: Mike Ridewood/epa/Corbis; p. 125: Dennis Chang - Singapore/Alamy Stock Photo

Chapter 6: p. 131: EXImages/Alamy Stock Photo

Chapter 7: p. 155: Pete Spiro/Shutterstock; p. 166: Robert McGouey/Landscape/Alamy Stock Photo; p. 170: Terry Vine/Blend Images/Alamy Stock Photo; p. 179: Public Domain/Wikipedia; p. 180: Photo Courtesy of Susan Athey

Chapter 8: p. 181: Wavebreakmedia/Shutterstock

Chapter 9: p. 205: Zoonar GmbH/Alamy Stock Photo; p. 214 (right): Dennizn/Shutterstock; p. 214 (left): Corbis/VCG/Getty Images; p. 225: Bettmann/Getty Images; p. 226: Photo courtesy of Steven D. Levitt

Chapter 10: p. 227: Norman Pogson/Alamy Stock Photo; p. 239 (left): Antenna/fStop Images GmbH/Alamy Stock Photo; p. 239 (right): ZUMA Press Inc/Alamy Stock Photo; p. 245: Jim West/Alamy Stock Photo

Chapter 11: p. 253: Seewhatmitchsee/Alamy Stock Photo; p. 263: Robert McGouey/Industry/Alamy Stock Photo;

p. 265 (left): Digital Vision/Photodisc/Getty Images; p. 265 (right): Elena Elisseeva/Shutterstock; p. 267: Olivia Stapley and Jack Parkin; p. 272: Urbanmyth/Alamy Stock Photo

Chapter 12: p. 279: Lisa Werner/Alamy Stock Photo; p. 294: Craig Joiner Photography/Alamy Stock Photo

Chapter 13: p. 305: Maksym Yemelyanov/Alamy Stock Photo; p. 308 (top left): All Canada Photos/Alamy Stock Photo; p. 308 (top right): Craig Ellenwood/Alamy Stock Photo; p. 308 (middle left): STEPHEN BRASHEAR/AP Images; p. 308 (bottom left): Copyright Airbus S.A.S; p. 308 (bottom right): Francis Vachon/Alamy Stock Photo; p. 315: Pearson Education, Inc.

Chapter 14: p. 325: Cunaplus/Fotolia; p. 337 (top): Copyright Airbus S.A.S; p. 337 (bottom): Boeing Corporation; p. 342: Steve White; p. 343: Paul Chiasson/The Canadian Press Images; p. 351: TopFoto/The Image Works; p. 352 Evanston Photographic Studios, Inc.

Chapter 15: p. 353: Bill Brooks/Alamy Stock Photo; p. 355: Trekandshoot/Alamy Stock Photo; p. 361 (left): David Pearson/Alamy Stock Photo; p. 361 (right): Patrick Jube/Getty Images Entertainment/Getty Images

Chapter 16: p. 375: Oleksiy Maksymenko Photography/Alamy Stock Photo; p. 380: Peter Langer/DanitaDelimont.com "Danita Delimont Photography"/Newscom; p. 382: Private CollectionPhoto © Christie's Images/Bridgeman Images; p. 383: Jeff Rotman/ Photonica/Getty Images; p. 395: David Joel Photography Inc.; p. 396: Courtesy of Caroline M. Hoxby/E.S. Lee

Chapter 17: p. 397: UrbanImages/Alamy Stock Photo; p. 407: Susana Gonzalez/Bloomberg/Getty Image; p. 407: Jamie Squire/Getty Images Sport/Getty Images

Chapter 18: p. 423: dpa picture alliance archive/Alamy Stock Photo; p. 447: World History Archive/Alamy Stock Photo; p. 448: Courtesy of Raj Chetty

Economics in the News

Economics in the News boxes show students how to use the economic toolkit to understand the events and issues they are confronted with in the media. An extended *Economics in the News* at the end of each chapter helps students think like economists by connecting chapter tools and concepts to the world around them.

1 The Invisible Hand 6
   The Internet for Everyone 14
2 Opportunity Cost of Kale 36
   Expanding Production Possibilities 50
3 The Markets for Chocolate and Cocoa 73
   The Market for Vanilla Bean 75
   Demand and Supply: The Market for Orange Juice 78
4 The Elasticity of Demand for Peanut Butter 94
   More Peanut Butter Demand Elasticities 97
   The Elasticity of Demand for Sugar-Sweetened Drinks 102
5 Making Traffic Flow Efficiently 124
6 Push to Raise the Minimum Wage 148
7 The U.S.–Canada Lumber Dispute 166
   The Cost of a Tariff 172
8 Consumer Choice with Unlimited Data 198
9 Student Budget and Choice 218
10 Checkout Cost Curves 238
   A Long-Run Decision for IKEA 246

11 Vinyl's Comeback 267
   The Falling Cost of Sequencing DNA 269
   Perfect Competition in Smartphone Apps 272
12 Microsoft Monopoly 294
   Is Google Misusing Monopoly Power? 298
13 Product Differentiation in Smartphones 318
14 Airbus Versus Boeing 337
   Oligopoly Games in Cellphone Service 344
15 A Carbon Reduction Plan 368
16 Maintaining the Transportation Infrastructure 388
17 The Growth of the Sharing Economy 410
   The Gig and Sharing Economy 414
18 The Rich-Poor Gap Widens in Canada's Most Unequal Places 440

Economics in Action

Economics in Action boxes apply economic theory to current events to illustrate the importance of economic forces in the world around us.

2 Hong Kong Overtakes Canada 46
4 Elastic and Inelastic Demand 93 ◆ Price Elasticities of Demand for Food 93 ◆ Necessities and Luxuries 95 ◆ Income Elastic and Inelastic Demand 96
5 Seeing the Invisible Hand 117
6 Rent Control Winners: The Rich and Famous 134 ◆ Workers and Consumers Pay the Most Tax 142 ◆ Rich High-Cost Farmers the Winners 145
7 We Trade Metals for Consumer Goods 156 ◆ Tariffs Almost Gone 162 ◆ Self-Interest Beats the Social Interest 167
8 Maximizing Utility from Recorded Music 194
9 Best Affordable Choice of Movies, DVD Rentals, and Streaming 214
10 How to Pull Up Your Average 234 ◆ Produce More to Cut Cost 245
11 A Temporary Shutdown 263 ◆ Entry and Exit 265
12 Two Information-Age Monopolies 281 ◆ Attempting Perfect Price Discrimination 293

13 Monopolistic Competition Today 309 ◆ The Cost of Selling a Pair of Shoes 315
14 Oligopoly Today 327 ◆ A Game in the Market for Tissues 334 ◆ Mergers Blocked 341 ◆ Cineplex Galaxy Acquires Famous Players 342 ◆ Price Fixing 343 ◆ Abuse of Dominant Position 343
15 Opposing Trends: Success and Failure 355 ◆ Taxing Carbon Emissions 360 ◆ A Global Prisoners' Dilemma 362 ◆ Education Efficiency and School Choices 366
16 Is a Lighthouse a Public Good? 380 ◆ The Original Tragedy of the Commons 382 ◆ One of Today's Tragedies of the Commons 383 ◆ ITQs Work 387
17 Wage Rates in Canada 404 ◆ The World and Canadian Markets for Oil 413
18 The Rich Get Richer 427 ◆ School Pays 428 ◆ How Long Does a Spell of Poverty Last? 429 ◆ Income Redistribution: Only the Richest Pay 438